100 Styles of French Cooking

100 Styles of French Cooking

Karl Wurzer

GROSSET & DUNLAP
A FILMWAYS COMPANY
Publishers • New York

Contents

Foreword

This is not simply another French cookbook. It is the book I have always wanted and couldn't find, a book that arranges the classic (and some not so classic) styles of French cooking in alphabetical order and then explains them fully.

It gives you the name of the cooking style first, then its phonetic pronunciation, literal meaning, history or background, and the characteristics or ingredients that make the style unique. It tells how to vary the recipes within the framework of the cooking style, for personal latitude in ingredients and flavorings. Then for each style there are its recipes, from steaks and sauces to tarts and tomatoes. Some styles deal only with a single type of dish, such as fish, while others cover the gamut from hors d'oeuvres to dessert.

This book will enable you to understand and use 100 categories of French cooking, from à l'Albigeoise to à la Zingara, and to find out just what makes each style different from the rest as well as how it resembles similar styles.

Did you know there is a cooking mode named after one of Napoleon's battles? Do you know what sets cooking à la Normande apart from virtually all other French cooking? You'll find points of interest such as these under the categories they apply to. I think it's fun to know some facts about the dishes you're cooking and to be able to talk intelligently about the dinner you're serving. And when eating out, if you've ever wondered what that exotic French word on the menu means, or how it's pronounced, or what it means the dish should contain, or how it came to be used as a cooking term, then this book is for you, because that's what it's about.

Introduction

In the past ten years, as an illustrator and art director in advertising, publishing and film, I've naturally been involved in commercial competition, which has spilled over into my social life. There, of course, the battlefield changes from studio to kitchen. This is not to downgrade the social aspects of commercial life. On the contrary: Entertaining has become a most important facet of contemporary life; and it's more fun to throw a party than to tackle the design for a new advertising campaign.

If you live and work in a creative field, however, it's not easy to compete successfully. Creative friends are always thinking creative thoughts and doing creative deeds. It's easy enough to fall in with the mob and try to be creative exactly as they are. This entails adopting a snobbish attitude toward everybody who is unfortunate enough to be in a noncreative field. However, it's difficult to be a good snob when you haven't the faintest idea what you're doing.

At first I was satisfied with serving guests a dish "à la Bourguignonne" or "à la Lyonnaise." If anyone had the temerity to ask, I could reel off the names of the various dishes. Gradually, however, my self-satisfied state gave way to a nagging curiosity. Just what *was* a Bouquetière, or a Jardinière? Exactly what qualities entitled a salad to be called a Salade Niçoise? I tried to learn more through the media, but the information I gleaned there was often contradictory. In fact, the more I found out the more confused I became. If one expert says a particular dish must always contain garlic and another makes the dish with no garlic, who is right?

I finally became aroused enough to undertake research on my own. But this turned out to be no easier. What I needed was a book that took the classic French modes of cooking and explained them to my satisfaction. What I found was a confusion of contradictory books by chefs and restaurateurs, by politicians and show biz people, by housewives and recipe collectors. There were books to teach me how to boil water and books bulging with awesome recipe lists. There were books on regional cooking, but not one comprehensive book on the classic French cooking modes treated separately and intelligibly. Nowhere could I quickly find the difference between cooking beef or bananas à l'Allemande and any other style. It was getting to be like trying to shoot a film without a script. So, since I couldn't find a book that came anywhere near the explanation in depth I wanted, I wrote one, and here it is.

GREATER AND LESSER STYLES

The cuisine of France is a bewildering kaleidoscope of styles. In this book I've included the truly great styles, such as Bourguignonne and Niçoise, as well as the truly unique styles, such as Amandine and Vigneronne, known for the use of almonds and grapes, respectively.

Styles such as Anna and Xérès are likewise important for their distinctive qualities: Anna for a particularly exquisite method for preparing potatoes (the name Anna also applies to any main course they are prepared or served with), Xérès for the use of sherry wine in the cooking of any dish. There can be no question as to the importance of these "lesser" categories in the French cuisine, for their distinctive qualities find expression throughout all the other categories. For instance, the "lesser" category Fines Herbes, meaning fine herbs, can be found in use throughout the French cuisine wherever herbal combinations are used as flavorings, which is practically everywhere. There are a host of these lesser styles: Poivrade (pepper), Soubise (onions), Crécy (carrots), Béchamel (Sauce Béchamel) and many more. Each is completely distinctive and as important to the whole of the French cuisine as any major cooking mode.

With this in mind, I have selected the 100 styles that represent the French cuisine in its greatest splendor as well as its widest variety and have described and illustrated each as fully as possible. Please don't think, though, that I expect you to follow this book religiously. Each of us has a different approach to cooking, and all of us have prejudices. Here are some of mine:

BUTTER

In my opinion, the French cooking "experts" simply use too much butter, particularly for finishing sauces. Most recipes use plenty of butter during the course of cooking, in such steps as sautéing and glazing. Then a beautifully balanced sauce is made by adding wine and a basic brown or white sauce to the cooking juices, often further enhanced with fresh herbs. Logically this sauce is complete. It has all the flavorings and essence of the dish enhanced by wine and herbs and extended with a great basic sauce to produce a masterpiece. But is it finished? No. We are asked by most French chefs to stir in a few tablespoons of "enrichment" butter.

I submit that this addition of butter to everything is not a finishing touch of refinement. The only reason a sauce without an overdose of butter tastes unfinished to many "experts" is because their palates are jaded. I further submit that constant enrichment with butter, leads to monotony.

HERBS

I like parsley. I love a salad with plenty of fresh parsley, especially with a lemony dressing, such as is popular throughout the Middle East. But I get sick of seeing chopped parsley strewn all over every roast and vegetable and in every soup. Has no one ever heard of chives? What's wrong with the magnificent flavor of chopped basil leaves or a little fresh or dried mint? Plumped in a bit of warm white wine, mint makes a much more appropriate garnish for lamb than parsley. Try different herbs and spices and decide what *you* like. Then use what you prefer.

To familiarize myself with the various herbs, I experimented with flavoring eggs. Each morning I made scrambled eggs with a little salt and pepper and one herb, such as tarragon. Then I noted my reactions so I could recall just how the herb had tasted. Next, I started using simple combinations, like basil and thyme. Soon, I felt comfortable using herbs in any combination, for any desired result. I suggest you try it, if only with a few herbs. Get to know them singly and you'll be able to combine them magnificently. I think you'll soon find yourself changing the old standard bouquet garni of parsley, thyme and bay leaf to suit your taste and achieve the result you want at that particular moment.

I think I dislike the words "bouquet garni" almost as much as "enrichment butter." Instead of the standard bouquet garni, which I admit is usable, though dull, in almost anything, give a bit more thought to the dish involved. A combination of celery leaves, oregano and caraway seed makes for a pungent pork or beef. Celery leaves with cardamom, coriander and chives go excellently with omelets and light meats. Celery leaves with crushed fennel seeds, fenugreek and basil render an unusual, pungent and almost sweet flavor to lamb. Grated lemon and orange rind with anise and tarragon make an interesting fruity combination. Celery leaves, coriander and fenugreek make a warm, very mild and unusual, currylike flavor. Try it instead of that abomination called curry powder. (There's no such thing as curry powder in culinary use in India; we Westerners invented it as a poor imitation of their wonderfully varied seasonings!)

TRUFFLES

Truffles are, unquestionably, a delicacy, particularly those from certain areas of France, such as Périgord or Lot. However, give the French (or any of us) a good thing and they'll beat it into the ground. Everywhere you look in French cooking you'll find truffles—including this book. They are fine, but I don't expect anyone to use them all the time just because they appear in recipes. I've kept them in most of the recipes here for authenticity. Feel free to substitute mushrooms, or simply ignore the truffles. But do try them sometime. Even though they don't grow here and are available only canned, they are exquisite.

COCKSCOMBS AND COCK'S KIDNEYS

This is another overused accompaniment to fine dishes that comes to us from the dim past when anything that was rare or hard to get was considered necessary in an important recipe. The old rule of thumb was: The rarer, the more expensive, the more desirable—regardless of taste. Certainly, give them a try sometime. Latch on to a cooperative farmer, talk nice, pay the price, and sample sautéed cockscombs and cock's kidneys. They're not bad. The point is, once again, that they don't have to be in every dish. When you find them in one of my recipes, use them if you want. If not, use something else, like small slices of veal kidney, sweetbreads, chicken hearts, pieces of chicken breast cooked gently in broth, or anything else you feel like at the moment.

You'll find other things popping up all too frequently too, like cream, artichoke hearts, and so on. But again, they're included (often in reduced amounts) for authenticity only. My aim is to clarify the classic French cooking styles, make them understandable and show how interesting they can be with a little background knowledge. Half the fun is knowing all about a dish and being able to talk about it intelligently, and this book tries to make that as easy as flipping a page.

HOW TO USE THIS BOOK

Any main course served with a particular category's sauce and garnishes becomes a dish *à la* that particular category. Recipes other than the category's garnishes, such as vegetables, however, are not necessarily appropriate with the category's main courses. For example, in the category Crème, cream finds its way into every dish. Personally, however, I wouldn't care for a dinner of Veal Chops à la Crème with Peas à la Crème and Potatoes à la Crème and Rice à la Crème for dessert. A category is a family, and some families get along well together while others don't. Nonetheless, they belong together as a family, for recognition and understanding by you, who will decide that the main course from an especially spicy category needs the foil of a bland accompaniment, such as a vegetable à la Crème, perhaps.

Generally, a given category is complete in itself. I've tried to keep cross-references to a minimum. All the ingredients, sauces, etc., that pertain to a particular category are included in its recipes. The exceptions are:
1. A few basic preparations, such as chicken stock, which are used in so many recipes they simply cannot be included over and over separately. These preparations are marked with an asterisk (*) and are found in the Appendix at the rear of the book.
2. Combinations of ingredients, or recipes, that are frequently used throughout

this book and pertain to a specific category listed in this book. For instance, a mirepoix of vegetables can be found under the general category Mirepoix, Sauce Allemande can be found under the category Allemande, and so on.

3. Particular recipes that are included in another category because they are an integral part of that category, such as potato croquettes, which are a standard garnish for dishes à l'Albigeoise. These will be noted as follows: (*see* Albigeoise Garnish #1).

Occasionally you will come across terms such as clarified butter or clear veal stock. If you are unfamiliar with how to make these items, the explanation will be found in the Appendix. The Appendix describes clarifying butter, clarifying stocks, stocks, consommés, blanching foods, glazing vegetables, slurries and *beurres maniés,* the proper way to cook eggs, preparing artichokes, how to peel tomatoes, various crusts, a few sauces that belong to no category and how to prepare canned truffles for use—in short, the basics. Some of these you may not need, but they are included just in case you do.

All items in the Appendix will be marked with an asterisk wherever they appear in this book's recipes.

I've taken for granted that you are familiar enough with cooking to taste a dish for seasoning before serving and make any necessary adjustments with salt and pepper as required at the end of each step, and that you are familiar with standard measurements. If not, all you need are measuring cups and spoons, which are clearly graded. The only measurements not necessarily found on these implements are: 8 ounces = 1 cup, 2 cups = 1 pint, 4 cups = 1 quart, 2 tablespoons = 1 ounce and 3 teaspoons = 1 tablespoon.

Finally, a note on the names of the various styles of French cooking. Most of the category names end in *e,* such as Ancienne, which is the feminine form of the word *ancien,* meaning old or ancient. This is true of regional terms, such as Alsacienne, Parisienne, etc. They are all feminine endings, as are most other category names. A few terms, such as Chasseur (meaning hunter), are masculine. The feminine ending would make it Chasseuse. Exceptions such as this seem only to accentuate the rule that French cooking categories have feminine endings. This is interesting, since virtually all the great French chefs were and are men.

Albigeoise

(ahl-bee-ZHWAZ)

From Albi, a city in southern France, near Toulouse. It was here that a religious sect arose at the end of the eleventh century. The adherents were the Albigenses and the sect spread throughout southern France in the thirteenth century. The Albigenses believed in two opposing creators and denied the resurrection of Christ. They condemned the procreation of children and praised death by suicide. Although their ideas were thought dangerous by their contemporaries, the only accounts of their doctrine come from their enemies, and not through members of the sect (not surprising if they all committed suicide).

The Albigenses became powerful enough to scare Pope Innocent III into initiating a crusade and inquisition against them in 1209. By then the sect had virtually divided France, north from south, and was a threat to the crown. This prompted King Louis VIII to join in the action, and by 1229 the Albigenses were defeated, and finally disappeared.

The cuisine named Albigeoise is typified by garnishes of Duchesse potato and ham croquettes and by tomatoes stuffed with duxelles. It generally includes a good bit of garlic, and ham in an accompanying role with the main-course meat. A plain salad dressed with olive oil, cider vinegar, salt and pepper would round out the meal nicely.

The mutton cutlet recipe would be fine for lamb chops, pork chops or even veal. The lamb shoulder could just as well be made with mutton shoulder or even a beef roast, cut with a large pocket and stuffed.

A fitting presentation for food à l'Albigeoise would be very simple and rustic. Perhaps a bare wooden table, with wood or earthenware bowls. For sound, how about French folk music?

SAUCE ALBIGEOISE
TO MAKE 2 CUPS

2 cups Demi-Glace Sauce
   (Sauce Alsacienne)

2-3 Tbs tomato purée

Cook the sauce and tomato purée together until lightly thickened.

This sauce can be used for both large and small cuts of meat.

ALBIGEOISE GARNISHES
TO SERVE 4

1. POTATO CROQUETTES À L'ALBIGEOISE

2 lbs potatoes, peeled	4 egg yolks
2 Tbs butter	½ cup cooked ham, minced
salt, white pepper, grated	3 Tbs oil (preferably peanut)
nutmeg	3 Tbs butter

Cook the potatoes in water until done, about 25 minutes. Drain and mash very smooth. Put them in a pot over lowest possible heat and stir to dry well without coloring; 5 minutes should do. Add the 2 tablespoons butter and season to taste with salt, pepper and nutmeg. Remove from heat and beat in the yolks thoroughly. Blend in the ham. (This mixture may be covered and chilled before sautéing.)

Heat the oil and 3 tablespoons butter in a pan. Shape small croquettes from the potato mixture (Duchesse potatoes plus minced ham) by using 2 spoons, or make the small oval shapes by hand. Sauté the croquettes in hot fat until golden on all sides, turning gently without breaking. As they are done, place them on a hot dish on paper towels, keeping them warm while you finish the others. Serve hot, discarding the draining towels, piled in a mound on a hot serving dish.

The potato croquettes may be deep-fried if desired.

2. STUFFED TOMATOES À L'ALBIGEOISE

8 small tomatoes	Swiss cheese, grated
1 cup duxelles	bread crumbs
salt	olive oil

Preheat oven to 300°. Cut the tops off the tomatoes and scoop out the insides. Turn the tomatoes upside down to drain. Season the tomatoes inside with salt. Drain the scooped-out tomato pulp and discard the seeds. Chop and mix with the duxelles and use to stuff the tomatoes. Put tomatoes in a buttered baking dish and sprinkle generously with cheese and crumbs. Sprinkle a little oil on the crumbs to moisten, and bake in the oven for about 30 minutes, until golden. Serve hot right in the dish.

LAMB SHOULDER À L'ALBIGEOISE
TO SERVE 4

1 lamb shoulder, boned	goose fat or butter
1 lb pork sausage meat	3 lbs potatoes, quartered
1 lb pig's liver (or beef liver),	12 garlic cloves, blanched for 30
minced	seconds in boiling water
2 garlic cloves, minced	salt and pepper
1 tsp chopped parsley	goose fat or butter, melted
1 tsp chopped chives	parsley and chives, mixed
salt and pepper	

Mix the sausage meat, liver, garlic, chopped parsley and chives and season well to taste with salt and pepper. Use this mixture to stuff the shoulder, and sew or skewer closed.

Preheat oven to 325°. Brown the stuffed shoulder in a casserole in goose fat until lightly browned on all sides. Add the potatoes and garlic, season to taste with salt and pepper and moisten with a little melted goose fat, if needed. Cover and cook in the oven for about 40 minutes per pound, or until done. Do not overcook lamb. Sprinkle with mixed parsley and chives, let stand a few minutes to set the juices and serve hot, right in the casserole.

If desired, a sauce may be made right in the casserole. Set the potatoes and garlic cloves aside and keep warm. Skim excess fat from the casserole. Blend in 1½ to 2 cups Sauce Alsacienne and 2 tablespoons tomato purée over direct heat until hot and thickened. Return the garlic and potatoes to the casserole, heat through for a moment and serve.

MUTTON CUTLETS or CHOPS À L'ALBIGEOISE
TO SERVE 4

8 mutton cutlets	1 cup Tomato Sauce* (prefera-
salt and pepper (optional)	bly homemade)
olive oil	olive oil
2 oz white wine	1 garlic clove, crushed
1 garlic clove, crushed	1 lb mushrooms, sliced

Season the cutlets lightly with salt and pepper, if desired, and sauté in oil until done. Arrange in a circle on a hot platter, leaving the center open, and keep hot. Drain excess fat from pan.

Add the wine and garlic to the pan and quickly boil down, scraping up the pan juices. Discard the garlic and add the tomato sauce, blending well. Pour over the mutton, reserving a few tablespoons.

Meanwhile, heat a little oil in a pan with the garlic and sauté the mushrooms lightly. Discard the garlic. Drain, and arrange the mushrooms in the center of the mutton platter in a neat pile. Top with remaining sauce and serve hot.

Algérienne

(ahl-zher-E'YEN)

From Algeria, an Arab country in North Africa that was for a time part of France. The capital is Algiers which is famous for its old section, the Casbah, with its maze of narrow alleys. Algeria was conquered by the French in the nineteenth century and remained a French colony until it became independent in 1962.

Algerian cooking, in France, is a dish garnished with small tomatoes cooked in oil and sweet potatoes sautéed in butter or made into croquettes. These garnishes are usually used with meat, and are especially good with pork roast. As is often the case when using garnishes, add some meat and you have a complete meal. Whatever the meat or meats, Sauce Algérienne makes a good gravy.

A fitting salad can be made with a head of lettuce, shredded and mixed with half a cup of orange juice and seasoned with salt and pepper. This is a bit different, and authentically North African. Or use any fresh salad with a simple oil and vinegar dressing.

A fine finale for any meal à l'Algérienne would be the Algerian Date Chew, and demitasse with lemon-peel twists.

SAUCE ALGÉRIENNE
TO MAKE 2 CUPS

2 cups veal stock* or gravy   salt and pepper
2 Tbs tomato purée or paste

Heat the stock with the purée and blend well. Season to taste with salt and pepper and serve hot.

This sauce is generally made with clarified* veal stock. It can be used for meats and poultry.

ALGÉRIENNE GARNISHES
TO SERVE 4

1. TOMATOES À L'ALGÉRIENNE

8 medium tomatoes   salt and pepper
4 Tbs olive oil

Quarter or slice tomatoes and discard seeds and juice. Sauté the tomatoes in hot oil, seasoning with salt and pepper to taste. Drain and serve hot.

This garnish is very attractive using whole peeled* cherry tomatoes.

2. SWEET POTATO CROQUETTES

2 lbs sweet potatoes, unpeeled   ½ tsp powdered nutmeg
8 Tbs ground cashews   ¼ tsp powdered cinnamon
4 Tbs butter   salt and pepper
                                        4 Tbs butter (more if needed)

Cook the potatoes in boiling water for 30 minutes, or until done and tender. Peel and mash. Meanwhile, sauté the cashews lightly in the butter and add to the mashed sweet potatoes. Blend in the nutmeg and cinnamon and season lightly with salt and pepper to taste. (This mixture may be chilled before sautéing.)

Shape the potato mixture into croquettes by rolling between two spoons, or by hand, and sauté in hot butter until golden on all sides. As the croquettes are done, drain them on paper towels on a hot dish, and keep warm while you finish the rest. Serve hot, discarding draining towels, piled in a mound on a hot serving dish.

BEEF FILLET À L'ALGÉRIENNE
TO SERVE 4

4 beef fillets	2 sweet potatoes, peeled, sliced
salt and paprika	and sautéed in butter, hot
butter	1 oz dry white wine
4 bread slices, crusts removed	1½ cups Sauce Espagnole or
1 recipe Algérienne Garnish	beef gravy
#1, hot	1 Tbs tomato paste

Season fillets with salt and paprika to taste and sauté in a little butter. Arrange on a hot platter on the bread (sautéed in butter, or buttered toast). Garnish with tomatoes and sweet potatoes and keep hot. Dilute the pan juices with the wine and bring to a boil. Blend in the Sauce Espagnole and tomato paste and heat. Pour over the fillets, or serve the sauce separately, hot.

LAMB CUTLETS or CHOPS À L'ALGÉRIENNE
TO SERVE 4

Proceed as for Beef Fillet à l'Algérienne, using 4 or 8 lamb cutlets in place of the beef fillets.

CHICKEN À L'ALGÉRIENNE
TO SERVE 4

1 chicken, cut up	2 tomatoes, peeled,* seeded
salt, pepper and paprika	and diced
flour	1 medium eggplant, peeled and
olive oil	diced
2 Tbs chopped onion	butter
2 garlic cloves, crushed	parsley sprigs (optional)
	1 recipe Algérienne Garnish #2,
	hot

Season chicken with salt, pepper and paprika to taste and dredge in flour, shaking off the excess. Sauté in oil over medium heat until browned, about 15 minutes. Reduce heat, add onion, cover and simmer 30 to 40 minutes, until done. Remove chicken and add garlic and tomatoes to pan. Cook 5 minutes, stirring gently. Return chicken to pan and simmer over low heat for 10 more minutes to reheat and absorb flavors.

Meanwhile, sauté eggplant in butter. Arrange the chicken on a hot platter and surround with the sautéed eggplant. Pour the pan juices over the chicken, garnish with parsley sprigs if desired and serve sweet potato garnish separately.

This pan juice, to be typically French, should be blended smooth and strained over the chicken through a sieve, or served strained separately. To by more typical of Algeria, however, the sauce should be mixed gently, retaining the vegetable pieces as much as possible.

DATE CHEW À L'ALGÉRIENNE
TO SERVE 4

1 lb dates	orange marmalade
3 oz chopped walnuts, toasted	sugar (preferably vanilla sugar)
2 oz chopped dried figs	

Split the dates enough to remove the pits without halving or breaking them in pieces. Mix the walnuts and figs with just enough marmalade so they stick together, and use to stuff the dates. Coat with sugar and store between layers of wax paper in a sealed jar. Store in a cool, dry place until used.

Allemande

(ahl-MAHND)

Means German. *Allemande* is used as the name of a basic white sauce, as *Espagnole* is used as the name of a basic brown sauce. However, the sauces did not originate in Germany and Spain, respectively, as their names would indicate, but were given these French names because of their color: Allemande, the white sauce, named after the blond Germanic peoples and Espagnole, the brown sauce, named after the darker-skinned and black-haired Spaniards.

Allemande is a hard cooking style to describe, because it is quite varied and somewhat confused. To begin with, Sauce Allemande is the same as Sauce Parisienne. While some Allemande recipes make use of vinegar, sour cream and horseradish, which is typically German, other recipes are fairly light, as a simple meat with Sauce Allemande/Parisienne, and these can just as well be called à la Parisienne. Either term is correct. This is not unusual in the French cuisine.

Vegetables of this cooking style are red cabbage, endive and cucumbers in oil, vinegar, water, salt and pepper, hot potato salad and cauliflower.

German wines are among the finest in the world and the variety is great. If you wish to serve a German wine with a dish à l'Allemande, simply pick the type and price you want. As with all imported wines, however, if your selection is a reasonably priced wine, your money would be better spent on a comparably priced American wine.

Some of the interesting cheeses of Germany to accompany this cuisine are Brandkäse, a sour-milk cheese ripened in old beer kegs; Altenburger, a very mellow, semisoft goat's milk cheese; and Hopfenkäse, which is cured between layers of hops and often blended with caraway seeds, milk or beer.

Experiment a bit with these recipes. Where a recipe calls for Sauce Allemande, consider adding a bit of sour cream to the sauce instead of the usual sweet cream. Try a few drops of vinegar on any vegetable for added spark. And don't forget horseradish; it can give zip to any roast, not to mention sauce.

Though this style of cooking doesn't rely heavily on herbs, sometime try a pork roast, well seasoned, and with a lot of caraway seed. Before cooking, insert some of the caraway seeds into the roast with a long thin knife, to get the flavor all the way through. Then serve with an Allemande sauce made with a bit of sour cream. Remove all the fat from the pan and blend the sauce with the cooking juices. Marvelous!

For décor, a fitting centerpiece could be made using beer steins as a focal point. Typical plants that could be used for decoration are ferns, cranberry heath, heathers, forget-me-nots and buttercups. Pine, fir and spruce boughs are typical of the higher German slopes, chestnuts and maple leaves of the lowlands. Chestnuts and acorns, with pinecones and bright maple leaves on evergreen boughs, surrounding various-size steins would make a fine decoration. For music, there are plenty of spirited German folk songs.

SAUCE ALLEMANDE
TO MAKE 2 CUPS

2 cups veal or chicken stock,* or broth
2½ cups Sauce Velouté*

2 egg yolks
1 oz butter, diced (optional)

Mix the stock and Velouté and cook down to 2 cups. Reduce heat, so the sauce is well below a boil, and blend in the yolks, whisking constantly. Cook, without allowing to boil, until thickened. Stir in the butter if desired.

This sauce can be used for meats, fowl, vegetables and eggs. Depending on the intended use, it can be seasoned with a little grated nutmeg for light dishes, or a little lemon juice to sharpen it, or a little grated cheese for the more robust dishes. Cream is also a standard addition, to be added or left out according to your preference.

SAUCE ALLEMANDE, MUSHROOM FLAVORED

Proceed as for Sauce Allemande, adding 2 to 3 ounces mushroom cooking liquor* or canned mushroom juice and, optionally, chopped mushroom skins or peelings during cooking. Strain finished sauce.

SALAD À L'ALLEMANDE
TO SERVE 4

1 lb potatoes, cooked in chicken stock* or broth, cubed
½ lb tart apples, diced
mayonnaise (preferably home-made)
½ cup sliced, cooked beets
½ cup sliced gherkins
½ cup sliced pickled herring fillets
parsley and/or chives
oil, vinegar, salt and pepper

Bind the potatoes and apples with enough mayonnaise so they will pile in a dome. Surround decoratively with beets, gherkins and herring and sprinkle with parsley and/or chives. Season the beets and gherkins with oil, vinegar, salt and pepper to taste and serve at room temperature.

POTATO SALAD À L'ALLEMANDE (Hot)
TO SERVE 4

2 lbs potatoes, unpeeled
a large salad bowl, preferably wooden, warmed
1 garlic clove, halved
1 onion, minced
1 garlic clove, minced
1 Tbs parsley
1 Tbs chives
1 Tbs celery leaves, chopped
salt and pepper
4 Tbs olive oil, warmed
4 Tbs vegetable oil, warmed
cider vinegar

Boil the potatoes in water until done. Drain and keep warm. (If necessary, use a barely warm oven.) Rub the halved garlic clove on the warmed bowl and discard. Put the onion, garlic, parsley, chives and celery in the bowl. Peel the warm potatoes and cut them into the bowl in bite-size pieces. Season with salt and pepper to taste and sprinkle with the warmed oils and a few drops of vinegar to taste. Toss lightly and serve at once, warm. (If the salad must be kept before serving, cover with a towel and hold in a barely warm oven.)

SAUERKRAUT SALAD À L'ALLEMANDE
TO SERVE 4

2 lbs sauerkraut
¾ lb tiny whole onions
1 qt chicken consommé* or broth
oil, vinegar, salt and pepper
½ Tbs wine vinegar
3 cups lightly salted water
¾ lb beets, peeled and sliced
4 eggs, hard-boiled and sliced

Blanch the sauerkraut and onions in boiling water for 30 seconds and drain. Add both to the consommé and simmer for 20 minutes. Drain the sauerkraut and onions well and put in a salad bowl. Let cool. Season to taste with oil, vinegar, salt and pepper. Toss lightly. Meanwhile, cook the beets in the vinegar and water for about 35 minutes. Drain and cool. Garnish the sauerkraut with egg slices and beets and serve at room temperature.

RED CABBAGE À L'ALLEMANDE
TO SERVE 4

2 Tbs butter
1 head red cabbage, shredded
1 tart apple, diced
1 bay leaf
¼ tsp ground cinnamon
3 juniper berries

salt and pepper
2 oz dry white wine
1 tsp sugar
2 Tbs vinegar (preferably white
  wine vinegar)

Melt the butter in a pan and add the cabbage and apple. Cook, stirring, for 2 minutes. Add the bay leaf, cinnamon, juniper berries and salt and pepper to taste. Mix well and cook, covered, for 10 minutes. Add wine and cook, covered, for 5 more minutes. Mix the sugar and vinegar, add to the pan and cook, covered, for 30 more minutes or until done. Discard bay leaf and juniper berries. Serve hot in a warmed bowl.

PUMPKIN À L'ALLEMANDE (Sweet and Sour)
TO MAKE 1 QUART

Pumpkin to fill a 1-quart jar,
  peeled and cubed
ground cinnamon, nutmeg,
  cloves, bay leaf, thyme,
  mixed in equal parts (about
  ¼-½ tsp each)

1 pt cider vinegar
4 Tbs sugar

Fill a quart jar with layers of pumpkin, seasoning each layer with a little of the mixed spice, until the jar is filled. Boil the vinegar and sugar for a couple of minutes and let cool. Pour into the pumpkin-filled jar, cover and refrigerate a week or two before using.

HAMBURGER STEAK À L'ALLEMANDE
TO SERVE 4

2 lbs lean ground beef
1 onion, chopped and lightly
  sautéed in butter
2 raw eggs
salt, pepper and grated nutmeg

flour
butter
1 small onion, sliced thin and
  lightly sautéed in butter, hot

Mix the beef, chopped onion and eggs and season to taste with salt, pepper and nutmeg. Shape into 4 hamburger patties. Dredge in flour, shaking off the excess, and sauté in a little butter, keeping them a bit underdone. They are said to be just right when little beads of blood form on the surface, but this depends on your taste. Serve on hot dishes topped with the sliced, sautéed onion.

VEAL BREAST À L'ALLEMANDE
TO SERVE 4

STUFFING

1 lb lean pork, ground	¼ tsp each thyme, basil, bay
1 lb pork fat, ground	leaf, sage, mace
1 tsp salt	*or*
½ tsp white pepper	2 lbs pork sausage meat

VEAL

1 veal breast, about 6 lbs	1½ lbs carrots, sliced
2 cups chicken stock* or broth	1 lb leeks, sliced
salt and pepper	1½ lbs potatoes, sliced

SAUCE

4 Tbs horseradish, grated	½ cup cream
½ cup chicken consommé* or	½ cup bread crumbs
broth	1 egg yolk mixed with 1 Tbs cold
1 Tbs butter	water
2 Tbs flour	salt and pepper
½ cup lightly salted water, boil-	¼ tsp dry mustard
ing	wine vinegar or cider vinegar
3 Tbs butter, diced	

Mix the pork, pork fat, salt, pepper and seasonings into a stuffing, or use the pork sausage meat for stuffing.

Preheat oven to 325°. Cut a pocket in the veal breast and stuff it. Sew or skewer closed. Season well and put in a pan with the stock. Cover and bake in the oven for 2 hours, turning and adding the vegetables after 1 hour.

Meanwhile, prepare horseradish sauce (also called Sauce Albert) by boiling the horseradish in the consommé for 20 minutes. While this is boiling, melt the 1 tablespoon butter in a pan, stir in the flour and blend. Slowly blend in the salted water. Add the diced butter and blend. When the horseradish has boiled for 20 minutes, add the flour mixture and blend well. Add the cream and crumbs and boil, stirring constantly, until thickened. Remove from heat and stir in the yolk blended with water. Season to taste, and add the mustard and a few drops of vinegar to taste. Put the veal on a hot platter and remove string or skewers. Surround with the baked vegetables and serve horseradish sauce separately, hot.

DUCK À L'ALLEMANDE
TO SERVE 4

1 duck, 4–5 lbs	½ cup seedless raisins
salt	(plumped in lukewarm dry
3 cups black pumpernickel	white wine)
crumbs	2 tsp sugar
½ cup diced apple	½ tsp salt
½ cup chopped dried figs	2 Tbs light rum

Clean the duck and remove all possible fat. Rub inside and out with salt. Preheat the oven to 350°. Combine all the remaining ingredients and use to stuff the duck. Sew or skewer closed. Truss the legs and wings to the body with string, prick all over with a fork to allow the fat to escape and place on a rack in a roasting pan. Roast the duck, uncovered, for about 2 hours, until done and tender. Discard the trussings and serve hot. (If the duck browns too quickly, cover loosely with a tent of aluminum foil.)

SOUP À L'ALLEMANDE (German Beer Soup)
TO SERVE 4

2 Tbs butter	1/16 tsp ground cloves
2 Tbs flour	2 egg yolks
1 qt beer or ale	2 oz dry white wine
salt	1 Tbs sugar
1 tsp ground ginger	1 orange rind, grated
¼ tsp ground cinnamon	8 bread slices, toasted and
⅛ tsp nutmeg	halved diagonally

Melt the butter in a casserole and stir in the flour, cooking gently for a few minutes. Stir in the beer slowly and blend well. Season with salt to taste. Add ginger, cinnamon, nutmeg and cloves and blend well. Cook, stirring, for 15 minutes.

Meanwhile, beat the yolks, wine, sugar and orange rind together until smooth. Add 1 tablespoon of slightly cooled soup and beat well. Add another tablespoon of soup and beat well. Lower heat so soup is just below a simmer. Add the yolk mixture, beating in well over low heat for 2 to 3 minutes. Do not allow to boil or the yolks will curdle. Serve hot, with the toast served separately.

CHOCOLATE PUDDING À L'ALLEMANDE
TO SERVE 4

¼ cup butter, softened	1 oz Kirsch brandy
6 Tbs sugar	½ cup ground almonds
4 eggs, separated	½ cup bread crumbs
1½ oz semisweet chocolate, melted	tiny pinch cream of tartar

Beat the butter until smooth and slowly add the sugar, blending well. In a separate bowl beat the 4 egg yolks and add to the butter and sugar. Beat until fluffy. Add the chocolate, Kirsch, almonds and crumbs and blend well. In a separate bowl, beat the egg whites with the cream of tartar until stiff (the cream of tartar helps produce beaten whites that will hold their form). Preheat oven to 325°. Fold the beaten whites gently into the chocolate mixture and pour into a well-buttered mold or casserole. Bake in a pan of water in oven until done, about 40 minutes. When done, run a knife around the inside of the mold, unmold on a heated serving dish and serve hot.

Alsacienne

(ahl-sah-S'YEN)

From the Alsace region of northeast France, bordering Germany. Here we see an interesting blend of substantial German fare and artistically refined French dishes. The distinguishing ingredients in cooking à l'Alsacienne are sauerkraut, ham and Strasbourg sausages. (Certain recipes are also based on pâté de foie gras.)

The Alsace region has at times been part of Germany and at other times part of France, as it is at present. Bordering on the Rhine, it's a land of rolling hills and narrow, stone-walled lanes. The towns that have survived the Second World War are incredibly picturesque, such as Riquewihr, hardly changed since the early 1700s. Under its narrow streets, long vaults are still stocked with the area's fine wines. Typical Alsatian wines are Riesling, Gewürztraminer (most typical of Alsatian wines) and Muscatel.

The Bénédictine monks of Alsace were the first to maintain ponds to keep live fish, and also the first to carefully breed pigs for the table. Strasbourg sausages, the fine, smoked, frankfurter-like sausages of the area, are one result of the monks' dedication to fine food. Alsace is most noted, however, for its especially fattened geese, whose livers yield the magnificent pâté de foie gras, Alsace's most famous food.

Alsace also produces the world's finest cabbages—hence the wide use of sauerkraut—and fine fruits as well. Alsatian cherries produce the best cherry liqueur found anywhere in the world, Kirsch. Finally, the freshwater fish of Alsace round out its remarkable larder: succulent salmon from the Rhine, river trout, eels, bream and crayfish from streams in the Vosges mountains. Alsace is one of the world's great areas in food production as well as cuisine.

Alsacienne is a fine example of a cooking category that makes full use of its garnishes. Any main dish served with Alsatian garnishes and sauce makes a fine dish à l'Alsacienne. Pâté de foie gras makes a fine garnish for almost anything, and goes especially well with Alsatian cooking, if it is available. Lacking this, the chicken liver pâté is a good substitute, as in Alsacienne Garnish #4. It will embellish any of the recipes here. The Alsatian garnishes could even make a meal in themselves.

For more variation, however, an occasional lighter vegetable might be included in lieu of one of the traditional listed garnishes. A good vegetable to go with just about anything à l'Alsacienne is cauliflower. Broccoli is also excellent, and its deep green color adds a fine touch to the whole table. Bright red cherries, stewed lightly in white wine, are also an interesting and colorful accompaniment. If using the cherries, omit the sauerkraut. (The cherries may be sweetened or not, as needed.)

Mashed potatoes mixed with chopped sauerkraut is another interesting variation, and fitting to the Alsatian style of cooking. I'm sure you'll find many of your own ways to use this versatile vegetable.

The proper décor for a meal à l'Alsacienne would lean more toward Germanic than French. This is the most "foreign" of any area in France, and the Alsatians resemble their relatives across the Rhine in Germany's Black Forest more than other Frenchmen. Think of a peasant table in the forest, carved wood and ironwork and you're on the right track. A large iron trivet to hold the steaming main dish, intricately carved wooden candleholders and simple cloths and tableware are appropriate.

SAUCE ALSACIENNE (Demi-Glace Sauce)
TO MAKE 2 CUPS

2 cups Sauce Espagnole
2 cups veal or beef stock*

2 Tbs Madeira wine (or sherry)

Mix the Sauce Espagnole and stock and cook down to half. Stir in the wine and serve hot. (If this is to be used to make a more complex sauce, especially one with other spirits in it, the Madeira may be omitted.)

This sauce is often cooked with a few ounces of mushroom skins and trimmings, and strained before use. As a basic brown sauce, it is used as the base for a great variety of sauces, for all foods.

ALSACIENNE GARNISHES
TO SERVE 4

1. SAUERKRAUT À L'ALSACIENNE

2 lbs sauerkraut
salt and pepper
1 cup sliced onions
4 Tbs butter
1 cup dry white wine
2 cups chicken stock* or broth
2 tsp parsley

½ tsp thyme
1 bay leaf
7 peppercorns
10 juniper berries
cheesecloth, washed
1 tsp caraway seeds (optional)

Drain the sauerkraut and soak in cold water for 10 minutes. Rinse well under cold running water and squeeze dry. Season with salt and pepper to taste. Preheat oven to 325°. Sauté the onions in the butter in a casserole lightly. Add the sauerkraut, wine and enough stock to cover and bring to a boil. Tie the parsley, thyme, bay leaf, peppercorns and juniper berries in cheesecloth and add. Add the caraway seeds, if desired (for me, they make the dish complete). Cover and bake in the oven for 2 hours. Check the pot occasionally to see if more stock is needed. Serve hot.

2. STRASBOURG SAUSAGES

Poach 4 Strasbourg sausages (or knackwurst or frankfurters) in chicken stock* or broth until done and slice for a hot garnish. Or poach them in sauerkraut juice for a bit more zip. Or poach in half sauerkraut juice and half white wine for a more rounded, mellow flavor.

3. BOILED POTATOES

Boil 2 pounds of potatoes, peeled and cut in equal rounds or cubes, in lightly salted water until just done. Do not overcook. Drain and serve hot.

For an interesting variation, use chicken stock* or broth for the cooking liquid. It's amazing what a difference in flavor it makes.

4. PÂTÉ DE FOIE GRAS

This exquisite garnish is available canned and imported—but read the label. It's surprising what odd things can find their way into a dish that should be primarily goose liver. Pâté de foie gras was invented in Strasbourg by the chef Jean Clause in the early 1760s. If this delicacy is not available or you feel the price is ridiculous (which it is), the following chicken liver pâté makes a fine substitute.

CHICKEN LIVER PÂTÉ
TO MAKE 1 CUP

½ lb chicken livers
1 Tbs butter
2 Tbs Madeira wine
1 garlic clove, minced
1 Tbs softened butter
1 Tbs heavy cream
$^1/_8$ tsp ground allspice
$^1/_8$ tsp ground thyme
1/16 tsp ground nutmeg
¼ tsp ground basil
1 tsp lemon juice
1 tsp brandy
salt and pepper

Sauté the livers in 1 tablespoon butter until just done. Remove from the pan and reserve. Add the Madeira to the pan off heat and scrape up the juices. Pour pan liquid into a blender and add garlic, softened butter, cream, allspice, thyme, nutmeg, basil, lemon juice and brandy. Cover and blend. Add livers, one at a time, and blend until smooth. Season with salt and pepper to taste. (If mixture is too dry, add a bit more cream or Madeira.) The pâté should be soft and semiliquid, and will firm up when chilled. Chill in a sealed pot or mold. Slice the chilled and set pâté and sauté lightly in butter. Serve hot. Or serve without sautéing, lightly chilled or at room temperature.

SALAD À L'ALSACIENNE
TO SERVE 4

Alsacienne Garnishes #1, 2 and 3, hot
olive oil, cider vinegar, salt and pepper

½ cup mayonnaise (preferably homemade)
½ lb lean bacon, sautéed crisp and drained

Drain the boiled potatoes and season to taste with oil, vinegar, salt and pepper while still warm. Mix with the mayonnaise. Slice the cooked Strasbourg Sausages and season with oil, vinegar, salt and pepper. Put the Sauerkraut à l'Alsacienne on a hot platter in a mound and surround with the potatoes and sausages, decoratively. Crumble the bacon over the sauerkraut and serve hot.

NOODLES À L'ALSACIENNE
TO SERVE 4

½ lb dry noodles
1 cup heavy cream
¼ cup Sauce Velouté*

1 tsp savory
salt and pepper

Cook the noodles in lightly salted water and drain. Meanwhile, mix the cream, Velouté and savory and boil down to half. Add the noodles as soon as they are drained. Season to taste with salt and pepper and serve hot.

For an excellent variation, mix ½ cup minced cooked ham with the noodles.

POTATO QUENELLES À L'ALSACIENNE (Dumplings)
TO SERVE 4

4 cups mashed potatoes
butter
2 eggs, beaten
½ cup flour

salt, pepper and grated nutmeg
4 oz butter
¼ cup bread crumbs

Mix the mashed potatoes with butter to taste. Add the eggs and flour and season to taste with salt, pepper and a little nutmeg. Mix well and shape into small dumplings. Cook in gently simmering, lightly salted water for about 10 minutes, depending on size. Drain and put in a warm, buttered serving dish. Meanwhile, cook the 4 ounces of butter in a pan until light brown and add the crumbs. Pour over the quenelles and serve hot.

These quenelles may be cooked in chicken consommé if desired.

GARNISHED SAUERKRAUT À L'ALSACIENNE
(Choucroute Garnie)
TO SERVE 4

1 recipe Alsacienne Garnish #1,
    hot
½ lb lean bacon, diced and
    blanched for 30 seconds in
    boiling water
4 pork chops (preferably
    smoked)

4 Strasbourg sausages, whole
    (or knackwurst or frank-
    furters)
4 thick ham slices
salt, if necessary
1 recipe Alsacienne Garnish #3,
    hot

Preheat oven to 325°. Add the bacon and pork chops to the Sauerkraut à l'Alsacienne and bake for 1 hour, covered. Add the sausages and ham and bake uncovered for 30 minutes more, letting the stock reduce. Season if necessary. Pile sauerkraut on a hot platter and decorate with meats and boiled potatoes. If desired, quickly boil down remaining juices to ½ cup or less and spoon over the sauerkraut.

This is most savory if the stock is all absorbed during cooking, by regulating the amount of time it cooks uncovered, except for a little stock at the end to moisten the dish.

EGGS À L'ALSACIENNE
TO SERVE 4

½ recipe Alsacienne Garnish #1,
    hot
4 ¼-inch-thick ham slices,
    cooked and hot

8 eggs, poached, soft-boiled or
    fried, fresh cooked and hot
1 cup Sauce Espagnole, or
    Demi-Glace (Sauce Alsa-
    cienne), or Madeira Sauce,
    hot

Arrange the sauerkraut on 4 hot plates and top with ham. Top ham with eggs and pour on the hot sauce, or serve plain. Sauce or not, it's a fine dish, and true to Alsatian cooking, you'll know you've eaten!

For a variation, try scrambling the eggs with chopped ham and/or cooking the sauerkraut with a good pinch of caraway seed.

OMELET À L'ALSACIENNE
TO SERVE 2

4 eggs
salt and pepper
goose fat, or butter
¼ cup cooked sauerkraut,
    drained

4 thin ham slices, folded in half
    or rolled, hot
¼ cup thick Sauce Espagnole
    (or beef gravy), hot
chives

Beat the eggs with salt and pepper to taste. Make the omelet* in very hot goose fat, and fill with the sauerkraut. Serve on a hot plate with the ham slices along the omelet's sides. Pour on the sauce, sprinkle with chives, and serve hot.

It's always a temptation to say garnish with watercress sprigs for any omelet, but here it would be out of place. Watercress doesn't fit with the Alsacienne spirit in cooking.

VEAL BREAST À L'ALSACIENNE
TO SERVE 4

1 veal breast	1 lb sauerkraut, blanched for 30
butter	seconds in boiling water and
white pepper	drained
salt, if necessary	¼ tsp caraway seed (or 3
1 cup chicken stock* or broth	juniper berries), optional

Preheat oven to 325°. Brown veal in butter in a casserole. Season with pepper and salt, if needed. Add stock and cook, covered, in the oven for 35 to 40 minutes per pound. One hour before meat is done, add the sauerkraut and the caraway seed or juniper berries if desired.

The veal breast is often made stuffed with the sauerkraut, and occasionally chopped ham, or sliced Strasbourg sausages (or knackwurst or frankfurters) or both are added to the stuffing.

PORK CHOPS À L'ALSACIENNE
TO SERVE 4

8 pork chops	Alsacienne Garnishes #1, 2 and
salt and pepper	3, hot
1 Tbs butter	1 oz dry white wine

Season the chops with salt and pepper to taste and sauté in butter until done. Arrange around the outside of a hot round or oval serving dish, filling the center with a mound of sauerkraut (Garnish #1), and decorate with sausages and potatoes (Garnishes #2 and 3). Keep hot. Pour excess fat from pan, add wine and scrape up the juices. Pour over the pork and serve hot.

It may seem odd to sauté pork chops in butter, since they are fatty themselves, but the butter lets the sautéing get started without hardening the chops before their own fat has a chance to melt and lubricate the pan. The fat is all removed before using the pan juices anyway. So the added butter does not make the dish greasier, just more tender.

HAM SLICES À L'ALSACIENNE
TO SERVE 4

1 ham, smoked
icing sugar

Alsacienne Garnishes #1, 2 and
3, hot

Soak ham in cold water in a large pot for several hours. Pour in fresh water to cover and bring to a boil (use no seasonings or flavorings). As soon as the boil is reached, lower heat to a gentle simmer, so that the water just shivers. Simmer for about 20 minutes per pound. Drain. Remove ham skin if desired, place on a baking sheet, sprinkle with sugar and glaze in a 350° oven for 20 minutes. Serve the ham surrounded with alternating piles of sauerkraut, potatoes and sausage (Garnishes #1, 2 and 3), hot.

HAM SLICES À L'ALSACIENNE
TO SERVE 4

Heat about 2 pounds of ham slices (or leftover pieces) and serve on a bed of sauerkraut garnished with boiled sausages and potatoes, hot

DUCK À L'ALSACIENNE
TO SERVE 4

1 4–5 lb duck
¼ lb bacon, sliced and blanched
    for 30 seconds in boiling wa-
    ter
1 carrot, chopped
1 onion, sliced thin
2 tsp parsley
½ tsp thyme

1 bay leaf
2 Tbs celery leaves
cheesecloth, washed
salt and pepper
1½ cups chicken stock* or broth
Alsacienne Garnishes #1, 2 and
    3, hot

Preheat oven to 400°. Prick duck all over with a sharp fork and truss. Put on a rack in a pan and brown in the oven for 15 minutes. Remove duck from pan and reduce heat to 350°. Place the bacon, carrot and onion, mixed, in the bottom of the pan. Add the parsley, thyme, bay leaf and celery tied in cheesecloth. Season well with salt and pepper. Place the duck on this braising bed, cover and cook in the oven for 20 minutes. Add the stock, cover and cook until done, about another 1½ hours.

Place the duck on a hot platter and surround with hot sauerkraut (Garnish

#1). Decorate the kraut with the bacon strips. Arrange the sausages and potatoes on the platter (Garnishes #2 and 3) and keep hot. Remove excess fat from the pan and pour the remaining juices through a strainer. Spoon a bit of this sauce over the duck and serve the rest separately, hot.

Duck à l'Alsacienne is often prepared stuffed with garlic-flavored sausage meat. If you decide on this, cook the stuffed duck about 40 minutes longer and omit the sausage garnish.

CORNISH GAME HENS À L'ALSACIENNE
TO SERVE 4

4 1-lb birds
salt and pepper
¼ cup butter
2 oz brandy, warm
2 lbs sauerkraut, cooked
1 cup dry white wine
½ cup water
1 cup pineapple chunks
4 Strasbourg sausages (or
    knackwurst or frankfurters),
    cooked

2 lbs potatoes, peeled and diced
¼ cup heavy cream
2 Tbs butter
salt and pepper
1 cup ham, in small strips, hot
1 cup Sauce Espagnole
chives

Preheat oven to 375°. Season the birds liberally with salt and pepper and brown in the butter in a casserole. Pour brandy over birds and flame, stirring until the fire dies. Cover the casserole and cook in the oven until done, about ½ hour.

Meanwhile, put the sauerkraut in a pan with the wine and water and heat. Add the pineapple and sausages and heat through. Boil the potatoes until done in lightly salted water. Mash the potatoes with the cream and butter, and season to taste with salt and a little pepper. (If desired, make rosettes of the potatoes and brown in the oven.)

Place the birds on a hot platter and decorate with ham strips. Surround with mounds of sauerkraut, sausages and potatoes, decoratively. Remove excess fat from the birds' pan, add the Espagnole and blend well and heat through quickly. Strain over the birds and potatoes and serve hot, sprinkled with chives. Or serve separately.

This recipe for Cornish game hens is applicable to any other birds, such as pheasant. Simply increase the cooking time if using larger birds. Cook birds about ½ hour per pound after browning and flaming.

FLOUNDER À L'ALSACIENNE
TO SERVE 4

2 lbs flounder fillets, salted lightly
1 Tbs lemon juice
¼ cup water
¼ cup dry white wine
2 garlic cloves, crushed
8 white peppercorns
¼ cup chopped onion
1 small head cabbage, trimmed
   and shredded
3 Tbs butter

salt and white pepper
2 Tbs dry white wine
1 Tbs butter
1 Tbs flour
1 cup milk
4 Tbs grated Parmesan cheese
1 Tbs heavy cream
grated Parmesan cheese
melted butter

Preheat oven to 350°. Place fillets in a buttered baking dish. Add lemon juice, water, ¼ cup wine, garlic, peppercorns and onion. Moisten fish with this mixture and cover loosely with foil or buttered wax paper. Put in the oven to braise for 15 minutes. Carefully remove fish without breaking fillets and keep hot. Reduce the braising liquids quickly to 2 tablespoons by boiling down.

Meanwhile, blanch the cabbage by placing it in cold water and bringing to a boil slowly. Drain well. Put in a pot with the 3 tablespoons of butter, salt and pepper to taste and 2 tablespoons of wine. Cover and simmer until tender, gently.

At the same time, melt the 1 tablespoon of butter in a pan. Lower heat and add flour and blend well. Season to taste with salt and white pepper and add milk. Cook, stirring, until the sauce thickens. Add the cheese and blend. Add the reduced liquid from braising the flounder and the cream and blend.

While you are blending the sauce, preheat the broiler. Spread the cooked cabbage on a hot ovenproof platter, lay the flounder fillets gently on the cabbage and cover with the sauce. Sprinkle liberally with cheese and a little melted butter to moisten and brown lightly under the broiler. Serve hot.

This is a fine recipe for any white fish fillets, especially flat fish like sole, halibut or brill.

COD À L'ALSACIENNE (Cold)
TO SERVE 4

2 lbs cod, in pieces, seasoned
1 cup dry white wine
1 medium onion, minced
2 garlic cloves, minced
1 tsp basil
½ tsp chervil
½ tsp thyme
cheesecloth, washed

1 Tbs olive oil
¼ cup shallots, chopped (or
   green onions)
1 Tbs flour
½ cup water
½ cup dry white wine
chives

Put the fish, 1 cup wine, onion and garlic in a bowl with the basil, chervil and thyme tied in cheesecloth. Cover tightly and marinate for 10 hours, or over-night, tossing occasionally. Remove fish gently from marinade, strain the marinade and reserve.

Heat the oil in a pan and cook the shallots until tender but not browned. Stir in the flour and blend well. Slowly add the water, ½ cup wine and reserved marinade and blend well. Bring to a boil. Lower heat, add fish and simmer very gently until done, about 15 minutes. Remove fish carefully and arrange on a platter. Cook the sauce down to half, pour over the fish and sprinkle generously with chives. Cover and chill thoroughly before serving. (This is best prepared ahead and served chilled the following day.)

CONSOMMÉ À L'ALSACIENNE
TO SERVE 4

1 qt chicken consommé*	2 Strasbourg sausages (or
1 cup coarsely chopped	knackwurst or frankfurters),
sauerkraut, cooked in	cooked, skinned and sliced
chicken broth and drained	thin

Heat the consommé. Add the sauerkraut and sliced sausages and simmer a few minutes to heat through and blend the flavors. Serve hot.

APRICOT TARTLETS À L'ALSACIENNE
TO SERVE 4

4 prebaked, caramelized tart	1 egg yolk
crusts,* empty	¼ cup flour
¼ cup sugar	1 egg
½ cup water	1¼ cups milk, brought to a boil
8 dried apricots	1 tsp banana extract
7 Tbs sugar	1 Tbs butter, softened (optional)

Cool and unmold the tartlet crusts. Melt the ¼ cup sugar in the water in a pan and add the apricots. Simmer for 10 minutes and let the apricots cool in the syrup.

Put the 7 tablespoons of sugar and egg yolk in a pan (do not use aluminum, as it will discolor the finished cream) and beat together with a whisk or wooden spoon until they are completely blended. The mixture should be thick, white and creamy. Add the flour and whole egg and beat until completely blended. Put over low heat, beating constantly, until warm but not hot. Add the boiling milk, stir-ring vigorously, and blend. Continue cooking and stirring. Do not let the mixture stick to the pan bottom. When it begins bubbling, cook for 2 minutes longer. Remove from heat and blend in the banana extract, and butter if desired. Cut the apricots, drained, into large pieces and place in the pastry shells. Pour over the creamy mixture, which is called Crème Pâtissière (*pâtissière* means pastrycook). Serve cool or semichilled.

Amandine

(ah-mahn-DEEN)

In cooking, a dish featuring almonds. The almond, generally thought of as a true nut, is actually the kernel from inside the pit of the almond tree fruit—similar to the kernel found inside the pit of a peach. The resemblance of the almond tree and fruit to the peach suggests a common remote ancestry. However, while the peach is native to China, the almond appears to have originated along the southern and eastern shores of the Mediterranean.

Amandine is not a regional style of cooking, but rather the use of a particular ingredient, almonds.

How and when you choose to use almonds is up to your taste at the moment. There is a general guideline, however. Since almonds have a distinctive flavor, they are generally most effective when used in otherwise fairly bland dishes, as reflected in the recipes here. For this reason, they are excellent accompaniments for chicken, eggs and fish.

Suprêmes de volaille (boneless skinless breasts) are very good made according to the recipe for sole fillets. Simply substitute 8 suprêmes, made from 4 large chicken breasts, for the 2 pounds of sole fillets, and proceed as directed.

BLANCHING ALMONDS

Blanch almonds by dropping into a pot of boiling water. Remove from heat and let stand 3 minutes. Drain and rinse under cold water and remove the brown skin.

ALMOND BUTTER
TO MAKE 1 CUP

½ cup almonds   ½ cup butter, softened

Blanch the almonds and mash to a fine paste with a few drops of water (the water will prevent the paste from becoming oily). Blend with the butter and strain through a fine sieve.

Almond butter is used as a garnish for cold hors d'oeuvres and as a flavoring in soups and sauces.

NOODLES AMANDINE
TO SERVE 4

½ cup almonds, blanched and
   slivered
1 Tbs butter
½ lb mushrooms, sliced
2 Tbs butter
1 Tbs grated onion

1 grated garlic clove
2 cups Cream Sauce, hot
1 lb noodles, freshly cooked,
   drained and hot
grated Parmesan cheese

Sauté the almonds in 1 tablespoon butter until browned. Sauté the mushrooms lightly in 2 tablespoons butter. Add the onion and garlic to the mushrooms and blend well. Blend the almond and mushroom mixtures and stir in the Cream Sauce. Toss the noodles in this sauce, sprinkle liberally with cheese and serve at once, hot.

BROCCOLI AMANDINE
TO SERVE 4

1½ lbs broccoli flowerets,
   cooked and hot
salt and pepper
1 fresh lemon, halved (or lemon
   juice)

½ cup almonds, blanched and
   shredded
1 garlic clove, minced fine
2 Tbs butter

Season the broccoli as desired with salt and pepper and squeeze several drops of lemon juice on to taste. Meanwhile, sauté the almonds and garlic in the butter until lightly browned. Pour over the broccoli and serve hot.

This is also excellent using green beans in place of the broccoli.

ASPARAGUS AMANDINE (With Sauce Smitane)
TO SERVE 4

1½ Tbs grated onion
1 Tbs butter
½ cup dry white wine
1 cup sour cream
salt and pepper

1½ lbs asparagus, cooked
¾ cup almonds, blanched and
   ground
¾ cup bread crumbs,
   moistened with 1½ Tbs
   melted butter

Sauté the onion very gently in the butter for 5 minutes, without browning. Add wine and cook until gone. Stir in the sour cream and blend. Bring to a boil, season to taste with salt and pepper and strain. This is Sauce Smitane.

Preheat broiler. Arrange the asparagus in a shallow buttered baking dish, and pour over the Sauce Smitane. Top with the ground almonds. Sprinkle with the crumbs. Run under the broiler to brown and serve hot, right in the baking dish.

Sauce Smitane is good with almost anything. Try it; I think you'll agree!

CHICKEN AMANDINE
TO SERVE 4

1 chicken
salt and white pepper
butter
2 oz Madeira wine mixed with 1 oz brandy, warmed
4 tomatoes, peeled* and sliced
2 tsp tomato paste
2 Tbs flour

salt and pepper
1 cup chicken stock* or broth
½ cup sour cream
¼ cup almonds, blanched and powdered in a blender
1 bay leaf
½ cup almonds, blanched and slivered
2 Tbs butter, melted

Preheat oven to 350°. Season the chicken inside and out with salt and white pepper and truss. Brown in butter in a baking pan. Discard excess fat, if any. Ignite the warm Madeira and brandy and pour over the chicken, spooning over until the fire dies. Set the chicken aside and add the tomatoes to the pan, simmering until limp. Remove from heat and blend in the tomato paste, flour and salt and pepper to taste. Blend in the stock. Return to heat and bring slowly to a boil. Reduce heat and blend in sour cream, a little at a time. Mix in the powdered almonds and bay leaf. Return the chicken to the pan and bake uncovered for 45 to 50 minutes, basting frequently.

When done, set chicken aside and heat broiler. Carve the chicken into serving pieces and arrange on a heat-proof serving platter. Spoon over the pan sauce. Sprinkle with the slivered almonds and butter and run under the broiler to brown the almonds and glaze. Serve hot.

CHICKEN MOUSSE AMANDINE
TO SERVE 4

1 envelope unflavored gelatin
2 cups chicken stock* or broth
¼ tsp paprika
white pepper
2 egg yolks, beaten
3 oz Madeira wine

½ cup almonds, blanched, toasted and powdered in a blender
1½ cups cooked chicken meat, ground several times
1 cup heavy cream, whipped

Put the gelatin and a little of the chicken stock in the top of a double boiler and cook until melted completely. Add remaining stock, paprika, a little white pepper to taste and yolks. Cook in the double boiler, stirring, until thickened.

Remove from heat, blend in Madeira and chill until the mixture begins to set. Fold in the powdered almonds, chicken and cream. Pour into a well-buttered mold and chill thoroughly. When firm, unmold and served chilled.

MUSHROOM OMELET AMANDINE
TO SERVE 2

1 tsp shallots, minced
4 Tbs tarragon butter (see Estragon)
¼ cup almonds, blanched and slivered
1 Tbs butter
4 eggs

1 oz Madeira wine
1 oz cream
salt and pepper
1 cup tiny mushroom caps, sautéed in butter and hot

Sauté the shallots in the tarragon butter until limp but not browned. In a separate pan, sauté the almonds in the butter slowly until browned. Drain and set aside. Beat the eggs lightly in a bowl. Add wine, cream and salt and pepper to taste and blend well. Pour the eggs into the pan with the hot tarragon butter and shallots and cook the omelet.* When ready, fill the omelet with the almonds and half the mushrooms. Slide onto a hot plate when done and garnish with the remaining mushrooms arranged in a line down the center of the omelet. Serve at once, hot.

SCRAMBLED EGGS are good topped with toasted slivered almonds.

POACHED EGGS or soft-boiled eggs are excellent served on hot buttered toast with a dollop of Almond Butter melting on top.

SOLE FILLETS AMANDINE
TO SERVE 4

2 lbs sole fillets
beer
flour
2 Tbs peanut oil
2 Tbs butter
salt and pepper
¼ cup blanched, slivered almonds

2 Tbs orange juice
2 Tbs dry white wine
2 Tbs heavy cream
2 Tbs chives
1 orange, peeled and sectioned, with thin skins and seeds removed

Dip the fillets in beer, then dredge in flour, shaking off the excess. Sauté in hot oil and butter until done and season to taste with salt and pepper. Arrange on a hot platter and keep hot. Add the almonds, orange juice, wine and cream to the pan juices and cook, stirring, until lightly browned. Pour over the fish, sprinkle with chives and decorate with the orange sections. Serve hot.

This recipe is excellent with any white-fleshed fish, with eel or with soft-shell crab.

For a variation, add ¼ cup of dry red wine (or red wine vinegar) in place of the orange juice and white wine. Blend with the pan juices and quickly boil down until almost gone. Then blend in ½ cup of heavy cream and cook to thicken lightly before pouring over the fish.

CHOCOLATE TART AMANDINE
TO SERVE 4–8

1 unbaked piecrust*
5 egg yolks
½ cup sugar
¼ cup almonds, toasted* and
   powdered

½ cup cocoa powder (un-
   sweetened)
5 egg whites, beaten stiff, with a
   small pinch of cream of tartar
slivered almonds, toasted*

Line a pie dish with the piecrust. Preheat oven to 350°. Beat egg yolks until light-colored. Slowly beat in the sugar and powdered almonds. Fold the cocoa into the beaten egg whites a spoonful at a time until mixed. Combine the 2 mixtures gently and pour into the pie dish. Sprinkle with slivered almonds to taste. Bake for about 25 minutes, or until the crust is done and the tart lightly browned. Serve cool.

Ancienne

(awn-SYEN)

Means old, ancient. In cooking, it means preparations according to the old school in France, usually elaborate and with mixed garnishes. Most recipes are braises or stews, cooked long and slowly to tenderize the tough meats typical of the day. Ragouts in pastry shells are also common fare here. The garnishes often feature cockscombs, kidneys, truffles and mushrooms. A characteristic dish is the Rump of Beef à l'Ancienne. The calf's head recipe seems the zenith of this style of cooking.

To round out any menu featuring an Ancienne main course, the Ancienne garnishes are more than adequate. However, you may wish to use a lighter-green vegetable like peas, beans or broccoli, simply cooked, in place of some of the heavier Ancienne garnishes. For wines, stick to the spirit of Ancienne cooking with the old standard reds and whites, which, incidentally, are still the finest in the world.

For décor, project yourself into the past of France. Elegantly decorated china, elaborate old serving dishes, frills and laces. Get in the mood, and scrounge around and see what you can find that fits. Something like old harpsichord music might be nice for background.

Many of these recipes, although time-consuming, are a great deal of fun. They recall an atmosphere of unhurried time and respect for a well-prepared dish —the opposite of today's scurrying to do five things at once, all poorly. These dishes virtually demand slowing down to spend a day in the kitchen. And even if you can find a way to make a complex dish à l'Ancienne while doing other things, I wish you wouldn't. I wish you'd take a whole day and let yourself slide back a few centuries while you work in the kitchen. It's an elixir; ask any doctor.

ANCIENNE SAUCE
TO MAKE 2 CUPS

¾ cup vegetable mirepoix
1 oz Madeira wine

1½ cups Sauce Suprême*
salt and pepper, if necessary

Heat the vegetable mirepoix with the Madeira for a few minutes and stir in the Sauce Suprême. Heat, season if necessary and serve hot with eggs, poultry or vegetables.

ANCIENNE GARNISHES
TO SERVE 4

1. CHICKEN FORCEMEAT (Stuffing) BALLS À L'ANCIENNE

1 lb raw chicken meat, ground
  or minced fine
salt and pepper to taste
¼ tsp ground cinnamon
⅛ ground nutmeg
1/16 ground cloves
2–4 Tbs truffles, minced (optional)

2 cups soft, white bread crumbs
¾ cup milk, scalded
¼ tsp ground sage
1 oz butter, softened
2 egg whites, well beaten
4 egg yolks, beaten (more if
  needed)
fat for deep frying, or chicken
  stock* or broth for simmering

Season the chicken with salt, pepper, cinnamon, nutmeg and cloves and mix with the truffles. Mix crumbs, milk and sage and pound in a mortar, making a smooth paste. Blend in the butter and chicken. Fold in the egg whites and mix gently but well. Form into walnut-size balls, dip in yolks and deep-fry in hot fat or simmer in hot stock or broth, gently, or cook in a medium (350°) oven until done and golden. Serve hot.

2. LAMB SWEETBREADS À L'ANCIENNE

1 lb lamb sweetbreads

1 cup veal stock* or chicken stock*

Soak the sweetbreads in cold water for 4 hours, changing water frequently. Place them in cold water to cover and slowly bring to a boil to blanch. Simmer for 2 minutes, drain and rinse thoroughly in cold water. Trim away all sinews and blood vessels, but do not remove enclosing membrane. Place the sweetbreads on a flat surface and weight lightly to flatten to an even thickness. They should become about ¾ inch thick after 15 minutes. Put the flattened sweetbreads in a large pan so they are in only 1 layer. If necessary, use 2 pans. Add the stock, cover and simmer for about 5 minutes. Uncover, cook the stock down rapidly to about 1 ounce and roll the sweetbreads in this thick, remaining semigel off heat to glaze. Serve at once, if possible, hot.

3. TRUFFLES

1 lb truffles, cut like olives	butter

Sauté the truffles lightly in butter to just semicook, and serve hot.

4. MUSHROOM CAPS

Sauté 8 mushroom caps lightly in butter and serve hot.

5. CRAYFISH TAILS À L'ANCIENNE

1 lb crayfish tails (or baby lobster tails)	salt and pepper
2 cups fish stock* or 1 cup clam juice plus 1 cup dry white wine	½ tsp basil or tarragon (optional)

Simmer the crayfish tails in the stock, lightly seasoned with salt and pepper and flavored with basil or tarragon if desired. As soon as the flesh firms and turns pink and opaque, they're done—about 5 minutes.

These crayfish tails are often cooked in water with a sliced carrot, a sliced onion, salt and pepper and 1 teaspoon parsley, ¼ teaspoon thyme and ¼ bay leaf tied in clean cheesecloth.

6. DUCHESSE POTATO NESTS À L'ANCIENNE

1 lb Duchesse potatoes	2–3 oz thick veal gravy
½ lb calf's kidneys, diced and sautéed in butter	salt and pepper
¼ lb mushrooms, diced and sautéed in butter	

Shape the Duchesse potatoes into small nests, like bird's nests. Mix the kidneys and mushrooms with enough veal gravy to bind and season to taste. Use to fill the potato nests. Brown quickly under a broiler and serve hot.

TURNIPS À L'ANCIENNE
TO SERVE 4

2 lbs turnips, peeled and diced
　large
1/8 tsp grated nutmeg (more if
　desired)
pepper
2 Tbs butter
1 Tbs flour

1 cup veal or chicken stock* or
　gravy
1 Tbs parsley or chives
1–2 tsp sugar (optional)
2 oz heavy cream
2 egg yolks

Cook the turnips in lightly salted water until just tender and done. Season with nutmeg and pepper to taste. Sauté in the butter in a pan slowly for 2 minutes, turning gently. Sprinkle in the flour and blend gently. Slowly stir in the stock. Try not to break up the turnip pieces. Add the parsley or chives, and the sugar if desired. Cover and cook slowly for 10 minutes. Remove from heat. Beat the cream and yolks lightly and blend with some pan juice. Then add to the pan and blend well. Let cook, but not boil, very slowly for a few minutes to heat the yolks and cream. Serve hot.

EGGS À L'ANCIENNE (Poached or Soft-Boiled)
TO SERVE 4

2 cups rice, cooked in beef
　stock*or broth, hot
8 eggs, poached or soft-boiled,
　hot

1/2 cup Sauce Velouté,* hot
1/4 cup truffles, cut in fine strips
　and simmered in 1/4 cup
　Madeira Sauce

Spread the rice on 4 hot plates. Put 2 hot, freshly cooked eggs on the rice on each plate. Spoon the Sauce Velouté over the eggs. Garnish with the truffles in Madeira Sauce and serve at once, hot.

RUMP OF BEEF À L'ANCIENNE
TO SERVE 4–8

1 5-lb rump roast, tied
4 Tbs butter or oil
2 onions, quartered
1 tsp thyme
1 bay leaf
1 garlic clove, crushed
pepper
1/2 cup dry red wine
1 cup beef stock* or broth

1 egg, beaten
bread crumbs
Parmesan cheese, grated
1 Tbs butter, melted
1/2 lb tongue, sliced
1/2 lb mushrooms, sliced
butter
1/4 cup Madeira wine

Preheat oven to 300°. Brown the roast in the butter in a pot large enough to cover. Add onions, thyme, bay leaf, garlic and pepper to taste. Brown. Add wine and stock, cover and braise in the oven for about 2 hours, removing beef before completely done, while it still has some firmness. Drain, saving the braising liquor, and fit into a deep, snug pot and weight the roast down heavily to cool to the shape of the pot.

When fully cool, trim out the roast's center, leaving 1-inch sides and bottom intact. Discard strings. Coat this hollow roast with beaten egg, and press crumbs and cheese into the meat. Put it in a pan, sprinkle with the melted butter and brown briefly at 350° in the oven. Keep hot. Meanwhile, slice the meat taken from the roast's center and sauté it along with the tongue and mushrooms, in a little butter. Discard fat from the reserved braising liquor and add 3 tablespoons of the juice to the sautéing meats along with the Madeira. Let it stew, but not boil, for 5 minutes. Strain before serving. To serve, arrange the sautéed meats in the hollowed roast. Place on a hot platter and serve with the sauce.

STUFFED CALF'S HEAD À L'ANCIENNE
TO SERVE 4–8

1 calf's head, cleaned and
   boned, with brain and tongue
   reserved
6 Tbs flour
1 Tbs salt
4 Tbs cider vinegar
2 onions studded with 4 cloves

2 Tbs parsley
1 tsp thyme
1 bay leaf
cheesecloth, washed
1 lb beef fat, chopped and
   soaked in cold water for 15
   minutes

STUFFING

salt and pepper
ground allspice
2 lb veal, ground
1 cup boiling water
4 Tbs butter

salt
1 cup flour
2 oz cream
4 oz truffles, chopped
2 bacon strips

COOKING

¼ lb bacon rinds
2 carrots, sliced
2 onions, sliced
1 Tbs parsley
¼ tsp thyme

½ bay leaf
1½ cups Madeira wine
2½ cups veal stock* or Jus de
   Veau* or chicken and veal
   stock* or broth

PRESENTATION

1 recipe each Ancienne Garnishes #1, 3, 4 and 5, hot
16 cockscombs, sautéed in
   butter and hot
16 cock's kidneys, sautéed in
   butter and hot

1 cup pitted green olives,
   blanched in boiling water 30
   seconds
1 cup pitted black olives,
   blanched in boiling water 30
   seconds

Boil the calf's head (if you can find a calf's head, you can find a butcher to clean and bone it) in a court bouillon made of the 6 tablespoons of flour mixed with ½ cup cold water and then stirred into 1 gallon of cold water (or enough to cover the head). Pour into a large, deep pot and season with salt and vinegar. Bring to a boil and add the onions studded with cloves, parsley, thyme and bay leaf. Immerse the calf's head (tied in cheesecloth to hold its shape), tongue and brain in the boiling stock. Add beef fat, which will melt and coat the head, keeping it from darkening. Cook for 20 minutes per pound. Remove the brain after 30 minutes and set aside. When done, drain the head, discarding the cheesecloth, and dry. Remove ears and reserve. Spread the head out flat, skin side down, and remove some of the inside lean meat and save. Cut the tongue along its bottom and remove and discard its thick skin.

Before stuffing, season with salt, pepper and allspice. Stuff the head with a forcemeat (stuffing) made of the ground veal mixed with a flour panada made of the boiling water with the 4 tablespoons of butter melted into it, lightly salted, and the cup of flour sieved in slowly while stirring briskly. Let the panada, or paste, cool before using. Mix with the veal and cream, plus the tongue and the flesh removed from the head, both chopped fine, and the chopped truffles. Stuff the head with this mixture, molding it back to its original shape, and sew closed. Cover the cuts made in removing the ears with bacon strips tied securely with string.

In a large braising pot or Dutch oven, brown the bacon rinds, carrots and onions. Add parsley, thyme and bay leaf and the calf's head and simmer slowly, covered, for 15 minutes. Add Madeira and cook down to half. Add stock and ears and finish cooking for 10 minutes per pound, removing ears after 15 minutes. When the head is done, remove from pot. Untie the bacon and replace the ears, holding in place with small skewers. Place the head on a large hot platter. Skim fat from pot and thicken juices by boiling down, if necessary, and pour over the head.

Meanwhile, slice the brains and sauté gently in butter, then arrange on the platter around the calf's head, along with the chicken forcemeat balls, truffles, mushrooms, crayfish, cockscombs, cock's kidneys and olives in separate piles. Serve hot.

Here's a recipe from the old days for the adventuresome. It's a lot of work, but worth it if you want something truly unusual. Your guests are bound to be utterly astounded!

VEAL CHOPS À L'ANCIENNE
TO SERVE 4

4 oz lamb's sweetbreads	4 or 8 veal chops, depending on
butter	size
2 oz cockscombs, diced	salt and pepper
2 oz cock's kidneys, diced	butter
4 oz mushrooms, diced	2 oz Madeira wine
1 oz truffles, diced	¾ cup Sauce Espagnole, or beef
2 oz Madeira wine	gravy
2 oz thick Sauce Velouté*	½ cup cream

Soak the sweetbreads in cold water for 4 hours, changing water often. Dice, and put in a pan with a little butter. Heat, add the cockscombs and kidneys and sauté until almost done. Add the mushrooms and finish cooking. Add truffles and toss lightly. Pour off excess butter, if any, and add Madeira and simmer until the wine is gone. Mix in the Velouté and keep hot.

Meanwhile, season the veal chops to taste and simmer in butter until done over low heat, without browning (a little extra butter in the pan will make it easier to cook the veal without browning). Arrange on a hot platter and garnish with the sweetbread mixture. Keep hot.

Pour butter from the veal pan and add the Madeira. Boil down until almost gone, scraping up the juices. Blend in the Espagnole and cream, cook down slightly to thicken, and strain a little over the chops. Serve the rest, strained, in a sauceboat, hot.

This is just as good with lamb chops, or any cut of veal or lamb suitable for pan-cooking.

LAMB SAUTÉ À L'ANCIENNE (or Veal)
TO SERVE 4

Proceed as for Veal Chops à l'Ancienne, using 2 pounds of lamb (or veal) in small chunks, lean. Use the cockscombs and kidneys, sweetbreads, truffles and mushrooms in bite-size pieces rather than diced, and sauté with the lamb, adding the cockscombs, kidneys and sweetbreads at the start and the mushrooms and truffles near the end of the cooking, since they take less time—particularly the truffles. At the end of cooking, add the Madeira, Espagnole and cream to the pan with the lamb, blending everything well. Let the sauce thicken lightly and serve everything in a hot bowl.

BLANQUETTE of LAMB À L'ANCIENNE (White Ragout)
TO SERVE 4–6

4 lbs lamb, trimmed and cut in
1½-inch pieces
1–2 cups chicken or veal stock*
or Jus de Veau*
2 carrots, quartered
2 medium onions
1 celery stalk
2 leeks, white part only (optional)
1 bay leaf
¼ tsp thyme
1 clove

cheesecloth, washed
salt, if needed
1 cup small onions, cooked in
lightly salted water
1 cup small mushrooms,
sautéed in butter
4 Tbs butter
5 Tbs flour
4 egg yolks
4 Tbs cream
1 pinch nutmeg
¼ tsp lemon juice

Blanch the lamb for 30 seconds in boiling water, rinse and dry. Arrange the lamb in a pan with enough stock to barely cover. Add carrots, onions, celery and leeks. Add the bay leaf, thyme and clove tied in cheesecloth. Season with a little salt if using unsalted stock. Bring to a boil and skim off the top. Cover and simmer gently for 1 hour. Remove lamb and strain and reserve the cooking stock, discarding the herbs and vegetables.

Return the lamb to the pan with the small onions and mushrooms. In a separate pan, make a roux by melting the butter and adding the flour, slowly blending over low heat. Do not allow to brown, since this is a white stew. Slowly add the strained cooking stock and simmer 15 minutes. Skim, strain and pour over the lamb mixture and simmer for 20 more minutes. Meanwhile, in a bowl, blend yolks, cream, nutmeg and lemon juice. Remove lamb from heat and whisk in egg-cream mixture to complete the ragout. Serve hot.

The carrots may be added to the stew at the end, rather than being discarded, or they may be used with the other vegetables simmered with the lamb in a soup.

BLANQUETTE of VEAL À L'ANCIENNE (or Chicken)
TO SERVE 4–6

The same as Blanquette of Lamb, using veal or chicken. This also yields excellent results using pork. However, the pork should only be washed, not blanched, and browned in butter before proceeding. This browning, of course, is dead set against the classic concept of a blanquette, or white stew, and would receive sneers from experts. But it makes a fine dish, so why not?

HAM in PASTRY À L'ANCIENNE
TO SERVE 4–8

1 ham, cooked and hot
piecrust dough* (enough for 3
   10-inch crusts)
1 cup vegetable mirepoix, hot
1 cup duxelles, hot

¼ cup truffles, chopped
2 eggs, beaten
½ cup Sauce Périgueux, hot
   (*see* Périgourdine)

Preheat oven to 450°. Remove skin from the ham, and most of the fat. Roll out the dough on a lightly floured board. Mix the mirepoix, duxelles and truffles and spread in the middle of the pastry, over an area the size and shape of the ham. Put the ham on this bed with its flattest side up, and wrap the pastry around the ham and seal. Turn the ham over onto a buttered baking dish, with the flat, sealed side down and the stuffed side on top. Make a small, circular hole in the crust at the top for the steam to escape, about ½ inch across. Brush the crust with beaten egg and bake for 45 minutes, or until nicely browned. Remove from the oven and pour the sauce in the hole in the crust. Serve on the baking dish, hot.

For an attractive presentation, decorate the pastry with fancy shapes and swirls made from scraps of the dough, before coating with egg and baking.

CHICKEN SAUTÉ À L'ANCIENNE
TO SERVE 4

2 young chickens, cut up
3 Tbs butter (more if needed)
½ cup chicken stock* or broth
1½ tsp flour blended with 1
   ounce cold water

½ cup cream
2 Tbs butter, softened (optional)
2 Tbs truffles, chopped and
   lightly sautéed in butter
½ cup port wine

Sauté chicken in butter until done over low heat, without browning any more than necessary. Add stock. Boil down to half and thicken with the flour-and-water slurry. Blend in cream, butter if desired, truffles and wine and heat quickly. Arrange chicken on a hot platter and serve sauce separately, hot.

FLOUNDER À L'ANCIENNE
TO SERVE 4

½ lb whiting (or pike or other
   light-fleshed fish), flaked
1 egg
¼ cup chopped mushrooms,
   sautéed in butter
2 lbs flounder fillets
salt and pepper
beaten egg
bread crumbs

butter (preferably clarified*)
1 lb small shrimp, cooked
½ lb button mushrooms
¼ lb truffles, diced
butter
¼ cup Sauce Velouté*
1½ cups Sauce Velouté
½ cup heavy cream
2 oz Madeira wine

Mix the whiting, egg and chopped mushrooms and spread on the flounder fillets. Fold the fillets in half with the mixture inside. Score the fillets where they fold so they won't unfold while cooking. Season to taste with salt and pepper and coat with beaten egg and crumbs. Sauté in butter until done and golden. Drain, arrange in a circle on a hot platter and keep hot.

Meanwhile, sauté the shrimp, button mushrooms and truffles together in a little butter. Mix with the ¼ cup Sauce Velouté and pile in the center of the circle of fish on the platter and keep hot.

Quickly add the 1½ cups Sauce Velouté to the fish sauté pan, along with the cream and Madeira. Boil down to thicken slightly, scraping up the juices. Strain into a sauceboat and serve with the fish, hot.

This is excellent with any other flat fish fillets, such as sole or halibut, or any delicate freshwater fish, such as trout, bass or perch.

CRAYFISH TIMBALE À L'ANCIENNE (Pie)
TO SERVE 4

piecrust for a 10-inch pie* (bottom and top crusts)	⅛ tsp pepper
½ lb pike, cooked and flaked	¼ lb chopped truffles, tossed in butter
½ lb beef fat, minced	1 recipe Crayfish à la Nantua, hot
2 eggs	
1 tsp salt	1 egg, beaten
½ tsp pepper	½ cup Sauce Nantua, hot

Preheat oven to 325°. Roll the dough out on a lightly floured board, making top and bottom crusts. Place the bottom crust in a 10-inch pie dish. Mix the pike, beef fat, eggs, salt, pepper, nutmeg and truffles. Spread half this mixture on the bottom piecrust. Fill the pie dish with the Crayfish à la Nantua, and top with the remaining half of the pike mixture. Cover with the top crust and cut a ½-inch hole in its center. Brush the crust (decorated with crust swirls and flowerets if desired) with the beaten egg and bake for about 1 hour, until browned and done. Remove from the oven, pour the Sauce Nantua in through the hole in the crust and serve hot. (If the crust browns too much, cover loosely with foil.)

APRICOT GENOISE À L'ANCIENNE (Cake)
TO SERVE 4–8

6 eggs	¼ cup butter (preferably clarified*), melted but cool
1 cup sugar	
1 tsp banana extract	1 cup apricot jam
1¼ cups flour	

FROSTING

4 egg whites	1 tsp banana extract
1 cup fine sugar	3 canned apricots, quartered lengthwise

Preheat oven to 350°. Beat the eggs and 1 cup sugar with a mixer on low speed in the top of a double broiler over (but not touching) simmering water. Beat until the mixture is hot to the touch. Remove from the heat and beat rapidly until cool, about 10 minutes. By now it should have tripled in volume and would form a ribbon if poured. Beat in the banana extract. Transfer gently to a large bowl. Add a little flour and fold in gently. Add a little butter and fold in gently. Alternate adding flour and butter until all is folded in. Pour into 2 9-inch layer-cake pans that are buttered and lightly dusted with flour. Bake in the oven until done, about 20 to 25 minutes. Turn onto a rack to cool as soon as the pans leave the oven. Raise oven to 500°.

Cook the jam quickly over high heat to melt, stirring. Rub through a fine sieve. Cut the cake, after fully cool, in halves horizontally, making 4 thin layers. Spread the layers with the hot apricot purée and stack to make a 4-layer cake.

Put the egg whites and fine sugar in the top of a double boiler and beat with a whisk over hot water until the eggs start to form soft peaks, about 7 or 8 minutes. Remove from heat and beat until just stiff, adding the banana extract bit by bit toward the end. Spread this meringue on the cake sides and top, and decorate with apricot quarters. Put in the 500° oven for 3 to 4 minutes to heat and toast lightly. Serve hot or cooled. Do not chill, and use as soon as possible.

Anglaise

(awn-GLEZ)

Means English or British. The French don't think much of English cooking, but then they don't think much of Italian cooking, German cooking, Russian cooking, Chinese cooking, Swedish, Indian, Hungarian . . .

Cooking à l'Anglaise is typically boiling, poaching or frying. Most dishes are relatively simple to prepare and often completely ungarnished. Very simple fare, by French standards. Vegetables cooked à l'Anglaise (boiled in lightly salted water) are also called au Naturel. Most typical are the recipes of breaded, sautéed meats, and vegetables dressed with Butter Sauce.

Any meats or vegetables may be prepared à l'Anglaise. Fried oysters are a common example. These dishes are so simple and direct, I really can't think of any way they could detract from other courses in different styles. Anglaise dishes make excellent accompaniments to almost any other dish, main course or otherwise. For instance, you might elect to serve Fish à l'Anglaise as a first course, then a salad course, then Beef à la Bourguignonne. Anglaise is great for this type of varied menu, and the possibilities are unlimited.

The wines of England are limited, the reason being that it was simpler to take the superior wines of France than to grow their own. Wine was produced in England on a large scale until the vineyards of Bordeaux became open to England by the marriage of Eleanor of Aquitaine to King Henry II of England in 1152. The queen's lands included the Bordeaux vineyards, the wines of which greatly overshadowed the English wines, so the English merely took the Bordeaux wines for their own use, and wine as a major agricultural industry in England was virtually dead for all time.

England's cheeses are varied and noteworthy, Banbury is a soft and pleasant cheese. Wensleydale is a firm, flaky cheese first made over 1,000 years ago in medieval abbeys in Yorkshire. Its pungent flavor is still a favorite with apple pie. England also gives us the great blue-green Stilton, with the subtle flavor so exquisite with bland crackers and port wine. And finally, cheddar, which originated in a Somerset village where cheese is no longer made at all!

In Anglaise cooking the idea is simplicity and elegance, and this should carry over into the décor for the occasion. A plain but fine white tablecloth with just a few roses for a centerpiece would be nice, with silver, fine china and crystal. Sherry or port would be fitting for after dinner, quite.

ANGLAISE (Egg Coating for Meats to Be Breaded)

1 egg	½ tsp salt
1½ tsp oil	⅛ tsp pepper
1 tsp water	white bread crumbs

Mix the ingredients by beating with a fork until well blended. To use, first dip the meat to be breaded in flour and shake off the excess. Next brush with a little Anglaise on one side, and invert the meat onto bread crumbs, Anglaise side down. Brush the second side with Anglaise. Sprinkle with crumbs and press lightly with wax paper so the crumbs will adhere. Shake off excess crumbs. The meats can be cooked at once, or kept for a short time in the refrigerator.

BREAD SAUCE (for Poultry and Game Birds)
TO MAKE 2 CUPS

2 cups milk	2 cloves
½ cup white bread crumbs	1 oz butter
salt and pepper	2 oz cream
2 small onions, quartered	

Bring the milk to a boil and add the crumbs, salt and pepper to taste, onions and cloves. Simmer 15 minutes. Add the butter and cream and cook 5 more minutes. Discard the onions and cloves and beat the sauce with a whisk over medium heat until smooth and thickened. Serve hot.

BUTTER SAUCE À L'ANGLAISE
TO MAKE 2 CUPS

4 Tbs butter
5 Tbs flour
2 cups boiling water
8 Tbs butter (1 stick), diced

salt and pepper
lemon juice
2–4 tsp capers, chopped

Blend the butter and flour in a pan over medium heat. Add the water and blend well. Incorporate the diced butter and season to taste with salt and pepper. Add a few drops of lemon juice to taste, stir in the capers and serve hot with vegetables and boiled foods, such as fish.

SAUCE ALBONI (for Game)
TO MAKE 2 CUPS

4 oz dry white wine
2 tsp parsley
½ tsp thyme
½ bay leaf
4 juniper berries

cheesecloth, washed
2 cups Sauce Espagnole
2–3 Tbs red currant jelly (more or
    less, to taste)

Put the wine in a rather small pan and add the parsley, thyme, bay leaf and juniper berries tied in cheesecloth. Simmer for 2 to 3 minutes slowly. Add the Espagnole and simmer 8 minutes more, or until properly thickened. Discard the herb bouquet. Stir in the red currant jelly and blend well. Serve hot.

ANGLAISE GARNISHES

The typical elaborate French garnishes are totally missing from this category. In their place, simple vegetables are served: carrots or turnips cut in oval shapes and cooked in chicken broth, or green beans, peas, brussels sprouts, onions, celery hearts or cauliflower similarly cooked and served with Butter Sauce.

RICE À L'ANGLAISE
TO SERVE 4

1 cup raw rice
5 qts hard-boiling, lightly salted
    water

salt and white pepper
2–3 Tbs butter, diced

Sprinkle the rice into the boiling water, a bit at a time so the water does not stop boiling. Stir once after all the rice is in to be sure none is sticking to the bottom. Boil 15 to 18 minutes, or until just done but still firm. Rinse under running water. Drain in a colander. When drained, set the colander and rice over boiling water, lightly covered with a towel, to steam for 10 minutes, or until fully tender. Pour the rice into a hot bowl, season to taste and blend in the butter by tossing lightly with forks. Serve at once, hot.

WHITE BEANS À L'ANGLAISE (Dried)
TO SERVE 4

1 Tbs parsley	cheesecloth, washed
½ tsp thyme	1 qt water, boiling rapidly
½ tsp chervil	salt and pepper
½ bay leaf	1 cup dried white beans

Tie the parsley, thyme, chervil and bay leaf in cheesecloth and put in the pot with the boiling water. Season to taste with salt and pepper. Add the beans and simmer until done and tender, 2 to 3 hours. Discard the herb bouquet and serve hot.

GREEN BEANS, BEETS, POTATOES, SPINACH À L'ANGLAISE
TO SERVE 4

Boil 1½ pounds of spinach, beans or beets, or 2 pounds of potatoes, in water until just done and tender. Season to taste and dress with a little butter. Serve hot.

Any vegetable prepared this way is a vegetable à l'Anglaise.

EGGS À L'ANGLAISE (Baked)
TO SERVE 4

12 bacon strips, fried and drained	butter
8 eggs	pepper

Preheat oven to 500°. Put 3 bacon strips in each of 4 buttered individual baking dishes. Break 2 eggs in each, being careful not to break the yolks. Season to taste with pepper. Bake on a high rack in the oven for 4 minutes, or until the whites are just set and the yolks still soft. Serve at once, hot, in the baking dishes.

EGGS À L'ANGLAISE (Fried)
TO SERVE 4

8 eggs	salt and pepper
8 bread slices	1 cup thick veal stock* or gravy, hot
butter	

Fry the eggs and the bread separately in butter. Place 2 bread slices on each of 4 hot plates and top with the eggs. Season to taste with salt and pepper and serve hot, with a little dab of stock on each egg.

This makes a nice presentation if the bread is cut in rounds and the eggs are trimmed of their ragged edges into rounds to fit the bread slices. Watercress makes a good garnish.

BEEF RIB ROAST À L'ANGLAISE
TO SERVE 4

1 standing rib roast of beef (at least 4 ribs)	salt and pepper

YORKSHIRE PUDDING

1 cup flour	2 eggs, beaten
1 cup milk	salt, pepper, grated nutmeg

Preheat oven to 325° and bake roast for 25 minutes per pound. Season with salt and pepper to taste when half done. This will yield perfect well-done outside ribs and rare inside ones. If desired, add 5 minutes per pound for medium inside ribs.

Make Yorkshire Pudding mixture by beating together flour, milk and eggs and seasoning to taste with salt, pepper and a little nutmeg. Fifteen minutes before roast is done, take it from the oven and pour its drippings into a pan about 9 inches square and 2 inches deep. Fill this pan with Yorkshire Pudding mixture, raise oven to 425° and return the roast and pudding to the oven. When the roast is done (in 10 minutes), remove from the oven and let stand in a warm place to set the juices. Let the pudding bake for 20 minutes more, or until done. Cut the pudding into squares and serve hot with the roast.

Test the Yorkshire Pudding as you would a layer cake for doneness, with a cake tester. If no dough sticks to the tester when the pudding is pricked, the pudding is done.

This is a dish of elegance and simplicity. I can't think of anything better in any style of cooking.

BEEF PIE À L'ANGLAISE
TO SERVE 4

3 lbs beef, cut in cubes	2 medium potatoes, cubed
1 onion, chopped	2 oz water
1 Tbs parsley	1 top piecrust* for an 8-inch pie
salt, pepper and grated nutmeg	

Preheat oven to 350°. Mix the beef with the onion and parsley and season to taste with salt, pepper and a little nutmeg. Put in a buttered casserole or deep pie dish and push the potatoes into the center of the beef. Add the water and cover with crust, pierced to allow steam to escape. Decorate the crust with pastry flowerets and designs if desired. Bake in the oven for 1½ to 2 hours, until browned and done, and serve hot. (If the crust becomes too brown, lay a piece of foil over to prevent further browning.)

This simple recipe is a nice change of pace for company, and the aroma while it's cooking is delightful.

VEAL ESCALOPES À L'ANGLAISE
TO SERVE 4

2 lbs veal cutlets	bread crumbs
salt and white pepper	butter
Anglaise, or beaten eggs	lemon juice

Flatten the escalopes with a mallet and season very lightly with salt and pepper. Dip in Anglaise, coat with crumbs and sauté in butter until just done —about 3 to 4 minutes per side. Do not overcook. Pile the cooked escalopes on a hot serving dish, sprinkle with hot noisette butter and serve at once, hot.

Noisette literally means hazelnut. Noisette butter is butter cooked in a pan until it turns a light-brown, or hazelnut, color. Add a few drops of lemon juice to the brown butter to taste and pour hot over the meat.

LEG of LAMB À L'ANGLAISE
TO SERVE 4–8

1 lamb leg, boned	1 clove
salt and pepper	1 Tbs parsley
muslin, or cheesecloth	½ tsp thyme
butter, softened	½ tsp chervil
flour	½ bay leaf
4 carrots, quartered	cheesecloth, washed
4 onions, quartered	2 garlic cloves

SAUCE

2–3 tsp capers, drained

1½ cups Beurre Maître d'Hôtel

Season the lamb with salt and pepper to taste, inside and out. Tie into original shape with string. Wrap in a clean, white piece of washed muslin cloth and tie. Spread with a little butter and dust lightly with flour. Put in a large pot. Add enough lightly salted water to just cover the lamb in the pot. Bring to a boil and add the carrots, onions and clove. Tie the parsley, thyme, chervil and bay leaf in cheesecloth and add to the pot. Add the garlic. Simmer, covered, for 18 minutes per pound. Drain the lamb and unwrap and untie it. Arrange on a hot platter with the carrots and onions. Keep hot.

Meanwhile, heat the Beurre Maître d'Hôtel and capers in a small pan. When the lamb is done, add ½ cup of its strained cooking liquid to the Beurre Maître d'Hôtel and blend well. Pour a little over the lamb, and serve the rest separately, hot.

Leg of Lamb à l'Anglaise is often served with a turnip purée. Mash well-cooked turnips and blend with cream or butter to taste. Season with a little salt and white pepper and serve hot. It's just like mashed potatoes.

LAMB BREAST À L'ANGLAISE
TO SERVE 4

1 tsp parsley	butter
¼ tsp thyme	2-lb boneless breast of lamb
¼ bay leaf	1 cup chicken stock* or broth
½ tsp basil	salt and pepper
cheesecloth, washed	beaten eggs
1 carrot, chopped	bread crumbs
1 onion, chopped	butter (preferably clarified*)
1 celery stalk, chopped	½ cup Beurre Maître d'Hôtel, diced

Tie the parsley, thyme, bay leaf and basil in cheesecloth and put in a pan. Brown the carrot, onion and celery in a little butter and add to the pan. Lay the lamb breast on this vegetable bed and add the stock. Season lightly with salt and pepper and simmer, covered, for 1 to 1½ hours, until done and tender. Remove the lamb to a plate and weight down to flatten as it cools. Cut the cooled, flattened lamb into 1½-inch square pieces. Dip in egg and crumbs and sauté until golden in butter. Serve hot, with pieces of Beurre Maître d'Hôtel melting on the lamb.

LAMB RAGOUT À L'ANGLAISE (Stew)
TO SERVE 4

1 tsp parsley	3 medium onions, sliced thick
½ tsp basil	2 cups chicken stock* or broth
¼ tsp thyme	salt and pepper
½ bay leaf	2 lbs lean lamb chunks
cheesecloth, washed	parsley sprigs
4 medium potatoes, sliced thick	

Tie the parsley, basil, thyme and bay leaf in cheesecloth and put in a pot with the potatoes, onions and stock. Season to taste with salt and pepper. Add the lamb, cover and simmer for 1½ hours. Remove cover and quickly boil down the liquid, if necessary, until just a little remains. Serve hot, decorated with parsley sprigs.

LAMB CHOPS À L'ANGLAISE
TO SERVE 4

8 thick lamb chops	bread crumbs
salt and pepper	3–4 Tbs butter
Anglaise, or 2 beaten eggs	

Season the lamb chops with salt and pepper to taste. Dip in Anglaise and crumbs and sauté in butter until done. Serve hot.

This dish is usually served with boiled potatoes and a green vegetable, both tossed in a little butter.

LEG of MUTTON À L'ANGLAISE
TO SERVE 4–8

Proceed as for Leg of Lamb à l'Anglaise, serving with a purée of celery instead of the turnip purée, if desired. Make celery purée by blanching the celery in boiling water for 1 minute, then simmering in a little butter until very tender. Rub through a sieve and blend with a little thick Sauce Béchamel to bind. Season with salt and white pepper to taste and serve hot.

MUTTON RAGOUT À L'ANGLAISE (Irish Stew)
TO SERVE 4

Proceed as for Lamb Ragout à l'Anglaise, using mutton in place of the lamb. Water may be used in place of the chicken stock★, but the flavor will not be as well rounded.

MUTTON CHOPS À L'ANGLAISE
TO SERVE 4

Proceed as for Lamb Chops à l'Anglaise, using 4 large double mutton chops in place of the 8 lamb chops.

CALF'S LIVER À L'ANGLAISE
TO SERVE 4

2 lbs calf's liver, sliced	2 lbs potatoes, peeled and of the
salt and pepper	same size (small)
flour	salt and pepper
butter	1 Tbs parsley
8 bacon strips	lemon juice

Season the liver slices with salt and pepper and dredge in flour, shaking off the excess. Sauté until done and golden in butter. Remove from the pan and drain. Arrange on a hot platter and keep hot. Add the bacon to the pan and sauté until done. Drain and arrange on the platter with the liver.

Meanwhile, boil the potatoes in lightly salted water until done and drain. Season to taste with salt and pepper and arrange with the liver and bacon on the platter. Sprinkle with the parsley and a few drops of lemon juice to taste. Pour the liver pan juices over the potatoes. Serve hot.

ROAST CHICKEN À L'ANGLAISE
TO SERVE 4

3 onions, unpeeled	salt and pepper
1 oz butter	2 small chickens
2 cups bread crumbs	salt and pepper
1 cup milk	8 bacon slices
½ cup veal fat, chopped	8 pork sausages
½ tsp sage	2 cups Bread Sauce, hot

Preheat oven to 375°. Prepare a stuffing by baking the onions in the oven for 15 minutes. Peel the onions and dice. Sauté in the butter until limp but not browned. Soak the crumbs in the milk and squeeze dry. Mix with the onions, veal fat and sage, and season with salt and pepper to taste.

Season the chickens inside and out with salt and pepper and stuff. Sew or skewer closed and truss the legs and wings to the body. Bake in the 375° oven for about 40 minutes per pound, or until done and golden. Meanwhile, sauté the bacon and sausages until done and drain. Keep hot. Put the birds on a hot platter and untruss. Surround with the bacon and sausages and serve hot, with the sauce separate.

CHICKEN CUTLETS À L'ANGLAISE
TO SERVE 4

4 chicken breasts, halved, skinned and boned	bread crumbs
salt and pepper	2 Tbs butter
Anglaise, or 2 beaten eggs	1½ cups veal gravy, hot

Season chicken with salt and pepper to taste. Dip in Anglaise and crumbs and sauté in butter until just done, about 3 to 4 minutes per side. Serve at once, with hot veal gravy served separately.

ROAST TURKEY À L'ANGLAISE
TO SERVE 4–8

Proceed as for Roast Chicken à l'Anglaise, doubling the ingredients and cooking time for a 6- to 8-pound bird.

ROAST DUCK À L'ANGLAISE
TO SERVE 4

6 medium onions, minced	1 tsp sage
3 Tbs butter	¼ tsp mace
4 cups bread crumbs	1 duck, about 5 lbs, all inner fat
milk	removed
salt and pepper	

Preheat oven to 325°. Sauté onions in butter until limp. Soak the bread crumbs in milk and squeeze almost dry. Mix with the onions, season with salt and pepper to taste and blend in the sage and mace. Use this mixture to stuff the duck. Sew or skewer duck closed, truss the wings and legs to the body and prick the skin all over to allow the fat to escape. Bake in the oven for 3 hours, or until done. Serve hot.

This duck is usually served with applesauce. Heat the applesauce with a little cinnamon to taste and serve warm.

GRILLED FISH À L'ANGLAISE
TO SERVE 4

2 lbs fish fillets, or small whole fish, cleaned	salt and pepper
	flour (for delicate fish)
¼ cup butter, melted, or oil	½ cup Beurre Maître d'Hôtel

Coat fish in butter or oil and season to taste with salt and pepper. (Delicate fish, such as flounder or sole fillets, should be dusted with flour before coating with butter.) Cook about 5 inches below a broiler until done. Fish is done when it flakes easily with a fork. Serve hot, with little pieces of Beurre Maître d'Hôtel melting over the fish.

This is a simple but effective way to deal with almost any small fish. If desired, the fish can be sautéed in a pan instead of grilled. In that case, it would be called Fish Sauté à l'Anglaise. The average fisherman who tosses his freshly cleaned catch into a hot, greased pan probably doesn't realize it, but he's cooking à l'Anglaise!

FLOUNDER FILLETS in MILK À L'ANGLAISE
TO SERVE 4

2 lbs flounder fillets	1 qt milk
salt and pepper	2 lbs boiled potatoes

Season the fillets with salt and pepper to taste and poach in simmering milk until done. Serve at once, with hot boiled potatoes seasoned to taste.

This recipe is applicable to any white-fleshed fish fillets.

MACKEREL À L'ANGLAISE
TO SERVE 4

1 cup dry white wine	1½ cups fish fumet* or ¾ cup
1 cup vegetable mirepoix	each white wine and clam
2 lbs mackerel slices	juice

SAUCE

½ oz butter	¼ tsp lemon juice
1 Tbs flour	1 oz butter
1 cup water, very lightly salted	½ cup gooseberries
and boiling	½ cup dry white wine
1 large egg yolk	3 Tbs powdered sugar
1 oz cream	

Mix the wine and vegetable mirepoix and boil down 1/3. Add the fish fumet and simmer for 10 minutes, making a court bouillon for poaching the mackerel. Poach the mackerel in the court bouillon until done. Carefully drain the slices and place on a hot platter without breaking. Keep hot.

Meanwhile, prepare Gooseberry Sauce, which is particularly good with poached mackerel. Melt the ½ ounce butter in a pan and blend in the flour. Blend the water in slowly, stirring and not allowing to reboil. Mix the yolk, cream and lemon juice and blend into the pan mixture. Blend in the 1 ounce butter, and you have a butter sauce. In a separate pan, containing boiling water, boil the gooseberries for 5 minutes and drain. Put the gooseberries in a pan with the wine and sugar. Cook gently, stirring, to make a smooth purée. Rub through a fine sieve into the pan containing the butter sauce. Blend well, and you have Gooseberry Sauce. Serve hot with the mackerel.

BOILED SALMON À L'ANGLAISE
TO SERVE 4

3-lb piece of salmon	2 cups Lobster Sauce,* hot

Poach the salmon in lightly salted water at a gentle simmer until done. Serve immediately with Lobster Sauce, hot.

This dish is customarily served with a cucumber salad. Prepare the salad using peeled, very thinly sliced cucumbers dressed with oil, vinegar, salt and pepper to taste and a little water. The salmon, Lobster Sauce and cucumbers make a fine flavor combination.

SMOKED HADDOCK À L'ANGLAISE
TO SERVE 4

2 lbs smoked haddock	white pepper (optional)
3 cups milk (more if needed)	2 cups Butter Sauce, hot

Put the haddock into a buttered casserole and add milk to cover. Bring to a simmer, lower heat and cook just under a simmer for about 15 minutes. Do not allow to boil. Do *not* add salt. Season with pepper, preferably white, if desired. Serve hot, with hot Butter Sauce.

This dish is customarily served with 1 poached egg per person and garnished with lemon wedges. Small boiled potatoes are also a standard accompaniment.

FROG'S LEGS À L'ANGLAISE
TO SERVE 4

8 pairs of frog's legs (16 legs)
salt and pepper
flour
Anglaise, or beaten eggs

bread crumbs
butter (preferably clarified*)
½ cup Beurre Maître d'Hôtel,
    diced
2 lbs boiled potatoes, hot

Season the frog's legs in salt and pepper to taste and dredge in flour, shaking off the excess. Dip in Anglaise and crumbs and sauté in butter until done and golden. Serve on a hot platter, with the pieces of Beurre Maître d'Hôtel melting on the frog's legs. Serve the potatoes separately, hot.

This dish is called Frog's Legs à l'Anglaise only because of the manner of cooking, that is, dipping in Anglaise and crumbs and sautéing.

CHICKEN SOUP À L'ANGLAISE
TO SERVE 4

½ chicken
1 qt chicken stock* or water
salt (if using unsalted stock or
    water)
1 small onion
1 clove
1 tsp parsley
½ tsp chervil
¼ tsp thyme

½ bay leaf
cheesecloth, washed
1 celery stalk
¼ cup raw rice
¼ cup diced onion
¼ cup diced carrot
¼ diced celery
butter

Put the chicken and stock in a pot and bring to a boil. Cook 15 minutes, skimming. Season with salt to taste if necessary. Add the onion and clove. Add the parsley, chervil, thyme and bay leaf tied in cheesecloth, and the celery and rice. Simmer slowly until well cooked. Take out the half chicken and dice the meat. Discard the skin and bones. Strain the broth and return to the pot with the diced chicken. Meanwhile, sauté the diced onion, carrot and celery in a little butter until limp and add to the soup. Simmer together for 5 minutes and serve hot.

OXTAIL SOUP À L'ANGLAISE
TO SERVE 4

1 lb oxtail
salt and pepper
½ small cabbage, chopped
5 small onions
1 carrot, sliced
1 turnip, diced

1 leek, white part only, sliced
    (optional)
1 Tbs sherry wine
4 chipolata sausages, or
    cocktail sausages, cooked
    and sliced thin

Cut the oxtail in chunks and put in a pot with water to cover. Bring to a boil and skim. Season lightly with salt and pepper and simmer covered for 2 hours. Add the cabbage, onions, carrot, leek and turnip and simmer covered another 2 hours. Add the sherry. Serve hot in a soup tureen, garnished with sliced sausages.

This is a very British soup, if oxtails can be considered to have a nationality.

CRÈME ANGLAISE
TO MAKE 2 CUPS

4 egg yolks	1½ cups scalded milk, hot
6 Tbs sugar	1½ tsp vanilla extract
⅛ tsp salt	

Mix yolks, sugar and salt well in a pan with a whisk, until the mixture is well beaten but not yet thick enough to ribbon. Add the milk very slowly, stirring over low heat. The mixture will foam. Continue stirring. The foam will turn into larger bubbles and finally the surface will be bubble-free and smooth. Remove from the heat and whisk rapidly to stop the cooking and cool the mixture. Beat in the vanilla. Chill. Serve chilled as a dessert sauce for fruits or molded desserts or in place of cream.

CUSTARD À L'ANGLAISE
TO SERVE 4

Proceed as for Crème Anglaise, adding ¾ envelope of unflavored gelatin melted in 2 tablespoons of water over low heat until all the crystals are dissolved. Add with the vanilla. Chill to set and serve topped with fruit. This custard is sometimes sprinkled with icing sugar as well.

Custard à l'Anglaise, or Crème Anglaise, may be flavored with 1 ounce of liqueur in place of the vanilla extract. Any flavored liqueur is delightful, but the color of cherry cordial is especially pleasing.

FRUIT TART À L'ANGLAISE
TO SERVE 4

1 cup water	pastry crust* for the bottom of a
1 cup sugar	9-inch pie dish
1 tsp vanilla extract	4 tart cooking apples, peeled,
1 cup peach slices	cored and sliced
1 cup banana slices	½ cup sugar
1 cup pear slices	

Mix the water and 1 cup sugar and bring to a boil. Add the vanilla and simmer for 6 to 7 minutes, forming a syrup. Add the fruits to the simmering syrup, a few pieces at a time, and cook for a few minutes to heat through the glaze. Put the glazed fruit in a bowl. Boil down the remaining syrup to a thick glaze, pour over the fruit and chill.

Meanwhile, preheat oven to 350°. Roll out the crust and use to make the bottom crust for a 9-inch pie dish. Chill. Fill with the chilled glazed fruit. Top with the apple slices. Sprinkle with the ½ cup sugar and bake for 35 minutes, or until done. Serve chilled.

This is a fine and fairly simple fruit tart and is excellent with almost any assortment of glazed fresh fruits, topped with the tart cooking apples and sugar.

ALMOND CUSTARD ANGLAISE
TO MAKE 2½ CUPS

2 cups Custard à l'Anglaise   ½ cup Almond Butter
¼ cup sugar

Prepare the Custard à l'Anglaise and let cool. Beat the sugar into the Almond Butter, and then little by little beat the almond mixture into the custard until blended. Pour into a well-buttered mold and chill. Unmold and serve chilled, alone or with fruits. Or serve in tart shells topped with fruit and whipped cream.

This is a fine flavorful custard in itself, and combined with fresh fruits makes an exquisite tart filling.

Anna

(ah-NAH)

The name given to a particular potato dish, Potatoes Anna, which was created by the great French chef Dugléré. The term Anna is also applied to foods served on a bed of Potatoes Anna.

Any simply cooked meats served on a bed of Potatoes Anna would be a dish Anna, as in the chicken recipe. The same would hold for vegetables, such as cooked asparagus served on a bed of Potatoes Anna.

Potatoes Anna are also a fine accompaniment for a great variety of main dishes, primarily because of their simplicity. If they are used with a major dish, such as Chicken Suprêmes à la Parisienne, then the major dish takes precedence. It would be Chicken Suprêmes à la Parisienne with Potatoes Anna.

We tend to think dishes such as Potatoes Anna have their origins in French antiquity. But potatoes, like tomatoes and corn, were unknown in Europe until fairly recently, all being native to South America. Potatoes only became widely used in Europe about 1750, in Germany.

Just think, a couple of hundred years ago, there were no potatoes for Salade Niçoise, nor tomatoes for all the other great Mediterranean dishes!

POTATOES ANNA
TO SERVE 4

2 lbs potatoes, peeled and
   sliced thin

¾ cup butter, melted
salt and white pepper

Preheat over to 400°. Butter a baking dish well. Sauté the potatoes very lightly in the butter and set aside. Put a thin layer of the potatoes in the baking dish, season lightly with salt and white pepper, and dribble with a little melted butter from the pan. Repeat this process, making several layers. Cover and bake about 30 minutes, until done and golden. Invert the baking dish, depositing the potatoes on a hot serving dish, and drain off the excess butter, if any. Serve hot.

This potato dish can also be cooked in a frying pan, like a large pancake. If so, turn the potatoes when half done, to brown both sides equally. To turn potatoes, put a plate over the pan and invert pan and plate together so that the potatoes fall to the plate. Then slide the potatoes back into the pan to finish the other side. This dish cooked with potatoes cut in very fine strips, or shredded, becomes Potatoes Annette.

Potatoes Anna baked in individual buttered baking dishes, instead of in one large dish, are called Potatoes Nina.

CHICKEN SAUTÉ ANNA
TO SERVE 4

2 small chickens, cut up
salt and white pepper
butter
1 recipe Potatoes Anna, hot
2 oz dry white wine
1 shallot, chopped

1½ cups Sauce Espagnole, or
   beef gravy
1 tsp parsley
½ tsp tarragon
½ tsp chervil
½ tsp lemon juice (or to taste)
1 Tbs butter (optional)

Season the chicken to taste with salt and white pepper and sauté in butter until done and golden. Put the Potatoes Anna on a hot platter and top with the chicken. Keep hot.

Discard excess fat from pan, if any, and add wine and shallot. Boil down quickly, scraping up the juices. Add the Espagnole, parsley, tarragon and chervil and simmer a few minutes. Add the lemon juice, and the 1 tablespoon of butter if desired. Heat well and strain a little sauce over the chicken pieces. Serve the rest in a sauceboat, hot.

This is an excellent place to use skinned chicken pieces. The result is less greasy and the taste a bit different. Simply remove all skin before sautéing, and the result will be more healthful as well as better tasting.

CORNISH GAME HENS ANNA
TO SERVE 4

Proceed as for Chicken Sauté Anna, using 4 whole 1-pound game hens. Bake basted with butter in a 375° oven for about 45 minutes. Serve on top of 4 individual Potatoes Anna patties, or surround the hens with rings of Potatoes Anna.

Anversoise

(ahn-vayr-ZWAZ)

From Anvers, meaning Antwerp, a city in northern Belgium. Antwerp is famous as the diamond center of the world. It is the country's second largest city, after Brussels, and is the leading port and commercial center.

Antwerp was overrun by the Normans in 836, when it was a small trading town. It remained relatively unimportant until the eleventh century, when it began a rise to prosperity as a port culminating during the reign of Charles V in the mid-1500s. It became the greatest seaport in Europe, even surpassing Venice. This fabulous prosperity came to a rude halt in 1576, when the Spanish destroyed the city in a religious uprising, also killing 6,000 of its citizens.

Antwerp today is important not only as a port, but in diamond cutting, sugar refining, distilling and shipbuilding. In foods, chocolate, biscuits and margarine are important commercially. Soap, candles and ivory are also marketed here.

The name Anversoise is generally applied to dishes of large or small meat chunks, calf's sweetbreads and eggs. The characteristic garnishes are potatoes cut like olives and deep-fried, and hop shoots cooked in lightly salted water and tossed in butter or cream. Hop shoots are a nice change of pace, if you can get them. New York and the western states are the prime producers. If you can't get hop shoots, try substituting artichoke hearts or white asparagus tips.

Any kind of meat, from a beef roast to chicken livers, cooked and tossed in butter can be a dish à l'Anversoise. When the meat is done, add a little white wine to the pan and scrape up the juices. Add some veal gravy, blend well and serve hot—a very straightforward cooking style. The trick is to find the hop shoots, which make the dish authentic. They also make this style unique, and with this in mind, beer suggests itself as a beverage, both in keeping with the hop-shoot garnish and the fact that the Low Countries do not produce wine.

Hop shoots are only available in the spring, for about three weeks, when the excess shoots are removed from each hill. For information write: Hop Growers of America Inc., 504 N. Naches Avenue, Suite 5, Yakima, Wash. 98901.

For décor, lots of candles would be fitting. A variety of shapes and sizes would make an interesting display. You might light the whole room with nothing but candles, and a few ivory holders would be a nice touch.

EGGS À L'ANVERSOISE (Poached or Soft-Boiled)
TO SERVE 4

3 Tbs butter
1 Tbs flour
1 cup milk
salt, pepper and grated nutmeg
¼ cup heavy cream

8 eggs, poached or soft-boiled,
    freshly cooked and hot
4 bread slices, trimmed,
    sautéed in butter and hot
½ lb hop shoots, simmered in
    butter or cream, hot

Make a Cream Sauce by melting the butter in a pan and stirring in the flour, blending well. Slowly add the milk, stirring over low heat. Season to taste with salt, pepper and nutmeg and cook slowly to thicken. Remove from heat and stir in the cream. Keep hot. To serve, place 2 eggs on each bread slice and top with hop shoots. Spoon over the Cream Sauce and serve hot.

ESCALOPES of VEAL À L'ANVERSOISE
TO SERVE 4

2 lbs veal cutlets
butter
salt and pepper
8 bread slices, trimmed, halved
    diagonally and sautéed in
    butter, hot

½ lb hop shoots, simmered in
    cream, hot
1 lb very small potatoes,
    sautéed in butter, hot
2 oz dry white wine
1½ cups veal gravy

Flatten the cutlets with a mallet and sauté in butter until done. Season with salt and pepper lightly and arrange on the bread sautéed in butter. Garnish with the hop shoots and potatoes and keep hot. Dilute the pain juices with the wine, scraping up the drippings, and blend in the gravy. Mix well, and heat through quickly. Strain into a sauceboat and serve hot.

CHICKEN À L'ANVERSOISE
TO SERVE 4

1 chicken, whole
hop shoots (¾ cup per lb of
    chicken)
cream
4 Tbs butter

4 cups potatoes trimmed to ol-
    ive shape
3 oz dry white wine
1½ cups veal gravy

Preheat oven to 375°. Stuff the chicken with the hop shoots partially cooked in cream. Sew or skewer closed and bake, uncovered, basting with the butter, in a casserole for 30 minutes per pound, or until done. When chicken is half done, add potatoes to the casserole and finish cooking together. When done, untruss the chicken and place on a hot platter surrounded by the potatoes. Keep hot. Add the wine to the casserole, and over direct heat quickly scrape up the drippings. Blend in the gravy and heat through. Strain into a sauceboat and serve hot.

Although meats cooked à l'Anversoise are usually in chunks, here we find a whole chicken, stuffed with hop shoots—apparently one of those exceptions that prove the rule.

Ardennaise

(ahr-den-NEZ)

From the Ardennes, a mountainous region in northern France, eastern Belgium and Luxembourg. The Ardennes is a region where old mountains have been worn down to plateaus, which now range from 1,500 to 2,000 feet in elevation. The land is suitable to little but lumbering and raising cattle. The old, flattened summits have little drainage and boggy areas abound, many covered with heather and blueberry bushes. It is a land of solitude, inhabited largely by Walloons, a sturdy, dark-skinned, French-speaking people.

In cooking, the term Ardennaise applies mostly to small birds such as thrushes or larks cooked in cocottes (casseroles) and flavored with juniper berries. The name is interchangeable with Liègeoise (lee'ezh-WAZ) after the city of Liège in eastern Belgium. The style is also used for other meats, such as pork and kidneys. Substitute veal chops for the pork chops if you wish, or lamb kidneys for the veal kidneys, or a chicken for the game birds. For vegetables, simply use whatever you like. These Ardennaise dishes are not overly delicate, so you need not fret about a vegetable dish taking the spotlight from the main course.

The Ardennes region is noted for its game and little else, save for an excellent cheese made in the Ardennes forest called Rocroi. The area is not fertile, and no producer of fine wines. Therefore, there are no local vintages to recommend. Since the dishes are traditionally game (I've included the pork and kidney recipes for a little variety), a sturdy wine would be best, such as Beaujolais or Gewürztraminer. For dessert, forget the light and wonderful French concoctions and stick to cheeses or fruits, or both.

For décor, heather and wild blueberry branches would be unusual, and very appropriate to the Ardennes.

PORK CHOPS À L'ARDENNAISE
TO SERVE 4

8 pork chops
salt and pepper
butter, or lard
2 lbs potatoes, sliced thick
1 cup onion, chopped
butter

½ lb bacon, diced
pepper
2 oz dry white wine
2–4 juniper berries, crushed
1½ cups Sauce Espagnole, or
    beef gravy

Season the chops with salt and pepper to taste and sauté slowly in butter until done and golden, basting constantly. Set on a hot platter in a circle and keep hot.

Sauté the potatoes in butter until done. Sauté the onions in butter until tender but not browned. Cook the bacon and drain. Mix the potatoes, onion and bacon and season with pepper to taste. Pile in the center of the chops on the platter and keep hot.

Pour excess fat from the pork sauté pan. Add the wine and juniper berries to the pan and boil down, scraping up the juices. Add the Espagnole, blend well and bring to a boil, cooking to thicken for a few minutes if necessary. Pour over the pork and serve at once, hot.

VEAL KIDNEYS À L'ARDENNAISE
TO SERVE 4

2 lbs veal kidneys
salt and pepper
4 Tbs butter
1 Tbs onion, minced
1 Tbs green pepper, minced
1 Tbs mushrooms, minced
2 oz dry white wine

3 juniper berries
2 oz warm brandy
1½ cups veal stock* or gravy,
    boiling
fresh crustless toast
paprika
chives

Trim membranes and skin from the kidneys and cut in ½-inch slices. Wash and dry and season lightly with salt and pepper. Melt the butter in a pan and add the onion and pepper. Sauté lightly and add the mushrooms. Mix and sauté lightly together. Meanwhile, put the wine and juniper berries in a separate small pan and boil until the wine is almost gone. Add this to the vegetables. Add the kidney slices, stirring to mix well and coat, and cook for 4 minutes, stirring. Add the brandy and flame, stirring until the fire dies. Add the stock and blend in well, scraping the bottom of the pan. Cover and simmer 10 minutes. Serve the kidneys on fresh toast. Strain the sauce over the kidneys, dust lightly with paprika and sprinkle with chives. Serve hot.

QUAIL À L'ARDENNAISE
TO SERVE 4

butter
2 onions, chopped
2 carrots, chopped
½ cup truffles, sliced
4 ¾-lb quail, boned*
quail livers, chopped
½ cup truffles, chopped
½ cup goose (or chicken) liver,
    chopped
2 cups black bread crumbs
milk
salt and pepper
4 bacon slices

bones and trimmings of birds
4 Tbs butter, melted
1 cup chicken stock* or broth
1 lb chicken livers
bacon fat
½ lb mushrooms, chopped
butter
salt and pepper
3 egg yolks
1 cup sherry wine
4 juniper berries, crushed
1½ cups Sauce Espagnole, or
    veal or beef gravy

In butter, sauté onions and carrots together and sliced truffles separately. Set aside. Preheat oven to 350°. To stuff quail, make a forcemeat of the birds' livers, chopped truffles, goose liver and the bread crumbs soaked in milk and squeezed almost dry. Season the forcemeat with salt and pepper to taste. Stuff the birds, forming back to their original shape before boning, and sew closed. Wrap each with a slice of bacon and secure with string or toothpicks. Put in a buttered baking pot with the bones and trimmings, and the sautéed onions and carrots (reserve the sliced truffles). Sprinkle with the melted butter and add the stock. Braise covered for 20 minutes and remove from oven. Take birds from pot and drain.

While the birds are braising, sauté the chicken livers in bacon fat and the mushrooms in butter. Chop chicken livers in a bowl, add mushrooms, season with salt and pepper to taste and add egg yolks. Mix well. Spread this mixture in a casserole to make a crustlike lining. Place the birds in the casserole. They should fit fairly snugly. Cook in the oven, uncovered, for about 20 minutes or until the birds are done and golden.

While the casserole is baking, place the pot with the trimmings, etc., on direct heat. Discard excess fat, if any. Add the sherry and juniper berries and cook down to half, scraping up the drippings. Add the Espagnole, blending in well, and let the sauce thicken lightly. Strain the sauce, add the reserved sliced truffles and keep hot. When the casserole is done, pour the sauce over the birds and serve in the casserole, hot.

This quail recipe was originally meant for European thrushes or larks. If birds similar to these are available, 8 should be used instead of the 4 quail. The recipe could be used for squab, Cornish game hens, or any other game birds.

Aurore

(or-ROHR)

The same as Aurora. Aurore in French means dawn, daybreak. Aurora is the Latin name for the Greek goddess of the dawn, Eos. Eos, or Aurora, is sometimes pictured with a pitcher in each hand, dispensing the dews of the morning. She was the lover of the hunter Orion.

In cuisine, the term is applied to any dish served with Sauce Aurore, or cooked with it. It is also the name of a stuffed egg dish and of a particular cheese produced in Normandy.

Sauce Aurore goes especially well with cauliflower. Celery, onions, cabbage and kohlrabi are also good with this sauce. Any fish, simply cooked, is fine served with Sauce Aurore, as are the lighter meats, such as veal, pork or rabbit.

Anything served with Sauce Aurore is a dish à l'Aurore. Strictly speaking, however, dishes served à l'Aurore should not be browned, but cooked without coloring. For example, if you wished to serve frog's legs à l'Aurore, the proper

way would be to cook the frog's legs by braising or simmering in chicken stock,*
not by sautéing, which would brown the frog's legs and make them unaccep-
table to a purist. Personally, I'm not much concerned with what the purists think.
I like fried chicken with Sauce Aurore.

SAUCE AURORE
TO MAKE 2 CUPS

2 cups Sauce Velouté*	2 tsp parsley, chives, chervil,
2–3 Tbs tomato paste or purée	basil or oregano (optional)

Bring the Velouté to a simmer and blend in the tomato paste and the herb
of your choice, if desired. Serve hot with eggs, fish, white meats or vegetables.

Sauce Aurore, if served with an herbal flavoring, should be simmered for 8 to
10 minutes to achieve full flavor, and may be strained or not, as desired. If you
use dried herbs, it should be strained. The herbs may also be combined to your
taste—1 teaspoon chives plus 1 teaspoon basil, for example.

EGGS À L'AURORE (Stuffed)
TO SERVE 4

8 eggs, hard-boiled	1 Tbs flour
2 Tbs butter	1 cup milk
1 tsp flour	½ cup heavy cream
¼ cup milk	salt, pepper and grated nutmeg
salt, pepper and grated nutmeg	¼ cup grated Parmesan cheese
¼ tsp parsley	¼ cup grated Gruyère cheese
⅛ tsp chervil	Parmesan cheese, grated
⅛ tsp marjoram	butter, melted
3 Tbs butter	1½ cups Tomato Sauce, prefer-
	ably homemade,* hot

Preheat oven to 400°. Shell eggs and halve lengthwise. Remove yolks and
chop. Make a Sauce Béchamel by melting the 2 tablespoons butter in a pan and
blending in the 1 teaspoon flour over low heat. Slowly blend in the ¼ cup milk,
season to taste with salt, pepper and a little nutmeg, and add the parsley, chervil
and marjoram. Mix with 2/3 of the chopped yolks and use to stuff the egg-white
halves. Reserve the remaining yolks.
Make a Sauce Mornay by melting the 3 tablespoons butter in a pan and
blending in the 1 tablespoon flour over low heat. Slowly blend in the 1 cup milk
and cream. Season to taste with salt, pepper and a little nutmeg and stir in the
2 cheeses. Pour this Sauce Mornay into a baking dish just large enough to hold
the stuffed eggs upright in a single layer, and arrange the eggs on the sauce.
Sprinkle the stuffed eggs generously with more Parmesan cheese and add a little
butter to moisten. Heat in the oven until golden brown. When hot and browned,
serve, sprinkled with the reserved chopped yolks. Serve the Tomato Sauce separately, hot.

CHICKEN À L'AURORE
TO SERVE 4

1 stewing chicken
2 qts chicken or veal stock* or
　broth

2 cups Sauce Aurore

STUFFING (Optional)

1 lb veal, ground
½ lb beef fat, ground
salt, pepper and grated nutmeg

1 egg beaten
2 egg yolks, hard-boiled,
　mashed
½ cup cream

If using the optional stuffing, stuff the bird. Sew or skewer closed and truss wings and legs to the body. Put it in a pot with enough stock to cover, and simmer covered for 4 hours. Check level of stock, and add water if needed to keep the chicken covered with liquid. If the bird is not stuffed, 3 hours will be sufficient cooking time.

Meanwhile, heat the Sauce Aurore. When the chicken is done, set on a hot platter and pour over the sauce, or serve separately, hot.

If you wish to stuff the chicken, begin 1 day in advance. Prepare Crème Quenelle forcemeat (stuffing) by mixing the veal and beef fat, seasoning to taste with salt, pepper and nutmeg and adding the egg and yolks. Spread the mixture on a board and refrigerate overnight. Before using for stuffing, mix once again, add the cream and blend well.

CONSOMMÉ À L'AURORE
TO SERVE 4

1 qt rich beef consommé*
2 Tbs tapioca
1 tsp parsley
1 tsp celery leaves

½ tsp chervil
cheesecloth, washed
1 Tbs tomato paste

Bring the consommé to a boil and add the tapioca by sprinkling in a bit at a time so the consommé does not stop boiling. Add the parsley, celery and chervil tied in cheesecloth. Boil about 15 minutes, stirring occasionally, until tapioca is done. Discard herb bouquet and strain. Blend in tomato paste and serve hot.

PEACHES À L'AURORE
TO SERVE 4

2 cups simple syrup (made by
　boiling 1½ cups of water and
　1½ cups of sugar together)
2 oz Kirsch brandy
2 cups fresh peach slices,
　peeled

1 cup strawberries, puréed in a
　blender
2 cups very stiff whipped cream
¼ lb powdered sugar
3 egg yolks
¾ cup dry white wine
2 oz Curaçao liqueur

Heat the Kirsch in 1 cup of the simple syrup and use to poach the sliced peaches. Let them cool in the syrup until chilled. Mix the remaining cup of simple syrup with the puréed strawberries (chilled), then fold into the whipped cream. Spread in the bottom of 4 serving dishes and freeze.

Meanwhile, shortly before serving, prepare a sabayon by whipping the sugar and yolks in a bowl until slightly whitened. Add wine and Curaçao and cook in a double boiler, whisking steadily, until it becomes 4 times its original volume and is firm and frothy. Chill. Just before serving the mousse, top with the peaches, then the sabayon, and serve at once.

Basquaise

(bahs-KEZ)

After the Basques, the lively and colorful people inhabiting the western end of the Pyrenees mountains in Spain and France. They are freedom-loving people, and apparently always have been. They were there when the Romans invaded and conquered Spain, but the Basques managed to maintain their independence. Later they fought just as fiercely against the Moors, and still later against the Franks. In 1202 they were finally incorporated into Castile (Spain), but only after being guaranteed immunity from taxation and conscription, and also a republican constitution.

The vigor and indomitable spirit of the Basques are reflected in their cuisine, which is colorful, flavorful and individualistic. Typical are spicy mixtures of tomatoes, peppers, mushrooms, ham and pimientos, with large chunks of meat. Olive oil is most widely used for cooking, probably because of the Spanish influence. There are more Spanish Basques than French. The Basques traditionally add a dash of vinegar at the table to whatever strikes their fancy, even soup. If you wish to add a bit of authentic zip to any of these recipes, try it.

Basque dishes are quite similar to the Mediterranean dishes of Provence. They all use olive oil, lots of tomatoes, and olives. The Basques, however, make much more use of peppers and pimientos, and it is this addition that gives cooking à la Basquaise a little added zip. As in all cooking, you may substitute ingredients. For example, any firm-fleshed white fish will do fine for the Fish Soup à la Basquaise. You could even make it Eel Soup à la Basquaise. Any suitable vegetable, such as peas or beans, cooked in a little olive oil with tomatoes, peppers and onions becomes a vegetable à la Basquaise. (Usually, the tomatoes, peppers and onions are simmered in a little oil until tender, then the main vegetable is added and simmered until just done.)

For variety in flavoring, rather than in ingredients, try using ½ cup of slivered almonds in place of the ham strips in the recipe for Chicken à la Basquaise, omitting the peppers since their flavor would conflict with that of the almonds. This omission makes the dish more Niçoise than Basquaise, but that's a pretty fine point. Serve it with a dash of vinegar at the table, and you're justified in calling it Basque. Anyway, the main thing about Basque cooking is vigor. So toss aside your chef's hat, don your beret, and cook up a Basquaise storm.

If you're serving wine, a hearty burgundy would be fine. The most noted wine of the Basque area, Jurançon, is excellent and hearty, but sweet. Only an inferior dry version is generally available in this country.

For décor, think of the Basque costume, berets, rope-soled shoes and the *makhila,* which is both a walking stick and weapon, and is carried by a leather thong. For music, folk dances are popular in Basque country, such as the *vztai dantza,* or *l'arkin,* the dance of the arches, where colorfully decorated half hoops are carried overhead by the dancers. Any European folk dances would fit well, because they all have in common something that typifies the Basques: liveliness. And a lively touch never hurt any party!

BASQUAISE GARNISHES

Basque garnishes are usually cooked with the dish, like pimientos, peppers, mushrooms and ham. The exception is Potatoes Anna, which is often an accompaniment to a dish à la Basquaise.

TOMATO FONDUE À LA BASQUAISE
TO SERVE 4

3 green peppers
olive oil
¼ lb prosciutto, or ham, diced
2 Tbs olive oil
4 garlic cloves, minced

1 medium onion, minced
1½ lbs tomatoes, peeled,*
    seeded and diced
salt and pepper
¼ tsp thyme

Brush the peppers with a little olive oil and scorch in a 500° oven. When well scorched, put under running cold water and remove scorched skin. Discard seeds and inner membranes, and cut in very thin, julienne strips. Cook the prosciutto in the oil in a casserole for a few minutes. Add the peppers, garlic cloves, onions and tomatoes. Season to taste with salt and pepper and add thyme. Stir. Cover and simmer very slowly, stirring occasionally, for 25 to 30 minutes. Uncover, bring to a boil and let fluids reduce. Serve hot or chilled.

POTATOES À LA BASQUAISE
TO SERVE 4

4 large, long potatoes
1 garlic clove, grated
½ cup sweet pimientos,
    chopped
½ cup ham, chopped
1 Tbs parsley
butter or oil

1 cup Basque Tomato Fondue,
    thick
butter, melted (or olive oil)
salt and pepper
bread crumbs
butter, melted
4 Tbs thick veal gravy, or Sauce
    Espagnole, hot

Preheat oven to 350°. Peel potatoes and hollow out lengthwise.

Boil in lightly salted water for 5 minutes. Drain and dry. Meanwhile, sauté the garlic, pimientos, ham and parsley in a little butter until tender. Add the Tomato Fondue and blend. Use to stuff the potatoes. Put the potatoes in a buttered baking dish and season to taste with salt and pepper. Sprinkle with a little melted butter and bake in the oven for 1 hour. Sprinkle potatoes with crumbs and a few drops of butter to moisten and return to brown in the oven, about 15 minutes. Spoon the gravy over the potatoes and serve hot in the baking dish.

SPINACH and POTATOES À LA BASQUAISE
TO SERVE 4

⅓ cup Parmesan cheese, grated
1 lb spinach, cooked in 1 cup of chicken broth and drained well
1 lb potatoes, peeled, sliced and boiled in chicken broth

1 Tbs anchovy paste
3 Tbs butter, softened
pepper to taste
¼ cup Parmesan cheese, grated
2 Tbs bread crumbs
3–4 tsp melted butter

Preheat over to 375°. Mix the cheese and spinach. Drain the potatoes. Blend the anchovy paste, softened butter and pepper into a smooth paste. Put half the potatoes in the bottom of a buttered baking dish. Spread with half the anchovy butter. Cover with half the spinach mixture. Repeat with remaining potatoes, anchovy butter and spinach. Sprinkle with cheese and crumbs, moisten by dribbling on a little melted butter and brown until golden in the oven, about 25 minutes. Serve hot.

PIPERADE (Basque Eggs)
TO SERVE 4

2 oz lean ham, diced
2 Tbs pure olive oil
1 small onion, minced
2 garlic cloves, minced
1 green pepper, seeded and minced
2 tomatoes, peeled,* seeded and chopped

1 tsp parsley
¼ tsp thyme
¼ tsp basil
cheesecloth, washed
salt and pepper
8 eggs, beaten lightly with a fork
3 Tbs pure olive oil

Brown the ham lightly in the 2 tablespoons of olive oil. Add the onion and garlic and lower heat. Cook, stirring, until tender but not browned. Add the pepper and simmer 5 minutes more. Add the tomatoes. Add the parsley, thyme and basil tied in cheesecloth and season well with salt and pepper. Simmer, covered, over very low heat for 15 minutes, until very tender. Uncover and cook, stirring, until you have a thick tomato sauce. Discard the herb bouquet. Mix the piperade sauce with the eggs and cook in hot olive oil, like scrambled eggs, over low heat, stirring until set.

There are probably as many variations of Piperade as there are Basques! Here are a few you might like to try:

1. Sauté a few tablespoons each of onions and sweet peppers in butter. Add a minced garlic clove and sauté gently for 5 minutes more. Add a peeled,* seeded and chopped tomato, season well with salt and pepper and toss lightly together. Sauté 8 ham slices separately. Scramble 8 eggs and serve on four hot plates, garnished with rolled-up ham slices and topped with the Piperade mixture.

2. Cook the vegetables as described in the main recipe, without the garlic. Sauté 4 thick ham slices with the garlic in butter. Remove the ham and keep hot. Add 2 tablespoons cider vinegar or white wine to the pan with the garlic and cook down to half. Mix the vegetables and eggs and scramble and serve on the hot ham slices, topped with the vinegar pan juices, discarding the garlic.

3. Simmer a pepper cut in large chunks, 4 ounces diced ham, 2 peeled* and seeded tomatoes cut in large chunks, 2 chopped garlic cloves and 1 coarsely chopped onion in ham fat. When limp but not browned, season well with salt and pepper. Stir in 8 beaten eggs and scramble. Be sure you have enough hot ham fat when you start, about 4 tablespoons.

If that's not enough, make up your own. You know the ingredients—ham, onion, sweet peppers, garlic, tomatoes and salt and pepper—and, of course, scrambled eggs. Or you may wish to bake the eggs, either mixed with the sautéed vegetables or topped with them.

CHICKEN À LA BASQUAISE
TO SERVE 4

2 small young chickens, cut up	½ lb mushrooms, sliced
3 Tbs olive oil	¼ lb ham, diced
3 tomatoes, peeled,* seeded and diced large	¼ cup dry white wine
3 green peppers, cored, seeded and cut in large dice	¼ cup chicken broth
1 small onion, chopped	salt and pepper
2 garlic cloves, minced	2 Tbs tomato paste
	1 Tbs parsley
	2 pimientos, cut in large strips

In a braising pot or Dutch oven, brown the chicken in the oil. Add tomatoes, peppers, onion and garlic and sauté for a few minutes. Add the mushrooms and ham and sauté a few minutes more. Add wine and broth, season well with salt and pepper, and simmer slowly, covered, for 45 minutes, or until tender. Set the chicken on a hot platter and keep hot. Add tomato paste, parsley and pimientos to the pot. Cook uncovered for 2 minutes, mixing gently. Pour over the chicken and serve hot.

VEAL À LA BASQUAISE
TO SERVE 4

Proceed as in Chicken à la Basquaise, substituting 2 pounds of veal chunks for the chicken.

PORK À LA BASQUAISE
TO SERVE 4

Proceed as in Chicken à la Basquaise, substituting 2 pounds of very lean pork chunks for the chicken and cooking about 15 minutes longer, or until done, depending on the size of the pork chunks.

COD À LA BASQUAISE
TO SERVE 4

2 lbs cod fillets
flour
¼ cup olive oil
4 large tomatoes, peeled,*
   seeded and cut in chunks
1 garlic clove, minced

salt and pepper
¼ cup green olives, pitted and
   sliced
¼ cup black olives, pitted and
   sliced
chives

Preheat oven to 350°. Dredge the cod in flour, shaking off the excess. Sauté in olive oil to brown lightly. Set in a baking dish. Add the tomatoes, garlic, and salt and pepper to taste to the sauté pan and cook and stir for 10 minutes. Add the green and black olives and cook 2 to 3 more minutes. Spoon this mixture over the cod and bake in the oven for 15 minutes, uncovered. Sprinkle with chives and serve hot.

FISH SOUP À LA BASQUAISE
TO SERVE 4

3 onions, sliced
3 oz olive oil
2 tomatoes, chopped coarsely
1 green pepper, seeded and
   minced
2 qts water
1 tsp parsley
¼ tsp thyme
½ tsp oregano

¼ bay leaf
cheesecloth, washed
salt and pepper
4 thick pieces of cod, boneless
1 garlic clove, crushed
4 slices French or Italian bread,
   crusts removed
chives

In a large pot, saute the onions in half the oil until lightly browned. Add tomatoes, green pepper and water. Add parsley, thyme, oregano and bay leaf tied in cheesecloth, and season to taste with salt and pepper. Bring to a boil, cover, and simmer for 15 minutes. Add the cod, re-cover, and simmer very slowly for 1 hour more.

Meanwhile, sauté the garlic in the remaining oil for 5 minutes. Discard the garlic. Sauté the bread in the garlic-flavored oil until golden and drain well. Carefully place the cod, when finished cooking, in a warm soup tureen. Add the bread and pour in the soup, discarding the herb bouquet. Sprinkle with chives and serve hot.

ALMOND CUSTARD À LA BASQUAISE
TO SERVE 4

¼ cup sugar
4 egg yolks
1 cup milk, scalded and hot
1½ oz semisweet baking chocolate, flaked
½ tsp almond extract

¼ lb butter, unsalted, softened
¾ cup almonds, powdered in a
   blender
½ tsp almond extract
2 Tbs Kirsch or Curaçao
2 cups whipped cream

Beat sugar into egg yolks a bit at a time, until well blended and pale yellow. Slowly add milk, in a very thin stream, beating until it is all blended in. Pour into a pan and cook over low heat until the custard thickens lightly, stirring continuously. Do not let the custard simmer or the yolks will curdle. Remove from the heat and beat in the chocolate and almond extract until blended. Cool.

Blend the butter and almonds until creamy. Slowly add the cool custard mixture and blend well. Blend in the almond extract and Kirsch or Curacao. Pour into a mold, or individual dishes, and chill. Serve the custard chilled, topped with whipped cream.

This is a fine dessert, and true to Basque form it has real zest!

Bayonnaise

(buy-yoh-NEZ)

From the city of Bayonne in the southwest corner of France near the Pyrennees and the Bay of Biscay. World famous are its Bayonne hams, fine preserved pork (*confit de porc*) and preserved goose (*confit d'oie*). The area's pork is the finest available, and its black puddings (blood puddings) rank above any others. There is good evidence to believe that the cold egg and oil sauce called mayonnaise was invented here, and so should be called Bayonnaise. (See Mayonnaise.)

Bayonne has been an important seaport since ancient times. It was a military post under the Romans. In the Middle Ages it was held by the Dukes of Aquitaine until 1154, then captured by the British, who held it until 1451, when it was finally occupied by the French. In June 1565, Catherine de' Medici and her son Charles IX of France met the Duke of Alva, who represented Philip II of Spain, at Bayonne. This meeting may have been the beginning of a joint attack on Protestantism which led to the St. Bartholomew Massacre of August 1572.

Bayonne is in Basque country, but the cooking mode à la Bayonnaise is primarily concerned with pork products, for which the area is justly famous. The spicy tomatoes, onions and peppers of Basque cooking are largely foregone here in favor of ham and pork. Nonetheless, Bayonnaise cooking, when it does use olive oil, tomatoes and garlic, becomes similar to Basquaise. Béarnaise cooking is also somewhat similar, which is understandable, since all three modes are of the same general area, southwest France (although the Basquaise style laps over the border into northern Spain).

Since mayonnaise might have originated here, it could be appropriate to serve a vegetable dressed in a little homemade mayonnaise; or a salad dressed with oil, vinegar, salt and pepper and topped with a dollop of mayonnaise.

Bayonne was known from early times for the manufacture of weapons, and gave its name to the bayonet. To amuse your guests, you may want to serve your after dinner cheeses with a bayonet-shaped knife.

TOMATOES À LA BAYONNAISE (Stuffed)
TO SERVE 4

4 tomatoes	meat of 3 chipolata sausages (or
salt and pepper	small pork sausages) cooked
3 Tbs butter	and crumbled
1 mild onion, halved and sliced	salt and pepper
thin	¼ cup grated Parmesan cheese
1 cup sliced mushrooms	¼ cup grated Gruyère cheese
1 cup chopped Bayonne or Virginia ham (or prosciutto)	bread crumbs
	2 Tbs butter, melted
1 tsp parsley	1 cup Tomato Sauce, preferably
1 tsp chives	homemade*

Cut tops off tomatoes, scoop out seeds and centers, and season inside with salt and pepper. Place each tomato in a cup shaped of aluminum foil around bottom and sides. This will help support the tomato during baking, and make for neat serving.

Preheat oven to 350°. Make a stuffing by sautéing the onion in the butter until limp. Add mushrooms and sauté lightly. Add ham, sausage meat, parsley and chives and simmer for a few minutes. Season to taste with salt and pepper. Use this mixture to stuff the tomatoes. Sprinkle the stuffed tomatoes with the cheeses. Top liberally with crumbs and dribble the melted butter on to moisten. Place on a baking pan and cook in the oven until done and golden. Meanwhile, heat the Tomato Sauce and serve hot, with the stuffed tomatoes.

To remove a tomato from the foil cup, place on a plate and tear the foil in half, so that it separates under the tomato, taking half out from under each side of the tomato.

PORK CHOPS À LA BAYONNAISE
TO SERVE 4

2 garlic cloves, slivered
8 pork chops, single thickness
salt and pepper
½ tsp thyme
olive oil
wine vinegar

1 lb new potatoes
lard
½ lb mushroom caps
olive oil
parsley and chives

Insert garlic slivers in pork chops with a sharp, thin knife. Season with salt, pepper and thyme. Sprinkle with oil and vinegar and let stand for 1 hour.

Preheat oven to 350°. Sauté potatoes in lard and sauté mushrooms in oil, and drain both. Brown chops briskly in lard. Place in a baking dish surrounded with the potatoes and mushrooms and finish cooking, uncovered, in the oven for 30 minutes, or until done. Sprinkle with parsley and chives and serve in the baking dish, hot.

HAM À LA BAYONNAISE
TO SERVE 4–8

1 good smoked ham, about 6
    lbs
1 cup Madeira wine
sugar (optional)
2 tomatoes, peeled,* seeded
    and chopped

½ lb small buttom mushrooms
butter
16 chipolata sausages, or small
    pork sausages

PILAF

6 Tbs butter
1 cup onion, chopped
1 lb rice
1 qt chicken broth

salt and pepper
3 Tbs butter, diced
2 cups Sauce Espagnole, or
    Demi-Glace (Sauce Alsa-
    cienne), or beef gravy

Desalt the ham by soaking in cold water for several hours. Place in a pot with water to cover and poach for 1½ hours. Remove from the pot and trim off the skin and surplus fat. Put in a braising pan or Dutch oven, add the Madeira and finish cooking in a 350° oven for ½ hour, covered. When done, sprinkle with a little sugar and glaze in the oven, uncovered, if desired.

Meanwhile, sauté tomatoes and mushrooms together in a little butter, and cook the sausages separately. Drain, put aside and keep hot. Make pilaf by putting the 6 tablespoons of butter in a separate pan and sautéing the onion until limp but not browned. Add the rice and cook, stirring, until the rice turns milky. Add the broth, season to taste with salt and pepper and cook, covered in a 350° oven (you can use the same oven as for the ham) for about 20 minutes, or until done. When done, stir in the 3 tablespoons of butter and the reserved tomatoes and mushrooms. Put the finished ham on a hot platter and surround with the rice mixture in piles. Garnish with the sausages and keep hot. Skim the fat from the braising pan and add the Espagnole, stirring up the drippings and heating through quickly. Strain the sauce and serve separately, hot.

This ham, cooked in Madiera and glazed in the oven, if served as is, without the pilaf and sausage garnish, is called Ham au Madère.

HAM TART À LA BAYONNAISE
TO SERVE 4

dough for 1 bottom pastry crust*
¾ lb Bayonne or Virginia ham
   (or prosciutto), in thin strips
3 Tbs flour
2 oz butter, softened
1 egg

1 egg yolk
ground nutmeg, cinnamon and
   cloves
1 cup milk
white pepper (optional)

Knead the dough well. Chill. Roll out on a floured board and use to line an 8-inch pie pan. Chill again. Preheat oven to 350°. Fill the pastry shell with the ham and bake for 15 minutes. Meanwhile, blend the flour with the butter until smooth, then blend in the egg, yolk, a little nutmeg and cinnamon and very little cloves, and the milk. Blend well and pour over the ham. (Season with a little white pepper if desired.) Bake 15 minutes more, or until done, and serve hot.

Béarnaise

(bayr-NEZ)

From the Béarn, a former French province along the central and western Pyrenees mountains in southwest France. According to some experts, this is where the great Sauce Béarnaise originated, at first made with the region's olive oil rather than butter, which is used today. The generally accepted derivation for Sauce Béarnaise, however, is that it was always made with butter, and originally conceived in the pavilion of Henry IV at Saint-Germain-en-Laye, about ten miles outside Paris, and so named in his honor since he was known as the "Great Béarnaise." At any rate, it's admitted by all to be one of the truly great French sauces, and any dish it adorns will be a delight to the palate.

The name Béarn was derived from the old Gallo-Roman city of Beneharnum, originally part of Roman Aquitaine. Béarn, being allied geographically with Basque country in southwest France, has similar cooking, except that butter is used more often, and Béarnaise cooking does not use the peppers and pimientos found in such profusion in cooking a la Basquaise.

Broccoli, asparagus, cauliflower and beans are all excellent served with Sauce Béarnaise. Just cook in a little water (with a dash of lemon juice in the water if desired) and serve with hot Sauce Béarnaise. Simple vegetables and salads always go well with Béarnaise main dishes, such as Potatoes Parisienne. Almost anything served with Sauce Béarnaise is excellent. Try a little on some heated leftover lobster, chicken or beef.

The wine typical of this area, which goes well with its dishes, is a fine *blanc de blancs*.

Any dish served with Sauce Béarnaise can be called a dish à la Béarnaise, no matter where one thinks the sauce originated.

SAUCE BÉARNAISE (For Eggs, Vegetables, Meats and Fish)
TO MAKE 2 CUPS

½ cup white wine	⅛ tsp white pepper
2 oz wine vinegar	3 egg yolks
2 Tbs shallots, minced	1 cup butter, melted and hot
1 tsp chervil	½ tsp tarragon
1½ tsp tarragon	1 tsp chervil
1½ tsp parsley	1 tsp parsley
½ bay leaf	a small pinch of red pepper
¼ tsp salt	(cayenne)
	1 Tbs boiling water

Place the wine, vinegar, shallots, herbs, salt and pepper in a pan and simmer down until less than 2 tablespoons of liquid are left. Lower heat below a simmer and whisk in yolks. Beat until thick. Remove from heat and add the butter slowly, blending well until all is incorporated. Strain. Meanwhile, place tarragon, chervil, parsley and red pepper in the boiling water and let soak (off heat). Then blend into the sauce well.

MUSHROOMS À LA BÉARNAISE (Hors d'Oeuvre or Side Dish)

mushroom caps, similar in size	bread crumbs (1 Tbs per
garlic slivers	mushroom cap)
salt and pepper	parsley
	olive oil

Insert 3 or 4 very thin slivers of garlic in each mushroom cap with a very fine knife. Season lightly with salt and pepper and grill on a buttered baking dish or over direct flame. Meanwhile, sauté crumbs and a little parsley in oil until golden. When the mushrooms are well grilled but not dried or too browned, top them with the hot sautéed crumbs and parsley. Serve hot.

This differs from a dish au Gratin by the addition of the crumbs to the finished mushrooms, rather than grilling the mushrooms already coated with crumbs.

EGGS À LA BÉARNAISE (Poached or Soft-Boiled)
TO SERVE 4

½ lb mushrooms, minced
2 Tbs minced onion greens
2 Tbs butter
1 Tbs flour
2 oz Madeira wine
¼ cup cream

¼ tsp salt
⅛ tsp white pepper
4 individual baked pastry
   shells*, hot
8 eggs, freshly poached or soft-
   boiled, hot
1 cup Sauce Béarnaise, hot

Sauté the mushrooms and onion greens in the butter lightly. Sprinkle in the flour and cook, stirring, for 3 minutes until blended. Add wine and boil for 1 minute. Add half the cream and blend well. Season to taste with salt and white pepper. Simmer for a few minutes, adding more cream if mixture is too thick. Put the hot mushroom mixture in the bottoms of the pastry shells and place 2 eggs in each. Top with Sauce Béarnaise and serve at once, hot.

This is excellent using ¼ pound sliced sweetbreads plus ¼ pound sliced mushrooms, in place of the ½ pound of mushrooms.

TOURNEDOS À LA BÉARNAISE (Beef Fillets)
TO SERVE 4

4 beef fillets
salt and pepper
butter and olive oil (optional)
4 thick bread slices, trimmed,
   sautéed in butter and hot
2 lbs potatoes, peeled and
   sliced

4 Tbs butter (or more if needed)
parsley
1 large bunch of watercress
1½ cups Sauce Béarnaise, hot

Season the steaks lightly with salt and pepper and grill. Or sauté in half butter and half olive oil until done to taste. Set on the bread slices on 4 hot plates and keep hot. Meanwhile, prepare Château Potatoes by sautéing the potatoes gently in the 4 tablespoons of butter until done, trying not to break up the slices or overbrown the potatoes. To do this, shake the pan occasionally, rather than stirring, to cook evenly. When done, arrange the steaks and potatoes on hot plates. Sprinkle with parsley and put a garnish of watercress with each steak. Top with Sauce Béarnaise and serve hot.

This recipe is fine with almost any meat, fish or poultry. Tournedos with Sauce Béarnaise are often prepared au Poivre (with pepper), also called Pepper Steaks. To prepare, coat raw steaks with melted butter and press crushed peppercorns into the steaks, completely coating them with crushed pepper. Chill between wax paper to set, and broil. Serve with hot Sauce Béarnaise.

BEEF DAUBE À LA BÉARNAISE (Stew)
TO SERVE 4–8

2 cups dry red wine
½ cup brandy
1 carrot, sliced
1 onion, sliced
1 tsp parsley
¼ tsp thyme
½ bay leaf
2 white peppercorns
1 clove
¼ cup olive oil (optional)
4 lbs beef, trimmed into lean 2-
   inch cubes
½ lb Bayonne or Virginia ham
   (or prosciutto), sliced

3 carrots, sliced thin
2 onions, sliced thin
lard, or goose fat
1 Tbs parsley
1 tsp chervil
½ tsp thyme
1 bay leaf
cheesecloth, washed
2 garlic cloves, crushed
½ cup Sauce Espagnole, or
   Demi-Glace (Sauce Alsacienne), or gravy
flour
French bread, warm and fresh

Mix first 10 ingredients and use to marinate the beef for 3 to 4 hours, turning occasionally. Line a braising pot or Dutch oven (with a tight-fitting cover) with the ham, and layers of carrots and onions sautéed in lard. Tie the parsley, chervil, thyme and bay leaf in cheesecloth and place in center of the pot. Preheat oven to 300°. Remove the meat from the marinade and dry on paper towels. Pour the marinade in a pan and bring to a boil. Add garlic and Sauce Espagnole and simmer gently for 15 minutes. Meanwhile, dredge the meat in flour, shaking off the excess, and place in the braising pot. Pour the marinade mixture over the meat, cover and cook in the oven for 4 hours. Check occasionally and add water or beef stock* if necessary to maintain fluid level in the pot. Remove from the oven when done and serve in the pot, after skimming off excess fat and discarding herb bouquet. Serve the French bread on a warm plate, separately.

In Béarn this *daube* was, and is, served with *broyo* instead of bread. *Broyo* is made of white corn flour cooked in water, lightly seasoned and served hot with a ladle. Or it's made ahead, chilled, sliced and sautéed until golden and served hot with the beef daube.

SOLE À LA BÉARNAISE
TO SERVE 4

4 ½-pound sole fillets
pepper (optional)
½ cup butter, melted

bread crumbs
½ cup Sauce Béarnaise, hot

Season the fish very lightly with pepper, brush liberally with butter and coat with crumbs. Grill under a broiler, turning once, until done and golden on both sides (6 to 8 minutes). Serve on a hot platter, with each fillet topped with a good dollop of hot Sauce Béarnaise.

Potatoes à la Parisienne go very well with this fish recipe, which can be made with any fish (or even eel) fillets.

OYSTERS À LA BÉARNAISE
TO SERVE 4

fat for deep frying
1 recipe frying batter au Xérès,
  lightly chilled

3 dozen oysters, shucked and
  washed
2 cups Sauce Béarnaise, hot

Have fat quite hot. Dip the oysters in the frying batter and deep-fry until lightly browned and done. Do not overcook. Drain on paper towels. Pile on a hot platter and serve the sauce separately, hot.

CABBAGE and BEAN SOUP À LA BÉARNAISE
TO SERVE 4

¾ lb potatoes, peeled and cut in
  chunks
1 lb smoked pork (in 1 piece)
1 onion stuck with 2 cloves
3 garlic cloves, crushed
2½ qts water
1 Tbs celery leaves
1 tsp parsley
¼ tsp thyme
½ bay leaf

6 peppercorns
cheesecloth, washed
1 cup dry white beans, soaked
  overnight in water and
  drained
2 lbs cabbage, coarsely
  chopped
2 carrots, peeled and in chunks
½ lb lean ham, in 1 piece
salt and pepper

Put the potatoes, pork, onion and garlic in a pot with the water and add the celery, parsley, thyme, bay leaf and peppercorns tied in cheesecloth. Bring to a boil. Cover and simmer over low heat for 1 hour. Add the beans, cabbage, carrots and ham and simmer, partially covered, for 1½ hours more. Season to taste with salt and pepper. Remove meats, trim and cut in serving pieces. Skim excess fat from the soup, if any, return meats and serve hot.

Béchamel

(bay-shah-MEL)

The name of a basic white sauce, used as the base for a variety of sauces. Originally, Béchamel was made by adding cream to a thick Sauce Velouté*, which makes an excellent rich sauce.

Sauce Béchamel has erroneously been attributed to the Marquis de Bechameil. He was a financier and lord steward of the royal household of Louis

XIV. Sauce Béchamel was actually invented, or at least perfected, by a chef working in the royal kitchen under Marquis Béchameil, and thus named in his honor.

Today, Sauce Béchamel is made much more simply, and consequently the taste suffers. The Marquis de Béchameil would hardly be honored by the Sauce Béchamel produced by most chefs today. Sauce Velouté is superior for virtually every use, Béchamel being used primarily as the base for more complex sauces, and also as a binding agent, a thickener for milk gravies and as a rather bland sauce for meats and vegetables.

Béchamel as a cooking mode is similar to Crème and Blanc. All are based on white sauces. But Crème, as the name implies, makes use of cream, usually added to the pan juices of the main course for a sauce, which is decidedly more flavorful than Sauce Béchamel. And Blanc, which in sauce means the same as Béchamel, also applies to a butter, Beurre Blanc, which is also zippier than Sauce Béchamel, and is used with meats or vegetables. Also, a Sauce Blanc is sometimes made as in the original Béchamel, that is, a thick Velouté with cream, and sometimes a touch of lemon juice for added zest. At any rate, the only distinguishing feature of Béchamel is its blandness.

For this reason, however, Béchamel is extremely versatile and will pick up any flavors it encounters. Béchamel is so basic, it will go well with any food, although not excellently.

The first recipe, for the simplest Sauce Béchamel, is virtually tasteless, for use only in an emergency, as to stretch a gravy when you're being invaded by starving, unexpected guests. The second recommended recipe is usable. Some people even enjoy it. Some actually prefer it to Velouté, which to me is incredible.

SAUCE À LA BÉCHAMEL (Simplest Recipe)
TO MAKE 1 QUART

8 Tbs butter	1 qt milk
8 Tbs flour	salt and pepper

Melt the butter in a pan, stir in the flour into a smooth roux. Slowly mix in the milk and cook very slowly until thickened. Season to taste with salt and pepper and serve hot.

SAUCE À LA BÉCHAMEL (Recommended Recipe)
TO MAKE 1 QUART

2 small onions, chopped	salt, pepper and grated nutmeg
2 small carrots, chopped	1 tsp parsley
1 celery stalk, chopped	½ tsp chervil
8 Tbs butter	¼ tsp thyme
8 Tbs flour	½ bay leaf
1 qt milk, scalded	

Sauté vegetables in butter until onion is transparent. Stir in flour, blending over low heat for a few minutes. Do not let brown. Slowly add milk, blending well, and bring back to a boil. Season to taste with salt, pepper and nutmeg, and add the parsley, chervil, thyme and bay leaf. Simmer slowly for 30 minutes, or more, until flavors are well blended and sauce thickened. Strain and use hot, or store or freeze.

Before serving, Sauce Béchamel can be enhanced by heating with 1 or 2 teaspoons of sherry or Madeira per cup. The addition of 1 ounce of cream and an egg yolk per cup will also help, but do not boil after adding yolks to sauce—they'll curdle. Usually a teaspoon or so of butter is whisked in to help enrich the Béchamel as well. This is one of the few cases where I'm all for the addition of enrichment butter at the end of making a sauce.

Sauce Béchamel is often flavored with meat. To do this, simply add 1 cup of chopped and sautéed veal to the sauce while it cooks, or ½ cup of veal and ½ cup of chicken. This will produce a more rounded flavor in the finished sauce, and consequently improve any sauce made with Béchamel as a base.

ARTICHOKE HEARTS À LA BÉCHAMEL
TO SERVE 4

1½ lbs artichoke hearts* butter	1½ cups Sauce Béchamel, hot

Cook the artichoke hearts in boiling lightly salted water for 30 seconds to blanch. Drain, and stew, covered, in a pan in a little butter until tender. Drain and place in a hot serving dish. Top with Sauce Béchamel and serve hot.

Sliced carrots, sliced celery, sliced beets, endive, leek whites and swiss chard can be cooked in this way also. Use 1½ pounds of the selected vegetable, or a combination, such as ½ pound of artichoke hearts plus ½ pound of carrots and ½ pound of celery. Your preferences in vegetables will lend the dish an individual touch.

DUCKLING STUFFED with OYSTERS À LA BÉCHAMEL
TO SERVE 4

1 duck, 4½–5 lbs	cheesecloth, washed
salt, pepper and powdered marjoram	1½ tsp salt
24 fresh oysters, cleaned	1 medium onion, chopped
1 tsp parsley	1 carrot, chopped
2 sprigs of celery leaves	2 leeks, white part only
1 bay leaf	½ white turnip, chopped
¼ tsp thyme	1 cup Sauce Béchamel
6–10 peppercorns	½ cup heavy cream
2 cloves	12 oysters, cooked
	salt and pepper, if necessary

Season the duck inside with salt, pepper and marjoram to taste. Stuff with the 24 oysters and sew or skewer closed. Put the duck in a large pot. Add the parsley, celery, bay leaf, thyme, peppercorns, and cloves tied in cheesecloth. Cover with water. Add the salt, onion, carrot, leeks and turnip. Bring to a boil, skim, cover tightly and simmer 2 hours, or until tender. Transfer to a hot platter, draining well. (Some water may remain in the duck if not carefully drained.) Untruss and keep hot.

Meanwhile, heat the Béchamel and cream, blending. Add the cooked oysters and serve hot with the duck, seasoning with salt and pepper if needed.

The stock from cooking the duck may be strained and chilled overnight in the refrigerator. The next day the fat will have risen to the top and solidified, and can be removed from the stock, which can then be used as a soup base or further thickened for a consommé.

FROG'S LEGS À LA BÉCHAMEL
TO SERVE 4

8 sets of frog's legs (16 legs),
   soaked in milk for 1 hour
salt and pepper
2 oz butter

2 oz dry white wine
1½ cups Sauce Béchamel
3 oz cream

Dry off the frog's legs and season to taste with salt and pepper. Simmer in a covered pan with the butter and wine for 10 to 15 minutes, or until tender. Meanwhile, put the Béchamel and cream in a pan and boil down to thicken fairly well. Pour over the frog's legs in their pan and mix well. Turn the frog's legs and sauce into a hot dish and serve at once, hot.

Bénédictine

(bay-nay-deek-TEEN)

This name is more famous as a liqueur than a cooking mode. Benedictine liqueur was invented by the Bénédictine monks at the abbey at Fécamp, a town in northern France on the coast of the English Channel.

The Bénédictine order consists of autonomous congregations professing the same way of life, and unlike other orders has no general superior. Even within the individual abbey, the abbot exerts only limited authority and the individual members may undertake any work that is not at variance with the community life of the monastery. Saint Benedict of Nursia (480–c. 547) founded the order when he was shocked by the licentiousness of Rome, where he was studying. He retired to the Sabine hills, joining a group of men who shared his desire for a life of quiet and prayer. There, he was the first to stabilize and organize the monastic life of Europe. He lived for three years in a cave as a hermit in poverty, hard labor and prayer, the three principal features of his future guideline, the Bénédictine Rule.

His reputation for sanctity and wisdom spread, and he agreed to become abbot of a neighboring monastery. But his ideals were so radically different from those of the monks there that an attempt was made to poison him, and he returned to his cave. So many people came to seek his guidance that eventually there were twelve monasteries in the area, each with twelve monks and a superior. Benedict lived in a thirteenth monastery as abbot with a few chosen disciples.

Bénédictine dishes are noted for a garnish of Brandade of Salt Cod with truffles. Considering the principles of the Bénédictines, décor and music to accompany a dish à la Bénédictine become the essence of simplicity. Don't have any.

BRANDADE of SALT COD with TRUFFLES
TO SERVE 4

1 lb salt cod	salt (optional)
1¼ cups olive oil	white pepper
1 garlic clove, grated	½ cup truffles, chopped
½ cup cream, boiled	butter

Soak the cod in cold water overnight to remove extra salt. Cut into small pieces and poach in boiling water for 5 minutes. Drain and flake, discarding any skin and bones. Heat ½ cup of the olive oil in a pan. Add the flaked cod and garlic, and work the mixture to a smooth paste with a wooden spoon. Turn the heat very low and add the rest of the oil and the cream, alternating and just a little at a time, stirring vigorously. Season with salt (only if necessary) and pepper to taste. Cook, stirring, until it has the consistency of mashed potatoes, keeping the heat low to avoid boiling or browning. The finished mixture should be a thick, smooth, white paste. Sauté the truffles in a little butter and blend in. Serve hot.

Once the cod has been desalted, boiled and flaked, it can be sautéed lightly in 2 tablespoons of olive oil, then mixed with 2 ounces of heavy cream and cooked to thicken. Then add lightly sautéed truffles. This makes an unusual fish dish which may be substituted for the Brandade of Salt Cod and is much less fattening, since the 1¼ cups of olive oil in the Brandade contains over 2,500 calories. The Brandade is, however, the distinctive Bénédictine garnish, and using this substitute, although it is excellent, could disqualify the dish from being called à la Bénédictine, depending on how strict you wish to be.

EGGS À LA BÉNÉDICTINE (Poached or Soft-Boiled)
TO SERVE 4

1 cup Sauce Béchamel	8 eggs, freshly poached or soft-boiled and hot
½ cup cream	
1 Tbs butter	2 cups Brandade of Salt Cod, hot
2 Tbs heavy cream	

Make a Cream Sauce by mixing the Béchamel and cream and boiling down by ⅓. Remove from heat and blend in butter and cream. Keep hot. Prepare the eggs as desired. Divide the Brandade of Salt Cod on 4 hot plates, place 2 eggs on each, top with Cream Sauce and serve hot.

SUPRÊMES de VOLAILLE À LA BÉNÉDICTINE
TO SERVE 4

Halve 4 chicken breasts and skin and bone. Season lightly with salt and pepper, if desired, and sauté in butter until just done. Serve hot with Cream Sauce and Brandade of Salt Cod as in the recipe for Eggs à la Bénédictine.

This approach gives excellent results with any light meats, like other poultry, pork or veal.

RASPBERRIES À LA BÉNÉDICTINE
TO SERVE 4

1 cup milk, scalded and hot
2 Tbs sugar
¹/₁₆ tsp salt
1–2 oz Bénédictine liqueur

3 egg yolks
2 oz heavy cream
3 cups raspberries, cleaned and
   chilled

Put the milk in the top of a double boiler over simmering water. Stir in the sugar and salt. Stir in the Bénédictine. Using a fork, beat the yolks and cream lightly. Add to the milk mixture, slowly. Stir until warmed through. Raise heat so the water in the bottom of the double boiler boils, and continue stirring the custard mixture steadily until it thickens lightly. (Do not let it get above 180°. If the custard gets too hot, it becomes granular.) Remove from heat and place the top of the double boiler in a pan of cold water. Continue stirring the custard until it cools. Arrange the raspberries in a serving dish or in 4 individual dishes. Top with the Bénédictine-flavored cream, chill and serve.

CUSTARD À LA BÉNÉDICTINE
TO SERVE 4

Prepare Custard à l'Anglaise, substituting 1 ounce Bénédictine liqueur for the vanilla extract.

Bercy

(bayr-SEE)

A former seigniory (domain) east of Paris and a port for wood and wines. The name Bercy dated from 1134. The domain included numerous country estates from the seventeenth century on: the house of Rapée, Grange-aux-Merciers, and Bercy castle. It was at Bercy castle that Le Vau, La Guepière and Le Nôtre collaborated on the design and construction of the Palace of Versailles. Bercy was established as a commune in 1790 and incorporated into Paris in 1860, subsequently forming a section of the twelfth district of Paris, which is divided into twenty districts. The area around Bercy on the banks of the Seine is quite colorful, and known for its nightclubs.

The wine warehouse of Bercy was developed at the beginning of the nineteenth century and is what gives the cooking category its name. Bercy dishes are noted for the use of a wine-based sauce or a wine-flavored butter, which is often made right in the main-course pan, after the meat or fish is removed. You can further enhance a particular dish by cooking down meat or fish stock to a glaze* and brushing some of this glaze on the hot food before topping with Bercy Butter. An interesting dinner can be made with a mixed grill of meats of your choice, served with Bercy Butter.

Bercy Butter can be made long ahead, then cut in small pieces to put atop any dish just before serving—a simple way to enhance a dish at the last moment without any extra work to keep you from your guests. For suitable vegetables, try deep-fried shoestring potatoes, or tomatoes, halved, seasoned, sprinkled with grated cheese and broiled, or sautéed mushroom caps, lightly seasoned and sautéed with a few drops of lemon juice. Any or all of these, plus a fresh salad, are heartily recommended.

SAUCE BERCY (For Fish)
TO MAKE 2 CUPS

2 tsp chopped shallots	1½ cups Sauce Velouté,* pref-
2 tsp butter	erably fish-based
1 cup dry white wine	2 Tbs butter
1 cup fish fumet* or clam juice	2 tsp parsley

Cook the shallots in the butter until limp but not browned. Add wine and fish fumet and cook down to ⅓. Add the Velouté and boil for 3 minutes. Stir in butter and parsley and serve hot.

This sauce is usually made right in the pan while cooking fish.

BERCY BUTTER (For Meat and Fish)
TO MAKE 1 CUP

2 tsp shallots, chopped fine	1½ tsp parsley
½ cup dry white wine	1 tsp lemon juice
3 oz butter, softened	½ tsp salt
¼ lb beef marrow, diced	⅛ tsp white pepper

Put shallots and wine in a pan and boil down to half. Let cool. When almost cold, add butter and blend. Meanwhile, poach the marrow in lightly salted water and drain dry. Add to the butter mixture. Add the rest of the ingredients and blend well.

This butter is generally served in little pieces, melting on the top of a hot piece of meat or fish. Any meat or fish served in this way can be called à la Bercy.

EGGS À LA BERCY (Baked)
TO SERVE 4

8 eggs	8 small pork sausages, cooked
salt and pepper	and hot
grated cheese	1½ cups Tomato Sauce, prefer-
	ably homemade* and hot

Preheat oven to 500°. Carefully break 2 eggs into each of 4 individual buttered baking dishes, without breaking the yolks. Season with salt and pepper and sprinkle liberally with grated cheese. Bake on a high rack in the oven for 4 minutes, or until whites are just set and yolks still soft. Put 2 sausages on each egg dish, top with Tomato Sauce and serve at once, hot.

OMELET À LA BERCY
TO SERVE 2

4 eggs	4 chipolata sausages (or small
½ tsp chervil	pork sausages), cooked and
¼ tsp chives	hot
¼ tsp tarragon	½ cup thick Tomato Sauce,
¼ tsp parsley	preferably homemade* and
4 Tbs butter	hot

Beat the eggs with the chervil, chives, tarragon and parsley. Heat the butter and prepare the omelet.* Serve the omelet at once on a hot dish, garnished with the sausages and topped with the thick Tomato Sauce.

BEEFSTEAK À LA BERCY (Entrecôte)
TO SERVE 4

¼ cup butter	3 oz dry white wine
4 steaks	¼ cup butter
salt and pepper	4 tsp parsley
3 Tbs chopped onion	lemon juice
1 garlic clove, minced	

Melt ¼ cup butter in a pan and sauté the steaks until done to taste. Put on a hot platter, season to taste with salt and pepper and keep hot. Add the onion and garlic to the pan and cook until limp but not browned. Add wine and boil down to half. Remove from heat and beat in ¼ cup butter a bit at a time to blend. Mix in the parsley and a few drops of lemon juice to taste. Pour over the steaks and serve at once, hot.

CALF'S LIVER À LA BERCY
TO SERVE 4

2 lbs calf's liver, sliced
salt and pepper
flour

butter
4 Tbs Bercy Butter, diced

Season the liver with salt and pepper lightly and dredge in flour, shaking off the excess. Sauté in butter until done, or grill. Serve on hot plates, with Bercy Butter melting on top.

FLOUNDER À LA BERCY
TO SERVE 4

butter
2 Tbs shallots, chopped
1 Tbs parsley
4 whole 1½-lb flounder, cleaned
  or 2 lbs fillets

salt and pepper
2 oz dry white wine
1 Tbs lemon juice
2 oz butter, diced

Preheat oven to 325°. Butter a baking dish well and sprinkle with the shallots and parsley. Season fish lightly with salt and pepper and place on the baking dish. Sprinkle with wine and lemon juice and top with butter pieces. Cook in the oven until just done, about 15 minutes, basting often. When fish flakes easily with a fork, it is done. Do not overcook. Serve hot, in the baking dish.

This recipe is fine with any fish or fish fillets, from sole or salmon to eel.

LOBSTER À LA BERCY
TO SERVE 4

1½ Tbs minced shallots
1 oz butter
½ cup dry white wine
½ cup fish stock* or clam juice
1 cup Sauce Velouté,* preferably fish-based
3 Tbs butter
2 tsp parsley

2 2-lb lobsters, cooked
3 Tbs butter
1 garlic clove, mashed
1 tsp parsley
¼ tsp thyme
¼ tsp chervil
2 oz Parmesan cheese, grated

Make a sauce by sautéing the shallots in the butter in a pan until limp but not browned. Add wine and stock and boil down to ⅔. Add Velouté and boil 3 minutes. Blend in the butter and parsley and set aside, keeping hot.

Split the lobsters lengthwise, reserving meat and juices. Clean out the shells. Chop the meat and sauté in the butter with the garlic, parsley, thyme and chervil. Meanwhile, add the juices to the sauce and cook down to thicken.

Preheat broiler. Fill the lobster shells with half the lobster meat and sprinkle with a tablespoon of cheese. Top with half the sauce. Add the remaining lobster meat and top with the remaining sauce. Sprinkle generously with cheese. Brown until golden under the broiler and serve hot.

Blanc

(blahng)

Means white. Foods prepared au Blanc are cooked without coloring, such as chicken simmered in chicken or veal stock* until done and served with a white sauce.

Any food that is white, or at least light, may be called Blanc. For example, plain cooked rice is called Rice au Blanc. The cooking mode Blanc is related to Béchamel and Crème. All use white sauces, and in many recipes the names are interchangeable.

For a beverage with a dish au Blanc, how about a good champagne, a *blanc de blancs,* perhaps?

An interesting motif for the décor would be the purest white linen and china set off by a few brilliant flowers and a vegetable or two like carrots or beets. The touch of color would accent the whiteness of the overall scheme.

SAUCE BLANC
TO MAKE 2 CUPS

½ cup Sauce Velouté*
3 oz white port wine, or dry white
   vermouth
2 cups heavy cream

salt and white pepper
lemon juice
chives, parsley or chervil, fresh
   (optional)

Mix the Velouté and port in a pan and boil down to half. Add the cream and cook to thicken. Remove from heat, season to taste with salt, pepper and a few drops of lemon juice, and serve hot, sprinkled with chives, parsley or chervil if desired, with meats, fish and vegetables.

This sauce is often made right in the main-course pan, right after the meat or fish has been set aside and kept hot. Add the Velouté and port to the pan and boil down while scraping up the juices. Then finish with the cream and seasonings.

BEURRE BLANC (White Butter)
TO MAKE 1 CUP

2 Tbs white wine vinegar
2 Tbs white wine, or lemon juice
1 Tbs minced shallots

⅛ tsp white pepper
1 cup butter, cut in ½-oz pieces

Put the vinegar, wine, shallots and pepper in a pan and boil liquid down to 1 tablespoon. Remove from heat and beat in 2 pieces of butter with a whisk. As soon as the butter blends with the liquid, set the pan on very low heat and beat in the rest of the butter piece by piece, until thick and creamy and an ivory color. Check flavor and add salt, white pepper and a few drops of lemon juice if needed. Serve hot with fish, eggs and vegetables.

ONIONS AU BLANC
TO SERVE 4

1½ lbs small onions
½ cup chicken stock*
½ cup dry white wine
2 Tbs butter
1 tsp parsley

¼ tsp thyme
¼ bay leaf
cheesecloth, washed
salt and white pepper

Put the onions, stock, wine and butter in a pot. Add the parsley, thyme and bay leaf, tied in cheesecloth, and season lightly with salt and pepper. Simmer very slowly, covered, shaking the pot occasionally, for 45 minutes. Remove cover and let the liquids thicken to glaze the onions. Discard herb bouquet and serve hot. (Check liquids once or twice during cooking, and add a little stock if needed.)

CABBAGE AU BLANC
TO SERVE 4

2 lbs cabbage, cut in pieces

½ cup Beurre Blanc, or Sauce Béchamel, hot

Cook the cabbage in lightly salted water until done and tender and drain well. Serve in a vegetable dish topped with Beurre Blanc, hot.

SWISS CHARD AU BLANC (or Other Green Vegetables)

See Artichoke Hearts à la Béchamel. The recipes are the same, and the names interchangeable. Actually this is a misnomer, since green vegetables are certainly never blanc, but the name appears in books and on menus nonetheless. To be correct, they should be called à la Béchamel. Or, if the vegetables are cooked and served with Sauce Blanc, they may be termed au Sauce Blanc.

VEAL ESCALOPES AU BLANC (Slices)
TO SERVE 4

2 lbs veal slices, similar in size
salt and white pepper
lemon juice
3 carrots, quartered
1 onion, quartered
2 celery stalks, quartered
1 cup chicken or veal stock* or
    broth

1 Tbs parsley
½ tsp thyme
½ bay leaf
½ tsp chervil
cheesecloth, washed
½ cup Beurre Blanc, hot

Season the veal slices lightly with salt, white pepper and a few drops of lemon juice. Put the carrots, onion and celery in a pot with the stock. Add the parsley, thyme, bay leaf and chervil tied in cheesecloth. Put the veal in on the vegetables and cook, covered, at a low simmer for about 40 minutes, or until the meat is done. Remove the meat, drain, and serve with hot Beurre Blanc.

The veal cooking liquids can be strained and used as stock for soup or for braising other light meats, such as chicken.

CALF'S SWEETBREADS AU BLANC
TO SERVE 4

Proceed as for Veal Escalopes au Blanc, replacing the veal with 2 pounds of calf's sweetbreads. Soak sweetbreads in cold water for 4 hours, changing waters often. Drain and slice, trimming away center tubes.

CHICKEN SUPRÊMES AU BLANC
TO SERVE 4

4 chicken breasts, halved,
    skinned and boned
salt and white pepper

lemon juice
butter
½ cup Beurre Blanc, hot.

Season the chicken lightly with salt, pepper and a few drops of lemon juice. Sauté gently in butter, without browning at all, until just done. Serve with Beurre Blanc, hot.

FLOUNDER, COD or SCALLOPS AU BLANC
TO SERVE 4

Proceed as for Chicken Suprêmes au Blanc. This is fine for any seafood; simply sauté gently in butter without browning and serve with Beurre Blanc, hot. Another method would be to poach in white wine with a little butter. Parsley, thyme and chervil may be added, if desired.

For a fun dish, combine your favorite seafoods, cook them as in the Chicken Suprême recipe and serve with hot Beurre Blanc. The result would be something like a mixed grill with meats. Another variation, for the adventuresome, is to combine seafoods with light meats like chicken or veal. You can make some exciting combinations, and if they're all cooked as in the Chicken Suprême recipe, they'll go together excellently.

Bonne Femme

(bun FAHM)

Bonne means good and *femme* means woman, so *Bonne Femme* means good woman, old, or rustic, woman, and many of these dishes are also called Grand-Mère, or Grandmother. In cuisine, this term covers a lot of territory, anything that signifies good old home-cooking, especially that which uses vegetables cooked with the main courses.

For poultry and meats, Bonne Femme generally means cooking potatoes, small onions, lean bacon and mushrooms with the main course. For fish, it means cooking them with thinly sliced mushrooms, although I prefer small button mushrooms. Bonne Femme cooking is excellent in its simplicity, and the main courses need little embellishment, save perhaps a green vegetable. Peas à la Française would be good, as would most vegetables.

There are many cooking modes that have vegetables as their hallmark, such as Fermière, Jardinière and Bouquetière. These modes, however, generally use a greater variety of vegetables. Bonne Femme is noteworthy for its simplicity, which makes it ideal for combining on a menu with a large variety of other dishes. The simpler a dish, the more versatile. With a dish à la Bonne Femme, a simple dry wine is in order. Not a fancy label, but the equivalent of the wine of the house, which is available in much of Europe. Reasonable but good, as a *Bonne Femme* would recommend.

For décor and general atmosphere, a dining room table set with rustic cloth and simple dishes.

BONNE FEMME GARNISHES
TO SERVE 4

1. TO BE COOKED WITH MEATS:

1½–2 lbs potatoes, trimmed like olives	½ lb very lean bacon, diced
1 lb small onions	½–1 lb button mushrooms

Cook all with the meat, or poultry, in the pan. Add potatoes for the final hour of cooking, onions and bacon for the final ½ hour and mushrooms for the last 10 to 15 minutes. The mushrooms should be lightly sautéed in butter before adding to the pan. The potatoes and onions may be blanched, before adding, in lightly salted boiling water for 5 minutes, if desired. The bacon should be lightly sautéed before adding to the pan, to bring out its flavor and remove some of its fat.

2. TO BE COOKED WITH FISH:

¾ lb thinly sliced mushrooms

Sauté lightly in butter and cook with the fish for the final 10 minutes of its cooking time.

POTATOES À LA BONNE FEMME
TO SERVE 4

2 lbs potatoes	1 onion, sliced thin
2 oz butter	pepper
¼ lb bacon, in thin slices	chives

Peel the potatoes and cut in ¼-inch slices. Melt the butter in a pan. Top with the bacon, then the onion, then the potatoes. Season lightly with pepper and cover. Cook over low heat without stirring for 25 minutes, or until tender, occasionally shaking the pan to prevent sticking. When done, transfer to a hot serving dish, tossing a bit to mix. Sprinkle with chives and serve hot.

This dish is very flavorful using unpeeled sliced potatoes, but then it should be called Potatoes in Their Skins à la Bonne Femme.

GREEN BEANS À LA BONNE FEMME
TO SERVE 4

1½ lbs green beans	1 Tbs butter (optional)
10 oz lean bacon, diced	parsley
3 oz thick veal stock* or gravy	

Boil the beans in lightly salted water until ¾ done. Drain thoroughly. Blanch the bacon in boiling water for 2 to 3 minutes and drain. Put the bacon in a pan and sauté lightly. Add the beans and stock and simmer slowly, covered, until the beans are cooked, about 10 minutes. Stir in the butter, if desired. Sprinkle with parsley and serve hot.

PEAS À LA BONNE FEMME
TO SERVE 4

1 Tbs butter	¾ cup chicken stock* or broth
12 small onions	1½ lbs peas
¼ lb lean bacon, diced and blanched in boiling water for 2 minutes	1 tsp parsley
	¼ tsp thyme
	¼ bay leaf
1 Tbs flour	cheesecloth, washed

Melt the butter in a pan. Add the onions and bacon and brown lightly. Remove the onions and bacon and add the flour. Cook, stirring, for a few minutes to blend (and remove the raw flour taste), but do not brown. Add the stock and boil for 5 minutes. Add the peas. Return the onions and bacon. Add the parsley, thyme and bay leaf tied in cheesecloth. Do not overcook. Discard herb bouquet and serve in a hot bowl.

TOMATOES À LA BONNE FEMME (Stuffed)
TO SERVE 4

4 tomatoes, halved and seeded
salt and pepper
olive oil, or vegetable oil
1 lb pork sausage meat
4 Tbs chopped onion, sautéed
   in butter

½ cup bread crumbs
2 garlic cloves
1 Tbs parsley
bread crumbs
oil

Preheat oven to 350°. Season the tomato halves well with salt and pepper and sauté in hot oil lightly. Mix the sausage meat with the onion and bread crumbs. Chop garlic and parsley together very fine and mix well with the sausage mixture. Pile this stuffing on the tomato halves. Put a foil cup around the sides and bottom of each stuffed tomato half to help hold the tomato's shape while it bakes. Arrange on a baking pan. Sprinkle the stuffed tomatoes liberally with crumbs and a few drops of oil to moisten and bake for 30 minutes, or until done. Serve hot.

OMELET À LA BONNE FEMME
TO SERVE 2

¼ cup potatoes, chopped
¼ cup lean bacon, chopped
¼ cup onion, chopped
butter

salt and pepper
4 eggs
4 Tbs butter
chives

Sauté the potatoes, bacon and onion in a little butter until lightly browned and done. Season with salt and pepper to taste. Keep hot. Prepare an omelet* in the 4 tablespoons of butter and fill with the potatoes, bacon and onion. When done, serve hot, sprinkled with chives.

BEEF ENTRECÔTE À LA BONNE FEMME (Steak)
TO SERVE 4

4 steaks
salt and pepper
butter
24 small onions, lightly sautéed

2 lbs potatoes, cut like olives
   and blanched in boiling water
   for 10 minutes
½ lb lean bacon, diced and lightly sautéed
1 cup beef stock* or gravy
parsley

Season the steaks to taste with salt and pepper and sauté in butter with the onions, potatoes and bacon. Arrange on a hot dish (an oval earthenware dish would be ideal) and keep hot. Quickly add the stock to the pan, scraping up the juices. Blend well and strain over the steaks. Sprinkle with parsley and serve hot.

This is a nice, straightforward dish, simple and hearty. Add a green vegetable and you have a complete meal!

MUTTON RAGOUT À LA BONNE FEMME
TO SERVE 4

3 lbs mutton, in pieces
salt and pepper
½ onion
butter
½ tsp sugar
4 Tbs flour
2 garlic cloves, crushed
1 qt clear beef stock* or broth
1 Tbs parsley
1 tsp basil

4 Tbs tomato paste, or 1 cup tomato pulp, seeded and peeled*
½ tsp thyme
½ bay leaf
cheesecloth, washed
2 lbs potatoes, cut like olives
24 small onions
½ lb lean bacon

Preheat oven to 325°. Season the mutton lightly with salt and pepper and brown with the ½ onion in a casserole in butter. Pour off excess fat. Add sugar and flour and blend. Add garlic and stir in the stock and tomato paste. Tie the parsley, basil, thyme and bay leaf in cheesecloth and add. Cover and cook in the oven for 1 hour.

Skim fat from the casserole and add the potatoes, small onions and bacon. Recover and cook in the oven for 1 hour more, or until meat and vegetables are done and tender. Discarb herb bouquet and serve in the casserole or on a hot earthenware dish.

LAMB RAGOUT À LA BONNE FEMME
TO SERVE 4

Proceed as for Mutton Ragout à la Bonne Femme, omitting the ½ onion in the beginning. When the casserole is done, stir 4 tablespoons tomato purée or sauce into the casserole juices. This dish may also be made using water in place of the beef stock.

LAMB LOIN À LA BONNE FEMME
TO SERVE 4

1 lamb loin
salt and pepper
butter
2 lbs potatoes, cut like olives and blanched in boiling water for 5 minutes
½ cup beef stock* or broth
1 tsp parsley
½ tsp basil

¼ tsp thyme
½ bay leaf
cheesecloth, washed
24 small onions
½ lb lean bacon, diced and lightly sautéed
parsley
chives

Preheat oven to 325°. Season lamb with salt and pepper lightly and brown well in a casserole or iron pot, in butter. Add the potatoes and stock to the casserole. Add the parsley, basil, thyme and bay leaf tied in cheesecloth, cover, and bake in oven for about ½ hour. Add the onions and bacon. Bake, covered, ½ hour more, or until meat and vegetables are done. Discard herb bouquet. Sprinkle with parsley and chives and serve hot, in the casserole.

PORK LOIN À LA BONNE FEMME
TO SERVE 4

Proceed as for Lamb Loin à la Bonne Femme, using chicken stock* in place of the beef stock and cooking longer. After browning, cook about 40 minutes per pound.

CHICKEN CASSEROLE À LA BONNE FEMME
TO SERVE 4

Proceed as for Lamb Loin à la Bonne Femme, using 2 small young chickens, cut up, and substituting chicken stock for beef stock.

QUAIL or CORNISH GAME HENS À LA BONNE FEMME
TO SERVE 4

Proceed as for Chicken Casserole à la Bonne Femme, using 4 whole 1-pound birds. Adjust cooking time to about ¾ hour. Blanch the potatoes for 10 minutes instead of 5, to assure their finishing with the birds.

SOLE À LA BONNE FEMME
TO SERVE 4

2 lbs fish fillets	½ cup fish fumet* or clam juice
salt and pepper	lemon juice
butter	2 Tbs butter, diced
½ lb mushrooms, chopped	1 Tbs butter kneaded with
coarse, or button	1 Tbs flour (this is a *beurre*
mushrooms	*manié*)
1 tsp parsley	2 lemons, cut in wedges, seeded
½ cup dry white wine	

Preheat oven to 350°. Season the fillets to taste with salt and pepper. Butter a casserole well. Add the mushrooms, sprinkle with parsley, and place the fillets on this bed. Add the wine and fish fumet, sprinkle each fillet with a few drops of lemon juice and dot them with the 2 tablespoons of butter. Bring to a boil on top of the stove, cover and bake in the oven for 10 minutes, or until fish flakes easily and is done.

Remove fillets carefully to a hot platter, without breaking them, and surround with the mushrooms. Keep hot. Add the *beurre manié* to the cooking juices and quickly boil to thicken over direct heat. Meanwhile, raise oven heat to broil. Coat the fish and mushrooms with the thickened juices and run under the broiler to glaze. Serve hot, with lemon wedges.

This is an excellent recipe for any white-fleshed fish. For a bit of variety, try serving lime wedges along with the standard lemon wedges.

MUSSELS À LA BONNE FEMME
AS AN HORS D'OEUVRE FOR 4

1 qt mussels, live and well
    cleaned
1 small onion, minced
2 oz sliced mushrooms
3 Tbs celery, slivered
½ tsp parsley
½ bay leaf
¼ tsp chervil
cheesecloth, washed

1 garlic clove
½ cup dry white wine
½ cup water
pepper
1 egg yolk beaten with 2 oz
    heavy cream
1 Tbs butter, softened
salt

Put the mussels, onion, mushrooms and celery in a kettle. Add the parsley, bay leaf and chervil tied in cheesecloth, and the garlic, wine and water. Season to taste with pepper. Cover tightly and simmer over moderate heat for about 10 minutes, shaking occasionally, or until the mussels are open and are done. Put the mussels and their shells aside and keep hot.

Discard herb bouquet and garlic and quickly boil down the cooking broth by ¼. Remove from heat and beat in the yolk and cream mixture and the softened butter. Season with salt to taste and pour over the mussels. Serve at once, hot.

This dish is often made using 1 cup of wine, rather than ½ cup of wine plus ½ cup of water, but it is less delicate.

SOUP À LA BONNE FEMME
TO SERVE 4

2 leeks, white part only,
    shredded
1 Tbs butter
1 qt chicken consommé*
1 cup potatoes, cut in small
    slices

salt and pepper
2 Tbs butter (optional)
1½ tsp chervil

Cook the leeks gently in the 1 tablespoon of butter in a covered pot until limp but not browned. Add the consommé and bring to a boil. Add the potatoes, season to taste with salt and pepper and simmer gently, covered, until the potatoes are done. Stir in 2 tablespoons butter, if you wish, and add the chervil. Remove from heat and let stand for 2 minutes. Serve hot.

This soup may be seasoned with a tiny pinch of dry mustard if desired, and is often thickened with 1 tablespoon of cream beaten with an egg yolk, which is stirred into the consommé off heat just before serving.

APPLES À LA BONNE FEMME
TO SERVE 4

4 cooking apples, cored	6 Tbs sugar
4 tsp butter, semisoftened	½ tsp cinnamon

Preheat oven to 375°. Peel a 1-inch strip of skin from around the middle of the apples to prevent their splitting while baking, or score the skins 6 or 8 times from top to bottom. Mix the butter, sugar and cinnamon and put in the apples' hollow centers. Stand the apples in ¼ inch of water in a baking dish and bake in the oven for 30 to 40 minutes, or until tender when poked with a fork. Spoon some of the pan syrup over the apples a few times during cooking. Serve hot, right in the baking dish.

Bordelaise

(bohr-duh-LEZ)

From Bordeaux, capital of the Department of Gironde, in southwest France, the land of fine wines and food to match. Bordeaux is a large city, today spreading westward, building right over the vineyards that have made it famous. It is located on the Garonne river, about fifty-five miles inland from the Bay of Biscay. Being near a coastal area, the people of Bordeaux make great use of seafood. The famous Marennes oysters and a whole spectrum of fish, shellfish and crustaceans, and the food and wines of Bordeaux were praised back in the fourth century by the Roman poet Decimus Magnus Ausonius.

As a cooking style, Bordelaise is quite varied. You'll find a great number of dishes in at least four subcategories, which often overlap or are combined: dishes characterized by Sauce Bordelaise, dishes cooked with Mushrooms à la Bordelaise, dishes cooked with a mirepoix of vegetables and/or meats and dishes with a garnish of artichokes and potatoes. The garnishes supply a well-rounded vegetable group to complement any dish à la Bordelaise.

There are a great many interesting recipes and variations for this style. For example, a veal or lamb breast can be stuffed with veal mousse* (or a stuffing of your choice) and roasted in a little dry red Bordeaux wine and water and served with Sauce Bordelaise. (The breast can be seasoned inside and out and marinated in brandy before stuffing and cooking.) Pork chops stuffed with veal mousse and served with Sauce Bordelaise are also excellent.

If the garnishes are discounted, Bordelaise becomes a fairly basic cooking style, using Bordeaux wine as the moistening liquid, much as the style Bourguignonne uses Burgundy wine. Other regional wines that lend their names to the dishes they are used in are: Champenoise (Champagne wine), Maconnaise (Macon wine) and Chambertin (Chambertin wine).

About 500 million bottles of Bordeaux are produced annually in France's Gironde department, and nothing could be more fitting to accompany a dish à la Bordelaise than a good Bordeaux wine. Bordeaux is a great name in wines, but the quality varies from the very finest to quite mediocre. As with all good imported wines, the prices are fairly high. For a domestic wine, red Bordeaux's equivalent here in the United States is claret.

SAUCE BORDELAISE
TO MAKE 2 CUPS

½ cup red Bordeaux wine
1 Tbs chopped shallots
¼ tsp pepper (or to taste)
½ tsp thyme

½ bay leaf
2 cups Sauce Espagnole
salt
2 Tbs beef marrow, minced fine

Put the wine, shallots, pepper, thyme and bay leaf in a pan and boil down until almost dry. Add Espagnole and season with salt to taste if necessary. Simmer for 10 minutes on very low heat. Strain sauce, add marrow, and simmer a few minutes longer. Serve hot with meats, especially steak and poultry.

BORDELAISE GARNISHES
TO SERVE 4

1. MUSHROOMS À LA BORDELAISE

½ lb mushrooms, sliced
2 Tbs butter
¼ tsp lemon juice
1 Tbs olive oil

salt and pepper
1 garlic clove, minced
½ tsp each of parsley, chervil,
    chives and tarragon

Stew the mushrooms in a pan in the butter and lemon juice until limp. Drain on paper towels. Put the oil in another pan and add the mushrooms, season to taste with salt and pepper, and sauté for a few minutes over low heat. Add the garlic, parsley, chervil, chives and tarragon and sauté until golden.

This is an attractive garnish, especially when done with whole tiny button mushrooms. Small, thin ham strips are often sautéed with the mushrooms. If adding the ham, add 2 to 3 ounces of small strips with the garlic and herbs and cook while the mushrooms finish.

2. 2 pounds of potatoes, cut like olives or thinly sliced, cooked in clarified* butter over very low heat until done and golden, but not overly browned or crumbling.

3. 1–1½ pounds tiny artichokes, trimmed* and simmered in butter until very tender.

4. 1½ pounds onion rings, dredged in flour, seasoned well with salt and pepper and sautéed until golden, or deep-fried.

EGGS BAKED À LA BORDELAISE
TO SERVE 4

1 recipe Garnish #1, hot
8 eggs
4 tsp butter, melted

1 recipe Tomatoes à la
    Provençale, hot, using small
    to medium tomatoes and
    halving the remaining ingre-
    dients (optional)

Preheat oven to 500°. Divide the Mushrooms à la Bordelaise between 4 individual baking dishes. Top with 2 eggs each, being careful not to break the yolks. Dribble the butter on the yolks and place on a high rack in the oven for 4 minutes, or until the whites are just set and the yolks still soft. Serve in the baking dishes, with the Provençale Tomatoes on the side if desired.

BEEF ENTRECÔTE À LA BORDELAISE (Steak)
TO SERVE 4

4 steaks
salt and pepper

8 slices of beef marrow,
    poached 10 minutes in lightly
    salted water, hot
2 cups Sauce Bordelaise, hot

Season the steaks lightly and grill or broil (or sauté in half butter and half olive oil). When done to taste, serve topped with marrow slices. Serve sauce separately, hot.

This recipe is excellent with Tournedos (fillets) of Beef, and is very often served with fried onion rings. An excellent combination.

LAMB LOIN À LA BORDELAISE
TO SERVE 4

½ lb mushroom caps
olive oil
2 cups Sauce Espagnole, or
    beef gravy
1½ Tbs tomato paste
1 garlic clove, crushed
1 Tbs butter

1 Tbs olive oil
1 lamb loin roast
1½ lbs potatoes, cut in small
    balls, or new potatoes
salt and red pepper
parsley

Preheat oven to 325°. Brown the mushrooms lightly and quickly in a little oil. Meanwhile, simmer the Espagnole with the tomato paste and garlic for 5 minutes, cover and set aside. Put the butter and oil in a casserole and brown the lamb. Add the mushrooms and potatoes. Season to taste with salt and red pepper and bake in the oven, uncovered, for 30 minutes. Raise heat to 350°. Pour the Espagnole mixture over the meat and cook for 20 minutes more, or until done, basting twice. Turn off oven and let meat stand in it for 5 minutes. Serve hot, in the casserole, sprinkled with parsley.

A double loin is called a rack, and serves 8.

CALF'S LIVER À LA BORDELAISE
TO SERVE 4

2 lbs calf's liver, sliced	butter
salt and pepper	1 lb ham, sliced
flour	2 cups Sauce Bordelaise, hot

Season the liver to taste with salt and pepper and dredge in flour, shaking off the excess. Sauté in butter until done. Meanwhile, sauté the ham lightly in butter, seasoned with pepper if desired. Arrange the liver and ham slices in an alternating and overlapping row on a hot platter and serve the sauce separately, hot.

CHICKEN SAUTÉ À LA BORDELAISE
TO SERVE 4

2 small tender chickens, cut up	2 Tbs butter (optional)
salt and pepper	3 cups sliced potatoes
butter and olive oil	4 artichoke hearts
1 garlic clove, crushed	2 medium onions, sliced in rings
1½ cups white Bordeaux wine	and dredged in well-sea-
2 cups thick veal stock* or	soned flour
Sauce Espagnole	butter
1½ Tbs tomato purée	parsley and/or chives

Season the chicken to taste with salt and pepper. Heat a little butter and oil in a pan with the garlic. Add the chicken and sauté until done and golden. Remove the chicken and keep hot. Discard the garlic. Add the wine to the pan and boil down, scraping up the juices. Add the veal stock and tomato purée and blend well. Add the butter, if desired, and keep hot.

Meanwhile, cook the potatoes in butter gently, without breaking, and keep hot. Cook the artichoke hearts in butter without browning and keep hot. Cook the onion rings in butter until done and golden and keep hot. When the chicken is done, arrange it on a hot platter surrounded with piles of potatoes and onion rings. Garnish with the artichoke hearts. Coat with the sauce, or serve the sauce separately. Sprinkle with parsley and/or chives and serve hot.

FLOUNDER À LA BORDELAISE
TO SERVE 4

2 lbs flounder fillets
salt and pepper
2 carrots, sliced
2 onions, sliced
1 Tbs parsley
½ tsp thyme
½ tsp chervil
½ bay leaf
cheesecloth, washed
1 cup red Bordeaux wine

½ lb button mushrooms,
    sautéed in butter, hot
½ lb tiny onions
2 cups water
1 Tbs sugar
3 Tbs butter
salt and pepper
½ cup Sauce Espagnole
1 Tbs butter (optional)

Season the fish lightly with salt and pepper. Put the carrots and onions in a buttered pan. Add the parsley, thyme, chervil and bay leaf tied in cheesecloth. Add the wine. Bring to a boil and cook for 15 minutes. Put the fish on this foundation and simmer, covered, for 10 minutes, or until just done. Drain the fillets and arrange on a hot platter with the mushrooms and keep hot.

Meanwhile, put the onions, water, sugar and butter in a pot and season very lightly with salt and pepper. Boil until the liquid is reduced to a glaze, and toss the onions in this glaze to coat. Put the glazed onions on the platter with the fish and mushrooms. Add the Sauce Espagnole (and the butter if desired) to the fish cooking liquids and boil down quickly to thicken lightly. Strain over the fish and serve hot.

This recipe is excellent with any white-fleshed fish fillets, or eel.

LOBSTER À LA BORDELAISE
TO SERVE 4

4 1½-lb lobsters
2 oz butter
salt, pepper, basil and tarragon
4 oz brandy, warm
1½ cups white Bordeaux wine

1½ cups vegetable mirepoix
3 egg yolks
1 oz butter
salt and pepper

Cook the lobsters in lightly salted boiling water until they are red and done. Drain, and carefully remove the meat from body, tail and claws without breaking in pieces. Slice the tail meat thickly. Discard shells and remains. Melt the 2 ounces of butter in a pan and toss the lobster meat gently for 5 minutes without breaking up. Season lightly with salt and pepper. Add a little basil and tarragon to taste, mix gently, and simmer 2 minutes more. Add the brandy and flame, stirring. After the flame dies, add the wine and vegetable mirepoix and cook, uncovered, for 20 minutes, letting the stock reduce and thicken. Remove the lobster pieces to a hot platter and keep hot. Take the pan from the heat and let cool to below a boil. Mix in the yolks, one at a time, and the 1 ounce of butter. Season to taste with salt and pepper, pour over the lobster and serve hot.

This dish can be made with shrimp instead of lobster, and is excellent. Use 3 pounds of raw shrimp and cook as directed for the lobster.

SCALLOPS À LA BORDELAISE
TO SERVE 4

1 onion, chopped
1 shallot, minced
4 Tbs butter
1½ lbs scallops, cleaned
2 oz brandy

1 large tomato, peeled,* seeded
  and chopped
1 garlic clove, minced
½ tsp chervil
salt and pepper
½ cup white Bordeaux wine

Sauté the onion and shallot in the butter until limp but not browned. Add the scallops and cook until light golden and almost done. Add the brandy and flame, stirring until the fire dies. Add the tomato, garlic and chervil. Season lightly with salt and pepper. Add the wine and simmer 5 minutes, stirring gently. Transfer the scallops to a hot platter and keep hot. Quickly cook down the pan juices to thicken lightly. Strain over the scallops and serve at once, hot.

Bouquetière

(boo-keh-T'YAYR)

Means flower girl, and is the name of a garnish of vegetables arranged to look like small separate flower bouquets surrounding a roast or fowl. The standard vegetables used are cauliflower flowerets, broccoli flowerets, small bunches of asparagus spears, held together and standing upright, and stuffed artichokes. Radish flowerets are occasionally included. Often carrots, potatoes or turnips are placed around the bottoms of the asparagus bunches, etc., to hold them. The idea is to surround the roast with a display of vegetables that look like small flower bouquets, and any way you do that entitles you to call the dish à la Bouquetière. Since this is not a true cooking mode but a method of garnishing large cuts of meat, the prime ingredient is not a food or foods, but your artistic ability in arranging the various vegetables around the roast.

An interesting addition to any display à la Bouquetière would be nasturtium flowers, since they are not only beautiful and colorful, but also tasty. The young flowers, stems and leaves are all edible, with a slightly peppery taste, quite good with any roast. Borage leaves and flowers can also be used, as can rose petals. All are edible, and would help make an unusual garnish for any dish.

There are other cooking styles that are characterized by garden vegetables, like Jardinière and Fermière, but Bouquetière stands apart. In Bouquetière, the display of the food must be as artistic as its preparation, which is a good idea in any category.

Décor cries for a centerpiece of different flowers in separate bouquets, as in a florist's shop, perhaps with many petals strewn around the tablecloth.

BEEF ROAST À LA BOUQUETIÈRE
TO SERVE 4

1 beef rib roast (4 ribs)	1 lb asparagus spears
salt and pepper	1 lb potatoes, cut like olives
1 lb artichoke hearts	butter
½ lb carrots, diced	4 oz Madeira wine
½ lb turnips, diced	2 cups Sauce Espagnole, or
1 lb cauliflower flowerets	beef gravy
	1½ cups Hollandaise Sauce, hot

Preheat oven to 325°. Season the roast with salt and pepper to taste and place on a rack. Bake for 25 minutes per pound, in a pan to catch the drippings, for rare inside cuts. For well done, bake 35 minutes per pound.

Meanwhile, blanch the artichokes, carrots, turnips and cauliflower separately in boiling water for 10 minutes. Drain. Sauté all the vegetables except the asparagus in butter, separately, if possible. Allow only the potatoes to brown lightly. Cook the asparagus in lightly salted water and toss in a little butter. Stuff half the artichoke hearts with carrots and the other half with turnips. Keep all the vegetables hot.

When the roast is done, place it on a platter and keep it hot. Dilute the roasting pan juices with the wine, scraping up the drippings, and add the Espagnole. Arrange the stuffed artichokes and cauliflower in bunches around the roast, using them to help support the asparagus. Alternate around the roast with piles of potatoes. Pour the Hollandaise Sauce over the asparagus, artichokes and cauliflower. Strain the pan sauce into a sauceboat and serve separately, hot.

This recipe is fine with any roast, but what makes Bouquetière an interesting style is the variety available. You can use all manner of vegetables that either look like flowers to begin with or that you can cut and arrange to look like flowers. In all cases, the vegetables are prepared entirely separate from the roast and the beauty of the display is as important as the quality of the cooking.

PORK ROAST À LA BOUQUETIÈRE
TO SERVE 4

Proceed as for Beef Roast à la Bouquetière, cooking the meat until well done, since it's pork.

CHICKEN À LA BOUQUETIÈRE
TO SERVE 4

Proceed as for Beef Roast à la Bouquetière, using a roast chicken or other fowl. Four small game hens can be used to make a very impressive display, since they can help hold up "bouquets" of asparagus, etc. This would be an interesting way to display a turkey at Thanksgiving—the traditional turkey, with a not-so-traditional vegetable garnish.

Bourgeoise

(boor-ZHWAZ)

Means of the middle class, or pertaining to the middle class, like a tradesman; *not* aristocratic.

In cooking, Bourgeoise usually applies to large cuts of meat, and always to a garnish of uniformly cut carrots, small, equal-sized onions and large, uniform squares of lean bacon. Bourgeoise dishes are sometimes called à la Mode. Bourgeoise is also similar to other styles that use vegetables, such as Fermière and Jardinière, but Bourgeoise also relies heavily on wine for its character and so is actually more a cross between a mode that uses vegetables and one that depends on a particular wine for its individuality.

Many foods, such as beef fillet, are often seen in cookbooks and on restaurant menus in recipes à la Bourgeoise. This is inaccurate. Beef fillet is simply not a middle-class food. Occasionally you'll also find olives, mushrooms or artichoke hearts in a dish à la Bourgeoise. Again, they don't fit in. Peas or equally cut green beans would be permissible, but leave the more exotic vegetables (olives are actually a fruit) for other cooking modes, of which the French have plenty. There's no point in having a Bourgeoise cooking style if you're going to fancy it up. Let's keep Bourgeoise bourgeois!

BEEF RUMP À LA BOURGEOISE
TO SERVE 4–8

1 6-lb beef rump roast	1 bay leaf
salt and pepper	1 garlic clove, crushed
2½ cups dry white wine	2 Tbs flour
1 lb lean bacon, in equal	½ cup dry white wine
squares	½ cup beef stock* or broth
1 Tbs butter	6 carrots, cut in uniform rounds
1 Tbs peanut oil	chicken broth
3 onions, quartered	16 small onions, equal in size
salt and pepper	1 Tbs butter
1 tsp thyme	

Preheat oven to 325°. Season the roast with salt and pepper and marinate in the 2½ cups of wine for 6 hours or more (optional). Blanch the bacon for 30 seconds in boiling water. Drain. Put the butter and oil in a braising pan or roaster. Put the pan over medium heat and add the bacon. Sauté a few minutes and add the quartered onions, salt if necessary, pepper to taste, thyme, bay leaf and garlic. Brown, and sprinkle with the flour, stirring to blend. Allow to brown a bit more. Add the ½ cup of wine and stock, and place the roast on this braising bed. Cover and cook in the oven for 2 hours.

Meanwhile, cook the carrots until about ⅔ done in broth, and sauté the onions briefly in the 1 tablespoon of butter to coat and glaze. Remove the meat from the braising pan and drain. Place it in a casserole with the carrots and onions. Add the bacon from the braising pan. Strain the braising liquid into the casserole, cover and replace in the oven for 1 hour. To serve, drain the meat, vegetables and bacon, slice the beef, and arrange on a platter. Keep hot. Quickly boil down the casserole juices to about ½ and serve separately, hot.

LAMB SHOULDER À LA BOURGEOISE (Stuffed)
TO SERVE 4–8

1 6–8-lb boned lamb shoulder roast	1 Tbs butter
1 onion, chopped	1 lb lean bacon, diced
1 tsp butter	1 cup dry white wine
1 tsp peanut oil	2 cups beef stock* or broth
1 Tbs parsley	1 Tbs parsley
1 lb pork sausage meat	½ tsp thyme
6 carrots, cut in uniform rounds	1 bay leaf
1 cup chicken broth	½ tsp chervil
16 small onions, equal in size	cheesecloth, washed

Preheat oven to 325°. Sauté onion in butter and oil until translucent, drain and mix with the parsley and sausage meat. Use to stuff the shoulder roast and tie securely with string. Brown in the oven. Cook the carrots in the broth until ⅔ done, and sauté the onions in the butter until glazed but not browned and remove from the pan. Put the bacon in the pan and brown.

Put the browned roast in a casserole with the wine and stock. Add the parsley, thyme, bay leaf and chervil tied in cheesecloth. Bring to a boil, cover and cook in the oven for 35 minutes per pound. Add the vegetables and bacon, recover and continue cooking in the oven for 40 minutes more. Remove meat to a hot platter and arrange the bacon and vegetables around it. Discard the trussing strings. Keep hot. Quickly boil down the casserole juices to half, discarding the herb bouquet and excess fat, if any. Pour in a sauceboat and serve hot with the roast.

This recipe may be followed for a boned, stuffed mutton shoulder, but discard excess fat before adding the vegetables for the final 40 minutes. It may also be used for Veal Tendrons (full breast) à la Bourgeoise, but the cooking time will be reduced to about 2 hours.

CALF'S LIVER À LA BOURGEOISE
TO SERVE 4–8

Proceed as for Beef Rump à la Bourgeoise, using a calf's liver. Lard the liver with ¼-inch square strips of bacon (2–3 inches long). Use about ¼ pound of bacon strips. Marinate the bacon strips in brandy for 2 hours, then season well with pepper. Roll the bacon strips in parsley. You can also roll the bacon strips in freshly ground fennel seed, if you like it. Lard the liver with the bacon, using a larding needle or a long, thin knife to insert the bacon strips. They will melt while the liver cooks, releasing their flavor and that of the brandy and spices from inside the cooking meat.

CHICKEN À LA BOURGEOISE
TO SERVE 4

1 large or 2 small young chickens
salt and pepper
butter and peanut oil, half and half
1 lb lean bacon, in squares
20 small onions, equal sized
20 small carrots, equal sized, lightly sautéed in butter
4 oz dry white wine
2 cups thick veal gravy
salt and pepper

Preheat oven to 375°. Season the chicken inside and out with salt and pepper. Put in a pot with about 2 ounces of mixed butter and peanut oil. Cover and bake for about 35 minutes per pound. When half cooked, add the bacon, onions and carrots and finish cooking together, basting frequently. Place the chicken and vegetables and bacon on a hot platter and keep hot. Remove excess fat from the pot, if any, and add the wine. Boil down quickly, scraping up the juices. Add the veal gravy and season with salt and pepper if necessary. Blend well, heat and strain over the chicken or into a sauceboat. Serve hot.

TURKEY DAUBE À LA BOURGEOISE (Stew)
TO SERVE 4–6

2 carrots, chopped
2 onions, chopped
2 celery stalks, chopped
1 turnip, chopped (optional)
1 oz butter
1 oz peanut oil
1 Tbs parsley
1 tsp thyme
1 tsp chervil
1 bay leaf
cheesecloth, washed
1 5–7-lb turkey, trussed
2 cups beef stock* or broth
1 lb lean bacon, in cubes
20 small onions, equal sized
20 small carrots, equal sized
butter

Preheat oven to 375°. Lightly brown the carrots, onions, celery and turnip in the butter and oil in a large pot. Add the parsley, thyme, chervil and bay leaf tied in cheesecloth. Place the turkey on this vegetable bed and add the stock. Cook the bird covered in the oven for about 35 minutes per pound. Meanwhile, lightly sauté the bacon, onions and carrots in a little butter. When the turkey has 1 hour left to cook, add these ingredients and finish cooking together, covered. Serve in the pot or on a hot platter.

CONSOMMÉ À LA BOURGEOISE
TO SERVE 4

⅓ cup carrots, diced	butter
⅓ cup turnips, diced	1 qt chicken consomme*
⅓ cup potatoes, diced	1 Tbs fresh chervil

Brown the vegetables lightly in butter, cooking until limp. Heat the consommé, garnish with the sautéed vegetables and chervil and serve hot.

Bourguignonne
(boor-gee-N'YOHN)

From Burgundy, a region in southeast France. The area's early inhabitants were the Burgondes, a Germanic tribe living in the valleys of the Saône and Rhône rivers. They were conquered by Julius Caesar in 54 B.C. They were then conquered by the Huns in 43 A.D., and later by the Franks in 534. The name Burgundy, or Bourgogne in French, was first applied to the early Teutonic kingdom in the fifth century.

Geographically, Burgundy is divided into two parts, the lowlands of the Saône and Rhône river valleys, and the mountainous section of the Alps and Jura mountains, containing some of the highest peaks in Europe. Burgundy is considered by many to be the home of France's finest food and wines. It was in its capital city, Dijon, that the first, and reportedly most magnificent, French gastronomical fair was organized.

The Burgundian cuisine is strong in foundation and rich in accompaniments and sauces. Much of this is probably a result of the rich larder in Burgundy. From Ain comes the finest poultry in the world. The cattle of Charolais yield excellent beef. Morvan contributes fine winged and ground game. The woodcock of the Dombes marshes are unequalled anywhere in the world. Burgundy's streams and ponds are rich with pike, char, trout and crayfish, and the escargots are as good as any in the world. The prized mushrooms called morels are found here, along with many other tasty varieties. (It's a culinary crime that the United States cultivates only one mushroom variety.) The black currants of Burgundy are used to make the famous liqueur Cassis, and of course Dijon mustard has been world renowned for centuries.

Cooking à la Bourguignonne is characterized by a red wine sauce with mushrooms and little onions. It is strong in flavor, but should be without any distracting harshness. Bourguignonne could well be the acme of strong, robust cooking styles. I think it is, and after you try it, you might agree.

Boiled potatoes are traditional with most Bourguignonne dishes, and peas or green beans are good as green vegetables. Burgundy produces a very unusual cheese called Epoisses. It is soft or semifirm, and sometimes flavored with pepper, cloves or fennel seeds, then soaked in white wine. For wine, a good, full-bodied Burgundy is as fine as there is. The Burgundy area is also noted for Chablis, Beaujolais and Côté d'Or.

Bourguignonne cooking is heavily reliant on the flavor of Burgundy wine for its character, just as cooking Bordelaise relies on the character of Bordeaux wine. The styles Xérès, Porto and Madère are somewhat similar in that respect, but their wines, sherry, port and Madeira, respectively, are fortified wines, not table wines as in Bourguignonne and Bordelaise. Bourguignonne dishes cooked with Chambertin wine or with Mâcon wine become dishes au Chambertin and à la Mâconnaise.

To fit with the Burgundian food, the atmosphere should be one of robust plenty. No small, delicate portions here, but a lavish table with lots of food. You don't have to worry about quality; if the food is Burgundian, it's excellent. For music you might try the "Song of the Vagabonds," by Rudolf Friml, a very robust, if not complimentary, song about Burgundy, or any other hearty song about the past, like "Stout Hearted Men," for instance. These might be a bit much for during dinner, but would be fine for a change of pace during cocktails.

SAUCE BOURGUIGNONNE (For Meat, Poultry and Eggs)
(Also Called Red Wine Sauce)
TO MAKE 2 CUPS

2 Tbs onion, chopped	½ bay leaf
butter	cheesecloth, washed
2 cups red Burgundy wine	1½ cups Sauce Espagnole, or
2 tsp parsley	Jus de Veau*
½ tsp thyme	2 Tbs butter (optional)
½ tsp chervil	

Sauté the onion in a little butter until limp but not browned. Add the wine. Add the parsley, thyme, chervil and bay leaf, tied in cheesecloth. Boil down to one quarter. Add the Espagnole and simmer for 5 minutes. Blend in the butter, if desired. Strain and serve hot.

SAUCE BOURGUIGNONNE (For Fish)
TO MAKE 2 CUPS

1 onion, chopped	1 tsp parsley
half a carrot, chopped	¼ tsp thyme
1 Tbs butter	½ bay leaf
bones and trimmings of the fish	cheesecloth, washed
½ cup mushroom skins (optional)	salt and pepper
1 qt red Burgundy wine	3 Tbs butter, kneaded with 3 Tbs flour

Brown the onion and carrot lightly in the 1 tablespoon of butter in a pan. Add the fish bones and trimmings and the mushrooms, if desired, and simmer very gently for 10 minutes. Add the wine and the parsley, thyme and bay leaf tied in cheesecloth. Season with salt and pepper to taste. Boil the liquid down to half. Strain the sauce and return to the heat, blending in the kneaded butter and flour to thicken. Serve hot.

This sauce is often made in the same pan used to prepare the fish.

BOURGUIGNONNE BUTTER (For Snails)
FOR 48 SNAILS

¾ lb unsalted butter
3 Tbs shallots, minced
1 garlic clove, ground to a paste

1 Tbs parsley
1½ tsp salt
⅛ tsp pepper

Blend all the ingredients well. Let stand for 1 hour before using, to allow the flavors to blend.

BOURGUIGNONNE GARNISHES
TO SERVE 4

1. One pound button mushrooms, sautéed in butter

2. One pound tiny onions, blanched in boiling water for 2 minutes and drained, then sautéed in ¼ cup of butter with 1 teaspoon of sugar until done and glazed. Season lightly with salt and white pepper.

KIDNEY BEANS À LA BOURGUIGNONNE
TO SERVE 4

1½ lbs dried red kidney beans,
   soaked in water for 12 hours
   and drained
2 cups red Burgundy wine
1 cup water
1 cup chicken stock*
1 tsp parsley
¼ tsp thyme
½ bay leaf

½ tsp chervil
½ tsp savory
cheesecloth, washed
1 garlic clove
1 onion, stuck with 3 cloves
2 oz ham fat, minced
2 oz very lean bacon
salt and pepper
1 Tbs butter

Put the beans, wine, water and stock in a casserole. Add the parsley, thyme, bay leaf, chervil and savory, tied in cheesecloth. Add the garlic, onion, ham fat and bacon and season to taste with salt and pepper. Simmer gently until the beans are tender. Remove the bacon, dice it, and sauté it in the butter. Drain the beans, discarding the herb bouquet, garlic and onion. Add the beans to the bacon in the sauté pan, mix well and serve hot.

EGGS À LA BOURGUIGNONNE (Poached)
TO SERVE 4

2 cups red Burgundy wine
salt and pepper
1 tsp parsley
¼ tsp thyme
¼ tsp chervil
1 garlic clove
4 bread slices, trimmed
butter

8 mushroom caps
½ lb very small onions, boiled
8 eggs
2 Tbs butter, softened and
    kneaded with 2 Tbs of flour
1 cup Sauce Espagnole, or Jus
    de Veau★ or beef gravy

Put the wine in a pot, season lightly with salt and pepper and add parsley, thyme, chervil and garlic. Bring to a boil and cook 5 minutes. Strain into an egg-poaching pot. Sauté the bread in a little butter and keep hot, or use buttered toast. Sauté the mushrooms and onions, but do not brown, and keep hot. Poach the eggs in the strained wine mixture. Put 2 eggs on each bread slice and garnish with mushrooms and onions. Keep hot. Quickly boil the poaching wine down to half. Blend in the kneaded butter and flour to thicken. Add the Espagnole and heat through. Pour over the eggs and serve hot.

I like this dish made with 1 cup of wine and 1 cup of beef stock* used in place of the 2 cups of wine. The flavor is much more mellow.

BEEF ENTRECÔTES À LA BOURGUIGNONNE (Steaks)
TO SERVE 4

8 mushroom caps
½ lb very small onions, boiled
butter
4 steaks

butter
1 cup red Burgundy wine
1½ cups Sauce Espagnole, or
    beef gravy

Sauté the mushrooms in butter, toss the cooked onions in butter and keep both hot. In the same pan, sauté the steaks until done to taste and keep hot. Quickly add wine and Espagnole to the sauté pan and cook down 1/3. Arrange the steaks on warm dishes and garnish with mushrooms and onions. Pour the sauce over the steaks and serve hot.

BEEF DAUBE À LA BOURGUIGNONNE (Stew)
TO SERVE 4

2 lbs beef, cut in 1-inch cubes
2 oz lean bacon, diced
2 oz oil
1 small onion, chopped
1 garlic clove, minced
1 tsp tomato purée
3 Tbs flour

1¼ cups red Burgundy wine
1½ cups beef stock* or broth
½ bay leaf
¼ tsp thyme
½ tsp chervil
salt and pepper

Brown the beef and bacon in the oil in a pot. Add the onion and garlic and cook, stirring, until browned. Add the tomato purée and flour and blend well. Add the wine, stock, bay leaf, thyme, chervil and salt and pepper to taste. Cover and cook over low heat for 2½ hours, stirring occasionally. Remove excess fat from the pot, if any, and serve the meat on a hot platter covered with the sauce, hot. (If you wish, strain the sauce. If not, discard the bay leaf and serve the sauce unstrained.)

BEEF RUMP À LA BOURGUIGNONNE
TO SERVE 4–6

1 6-lb rump roast of beef	1 bay leaf
1 cup brandy	1 garlic clove, crushed
2 Tbs butter	2 Tbs flour
2 carrots, quartered	1 cup red Burgundy wine
2 onions, quartered	1 cup beef stock* or broth
salt and pepper	12 mushroom caps
1 Tbs parsley	¾ lb very small onions, boiled
1 tsp thyme	butter

Marinate the roast in the brandy, basting and turning, for 6 hours (optional). Preheat oven to 325°. Put the butter in a braising pan or Dutch oven and place over low heat. Add the carrots and onions, salt and pepper to taste, parsley, thyme, bay leaf and garlic. Sauté until browned. Sprinkle with flour and blend, letting it brown a bit more. Add the wine and stock, and place the drained roast on this braising bed. Cover and cook in the oven for 2½ hours.

Meanwhile, sauté the mushrooms and onions separately in butter. When the roast has cooked, remove it from the braising pan and put it in a casserole. Add the sautéed mushrooms and onions and the strained braising stock. Cover and return to the oven for 30 minutes more. When finished cooking, place the roast on a hot platter, surround with the mushrooms and onions, skim the fat from the casserole and pour the remaining sauce over the roast and serve hot. Or serve the sauce separately.

My preference with this dish is to omit the garlic from the sauce and instead use a slivered garlic clove inserted into the roast with a fine sharp knife, to get the garlic flavor through the roast. Any way you make it, it's a simple way to make an elegant dish.

VEAL CHOPS À LA BOURGUIGNONNE
TO SERVE 4

8 veal chops	1 cup red Burgundy wine
salt and pepper	1 Tbs butter kneaded with 1 Tbs
butter	flour
24 small onions	1 cup beef stock* or unsalted
½ lb bacon, diced	broth, boiled down to ⅛ (1 oz)
24 button mushrooms	1 Tbs butter (optional)

Season the veal to taste with salt and pepper and sauté slowly in butter. Meanwhile, blanch the onions and bacon in boiling water for 30 seconds and drain. When the veal is about ½ cooked, add the onions, bacon and mushrooms and finish together. Set the meat and vegetables on a hot platter and keep hot.

Add the wine to the sauté pan and quickly boil, scraping up the juices. Add the kneaded butter and flour and reduce heat to a simmer. Blend well and thicken. Stir in the reduced beef stock (beef glaze). Stir in the butter, if desired, and strain the sauce over the meat and vegetables and serve hot, or serve the sauce separately.

HAM À LA BOURGUIGNONNE
TO SERVE 4

1 ham, soaked in water for several hours to desalt, drained well
1 onion stuck with 5 cloves
2 carrots, quartered
6 peppercorns
2 or 3 sprigs celery leaves
½ tsp basil
¼ tsp thyme
½ bay leaf
cheesecloth, washed
1½ cups red Burgundy wine
2 Tbs cornstarch blended with 2 Tbs red Burgundy wine

Put the ham, onion and carrots in a pot. Add the peppercorns, celery, basil, thyme and bay leaf, tied in cheesecloth. Just cover with fresh water and simmer for 1 hour. Meanwhile, preheat the oven to 325°. Drain the ham, and remove skin and excess fat. Put the ham in a casserole with the wine and 2 cups of the cooking liquid, and bake for 1 hour in the oven, basting occasionally. Put the ham on a hot platter and keep hot. Strain the casserole juices into a pan and add the cornstarch-wine slurry, blending well and bringing to a boil. Boil down to thicken lightly. Carve the ham, arranging the slices around the remaining ham on the platter. Strain a little sauce over the slices in a ring and serve the rest in a sauceboat, hot.

CALF'S LIVER À LA BOURGUIGNONNE
TO SERVE 4

Proceed as for Beef Entrecôtes à la Bourguignonne, using 2 pounds of sliced calf's liver lightly dredged in flour.

CHICKEN SAUTÉ À LA BOURGUIGNONNE
TO SERVE 4

3 lbs chicken pieces
salt and pepper
butter
20 small onions
½ lb lean bacon, diced
20 button mushrooms
1 cup red Burgundy wine
1 garlic clove, crushed
2 cups Sauce Espagnole, or beef gravy
8 heart-shaped croutons of bread, sautéed in butter (optional)

Season the chicken to taste with salt and pepper and sauté in butter slowly. Meanwhile, blanch the onions and bacon in boiling water for 30 seconds and drain. When the chicken is about ⅔ cooked, add the onions, mushrooms and bacon and finish cooking together. Remove the meats and vegetables to a hot platter and keep hot. Discard excess fat from the pan. Add the wine and garlic to the pan and boil until almost gone, scraping up the juices. Add the Espagnole and cook for a few minutes. Strain over the meat and serve, hot, garnished with the croutons if desired.

This may be flamed with brandy, for an added touch. After the chicken first browns, add 2 ounces of brandy to the pan and flame, stirring until the fire dies. Then proceed with the cooking as in the recipe.

SOLE À LA BOURGUIGNONNE (Often Called Sole in Red Wine)
TO SERVE 4

1 5–6-lb sole, whole and cleaned	2 tsp parsley
salt and pepper	½ tsp thyme
20 small onions	¼ tsp fennel seed, crushed
20 button mushrooms	cheesecloth, washed
¾ cup red Burgundy wine	2 Tbs butter kneaded with 2 Tbs
1¼ cups fish fumet* or clam	flour
juice	½ cup Sauce Espagnole, or 4
	Tbs butter

Preheat oven to 350°. Season the fish inside and out to taste with salt and pepper. Place in a buttered baking dish on top of the onions and mushrooms, and add the wine and stock. Add the parsley, thyme and fennel tied in cheesecloth, and slide under the fish. Bring to a boil on top of the stove, cover and braise in the oven for 40 minutes or until the fish flakes easily with a fork and is done. Place the sole on a hot platter with piles of onions and mushrooms and keep hot. Quickly add the kneaded butter and flour to the pan and thicken the juices over direct heat. Add the Espagnole, stir to blend well and strain over fish. Serve hot.

TROUT À LA BOURGUIGNONNE
TO SERVE 4

Proceed as for Sole à la Bourguignonne, using 4 trout, whole and cleaned, and adjusting cooking time to about 30 minutes.

FISH FILLETS À LA BOURGUIGNONNE
TO SERVE 4

Proceed as for Sole à la Bourguignonne, using 2 pounds of any white-fleshed fish fillets, and adjusting cooking time to about 15 minutes. Blanch the onions for 5 minutes in lightly salted water before adding to the baking dish.

This is a fine recipe for any white-fleshed fish, whole or in fillets. Just adjust the cooking time to suit the fish's size.

GRAPE TARTS À LA BOURGUIGNONNE
TO SERVE 4

1½ cups of grapes
3 oz red Burgundy wine
1½ Tbs brandy
2 tsp cornstarch
5 Tbs sugar (more or less, depending on sweetness of the grapes)

4 prebaked individual empty pastry shells*
4 Tbs apple jelly
whipped cream

Put the grapes and wine in a pan and heat slowly, until the grapes burst and the seeds come to the top. Remove and discard the seeds. Blend the brandy with the cornstarch well and mix in with the grapes. Add sugar to taste and cook, stirring constantly, until thick. Remove from heat. Spread the apple jelly in the bottoms of the tart shells and top with the grape mixture. Chill and serve, topped with whipped cream.

APPLES and PEARS À LA BOURGUIGNONNE
TO SERVE 4

1 cup sugar
½ cup water
4 apples, peeled, seeded and cut in eighths

4 pears, peeled, seeded and cut in eighths
½ cup red Burgundy wine
¼ tsp cinnamon (optional)

Put the sugar in a pan with the water and cook, making a syrup. Add the apples and pears and simmer, covered, for 10 minutes. Add the wine and cinnamon and simmer for 7 to 8 minutes more. Remove the apples and pears and arrange on a serving dish. Cook the wine-flavored syrup down until thick, pour over the fruit and chill. Serve chilled.

Brabançonne

(brah-bahn-SOHN)

After the Belgian province of Brabant, a part of the old duchy of Brabant. Brabant is the central and most metropolitan province in Belgium and consists of an undulating plateau averaging 400 feet in elevation, with intensively cultivated, fertile, loamy soil. Market gardening is an important industry, particularly of chicory, early vegetables and fruits. The central part of the Brabant plateau, near the city of Waterloo, was the scene of Napoleon's defeat in 1815.

Cooking à la Brabançonne is often confused with the modes Bruxelloise and Flamande, which is understandable since they are all of Belgium. However, Brabançonne is distinguished by the use of endive. If you see a dish labeled à la Bruxelloise or Flamande that has endive as a prime ingredient, it is mislabeled. Bruxelloise dishes feature brussels sprouts, not endive. (In French, Bruxelles means Brussels.) Flamande means Flemish, and in cooking means the use of braised cabbage, glazed carrots and turnips. Any main course that features endive and Potato Croquettes à la Brabançonne in a dish à la Brabançonne.

A fitting beverage for a dish à la Brabançonne would be beer, since Belgium is not a wine-producing country, but you needn't be hindered by that unless you want beer for a change of pace. Belgium does produce a nice variety of cheeses, however, from the rank-smelling but smooth and tasty Limburger to the velvet-smooth dessert cheese called Ardennes Herve. Somewhere in between would fall Herve, a soft cheese somewhat similar to Limburger but flavored with tarragon, parsley and chives.

In cuisine, Brabançonne pertains to two garnishes for large pieces of meat, endive (Belgian, of course) and potato croquettes. Occasionally the garnish is enhanced with creamed or sautéed hop shoots, although the hop shoots are more typical of dishes à l'Anversoise, from Antwerp, a city in Belgium.

The Low Countries (Belgium and Holland) were the forerunners in the perfection of carillons, principally due to the skill of Josef Denyn, considered the greatest carillonneur of all time. In the eighteenth century, nearly every town in the Low Countries had its own bell tower and *carillonneur.* So, bells would make for a different musical theme, and could be incorporated in the décor as well.

SAUCE BRABANÇONNE

Mildly seasoned, thick veal gravy is used as Sauce Brabançonne. It is suitable with beef, pork, veal, poultry and eggs.

ENDIVE À LA BRABANÇONNE
TO SERVE 4

4 small heads endive	1 tsp lemon juice
4 Tbs butter	1 Tbs dry white wine
¼ tsp salt	⅛ tsp sugar
pepper to taste	¾ cup chicken stock* or broth

Put all the ingredients in a pot, cover and bring to a boil. Lower heat and simmer gently for 45 minutes. Drain endive and arrange on a hot serving dish. Keep hot. Quickly boil down the cooking juices to ½ cup. Pour over the endive and serve hot.

POTATO CROQUETTES À LA BRABANÇONNE
TO SERVE 4

1½ lbs potatoes, peeled and
    cooked in lightly salted water
3 Tbs butter
salt, white pepper and grated
    nutmeg
3 egg yolks

½ recipe Endive à la Braban-
    çonne, without the sauce,
    minced and squeezed dry
3 Tbs oil, preferably peanut
3 Tbs butter

Mash the potatoes until very smooth. Put them in a pot over very low heat and stir to dry without coloring. Add the butter and season to taste with salt, pepper and nutmeg. Remove from heat and beat in the yolks one at a time. Add the endive and blend well. Cover and chill. (The mixture may not take all the endive.)

Heat the oil and butter in a pan. Shape small croquettes from the potato mixture by using 2 spoons, or simply by forming small ovals by hand. Sauté the croquettes in the hot fat until golden on all sides, turning gently without breaking. As the croquettes are done, place them on paper towels to drain, keeping them hot while you finish the others. Discard the paper draining towels and pile the croquettes in a mound on a hot platter. Serve hot.

SALAD À LA BRABANÇONNE
TO SERVE 4

1 recipe Endive a la Braban-
    çonne, drained and without
    sauce
¾ lb boiled potatoes, sliced
1 onion, chopped and browned
    in the oven

salt, pepper, oil, vinegar
20 small fillets of salt herring, or
    anchovies
2 Tbs chives
1 tsp chervil

Season the endive, potatoes and onion with salt, pepper, oil and vinegar to taste. Arrange, mixed, in a dome on a serving dish. Decorate with herring fillets. Sprinkle with chives and chervil and serve at room temperature or slightly chilled.

EGGS À LA BRABANÇONNE (Poached or Soft-Boiled)
TO SERVE 4

8 eggs, freshly poached or soft-
    boiled and hot

1 recipe Endive à la Brabançonne, hot
1½ cups Sauce Allemande, hot

Arrange the endives on 4 hot plates and top each with 2 freshly cooked eggs. Spoon the Sauce Allemande over the eggs and serve hot.

This was once very popular as a Lenten dish, the Sauce Allemande being replaced with Sauce à la Crème, which is meatless.

ROAST À LA BRABANÇONNE

Prepare a roast of beef, or pork or lamb, as you like, but preferably simply (that is, not highly seasoned), and serve with thick veal gravy. Serve Potato Croquettes and Endive à la Brabançonne as garnishes. This can be applied to any meat, in large or small cuts, but the most typical is a beef roast.

HAM and ENDIVE ROLLS À LA BRABANÇONNE
TO SERVE 4

8 small heads of Belgian endive	Swiss or Gruyère cheese,
8 ham slices	grated
2 cups Sauce Mornay, hot	chives

Preheat oven to 350°. Blanch the endive in boiling water for 3 minutes. Drain. Rinse under running cold water and drain very dry. Roll each head of endive up in a ham slice and place in a buttered baking dish. Cover the ham and endive rolls with the Mornay Sauce, sprinkle generously with grated cheese and bake in the oven for about 25 minutes, until golden brown. Serve hot, sprinkled with chives.

BAKED PEARS À LA BRABANÇONNE
TO SERVE 4

4 large, perfect pears, not overly	butter, softened
ripe	vanilla sugar*

Preheat oven to 300°. Coat pears well with butter and place on a buttered baking sheet. Bake for 40 minutes. Raise oven heat to 450°. Sprinkle generously with vanilla sugar and return to the oven briefly to glaze. Serve hot or chilled.

This dish is often accompanied by a vanilla custard.

LEEK SOUP À LA BRABANÇONNE
TO SERVE 4

½ lb white part of leeks, sliced	salt and pepper
2 Tbs butter	¼ cup cream
¾ lb potatoes, cubed	bread cubes, toasted (optional)
4 cups beef stock* or broth	chives

Sauté the leeks in the butter for 3 minutes. Add the potatoes and stock. Season with salt and pepper if necessary. Bring to a boil, lower heat and simmer for 40 minutes, stirring occasionally. Remove from heat. Stir in the cream and serve hot, garnished with toasted bread cubes and chives.

Bretonne

(bruh-TOHN)

From Brittany, the westernmost part of France, pointing out toward the Atlantic Ocean like a blunt finger, with the Bay of Biscay on the south and the English Channel and England to the north. Many of the inhabitants still speak Breton, the Celtic language of Brittany, which was brought to Brittany in the fifth and sixth centuries by immigrants from Cornwall and South Wales. These were Bretons fleeing from the Saxon invaders, and since that time the area has been known as little Britain, or Brittany. The immigrants apparently brought with them a rich vocal literature, for their minstrels' songs and tales are the basis of the legends of King Arthur, the Holy Grail, and the knights of the Round Table. These folk tales, adapted to French tastes and recited in French, fascinated western Europe, and by the late twelfth century, French, Anglo-Norman and German poets were moved to compose stories based on them. Much of the wandering minstrels' repertoire was in song, accompanied by harp, fiddle or lyre.

Brittany is noted for its scenery, but aside from the view the land is not very productive, with mostly barren, rocky soil. Along the coast the dense population is supported by fishing and intense cultivation of fruits and vegetables fertilized by seaweed.

In food, Bretonne means the use of white beans as a vegetable, in purée as a garnish for meat or as a soup course. Specifically, it's a white bean garnish for large pieces of meat, especially mutton. If White Beans à la Bretonne is the outstanding characteristic of a dish, the dish may be called à la Bretonne.

The typical wine of the area is Muscadet, a light, tart wine that goes especially well with seafood, which is a happy coincidence since seafood is a staple in Brittany. Actually, the more common drink here is cider, which makes a typical meal in Brittany similar to a meal in neighboring Normandy, and quite different from anywhere else in France.

Brittany has long been noted for fine cheeses. An excellent cheese is made near Nantes, and called Nantais. Port Salut is a smooth, semisoft cheese made by the Trappist monks of Notre Dame since 1816, and Vendômois comes in both a soft blue and a goat's milk cheese, both covered with vine ashes.

There is a wealth of ideas for décor and music here: china and lace, naval construction, fishing fleets, wandering minstrels, King Arthur's court, the Holy Grail, the music of harp, fiddle and lyre.

SAUCE BRETONNE
TO MAKE 2 CUPS

1 small onion, cut in thin strips
2 leeks, white part only, cut in
   thin strips
½ small celery heart, cut in thin
   strips
¼ tsp salt
⅛ tsp sugar

4 tsp butter
4 Tbs mushrooms, cut in thin
   strips
½ cup dry white wine
1½ cups Sauce Velouté*
2 Tbs butter (optional)
2 Tbs heavy cream

Cook the onion, leek and celery with the salt and sugar in the 4 teaspoons of butter slowly, until limp but not browned. Add the mushrooms and cook slowly 5 minutes more, or until just limp. Add the wine and boil until it is gone. Add the Velouté and boil for 3 minutes. Add the 2 tablespoons of butter, if desired. Add the cream and cook to thicken lightly if necessary. Serve hot with eggs, fish, poultry and white meats.

If this sauce is to be used with braised fish, the fish should be braised in the julienne vegetables and moistened with a little fish fumet* or white wine. When the fish is cooked and removed from the pan, the sauce is finished as directed. Allow 1 recipe of Sauce Bretonne for 2 pounds of fish to be braised.

WHITE BEANS À LA BRETONNE
TO SERVE 4

½ lb lean bacon, in 1 piece
1 carrot, quartered
1 onion, quartered
2 tsp butter
2 qts boiling water, or meat
   stock* or broth
1 tsp parsley

½ tsp thyme
½ bay leaf
cheesecloth, washed
salt
2 cups dry white beans
1 cup Sauce Bretonne, hot

Blanch the bacon in boiling water for 10 minutes and drain. In a large pot, brown the carrot and onion in the butter lightly. Add the water. Add the parsley, thyme and bay leaf tied in cheesecloth. Season to taste with salt and add the bacon. Bring to a boil, skim and cook for 25 minutes, boiling slowly. Strain the liquid and reserve the bacon. Add the beans to the liquid, bring to a rapid boil for 2 minutes, reduce heat and simmer covered for 2 hours, adding water if necessary. When the beans are done and tender, drain them and stir in the Sauce Bretonne gently. This is served hot, generally as a garnish for a roast, and the bacon is served hot, sliced, as an added garnish.

WHITE BEAN PURÉE À LA BRETONNE
TO SERVE 4

Prepare White Beans à la Bretonne and purée in a food mill or blender. Serve hot, as a vegetable. If necessary, thicken over low heat, stirring constantly to avoid sticking.

EGGS À LA BRETONNE (Poached or Soft-Boiled)
TO SERVE 4

4 bread sliced, trimmed
butter

8 eggs, freshly poached or soft-
boiled and hot
1½ cups Sauce Bretonne, hot

Sauté the bread in a little butter until golden and place on 4 hot plates. Top each with 2 hot, freshly cooked eggs and spoon the hot sauce over the top. Serve at once, hot.

Sauce Bretonne makes a fine topping for any eggs, from scrambled to baked. A side dish of Bretonne White Bean Purée makes an interesting and unusual accompaniment, and the bacon fits right in.

MUTTON LEG À LA BRETONNE
TO SERVE 4–8

2 garlic cloves, slivered
1 6–8-lb mutton leg roast
½ tsp rosemary or thyme,
ground

¼ tsp powdered ginger
salt and pepper
1½ recipes White Beans à la
Bretonne

Preheat oven to 450°. Insert the garlic slivers in the mutton with a thin knife so their flavor will spread through the meat from the inside. Rub the roast with the rosemary or thyme, ginger, and salt and pepper to taste. Roast for 15 minutes to brown. Reduce heat to 350° and cook for about 30 minutes per pound with the bone in, or 40 minutes per pound for a boned roast. Serve on a hot platter with piles of the white beans, garnished with bacon slices. For 8 people, use 2 recipes of White Beans.

ROAST of LAMB, BEEF or PORK À LA BRETONNE

Proceed as for Mutton Leg à la Bretonne, using the roast of your choice served with White Beans à la Bretonne. Any type of roast may be used.

MUTTON CHOPS À LA BRETONNE
TO SERVE 4

1 recipe White Beans à la
    Bretonne, hot
8 mutton chops
salt and pepper

butter
½ cup chicken or veal stock* or
    broth

Pile the beans in the center of a hot platter and keep hot. Season the mutton with salt and pepper to taste and sauté until done in butter. Arrange around the beans like the spokes of a wheel and keep hot. Discard excess fat from the sauté pan and add the stock. Heat quickly, scraping up the juices. Strain over the chops and serve hot, garnished with bacon slices.

This is a fine method for any other meat in small cuts, like pork chops. Beef steaks make an interesting dish cooked this way. The beans make an unusual combination with the steak.

FLOUNDER À LA BRETONNE
TO SERVE 4

2 lbs flounder fillets
salt and pepper
1 cup Vegetable Fondue*

1 cup fish fumet* *or* ½ cup each
    dry white wine and clam juice
2 oz cream

Preheat oven to 350°. Season the fillets lightly with salt and pepper. Put the vegetable fondue in a buttered baking dish. Lay the fish fillets on the fondue. Add the fish fumet and cook, partially covered, in the oven for 15 minutes, or until the fish flakes easily with a fork and is done. Baste frequently while the fish is cooking. When done, place the fillets carefully on a hot platter, trying to keep them intact. Quickly blend the cream with the fondue and stock, pour over the fish and serve hot.

This is a fine recipe for any fish, large or small, whole or filleted, because of its simplicity. The flavor achieved by using the vegetable fondue and fish fumet is excellent. This dish, or any similar approach using cooked vegetables and fish fumet, should be in every cook's repertoire.

WHITE BEAN SOUP À LA BRETONNE
TO SERVE 4

Prepare 1 recipe of White Beans à la Bretonne and purée in a food mill or blender, adding chicken broth to get the consistency you prefer. Serve hot, garnished with chives.

BOUILLABAISSE À LA BRETONNE (Also Called Cotriade)
TO SERVE 4

2 Tbs butter
½ lb button mushrooms
2 onions, quartered
1 Tbs flour
2 cups dry white wine
2 cups water
1 Tbs parsley
½ tsp chervil
¼ tsp thyme
½ bay leaf

cheesecloth, washed
½ lb potatoes, cubed
salt and pepper
2 garlic cloves, minced
½ tsp curry powder blended
   with 1 Tbs lemon juice
1 lb flounder, in 1-inch squares
2 bread slices, trimmed, toasted
   and diced
2 Tbs chives

Melt the butter in a pan and sauté the mushrooms. Set aside, and sauté the onions in the same pan. Blend in the flour and cook a few minutes. Return the mushrooms to the pan and add the wine and water. Add the parsley, chervil, thyme and bay leaf, tied in cheesecloth. Add the potatoes. Season lightly with salt and pepper and simmer for 15 minutes. Add the garlic and the curried lemon juice. Blend in well. Add the fish and simmer 15 minutes more. Discard the herb bouquet. Place the fish and potatoes in 4 individual hot bowls and pour in the soup. Garnish with diced toast and chives and serve at once, hot.

RAISIN CUSTARD À LA BRETONNE
TO SERVE 4

¾ cup flour
1 cup cold milk
3 cups milk flavored with 1 tsp
   vanilla extract
4 eggs, beaten

¾ cup sugar mixed with 1/16 tsp
   salt
3 oz seedless raisins, plumped
   in hot rum and drained

Preheat oven to 325°. Blend the flour with the cold milk, adding a bit at a time, making a large slurry. Scald the 3 cups of milk flavored with vanilla, then blend in the flour and cold milk slurry slowly and cook to thicken, stirring. Remove from heat. Add the sugar to the beaten eggs gradually, beating until well mixed and fluffy. Gradually add the flour and milk mixture, blending over low heat. Do not allow to boil. Pour half this custard mixture into a buttered and lightly floured baking dish, sprinkle on the raisins, pour the remaining custard on top and bake set in a pan with 1 inch of water, until done, about 50 minutes. Serve hot or at room temperature.

Bruxelloise

(brook-sel-WAZ)

From Brussels, the capital and largest city of Belgium. The name is generally applied to dishes containing Brussels sprouts, *choux de Bruxelles* in French. Brussels was built on islands in the Senne River originally, which provided good defensive sites for the early inhabitants.

Bruxelloise is an easy cooking style to spot. It's the only one that features Brussels sprouts. Similar categories are Alsacienne and Flamande, both of which use cabbage in one form or another extensively. Cabbage is related to Brussels sprouts, as are cauliflower, broccoli, kale, collard and kohlrabi. Frequently kale is used in dishes à la Bruxelloise in place of the Brussels sprouts, especially in egg recipes.

Brussels sprouts were developed from a wild cabbage native to the northwestern shores of Europe. They are extremely hardy, and will withstand snow and freezing temperatures.

Brussels has been a famous name in the production of fine laces for centuries, and a lace tablecloth would be ideal décor for a dish à la Bruxelloise.

BRUXELLOISE GARNISHES
TO SERVE 4

1. One and a half pounds of Brussels sprouts, cooked and tossed in butter.

2. Two pounds of olive-shaped potatoes, cooked and tossed in butter.

EGGS À LA BRUXELLOISE (Poached or Soft-Boiled)
TO SERVE 4

½ lb Brussels sprouts, chopped
½ cup Sauce Béchamel
salt, pepper and grated nutmeg
4 individual baked pastry
   shells,* hot

8 eggs, freshly poached or soft-
   boiled and hot
1 cup Cream Sauce, hot

Cook the Brussels sprouts in lightly salted water and drain well. Mix with the Sauce Béchamel and season to taste with salt and pepper and a little nutmeg. Put this mixture in the bottoms of the 4 pastry shells. Top the Brussels sprouts with 2 eggs per pastry shell. Spoon over the Cream Sauce and serve the tartlets hot.

For baked eggs, put the cooked Brussels sprouts and Béchamel mixture in a casserole and top with 8 fresh eggs, being careful not to break their yolks. Season to taste with salt, pepper and grated nutmeg and top with the Cream Sauce. Bake in a 500° oven on a high rack for 4 minutes, or until the whites are just set and the yolks still soft.

OMELET À LA BRUXELLOISE
TO SERVE 2

4 eggs	¼ lb very small Brussels
salt and pepper	sprouts, cooked, drained,
4 Tbs butter	sliced and tossed in butter
	¼ cup Sauce Demi-Glace
	(Sauce Alsacienne) hot

Season the eggs to taste and beat with a fork. Heat the butter very hot and use to cook the omelet.* Serve at once, surrounded by hot Brussels sprouts and topped with Sauce Demi-Glace.

This omelet is often prepared with a stuffing of half the sliced Brussels sprouts.

MUTTON CHOPS À LA BRUXELLOISE
TO SERVE 4

8 mutton chops	2 cups Sauce Demi-Glace
salt and pepper	(Sauce Alsacienne) or veal
butter	gravy
2 oz dry white wine	1½ lbs Brussels sprouts
	butter
	salt and pepper

Season the chops to taste with salt and pepper and sauté in a little butter until done. Set on a hot platter in a ring, leaving the center empty, and keep hot. Remove excess fat from pan, if any. Add the wine to the pan and boil down, scraping up the juices. Blend in the Sauce Demi-Glace well.

Meanwhile, cook the Brussels sprouts in boiling, lightly salted water until just done. Drain, toss in butter and season with salt and pepper. Pile in the center of the mutton chops and serve hot, with the sauce poured over the chops or served separately.

STEAK À LA BRUXELLOISE
TO SERVE 4

Proceed as for Mutton Chops à la Bruxelloise, using 4 beefsteaks.

PORK or LAMB CHOPS À LA BRUXELLOISE

Proceed as for Mutton Chops à la Bruxelloise, using 8 pork chops or 12 lamb chops.

HAM À LA BRUXELLOISE
TO SERVE 4

Proceed as for Mutton Chops à la Bruxelloise, seasoning the ham with pepper only, and replacing the Sauce Demi-Glace with Velouté.* You may also use Madeira instead of dry white wine. Use 2 pounds of ham in rather thick slices or in a large single steak. Chives make a nice garnish for ham cooked in this manner. Serve the chives in a little bowl with its own spoon, to be passed at the table with the sauce.

CHICKEN BREASTS À LA BRUXELLOISE
TO SERVE 4

Proceed as for Mutton Chops à la Bruxelloise, using 6 halved chicken breasts and substituting Sauce Velouté* for the Demi-Glace. If you skin and bone the breasts, the dish becomes Chicken Suprêmes à la Bruxelloise.

EEL À LA BRUXELLOISE
TO SERVE 4

2 lbs eel, cleaned and cut in pieces	½ cup watercress leaves, minced (optional)
1 oz butter	2 tsp parsley
1 Tbs chopped onion	½ tsp chervil
1 Tbs chopped celery leaves	¼ tsp each of sage, savory and mint
½ cup dry white wine	
salt and pepper	cheesecloth, washed
¼ tsp ground thyme	3 egg yolks
⅛ tsp ground cloves	3 oz heavy cream

Cook the eel in the butter with the onion and celery for 5 minutes over a brisk heat, stirring gently. Add wine, season to taste with salt and pepper and add thyme and cloves. Stir in the watercress. Add the parsley, chervil, sage, savory and mint, tied in cheesecloth. Cook, stirring gently, for about 12 minutes, until just done. Remove from heat. Beat the yolks and cream together until well blended. Put the eel on a hot platter and keep hot. Discard the herb bouquet and add the yolk-cream mixture to the pan and blend well. Pour over the fish and serve hot.

This recipe is excellent for any white-fleshed fish, especially cod or haddock. It is usually served with both the Bruxelloise Garnishes, but always with the Brussels sprouts.

Catalane

(kah-tah-LAHN)

Means Catalonian. Catalonia was a province in northeastern Spain on the Mediterranean Sea, separated from France by the Pyrenees mountains. Catalonia was one of the first Roman possessions in Spain. In the fifth century it was occupied by the Goths. In 712 it was taken by the Moors. Charlemagne began the reconquest of Catalonia in the later eighth century, and by 801 it was incorporated into the kingdom of the Franks. Catalonia's soil is fertile, and it produces excellent olive oil and wine and is an important producer of cork. Textiles, flour and chocolate are also important products, as are oil, paper and steel, making Catalonia the most important industrial area of Spain. The Mediterranean ports are busy, especially Barcelona, where industry flourishes.

In cooking, Catalane means a garnish of sautéed eggplant and rice pilaf, generally used with large cuts of meat.

Catalane is a Mediterranean cooking mode and uses tomatoes, olive oil, peppers, etc., as do many others, such as Niçoise or Grecque. But what sets Catalane apart is garlic. Garlic is more emphasized in Catalane cooking than any other cooking mode.

It can be argued that Sauce Aïoli, the very garlicky mayonnaise, should belong under cooking à la Catalane, but Aïoli was originated in Provence and belongs there regardless of its garlic flavor.

You might wish to substitute other ingredients for the main courses listed here. Boneless steaks of mutton, lamb, veal or pork work fine in the Beef Daube recipe. Any kind of bird will yield excellent results in the chicken recipe. Of course, it will help if the birds are young and tender.

There are several well-known wines produced in this area. One is the white Alella, which is served in some of the best of Barcelona's fine seafood restaurants. A dry or sweet white wine, is Panades; most of it is used to produce Xampan, a sparkling wine. Panades is always fairly strong, which is fine for a dish à la Catalane. Tarragona is another white wine of the area but has little virtue except its low cost.

SAUCE CATALANE

Sauce Catalane is Sauce Demi-Glace (Sauce Alsacienne), highly flavored with garlic and a little tomato paste.

CATALANE GARNISHES
TO SERVE 4

1. EGGPLANT À LA CATALANE

2 garlic cloves, crushed
2 oz olive oil

2 lbs eggplant, peeled and diced
    coarsely
salt and pepper

Sauté the garlic in the olive oil until well done and discard. Add the eggplant and sauté in the same oil until golden, adding a bit more oil if needed. Season to taste with salt and pepper and serve hot.

2. RICE PILAF À LA CATALANE

½ cup uncooked rice
½ onion, minced
4 garlic cloves, crushed
1½ tsp olive oil
3 Tbs butter
¾ cup chicken stock* or broth

salt and white pepper
1 tsp parsley
¼ tsp thyme
¼ bay leaf
cheesecloth, washed

Wash the rice well under running cold water and drain. Sauté the onion and garlic slowly in the oil and butter in a casserole, until golden and translucent. Discard garlic. Add the rice and sauté gently, stirring, until golden. Add the stock, season to taste with salt and pepper and add the parsley, thyme and bay leaf tied in cheesecloth. Cover and cook over very low heat for 20 minutes, or until tender and done. Discard the herb bouquet and serve hot.

CHICK PEAS À LA CATALANE
TO SERVE 4

1 lb drained canned chick peas
salt and pepper
4 chorizo or garlic sausages
1 pepper, seeded and minced
1 onion stuck with 2 cloves
1 carrot, diced
1 tsp parsley
¼ tsp thyme

½ bay leaf
cheesecloth, washed
¼ lb good ham (Bayonne, Virginia), or prosciutto
3 Tbs tomato paste
3 garlic cloves, grated
fresh chopped basil and/or
    chives

Put the chick peas in a pan and barely cover with water. Season to taste with salt and pepper. Add the sausages, pepper, onion and carrot. Add the parsley, thyme and bay leaf tied in cheesecloth, and the ham. Bring to a boil, lower heat and simmer for 30 minutes, adding a little water if needed. Discard the herb bouquet, onion and excess fat. Remove sausages and ham and cut in small cubes. Return to the pan and add the tomato paste and garlic. Blend gently, trying not to crush the chick peas. Continue simmering for 1 hour more, adding water if needed. Drain and serve hot, sprinkled with basil and/or chives.

STUFFED ONIONS À LA CATALANE
TO SERVE 4

8 medium onions
2 cups rice, cooked in beef
   stock* or broth
1 cup sweet pimientos, sautéed
   in olive oil and chopped
1 Tbs parsley

½ tsp basil
¼ tsp thyme
salt and pepper
beef stock* or broth
bread crumbs
butter, melted

Remove the brown onion skins and cut off the top third of the onions and discard. Blanch the trimmed onions in boiling, lightly salted water for 10 minutes. Drain. Preheat oven to 375°. Remove the inside of the onions, leaving the outer 2 layers intact. Chop half the removed inner layers of onions and mix with the rice, pimientos, parsley, basil and thyme. Season with salt and pepper to taste. Use this mixture to stuff the onions, and place them in a buttered baking dish with just a little room around them; they should almost fill the dish. Pour in enough beef stock to half-cover the stuffed onions, bring to a boil on direct heat and put in the oven to simmer for 15 minutes. Drain, top generously with the crumbs and a little butter to moisten, brown in the oven and serve hot.

EGGS À LA CATALANE (Scrambled)
TO SERVE 4

4 garlic cloves, crushed
olive oil
2 tomatoes, peeled* and halved
salt and pepper
4 ½-inch slices of eggplant,
   peeled

parsley sprigs
4 Tbs butter
8 eggs, lightly beaten
4 Tbs heavy cream (optional)
salt and pepper

Sauté the garlic in a little olive oil in a pan until golden. Add the tomatoes, season lightly with salt and pepper and sauté until well done but not mushy. In a separate pan, sauté the eggplant, lightly seasoned, in oil until golden. Arrange the tomatoes and eggplant, alternating, around the outside of a hot serving dish and keep hot. Decorate with parsley sprigs. Melt the butter in a pan. Mix the eggs and cream and season to taste with salt and pepper. Scramble the eggs in hot butter and slide into the open center of the tomato and eggplant platter. Serve at once, hot.

BEEF DAUBE À LA CATALANE (Stew)
TO SERVE 4

4 garlic cloves, crushed
3 Tbs butter
3 Tbs olive oil
4 boneless steaks
2 carrots, minced
2 onions, diced
1 cup Madeira wine
3 Tbs tomato paste

1 tsp parsley
¼ tsp thyme
½ bay leaf
½ tsp basil
cheesecloth, washed
salt and pepper
4 medium potatoes, minced

Cook the garlic in the butter and oil in a casserole until well browned. Discard the garlic. Quickly brown the steaks, and set aside. Sauté the carrots and onions in the casserole until soft. Return the steaks to the casserole and add the wine and tomato paste. Add the parsley, thyme, bay leaf and basil tied in cheesecloth. Season with salt and pepper to taste and sprinkle the potatoes on top. Cover the casserole and simmer over low heat for 1 hour. Discard the herb bouquet and serve hot, in the casserole.

MUTTON DAUBE À LA CATALANE (Stew)
TO SERVE 4

3 lbs mutton, in pieces
salt and pepper
½ onion
butter
½ tsp sugar
4 Tbs flour
4 garlic cloves, crushed
1 qt clear beef stock* or broth

4 oz tomato purée, or sauce
  (preferably homemade*)
1 Tbs parsley
½ tsp thyme
½ bay leaf
cheesecloth, washed
1½ lbs chick peas, cooked

Preheat oven to 325°. Season the mutton with salt and pepper to taste and brown with the onion in a casserole in butter. Remove excess fat. Add the sugar and flour and blend well. Add the garlic, stock and tomato purée. Add the parsley, thyme and bay leaf tied in cheesecloth, cover and cook in the oven for 1 hour.

Skim excess fat from the casserole, if any, and add the chick peas. Recover and cook in the oven for 1 hour more. Discard the herb bouquet and set the mutton and chick peas on a hot serving dish. Blend the cooking juices well and strain over the mutton. Serve hot.

MUTTON SHOULDER À LA CATALANE
TO SERVE 4–6

1 boned shoulder of mutton,
   tied
1 large slice of ham
1 onion, sliced
1 carrot, sliced
salt and pepper
2 Tbs goose fat, or butter
2 Tbs flour
1 cup dry white wine
2 cups beef stock* or broth

25 cloves of garlic, blanched 30
   seconds in boiling water,
   drained
1 Tbs parsley
1 tsp thyme
1 tsp chervil
1 bay leaf
1 1x2-inch strip orange peel
cheesecloth, washed

Put the mutton, ham, onion and carrot in a pot and season to taste with salt and pepper. Melt the fat and pour in the pot. Cover and cook very gently for 30 minutes.

Preheat oven to 350°. Remove the mutton and ham from the pot and discard any excess fat. Add the flour to the pot and stir in well. Cook for 3 minutes. Add the wine and stock and mix well, heating through. Strain the pot juices and return to the pot. Return the mutton to the pot. Add the garlic, and the parsley, thyme, chervil, bay leaf and orange peel tied in cheesecloth. Dice the ham and return to the pot. Cover and cook in the oven for about 30 minutes per pound, or until the mutton is done. To serve, drain and untie the shoulder and place on a hot platter. Let stand 10 minutes. Discard the herb bouquet and pour the sauce and garlic cloves over the roast. Serve hot.

This sauce is sometimes thickened with white bread crumbs, which is the custom in western Languedoc, just across the Pyrenees from Catalonia, in southern France.

Mutton Leg or Shoulder en Pistache is the term generally used to describe this dish. However, to be accurate, that term applies only to meat garnished solely with sauce and garlic cloves. This recipe would not quite qualify because of the diced ham in the sauce.

LAMB SHOULDER À LA CATALANE
TO SERVE 4–6

Proceed as for Mutton Shoulder à la Catalane.

CHICKEN À LA CATALANE
TO SERVE 4

2 young chickens, cut up
salt and pepper
2 oz olive oil
1 oz butter
1 cup dry white wine
2–4 garlic cloves, crushed
2 cups Sauce Espagnole, or
   beef gravy

½ cup tomato purée
½ lb button mushrooms,
   sautéed in butter
24 tiny onions
4 tomatoes, cubed
8 chorizo or garlic sausages,
   browned

Preheat oven to 325°. Season the chickens to taste with salt and pepper. Sauté in oil and butter in a casserole until browned. Add the wine and garlic and cook until the wine is gone. Add the Espagnole and tomato purée and cook in the oven for 45 minutes, covered. Remove the chickens, discard excess fat, if any, and strain the sauce. Return the chickens and sauce to the casserole. Add the mushrooms, onions, tomatoes and sausages to the casserole. Cook, uncovered, for 25 to 30 minutes in the oven and serve hot, in the casserole.

COD or TROUT À LA CATALANE
TO SERVE 4

2 lb cod or trout fillets
salt and pepper
beaten eggs
2 cups bread crumbs mixed
   with 2 Tbs finely minced
   fresh basil (or 2 tsp dried)
olive oil

butter
3 garlic cloves, grated
1½ cups Tomato Fondue*
3 cups peeled, diced eggplant
salt and pepper
olive oil
lemon slices

Season the fish to taste with salt and pepper. Dip in beaten eggs and crumbs and sauté in half olive oil and half butter until done and golden. Drain on paper towels and keep hot. Meanwhile, cook the garlic in the tomato fondue. Season the eggplant with salt and pepper and sauté in oil until tender. Drain on paper towels. Arrange the fish on a hot platter with the eggplant and top with the garlic-flavored Tomato Fondue. Serve hot, garnished with lemon slices.

This recipe is excellent with any white-fleshed fish, or eels.

LOBSTER À LA CATALANE
TO SERVE 4

1 Tbs parsley
1 tsp chervil
½ tsp tarragon
¼ tsp thyme
1 bay leaf
salt and pepper to taste
1 celery stalk, sliced
1 onion, sliced
1 carrot, sliced
4 cloves
4 garlic cloves
6 cups water

4 1½-lb lobsters, preferably live
1 small lettuce head, shredded
½ cup chopped watercress
1 cup mayonnaise, preferably
    homemade*
salt and pepper
4 tomatoes
2 sweet red peppers, peeled,*
    seeded and diced
2 hard-boiled eggs, quartered
    lengthwise
olive oil, vinegar, salt and pep-
    per

Make a court bouillon by mixing the first 12 ingredients and simmering covered for 30 minutes. Strain. Bring the strained liquid to a boil and use to cook the lobsters. Let the lobsters cool in the liquid. Meanwhile, mix the lettuce and watercress with ¼ of the mayonnaise and season with salt and pepper. Cut the tops off the tomatoes and scoop out the seeds and insides, leaving the skin and pulp intact. Turn upside down to drain. Fill the tomatoes with ½ the lettuce-watercress mixture. Remove all the meat from the lobsters and set the large claw meat aside whole. Dice the rest of the meat. Mix the diced lobster with the peppers and remaining mayonnaise and season to taste with salt and pepper. Pile this lobster mixture in the center of a serving platter and surround with the tomatoes. Top the tomatoes with the whole claw meat. Put the remaining lettuce-watercress mixture in piles between the tomatoes. Garnish the platter with the egg wedges seasoned with a little oil, vinegar, salt and pepper. Serve at room temperature or lightly chilled.

SOUP À LA CATALANE
TO SERVE 4

3 oz ham, minced
1½ Tbs olive oil
1½ cups diced onions
1½ cups leek whites, sliced thin
¾ cup green peppers, diced
6 garlic cloves, minced very fine
2 tsp flour
2 cups water, hot

3 cups beef stock* or broth, hot
3 Tbs raw rice
½ tsp basil
½ tsp turmeric
salt and pepper
1 egg yolk
1 oz olive oil
chives

Sauté the ham in the oil until lightly browned. Add onions, leeks, peppers and garlic and cook slowly, stirring, until tender but not browned. Blend the flour in well and remove from heat. Blend the water in slowly. Add the stock and return to heat and bring to a simmer. Add the rice, basil, turmeric and salt and pepper to taste. Simmer partly covered for 25 minutes.

Beat the yolk until pale yellow, and beat in the oil drop by drop until all blended. Slowly dribble 1 cup of the hot (but not boiling) soup into the egg and oil mixture, beating to absorb and blend. Mix with the rest of the soup off heat and serve hot, garnished with chives.

Cévenole

(say-ven-NOHL)

From the Cévennes, a sparsely populated mountain chain in southeast France. The mountains average over 3,000 feet in height, and heavy sudden rains feed torrential rivers, which have cut deep ravines throughout the mountain chain. Travel is very difficult here, and to make matters worse, the winters are cold and floods common. This is a rugged and inhospitable region, although on the southern slopes olive trees are cultivated on artificial terraces. The mountainsides host chestnut and mulberry trees, and the mulberry leaves have been used in silkworm culture in some of the valleys, but mulberry growing is now largely abandoned.

Cévenole is typified by chestnuts, onions and chipolata sausages as garnishes. Virtually any meat can be prepared à la Cévenole using the mutton recipe. Use the Cornish game hen recipe for birds. Simply adjust the cooking time for the particular meat involved. Dishes à la Cévenole are often served with a chestnut purée. (Chestnut purée is made with shelled and skinned chestnuts* simmered in white sauce such as Allemande or Béchamel, flavored with a little chopped celery. Purée chestnuts when tender with a little sauce in a blender. A little butter or cream may be added.) The main dish is braised and served on a bed of chestnut purée garnished with glazed onions, and sauce is made by adding Espagnole or Velouté* to the braising liquids and boiling down quickly to thicken. Cévenole is similar to the cooking mode Limousine in that they both make use of chestnuts as an important ingredient.

A bowl of shiny uncooked chestnuts or mountain laurel, if it's available, would make an appropriate centerpiece.

ARTICHOKE HEARTS À LA CÉVENOLE (Stuffed)
TO SERVE 4

12 chestnuts	2 Tbs heavy cream (or more if
8 small artichoke hearts	needed)
2 Tbs butter	2 Tbs *soubise,* or sautéed
1 cup chicken or veal stock* or	minced onions
broth, hot	Parmesan cheese, grated
1 sprig celery leaves	butter, melted

Score the chestnuts deeply with a knife and boil in water for 10 minutes. Cut open and remove the chestnut meat. Blanch the artichokes in boiling, lightly salted water for 30 seconds. Drain. Put in a pan with the butter and cook until just tender. Preheat oven to 400°. Put the chestnut meat in the hot stock with the celery and simmer 20 minutes. Strain. Discard the celery and rub through a sieve. Blend with the cream to make a thick purée and mix with the *soubise*. Use this to stuff the artichokes. Place on a buttered baking sheet, sprinkle generously with cheese and a little melted butter to moisten and brown in the oven. Serve hot.

You may boil down the stock used to simmer the chestnut meats (if it isn't too salty) until only 1 ounce is left, and add it to the chestnut purée. This will give the purée a well-rounded flavor.

Any dish browned like this becomes a *gratin,* so this dish could be called Artichoke Heart Gratin à la Cévonole, or Gratin of Artichoke Hearts à la Cévenole. If this dish is garnished with chopped cockscombs and truffles, lightly sautéed in butter and bound with a little thick Sauce Allemande, it becomes Artichokes à la Chalonnaise.

MUTTON CHOPS À LA CÉVENOLE
TO SERVE 4

8 mutton chops
salt and pepper
1 carrot, quartered
1 onion, quartered
1 celery stem, quartered
1 tsp parsley
¼ tsp thyme
¼ bay leaf

cheesecloth, washed
2 cups chicken stock* or broth
24 chestnuts, scored with a knife, boiled 10 minutes and shelled
16 small onions, glazed*
12 small chipolata sausages, or pork sausages, cooked in butter

Season the chops to taste with salt and pepper. Put the chops, carrot, onion and celery in a pot with the stock. Add the parsley, thyme and bay leaf tied in cheesecloth. Bring to a boil, then reduce the heat to simmer gently. Cover and cook until chops are almost done.

Add the chestnuts and onions and cook 10 minutes more. Add the sausages and cook 5 minutes more. Arrange the chops in a ring on a hot platter. Fill the center of the ring with the onions, chestnuts and sausages and keep hot.

Discard the herb bouquet, skim off excess fat, and quickly boil the stock down to half, mashing the braising vegetables into the stock. Strain over the mutton and serve hot.

CORNISH GAME HENS À LA CÉVENOLE
TO SERVE 4

4 1-lb birds
2 cups pork sausage meat
½ cup chopped chicken livers
2 Tbs chopped truffles
2 eggs
1 tsp salt
½ tsp white pepper
⅛ tsp grated nutmeg
¼ tsp basil
¼ tsp thyme
¼ tsp coriander
¼ tsp sage

salt and pepper
butter
12 chestnuts, scored with a
    knife, boiled 10 minutes and
    shelled
8 mushrooms, sautéed in butter
2 oz madeira wine
1 Tbs brandy
2 cups veal gravy, or Sauce
    Espagnole
2 oz flour
water

Mix the sausage meat with the chicken livers, truffles, eggs, salt, pepper, nutmeg. basil, thyme, coriander and sage. Stuff the birds with this mixture and sew or skewer closed.

Preheat oven to 400°. Truss the wings and legs to the birds with string and season with salt and pepper to taste. Brown the birds well in butter in a casserole. Add the chestnuts and mushrooms. Pour the madeira and brandy over the birds and flame. Add the gravy. Make a pastelike dough of the flour mixed with just a little water and use to seal the cover on the casserole. Bake in the oven for 45 minutes, or until done. Remove the trussings and serve the birds right in the casserole, hot.

Champenoise

(shahm-pen-WAZ)

Champagne was formerly a province in northeastern France. The name Champagne was derived from the Latin *campania*, meaning a flat, monotonous plain. This flat chalk plain covers most of the province, not very inspiring for sightseers, but the chalky soil is fine for growing grapes that yield a clean, dry white wine.

Being so far north, the grapes need all the sun they can get, and are harvested late. But even so they contain less sugar than grapes grown to the south. This causes them to ferment more slowly, and they are still in the process of fermentation when winter comes and the cold temporarily stops the process. When spring comes and the fermentation resumes, the result is a sparkling wine, or champagne. The gasses, a by-product of fermentation, are held in the bottles by the tight-fitting corks, whereas in still table wines the fermentation is completed before bottling.

As a cooking mode, Champenoise is similar to any other that relies on a particular wine for its character, like Bordelaise or Bourguignonne, except it is much more delicate than modes like Bourguignonne with its robust flavor of red Burgundy.

In these recipes, champagne is the distinguishing ingredient. Most main courses can be cooked successfully in champagne, with a little seasoning. For sauce, thicken the pan juices to suit your taste with Velouté,* Cream or even Espagnole or Demi-Glace (Sauce Alsacienne). Usually, dishes à la Champenoise are served with mushrooms. The recipes for flounder and Cornish game hens can be used for any fish or fowl, respectively.

The Champagne district also produces a very fine cheese, Carré de l'Est, a soft cream cheese that is always packed in boxes. Champenoise is a stylish cooking style, and the wine you cook with is always a good accompaniment, so serve champagne with a Champenoise dish. Or, if you wish to change the standard a bit, serve a very dry white wine.

The flavors in these dishes are subtle, so keep that in mind when planning vegetables and the rest of the menu.

For décor, you might round up a few interesting champagne bottles of different sizes and use some for candle holders and others for flowers. To make a champagne cocktail, place a lump of sugar and 2 dashes of bitters in a champagne glass, fill with chilled champagne and add a lemon twist.

TRUFFLES or MUSHROOMS À LA CHAMPENOISE
TO SERVE 4

1 lb truffles or mushrooms	½ cup Jus de Veau,* veal stock*
salt and white pepper	or veal gravy
1½ cups champagne	

Season the truffles lightly with salt and white pepper and cook, covered, in the champagne for 10 to 15 minutes. Remove the truffles with a slotted spoon to a hot platter and keep hot. Quickly boil down the champagne until almost gone, add the Jus de Veau, heat through and blend. Strain over the truffles and let stand for 10 minutes without cooling. Serve hot.

TURNIPS or RUTABAGAS À LA CHAMPENOISE
TO SERVE 4

2 lbs turnips, peeled and cubed	¾ cup beef stock* or broth
¼ lb lean bacon, diced	⅛ tsp sugar
½ cup minced onion	pepper
1 Tbs butter	½ tsp basil
1 Tbs flour	1 tsp grated lemon rind
	chives

Blanch the turnips in boiling, lightly salted water for 4 minutes and drain. Blanch the bacon in unsalted water at a gentle simmer for 5 minutes and drain. Sauté the bacon and onion in the butter until lightly browned. Add the flour and blend well. Remove from heat and slowly blend in the stock, sugar, pepper to taste, basil and lemon rind. Bring back to a simmer and mix in the turnips. Simmer gently until tender, covered, about 25 minutes. Uncover and simmer to thicken the sauce. Sprinkle with chives and serve hot.

SAUERKRAUT À LA CHAMPENOISE
TO SERVE 4

3 oz Canadian bacon or ham, diced	1½ lbs sauerkraut
3 Tbs butter	¾ cup champagne
1 onion, chopped	2 tsp sugar
	½ tsp white pepper

Sauté the bacon gently in the butter for a couple of minutes. Add the onion and cook until tender but not browned. Meanwhile wash the sauerkraut and squeeze dry. Add the sauerkraut to the sautéing pan. Add the champagne and enough water to just cover. Sprinkle with the sugar and white pepper. Cover and cook gently for 1 hour. Serve hot. If necessary, remove the cover toward the end of cooking to reduce the liquid, which will enhance the flavor of the dish.

EGGS EN COCOTTE À LA CHAMPENOISE (Casserole)
TO SERVE 4

1 oz butter	white pepper
1½ cups Brie cheese, sliced thin	1 Tbs chives
½ cup champagne	6 eggs
⅛ tsp nutmeg, ground	Parmesan cheese, grated

Preheat the broiler. Melt the butter in a casserole. Add the Brie and champagne and heat gently, stirring until the cheese melts. Add the nutmeg, pepper to taste and the chives. Mix well. Break the eggs carefully on top, and cook without stirring until almost done. Sprinkle lightly with Parmesan cheese and run under the broiler for 1 or 2 minutes. Serve hot, in the casserole. (You may wish to use 8 eggs instead of 4, depending on your guests' appetites.)

CORNISH GAME HENS À LA CHAMPENOISE
TO SERVE 4

4 1-lb birds	4 bread slices, trimmed
salt and pepper	butter
1½ lbs goose liver, diced (or chicken liver)	pâté de foie gras
4 Tbs brandy	1½ cups champagne
2 oz butter	½ cup cream
16 mushroom caps	3 Tbs truffles, shredded
	butter

Season the birds lightly inside and out with salt and pepper. Mix the liver with the brandy and season lightly. Use to stuff the birds, and sew or skewer closed. Brown the birds in the butter in a casserole. Lower heat and finish cooking slowly, partly covered, for 1 hour. Put the mushrooms in the casserole for the final 20 minutes.

Meanwhile, sauté the bread in a little butter until golden on both sides, drain and spread generously with pâté. Place 1 slice on each of 4 hot plates.

Put the cooked birds (untrussed) on the bread slices. Surround with the mushrooms and keep hot. Remove excess fat from the casserole, if any, and add the champagne. Quickly boil down to half, scraping up the juices. Add the cream and boil for a few minutes to thicken lightly. Toss the truffles in a little hot butter. Strain the sauce and add the truffles. Pour over the birds and serve hot.

FLOUNDER FILLETS À LA CHAMPENOISE
TO SERVE 4

4 ½-lb flounder fillets	cheesecloth. washed
½ cup chopped onion	salt
1 minced garlic clove	white pepper
1 cup champagne, preferably	½ cup champagne
dry	1 oz butter (optional)
½ cup heavy cream	16 small sautéed mushroom
1 tsp parsley	caps, hot
½ tsp basil	16 small shrimp, cooked,
¼ tsp thyme	shelled, cleaned and hot
½ bay leaf	chives

Preheat oven to 350°. Put the fish, onion, garlic, 1 cup of champagne and cream in a buttered baking dish. Add parsley, basil, thyme and bay leaf tied in cheesecloth. Season to taste with salt and a little white pepper. Bring to a boil over direct heat, then bake in the oven for 12 minutes, or until done. Remove the fillets carefully to a hot platter and keep hot. Quickly boil the sauce down to ¹/₃. Stir in the ½ cup of champagne and butter, if desired, and pour over the fillets. Garnish with the mushroom caps and shrimp, sprinkle with chives and serve hot.

This recipe is excellent with any white-fleshed fish, or eel.

SOUP À LA CHAMPENOISE
TO SERVE 4

4 cups water	2 small turnips, peeled
2 cups chicken stock* or broth	1 very small cabbage, chopped
(preferably unsalted)	coarsely
½ lb lean bacon	3 potatoes, peeled
1½ lbs smoked ham	3 leeks, white parts only
2 carrots, peeled	salt and pepper

Put the water, stock, bacon and ham in a soup kettle, bring to a boil, cover and simmer 1 hour. Add the carrots and turnips and simmer 20 minutes more. Add the cabbage, potatoes and leeks and simmer until done, about 40 minutes more. Season with salt and pepper to taste (it may need no salt). Remove the meats and vegetables, cut in bite-size pieces and put in a hot soup tureen. Add the broth, skimming off fat if necessary, and serve hot.

CRÈME À LA CHAMPENOISE
TO SERVE 4

2 cups champagne, hot
1 Tbs cherry liqueur

½ cup sugar (or to taste)
8 eggs, separated

Mix the hot champagne with the cherry liqueur and stir in the sugar until dissolved. Beat the egg yolks in a bowl until pale yellow, and slowly blend into the champagne mixture. Pour into the top of a double boiler and cook very slowly, beating with a whisk, until thickened. Chill. Beat the egg whites very stiff just before serving, and fold into the chilled champagne cream. Serve at once.

Chasseur

(shah-SEWR)

Means hunter. The feminine form is Chasseuse. The term is applied to any dish served with Sauce Chasseur.

Dishes Chasseur are hearty in flavor, as they should be. No mighty hunter wants to come home to a bland meal! As a cooking mode, Chasseur is similar to Bordelaise. They both rely heavily on wine for flavor and on mushrooms as a garnish. There are other styles that rely on wine, like Madère or Bourguignonne, but they are not as similar to Chasseur as is Bordelaise.

Chasseur dishes are generally meats with sauce, which is fitting for a category named Hunter. Any meat can be successfully prepared in this manner, that is, browned in butter or oil and then cooked covered with mushrooms, shallots (or onions), parsley, chervil, tarragon, wine and Sauce Espagnole (or beef gravy). Naturally, it is an excellent method for cooking game. Rabbit can be prepared the same as the Tournedos Chasseur using red wine in place of the Madeira. Squab or Cornish game hens can be prepared as in the chicken recipe, first seasoning the birds inside and placing ½ garlic clove in each before trussing. Once you are familiar with the recipes here, you can adapt them to any meat, large or small, and for a fine accompaniment use sautéed chicken livers. Actually, Eggs Caruso are Eggs Chasseur without the sauce.

When I think of décor for this mode, the problem isn't what to use, but what not to use. There's all sorts of hunting gear—a quiver of arrows, bolas, boomerangs, slings, etc. There is the goddess of the hunt, Diana, of mythology. There is the constellation of Orion, the mighty hunter of Greek mythology, containing the giant red star Betelgeuse. There are duck decoys, there are bugles, which were originally hunting horns and are still prominent in the good old fox hunt.

For music, something with horns might be appropriate. Mozart's Quartet in

B-Flat Major, known as the "Hunt Quartet," opens with a theme that has the quality of a hunting horn. Or there is Handel's "Water Music," with a transcription by Sir Hamilton Harty that is scored for four horns.

CHASSEUR SAUCE (for Meats and Eggs)
TO MAKE 2 CUPS

¼ lb mushrooms, chopped
1 Tbs butter
1 Tbs minced shallots
½ cup dry white wine
1½ tsp parsley
1 tsp chervil
½ tsp tarragon

½ cup tomato sauce, or ½ cup tomatoes, peeled,* seeded and chopped
1 cup Sauce Espagnole, or beef gravy
2 Tbs butter, diced (optional)
salt and pepper

Sauté the mushrooms in 1 tablespoon of butter. When they are ¾ done, add the shallots and finish sautéing. Put the wine, parsley, chervil and tarragon in a separate pan. Boil down to half. Add the tomato sauce and Espagnole and boil a few minutes to blend flavors. Mix in the mushrooms and shallots. Add the butter, if desired. Season to taste with salt and pepper, if necessary, and serve hot.

POTATOES CHASSEUR (Stuffed)
TO SERVE 4

4 potatoes, baked and halved lengthwise
salt and pepper
½ lb chicken livers, sautéed in butter and chopped

¼ lb mushrooms, chopped and sautéed in a little butter
1 cup Sauce Chasseur

Preheat oven to 375°. Hollow out the potatoes, leaving about ½ inch of flesh around the skins. Mash the removed pulp. Season the potato shells with salt and pepper. Mix the mashed potato pulp with the livers and mushrooms. Use this mixture to stuff the potato shells. Top with sauce and brown in the oven. Serve hot.

EGGS CHASSEUR (Poached or Soft-Boiled)
TO SERVE 4

8 chicken liver halves
butter
salt and pepper
4 individual baked pastry shells,* hot

8 eggs, freshly poached or soft-boiled, hot
1 cup Sauce Chasseur
parsley or chives

Sauté the livers in a little butter. Season lightly with salt and pepper and place in the bottoms of the pastry crusts. Top with 2 eggs in each, and spoon over the sauce. Sprinkle with parsley or chives and serve at once, hot.

EGGS CHASSEUR (Baked)
TO SERVE 4

8 chicken livers	8 eggs
butter	1 cup Sauce Chasseur, hot
salt and pepper	parsley

Sauté the chicken livers in a little butter until just done and season lightly with salt and pepper. Keep hot. Preheat oven to 500°. Break 2 eggs in each of 4 individual buttered baking dishes, being careful not to break the yolks. Place on a high rack in the oven for 4 minutes, or until the whites are just set and the yolks still soft. Serve in the baking dishes, garnished with the chicken livers and sauce. Sprinkle with a little parsley and serve hot.

TOURNEDOS CHASSEUR (Beef Fillets)
TO SERVE 4

4 beef fillets	1 tsp parsley
butter	½ tsp chervil
½ lb mushrooms, sliced	½ tsp tarragon
1 tsp chopped shallot	1–2 tsp tomato paste or sauce
salt and pepper	(optional)
1 cup Madeira wine	
1 cup Sauce Espagnole, or beef	
gravy	

Sauté the beef fillets in a little butter until done to taste. Set aside and keep hot. Into the same pan put the mushrooms, shallot and salt and pepper to taste. Sauté until lightly browned. Add the wine and Espagnole and cook down to half quickly. Add the parsley, chervil and tarragon. Add the tomato paste if desired. Blend well. Pour over the fillets and serve hot.

Since the sauce step takes several minutes, this may raise problems with the steaks. If you like your steaks fresh from the grill or pan and not kept hot even for an instant longer than necessary, as I do, then prepare a cup of Sauce Chasseur ahead and have hot. Sauté the tournedos to taste and place on hot plates, pour the sauté into the sauté pan, blend with the juices, and pour right over the steaks. The whole process of blending the sauce with the pan juices is reduced to a few seconds, rather than minutes.

Tournedos Chasseur are often served on bread rounds, cut to the same size as the tournedos and sautéed in a little butter on both sides, making golden croutons.

VEAL CHOPS CHASSEUR
TO SERVE 4

Proceed as for Tournedos Chasseur, using veal chops in place of the beef fillets.

LAMB NOISETTES CHASSEUR (Thin Fillets)

Proceed as for Tournedos Chasseur, using 8 lamb noisettes in place of the beef and sautéing in half butter and half olive oil.

MUTTON CHOPS CHASSEUR
TO SERVE 4

Proceed as for Tournedos Chasseur, using 8 mutton chops or small cutlets in place of beef. After sautéing the chops, remove excess fat from the pan before continuing. Omit the parsley and increase the chervil and tarragon to 1 teaspoon each. In this sauce, the tomato paste or sauce is not optional; its flavor is necessary with the mutton.

VEAL DAUBE CHASSEUR (Stew)
TO SERVE 4

3-lb veal steak or roast	1 Tbs tomato paste
¾ lb button mushrooms	1 tsp parsley
3 Tbs butter	½ tsp chervil
3 Tbs olive oil	½ tsp tarragon
1 Tbs chopped shallots	cheesecloth, washed
¾ cup dry white wine	salt and pepper
¾ cup Sauce Espagnole, or veal	chives
stock* or gravy	fresh chervil, if available

Preheat oven to 325°. Brown the veal and mushrooms in the butter and oil in a braising pan or roaster. Set aside and brown the shallots in the same pan. Return the veal and mushrooms to the pan. Add the wine, Espagnole and tomato paste to the pan. Add the parsley, chervil and tarragon tied in cheesecloth. Season to taste with salt and pepper, cover and simmer in the oven for 1½ hours. Remove herb bouquet and discard. Put the roast in a hot serving dish with the mushrooms and pour over the pan sauce. Sprinkle with chives and fresh chervil and serve hot.

This is excellent with lamb or beef, or even pork or mutton, but with pork or mutton, the excess fat must be spooned from the pan before serving the sauce.

CHICKEN DAUBE CHASSEUR (Stew)
TO SERVE 4

Proceed as for Veal Daube Chasseur, using 2 small, cut-up chickens. After browning the chicken pieces, flame them in brandy (about 2 ounces), stirring until the fire dies. Finish the recipe in the same manner, reducing the oven time to about 45 minutes.

Chaud-Froid

(shoh-FWAH)

Literally means hot-cold. It is a dish prepared hot and served cold. Some people who should know better have attributed this mode of food preparation to a man named Chafroix, who served outstandingly in the royal kitchens of Louis XV. This derivation, however, is incorrect. There are records of "hot-cold" dishes as far back as Roman times. At the excavations of Pompeii a vase was unearthed which still held pieces of meat in jelly, and was inscribed *calidus-frigidus,* which can be translated to the French equivalent Chaud-Froid. This meat may not have been cooked as in the classic French manner, but it was unquestionably the same idea. Therefore, France may not claim the origin of Chaud-Froid as a cooking idea, nor could Chaufroix have invented a dish centuries older than himself.

At any rate, you're likely to see this type of dish spelled Chaufroix, or Chauds-Froids (the plural), neither of which is correct. While the French didn't originate the idea of serving food cooked, then cooled in jellied stock, the *modern* Chaud-Froid comes to us from the Château Montmorency, and was given its name by the Maréchal de Luxembourg in 1759. His table at Montmorency was known as one of the finest in France.

There are all kinds of variations on Chaud-Froid Sauce, and the choice in variation is yours. You might decide to use Sauce Allemande in place of the Velouté in the recipe for White Chaud-Froid Sauce #1, for instance, or any other sauce in the appropriate Chaud-Froid Sauce recipe, such as Sauce Chasseur in place of the Espagnole in the Brown Chaud-Froid. This sauce is excellent with beef. The rule of thumb is, if you like a sauce with a particular meat or fish, then it's fine to use as a base in making a Chaud-Froid Sauce for use with that main dish. This rule applies to virtually any food that can be served chilled.

Often foods are coated just with aspic* jelly. These dishes are called en Gelée. The aspic must be made with perfectly clear* stock, and can be colored. For a reddish-amber coloring, cook some dry sugar gently until melted, and let color. It will turn amber with a reddish cast. Add a little water and boil a few minutes, then mix with clear stock and unflavored gelatin for a beautifully colored aspic. For green, try condensed cooking juices from spinach. For a beautiful, deep, dark red, use beet juice. Artificial vegetable colors can also be used, of course, but sparingly. The aspics should be richly colored, but not garish, which is the tendency with artificial food coloring.

WHITE CHAUD-FROID SAUCE #1 (For Eggs, White Meats and Poultry)
TO MAKE 1 CUP

½ envelope unflavored gelatin mixed with 1 oz each dry white wine and chicken stock*

¾ cup Sauce Velouté* (or Béchamel)
1 oz chicken glaze*
¼ cup heavy cream

Let gelatin soak in the wine and stock for several minutes. Bring the Sauce Velouté, chicken glaze and cream to a boil. Heat the gelatin mixture and blend with the Velouté mixture. Return to a boil and simmer a few minutes, until the gelatin granules are completely dissolved. Cool until lightly thickened. Use to coat cold foods, usually with several layers. Each time the food is coated it should be put into the refrigerator to chill and set quickly while the remaining Chaud-Froid Sauce is kept just cool to remain semiliquid.

White Chaud-Froid Sauce can be colored and flavored with 1 or 2 tablespoons of tomato paste.

WHITE CHAUD-FROID SAUCE #2 (for Fish and Shellfish)
TO MAKE 1 CUP

Proceed as for White Chaud-Froid Sauce #1, using fish-based Velouté,* and fish glaze* in place of the chicken glaze.

It isn't mandatory to use the fish-based Chaud-Froid Sauce #2 for fish. Only a purist would throw a tantrum if you served a fish with a chicken-based Chaud-Froid sauce. I happen to like the combination.

BROWN CHAUD-FROID SAUCE (for Beef, Lamb and Mutton)
TO MAKE 1 CUP

Proceed as for White Chaud-Froid Sauce #1, using 1 cup of Sauce Espagnole in place of the Velouté and cream, beef glaze* in place of the chicken glaze, and port wine and beef stock* to melt the gelatin.

VEAL CHOPS EN CHAUD-FROID
TO SERVE 4

8 veal chops
salt and pepper
butter
1 recipe White Chaud-Froid Sauce #1, cool but not quite set
1 oz Madeira wine

1 oz truffles, minced fine
2 oz lean ham, in small, thin strips
1 Tbs fresh tarragon leaves
2 cups clear veal stock*
1 pkg unflavored gelatin

Season the veal with salt and pepper to taste and sauté in a little butter until done. Do not overcook. Drain and let cool. Arrange on a platter. Mix the

Madeira and truffles into the Chaud-Froid Sauce and use to coat the chops. Chill to set. Decorate the coated chops with the ham strips and tarragon leaves, or other fresh herb leaves of your choice. Meanwhile, soak the gelatin in the stock for 5 minutes and slowly bring to a boil. Boil 5 minutes, until the gelatin granules are completely dissolved. Brush this over the decorated chops and chill to set. Chill the remaining jellied veal stock separately, and when set, chop and put around the coated chops to garnish. Serve chilled.

A typical accompaniment for this dish would be a mixed, cooked vegetable salad bound with mayonnaise and piled in the center of a serving dish, garnished with hard-boiled egg quarters and tiny lettuce hearts, seasoned with oil, vinegar, salt and pepper and chilled.

BEEF NOISETTES EN CHAUD-FROID (Thin Fillets)
TO SERVE 4

Proceed as for Veal Chops en Chaud-Froid, using 2 pounds of thin beef fillets, and Brown Chaud-Froid Sauce. Use strips of pâté de foie gras in place of the ham to decorate the dish.

HAM EN CHAUD-FROID
TO SERVE 4

Proceed as for Veal Chops en Chaud-Froid, using cooked ham. Decorate with mushroom and truffle slices and thin hard-boiled egg slices, before coating with the final veal gelatin.

CHICKEN SUPRÊMES EN CHAUD-FROID
TO SERVE 4

Proceed as for Veal Chops en Chaud-Froid, using 4 chicken breasts, skinned, boned and simmered until done in chicken stock* or in 1 quart of water, lightly salted and blended with 1 tablespoon flour. Decorate the chicken after coating with White Chaud-Froid Sauce with thinly sliced olives and leek whites, then glaze with gelatin made with chicken stock* instead of veal stock.

This can be a very attractive dish with whole small birds, like quail, squab or Cornish game hens. Poach them until done and decorate just as in the Chicken Suprêmes. Sliced truffles could be added to the garnish.

FLOUNDER EN CHAUD-FROID
TO SERVE 4

1 5-lb flounder, cleaned but whole
salt and white pepper
1 cup bread crumbs
1 cup cooked crabmeat chunks
3 oz chicken stock* or broth
1 tsp parsley
1 tsp chives
½ tsp basil

¼ tsp thyme
4 cups fish fumet* or 2 cups each clam juice and dry white wine
2 cups White Chaud-Froid Sauce #2, half set
truffle slices
pimiento strips
2 envelopes unflavored gelatin

Preheat oven to 375°. Season the fish inside and out with salt and white pepper to taste. Mix the crumbs, crabmeat, stock, parsley, chives, basil and thyme and season to taste. Use to stuff fish. Secure with string to just hold in shape, not too tight. Place on a well-buttered foil sheet in a baking dish and add the fish fumet. Bring to a boil over direct heat, cover and bake in the oven for 30 minutes, or until done. Do not overcook. Remove the fish by lifting out with the foil and reserve the fish stock. Set carefully on a platter and gently split the foil under the fish so it can be slid out from under. Discard trussing strings and chill the fish.

Coat the chilled fish with the half-set Chaud-Froid Sauce and return to the refrigerator to chill and set. Repeat several times, using up the Chaud-Froid Sauce. Decorate the coated fish with truffle slices and pimiento strips. Meanwhile, soak the gelatin in a little cool, strained fish stock, which you have reserved, for a few minutes to dissolve. Mix with the remaining cooking stock, strained, and bring to a simmer. Simmer 5 minutes to completely dissolve the gelatin granules, and cool until half set. When half set, use to coat the fish and its decorations. Chill to set. Chill the remaining stock, or aspic, until fully set and chop and arrange around the fish. Serve chilled.

SALMON EN CHAUD-FROID
TO SERVE 4

2 carrots, sliced
1 onion, sliced
1 celery stalk, sliced
1 bay leaf
¾ cup dry white wine
1½ cups water

½ tsp salt
4 salmon steaks, ½ lb each
1 cup White Chaud-Froid Sauce #2, half set
8 thin black truffle slices
parsley sprigs

Combine the carrots, onion, celery, bay leaf, wine, water and salt and simmer for 30 minutes. Strain. This is a court bouillon. Heat the court bouillon to a boil, lower heat, add salmon and simmer gently for 12 to 15 minutes, until done. Let salmon cool in the court bouillon. Carefully remove the salmon and discard the skin and bones, leaving 8 cutlet-shaped salmon pieces. Arrange these salmon cutlets on a platter and coat with the Chaud-Froid Sauce. Chill a few minutes to set. Repeat several times, using all the sauce. The salmon cutlets should now be smooth and shiny. Decorate with truffle slices and put the parsley sprigs around the cutlets. Serve chilled.

SALMON MOUSSE EN CHAUD-FROID
TO SERVE 4

2 lbs salmon, cooked in fish
    stock* and drained
2 egg whites
salt and white pepper
1 cup heavy cream, cold
2 egg whites, beaten
1 pkg unflavored gelatin dis-
    solved and simmered in 2 oz
    dry white wine

2 cups White Chaud-Froid
    Sauce #2 made with 1½ cups
    Velouté* and ½ cup sour
    cream
peas, just cooked
caviar, preferably salmon

Skin, bone and mash the salmon in a bowl with a pestle or wooden spoon until very fine. Incorporate the egg whites into the salmon little by little. Place the bowl in ice water and ice cubes coming ¾ up the bowl's outside to chill the salmon, and work with a wooden spoon to a smooth paste, about 10 minutes. Season lightly with salt and white pepper. Rub through a fine sieve and return to the bowl in the ice water and let stand for 30 minutes to chill, stirring occasionally.

Slowly beat in a little cream, then a little beaten egg white, and alternate until the cream and egg whites are all blended in. Mix in the gelatin, softened until the granules are completely dissolved, and blend. Pour into a mold coated with clear fish aspic* and chill thoroughly.

Unmold on a serving dish and coat with a thin coating of Chaud-Froid Sauce and chill quickly. Repeat several times, until all the Chaud-Froid is used. Decorate with peas arranged in a pattern, pressed lightly into the Chaud-Froid, and with little clumps of caviar. Serve chilled.

This is excellent with other meats also. Try substituting chicken for the salmon and decorate with whatever you like—peas and small ham strips, for instance. Sweetbreads also make a fine mousse, as does any white-fleshed fish.

Chipolata

(shee-poh-LAH-tah)

The name of small cocktail sausages made in sheep's casings. They have a soft texture, similar to a hot dog, but are made primarily of pork. In French, *chipolata* means small sausage. It also means onion stew, for a chipolata was originally an

Italian ragout based on onions. In the French cuisine it is now a garnish of chipolata sausages, glazed carrots, diced breast of pork and tiny glazed onions. Sometimes chestnuts and mushrooms braised in veal stock are added.

Any main course garnished with chipolata sausages, with or without one or more of the other chipolata garnishes, is a dish Chipolata. It's a good idea to precook the sausages and then add them to the main course for the final several minutes of cooking to let the flavors blend.

Use another sausage, such as chorizo sausages, with the same garnishes listed here and you would have a dish chorizo. Or, if you used Gehirnwurste, the dish would be a dish Gehirnwurste, and so on. A dish garnished with a mixture of different sausages is a dish à la Bouchère (boo-SHAYR). *Bouchère* means butcher's wife.

CHIPOLATA GARNISHES
TO SERVE 4

1. GLAZED ONIONS OR CARROTS

1 lb tiny onions, or carrots cut in equal rounds	2 tsp salt
1 qt water	4 oz butter
	2 Tbs sugar

Put all the ingredients in a pot and boil until almost all the liquid is gone, leaving a syrupy glaze. Shake the pot to glaze the vegetable evenly.

2. CHIPOLATA SAUSAGES

Put 12 chipolata sausages, or small pork sausages, in a pan with ¼ inch of water and simmer until the water is gone. Then brown the sausages lightly in their own fat, drawn out by the water. This should be done slowly, and takes about 15 minutes.

3. BRAISED CHESTNUTS

1 lb chestnuts	cheesecloth, washed
½ tsp parsley	salt and pepper
1 tsp celery leaves	2 cups veal stock* or thin gravy
⅛ tsp thyme	
⅛ bay leaf	

Preheat oven to 350°. Cut through the domed side of the chestnuts with a sharp knife and boil in water for 5 minutes. Peel. Put the peeled chestnuts in a pot with the parsley, celery, thyme and bay leaf tied in cheesecloth. Season lightly with salt and pepper. Add the stock and bake in the oven, covered, for 30 minutes, or until tender. More time may be needed, depending on the chestnuts.

EGGS CHIPOLATA (Baked)
TO SERVE 4

4 Tbs chopped onion, sautéed
  in butter
8 eggs
salt and pepper
8 chipolata sausages, or small
  pork sausages, precooked

1 cup veal gravy, or Sauce
  Espagnole, hot
chives

Preheat oven to 500°. Put 1 tablespoon of onion in each of 4 buttered individual baking dishes. Top with 2 eggs each, being careful not to break their yolks. Season to taste with salt and pepper. Place 2 sausages at the sides of each dish and bake in the oven for 4 minutes on a high rack, or until the whites are just set and the yolks still soft. Pour the gravy over the yolks, sprinkle with chives and serve at once, hot.

PORK LOIN CHIPOLATA
TO SERVE 4

1 pork loin roast (about 6 lbs)
salt and pepper

chipolata sausages, chipolata
  garnishes and sautéed
  mushrooms

Season the pork well with salt and pepper and roast in a 325° oven for about 35 minutes per pound. Serve on a hot platter surrounded by 16 chipolata sausages, 1½ pounds of glazed carrots, 1 pound of tiny glazed onions and ½ pound of sautéed mushroom caps. Include 1 pound of braised chestnuts, if desired and in season. Serve hot.

MUTTON or LAMB SHOULDER CHIPOLATA
TO SERVE 4–8

Proceed as for Lamb Shoulder (Stuffed) à la Bourgeoise, adding 12 cooked chipolata sausages (or small pork sausages) to the garnish.

SQUAB or CORNISH GAME HENS CHIPOLATA
TO SERVE 4

4 1-lb birds
salt and pepper
butter

chipolata sausages, chipolata
  garnishes and sautéed
  mushrooms

Preheat oven to 350°. Season the birds inside and out with salt and pepper to taste and truss the wings and legs to the bodies with string. Brown lightly in butter in a casserole. Cook in the oven, basting with butter occasionally, until done—about 40 minutes. When nicely browned, cover and finish cooking. Serve on a hot platter surrounded by 12 cooked chipolata sausages, glazed onions and carrots and sautéed mushroom caps. Braised chestnuts would also be nice, if in season. Serve hot.

Choron

(sho-ROHN)

After Alexandre Choron, a French musicologist born at Caen in 1772. He edited the *Principles of Composition of the Schools of Italy* in 1808 and collaborated with Fayotte in editing the *Dictionary of Musicians* in 1810. Choron was named director of the Paris Opera in 1816 and in 1817 was put in charge of a school of chant song which later became the Religious Music School. He died in 1834.

An excellent, tomato-flavored Sauce Béarnaise is named in honor of Choron. Sauce Choron is used primarily with steaks, chicken, eggs and fish. It is also good with some vegetables, such as peas and asparagus, and the cauliflower and artichokes listed in the recipes. Any vegetable that goes well with Sauce Béarnaise and does not conflict with the tomato flavoring is excellent with Sauce Choron, as are all meats.

Choron also applies to a garnish of artichoke hearts stuffed with peas or asparagus, and potato balls browned in butter. Although not mentioned in the recipes, dishes Choron are usually accompanied by the browned potato balls (Choron Garnish #2).

SAUCE CHORON
TO MAKE 2 CUPS

Blend 2 cups of Sauce Béarnaise with 4 to 6 tablespoons of tomato purée or paste and serve hot.

CHORON GARNISHES
TO SERVE 4

1. STUFFED ARTICHOKE HEARTS

8 artichoke hearts, cooked and tossed lightly in butter

1 cup peas, cooked and dressed with a little butter

1 cup asparagus tips, cooked and dressed with a little butter

Stuff 4 of the artichoke hearts with peas and the other 4 with asparagus. Serve hot.

2. POTATO BALLS

2 lbs potatoes, cut in balls
butter

salt and white pepper

Cook the potato balls in butter until done and browned, without breaking. Season lightly with salt and white pepper, and serve hot.

CAULIFLOWER CHORON
TO SERVE 4

2 lbs cauliflower flowerets   1½ cups Sauce Choron, hot
salt and white pepper

Cook the cauliflower in water until tender and drain. Season to taste with salt and white pepper. Arrange in a serving dish, top with the sauce and serve hot.

The cauliflower is often put in a casserole, or heat-proof serving dish, topped with the sauce and run under the broiler to brown lightly before serving.

ARTICHOKE HEARTS CHORON
TO SERVE 4

8 artichoke hearts, cooked   ¼ lb pâté de foie gras (or
2 Tbs butter   chicken liver pâté) in 8
1 Tbs olive oil   slices or patties
                                     ½ cup Sauce Choron

Simmer the artichokes gently in the butter and oil to heat through. Do not brown. Place on a flat, buttered baking dish, top with foie gras slices, and top the foie gras with the sauce. Brown under a broiler and serve hot.

EGGS CHORON (Poached or Soft-Boiled)
TO SERVE 4

4 bread slices, trimmed   1½ cups Sauce Choron, hot
butter   2 cups cooked peas, tossed in
8 eggs, freshly poached or soft-   butter and lightly seasoned,
   boiled, hot   hot

Sauté the bread in a little butter until golden on both sides and drain. Place on 4 hot plates and top each bread slice with 2 eggs. Spoon the sauce over the yolks and serve the peas in 2 little piles on each plate, hot.

TOURNEDOS CHORON (Beef Fillets)
TO SERVE 4

4 bread slices, trimmed round   2 oz dry white wine
butter   2 oz veal gravy, or Sauce
4 beef fillets   Espagnole
Choron Garnish #1, hot   2 oz Sauce Choron, hot

Sauté the bread in a little butter until golden on both sides and drain. Meanwhile, sauté the beef fillets separately in butter until done to taste. Arrange the bread rounds in a row on a hot platter topped by the fillets. Put a row of pea-stuffed artichoke hearts on one side of the fillets and a row of asparagus-stuffed artichoke hearts on the other. Keep hot. Add the wine to the beef sauté pan and cook, scraping up the juices. Blend in the gravy. Top the fillets with the Sauce Choron and place a dab of strained pan gravy in the center of the Sauce Choron on each fillet. Serve at once, hot.

CHICKEN CHORON
TO SERVE 4

4 chicken breasts, halved	3 oz dry white wine
salt and pepper	2 cups Sauce Choron
butter	Choron Garnish #1, hot

Season the chicken lightly with salt and pepper and sauté in butter until done. Set on a hot platter and keep hot. Add the wine to the sauté pan and boil down, scraping up the juices. Blend in the sauce and heat well. Strain over the chicken and serve hot, garnished with the stuffed artichokes.

This dish is often served on bread croutons, as in the Tournedos recipe, and using boned and skinned chicken breasts (suprêmes). It is then called Chicken Suprêmes Choron.

SOLE FILLETS CHORON (or Other White-Fleshed Fish)
TO SERVE 4

Proceed as for Chicken Choron, using 2 pounds of fillets.

Clamart

(klah-MAR)

A suburb about three miles southwest of Paris.

In cuisine, Clamart means the use of peas somewhere, usually in purée. A dish Clamart is typically garnished with artichoke hearts tossed in butter and stuffed with peas, plus potato balls browned in butter—just like the garnish typical of Choron. Or it may have a garnish of artichoke hearts filled with a purée of peas, which is also called a garnish à la Saint-Germain. The terms are used interchangeably, something the French have a penchant for doing. Furthermore, in Clamart the peas are a prime ingredient, while in Choron they may not be in a recipe at all. Any dish served with a pea purée is either Clamart or Saint-Germain (San-zhayr-MEHN) after the city of Saint-Germain-en-Laye, about fourteen miles west of Paris. If it also has a tomato-flavored Sauce Espagnole, it's a dish Clamart.

Wherever a recipe Clamart calls for Peas à la Française, a pea purée can be substituted. It will have less flavor, but be more accurate. To achieve both accuracy and flavor, simply purée the Peas Française and proceed with the recipe.

However, there is a difference between these cooking modes. Choron dishes use tomato-flavored Béarnaise Sauce. Clamart dishes use tomato-flavored Espagnole Sauce. Dishes à la Saint-Germain might use almost any sauce, Espagnole, Béarnaise or veal gravy, but no tomato flavoring.

CLAMART GARNISHES
TO SERVE 4

1. CROUTES CLAMART

1 lb peas, cooked and very light-
    ly seasoned with salt and
    white pepper

heavy cream

A croûte is a crust or a dab. In this case it is a dab, or a group of dabs—like rosettes—used as a garnish. Prepare the rosette mixture by puréeing the peas. Mash and rub through a sieve. Mix with enough heavy cream to bind (a couple of ounces) and pipe in rosettes or in a border around the main dish. This is an especially nice garnish for eggs, and quite unusual.

2. ARTICHOKE HEARTS CLAMART

8 artichoke hearts, cooked and
    tossed in butter, hot

2 cups pea purée (as in Croutes
    Clamart), hot

Stuff the artichoke hearts with the pea purée and serve hot.

3. POTATO BALLS

2 lbs potatoes, cut in balls

butter

Simmer the potatoes in butter until done and browned, without breaking the potatoes. Shake the pan from time to time, rather than stirring, to help keep the potato balls whole. Serve hot.

EGGS CLAMART (Poached or Soft-Boiled)
TO SERVE 4

4 baked pastry shells,* hot
½ recipe Peas à la Française,
    hot

8 eggs, freshly poached or soft-
    boiled, hot
1 cup Cream Sauce, hot

Put the peas in the bottoms of the pastry shells, top with 2 freshly cooked eggs each, and spoon the sauce over the eggs. Serve at once, hot.

This dish is often made using pea purée (as in Clamart Garnish #1) instead of the Peas Française.

OMELET CLAMART
TO SERVE 2

3 oz Peas à la Française or
    pea purée (as in Clamart
    Garnish #1), hot

4 eggs, lightly beaten
salt and pepper
4 Tbs butter

Prepare the omelet,* using lightly seasoned eggs, in very hot butter and fill with the peas. Serve at once, hot.

This omelet is attractive decorated with a line of individual peas down its center. A little cooked, shredded lettuce is sometimes added to the filling of peas.

TOURNEDOS CLAMART (Beef Fillets)
TO SERVE 4

4 beef fillets
salt and pepper
butter (optional)

1 recipe Clamart Garnishes #1
    and #3, hot

Season the fillets lightly with salt and pepper and sauté in butter until done to taste, or broil. Serve hot, surrounded with a piping of pea purée (Garnish # 1) and little groups of browned potato balls (Garnish #3).

VEAL SAUTÉ CLAMART
TO SERVE 4

2 lbs veal cutlets, pounded thin
salt and pepper
butter

1 recipe Peas à la Française,
    cooked and hot

Preheat oven to 350°. Season the veal to taste with salt and pepper and sauté in butter in a casserole until ¾ done. Drain most of the fat from the casserole, and cover the veal with the peas. Cover and bake in the oven for 20 minutes, or until done. Serve in the casserole, hot.

LAMB LOIN CLAMART
TO SERVE 4–6

1 lamb loin
salt and pepper
butter

1 recipe Peas à la Française,
    hot

Preheat oven to 325°. Season the lamb well with salt and pepper. Brown in butter in a casserole. Cover and bake in the oven for about 40 minutes per pound, or until done. Remove excess fat from the casserole and add the peas. Recover and bake in the oven for 5 minutes more. Serve in the casserole, hot.

CHICKEN CLAMART
TO SERVE 4

2 small chickens
salt and pepper
butter

1 recipe Peas à la Francaise
(¾ cooked)

Season the chickens lightly with salt and pepper, inside and out. Truss legs and wings to the birds with string. Brown in butter in a casserole. Lower heat, cover, and simmer for 30 minutes. Meanwhile, preheat oven to 375°. When chickens have simmered for 30 minutes, untruss and remove excess fat from the casserole, if any. Add the peas, over and around the birds. Cover and bake in the oven for 30 to 40 minutes, or until done. Serve in the casserole, hot.

CREAM PEAS and LETTUCE SOUP CLAMART
TO SERVE 4

3 cups peas, preferably freshly
    shelled
1 cup chicken stock* or broth
1½ cups scalded milk
1 Tbs flour blended with 2 Tbs
    cold milk
¼ tsp sugar

salt and white pepper
2 egg yolks
3 Tbs heavy cream blended with
    2 Tbs dry white wine
2 bright-green lettuce leaves,
    shredded

Cook the peas in lightly salted water until done. Drain and rub through a sieve to purée. Put the pea purée in a pan with the stock and scalded milk and cook, stirring, until very hot and blended. Remove from heat, stir in the flour and milk slurry and blend well. Add the sugar and the salt and pepper to taste and simmer very gently, stirring, for 15 minutes. Remove from heat. Beat the yolks and cream and pour into a warm soup tureen. Slowly blend in the soup. Garnish with the shredded lettuce and serve at once, hot.

CRÊPES CLAMART
TO SERVE 4

½ recipe Clamart Garnish #1,
    hot

cream, hot
12 cooked crêpes,* hot

Thin the pea purée with a little cream. Set 3 crêpes on each of 4 hot plates, top with the thinned purée and serve at once, hot.

Colbert

(kohl-BARE)

After Jean-Baptiste Colbert, minister of finance to Louis XIV. In the 1670s he encouraged emigration to Canada to form the colony of New France in modern-day Quebec. As secretary of state for the king's household, Colbert became deeply involved in beautifying the towns of France and in the protection of scholars and writers. He founded the Académie des Sciences in 1666 and the Académie Royale d'Architecture in 1671, which laid down the rules for refining the taste of French architecture.

In cooking, Colbert is the name of a versatile sauce for meat, fish and vegetables and of a compound butter for meat and fish. Sauce Colbert is excellent with most vegetables, especially cauliflower. Carrots are also good with Sauce Colbert, as are most green vegetables, from peas and beans to the more exotic artichokes and asparagus. Sauce Colbert is also good on any meats, fish or eggs.

Colbert Butter is good on meats, too. Try a dollop of it melting over any meat, especially grilled meat. Liver smothered with onions and topped with melting Colbert Butter makes a fine and simple variation on an old theme.

Offhand, I can't think of a single fish that Colbert Butter would not improve, especially when further enhanced with small piles of caviar. The same goes for eggs. Colbert Butter with a vegetable mirepoix is great on meats. In fact, it's a good idea to whip up a small batch of Colbert Butter and the next time you cook any meat or fish, serve a dab of it on top. You'll be glad you did.

SAUCE COLBERT
TO MAKE 2 CUPS

2 oz beef glaze*
1 oz dry white wine

2 cups Sauce Béarnaise

Simmer the beef glaze with the wine for a few minutes to remove the raw alcohol flavor. Blend into the Sauce Béarnaise and serve hot with meats, fish, vegetables or eggs.

COLBERT BUTTER
TO MAKE 1 CUP

6 oz butter, softened
4 tsp parsley
1 tsp salt
2 tsp tarragon

pepper
lemon juice
1 oz beef glaze,* hot

Blend butter, parsley, salt and tarragon with a fork. Season with pepper and lemon juice to taste. Blend in the beef glaze and serve lightly chilled (just below room temperature), on meats, fish, vegetables or eggs.

LETTUCE COLBERT
TO SERVE 4

2 medium lettuce heads
butter
beaten eggs

bread crumbs
1 cup Sauce Colbert, hot

Preheat oven to 325°. Melt about 1 ounce of butter in a pan and add the lettuces, halved, with outer leaves and inner stalks removed. Cover the pan and cook in the oven for 35 minutes. Drain, and squeeze the lettuce halves as dry as possible without breaking. Roll each lettuce half up separately and secure with string or toothpicks. Dip in beaten egg and coat with crumbs. Sauté in butter until golden, or deep-fry. Remove string or toothpicks and serve with Sauce Colbert spooned over the top, hot.

Instead of rolling up the entire halves of lettuce in 1 roll, several leaves may be rolled together, making smaller roles. Or single leaves may be rolled and cut in 1½-inch lengths, skewered with toothpicks and prepared as hors d'oeuvres, hot.

EGGS COLBERT (Poached or Soft-Boiled)
TO SERVE 4

2 oz turnips, diced	½ cup Sauce Colbert, hot
2 oz green beans, diced	8 eggs, freshly poached or soft-
2 oz asparagus, diced	boiled, hot
2 oz small green peas	4 pastry shells,* freshly baked
2 oz carrots, diced	and hot

Boil all the vegetables separately in lightly salted water until tender. Drain well, mix and blend with the Sauce Colbert, making a Macédoine of Vegetables Colbert. Put 2 freshly cooked hot eggs in each of the pastry shells, top with the vegetable macédoine and serve at once, hot.

Eggs Colbert are often served on bread croutons, (bread sautéed in butter) or buttered toast, topped with Sauce Colbert or Colbert Butter and garnished with parsley or chives.

TROUT COLBERT
TO SERVE 4

2 lbs fish fillets	beaten eggs
milk	bread crumbs
salt and pepper	butter
flour	½ cup Colbert Butter, diced

Soak the fillets in cold milk for 10 minutes. Drain. Season to taste with salt and pepper and dredge in flour, shaking off the excess. Dip in beaten egg and crumbs and sauté in butter until done and golden. Serve on a hot platter topped with the diced Colbert Butter, melting over the fish as they are served.

This is a fine and simple way to prepare and present any fish fillets, scallops or small whole fish.

SAUTÉED OYSTERS COLBERT

oysters, live preferably   butter
beaten eggs   Colbert Butter, diced
bread crumbs

Poach the oysters in lightly salted water until the shells open and they are done. Drain and cool. Dip in egg and coat with crumbs. Sauté in butter until golden. Serve on a hot platter, or individual plates, dotted with Colbert Butter, melting as they're served.

CONSOMMÉ COLBERT
TO SERVE 4

1 qt chicken consommé*   4 Tbs mixed, minced spring
4 tiny pullet eggs, freshly   vegetables (beans, carrots,
   poached   onions, turnips, etc.), lightly
2 tsp chervil   sautéed in butter

Serve the consommé hot, garnished with eggs, vegetables and chervil.

Crécy

(KRAY-see)

Named after the little town of Crécy-en-Ponthieu, in northern France, near the English Channel.

Crécy was the scene of a decisive battle, on August 26, 1346, in the Hundred Years War. More than 1,500 French nobles and uncounted thousands of lower birth died at the hands of the British under Edward III, who lost only about fifty men altogether. The Battle of Crécy marked the first use on the European continent of the longbow, and the emergence of England as a first-rank military power. According to local lore, after the cutting and slashing of the battle were over, there was little left but the famous soup of the area, Purée Crécy. A pretty gruesome analogy, but that's history for you.

In cooking, the term Crécy, like Vichy, means you'll find carrots in the recipe somewhere. The names are practically interchangeable. Usually, a sliced carrot dish is called à la Vichy, and so are recipes that use it as a garnish. Dishes à la Crécy are also garnished with carrots, but usually in purée.

Any meat, vegetable, egg or even fish served with Carrots à la Crécy can be called a dish à la Crécy. Sometimes the carrot purée is enriched by adding a Béchamel or Velouté sauce. The same dish served with sliced carrots becomes a dish à la Vichy.

An appropriate wine for Crécy would be champagne, for the Champagne region is the closest wine-producing area to Crécy.

POTATOES À LA CRÉCY
TO SERVE 4

Prepare Potatoes Anna, but use ½ potatoes and ½ carrots in alternating layers.

CARROTS À LA CRÉCY
TO SERVE 4

2 lbs carrots, sliced	2 Tbs sugar
1 qt water	6 Tbs butter
1 tsp salt	parsley
⅛ tsp white pepper	

Cook the carrots in the water with the salt, pepper, sugar and butter, occasionally stirring gently, until the liquid is almost gone, leaving the carrots glazed. Sprinkle with parsley and serve at once, hot.

This recipe is the same as that for Carrots à la Vichy.

ARTICHOKES À LA CRÉCY
TO SERVE 4

12 very young artichokes, trimmed*	½ tsp salt
2 cups carrot slices	2 tsp sugar
2 oz butter	1 oz water

Put everything in a pot and simmer gently, covered, for 20 minutes, or until tender. Remove lid and continue cooking to evaporate excess moisture, and glaze the vegetables by shaking the pan. Serve in a hot vegetable dish at once, hot.

CARROT PURÉE À LA CRÉCY
TO SERVE 4

2 lbs carrots, peeled and sliced	white pepper (optional)
½ lb potatoes, peeled and sliced	3 oz butter, diced
½ tsp sugar	

Cook the carrots and potatoes in lightly salted water with ½ teaspoon of sugar until done and tender. Drain well and mash the carrots and potatoes together. Season with a little white pepper if desired. Blend in the butter. (If the puree is too thick, add a bit of the cooking liquid.) Serve hot.

EGGS À LA CRÉCY (Poached or Soft-Boiled)
TO SERVE 4

½ recipe Carrot Purée à la Crécy, hot	8 eggs, freshly poached or soft-boiled and hot
1 cup thick Cream Sauce, hot	

Place ¼ of the carrot purée on each of 4 hot plates. Top with the eggs, and pour the sauce on top. Serve hot.

OMELET À LA CRÉCY
TO SERVE 2

4 eggs
salt and white pepper
4 Tbs butter
3 Tbs Carrot Purée à la Crécy

8 carrot slices, sautéed in butter, hot
½ cup thick Cream Sauce, hot

Season the eggs lightly with salt and white pepper and beat. Prepare the omelet* in very hot butter, filling with the carrot purée. Place on a hot platter, topped with a row of sauteed carrot slices and the Cream Sauce, and serve hot.

VEAL CHOPS À LA CRÉCY
TO SERVE 4

12 veal chops
salt and white pepper
butter

1 recipe Carrots a la Crécy, hot
2 oz dry white wine

Season the chops with salt and white pepper lightly and sauté gently in butter until done. Just before the chops are done, add the carrots to the pan and finish cooking together for the final 3 to 4 minutes. Place on a hot serving dish and keep hot. Add the wine to the sauté pan and boil down, scraping up the juices. Strain over the veal and carrots and serve hot.

CHICKEN À LA CRÉCY
TO SERVE 4

2 small chickens, cut up
salt and white pepper
butter

1 recipe Carrots à la Crécy, half cooked
4 oz Jus de Veau, or veal stock* or gravy

Preheat oven to 375°. Season the chicken lightly with salt and white pepper and sauté in butter in a casserole until browned. Add the carrots and finish cooking together in the oven, covered, for about 30 minutes. Add the Jus de Veau to the casserole juices and blend. Arrange the chicken on a hot platter and cover with the carrots and sauce. Serve hot.

SOLE À LA CRÉCY
TO SERVE 4

2 lbs sole fillets
salt and white pepper
lemon juice
1 cup fish fumet* or ½ cup each white wine and clam juice

4 Tbs Sauce Velouté* or Sauce Béchamel
4 Tbs Carrot Purée à la Crécy

Season the fillets with salt and pepper to taste and sprinkle with a little lemon juice. Put in a pan and add the fish fumet. Cover and simmer for 10 minutes, or until the fish flakes easily with a fork and is done. Drain the fillets and arrange on a hot platter. Keep hot. Quickly boil down the cooking liquid to half and add the Velouté and carrot purée, blending well. Strain over the fish and serve hot.

CARROT SOUP À LA CRÉCY
TO SERVE 4

4 carrots, peeled and sliced
3 Tbs butter
2 Tbs chopped onion
1/8 tsp salt
1/4 tsp sugar
1 qt chicken consommé* or
  broth

1/3 cup rice
4 Tbs butter, diced (optional)
2 bread slices, trimmed, diced
  and sautéed in butter
chives and parsley
white pepper (optional)

Cook the carrots until almost done in the butter in a pan. Add the onions, salt and sugar and finish cooking, covered. Add the consommé and rice, cover again and cook until the rice is soft. Purée in a blender or food mill, or by rubbing through a sieve. Stir in the butter if desired. Serve hot with the bread croutons and garnished with parsley and chives. If desired, season lightly with white pepper.

This soup is often enriched with cream.

Crème

(KREM)

The name given to dishes of meat or vegetables, often cooked in a pan, which are mixed with cream to make a Cream Sauce, or Cream Gravy.

Cream is an emulsion of fat and water, containing mineral salts, casein and lactose. Cream is also full of calories, mostly fat, but it's interesting to note that the difference between light and heavy cream in total calories is not as much as you might expect. A 100-gram serving (3½ ounces), of light coffee cream has 211 calories, while the same amount of heavy whipping cream has 352. That's a difference of 141 calories. In making a sauce, however, you would need a good deal more of the light cream than the heavy. The light cream, containing more water, would have to be cooked down much more than the heavy, so you'd have to use more to start with, and in the end you wouldn't be ahead at all as far as calories go. Also, the flavor would be improved by using heavy cream. Besides, if you're worrying about calories, you shouldn't cook a dish à la Crème anyway. So, if you're making a dish à la Crème, use heavy cream.

Dishes à la Crème are often cooked together, such as boned, skinned chicken breasts (suprêmes) and oysters. The chicken breasts would be sautéed in butter with a little white wine and shallots until half done. The oysters and their liquor would be added to the pan and simmered with the chicken until done. Cream would be added and simmered to thicken (after setting the chicken and oysters on a hot platter and keeping hot). The sauce would be seasoned lightly with salt, white pepper and lemon juice, possibly with a dash of tabasco sauce. The sauce would then be strained over the chicken and oysters and served hot. This basic approach would apply to almost any foods.

Dishes à la Crème are usually seasoned with lemon juice, orange juice, paprika, red pepper, tarragon, parsley, savory or chives according to personal preference. Mushrooms, previously sautéed, are often added toward the end of cooking a dish, as are tiny glazed* onions. One or more beaten egg yolks are often added to the finished sauce off heat to enrich it.

Many vegetables are simply seasoned, sautéed in butter and dressed with Sauce Béchamel and called à la Crème, which is acceptable but not wholly accurate. To merit the name, the Sauce Béchamel should be enriched with extra cream and boiled down to thicken. Often a dish à la Crème is sprinkled with grated Parmesan or Gruyère cheese and browned in the oven before serving.

As a general rule, when a dish is finished à la Crème, that is, the Cream Sauce is done and ready to serve, a little fresh cream is added just before serving. This improves the whole dish, adding a fresh taste to the sauce. Use just 1 or 2 tablespoons, not enough to thin or cool the sauce unduly.

CRÈME SAUCE (Cream Sauce)
TO MAKE 2 CUPS

1½ cups Sauce Béchamel	3 oz cream
¾ cup cream	salt and white pepper (optional)
3 Tbs butter	

Mix the Béchamel and ¾ cup of cream and cook down to 1½ cups. Stir in the butter and 3 ounces of cream, season with salt and white pepper if necessary and serve hot on vegetables, fish, eggs or white meats.

MUSTARD DRESSING À LA CRÈME (for Salads)
TO MAKE ¾ CUP

1 oz prepared mustard	lemon juice
5 oz cream	salt and white pepper

Blend the mustard and cream and season with lemon juice and salt and white pepper to taste.

ARTICHOKE HEARTS À LA CRÈME
TO SERVE 4

1½ lbs artichoke hearts	1 oz butter (optional)
1 cup vegetable mirepoix	salt and white pepper
1 cup cream, boiling	

Simmer the artichoke hearts in lightly salted water with the vegetable mirepoix until almost done and drain. Set in a pan and pour the boiling cream over them, and cook until the cream is reduced by half. Place the artichokes on a hot dish and keep hot. Add the butter to the cream in the pan, if desired, and season lightly with salt and white pepper if necessary. Mix and pour over the artichokes. Serve hot.

BEET SALAD À LA CRÈME
TO SERVE 4

1½ lbs beets, cooked and sliced
½ recipe Mustard Dressing à
    la Crème

small, thin onion rings (optional)

Arrange the beets in a serving dish and top with the dressing. Serve at room temperature. Garnish with onion rings if desired.

This salad is often prepared using cooked celery or endive in place of the beets. Since some people prefer more dressing than others, it might be a good idea to serve extra Mustard Dressing separately.

CARROTS À LA CRÈME
TO SERVE 4

1½ lbs carrots, cut in equal
rounds, glazed* and hot

1 cup cream, boiling
1 Tbs butter

Put the glazed carrots and cream in a pot and boil down to thicken lightly. Stir in the butter and serve hot.

CELERY À LA CRÈME
TO SERVE 4

1 large bunch of celery
salt and white pepper
chicken stock* or broth

½ cup Sauce Béchamel
½ cup cream
1 Tbs butter (optional)

Wash the celery and trim. Cut in 3-inch-long sticks. Blanch for 30 seconds in boiling, lightly salted water and drain. Place in a buttered casserole and season lightly with salt and white pepper. Add enough stock to just barely cover, bring to a boil, lower heat and simmer covered for 1 hour. Remove the celery with a slotted spoon to a hot vegetable dish and keep hot. Strain the cooking liquid and add the Béchamel and cream. Quickly boil down to thicken. Stir in the butter if desired, pour over the celery and serve hot.

EGGPLANT À LA CRÈME
TO SERVE 4

2 eggplants, peeled (small)
salt
butter

1 cup Cream Sauce, hot
1 cup cream, hot
1 Tbs butter (optional)

Cut the eggplants in ¼-inch-thick slices and sprinkle liberally with salt. Let stand for 30 minutes. Wash off the salt and dry. Simmer the slices in a little butter until done and tender. Arrange on a hot vegetable dish and top with the Cream Sauce, being careful to mix without breaking the eggplant slices. Add the hot cream to the sauté pan and quickly boil down to half or less, until quite thick. Stir in the butter, if desired, pour over the eggplant and serve hot.

ENDIVE À LA CRÈME
TO SERVE 4

4 small heads endive
2 Tbs butter
¼ tsp salt
1 tsp lemon juice

½ cup water
1 cup cream, boiling
1 Tbs butter (optional)

Wash the endive well and trim off the bottoms. Put in a pan with the butter, salt, lemon juice and water. Cover, bring to a boil and simmer slowly for 45 minutes. Drain off the endive well and chop. Add to the boiling cream and cook the cream down to half. Stir in the butter, if desired, and serve hot.

GREEN BEANS À LA CRÈME
TO SERVE 4

1½ lbs green beans
butter
1 cup cream, boiling

salt and white pepper
fresh minced savory, tarragon,
parsley or chives (optional)

Cook the beans in lightly salted water until ¾ done. Drain and toss in a little butter. Add them to the boiling cream and cook the cream down to ½. Season lightly with salt and white pepper if needed and serve hot, sprinkled with fresh herbs.

This recipe can also be used for peas, Brussels sprouts, broccoli, cauliflower or asparagus.

MUSHROOMS À LA CRÈME
TO SERVE 4

1 lb mushrooms, sliced
2 Tbs butter
2 Tbs oil
2 Tbs minced green onions

1 tsp flour
1 cup cream
salt and white pepper
2 Tbs cream

Sauté the mushrooms lightly in the butter and oil. Add the green onions and simmer 3 minutes more. Stir in the flour and cook 2 minutes more. Add the 1 cup of cream, season to taste with salt and white pepper and cook until the cream is reduced by ½. Remove from heat, stir in the 2 tablespoons of fresh cream and serve at once, hot.

OKRA À LA CRÈME
TO SERVE 4

1½ lbs okra	2 oz chicken stock* or broth
butter	½ cup Cream Sauce, hot
salt and pepper	

Blanch the okra in boiling water for 30 seconds and drain. Repeat in fresh boiling water 3 more times to remove the stickiness of the okra. Put the okra in a pan with a little butter, season to taste with salt and pepper, cover and simmer for 15 minutes. Add the chicken stock and simmer gently uncovered, until fluid is almost gone. Put in a hot vegetable dish, top with Cream Sauce and serve hot.

POTATOES À LA CRÈME (or Sweet Potatoes)
TO SERVE 4

2 lbs potatoes (or sweet potatoes), washed and un-peeled	salt, white pepper and grated nutmeg
2 cups heavy cream, boiling	2 Tbs cream

Boil the potatoes until done. Peel. Cut into thick slices and put in a large pan. Pour in the boiling cream and cook until the cream is reduced to less than ½ and thickened. Season to taste with salt, white pepper and a little nutmeg. Stir in the 2 tablespoons of fresh cream and serve hot.

POTATO PURÉE À LA CRÈME (Mashed Potatoes)
TO SERVE 4

Prepare 2 pounds of mashed potatoes, seasoned with salt and white pepper. Blend in 4 ounces of butter and 4 ounces of cream. Serve hot.

SPINACH À LA CRÈME (or Swiss Chard)
TO SERVE 4

1½ lbs spinach (or Swiss Chard), chopped	salt and pepper
butter	½ cup Cream Sauce, hot (or more if desired)

Simmer the spinach in a little butter in a pan until limp and well mixed. Season lightly with salt and pepper. Serve hot, topped with the Cream Sauce.

WHITE BEANS À LA CRÈME
TO SERVE 4

½ lb lean bacon
1 carrot, quartered
1 onion, quartered
1 Tbs butter
2 qts water
1 tsp parsley
¼ tsp thyme

½ bay leaf
cheesecloth, washed
1½ tsp salt (or to taste)
2 cups dry white beans
2 cups cream
2 Tbs cream

Blanch the bacon in boiling water for 10 minutes and drain. In a large pot, brown the carrot and onion lightly in the butter. Add the water. Add the parsley, thyme and bay leaf tied in cheesecloth. Add the salt and bacon. Bring to a boil, skim, and boil slowly for 25 minutes. Strain the liquid and reserve the bacon. Add the beans to the strained liquid, bring to a rapid boil for 2 minutes, reduce heat, cover and simmer for 2 hours, adding water occasionally if needed. Dice the bacon. When the beans are done and tender, drain. Add the bacon and the 2 cups of cream and boil down to ½. Remove from heat, stir in the 2 tablespoons of fresh cream and serve at once, hot.

If you wish to hold this dish for any length of time, keep hot, covered, stirring in the 2 tablespoons of fresh cream just before serving.

EGGS À LA CRÈME (Poached or Soft-Boiled)
TO SERVE 4

8 eggs, freshly poached or soft-
    boiled and hot
4 bread slices, trimmed and
    sauteed in butter and
    drained, hot

salt and white pepper
1 cup Cream Sauce, hot
chives

Put the bread slices on 4 hot plates and top each with 2 hot eggs. Season lightly with salt and white pepper, top with sauce and serve hot, sprinkled with chives.

MUSHROOM OMELET À LA CRÈME
TO SERVE 2

4 eggs
salt and pepper
4 Tbs butter

2 oz Mushrooms à la Crème,
    hot
½ cup Cream Sauce, hot

Beat the eggs with salt and pepper to taste and make an omelet* in very hot butter, filling with the mushrooms. Top with the Cream Sauce and serve at once, hot.

VEAL CHOPS À LA CRÈME
TO SERVE 4

4 veal chops, or steaks
salt and white pepper
butter
½ lb raw button mushrooms
  (optional)

2 oz dry white wine, or Madeira
1 cup cream
½ tsp mint, tarragon or basil
1 oz Sauce Velouté* (optional)

Season the veal lightly with salt and white pepper and sauté in a little butter until done. If using the mushrooms add halfway through the cooking. Remove from the pan to a hot platter and keep hot. Add the wine to the pan and boil down, scraping up the juices. Lower heat and add the cream and mint and cook down to thicken. Stir in the Velouté, if desired, strain over the veal and serve hot.

Tiny glazed onions* make an excellent accompaniment to this veal. If you use them, add them to the sauté pan for the final few minutes of cooking, and set them on the platter with the veal while you make the cream sauce in the sauté pan.

Pork may be used in place of veal in any recipe à la Crème, but change the seasoning from mint to either basil or marjoram.

LAMB or VEAL SAUTÉ À LA CRÈME
TO SERVE 4

2 lbs lean lamb (or veal),
  trimmed, in square pieces
salt and paprika
butter

2 oz dry white wine
½ tsp mint (or more to taste)
1½ cups cream

Season the lamb with salt and paprika to taste and sauté in a pan in a little butter until done. Set on a hot platter and keep hot. Add the wine and mint to the pan and boil down, scraping up the juices. Add the cream and cook down to thicken. Strain over the lamb and serve hot.

HAM À LA CRÈME
TO SERVE 4

4 ham steaks, or 1 large, thick
  ham steak (2–3 lbs)
1 cup vegetable mirepoix

1 cup Madeira wine
2 cups cream

Preheat oven to 325°. If the ham is salty, soak it in cold water (or milk) for 10 to 20 minutes, rinse off and dry. Put the mirepoix in a pot with the Madeira and lay the ham on top. Cover partly with foil and cook in the oven for about 30 minutes for individual steaks or about 1 hour for a single large steak. Check occasionally, adding a bit more wine or water if needed. When done, set the ham on a hot platter and keep hot. Discard excess fat from the pan, if any. Add the cream to the pan and quickly boil down to thicken and blend with the pan juices. Strain over the ham and serve hot.

BEEFSTEAKS À LA CRÈME
TO SERVE 4

Proceed as for Veal Chops à la Crème, substituting parsley for the mint, and serve with a sprinkling of chives on the sauce.

CHICKEN À LA CRÈME
TO SERVE 4

Proceed as for Veal Chops à la Crème, using 2 very small cut-up chickens in place of the veal. Substitute ½ teaspoon parsley and ½ teaspoon tarragon for the mint.

COD À LA CRÈME
TO SERVE 4

2 lbs cod steaks	cream (about 1½ cups)
salt and white pepper	2 Tbs butter (optional)
butter	

Season the cod to taste with salt and white pepper and sauté in a little butter in a pan until half done. Add enough cream to half cover the cod, cover the pan and simmer until done. Remove the cod carefully to a hot platter and keep hot. Boil down the cream to thicken and add the butter, if desired. Strain over the fish and serve hot.

Any white-fleshed fish makes a fine dish à la Crème, especially the firmer-fleshed fish, like cod, listed here, or haddock.

PIKE QUENELLES À LA CRÈME (Dumplings)
TO SERVE 4

¾ cup milk	1 whole egg
3 cups soft white bread crumbs	1 egg yolk (if needed)
1 lb pike flesh, flaked	boiling lightly salted water
2 tsp salt	8 bread slices, trimmed and
½ tsp white pepper	sautéed in butter, drained
⅛ tsp grated nutmeg	and quartered
2 Tbs butter, softened	2 cups Cream Sauce, hot

Make a bread panada (thickening paste) by pounding the milk and crumbs in a bowl. Pound the fish with the salt, pepper and nutmeg in another bowl, using a pestle or other blunt shaft, like a wooden spoon, until well blended. Add the fish to the panada along with the butter and blend well. Then add the whole egg. Add the yolk if the mixture will take it without becoming too liquid to form quenelles. Blend well. Shape the mixture into 1½-inch quenelles and place in a buttered pan. Cover gently with boiling, lightly salted water and simmer very gently over direct heat until done—about 10 minutes. Drain on paper towels and serve on the bread croutons topped with Cream Sauce, hot.

FROG'S LEGS À LA CRÈME (or Salt Cod)
TO SERVE 4

Proceed as for Frog's Legs à la Béchamel, adding more cream, to taste, to cook down and thicken with the sauce.

SALMON CÔTELETTES À LA CRÈME (Cutlets)
TO SERVE 4

4 large salmon steaks, skinned and boned (leaving 8 cutlet-shaped pieces, or cotelettes)	24 button mushrooms
	2 oz Madeira wine
	1½ cups Cream Sauce
salt and white pepper	½ tsp mint, or chervil or tarragon
flour	
butter	1 oz Sauce Velouté* (optional)

Season the salmon côtelettes lightly with salt and white pepper and dredge in flour, shaking off the excess. Sauté gently in a little butter until ½ done. Add the mushrooms and finish sautéing together. Arrange the finished salmon gently on a hot platter with the mushrooms and keep hot. Add the Madeira to the pan and boil down, scraping up the juices. Add the Cream Sauce, mint and Velouté if desired, and boil down to thicken lightly. Strain over the fish and mushrooms and serve hot.

LOBSTER À LA CRÈME
TO SERVE 4

4 1-lb lobsters, preferably live	salt and a little red pepper (cayenne)
butter	
4 Tbs good brandy	3 Tbs butter
2 cups cream	lemon juice

Kill the lobsters, using a heavy, pointed knife. Thrust it deep into the cross just behind the head, or make a quick cut down between the body and first tail segment, severing the spinal cord. Cut the tails in neat slices, following the shell segments. Cut off all the claws and crack. Split the bodies lengthwise. Remove and discard the gritty stomach sacs in the heads and the intestinal tubes (these also run the length of the tail). Cut off the tail shell tips and discard. Remove and reserve the coral (roe) from the females and the livers, and reserve the water from the lobsters (trim them in a pan to save the water inside their shells).

Sauté the lobster pieces in a little butter until the shells are bright red. Drain off the butter. Pour the brandy over the lobster and flame, stirring until the fire dies. Add the lobster water, cream and salt and pepper to taste. Simmer covered for 10 minutes. Put the lobster pieces on a hot platter and keep hot. Add the coral and liver, mashed, to the pan juices along with the butter, and cook down quickly to half. Add a few drops of lemon juice to taste, pour over the lobster and serve hot.

MUSSELS À LA CRÈME
TO SERVE 4

Proceed as for Mussels à la Marinière, adding a cup of Béchamel Sauce to the cooking stock along with 2 to 4 tablespoons of cream, and thickening by boiling down. Pour the sauce over the mussels and serve hot.

CLAMS or OYSTERS À LA CRÈME
TO SERVE 4

24 clams or oysters
1½ cups cream (or to taste)
rock salt

Parmesan cheese, grated
butter, melted

Detach the clams or oysters from their shells and clean. Reserve a half shell for each. Set each clam or oyster in a half shell with 1 tablespoon of cream. Set on rock salt on a baking pan (the rock salt will hold the clams erect while grilling). Sprinkle with grated cheese to taste and a little butter to moisten. Grill until the clam or oyster edges begin to curl and serve at once, hot.

RICE À LA CRÈME
TO SERVE 4

1¾ cups milk
1 tsp vanilla extract (or 1 tsp grated orange or lemon peel)
2 Tbs sugar

⅛ tsp salt
½ cup raw rice, blanched a few seconds in boiling water, drained
½ cup cream

Mix the milk and vanilla in a pot and bring to a boil. Remove from heat and blend in sugar and salt. Return to very low heat, stir in the rice and cook very gently until done, covered—about 35 minutes. Do not disturb while cooking. The rice should be soft and absorb all the milk. Add the cream and boil quickly, stirring, until absorbed also. Serve hot or cold. This is usually used as a bed for fresh fruits, or served in a pile surrounded by fruit, for dessert.

Dauphine

(doh-FEEN)

From the Dauphine region of France, which stretches from the Alps to the

Rhône valley in the west, and from the Lyonnaise district in the north to Provence in the south, with no clear-cut line of demarcation. The region has great diversity of terrain and climate, so naturally its larder is quite varied. Toward the Rhône valley the climate is good for vegetables and orchards, especially peaches and apricots. Its sunlit slopes bear the famous Rhône vineyards. In the south, bordering Provence, olives are grown. The valleys of the Alps provide pasture for cows and account for a high yield of dairy products, as well as fine groves of chestnut and hazelnut trees. Honey is also produced in these upland areas. The lakes and streams are well known for trout and crayfish, and truffles are found in some places, as well as the tasty morel mushroom, which is common in the woods. Thanks to the extensive dairying here, excellent cheeses are produced. Among the better known are Sassenage, Saint-Marcellin, Champoléon, Pelvoux and Briancon.

Any meat or fish prepared simply and served with Dauphine Potatoes (usually with the pan juices defatted and extended with veal gravy for sauce) is a dish à la Dauphine. The Trout à la Dauphine recipe, listed here, is a different matter. It can be applied to any white-fleshed fish, but really is a variation of the cooking mode Nantua. This variation is called Daumont. While Daumont usually applies to whole fish, it would apply to the trout fillets listed here because of the garnishes of pike quenelles and mushrooms. Calling this dish Trout à la Dauphine is incorrect, but I list it here because it continually pops up with this title—just another example of the confusion in the names of French dishes.

A good deal of wine is produced in the Rhône valley, but the quality is poor by French standards. You may find a Côtes du Rhône red, but you probably won't find one aged the necessary twenty years. You'll find a harsh dark red wine of low quality—better than nothing.

For décor, there's much to choose from—the grapes and fruits of the Rhône valley, as well as blossoms in the spring. Cheeses and chestnuts and olives and morel mushrooms are all applicable, and with wild flowers could make interesting displays. For music, you can draw on the wealth of European folk music. A medley of different types would be appropriate to this varied region, even including yodeling.

DAUPHINE POTATOES (Dauphine Garnish)
TO SERVE 4

½ cup milk or water	1 egg
1½ Tbs butter	1 lb Duchesse Potatoes
⅛ tsp salt	flour
½ cup flour	fat for deep-frying

Prepare Chou Paste by putting the milk, butter and salt in a pot and bringing to a boil. Remove from heat and blend in the flour. Return to heat and cook, stirring with a wooden spoon, until it dries somewhat and comes away from the sides of the pot. Remove from heat and blend in the egg. Mix this Chou Paste with the Duchesse Potatoes, form into balls, roll in flour and deep-fry until golden. Serve hot.

These potatoes can be molded into various shapes before deep-frying. They can also be dipped in beaten eggs and bread crumbs before frying. If they are shaped like small crescents and deep-fried until golden, you have Potatoes Lorette.

BEEF FILLET À LA DAUPHINE
TO SERVE 4

Prepare a beef fillet, or fillet steaks, as you prefer and serve with Potatoes à la Dauphine, hot. For sauce, use fillet pan juices.

TROUT À LA DAUPHINE
TO SERVE 4

2 lbs trout fillets
salt and white pepper
2 cups Madeira wine
1 cup truffles and mushrooms,
　　sliced very thin
½ cup Sauce Villeroi
1 Tbs butter pounded to a paste
　　with 1 Tbs shredded crayfish
　　or lobster
white bread crumbs
butter, preferably clarified*
½ cup flour
2 egg yolks
3 Tbs butter, melted
5 oz boiling milk
½ lb beef fat, minced

2 egg whites
½ lb pike flesh, flaked
1 tsp salt
½ tsp white pepper
⅛ tsp grated nutmeg
½ lb mushrooms, sautéed in
　　butter, hot
1 lb crayfish or lobster meat in
　　chunks, cooked and hot
¼ lb truffles, sliced and lightly
　　sautéed in butter, hot
½ cup very thick Sauce
　　Velouté,* hot
1½ cups Sauce Nantua, hot

Season the fillets to taste with salt and white pepper and roll up. Tie with string, 2 or 3 loops, to keep the fillets rolled up during cooking. Put the truffles and mushrooms in the Madeira and simmer 5 minutes, in a flat pan just large enough to hold the rolled fillets comfortably. Add the fillets and simmer gently for 10 minutes. Let the fillets cool in the cooking stock. Drain the fillets and discard the string. Coat the fillets with a mixture of the Sauce Villeroi, 2 tablespoons of the cooking liquid and the butter and crayfish paste. Coat again with crumbs and sauté in a little clarified butter until golden. Drain and arrange in a circle on a hot platter and keep hot.

Meanwhile, mix the flour and yolks in a pan over very low heat, so the eggs will blend with the flour but not solidify. Stir in the melted butter. Stir in the milk, blending well. Place in a mortar or bowl and add the beef fat, pounding with a pestle into a smooth paste. Add the egg whites and blend. Add the pike and pound smooth. Blend in the seasonings. Work with a spoon or spatula until very smooth. Shape into small quenelles (dumplings) and simmer very gently in lightly salted water for 10 minutes. Drain and arrange with the cooked fish in another ring on the platter and keep hot.

Mix the mushrooms, crayfish chunks and truffle slices with the Sauce Velouté and pile in the center of the platter. Serve hot, with a little of the Sauce Nantua spooned over the quenelles, and the rest served separately.

Diable

(dee-AHBLA)

Means devil. In cooking, Diable usually pertains to foods served with Sauce Diable. As you might expect, this is a spicy sauce, depending on the maker's taste. It can be, and often is, hot as well. Diable shares the use of mustard as a flavoring with the cooking mode Dijonnaise and with Moutarde (moo-TAHRD), which means mustard and can be applied to any dish using mustard.

Sauce Diable is good with virtually any main course and, if you like highly seasoned food, makes a fine change of pace and flavor. Any white-fleshed fish can be prepared following the eel recipe. Poached eggs with Sauce Diable become Poached Eggs à la Diable. Pork chops served with Sauce Diable become Pork Chops à la Diable, as does any meat.

Fowl cooked à la Diable differs from that cooked à la Crapaudine only in the use of crumbs and mustard and in the addition of lemon slices to the garnish. The name Crapaudine is given to birds cooked in this manner because when finished, the birds resemble toads. There is a difference of opinion as to the origin of the term. Some experts hold that the word comes from the French word *crapaud,* meaning toad. Others maintain that the term comes from an ancient ordeal called *crapaudine,* in which men belonging to disciplinary orders were made to assume an uncomfortable position and stay in it, which made *them* resemble squatting toads. Birds prepared in this way are often embellished with round, black truffle slices, or hard-boiled egg slices, to resemble eyes, placed on a purée of peas (see Clamart Garnish #1) shaped like a lily pad and decorated with nasturtium flowers (which are edible)—all to enhance the resemblance to toads in the finished dish.

This is a fun mode as far as décor is concerned. Think of the devil, of hell, of Dante's *Inferno* and the magnificent steel engravings by Doré. You might try dim, red, indirect lighting, from behind plants or the like (coming up from below instead of down from the ceiling really changes the effect of lighting). Red candles would be fine, and so would a red tablecloth and napkins. Red lights are easy to get—just go to your nearest photography store. Add some appropriate background music, like "Danse Macabre" by Saint-Saens, for instance, and you could have quite an effect!

SAUCE DIABLE (for Meats, Eggs, Fish)
TO MAKE 2 CUPS

1 cup dry white wine
2 Tbs chopped shallots
¼ tsp thyme
⅛ tsp pepper

1½ cups Sauce Espagnole, or
    veal or beef gravy
1½ tsp parsley
red pepper (cayenne)

Mix the wine and vinegar and boil down to 3 ounces. Add the shallots, thyme and pepper and simmer a few minutes. Stir in the Espagnole and boil a few minutes more. Add the parsley, and red pepper to taste. Serve hot.

ARTICHOKES À LA DIABLE
TO SERVE 4

8 small artichokes, trimmed*
1½ cups bread crumbs
2 garlic cloves, minced fine
1 Tbs capers, minced
1 Tbs parsley

½ tsp salt
¼ tsp pepper
olive oil
salt and pepper

Preheat oven to 375°. Blanch the artichokes in boiling, lightly salted water for 30 seconds and drain well. Mix the crumbs, garlic, capers, parsley, salt and pepper and use to stuff the artichokes. Oil a baking pan and put the artichokes on it, packed lightly together. Sprinkle with a few drops of oil and season with salt and pepper to taste. Bake in the oven until the artichoke tips are crisp, basting frequently. Serve at once in the baking dish, or on a hot platter.

EGGS À LA DIABLE (Fried)
TO SERVE 4

8 eggs
4 Tbs butter

salt and pepper
1 Tbs vinegar

Sauté the eggs in the butter, turning without breaking the yolks to brown on both sides. Use a high heat. Put the eggs on 4 hot plates. Season to taste with salt and pepper. Add the vinegar to the pan juices, mix and spoon over the eggs. Serve hot.

This dish, spiced with a dash of vinegar, is similar to Lyonnaise cooking, where a dash of vinegar is a standard addition.

BOILED BEEF À LA DIABLE
TO SERVE 4

2 lbs beef, boiled
prepared mustard
melted butter or olive oil

bread crumbs
2 cups Sauce Diable, hot

Cut the beef into ½-inch slices. Spread lightly with mustard. Sprinkle with a little melted butter and coat both sides with crumbs. Grill or broil until golden. Serve hot, with the sauce served separately.

LAMB BREAST À LA DIABLE
TO SERVE 4

1 lamb breast, simmered in
   chicken stock* or broth until
   done, boned
prepared mustard
red pepper (cayenne)

melted butter
bread crumbs
watercress
2 cups Sauce Diable, hot

Preheat oven to 350°. Cut the lamb into small squares. Spread lightly with mustard and season with a very little red pepper. Brush with melted butter and coat with crumbs. Brown in the oven. Arrange the lamb on a hot platter and garnish with watercress. Serve the sauce separately, hot.

HAM À LA DIABLE
TO SERVE 4

8 ¼-inch-thick ham slices
1 Tbs Dijon mustard
1 Tbs chutney (optional)
lemon juice
olive oil

4 bread slices, trimmed and
   lightly sautéed in butter, hot
4 mushroom caps, sautéed in
   butter, hot
½ cup Sauce Diable, hot

Preheat the broiler. Mix the mustard, chutney and a few drops of lemon juice to taste and spread on 4 of the ham slices. Top with the remaining 4 ham slices, brush with oil and grill under the broiler for a few minutes. Arrange the bread on a hot platter, top with ham, top the ham with the mushrooms, spoon over the sauce and serve hot.

CHICKEN À LA DIABLE
TO SERVE 4

1 large chicken or capon
2 Tbs butter, melted
salt and pepper
2 Tbs prepared mustard
red pepper (cayenne)

bread crumbs
2 oz butter, melted
1 lemon
8 gherkins, sliced lengthwise
2 cups Sauce Diable, hot

Preheat oven to 350°. Split the chicken through the back but not through the chest. Spread open and flatten. Brush with the melted butter and season to taste with salt and pepper. Roast in the oven for 30 minutes. Mix the mustard with red pepper to taste. Smear the mustard on the chicken, coat with crumbs and sprinkle with the butter. Roast for 30 minutes more, letting it brown well. Set the chicken on a hot platter. Halve the lemon lengthwise, slice and discard the seeds.

Arrange the lemon slices and gherkins around the chicken and serve the sauce separately, hot.

Chicken Diable is often served with a tablespoon or two of red currant jelly added to the Diable Sauce, or with melted red currant jelly served separately.

CORNISH GAME HEN À LA DIABLE
TO SERVE 4

Proceed as for Chicken à la Diable, using 4 1-pound hens and adjusting the total cooking time to about 40 minutes.

SQUAB À LA DIABLE
TO SERVE 4

Proceed as for Chicken à la Diable, using 8 small squabs and adjusting total cooking time to about 30 minutes.

SALMON À LA DIABLE
TO SERVE 4

4 oz butter, softened
1 Tbs Dijon mustard
2 tsp lemon juice
red pepper (cayenne)
1 Tbs parsley

1 Tbs chives
4 ½-pound salmon steaks
olive oil
salt and pepper

Preheat broiler. Blend the butter, mustard, lemon juice, a little red pepper, parsley and chives. This is Diable Butter. Chill. Brush the salmon lightly with oil and season to taste with salt and pepper. Grill 4 to 6 minutes on each side, until done. Serve hot, topped with little dollops of Diable Butter melting over the hot salmon.

EELS À LA DIABLE
TO SERVE 4

4 eels, cleaned and skinned
1 cup dry white wine
1 cup vegetable mirepoix
1½ cups fish fumet,* or ¾ cup
    each clam juice and white
    wine
prepared mustard

bread crumbs
butter, melted
gherkins, sliced
lemon slices, halved, seeds dis-
    carded
2 cups Sauce Diable, hot

Mix the wine with the mirepoix and cook until wine is 2/3 gone. Add the fish fumet and boil for 10 minutes. Add the eels and simmer covered for 20 minutes, or until done. Let the eels cool in the cooking liquid. Spread the eels lightly with mustard. Coat with crumbs and sprinkle with a little moistening butter. Grill under a gentle heat until golden. Arrange on a hot platter with the gherkin and lemon slices. Serve the Sauce Diable separately, hot.

CLAMS or OYSTERS À LA DIABLE
TO SERVE 4

32 clams or oysters, poached in
    lightly salted water, drained,
    cleaned and seasoned
8 small skewers
melted butter seasoned with a
    little lemon juice

bread crumbs
red pepper (cayenne)
1 cup Sauce Diable, hot

Thread the clams or oysters on the skewers, brush with butter and coat with crumbs. Season very lightly with red pepper and grill or broil until golden. Serve the sauce separately, hot.

These are also called deviled clams or oysters.

Dieppoise

(dee-P'WAZ)

From the town of Dieppe, a seaport in northwestern France at the mouth of the Arques River on the coast of the English Channel. The name is of Scandinavian origin, *diep* meaning inlet in Norwegian.

Dieppe has been an active port since the 1100s. In the early 1500s it was a flourishing city of over 60,000 people, but today the population is much smaller. It is still a fishing port, but unlike the typical fishing port that comes to mind with nets and old fishing boats all around, Dieppe's waterfront has buildings that are medieval in character and have been in use for hundreds of years. There is also a restored fifteenth-century castle. Dieppe has been well known for the manufacture of lace and ivory objects. It was heavily bombed by the British in World War II, and finally taken by them on September 1, 1944.

In cooking, the name Dieppoise applies mainly to seafood, characterized by White Wine Sauce and a garnish of mussels, crayfish and mushrooms. It has many relatives, such as Marinière, Nage and Nantua, that use seafood as a prime feature. What makes Dieppoise unique is its garnish, which can be very good with other foods, such as beef fillets. It makes an excellent, and somewhat surprising, variation for beef and other meats. The Dieppoise Garnish is also good with any eggs, or just on toast.

There is a good cheese produced in Picardy, east of Dieppe, called Maroilles. Its distinctive taste and aroma made it the favorite of Charles V. Since the area around Dieppe produces no wine, a suitable drink with dinner would be cider, hard or sweet.

For décor, Dieppe presents an interesting face, for while anything that pertains to fishing is appropriate, so are laces. A combination of laces and rough fishing floats, for example, would make an unusual start for a centerpiece. For music, take your pick, from sounds of the sea to medieval folk music.

DIEPPOISE GARNISH (for Seafood or Eggs)
TO SERVE 4

1 qt mussels, opened and
    steamed in their own liquid
    and 2 oz dry white wine
1 lb crayfish or lobster tails,
    cooked, shelled and cleaned

½ lb button mushrooms,
    sautéed in butter
1 cup White Wine Sauce* (or
    more to taste)

Mix all the ingredients together and heat. Serve hot.

MUSSEL OMELET À LA DIEPPOISE
TO SERVE 2

4 eggs
salt and pepper
4 Tbs butter
1 qt mussels, shelled and
    steamed in their own juices
    and a little dry white wine,
    then lightly sauteed in butter,
    hot

1 Tbs melted butter
Parmesan cheese, grated
¼ cup Tomato Sauce, prefera-
    bly homemade,* hot
chives

Preheat broiler. Beat the eggs with salt and pepper to taste and prepare an omelet* in very hot butter. Fill with half the cooked mussels. When finished, brush with the melted butter, sprinkle liberally with cheese and run under the broiler to brown lightly. Serve topped with the remaining mussels and Tomato Sauce. Sprinkle with chives and serve hot.

FLOUNDER À LA DIEPPOISE
TO SERVE 4

1½ Tbs minced shallots
2 lbs flounder fillets
salt and pepper
1½ Tbs butter, diced
1½ cups fish fumet* or ¾ cup
    each clam juice and white
    wine

1 lb mussels
1 cup white wine
½ lb shrimp, small
2 egg yolks
½ cup butter, melted
salt, pepper and lemon juice

Preheat oven to 350°. Sprinkle the shallots in a buttered baking pan. Place the fillets on the shallots and season to taste with salt and pepper. Dot the fish with the butter and pour in the fish fumet. Bring to a boil over direct heat. Cover the fish with a loose foil tent and braise in the oven for about 10 minutes, or until done.

Meanwhile, open the mussels and cook in their own liquid with the wine. Cook the shrimp in lightly salted water until pink and done. Drain both and keep hot.

When the flounder is done, arrange carefully on a hot platter, without breaking the fillets. Surround with the mussels and shrimp and keep hot. Meanwhile, remove the braising pan from the heat and let cool slightly. Beat the yolks into the braising pan's juices until thickened. Beat in the melted butter, little by little. Season this sauce with salt, pepper and a little lemon juice to taste. Strain over the fish and serve at once, hot.

Some of the mussel cooking liquid may be added to the liquids in the braising pan and quickly cooked down to 1½ cups before adding the yolks, etc. This will give a stronger flavor to the sauce.

This recipe is excellent for any white-fleshed fish fillets, or for sliced eel.

FISH SOUP À LA DIEPPOISE
TO SERVE 4

1 onion, minced	cheesecloth, washed
2 leek whites, minced	1 garlic clove, crushed
1 small celery stalk, minced	4 small sole fillets
2 Tbs butter	4 very small whole freshwater
1 Tbs olive oil	fish (perch, bass, etc.),
1 qt mussels	cleaned
½ cup water	salt and pepper
½ cup dry white wine	2 tsp cornstarch blended with 2
3 cups fish fumet* or 1½ cups	Tbs dry white wine
each clam juice and white	1 Tbs fresh basil, or 1 tsp dried
wine	4 bread slices, trimmed and cut
1 tsp parsley	in croutons and sautéed, or
½ tsp basil	buttered and browned in the
½ bay leaf	oven

Sauté the onion, leeks and celery in the butter and oil until tender. Scrub the mussels clean and steam in the water and wine until they open and are done. Drain. Strain the liquid and save. Set the mussels aside, discarding the shells. Put the mussel liquid in a pan and add the fish fumet, the sautéed vegetables, the parsley, basil and bay leaf tied in cheesecloth and the garlic. Bring to a boil, lower heat and simmer covered for 20 minutes. Strain and reserve the liquids.

Preheat oven to 350°. Put the fish fillets and whole fish in a buttered baking dish and season lightly with salt and pepper. Add the strained stock, bring to a boil, and cook in the oven for 10 minutes, partly covered with foil. Place 1 fish fillet piece, 1 whole fish, and ¼ of the mussels in each of 4 hot soup dishes and keep hot. Put the poaching liquids on direct heat and bring to a boil. Stir in the cornstarch-wine mixture and blend to thicken. Add the fresh basil and remove from the heat. Pour the hot soup over the fish, garnish with croutons and serve hot.

Dijonnaise

(dee-Zhohn-NEZ)

From Dijon, the capital city of the ancient province of Burgundy. Dijon is probably best known for its mustard, but is also famous for gingerbread and the cassis liqueur made from its black currants. Since Dijon has become synonymous with mustard, liberties have been taken with the term à la Dijonnaise. It gets applied to all sorts of things as long as they are smeared with mustard. But, believe me, a hot dog with mustard is not a hot dog à la Dijonnaise! Dijonnaise means of Dijon. And Dijon is a city, not a mustard factory.

Dijon was originally built by the Lingones, a Celtic tribe, but became important only after the Mongol invasion in the fifth century headed by Attila. Dijon became Burgundy's capital in the twelfth century, and the prosperity of the dukes of Burgundy made the court of Dijon a rival to the royal court of Paris. Dijon has large blocks of new flats and houses. The commercial center is still in the old section of the city. Along narrow, winding streets are wooden fifteenth-century houses together with the bourgeoise dwellings of the sixteenth century with their sculptured façades. In the center of the old city stands the magnificent group of buildings that was the palace of the dukes of Burgundy and is now the Hôtel de Ville (Town Hall). This former palace was built in the fourtenth and fifteenth centuries and expanded in the seventeenth and eighteenth. Two towers, the kitchen and the guardroom, still survive from the old buildings.

In food, Dijonnaise means you can expect the use of mustard as a flavoring— a flavoring to enhance the dish, not to overwhelm it, as many recipes with this name do. For its particular quality, Dijonnaise relies on a mustard-flavored cream sauce. Diable is another category that uses mustard as an important ingredient. However, Diable uses mustard directly on the dish being prepared or, occasionally, mixed with the pan juices. Dijonnaise is more subtle, in combining the mustard in a cream sauce.

East of Dijon, in the Franche-Comté region, several fine cheeses are produced: Cancoillotte, flavored with wine and herbs; Morbier, with its black sooty streaks from smoking; and the ivory-colored Comté.

DIJONNAISE SAUCE
A Mustard-Flavored Mayonnaise
TO MAKE 2 CUPS

4 egg yolks, hard-boiled
4 tsp Dijon mustard
½ tsp salt

¼ tsp white pepper
1½ cups oil (½ olive and ½ corn)
lemon juice

Mash the yolks well and force through a sieve. Blend in the mustard, salt and pepper. Add the oil, drop by drop, blending well and gradually adding it faster until it is all incorporated. Season to taste with lemon juice.

For a stronger and more distinctive Dijonnaise Sauce, increase the yolks and mustard.

OMELET À LA DIJONNAISE
A Dessert Omelet
TO SERVE 2

1 oz flour	1 Tbs crushed macaroons
1½ oz sugar	1 Tbs heavy cream
⅛ tsp salt	4 Tbs butter
¾ tsp butter	2 egg whites
½ cup milk, boiling	tiny pinch of cream of tartar
¼ tsp vanilla extract	¼ tsp salt
1 Tbs ground almonds	5 Tbs confectioners' sugar
1 Tbs black currant jam	icing sugar
4 eggs	2 oz black currant jam, melted
1 tsp sugar	

Put the flour, sugar, salt and butter in a thick-bottomed pan and blend over very low heat until smooth. Mix the boiling milk with the vanilla and slowly blend into the pan mixture. Bring it to a boil for 2 minutes, stirring, and remove from the heat. Stir in the almonds and 1 tablespoon of jam and chill, making a vanilla-flavored pastry cream.

Beat the eggs, sugar, macaroons and cream. Melt half the 4 tablespoons of butter in a pan and make a pancake omelet* with half the egg mixture. Place on a hot plate and keep hot. Repeat with the remaining half of the butter and eggs, making another equal-sized pancake omelet. Spread the chilled pastry cream on the first omelet and top with the second omelet.

Meanwhile, preheat the oven to 450° and make a meringue by beating the egg whites with the cream of tartar until stiff. As soon as it holds a peak well, stir in the salt and sugar gently. Coat the omelet sides and top with this meringue and sprinkle with icing sugar. Glaze quickly in the oven, decorate with a fine ring of melted jam and serve hot.

VEAL À LA DIJONNAISE
TO SERVE 4

2 lbs veal in slices	1 Tbs minced onion
salt and pepper	1 tsp parsley
1 oz butter	1 tsp chives
1 cup mushrooms, sliced	1 tsp lemon juice
½ cup heavy cream	salt and red pepper (cayenne)
1 Tbs Dijon mustard	

Preheat oven to 350°. Season the veal with salt and pepper to taste and brown in the butter in a casserole. Add the mushrooms and brown. Combine the cream, mustard, onion, parsley, chives, lemon juice and salt and red pepper to taste and pour over the veal and mushrooms. Bake in the oven for 15 to 20 minutes or until done. Serve hot.

KIDNEYS or SWEETBREADS À LA DIJONNAISE
TO SERVE 4

Proceed as for Veal à la Dijonnaise, using 2 pounds of sliced kidneys (soaked in cold water for 15 minutes, cleaned of veins and membranes) or sweetbreads (soaked in cold water for 4 hours, water changed often, and trimmed of central tubes).

Pork, lamb, mutton or even chicken can be made using the Veal à la Dijonnaise recipe. Just use 2 pounds of lean meat in chunks and cook until done as directed, cooking longer for pork or chicken to be sure it is fully cooked.

FLOUNDER À LA DIJONNAISE
TO SERVE 4

Prepare 2 pounds of flounder (or any other white-fleshed fish) fillets as desired and serve with Sauce Dijonnaise.

CUCUMBERS À LA DIJONNAISE
TO SERVE 4

2 cucumbers	1 Tbs white wine vinegar
1 qt lightly salted water	¼ tsp salt
¼ tsp white wine vinegar	¼ tsp paprika
2 Tbs olive oil	2–4 tsp Dijon mustard

Peel the cucumbers and quarter lengthwise. Slice the cucumber quarters crosswise into ½-inch slices, making little pie shapes. Bring the salted water to a boil with the ¼ tsp of vinegar, add the cucumbers and boil 2 minutes. Rinse under running cold water and drain well. Put the oil, vinegar, salt and paprika in a casserole and blend over heat. Add the cucumbers and simmer for about 10 minutes. Blend well without breaking the cucumber pieces. Remove from heat and toss with the mustard to blend well. Serve lightly chilled.

PEARS À LA DIJONNAISE
TO SERVE 4

1½ cups water	2 cups raspberries
1 cup sugar mixed with ½ tsp ground cinnamon	2–4 Tbs black currant jam
1 tsp vanilla extract	1½ oz cassis liqueur
4–6 ripe pears, peeled, cored and quartered	¾ cup heavy cream
	1 cup raspberries, preferably fresh

Heat the water, sugar and vanilla to make a syrup. Use this syrup to poach the pears. Drain and arrange on a serving platter in a ring with an open center. Purée the 2 cups raspberries in a blender or food mill and mix with the black currant jam to taste and ½ ounce of the cassis. Strain. Whip the cream until fairly stiff and blend in the remaining cassis. Pile the cassis-flavored whipped cream in the center of the pear dish and decorate with the remaining raspberries. Serve the raspberry-currant jam purée separately.

Duchesse

(dew-SHESS)

Means Duchess. It is also the name of a particularly luscious fall-ripening pear. A duchess is the consort of a duke, or his widow, or one who has sovereignty of a duchy in her own right.

In cuisine, Duchesse applies to a particular potato dish and to anything that dish, Duchesse Potatoes, is served with as the featured accompaniment or ingredient. Duchesse is much like the categories Anna and Dauphine. They all revolve around a particular potato dish, such as Potatoes Anna, that is the distinguishing characteristic of the category. Duchesse stands apart from the others only in the type of potatoes used, mashed potatoes enriched with cream and egg yolks.

For décor and music, you know what duchesses like—pomp and circumstance. I've never met a duchess who didn't.

SAUCE DUCHESSE
TO MAKE 2 CUPS

Sauce Duchesse is prepared by adding 2 cups of Jus de Veau* or veal gravy to the main course's pan juices, thickening lightly and serving hot. It is used for meats, fowl and eggs.

POTATOES À LA DUCHESSE
TO SERVE 4

2 lbs potatoes, peeled and cut in
   pieces
2 Tbs butter
salt, pepper and grated nutmeg

4 egg yolks
4 Tbs heavy cream (optional)

Boil potatoes in lightly salted water until done. Drain and force through a sieve or mash well with an electric mixer or food mill. Beat in the butter, season to taste with salt, pepper and grated nutmeg and mix in the yolks and cream. Serve hot.

Duchesse Potatoes are often flavored with grated cheese to taste, usually Parmesan. By adding 1 teaspoon of chervil to the Duchesse Potatoes and shaping them into croquettes, dipping in beaten egg and bread crumbs and deep-frying, you make Potatoes à la Chevreuse.

Duchesse Potatoes are often accompanied by tender asparagus tips.

POTATO PANCAKES À LA DUCHESSE
TO SERVE 4

1 recipe Duchesse Potatoes, chilled	bread crumbs (optional) butter

Shape the Duchesse Potatoes into small pancakes and sauté in butter until golden. If using the crumbs, first press them into the potato patties, then sauté until golden. Either way, do not overbrown. They should be a nice golden color since the slightest hint of burnt taste will destroy their delicate flavor.

EGGS À LA DUCHESSE (Poached or Soft-Boiled)
TO SERVE 4

½ recipe Duchesse Potatoes 8 eggs, freshly poached or soft-boiled and hot salt and pepper (optional)	¾ cup very thick veal stock* or gravy, hot 1 Tbs butter (optional)

Preheat oven to 350°. Shape the potatoes into 4 patties and place on a buttered baking sheet. Bake in the oven until golden and arrange on 4 plates. Top each with 2 fresh-cooked, hot eggs. Season with salt and pepper if desired. Top the eggs with the veal stock (mixed with the butter, if desired) and serve hot.

BEEF FILLET À LA DUCHESSE
TO SERVE 4

½ beef fillet, whole salt and pepper 1 recipe Duchesse Potatoes, hot	2 oz Madeira wine 2 cups Jus de Veau, veal stock* or veal gravy

Season the fillet with salt and pepper to taste and broil over a dripping pan until done to taste. Set on a hot, oven-proof platter. Surround the fillet with a piped border of Duchesse Potatoes, or arrange the potatoes in little piles around the roast, and brown lightly in the oven. Meanwhile, add the wine to the dripping pan and scrape up the juices over direct heat. Blend in the Jus de Veau, heat through and strain over the beef or serve separately, hot.

This is generally accompanied by cooked asparagus spears tossed in butter. Any steaks or chops of beef, pork, veal, lamb or mutton can be prepared in this way. If using fatty meat, like mutton, be sure to remove excess fat from the dripping pan before adding wine, etc., for the sauce.

CORNISH GAME HENS À LA DUCHESSE
TO SERVE 4

4 1-lb birds, trussed
salt and pepper
butter
2 cups Sauce Espagnole, or veal
    gravy

1 recipe Duchesse Potatoes, hot
1½ lbs asparagus tips, cooked,
    tossed in butter and lightly
    seasoned, hot

Preheat oven to 375°. Season the birds inside and out with salt and pepper and brown in butter in a casserole. Cover and cook in the oven for about 45 minutes, or until done. Remove from casserole, discard trussing strings and arrange on a hot platter and keep hot. Add the Espagnole to the casserole over direct heat, and scrape up the cooking juices. Arrange the Duchesse Potatoes on the platter with the birds decoratively. Garnish with the asparagus. Strain the sauce over the birds or serve separately, hot.

MOLDED CRÈME À LA DUCHESSE
TO SERVE 4

3 egg yolks
2 Tbs sugar
$1/16$ tsp salt
1 oz Grand Marnier
½ tsp vanilla extract

2 cups whipped cream
8 ladyfingers, split lengthwise
Curaçao liqueur
icing sugar

Put the yolks in the top of a double boiler with the sugar and salt and cook, beating, until very thick. Slowly blend in the Grand Marnier. Rethicken if necessary. Remove from heat, blend in the vanilla and pour in a bowl. Chill until almost firm and old in $2/3$ of the whipped cream. Sprinkle the ladyfinger halves liberally with Curaçao and with icing sugar to taste, and put 4 in each of 4 sherbert glasses. Fill the glasses with the custard mixture, top with the remaining whipped cream and serve lightly chilled.

Duxelles

(dewk-SEL)

The name of a mushroom hash created by the chef La Varenne while an official of the household of the Marquis d'Uxelles. Hence the honorary name Duxelles for his dish. This mushroom hash, with onions and shallots, has a great many uses. It is found in stuffings, sauces and as garnishes for all sorts of dishes.

Duxelles may be made with mushrooms plus any other ingredient of your choice, as in the Chicken Liver Duxelles recipe. For example, Carrot Duxelles is made by cooking minced carrots in butter until limp, and then using in place of the chicken livers in Chicken Liver Duxelles. Carrot Duxelles go very well with eggs and light meats. You may wish to substitute a favorite ingredient of your own for the chicken livers in the Chicken Liver Duxelles recipe. Just be careful of the cooking time. In Carrot Duxelles, the carrots have to be cooked well before using because they take so long to tenderize, while the chicken livers only need be mixed with the mushrooms and sautéed together, since they cook in the same amount of time.

Using your judgment for cooking time, you can make Celery Duxelles, Tomato Duxelles, Egg-White Duxelles (with hard-boiled egg whites)—the variations are endless.

Any steak can be used in the Veal aux Duxelles recipe. Any fowl, or veal or lamb breast, can be used in the recipe for Stuffed Chicken aux Duxelles.

For this category, we might look to the world of mushrooms for help in décor. They make an interesting display with flowers, and come in so many assorted shapes and colors it's almost unbelievable. I once found twenty-six different varieties on a single small island in the St. Lawrence River's Thousand Islands. They ranged in color from almost black to pure white, with brights reds, dull reds, a brilliant orange and one that was an absolutely startling golden yellow. Some were spotted, some plain, but what a variety!

DUXELLES (Mushroom Hash)
TO MAKE 1 CUP

½ onion, chopped fine	salt, pepper and grated nutmeg
3 Tbs butter	2 oz Madeira wine (optional)
2 shallots, chopped fine	2 oz beef stock* or broth (op-
½ lb mushrooms, chopped fine and squeezed of all juice	tional)

Sauté the onion in the butter until just limp. Add the shallots and sauté until they are just limp. Add the mushrooms and sauté until tender and very lightly browned. Season to taste with salt, pepper and nutmeg. For a richer-tasting Duxelles, add the wine and stock and boil down until the liquids are totally absorbed.

This may be made ahead of time and refrigerated or frozen. It's a good idea to make this in a large amount and freeze in ice cube trays, then store the cubes in the freezer in plastic bags until needed, if you have the room. This is a good idea for sauces as well, especially sauces like Espagnole or Velouté, which you often need in small quantities, but which are much too complex to make in small amounts.

CHICKEN LIVER DUXELLES
TO MAKE 1 CUP

¼ lb mushrooms, chopped
¼ lb chicken livers, chopped
1½ Tbs butter
1 oz chopped onions
¼ garlic clove, grated
¼ bay leaf
¼ tsp chervil
¼ tsp basil

pepper
tiny pinch paprika
tiny pinch thyme
1 oz Madeira wine
2 tsp flour
1½ oz Jus de Veau,* veal stock*
    or veal gravy
1 Tbs heavy cream

Mix the mushrooms and livers and sauté in the butter with the onions, garlic, bay leaf, chervil, basil, pepper to taste, paprika and thyme. When well browned, pour on the wine and flame. Cook liquid down to half. Stir in the flour and blend well. Blend in the Jus de Veau. Mix in the cream and simmer a few minutes to thicken. Remove from heat and cool. Discard bay leaf.

SAUCE DUXELLES
TO MAKE 2 CUPS

1 cup dry white wine
4 Tbs Mushroom Duxelles
1½ cups Sauce Espagnole, or
    beef gravy

½ cup tomato purée
2 Tbs parsley

Mix the wine and Duxelles in a pan and cook down until the wine is almost gone. Add the Espagnole and tomato purée and simmer for 5 minutes. Add the parsley and simmer a few minutes more. Serve hot with eggs, fish, poultry or meats.

MUSHROOM BUTTER
TO MAKE 1 CUP

¾ cup mushrooms, sliced
1 oz butter

salt and pepper
4 oz butter

Sauté the mushrooms in the 1 ounce of butter lightly, season to taste with salt and pepper, and force through a sieve. Blend with the remaining butter into a smooth paste. Use as is or chilled in sauces and as a garnish for cold hors d'oeuvres.

RICE AUX DUXELLES
TO SERVE 4

Mix 3 cups of cooked rice with 1 cup of Duxelles and serve hot.

POTATOES, STUFFED, AUX DUXELLES
TO SERVE 4

4 baking potatoes
1 recipe Duxelles, hot
2 Tbs butter, melted

salt and pepper
Parmesan cheese, grated
butter, melted

Bake the potatoes in a 375° oven until done. Halve lengthwise and scoop out the pulp, leaving about ½ inch around the sides. Mash the removed pulp with the Duxelles and 2 tablespoons of melted butter. Season the insides of the scooped-out potatoes with salt and pepper to taste. Stuff with the Duxelles mixture. Sprinkle generously with cheese and a few drops of melted butter and brown in the oven until golden. Serve hot.

Browning this dish in the oven with the cheese makes it au Gratin, and it could be called Duxelles Stuffed Potatoes au Gratin.

TURNIPS, STUFFED, AUX DUXELLES
TO SERVE 4

4 fairly large turnips, peeled
1 cup chicken broth
1 recipe Duxelles
2 oz butter
salt and pepper

2 oz clear chicken or veal stock*
  or broth
bread crumbs
butter, melted

Preheat oven to 350°. Cut the base off the turnips and scoop out the pulp, leaving about ½ inch around the sides. Parboil the scooped-out turnips until fairly tender in lightly salted water. Meanwhile, cook the scooped-out pulp in the chicken broth until tender and purée, or mash. Mix with the Duxelles and butter, season to taste with salt and pepper and use to fill the shells. Moisten with the stock, sprinkle with bread crumbs liberally, add a little melted butter to moisten and place on a buttered baking pan. Bake in the oven until golden and serve hot.

ARTICHOKE HEARTS, STUFFED, AUX DUXELLES
TO SERVE 4

8 small artichoke hearts
butter
1 recipe Duxelles

Parmesan cheese, grated
butter, melted

Preheat oven to 400°. Blanch the artichokes in boiling, lightly salted water for 30 seconds. Drain and sauté in a little butter until tender. Stuff with the Duxelles and place on a buttered baking sheet. Sprinkle generously with cheese and a little butter to moisten and brown in the oven. Serve hot.

EGGS AUX DUXELLES (Poached or Soft-Boiled)
TO SERVE 4

4 bread slices, trimmed and
  lightly sautéed in butter (or
  buttered toast, hot)
4 ham slices, lightly sautéed in
  butter, hot

8 eggs, freshly poached or soft-
  boiled, hot
salt and pepper
1½ cups Sauce Duxelles, hot
parsley or chives

Put a slice of bread on each of 4 hot plates. Top with ham slices. Top ham with 2 eggs each. Season the eggs lightly with salt and pepper, pour the sauce over them, sprinkle with parsley or chives and serve hot.

OMELET AUX DUXELLES
TO SERVE 4

¼ cup Sauce Espagnole
1 Tbs tomato purée
4 eggs
salt and pepper

4 Tbs butter
⅓ cup Duxelles
1 oz cooked ham, diced and
  sautéed
chives

Mix the Espagnole and tomato purée and heat. Beat the eggs with salt and pepper to taste. Prepare the omelet* in very hot butter, filling with a mixture of the Duxelles and ham. Serve on a hot plate with the sauce poured along the top and sprinkled with chives, hot.

VEAL AUX DUXELLES
TO SERVE 4

4 veal steaks
salt and pepper
2 recipes Chicken Liver Duxelles

salt and pepper
¼ cup Gruyère cheese, grated
chives and parsley (optional)

Season the veal very lightly with salt and pepper and cook under a broiler. Remove, lower heat to 250°. Cover the veal steaks with the Duxelles. Season with salt and pepper to taste, sprinkle with the cheese and put in the oven for 5 minutes, or until the cheese melts. Serve at once, hot, sprinkled with chives and parsley, if desired.

MUTTON CHOPS or CUTLETS AUX DUXELLES
TO SERVE 4

8 mutton chops
salt and pepper
butter, or ½ butter and ½
  olive oil

2 oz dry white wine
1½ cups Sauce Duxelles
parsley

Season the chops lightly with salt and pepper and sauté in a little butter until done and golden. Arrange on a hot platter and keep hot. Discard the excess fat from the pan and add the wine. Quickly boil down, scraping up the juices. Add the Sauce Duxelles and blend in well until heated. Pour over the chops, sprinkle with parsley and serve at once, hot.

HAM AUX DUXELLES
TO SERVE 4

Proceed as for Mutton Chops aux Duxelles, seasoning with pepper only. Use individual ham steaks or slices, or a single large 2-pound slab.

ATTEREAUX (Small Skewers) of CHICKEN LIVERS AUX DUXELLES
TO SERVE 4

1 lb chicken livers, halved and lightly sautéed in butter
½ lb small mushroom caps
1 cup Sauce Duxelles

eggs, beaten
bread crumbs
butter

Thread the livers and mushrooms on small skewers, alternating. Coat with Sauce Duxelles and chill. Coat with beaten egg and crumbs and sauté in butter until done and golden. Drain on paper towels and serve hot.

This makes an excellent hors d'oeuvre on toothpicks with just 1 liver piece and 1 mushroom cap each, coated and sautéed, hot.

CHICKEN AUX DUXELLES
TO SERVE 4

Proceed as for Mutton Chops aux Duxelles, using 2 small, cut-up chickens or 8 boned and skinned chicken-breast halves. These breasts are called suprêmes.

CHICKEN, STUFFED, AUX DUXELLES
TO SERVE 4

2 plump pullets (about 2–3 lbs each)

4 cups Chicken Liver Duxelles
butter, melted

Stuff the pullets with the Duxelles and truss. Bake in a 375° oven until done, basting with butter—about 1¼ hours. Serve hot.

SOLE AUX DUXELLES
TO SERVE 4

2 lbs sole fillets
salt and pepper
butter and oil, ½ and ½
1 cup Duxelles

2 oz Tomato Sauce, preferably
   homemade*
parsley
2 lemons, cut in wedges

Season the fillets to taste with salt and pepper and sauté in hot butter and oil until done. Drain and keep hot. Meanwhile, mix the Duxelles and Tomato Sauce and heat. Divide the Duxelles mixture on 4 hot plates, top with the sautéed fish, sprinkle with parsley and serve with lemon wedges, hot. The pan juices, sizzling hot, can also be poured over the fillets, if desired.

SOLE EN BROCHETTES AUX DUXELLES (Skewers)
TO SERVE 4

4 egg yolks, hard-boiled and
   mashed
4 Tbs bread crumbs
1 Tbs parsley
1 oz butter, melted
2 lbs sole fillets, cut in small
   squares, seasoned with salt
   and pepper

½ lb mushroom caps, 2 inches
   in size
2 oz butter, melted (or as
   needed)
bread crumbs
1 cup Duxelles, hot
½ cup Sauce Velouté* hot

Mix the yolks, 4 tablespoons of bread crumbs, parsley and 1 ounce of melted butter. Spread on ½ the fish squares and cover with the other ½. Dip the mushroom caps in the 2 ounces of melted butter. Thread the fish and mushrooms on skewers, alternating. Brush with the remaining butter and coat with crumbs. Grill until done and golden. Serve with the Duxelles and Velouté mixed as a topping sauce, hot.

Any white-fleshed fish, like cod, etc., can be used with this recipe.

Espagnole

(es-spah-N'YOHL)

Means Spaniard, Spanish language. It is the name given to a basic brown sauce, Sauce Espagnole. This sauce is also called Sauce-Mère, which means mother sauce, since it is used as the base for many derivative brown sauces, often called "lesser" sauces. This can be quite misleading and is a misnomer, for they are, if anything, more, not less than the parent sauce.

Some gastronomes regard Sauce Espagnole as inferior. But, if properly made, it is exquisite in its perfect balance of meat and vegetable flavors and in its velvet smoothness. It should not have any single noticeable characteristic, like a taste of onion, for example, but should be rich in perfectly balanced flavor. As far as I'm concerned, this makes it a perfect sauce for any food whose taste you don't want to disguise, such as a fine steak or a perfect omelet.

There is, of course, one characteristic of Espagnole that certain gastronomes find undesirable. There is no fat or butter in it, unless you add some while reheating, because in the process of making Espagnole all the fat is removed, leaving just the rich flavors and fatless juices of meats, bones, trimmings and vegetables. Most experts prefer butter in everything, and if you *must* have butter in everything you need a fairly distinctive flavor in the sauce to fight back. The succulent, but mild, Espagnole really can't do this. It's a straightforward fine taste, without grease, and so are most fine sauces before being mixed with "enrichment butter." There are exceptions to this, like Cream Sauce, or a sauce based on cream. There you automatically get the fat of the cream. This is fine. It has a reason and if you don't want any fat, you don't make cream sauces.

With the simple addition of a little Port or Madeira, Espagnole becomes Sauce au Porto and Sauce au Madère, two classic and magnificent sauces. Then there are the more complex and exotic sauces based on Espagnole, from the spicy Diable to the tomatoey Languedocienne.

Any dish served with Sauce Espagnole as its hallmark is a dish à l'Espagnole.

Cooking à l'Espagnole is similar to other Mediterranean styles, like Provençale, in the use of olive oil as the standard fat and tomatoes and olives as standard ingredients. The use of red pepper and pimientos is the distinguishing feature here, especially pimientos, which may be incorporated in virtually any recipe a l'Espagnole, if they're not already there. The other distinguishing feature of a dish à l'Espagnole is the use of sautéed onion rings as a standard garnish.

Spain is not noted for producing fine wines, but if you're adventuresome, be ready for a strong, rather harsh wine. The best thing I can say for Spanish wines is that they're reasonable as imported wines go. Spain does produce some good cheeses, however, and if you're interested, try Manchego, a very fine, firm cheese made from sheep's milk. It's creamy smooth and luscious.

Décor fitting to a dish à l'Espagnole is, of course, Spanish: ironwork, iron kettles, laces and warm, brilliant colors set off by black. Black lace napkins or placemats on a hot yellow or orange tablecloth would be striking. And, of course, Spanish music.

SAUCE ESPAGNOLE
TO MAKE 1½ QUARTS

3 carrots, quartered
2 onions, halved
½ celery stalk, quartered
½ cup veal, diced (optional)
3 Tbs butter
¾ cup butter, preferably
   clarified*
1¼ cups flour

5 qts brown stock* (beef stock)
1 tomato, chopped
1 cup dry white wine
1 tsp parsley
¼ tsp thyme
¼ bay leaf
cheesecloth, washed

Brown the carrots, onions, celery and veal lightly in the 3 tablespoons of butter. Cook the clarified butter and flour together slowly, stirring until browned. Be very careful not to burn. Beat 4 quarts of stock into the butter and flour slowly to blend, and bring to a boil. Add the browned vegetables, the tomato, wine and the parsley, thyme and bay leaf tied in cheesecloth. Simmer 2 to 3 hours, skimming as well as possible. Strain into a bowl and refrigerate overnight.

The next day, remove the layer of butter on top of the sauce. This may be saved for use on vegetables, if desired. Put the sauce in a pot, add the remaining 1 quart of cold stock, bring to a boil and skim again. Let it simmer down to about 1½ quarts (6 cups). Skim repeatedly. The finished sauce should be clear and coat a spoon lightly. It should be fat-free. Let the sauce cool and strain into containers to store or freeze. The frozen sauce can be used without defrosting. Cut the amount you need from the container with a short, strong knife and return the rest to the freezer.

This basic brown sauce can be used with virtually anything, but is usually flavored with herbs and wines to suit a particular dish.

CREAM SAUCE ESPAGNOLE
TO MAKE 2 CUPS

2 cups Sauce Espagnole

½ cup cream, or to taste

Cook the Espagnole and cream down to 2 cups and serve hot with eggs, meats or vegetables.

This is an exquisite cream sauce, especially good on light meats like veal, pork, chicken or turkey.

PEPPER RAGOUT À L'ESPAGNOLE
TO SERVE 4

½ cup sliced onion
olive oil
6 sweet peppers, seeded and
   cut in 1-inch cubes
salt and red pepper (cayenne)

2 garlic cloves, crushed
2 Tbs flour
1½ cups beef stock* or broth
2 Tbs tomato purée
chives

Sauté the onion lightly in a little oil and add the pepper quarters. Season well with salt and a little red pepper. Add the garlic and sprinkle in the flour, stirring to blend well. Slowly add the stock, blending in well. Add the tomato purée and simmer gently for 35 minutes. Serve hot in a vegetable dish (crockery would be nice), sprinkled with chives.

ASPARAGUS À L'ESPAGNOLE
TO SERVE 4

1½ lbs asparagus spears
salt and pepper
1 garlic clove, crushed

1 oz butter
1 cup Sauce Espagnole

Cook the asparagus in water until just tender and drain. Season the asparagus lightly with salt and pepper, arrange on a hot dish and keep hot. Meanwhile, cook the garlic in the butter until browned and discard the garlic. Add the Espagnole to the garlic-flavored butter and quickly heat through, blend and thicken. Pour over the asparagus and serve hot.

EGGS À L'ESPAGNOLE (Fried)
TO SERVE 4

4 tomatoes, halved
salt and pepper
8 eggs
2 cups onion rings

olive oil
2 Tbs pimientos, diced fine
1 cup Tomato Sauce, preferably
   homemade,* hot

Season the tomato halves well with salt and pepper. Sauté the tomatoes, eggs and onions separately in a little oil. Season the eggs lightly. Arrange the onion rings in the center of a hot platter in a pile and surround with alternating eggs and tomatoes. Mix the pimientos with the Tomato Sauce and pour over the eggs and tomatoes. Serve at once, hot.

EGGS À L'ESPAGNOLE (Poached or Soft-Boiled)
TO SERVE 4

Proceed as for Eggs à l'Espagnole, fried, using freshly poached or soft-boiled eggs.

EGGS À L'ESPAGNOLE (Baked)
TO SERVE 4

1 onion, sliced thin
butter
red pepper (cayenne)
8 eggs

salt and red pepper (cayenne)
½ cup Tomato Sauce, preferably homemade*
1 Tbs chopped pimiento

Preheat oven to 500°. Sauté the onion lightly in a little butter and season lightly with red pepper. Use to line 4 individual buttered baking dishes. Break 2 eggs into each dish without breaking the yolks. Season lightly with salt and red pepper. Top with the Tomato Sauce mixed with the pimiento. Bake for 4 minutes on a high rack, or until the whites are just set and the yolks still soft. Serve at once in the baking dishes, hot.

EGGS À L'ESPAGNOLE (Scrambled)
TO SERVE 4

2 oz pimientos, chopped
4 oz tomato, peeled,* seeded
   and chopped
butter

salt and pepper
8 eggs
1 onion, sliced thin, sautéed in
   butter, hot

Simmer the pimento and tomato in a little butter until soft and season to taste with salt and pepper. Keep hot. Beat the eggs with salt and pepper to taste and scramble in hot butter. Arrange on a hot platter. Top with the pimientos and tomatoes and strew the onions across the top. Serve at once, hot.

OMELET À L'ESPAGNOLE
TO SERVE 2

4 eggs
1 oz pimientos, diced and
   sautéed in butter, drained
1 garlic clove, chopped fine with
   2 tsp parsley

salt and pepper
4 Tbs butter

Beat the eggs with the pimientos and the garlic and parsley and season to taste with salt and pepper. Use to prepare a flat, or pancake, omelet* in hot butter. Serve as soon as done, hot.

STEAK À L'ESPAGNOLE
TO SERVE 4

4 boneless beefsteaks
salt and pepper
½ tsp ground cloves
1 tsp ground thyme
1 tsp garlic powder
olive oil
1 green pepper, chopped
24 small stuffed green olives
2 tomatoes, peeled,* seeded
   and sliced
12 small mushrooms

1 tsp parsley
1 tsp celery leaves
2 cloves
1 bay leaf
¼ tsp thyme
cheesecloth, washed
2 cups beef stock* or broth
2 oz sherry wine
1-2 Tbs cornstarch blended with
   1 oz cold water (optional)

Season the steaks with salt and pepper to taste. Mix the cloves, thyme and garlic powder and rub on the steaks. Brown the steaks well in a little oil and transfer to an oiled casserole.

Preheat oven to 350°. Put the pepper, olives, tomatoes and mushrooms in the beef sauté pan with the parsley, celery, cloves, bay leaf and thyme wrapped in cheesecloth. Add the stock, cover and bring quickly to a boil. Pour this mixture over the beef in the casserole, cover and braise for 1½ hours in the oven. When done, discard the herb bouquet, stir in the sherry and serve in the casserole. If desired, thicken the juices with the cornstarch slurry over direct heat, then serve hot.

LAMB, PORK or MUTTON STEAKS À L'ESPAGNOLE
TO SERVE 4

Proceed as for Steak à l'Espagnole, using 4 to 8 boneless steaks of your choice, but remove any excess fat from the pan before thickening the juices or serving.

CHICKEN SAUTÉ À L'ESPAGNOLE
TO SERVE 4

2 small chickens, cut up
salt and pepper
olive oil
2 cups rice cooked in chicken
   stock* or broth and well seasoned
½ green pepper, diced and
   sautéed in olive oil, drained

½ cup pimientos, lightly sautéed
   in oil and drained
¼ lb cooked peas
4 chorizo sausages (or garlic
   sausages), cooked and
   sliced
4 tomatoes, halved, well seasoned and grilled, hot

Season the chicken to taste with salt and pepper and sauté until done and golden in a little oil. Remove from the pan, drain, and keep hot. Add the rice to the pan with the peppers, pimientos, peas and sausages. Cover and simmer gently 8 to 10 minutes. Put the chicken pieces on a hot platter, top with the rice mixture, garnish with the tomato halves and serve hot.

FLOUNDER À L'ESPAGNOLE
TO SERVE 4

3 tomatoes, peeled,* seeded
   and coarsely chopped
salt and paprika
1 garlic clove, crushed
olive oil

1 cup pimientos, cut in strips
1 onion, sliced in rings
flour
2 lbs flounder fillets
salt and paprika

Season the tomatoes well with salt and paprika and sauté with the garlic in a little oil. Discard the garlic. Sauté the pimientos in a little oil and drain. Dredge the onion rings in flour and sauté in a little oil until done and golden and drain. Season the fish fillets with salt and paprika to taste, dredge lightly in flour and sauté in a little oil until done and golden and drain. Arrange the fish on a bed of the tomatoes on a hot platter. Put the pimientos in a pile at each end of the platter and arrange the onion rings on top of the fish. Serve at once, hot.

This is an excellent way to prepare any white-fleshed fish fillets. The fillets are often dipped in beaten egg and coated with crumbs before sautéing.

Estragon

(es-trah-GOHN)

Means tarragon. In cooking, the term denotes dishes making use of tarragon as a prime flavoring herb. Tarragon is one of the truly great herbs in its distinctiveness, and is related botanically to wormwood, southernwood and mugwort. Its botanical name is *Artemesia dracunculus*. "French" tarragon is considered the finest, but seldom produces usable seed, and must be grown from cuttings or root division. Therefore, if you buy seed to raise your own tarragon, you're buying the seed of an inferior variety of tarragon commonly known as "Russian" tarragon. The botanical name for Russian tarragon is *Artemesia dracunculoides*. Tarragon is a bushy perennial, growing up to 3 feet high, with small grey-green flowers. It grows best in well-drained soil, in sun or partial shade.

There are a great many dishes to use tarragon in, provided you like it. I *love* it! Any simply sautéed meat can be greatly enhanced by the addition of tarragon, wine and meat stock, as explained in Tarragon Sauce #2. The time involved is virtually nil. You have to cook the stuff anyway, and with a small added effort you have a dish that is a delight. Another favorite of mine is basil, and if it is used in place of the tarragon in these dishes, they would be called à la Basilic.

TARRAGON SAUCE #1
TO MAKE 2 CUPS

1 cup dry white wine
4 tsp tarragon

2 cups Sauce Espagnole, or
    Sauce Demi-Glace (Sauce
    Alsacienne)

Put the wine and tarragon in a pan and boil down until the wine is virtually gone. Add the Espagnole and simmer 5 minutes. Serve hot.

TARRAGON SAUCE #2
TO MAKE 2 CUPS

Sauté the meat or meats (for 4) in butter and set aside and keep hot. Drain excess fat from the sauté pan, if any. Add 1 cup of dry white wine and 4 teaspoons of tarragon to the pan and boil down, scraping up the juices, until the wine is almost gone. Add 2 cups of thick chicken stock* for dark meats, or Jus de

Veau* or veal stock* for any meats. Simmer for 5 minutes, strain and serve hot. (Thicken with about 2 tablespoons each of flour and butter kneaded together, if desired.)

These sauces are best made with fresh tarragon, in which case use 4 tablespoons and when it is cooked, strain, garnish with 1 tablespoon of fresh, minced tarragon and serve hot with eggs or meat.

TARRAGON BUTTER
TO MAKE 1 CUP

6 Tbs fresh tarragon (or 3 Tbs dried, plumped in a little hot dry white wine)

1 cup butter, softened

Grind the tarragon in a mortar and slowly blend in the butter, making a smooth paste. Use for grilled meats and fish.

BEETS À L'ESTRAGON
TO SERVE 4

2 good bunches of baby beets with greens
2 Tbs butter
salt and pepper
½ tsp sugar

1 oz tarragon vinegar
2 oz sour cream
1 Tbs fresh tarragon, chopped (or 1 tsp dried, plumped in hot white wine)

Cut tops off beets and wash well. Cook the beets in boiling, lightly salted water until done and peel. Cook the beet tops in a pan with a little salted water until they are limp and squeeze dry. Grind the greens or chop very fine. Melt the butter in a pan and add the peeled beets, salt and pepper to taste, sugar and vinegar. Warm slowly, shaking the pan occasionally. When hot, add the beet greens, sour cream and tarragon. Blend off heat, pour in a hot serving dish and serve at once, hot.

VEAL ESCALOPES À L'ESTRAGON (Slices)
TO SERVE 4

8 veal cutlets, pounded thin
salt and pepper
1 lb pork sausage meat
4 Tbs fresh tarragon, or 4 tsp dried, minced
2 oz butter
1 Tbs flour

¾ cup dry white wine
1 onion, cut in eighths
½ tsp tarragon
½ tsp chervil
½ tsp chives
cheesecloth, washed
salt and pepper

Season the cutlets to taste with salt and pepper. Blend the sausage meat with the tarragon, spread on the cutlets and roll them up. Secure with string. These are sometimes called veal birds. Brown the veal in butter on all sides. Blend in the flour. Slowly blend in the wine. Bring to a boil and add the onion. Add the tarragon, chervil and chives tied in cheesecloth. Season to taste with salt and pepper. Simmer covered over low heat for 20 minutes, or until done. Arrange the veal on a hot platter, discarding the strings. Strain the sauce over the veal and serve hot.

CHICKEN SAUTÉ À L'ESTRAGON
TO SERVE 4

1 4–5-lb chicken, cut up
3 oz butter
1½ cups Jus de Veau* or veal
   stock* or gravy

3 Tbs fresh tarragon sprigs
   (or 2–3 tsp dried)
½ cup heavy cream

Brown the chicken in the butter and remove the excess fat from the pan.

Add the Jus de Veau and the tarragon sprigs tied together (or the dried tarragon tied in washed cheesecloth). Cook covered for 30 minutes, or until done. Arrange the chicken on a hot platter and keep hot. Discard the tarragon. Blend the cream into the sauce, heating through quickly. (Add a little chopped fresh tarragon, if desired.) Coat the chicken with a little sauce and serve the rest separately, hot.

Chicken or other birds may be prepared à l'Estragon by roasting with a good dollop of tarragon butter in their cavities and also using tarragon butter, melted, for basting.

CORNISH GAME HENS À L'ESTRAGON
TO SERVE 4

4 1-lb birds
salt and pepper
2 Tbs fresh tarragon, or 2 tsp
   dried
3 carrots, chopped
2 onions, chopped
4 celery stalks, chopped
2 cups Jus de Veau,* veal stock*
   or veal gravy

¾ cup dry white wine
¾ cup Jus de Veau,* veal stock*
   or veal gravy
1 Tbs fresh tarragon, chopped,
   or 1 tsp dried
3 Tbs butter

Preheat oven to 375°. Season the birds lightly inside and out with salt and pepper. Put ½ tablespoon of tarragon in each bird and truss. Simmer the carrots, onions and celery in the 2 cups of Jus de Veau for 10 minutes. Put the birds in a roasting pan and pour the vegetables and Jus de Veau over them. Cook in the oven for about 25 minutes, or until almost done.

Meanwhile, heat the wine, ¾ cup Jus de Veau, 1 tablespoon tarragon and butter. When the birds are almost done, pour this mixture over them and cook in the oven for about 10 minutes more, until done. Arrange the birds on a hot platter. Untruss and strain the sauce over them and serve hot.

LOBSTER À L'ESTRAGON
TO SERVE 4

Serve freshly cooked hot lobster meat with little pieces of Tarragon Butter melting on top of the lobster, or serve the lobsters freshly cooked and whole, with Tarragon Butter on the side.

Fermière

(fayr-M'YAYR)

Means farmer's wife. This is the French version of good old farm cookin'. Usually it's a pot roast of some kind served with a vegetable fondue of carrots, turnips, celery and onions cooked in butter. This garnish is sometimes made of artichoke hearts filled with vegetable fondue, and braised lettuces. The braised lettuces might fit with farm cooking, since farms have been noted for keeping stockpots cooking continuously, and thus would have a handy stock available to cook lettuces fresh from the field. But the artichokes stuffed with vegetable fondue seems to be stretching things. It just doesn't belong with farm cooking.

Fermière belongs to a family of cooking styles that all use garden fresh vegetables in one way or another. Some of the other members of the family are Bouquetière, which arranges the vegetables like flower bouquets; Bourgeoise, which uses uniformly shaped vegetables as a garnish; and Bonne Femme, which uses potatoes and mushrooms more widely and often adds bacon, rather than the ham used in Fermière.

The hallmark of a dish à la Fermière is a mixture of vegetables, usually diced, sautéed in butter, then added to the main course to finish cooking together. Carrots, onions and celery are the standards. This isn't a category with much in the way of variations. Stick to the straightforward recipes that fit with farm cooking. They should be dishes that are relatively simple, and always hearty; no hard-working farmer ever looked forward to a delicate dinner! While you will see recipes listed as à la Fermière that are less wholesome but fancier than those listed here, they're wrong as far as I'm concerned.

Dishes Fermière are sometimes called Paysanne (payee-ZAHN), meaning peasant. The names are interchangeable.

For ideas in décor, just think of a country kitchen, with its stockpot on the stove. Country music would be nice, either French or any other kind for variety.

SALAD À LA FERMIÈRE
TO SERVE 4

1 cup potatoes, cut in small pieces	1 cup celery, cut in small pieces
1 cup beets, cut in small pieces	1 cup Cream Sauce
1 cup green peppers, cut in small pieces	1 Tbs prepared mustard, mild
	1 tsp parsley (optional)
	1 tsp chives (optional)

Boil the vegetables separately in lightly salted water until done. Drain. Mix and pile on a hot serving dish, preferably crockery, and keep hot. Meanwhile, prepare Mustard Sauce by blending the Cream Sauce and mustard in the top of a double boiler over simmering water. Mix in the parsley and chives, if desired, but do not allow to boil. Pour the sauce over the vegetables and serve hot.

Salad à la Fermière can be made with any garden vegetables. The choice is yours. Mustard Sauce is the usual dressing.

POTATOES, STUFFED, À LA FERMIÈRE
TO SERVE 4

4 potatoes, baked and halved	Parmesan cheese, grated
2 cups mirepoix of vegetables	butter, melted
salt and pepper	

Preheat oven to 375°. Scoop out the potato halves, leaving about ½ inch of potato pulp around the sides. Mash the removed pulp and mix with the vegetable mirepoix. Season the potato shells inside, mostly with salt. Stuff the potatoes with the vegetable mixture. Sprinkle generously with cheese and a little butter to moisten, and brown in the oven. Serve hot.

DANDELIONS À LA FERMIÈRE
TO SERVE 4

2 lbs dandelion greens	salt and pepper
¼ cup bacon drippings	2 Tbs grated onion
4 potatoes, boiled and sliced	4 freshly poached eggs, hot
¼ cup cider vinegar	8 cooked bacon strips, drained and hot
¾ tsp sugar	

Wash the greens and drain. Chop. Simmer the greens in the bacon drippings until almost tender. Add the potatoes, vinegar and sugar and heat through well. Season to taste with salt and pepper and stir in the grated onion. Serve hot, topped with the poached eggs and bacon strips.

This is an excellent method for preparing any greens, like mustard greens, beet greens, etc.

PEAS À LA FERMIÈRE
TO SERVE 4

½ lb small new carrots (or carrots sliced thick)
12 very small onions
2 cups water (or enough to barely cover vegetables)
1 tsp salt
1 Tbs sugar
4 Tbs butter

2 cups peas
½ head lettuce, quartered
1 tsp parsley
½ tsp chervil
1 bay leaf
cheesecloth, washed
1 Tbs water
butter (optional)

Put the carrots and onions in a pot with the water, salt, sugar and butter. Simmer until the liquid is almost gone and shake the pan to glaze the vegetables. Add the peas and lettuce. Add the parsley, chervil and bay leaf tied in cheesecloth. Add the water, cover, and simmer 10 more minutes, or until just done. Discard herb bouquet and add a little butter, if desired. Serve at once, hot.

There are a lot of variations on this recipe. Here are some popular ones: Add ½ cup of diced cooked ham with the peas and lettuce. Or sweeten with honey rather than sugar. Or use chicken stock* in place of the water. Or add ½ cup of minced green pepper with the carrots and onions. Finally, the vegetables are often served with cooked sausages, as a complete meal.

EGGS À LA FERMIÈRE
TO SERVE 4

This name is generally applied to eggs of the style of your choice served with dandelion greens, or any other greens. See Dandelions à la Fermière, and use ¼ of the recipe with 8 eggs.

OMELET À LA FERMIÈRE
TO SERVE 2

1 Tbs chopped onion
1 Tbs chopped carrot
1 Tbs chopped celery
butter
salt and pepper

4 eggs
2 Tbs cooked, diced ham
butter
chives

Lightly sauté the onion, carrot and celery in a little butter. Drain and season to taste with salt and pepper. Beat with the eggs. Sauté the ham lightly in a little butter, drain, mix with the eggs and prepare a flat omelet* in 4 tablespoons of butter. Serve at once, sprinkled with chives, hot.

BEEF ENTRECÔTES À LA FERMIÈRE (Steaks)
TO SERVE 4

4 steaks, thick	4 celery stalks, sliced thin
butter	salt and pepper
1 lb carrots, sliced thin	4 oz dry white wine
½ lb small onions, halved	2 cups Sauce Espagnole, or veal
½ lb turnips, sliced thin	or beef gravy

Brown the steaks in a little butter in a large pan. Meanwhile, blanch all the vegetables in boiling water for 30 seconds and drain. When the steaks are well browned, add the vegetables to the pan and season to taste with salt and pepper. Finish cooking together, covering when the vegetables are browned. Add a bit more butter, if needed, during cooking. When the steaks are done, set on a hot platter, or perhaps a large board or pottery bowl for a more farmlike atmosphere, surround with the vegetables and keep hot. Add the wine to the pan and boil down, scraping up the juices. Add the Espagnole, mix and heat through, and pour over the meat and vegetables. Serve hot.

Diced cooked ham, ½ cup or more, is often added with the vegetables.

VEAL CHOPS À LA FERMIÈRE
TO SERVE 4

Proceed as for Beef Entrecôtes à la Fermière, using large, thick veal chops.

BEEF ROAST À LA FERMIÈRE
TO SERVE 4

Prepare a roast in a pot. Toward the end of the cooking time, add the vegetables as in Beef Entrecôtes à la Fermière, so they will be done when the meat is. Skim off excess fat if necessary, and follow the procedure in the Entrecôte recipe for seasonings and sauce.

CHICKEN SAUTÉ À LA FERMIÈRE
TO SERVE 4

Proceed as for Beef Entrecôtes à la Fermière, using 2 small, cut-up chickens.

MEAT LOAF À LA FERMIÈRE
TO SERVE 4

3 Tbs butter
3 Tbs flour
salt and pepper
¾ cup milk
1 lb ground meat (beef, veal,
    pork, chicken, ham, or even
    fish)

1 egg, beaten
salt, pepper, grated nutmeg,
    ground cloves
¼ cup light cream
2 cups Velouté Sauce,* hot
    (optional)

Melt the butter in a pot. Remove from heat and stir in the flour. Add salt and pepper to taste. Blend until smooth. Add the milk over low heat, stirring until it boils and thickens. Chill. Preheat oven to 350°. Mix the meat into the chilled white sauce and blend thoroughly. Add the egg and blend again. Season to taste with salt, pepper, nutmeg and a tiny pinch of cloves. Blend in the cream. Pour into a buttered loaf pan, cover with foil, place in a pan of hot water and bake in the oven until done—about 40 minutes. Unmold and serve on a hot dish, with the Velouté Sauce served separately, if desired.

This dish may be garnished with any farm-fresh vegetables, braised in stock* or boiled, drained and tossed in a little butter.

TROUT À LA FERMIÈRE
TO SERVE 4

2 lbs trout fillets (or any other
    freshwater fish)
salt and pepper
4 Tbs each carrots, onions,
    leeks and celery, shredded

butter
½ cup dry white wine
2 Tbs butter, diced
½ cup cream

Preheat oven to 350°. Season the fillets lightly with salt and pepper. Sauté the shredded vegetables in a little butter until limp, and put half in the bottom of a buttered baking pan. Put the fish on this bed and cover with the remaining vegetables. Add the wine and dot the fish with the diced butter. Bring to a boil on the stove and put in the oven for 10 to 15 minutes, until the fish flakes easily with a fork and is done. Baste frequently while cooking. Place the fish on a hot platter and keep hot. Add the cream to the pan juices and vegetables and blend over high heat to thicken quickly. Pour over the fish and serve hot.

This recipe is very often given for sole or other ocean fish. While the results are fine, ocean fish just don't seem to fit well with farm cooking, whereas freshwater fish can be had in most streams and are often kept stocked in ponds on farms.

You will also come across this recipe for fish, or a similar one, using red wine. That is *definitely* wrong. Fish cooked in red wine belong in categories like Bourguignonne, or Chambertin, which are named after red wines.

VELOUTÉ SOUP À LA FERMIÈRE
TO SERVE 4

2 Tbs dry white beans
4 cups water
3 Tbs butter
3 small carrots, shredded
1 small turnip, shredded
4 Tbs leek whites, shredded

4 Tbs onions, shredded
½ cabbage heart, shredded
salt and pepper
3 cups chicken consommé* or
   broth
½ cup cream
1 tsp chervil

Cook the beans in the water at a simmer until done, adding a little water if necessary. Drain, reserving the cooking water that has not been absorbed. Meanwhile, melt the butter in a pot and add all the shredded vegetables. Season lightly with salt and pepper, cover and simmer slowly until limp but not browned. Add the bean water and consommé to the vegetables and simmer for 1½ hours more. Add the cream, the white beans and the chervil and simmer 5 minutes more. Serve hot.

NUT CREAM PIE À LA FERMIÈRE
TO SERVE 4–8

½ cup sugar
3 eggs, beaten
1 cup dark corn syrup
¼ cup melted butter
salt
½ tsp vanilla extract
¼ tsp ground cinnamon

⅛ tsp ground nutmeg
1/16 tsp ground cloves
1 cup unsalted nuts, chopped
   (almonds, pecans, walnuts,
   etc. or any combination)
1 unbaked 8–9 inch piecrust*
heavy cream

Preheat oven to 450°. Beat the sugar into the eggs. Blend the corn syrup with the melted butter and beat into the egg-sugar mixture little by little. Stir in a pinch of salt, the vanilla, cinnamon, nutmeg, cloves and nuts and pour into the piecrust. Bake in the oven for 10 minutes, lower heat to 350° and bake for 25 minutes more, or until done. If serving hot or warm, top with a little heavy cream, thickened by boiling down. If serving cool or chilled, top liberally with whipped cream.

Financière

(fee-nahn-S'YAYR)

Means financier. These dishes are very similar to dishes à la Banquière (bahn-K'YEHR), meaning banker, which isn't surprising. The difference is that Financière dishes are richer and more elaborately garnished than Banquière dishes, just as a man of "finance" is supposedly richer than a mere banker.

A dish à la Banquière is garnished with quenelles (dumplings), truffles and mushrooms. A dish à la Financière is garnished with quenelles, truffles and mushrooms *and* cockscombs, cock's kidneys and olives; sometimes with lamb's sweetbreads and occasionally even with crayfish.

Its elaborate and specific garnish is the distinguishing feature of Financière. Any food served with Sauce Financière and Garnishes is a dish à la Financière. That's all there is to it. Contrarily, any food served without Financière Garnishes is *not* a dish à la Financière, no matter what a menu or recipe book might say.

For wines with a dish à la Financière, you might as well go all the way with a very good wine or champagne.

The proper setting for a dish à la Financière is your most expensive napery, silver and crystal.

SAUCE FINANCIÈRE (for Eggs, Meats or Fowl)
TO MAKE 2 CUPS

2 cups Sauce Espagnole or Sauce Demi-Glace (Sauce Alsacienne)

2 oz Madeira wine
1 oz truffle juice

Heat the sauce, wine and truffle juice together and cook to thicken lightly. Serve hot.

FINANCIÈRE GARNISHES
TO SERVE 4

1. CHICKEN QUENELLES

½ lb chicken or veal, ground
¼ lb beef fat, ground
1 egg, beaten

1 egg yolk
salt, white pepper, grated nutmeg
2 cups chicken broth

Begin 1 day in advance. Mix the chicken, fat, beaten egg and egg yolk and season to taste with salt, pepper and nutmeg. When well blended, spread on a board or plate and refrigerate overnight. The next day, shape the mixture into small quenelles (dumplings) and simmer gently in the chicken broth for 15 to 20 minutes, until done. Drain. Serve hot.

2. COCKSCOMBS, ETC.

¼ lb cockscombs
¼ lb cock's kidneys
8 mushroom caps
8 truffle slices

butter
½ lb black olives, pitted
salt and pepper

Sauté the cockscombs, kidneys, mushrooms and truffles in a little butter. When half done, add the olives and finish together. Season to taste with salt and pepper and serve hot. Or, sauté all the ingredients separately and serve separately, garnishing the main dish, hot.

LAMB CHOPS À LA FINANCIÈRE
TO SERVE 4

12 lamb chops
salt and pepper
butter
1 8–9 inch puff pastry shell* or
   baked pie shell,* hot
1 recipe Financière Garnish
   #2, hot

1 cup Sauce Financière, hot
1 recipe Financière Garnish
   #1, hot
2 oz Madeira wine
2 cups beef stock*

Season the lamb chops lightly with salt and pepper and sauté in a little butter until done. Place in the pastry shell, arranging around the outside. Fill the center with the cockscombs, etc. (Garnish #2) bound with the Sauce Financière. Place the quenelles (Garnish #1) on top of the cockscombs, etc. and keep hot. Put the Madeira in the lamb saute pan and quickly boil down, scraping up the juices. Add the beef stock and quickly boil down to ⅛, making a glaze. Strain this glaze over the filled pastry and serve at once, hot.

VEAL CHOPS À LA FINANCIÈRE
TO SERVE 4

Proceed as for Lamb Chops à la Financière, using veal chops in place of the lamb chops.

TOURNEDOS À LA FINANCIÈRE (Beef Fillets)
TO SERVE 4

Proceed as for Lamb Chops à la Financière, using 8 beef fillets about 1 inch thick in place of the lamb chops.

CHICKEN À LA FINANCIÈRE
TO SERVE 4

Proceed as for Lamb Chops à la Financière, using 12 chicken suprêmes, (boneless, skinless chicken breasts).

All these recipes following the lamb chop recipe can be served on bread croutons, rather than in a pastry shell, if desired.

HAM À LA FINANCIÈRE
TO SERVE 4

1 8-lb ham
2 turnips, quartered
2 carrots, quartered
2 celery stalks, quartered
2 onions, stuck with 4 cloves

pepper
2½ cups Madeira wine
icing sugar
Financière Garnishes #1 and
   2, hot

Soak the ham in cold water for at least 6 hours. Put the turnips, carrots, celery and onions in a pot with 1 quart of water and season with pepper. Boil for 10 minutes. Add the ham and simmer gently for 1 hour. Add a little water if necessary to just cover the ham. (The ham should almost fill the pot, so you don't need too much water.) Skim toward the end of the cooking. Drain the ham, setting the cooking liquid aside and reserving.

Put the ham back in the same pot (which is clean and empty now), add the Madeira, cover and simmer gently for 1 hour. Drain, reserving the cooking liquid, and remove skin and excess fat and discard. Sprinkle the ham with sugar and glaze in the oven or under a grill. Put the glazed ham on a hot platter and decorate with the Financière Garnishes #1 and 2. Keep hot. Quickly cook down the ham cooking liquids, skimming off excess fat. When reduced to about ¼, strain into a sauceboat and serve hot with the ham.

CORNISH GAME HENS À LA FINANCIÈRE
TO SERVE 4

4 1-lb birds	Financière Garnishes #1 and
salt and pepper	2, hot
butter	2 cups Sauce Financière, hot

Preheat oven to 375°. Season the birds inside and out with salt and pepper to taste and truss with string. Brown in butter in a casserole and bake in the oven for 45 minutes, or until done. When the birds are almost done baking, add the Financière Garnishes and Sauce and finish cooking together. Discard the trussing strings and serve hot, in the casserole.

Fines Herbes

(FEEN ZAYRB)

Refers to a mixture of chopped herbs, generally parsley, chives, chervil and tarragon. Sometimes one or more of the following is added: basil, fennel, sage, oregano. In the earlier days of cooking, Fines Herbes included chopped mushrooms and truffles.

Many people mix a batch of their own "secret" combination and use it as a general seasoning. How *monotonous!*

Again, this is a very simple cooking category. Any food that is cooked in a pan in butter with herbs of your choice is a dish aux Fines Herbes. This is an excellent way to cook meats and fish. Any vegetable may be cooked by following the carrot, artichoke or asparagus recipes. Steaks are splendid grilled and served with Fines Herbes Sauce.

SAUCE FINES HERBES (for Eggs, Meats or Fowl)
TO MAKE 2 CUPS

1 cup dry white wine
2 Tbs parsley
1 Tbs chervil

2 tsp tarragon
2 cups Sauce Demi-Glace
    (Sauce Alsacienne) or Sauce
    Espagnole, or gravy

Heat the wine in a pan. Grind the herbs together in a mortar, if you have one, and add to the pan. Boil down until the wine is almost all gone. Add the Sauce Demi-Glace and cook to thicken lightly. Serve hot.

SALAD DRESSING AUX FINES HERBES
TO MAKE 1 CUP

2 oz wine vinegar
6 oz oil
1½ tsp salt
½ tsp white pepper
1 tsp parsley

1 tsp chives
½ tsp tarragon
½ tsp chervil
½ tsp celery leaves
½ tsp thyme

Combine all the ingredients and use for salads, or for seasoning vegetables and meats.

CARROTS AUX FINES HERBES
TO SERVE 4

1½ lbs carrots, in equal-size
    pieces
1 tsp salt
1 Tbs sugar
2 oz butter
1 qt water
½ tsp parsley

½ tsp chives
¼ tsp tarragon
¼ tsp chervil
¼ tsp celery leaves
¼ tsp thyme

Put the carrots, salt, sugar and butter in the water and bring to a boil. Cover loosely. Simmer until the carrots are almost done, then uncover and cook until the water is almost all gone. Toss the carrots in the remaining syrup to glaze. Mix the herbs. Put the glazed carrots in a hot serving dish, sprinkle with the herbs and serve hot.

MUSHROOMS AUX FINES HERBES
TO SERVE 4

1 lb mushrooms, sliced (or but-
    ton mushrooms)
butter
½ tsp parsley

½ tsp chervil
¼ tsp oregano
¼ tsp celery leaves
salt and pepper

Sauté the mushrooms in a little butter with the parsley, chervil, oregano and celery leaves. Season lightly with salt and pepper and serve hot.

ASPARAGUS AUX FINES HERBES
TO SERVE 4

2 lbs asparagus, cooked and hot   ¾ cup Salad Dressing aux Fines
                                         Herbes

To serve hot: Arrange the asparagus on a hot dish, top with dressing and serve.

To serve cold: Chill asparagus and dressing separately and serve on a chilled platter.

ARTICHOKE HEARTS AUX FINES HERBES
TO SERVE 4

8 artichoke hearts   1 tsp parsley
butter   ½ tsp chervil

Blanch the artichokes in boiling, lightly salted water for 30 seconds. Drain. Sauté in a little butter with the parsley and chervil until tender. Serve at once, hot.

For a nice variation, sauté the artichokes without the parsley and chervil. When tender, set aside and keep hot. Quickly add 1 ounce of white wine to the sauté pan with ¼ teaspoon each of parsley, chervil and tarragon. Boil until the wine is almost gone and add 2 to 3 ounces of Sauce Espagnole or veal gravy. Season with salt and pepper, if necessary, and pour over the artichokes. Serve hot.

OMELET AUX FINES HERBES
TO SERVE 2

4 eggs   ½ tsp tarragon
1 tsp parsley   1 tsp chives
½ tsp chervil   4 Tbs butter

Beat the eggs and herbs and prepare the omelet* in very hot butter. Serve at once, hot.

A few tablespoons of chopped, sautéed mushrooms are an excellent addition to this omelet. Just drain the mushrooms and beat with the eggs and herbs. Another variation would be to cook the herbs in 2 ounces of Madeira wine until the wine is almost gone, then mix in a few tablespoons of sautéed mushrooms and use as a filling for the omelet. Scrambled eggs are also excellent if first mixed with the herbs, then scrambled.

VEAL CHOPS AUX FINES HERBES
TO SERVE 4

8 veal chops	2 cups Sauce Espagnole, or veal
salt and pepper	gravy
butter	½ Tbs parsley
¼ cup dry white wine	½ Tbs chervil
1 tsp chopped shallot	½ Tbs tarragon

Season the veal to taste with salt and pepper and sauté until done and golden in a little butter. Set on a hot platter and keep hot. Add the wine and shallot to the pan and cook down, scraping up the juices. Add the Espagnole, parsley, chervil and tarragon and simmer for a few minutes to develop the flavors. Pour over the veal and serve hot.

Don't let the recipe here limit your choice of herbs. Basil, chives, fenugreek, marjoram, mint, oregano, savory and thyme all go well with veal. An excellent combination is chives, parsley and savory. Mint, tarragon and chives is also very good, and unusual. Try a few combinations; you're certain to find your own favorites.

LAMB SAUTÉ AUX FINES HERBES
TO SERVE 4

1 Tbs chopped shallots	½ Tbs tarragon
butter or oil	lemon juice
2 lbs lamb slices	3 oz dry white wine
½ Tbs parsley	2 cups veal gravy
½ Tbs chervil	

Sauté the shallots in a little butter or oil very briefly and add the lamb. Sauté until the lamb is just done. Set on a hot platter and keep hot. Add the parsley, chervil, tarragon and a few drops of lemon juice to the pan. Add the wine and stir, scraping up the juices. Boil down to ½. Add the gravy and cook to heat and thicken lightly. Pour over the lamb and serve hot.

For this dish there are plenty of other Fines Herbes combinations you might try. Celery leaves, crushed fennel seeds, fenugreek and basil make an excellent combination with lamb. Or, for a warm, slightly sweet, milk currylike flavor you might try celery leaves, cardamom, coriander and chives. The only way to find what you like best is to try a few variations of your own!

Some experts may say that spices like crushed fennel seeds don't belong in Fines Herbes. I say you can use any herbs you want and call them Fines Herbes, since the French themselves have conflicting views on just what is meant by Fines Herbes. One view is that it applies to the use of parsley alone! Since the term has no specific meaning, it seems only fair that you judge what Fines Herbes are for yourself, according to taste.

LIVER AUX FINES HERBES
TO SERVE 4

2 lbs liver, in equal ¼-inch-thick
   slices
milk
flour, seasoned well with salt
   and pepper
butter, preferably clarified*
salt and pepper
1 tsp parsley
1 tsp tarragon

1 oz butter
1–2 tsp lemon juice
1 tsp minced shallot
1 tsp chervil
8 bacon strips, cooked, drained
   and hot
4 small bunches watercress (optional)

Dip the liver in milk, dredge in flour, shaking off the excess, and sauté gently in a little butter until done. Arrange on a hot platter and season lightly with salt and pepper. Keep hot. Meanwhile, cook the parsley and tarragon in the butter gently for 3 minutes. Add the lemon juice and simmer 1 minute more. Add the shallot and chervil and simmer 1 minute more, blending well. Pour over the liver, garnish with bacon and watercress and serve hot.

CHICKEN SAUTÉ AUX FINES HERBES
TO SERVE 4

Proceed as for Lamb Sauté aux Fines Herbes. For seasonings, you might try celery leaves, cardamom, coriander and chives in place of the parsley, chervil and tarragon. A little grated lemon and orange rind with anise and tarragon is also interesting. Experiment with your own combinations. If you do, you'll soon *know* what will make a good and unusual combination to enhance any kind of dish.

OYSTERS AUX FINES HERBES
TO SERVE 4

½ lb butter
6 shallots, grated
1 Tbs parsley
2 tsp tarragon
1 Tbs chives

2 Tbs stale bread crumbs
1–2 tsp lemon juice
rock salt
24 oysters on the half shell

Preheat oven to 500°. Blend the butter, shallots, parsley, tarragon, chives, crumbs and lemon juice into a smooth paste. Put a dollop of this paste on each oyster. Line each of 4 baking dishes with rock salt. (The rock salt will hold the oysters erect while cooking and retain the heat when serving.) Place the dishes in the oven for a few minutes to heat well. Put 6 oysters on each baking dish and return the dishes to the oven until the oysters plump up and curl at the edges. Serve at once, hot.

Flamande

(flah-MAHND)

Means Flemish, and applies to the people of Flanders, in western Belgium. Flanders originally applied only to the area around Bruges, Belgium, but in the eighth and ninth centuries it expanded to include the territory from Calais, France, to the southern part of the province of Zeeland in Holland. In the Middle Ages, Flanders was a feudal country divided into two areas, one centering in Bruges, the other in Ghent. Today, these are the capitals of the provinces of West and East Flanders, respectively.

Modern Flanders comprises an area of lowland and dunes along the coast of the North Sea called the polders. These polders are largely reclaimed from the sea and protected by dikes, as in Belgium's northern neighbor Holland. Inland from the polders, Flanders is industrial and agricultural. In World War I part of the polders was flooded to stop the advancing Germans, but in World War II the tables were reversed, as the Germans flooded the entire polders themselves.

In cuisine, Flamande applies to a garnish of braised cabbage, carrots, bacon and potatoes. It also applies to a particular method for preparing asparagus and to a particular kind of *hochepot* (soup). Cooking à la Flamande is similar to the style Alsacienne, among others, in that they both use cabbage in one form or another. Flamande, however, generally uses red cabbage. Flamande is also typified by the use of beer in cooking, rather than wine. This is because wine is not a product of Belgium, as a result of its chilly climate.

Any main-course meat can become a dish à la Flamande by cooking it in beer, with a bit of brown sugar and with a dash of vinegar at the end to add zest. Follow the general procedure under Beef Entrecôtes à la Flamande, substituting the meat of your choice.

For a beverage typical of Belgium, or Flanders, beer would be the logical choice, but there's no rule that says you have to serve a particular beverage just because it's made in the same area as the dish it accompanies. Often they do go well together, but not always. Beer does go well with most foods cooked à la Flamande, however, since it is often an ingredient. If you use a particular wine or beer in cooking a dish, it always makes a fine accompanying beverage.

SAUCE FLAMANDE

This is made by adding Sauce Demi-Glace (Sauce Alsacienne) or veal gravy to the pan used to cook the main-course meat, seasoning to taste, skimming off excess fat and straining. It is served hot with the meat, usually with a little poured over the meat and the rest separately.

FLAMANDE GARNISHES
TO SERVE 4

1. RED CABBAGE A LA FLAMANDE

1 red cabbage, cored and shredded salt and pepper cider vinegar	2 oz butter 3 tart apples, peeled, cored and sliced 1 Tbs brown sugar

Season the cabbage to taste with salt and pepper and a little vinegar. Put it in a casserole or pot and simmer gently with the butter, covered, for an hour. Stir in the apples and sugar and cook about 10 minutes more, until done and tender. Serve hot.

2. CARROTS (or Turnips) À LA FLAMANDE

8 carrots, cut in small, equal pieces ¼ cup water 2 Tbs butter salt and sugar 1 egg yolk	¼ cup heavy cream 1 oz cider 1 Tbs butter, softened lemon juice chives

Blanch the carrots in boiling water for 2 to 3 minutes. Drain. Put in a buttered casserole and add the water and butter. Season to taste with salt and a little sugar. Cover, bring to a boil and simmer until tender. (Shake occasionally to prevent sticking.) Meanwhile, blend the yolk, cream, cider and butter well. When the carrots are done, remove from heat and stir in the yolk mixture. Blend in lemon juice to taste, sprinkle with chives and serve hot.

ASPARAGUS À LA FLAMANDE
TO SERVE 4

1½ lbs asparagus 4 eggs, hard-boiled and halved lengthwise, hot	4 oz butter, melted and hot salt and white pepper

Cook the asparagus in water until done. Serve hot, with individual butter dishes and egg halves. Your guests mash the eggs in their butter with forks, season, then dip their asparagus into the mixture.

CARROT FLAN À LA FLAMANDE
TO SERVE 4

1½ lbs carrots, minced 2 Tbs butter ½ tsp sugar salt and white pepper 1 egg	2 Tbs cream 1 tsp cornstarch 1 baked piecrust* (lightly browned) icing sugar

Preheat oven to 350°. Boil the carrots in water until done with the butter, sugar and salt and pepper to taste. Drain. Beat the egg and cream together, mix in the cornstarch and mix with the carrots. Fill the pastry crust with this carrot mixture and bake in the oven for about 10 minutes. Sprinkle with icing sugar, return to the oven to glaze and serve hot.

BEEF ENTRECÔTES À LA FLAMANDE (Steaks)
TO SERVE 4

4 steaks, or 2 lbs of lean beef chunks, seasoned	2 tsp brown sugar
3 Tbs butter	1 Tbs celery leaves
1 lb milk onions, sliced	1 tsp parsley
3 garlic cloves, crushed	½ tsp basil
salt and pepper	1 bay leaf
1 cup beer	cheesecloth, washed
1 cup beef stock* or broth	2 Tbs cornstarch blended with 2 Tbs cider vinegar

Preheat oven to 350°. Brown the steaks well in hot butter and set aside in a casserole. Brown the onions in the same pan with the garlic, and season to taste with salt and pepper. Put the onion mixture on the steaks in the casserole. Mix the beer and stock, blend in the sugar and pour into the casserole. Add the celery, parsley, basil and bay leaf tied in cheesecloth. Cover and bake in the oven for 1½ hours. Discard the herb bouquet and garlic and put the casserole on direct heat. Slowly add the cornstarch blended with vinegar, a few drops at a time, while stirring the sauce. Cook until thickened (you may not need all of the cornstarch slurry) and serve in the casserole, hot.

CIVET of RABBIT À LA FLAMANDE (Red Wine Stew)
TO SERVE 4

1 rabbit cut in pieces (fresh-killed if possible), with liver and blood reserved	3 Tbs brown sugar
salt and pepper	1 Tbs parsley
butter	1 tsp thyme
2 Tbs flour	1 bay leaf
1 qt dry red wine	cheesecloth, washed
½ cup wine vinegar	4 onions, sliced and lightly sautéed in butter

Season the rabbit pieces with salt and pepper to taste and brown in a pot in butter. Sprinkle with the flour and cook, stirring, for 3 minutes. Add the wine. Add the vinegar and brown sugar. Add the parsley, thyme and bay leaf tied in cheesecloth. Cover and simmer 15 minutes. Add the onions, recover, and finish cooking (about 45 minutes, or until tender). Drain the rabbit pieces and put in a hot bowl. Keep hot. Strain the cooking juices through a sieve, forcing the onions through. Discard the herb bouquet and boil down quickly to thicken lightly. Add the blood and the liver, forced through a sieve, and simmer the sauce for a couple of minutes, stirring. Pour over the rabbit and serve hot.

For an added touch, serve this dish with buttered, heart-shaped bread croutons spread with red currant jelly.

COD À LA FLAMANDE
TO SERVE 4

2 lbs cod, in 8 equal pieces
salt and pepper
1 Tbs chopped shallots
1 Tbs parsley

dry white wine
8 lemon slices, seeded
1 Tbs butter
fresh parsley, chopped (optional)

Preheat oven to 350°. Season the cod with salt and pepper to taste and place in a buttered baking pan, fitting fairly tightly. Sprinkle the fish with the shallots and parsley and add wine to just cover. Place a lemon slice on each piece of fish and bring to a boil over direct heat. Put in the oven for about 12 minutes, or until the fish flakes easily and is done. Arrange the fish on a hot platter. Add the butter to the pan juices and bring to a boil. Strain over the fish, sprinkle with parsley if desired and serve hot.

This is excellent with any white-fleshed fish, especially firm-fleshed fish like haddock or swordfish.

CANAPÉS À LA FLAMANDE
TO SERVE 4

1 cup cottage cheese, drained if too moist
½ cup cooked ham, minced fine
1 Tbs horseradish, drained
¼ cup sour cream
½ cup watercress, chopped
2 Tbs chives
1 tsp onion, grated

salt and red pepper (cayenne)
fresh brown bread, trimmed into 16 rounds
thin mayonnaise (optional)
32 anchovies, split in half lengthwise, washed and dried (to desalt)
16 large capers
16 small lettuce leaves

Mix the cottage cheese, ham, horseradish, sour cream, watercress, chives and onion and season to taste with salt and red pepper. Spread on the bread and coat with a layer of thin mayonnaise, if desired. Put 2 of the split anchovy strips across each canapé, and cross them with 2 more strips. Put a large caper in the box formed by the crossed anchovies and serve on individual lettuce leaves.

HOCHEPOT À LA FLAMANDE (Hotchpotch)
TO SERVE 4–6

10 oz beef brisket	1 tsp salt
10 oz mutton	1 carrot, sliced
1 pig's tail (optional)	1 small onion, sliced
½ lb pig's feet	2 leek whites, sliced (optional)
1 pig's ear (optional)	½ head of cabbage, sliced
¼ lb lean bacon	2 potatoes, sliced
2 qts water	6 chipolata sausages, or small pork sausages

Put all the meats, water and salt in a pot. Bring to a boil and skim. Cover and simmer gently for 2 hours. Check water level occasionally and add a bit if necessary. Add all the vegetables and simmer about 1½ hours more. Add the sausages and simmer until done, about 30 minutes more. Skim off excess fat. Serve the broth of the soup in a hot tureen and the meats and vegetables on a hot platter.

Florentine

(flohr-ahn-TEEN)

From the city of Florence in Italy. It also means a kind of heavy silk fabric, usually with a figured pattern.

Florence is one of the most important artistic centers of the world, in tradition as well as in actual artistic treasures. In Florence we find the great art treasures of the Uffizi, Italy's most important collection. Florence also has more than its share of Gothic churches, and the noteworthy palaces of Corsini, Ferroni, Strozzi and Rucellai. In the old part of town is the original headquarters of the chief constable, the Palazzo del Podesta, with an extensive collection of terra-cottas, paintings, tapestries and sculpture, notably by Michelangelo. Here we also find the remarkable Pitti Palace, which was extensively damaged during World War II. The list is virtually endless.

Florence's local gardens and fields produce such an abundance of flowers that Florence is known as La Citta del Fiore (the city of the flower). The city's emblem is a flower, which also was struck on the Florentine gold coins, hence known as florins.

Florence is noted for artistic crafts, statuettes, art reproductions, gold and silver wares, Florentine mosaics, ornamental glass and pottery, leatherwork, wrought iron, embroidered linen and plaited straw goods. Fashion shows at the Pitti Palace attract buyers from all over Europe and even America. The beautiful city has about a million tourists each year, the greatest number from the United States.

Florence was established as a city in about 200 B.C. Most of the city lies along the north bank of the river Arno, since the south is hilly. It was built in successively expanding walled towns, growing ever larger around the old center. This is still apparent as you travel into the central, oldest section of the city. The closer you get to the old section, the more colorful and medieval the buildings.

Florentine is a distinctive cooking mode. Spinach is its hallmark, and there is no other French mode like it. Virtually anything can be served on a bed of spinach, or placed on a bed of spinach and topped with Sauce Mornay and grated cheese and browned in the oven. If prepared in this manner, it's a dish à la Florentine.

For wine of the Florence area, the name is very familiar: Chianti. Chianti is the red wine of the hills between Florence and Siena. It varies greatly in quality, from a light, coarse-flavored wine (which is what is commonly seen in the stores here) to a fine, smooth, perfumy wine called Reservas, which is second to none in Italy. Reservas, to be at its best, should be aged for seven or eight years in oak casks, and appears on the market not in the familiar round-bottomed Chianti bottle, but in a tall, narrow bottle similar to the ones used for good Bordeaux.

The farmers in this area still cultivate their wine by planting various vines among their olive trees and vegetables patches, using whatever grapes they can get, tossing them, stalks, pips, skins and all, into a barrel and forgetting all about them while they ferment. Of course, this approach doesn't apply to the commercial wines that are exported, but it accents the tremendous variation in different Chianti wines. I wouldn't recommend Chianti as an accompaniment for any but beef dishes, however. For the lighter Florentine dishes, use a strong white, like a full-bodied white Burgundy.

The setting of Florence, with the city on the plain of the river Arno, spreading up into the southern hills which are dotted with beautiful villas, is very atmospheric, especially as the sun sinks toward evening. Let's picture this, with ourselves on a villa's balcony lazily looking out across the old city at twilight. Then bring on the food!

POTATOES À LA FLORENTINE (Stuffed)
TO SERVE 4

4 potatoes, baked and halved lengthwise	salt and pepper
2 cups spinach, chopped	1 cup Sauce Mornay
butter	Parmesan cheese, grated

Preheat oven to 350°. Hollow out the potatoes, leaving about a half inch of pulp around the sides. Mash the removed pulp. Meanwhile, stew the spinach in a little butter until done, drain, and mix with the mashed potato pulp. Season to taste with salt and pepper. Lightly season the insides of the potatoes. Stuff the potatoes with the spinach mixture. Place them on a buttered baking pan, top with the Sauce Mornay, sprinkle with cheese liberally and brown in the oven. Serve hot.

ARTICHOKE HEARTS À LA FLORENTINE (Stuffed)
TO SERVE 4

8 artichoke hearts	salt and pepper
butter	1 cup Sauce Mornay
½ lb spinach, chopped	Parmesan cheese, grated

Preheat oven to 350°. Blanch the artichokes in boiling, lightly salted water for 30 seconds and drain. Simmer in a little butter in a covered pan until tender but not limp. Meanwhile, sauté the spinach in a little butter until limp and done and season to taste with salt and pepper. Drain and use to stuff the artichokes. Arrange the stuffed artichokes on a buttered baking pan, top with the Sauce Mornay and sprinkle liberally with cheese. Brown in the oven and serve hot.

EGGS À LA FLORENTINE (Poached or Soft-Boiled)
TO SERVE 4

1 lb spinach, coarsely chopped	8 eggs, freshly poached or soft-boiled and hot
1 Tbs butter	1 cup Sauce Mornay
salt and pepper	Parmesan cheese, grated

Preheat oven to 450°. Cook the spinach in water until done and drain. Mix in the butter and season to taste with salt and pepper. Put the spinach in a buttered baking dish. Top with the eggs, then the Sauce Mornay. Sprinkle with a liberal amount of cheese and brown in the oven. Serve hot.

OMELET À LA FLORENTINE
TO SERVE 2

4 eggs	2 oz spinach, simmered in butter until done and drained
salt and pepper	3–4 oz thick Sauce Velouté,* hot
4 Tbs butter	

Beat the eggs with salt and pepper to taste. Make the omelet* in very hot butter, filling it with the spinach. Top with the Velouté and serve at once, hot.

This dish may also be prepared omitting the Sauce Velouté. Instead, top with Sauce Mornay and a sprinkling of grated Parmesan cheese and brown quickly in the oven before serving.

BEEF ENTRECÔTES À LA FLORENTINE (Steaks)
TO SERVE 4

4 lean steaks	1 lb spinach, cooked, drained, chopped, seasoned and
salt and pepper (optional)	tossed in a little butter, hot
1 recipe Duchesse Potatoes, hot	

Season the steaks with salt and pepper to taste, if desired, and grill or broil until done to taste. Arrange the spinach on a hot platter, top with the hot steaks, surround with rosettes of Duchesse potato and serve at once, hot.

This dish is often browned quickly under a broiler before serving.

PORK CHOPS À LA FLORENTINE
TO SERVE 4

8 pork chops or steaks
salt and pepper
flour
butter

1½ lbs cooked spinach,
   chopped, seasoned and
   tossed in a little butter, hot
2 egg yolks
1½ cups thick Sauce Béchamel,
   or Sauce Velouté*
Parmesan cheese, grated

Preheat broiler. Season the pork with salt and pepper to taste. Dredge in flour, shaking off the excess. Brown in a little hot butter in a pan, lower heat, cover and simmer gently until done. Arrange on a bed of the spinach in a buttered baking dish. Meanwhile, beat the yolks and blend with Sauce Béchamel. Pour over the pork, sprinkle liberally with cheese and brown under the broiler until the cheese melts and is bubbly. Serve at once, hot.

HAM MOUSSELINE QUENELLES À LA FLORENTINE
(Dumplings)
TO SERVE 4

1½ lbs cooked ham, diced
pepper and grated nutmeg
3 egg whites
heavy cream
2 cups almost simmering
   chicken stock* or broth

1½ lbs cooked spinach,
   chopped, seasoned and
   tossed in a little butter, hot
1½ cups Sauce Allemande
2 oz grated Parmesan cheese

Season the ham to taste with pepper and nutmeg and grind until reduced to a paste. Gradually beat in the egg whites. Blend thoroughly, strain through a fine sieve into a bowl and place the bowl in a larger bowl containing ice water and ice cubes to chill the ham mousseline mixture. Work the mixture with a wooden spoon or your hands, and gradually add cream until the mixture is well moistened. Add as much cream as the mixture will absorb without becoming too soft to make the quenelles. Shape the mousseline mixture into little balls and cook gently in the stock, draining on paper towels as they are finished. Keep hot.

Preheat oven to 500°. Arrange the spinach on a buttered baking dish and top with the ham quenelles. Mix the Sauce Allemande with the cheese and pour over the top. Brown quickly in the oven and serve hot.

CHICKEN SUPRÊMES À LA FLORENTINE
TO SERVE 4

8 whole chicken breasts, halved,
skinned and boned
1 qt veal or chicken stock* or
broth
1 lb cooked spinach, drained
and seasoned

1 cup Sauce Mornay
Parmesan cheese, grated

Preheat oven to 400°. Poach the chicken breasts in the stock until just cooked. Drain. Arrange the spinach on a buttered baking pan. Top with the chicken. Coat with the Sauce Mornay and sprinkle liberally with cheese. Brown in the oven until done and golden and serve hot.

SOLE À LA FLORENTINE
TO SERVE 4

2 lbs sole fillets
lemon juice
salt and pepper
2 oz butter
salt and pepper

1½ lbs spinach, coarsely
chopped
1½ Tbs butter
1 cup Sauce Mornay
Parmesan cheese, grated

Preheat oven to 450°. Season the fish with lemon juice and salt and pepper to taste. Melt the 2 ounces of butter in a pan and cook the fish in it slowly, covered, until done. Meanwhile, cook the spinach in water until done and drain. Season to taste with salt and pepper and stir in the 1½ tablespoons of butter. Spread the spinach in a long baking dish and top carefully with the fish. Pour the Sauce Mornay over the fish, sprinkle with a generous amount of cheese, brown well in the oven and serve in the baking dish, hot.

This dish is excellent for any white-fleshed fish fillets, or even eel.

COD TARTLETS À LA FLORENTINE
TO SERVE 4

½ lb cooked chopped spinach,
drained, seasoned and
tossed in a little butter
4 baked individual tart shells*
2 lbs cooked cod, in chunks
salt and pepper

4 medium-size mushroom caps,
lightly sautéed in butter
1 cup Sauce Mornay
bread crumbs
butter, melted

Preheat oven to 400°. Put the spinach in the bottoms of the pastry shells. Season the cod with salt and pepper to taste and arrange on the spinach. Top with a mushroom cap in each tartlet. Cover with the Sauce Mornay, sprinkle generously with crumbs and a little melted butter to moisten and brown in the oven. Serve hot.

This is also an excellent recipe for any white-fleshed fish, especially firm-fleshed fish like haddock.

SALMON CÔTELETTES À LA FLORENTINE (Cutlets)
TO SERVE 4

4 ½-lb salmon steaks
salt and pepper
1½ cups fish fumet* or half clam
    juice and half dry white wine
1½ cups Sauce Mornay

1 lb spinach, cooked and
    drained, chopped and sea-
    soned
bread crumbs
butter, melted

Halve the salmon steaks by removing the center bones and skins. You will then have 8 cutlet-shaped pieces of salmon called cotelettes. Season the cotelettes with salt and pepper to taste and simmer in the fish fumet until just done but not falling apart. Carefully arrange the cotelettes on a bed of spinach on a hot, oven-proof dish. Top with the Sauce Mornay, sprinkle with crumbs to taste and a little melted butter to moisten and brown in a medium oven. Serve hot.

PIKE QUENELLES À LA FLORENTINE (Dumplings)
TO SERVE 4

Proceed as for Pike Quenelles à la Crème, omitting the croutons and sauce. Then continue as for Sole à la Florentine, using the pike quenelles in place of the sole fillets.

OYSTERS or CLAMS À LA FLORENTINE
TO SERVE 4

24 oysters (or clams), poached
    in their own juice*
24 oyster half shells (bottoms)
1½ cups Sauce Mornay

1 lb chopped spinach, cooked,
    drained, seasoned and
    tossed in butter, hot
Parmesan cheese, grated

Preheat oven to 500°. Divide the spinach among the shell bottoms, making little beds. Place the oysters on these little beds of spinach and top with the Sauce Mornay. Sprinkle generously with cheese. Brown in the oven and serve hot.

SOUP À LA FLORENTINE (Cream of Spinach Soup)
TO SERVE 4

¼ cup onion, sliced thin
1 Tbs butter
1 lb spinach, chopped
3 cups chicken stock* or broth
¼ cup raw rice

salt, pepper and grated nutmeg
3 oz heavy cream
1 egg yolk
lemon juice
1 Tbs butter, softened (optional)

Sauté the onion in the butter until limp but not browned. Stir in the spinach, cover and simmer for 5 minutes, stirring once or twice. Add the stock, bring to a boil, and add the rice. Season to taste with salt, pepper and nutmeg. Simmer, partly covered, for 30 minutes and purée in a blender. Beat the cream and yolk together. Slowly (by drops) blend in some of the purée. Add the yolk mixture to the rest of the purée and blend over low heat without boiling. Add lemon juice to taste and a little butter, if desired. Blend well and serve hot.

Française

(frahn-SEZ)

Means French. So, a dish cooked à la Française is a dish cooked à la French. France is a complex country, in every respect. It's no wonder the food of France is so varied. Even the racial origins of the French are complicated. In France's Central Plateau valleys there are still remnants of prehistoric Cro-Magnon man, who possessed a larger brain than the average modern man. The Celtic types are still prevalent, with round heads and brown hair and eyes, as well as the Germanic peoples, with their longer heads and blond hair and blue eyes, and in the south the Mediterranean types are quite evident, smaller and darker in skin, hair and eyes.

The language is just as complex. While French is the language generally, several patois survive, especially in the southern agricultural districts. About 150,000 Basques speak a language of unknown origin called Euskera. A million Bretons use a Celtic language. Nearly a million Alsatians speak a dialect closely related to German, or German itself. A quarter of a million Corsicans speak an Italian dialect, and Italian itself is spoken in a section of the MaritimeAlps. Around Dunkirk, near the border of Belgium, on the English Channel, a couple of hundred thousand Frenchmen speak Flemish.

In food, Française is a general cooking category, as its name implies, of cooking as the French cook. It is most often distinguished by the use of sliced green olives, pitted or stuffed, as an adjunct to the sauce or gravy. The Française Garnishes are not especially unique, the most individual being the Duchesse Potatoes nests filled with vegetable mirepoix (Garnish #1).

Virtually anything can be cooked following these recipes, and served with Peas or Green Beans à la Française, or Cabbage à la Française, or one or more of the garnishes, plus Française Sauce. Roasts, chops, large cuts, small cuts, any fish served with Sauce Française and some of the vegetables or garnishes listed here becomes a dish à la Française.

The term Française also applies to a food-serving procedure. In the past, serving à la Française was typified by a large selection of dishes at each course. For instance, four or more soups would be placed on the table at once, to be removed when the diners were through. For another course, thirty or more entrées might be served, and so on through all the courses of the dinner. In the mid 1800s this method was gradually replaced by serving à la Russe (ROOss) which had one waiter serve a soup to the guests, another waiter serve the meat course, etc. Obviously this reduced the number of dishes that could be served per course, since four soups or thirty entrées served individually would be unmanageable.

A dish à la Française naturally deserves a good French wine as accompaniment.

For music and décor there's too much to list, and I'm sure you need no help. There are a few special things worth mentioning, however. The fleur-de-lis is usually associated with the royal house of France, which adopted it as its emblem in the twelfth century. The fleur-de-lis is a symbolic representation of the white lily, hence the lily banners, etc. A few of the great composers of French origin are Claude Debussy, Georges Bizet and Maurice Ravel. In art, the French Impressionists come first to mind, but there's much, much more to choose from.

SAUCE FRANÇAISE (for Meats, Eggs or Fowl)
TO MAKE 2 CUPS

Heat 2 cups of Sauce Demi-Glace (Sauce Alsacienne) and add ½ cup of thinly sliced green pitted olives. Serve hot.

SAUCE FRANÇAISE (for Fish)
TO MAKE 2 CUPS

2 cups Sauce Béchamel, preferably based on fish stock*
1 garlic clove, crushed
nutmeg, grated

2 oz mushroom juice (from cooking mushrooms, or canned mushrooms)
2 Tbs butter kneaded with 2 Tbs shredded, cooked pink shellfish

Bring the Béchamel almost to a boil. Add the garlic, a little nutmeg to taste and the mushroom juice. Boil for a few minutes to thicken lightly. Just before serving, stir in the shellfish butter, which will give the sauce a delicate, pinkish color. Serve hot.

Tiny shelled shrimp or crayfish tails and peeled button mushrooms, both cooked, are sometimes added to this sauce.

FRANÇAISE GARNISHES
TO SERVE 4

1. 1½ pounds of Duchesse Potatoes, formed into 4 very thick patties with partly hollowed centers to form cups, spread with melted butter and bread crumbs and deep-fried in hot oil until light golden, drained and filled with a mirepoix of vegetables. Or filled with any vegetables, diced, cooked, lightly seasoned and tossed in a little butter.

2. 1½ pounds of cooked asparagus tips in little bunches, seasoned and dressed with a little butter.

3. 8 tiny lettuces braised in chicken stock,* well seasoned and drained.

4. 1½ pounds cauliflower flowerets, cooked, very lightly seasoned and coated with 1 cup of Hollandaise Sauce (or to taste).

PEAS À LA FRANÇAISE
TO SERVE 4

1½ lbs peas	2 tsp sugar
1 small lettuce heart, shredded	2 oz cold water
8 very small new onions (optional)	1 tsp parsley
	¼ tsp chervil
1 oz butter	cheesecloth, washed
½ tsp salt	

Put everything in a pot, with the parsley and chervil tied in cheesecloth. Bring to a boil. Cover. Lower the heat and simmer gently until tender, about 20 minutes. Discard the herb bouquet, and serve hot.

This is one of the finest possible ways to prepare peas. These peas are usually served in a mound in the center of a hot dish, garnished with the onions and surrounded with the shredded lettuce. Often the lettuce is cut in quarters, rather than shredded, and tied with string to hold together while cooking, and the peas are served in a pile with a lettuce quarter (untied) on four sides of the peas, and the onions between the lettuce quarters.

GREEN BEANS À LA FRANÇAISE
TO SERVE 4

Proceed as for Peas à la Française, using cut green beans in place of the peas.

CABBAGE À LA FRANÇAISE
TO SERVE 4

1 head of cabbage, cleaned and cut in large pieces	1 Tbs chives
2 bacon strips, chopped	salt, pepper and grated nutmeg
3 Tbs onion, grated	½ cup cream, scalded
1 tsp shallot, grated (optional)	

Cook the cabbage for 10 minutes in boiling, lightly salted water. Drain and chop. Cook the bacon gently in a pan with the onion, shallot and chives until lightly browned, stirring constantly. Stir in the cooked cabbage and season to taste with salt, pepper and nutmeg. Add the cream, or as much as is needed to just hold the mixture together. Heat through well and serve hot.

VEAL with OLIVES À LA FRANÇAISE
TO SERVE 4

¼ lb pork sausage meat
¼ lb lean veal, ground
1 tsp parsley
1 tsp celery leaves, minced
1 tsp green pepper, minced fine
1 tsp onion, minced
salt and pepper

4 ham slices
4 veal cutlets, about ¼ lb each,
    pounded thin
1–2 oz butter
2 cups Sauce Espagnole
½ cup Madeira wine
2 lbs Duchesse Potatoes, hot
½ cup pitted green olives, sliced

Brown the pork sausage meat in a pan, stirring to break into the smallest pieces possible. Remove excess fat and add veal, parsley, celery, pepper and onion. Season to taste with salt and pepper and sauté until the meats are cooked. Cool.

Lay the ham slices on the veal cutlets. Top with the cooled ground-meat mixture and roll up, securing with string. Brown in the butter in a pan. Add the Espagnole and Madeira and bring to a boil. Lower the heat and simmer for 3 minutes, then cover and simmer very gentlyfor 1 hour. Serve the rolls on a bed of the hot Duchesse Potatoes, add the sliced olives to the cooking sauce, stir and pour over the veal rolls, or serve separately, hot.

LAMB CUTLETS À LA FRANÇAISE
TO SERVE 4

8 boneless lamb cutlets
salt and pepper
butter
½ lb chicken meat
¼ lb chicken fat

1 egg
salt, pepper and grated nutmeg
2 eggs, beaten
1 oz butter, melted

CROUSTADE

French bread (large loaf)
fat for deep-frying
½ lb lamb's sweetbreads
    (soaked in cold water for 4
    hours and changed often)

¼ lb truffles, sliced
butter

Season the cutlets lightly with salt and pepper and sauté in a little butter until done. Let cool under weights to flatten. Grind the chicken meat with the fat. Mix in the egg and season with salt, pepper and nutmeg to taste. Blend well. Arrange the pressed lamb cutlets on a buttered baking sheet and spread with the chicken mixture. Preheat oven to 350°. Coat the cutlets (spread with the chicken mixture) with the beaten eggs. Bake in the oven for about 15 minutes, or until done, brushing twice with melted butter. Keep hot.

Cut a 2½-inch-thick slice from the loaf of French bread and remove the crust. Dig out all the inside, leaving ¾ inch on the sides and bottom. Deep-fry this cup-shaped bread croustade in very hot fat until golden. Drain. Put this croustade in the center of a hot platter and keep hot. Slice the sweetbreads and remove any central tubes or sinews. Sauté these sweetbread slices in a little butter and drain. Fill the croustade with the sautéed sweetbreads and truffles. Surround with the lamb cutlets and serve hot.

Sauce Française with green olives is often served with this dish.

BEEF FILLETS or BONELESS STEAKS À LA FRANÇAISE
TO SERVE 4

Proceed as for Lamb Cutlets à la Française, using beefsteaks in place of the lamb.

LIVER À LA FRANÇAISE
TO SERVE 4

1 2-lb piece of liver
½ tsp salt
¼ tsp each, ground pepper,
   nutmeg and cinnamon
1–2 oz butter
2 cups beef stock* or broth, hot
1 bay leaf
2 cloves

2 garlic cloves
16 very small white onions
12 whole mushrooms
1 cup celery, in ½-inch diagonal
   slices
1 oz Madeira wine
2 Tbs cornstarch blended with 2
   Tbs Madeira wine
chives

Preheat oven to 350°. Rub the liver with a mixture of the salt, pepper, nutmeg and cinnamon. Brown in the butter in a pan well. Place the browned liver in a buttered baking dish. Add the stock, bay leaf, cloves, garlic, onions, mushrooms, celery and Madeira and cover. Bake in the oven for 1½ hours. Place the liver on a hot platter and surround decoratively with the onions, mushrooms and celery. Keep hot. Strain the cooking liquids and thicken over direct heat with the cornstarch-wine slurry. Pour over the meat and vegetables, sprinkle with chives and serve hot.

Sliced green olives are often added to this sauce.

COFFEE À LA FRANÇAISE (Café Filtre)

Prepare coffee twice as strong as American coffee, preferably in a cone-filter-type drip coffeemaker. Serve black in demitasse cups or with sugar and cream if desired.

This beverage is also served with 1 part hot milk (seasoned with a few grains of salt) to 2 parts of hot coffee, with sugar if desired. This is France's traditional breakfast coffee, and is called Café au Lait (*lait* means milk).

Gauloise

(goh-L'WAZ)

Means Gaulish, old-fashioned. It derives from the Celts, who were called Gauls by the Romans. Gaul was a Roman possession (actually it was known as Gallia), consisting of all of France and Belgium plus parts of Germany, Switzerland and Holland. According to the well-known dictum of Julius Caesar, Gallia was divided into three parts: the land to the southwest below the Garonne River inhabited by the Aquitanians, the land to the northeast above the Marne and Seine rivers inhabited by the Belgae and the remaining area inhabited by the Gauls. These rough divisions were later known as Aquitania, Belgica and Lugdunensis. The long Roman occupation, of about 500 years, resulted in the complete Romanization of Gaul in custom and language. In the latter days of the Roman Empire, Gaul could hardly be distinguished from Italy in its culture.

In cooking, the name Gauloise denotes a particular garnish of sautéed cockscombs and cock's kidneys. Often the dishes will include pickled tongue, mushrooms and truffles. For fish, the garnishes change to carp's milt, artichoke hearts, truffles and crayfish. Either way, it's a conglomeration, and you'll see a lot of variations, depending, apparently, on what different experts think the old Gauls would have considered respectable food. There are other styles that are similar in this respect. Ancienne is most similar in spirit, because it has elaborate garnishes and also connotes the past.

Any light meat, such as sweetbreads, can be used in the chicken aspic recipe in place of the chicken. Any fish can be used in the eel recipe. Also, any meats that are served with sautéed cockscombs and cock's kidneys, truffles and mushrooms are dishes à la Gauloise. Generally, the garnishes are cooked for the final few minutes with the main course and the whole is decorated with small slices of tongue, sometimes pickled tongue.

Sauce is usually made by removing the excess fat from the cooking pan and adding 2 ounces of dry white wine and cooking down while scraping up the juices, then adding 1 to 2 cups of stock. Generally this is cooked down to thicken lightly and is served more as a juice than a thick sauce. If you wish, you can thicken the sauce with a little butter kneaded with an equal amount of flour, or with a slurry of cornstarch blended with cold water added to the cooking stock. The thickening, however, should be light for Gauloise dishes.

To get into the proper spirit for a dish à la Gauloise, you might try thinking like the Romans, because they are the ones the Gauls would have copied. A lavish table would fit. More than one main course might be an idea, served with the appropriate garnishes, of course. Also, bread, cheese, figs and olives would make fitting accompaniments, as they were important in the Roman menu.

CHICKEN ASPIC À LA GAULOISE
TO SERVE 4

4 cups rich chicken stock*
2 envelopes unflavored gelatin
3–4 oz truffles, sliced thin
8 chicken breasts, boned, skinned and sautéed
1 cup Brown Sauce Chaud-Froid

½ lb cockscombs, sautéed
½ lb cock's kidneys, sautéed
½ cup White Sauce Chaud-Froid
½ lb tongue, cooked and cut in oval slices

Cook the chicken stock and gelatin at a low simmer for 5 minutes, until all the gelatin granules are completely melted and blended. Let this aspic cool until half-set. Use the aspic to coat an ornamental mold and chill quickly to set, keeping the rest of the aspic just barely warm so it remains about half-set. Coat again and chill to set again. Place the truffle slices around the aspic lining of the mold decoratively; these will be part of the decoration of the outside of the finished unmolded dish. Coat 4 chicken breasts with Brown Sauce Chaud-Froid and chill to set quickly. Line the bottom of the mold with them. Meanwhile, coat ½ the cockscombs with the Brown Sauce Chaud-Froid and chill to set. Add them to the bottom of the mold between the chicken. Coat them both with aspic liberally. Coat ½ the cock's kidneys with White Chaud-Froid and chill to set. Add them to the mold. Add half the sliced tongue and coat the kidneys and tongue with aspic. Repeat with the remaining ingredients and chill. Unmold on a serving platter. Meanwhile, chill the remaining aspic separately; there should be about 2 cups left. When fully set, chop and pile in a ring around the chicken mold on the platter. Serve chilled.

EEL À LA GAULOISE
TO SERVE 4

1 lb cooked whiting, flaked (or other light-fleshed fish)
¼ lb truffles, diced
4 1-lb eels, whole and cleaned
salt and pepper
1 cup fish fumet* or ½ cup each white wine and clam juice
4 bread slices, trimmed and halved
butter

8 small artichoke hearts
butter
8 oz carp's soft roe (milt)
white pepper (optional)
4 cooked individual pastry shells,* hot
1 lb lobster or crayfish à la Nantua, hot
½ cup Sauce Espagnole

Preheat oven to 350°. Mix the whiting and truffles and season to taste with salt and pepper. Season the eels inside and out lightly. Stuff with the whiting mixture and place in a buttered baking dish. Add the fish fumet and cook, covered, in the oven for about 15 minutes, or until done. Meanwhile, sauté the bread pieces in a little butter until golden on both sides. Drain and arrange on a hot platter. Top with the cooked stuffed eels and keep hot.

Meanwhile, simmer the artichoke hearts in lightly salted water until almost done. Simmer in a little butter for a few minutes to finish the cooking. Cook the carp's milt in a little butter slowly until done and use to stuff the artichoke hearts. Season lightly with white pepper if desired. Fill the pastry shells with the lobster Nantua. Arrange the stuffed artichokes and filled pastry shells around the eel on the platter and keep hot. Quickly reduce the eel cooking liquid to half and add the Espagnole. Continue boiling to thicken lightly and strain over the eel. Serve hot.

Gratin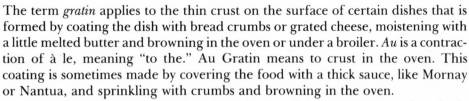

(grah-TEN)

The term *gratin* applies to the thin crust on the surface of certain dishes that is formed by coating the dish with bread crumbs or grated cheese, moistening with a little melted butter and browning in the oven or under a broiler. *Au* is a contraction of à le, meaning "to the." Au Gratin means to crust in the oven. This coating is sometimes made by covering the food with a thick sauce, like Mornay or Nantua, and sprinkling with crumbs and browning in the oven.

A Gratin does not necessarily include the use of cheese. There are three basic variations of Gratin: (1) Bread and/or cheese crumbs sprinkled with melted butter to top a dish to be browned. (2) A thick sauce, such as Mornay, to top the dish to be browned (with or without crumbs and/or cheese and butter). Any meat, fish or vegetable can be browned in one of these two ways for a fine Gratin dish. (3) Fruits poached in syrup, coated with praline, sprinkled with sugar icing and lightly browned, as in the apricot recipe.

This is an excellent way to use leftovers, and the variations you can achieve, using these methods, are endless. Take what leftovers you have and select a combination you think you will like and prepare them au Gratin. If the foods go well together when freshly cooked, they will be just as good as leftovers combined in a Gratin! Generally a Gratin is served right in its baking dish, hot.

MACARONI AU GRATIN
TO SERVE 4

1 lb macaroni, cooked and hot
1 cup Sauce Béchamel, hot
Parmesan cheese, grated

½ cup bread crumbs mixed with
    ½ cup grated Parmesan
    cheese
butter, melted

Preheat oven to 375°. Mix the macaroni and Béchamel and put in a buttered baking dish. Sprinkle with cheese to taste. Top with the cheese-crumb mixture, sprinkle with a little melted butter to moisten and brown in the oven until golden. Serve at once, hot.

POTATOES AU GRATIN
TO SERVE 4

1 recipe Duchesse Potatoes, hot   butter, melted
Parmesan cheese, grated

Preheat oven to 350°. Mix the potatoes with a liberal amount of grated cheese, to taste. Put in a buttered baking dish and smooth the top. Sprinkle generously with more grated cheese and with a little melted butter to moisten, and brown in the oven until golden. Serve at once, hot.

SWEET POTATOES AU GRATIN
TO SERVE 4

Proceed as for Potatoes au Gratin, using Duchesse Potatoes made with sweet potatoes instead of white potatoes.

TURNIPS AU GRATIN
TO SERVE 4

Proceed as for Cauliflower Mornay, using sliced turnips. Many dishes au Gratin are the same as dishes à la Mornay. Any dish that is coated with Sauce Mornay and a sprinkling of crumbs or cheese and browned in the oven can be called either au Gratin or Mornay.

MUSHROOMS AU GRATIN
TO SERVE 4

12 good-sized mushrooms   1 Tbs parsley
salt and pepper (optional)   1 garlic clove, shredded
butter   salt and pepper
6 Tbs bread crumbs   bread crumbs
2 Tbs chopped onion   butter, melted
butter

Separate the stems from the mushroom caps. Season the caps with salt and pepper lightly, if desired, and sauté in a little butter until just done. Preheat oven to 350°. Chop the mushroom stems, mix with the crumbs and onion and sauté in a little butter until the onions are limp. Mix with the parsley and garlic well and season to taste with salt and pepper. Use this mixture to stuff the mushroom caps. Butter a baking dish and set the stuffed mushrooms on it. Top each with bread crumbs generously. Sprinkle on a little melted butter to moisten and bake in the oven until golden brown. Serve at once, in the baking dish, hot.

EGGPLANT AU GRATIN
TO SERVE 4

2 small eggplants
salt
olive oil
1 recipe Duxelles, hot

1 Tbs parsley
salt and pepper
bread crumbs
butter, melted

Cut the eggplants in half lengthwise and sprinkle generously with salt. Let stand for 30 minutes. Wash off well and dry. Preheat oven to 350°. Sauté the eggplant halves until cooked in a little oil, without damaging the skin. Drain and scoop out most of the pulp, leaving the skin intact. Mash the scooped-out pulp with the Duxelles and parsley. Season to taste with salt and pepper. Use this mixture to stuff the eggplant shells. Place them on a buttered baking dish. Sprinkle generously with bread crumbs and with a little melted butter to moisten. Brown in the oven until done and golden. Serve at once, hot.

This dish is often served with Espagnole or Sauce Demi-Glace.

GREEN BEANS AU GRATIN
TO SERVE 4

1½ lbs green beans
2 tsp butter
2 cups cream

salt and pepper
Parmesan cheese, grated
butter, melted

Preheat oven to 350°. Boil the beans in water until about ¾ done. Drain beans and toss in the 2 teaspoons of butter. Put in a pot with the cream and simmer until the cream is reduced by half or more, stirring occasionally. Season lightly with salt and pepper. Butter a baking dish and sprinkle it with a little cheese. Add the beans and cream. Top the beans with grated cheese liberally. Sprinkle with a little melted butter to moisten and brown it in the oven. Serve in the baking dish, hot.

SWEET PEPPERS AU GRATIN
TO SERVE 4

1 cup Sauce Mornay, hot
6–8 sweet peppers
butter
2 Tbs onion, chopped

butter
Parmesan cheese, grated
butter, melted

Preheat oven to 350°. Use ⅓ of the Sauce Mornay to line a baking dish. Quarter the peppers lengthwise and discard the seeds, etc. Sauté in a little butter until done and limp but not browned. Sauté the onion in a little butter and sprinkle in the sauce-lined dish. Add the peppers. Top with the remaining sauce, sprinkle generously with cheese and a little melted butter to moisten and brown in the oven until golden. Serve hot.

CUCUMBERS AU GRATIN
TO SERVE 4

1½ lbs cucumbers, peeled and
    sliced
butter

Parmesan cheese, grated
butter, melted

Preheat oven to 350°. Blanch the cucumber slices in lightly salted, boiling water for 30 seconds and drain. Sauté until limp but not browned in a little butter. Butter a baking dish and sprinkle lightly with cheese. Arrange the cucumber slices on this dish, sprinkle generously with cheese and with a little melted butter to moisten and brown until golden in the oven. Serve in the baking dish, hot.

ENDIVE AU GRATIN
TO SERVE 4

2 heads endive
3 Tbs butter
3 Tbs flour
salt and pepper
⅛ tsp sugar

grated nutmeg
2 cups chicken consommé* or
    broth
1 cup thick Sauce Béchamel*
Parmesan cheese, grated
butter, melted

Preheat oven to 325°. Trim the endive of tough outer leaves and remove the center core, leaving the leaves loose. Wash several times in cold water and squeeze dry. Blanch in boiling, lightly salted water for 10 minutes. Drain, rinse under running cold water, squeeze dry and chop fine. Melt the butter in a casserole and add the flour, blending well without browning. Add the chopped endive and mix. Season with salt and pepper to taste. Add the sugar and a little grated nutmeg to taste. Add the consommé, bring to a boil on the stove, cover and cook in the oven for 1½ hours, adjusting the heat to allow the stock to just simmer gently. When done, drain.

Put the endive in a buttered baking dish and cover with the Sauce Béchamel. Sprinkle generously with cheese, dribble on a little butter to moisten and brown in the oven. Serve in the baking dish, hot.

LEEKS AU GRATIN
TO SERVE 4

Proceed as for Cucumbers au Gratin, using 1½ pounds of leek white parts.

SPINACH AU GRATIN
TO SERVE 4

1½ lbs spinach
2 oz butter
1 cup Parmesan cheese, grated

salt and pepper
Parmesan cheese, grated
butter, melted

Blanch the spinach for 30 seconds in boiling, lightly salted water. Drain, and simmer gently in the 2 ounces of butter until done and tender. Mix in the cheese, off heat. Season to taste with salt and pepper. Preheat oven to 350°. Put the spinach mixture in a buttered baking dish, sprinkle generously with cheese and a little melted butter to moisten and brown until golden in the oven. Serve in the baking dish, hot.

ASPARAGUS AU GRATIN
TO SERVE 4

1½ lbs asparagus spears
salt and pepper
butter

1 cup Sauce Mornay, hot
Parmesan cheese, grated

Cook the asparagus in water until just done and drain. Season very lightly with salt and pepper and toss in just a little butter. Meanwhile, preheat oven to 375°. Put the asparagus in a buttered baking dish. Top with Sauce Mornay and sprinkle liberally with cheese. Brown until golden in the oven and serve hot.

Since asparagus is a delicate vegetable with a very distinctive flavor, bread crumbs are often mixed with the grated cheese in this dish, to make the cheese flavor a little less competitive.

EGGS AU GRATIN
TO SERVE 4

Proceed as for Eggs à la Mornay. This is simply another name for the same dish.

OMELET AU GRATIN
TO SERVE 2

4 eggs
1 oz heavy cream
salt and white pepper
4 Tbs butter

½ cup omelet filling of your
  choice, hot (cooked lobster,
  asparagus, mushrooms, etc.)
Parmesan cheese, grated
butter, melted

Preheat oven to 450°. Beat the eggs and cream and season to taste with salt and white pepper. Prepare an omelet* in hot butter and fill with the hot filling of your choice. Put on a buttered baking pan as soon as it is finished, sprinkle liberally with cheese and a little melted butter to moisten and brown quickly in the oven. Serve at once, hot.

BEEF AU GRATIN
TO SERVE 4

2 lbs boiled or leftover beef,
  diced and hot
salt and pepper
beef stock* or broth (optional)

1 recipe Duchesse Potatoes, hot
grated Parmesan cheese
butter, melted

Preheat oven to 350°. Season the beef to taste with salt and pepper. Moisten with a little stock if desired. Line a large casserole with Duchesse Potatoes on the sides and bottom. Fill the center with the beef. Top liberally with cheese and a little melted butter. Brown in the oven and serve hot, in the casserole.

This casserole can be made in any number of ways, depending on your taste. For instance, line the casserole with sliced, cooked potatoes (like home fries) and fill with sliced beef and mushrooms. The beef can be moistened with a few ounces of Sauce Espagnole cooked with 1 tablespoon of cooked diced ham and seasoned with parsley, chervil and tarragon to taste (this is Sauce Italienne). There are any number of other variations, using whatever potatoes you like with beef cooked in any manner, with or without a little sauce of your choice, then topping with cheese and butter as in the recipe and baking until golden in the oven.

SOLE AU GRATIN
TO SERVE 4

4 Tbs chopped onion
1 Tbs parsley
½ cup dry white wine
1 tsp lemon juice
2 lbs fish fillets, or four ¾-lb
  whole fish, cleaned
salt and pepper
4 Tbs butter, diced
1 cup chopped mushrooms

1 Tbs chopped onion
1 tsp chopped shallot
2 Tbs butter
1 Tbs tomato purée
12 mushroom caps, sautéed in
  butter (optional)
1 cup bread crumbs
butter, melted

Preheat the oven to 450°. Butter a baking dish and line with the 4 table-spoons of onion. Sprinkle with the parsley. Add the wine and lemon juice. Season the fish with salt and pepper and place in the dish. Dot with the diced butter and cook in the oven for 5 minutes. Lower the heat to 350° and carefully remove the fish from the baking dish and keep hot. Put the dish on direct heat and quickly boil down its liquid to ⅓. Meanwhile, sauté the chopped mushrooms, 1 table-spoon onion and shallot in the butter lightly. When the liquids are boiled down to ⅓, mix in the mushrooms, onion, shallot and the tomato purée, making a sauce.

Return the fish to the baking dish and garnish with the sautéed mushroom caps. Spoon the sauce in the baking dish over the fish and mushroom caps.

Sprinkle with the bread crumbs and a little butter to moisten. Cook in the oven for about 25 minutes. If the dish is browning too much, lay a piece of foil loosely across the top for the rest of the cooking time. Serve hot.

This recipe is good for any white-fleshed fish.

SALMON AU GRATIN
TO SERVE 4

1 recipe Duchesse Potatoes, hot	butter
1 cup Sauce Mornay, hot	1 egg, beaten
2 lbs salmon fillets	Parmesan cheese, grated
salt and pepper	butter, melted (optional)

Pipe the potatoes in a ring around a buttered baking dish. Put ¼ cup of the Sauce Mornay in the center of the dish and spread out across the dish's center. Season the fish lightly with salt and pepper and sauté until just done in a little butter, without breaking the fillets. Carefully transfer the fillets to the potato-lined dish and place on the Sauce Mornay in its center. Preheat the oven to 350°. Brush the potato border with the beaten egg. Pour the remaining Sauce Mornay over the fish, top generously with cheese and sprinkle with a little melted butter to moisten if desired. Put in the oven until golden brown and serve in the baking dish, hot.

This is a fine recipe for any fish. Any cooked fish can be placed on a buttered baking dish and topped with the grated cheese of your choice and a little melted butter to moisten and browned in the oven, and you have Fish au Gratin.

FROG'S LEGS AU GRATIN
TO SERVE 4

1 cup Cream Sauce, hot	½ lb mushrooms, cut in thick
2 lbs frog's legs, cleaned	strips
salt and pepper	butter
butter	1 cup bread crumbs
	butter, melted

Preheat oven to 350°. Use ⅓ of the Cream Sauce to coat a baking dish. Season the frog's legs with salt and pepper to taste and sauté in a little butter until done and golden. Arrange on the sauce-coated baking dish and keep hot. Sauté the mushrooms in a little butter and arrange around the frog's legs. Top the frog's legs and mushrooms with the remaining sauce. Sprinkle with the crumbs and a little butter to moisten and brown in the oven. Serve hot, in the baking dish.

LOBSTER or SHRIMP AU GRATIN
TO SERVE 4

4 carrots, sliced
2 onions, sliced
2 bay leaves
2 cups dry white wine
6 cups water
1½ tsp salt
4 1-lb lobsters, or 2 lbs large
   shrimp

¼ cup butter, preferably
   clarified*
2 oz brandy
2 cups Sauce Nantua
salt and pepper
lemon juice
Parmesan cheese, grated

Combine the first 6 stock ingredients and simmer for 30 minutes. Bring the simmering stock to a boil and use to cook the lobsters. When the shells turn bright red, they are done. Drain the lobsters and remove all their meat. Dice the lobster meat. If using shrimp, halve lengthwise and remove the central vein (intestine).

Preheat broiler. Melt the butter in a pan and add the lobster meat or shrimp. Sauté for 5 minutes. Pour on the brandy and flame, stirring until the fire dies. Cook until the brandy is absorbed. Blend in the Sauce Nantua and season with a little salt and pepper if needed. Add lemon juice to taste (½ to 1 teaspoon) and pour into a buttered baking dish. Sprinkle with cheese liberally and brown under the broiler. Serve at once, hot.

This is an excellent company dish, since it can be made ahead except for sprinkling with the cheese and browning, which must be done just before serving.

CRAYFISH TAILS AU GRATIN
TO SERVE 4

Proceed using Crayfish à la Nantua. Put the mixture in a buttered baking dish, sprinkle with grated Parmesan cheese and a little melted butter and brown in a 350° oven. Serve in the baking dish, hot.

SCALLOPS AU GRATIN

1 cup Sauce Duxelles
1 Tbs tomato purée
2 lbs scallops
2 eggs, beaten
bread crumbs
butter

1 cup chopped mushrooms
1 Tbs chopped onion
1 tsp shallot, minced fine
2 Tbs butter
1 cup bread crumbs
butter, melted (more if needed)

Mix the Sauce Duxelles and tomato purée. Preheat oven to 350°. Dip the scallops in the egg and bread crumbs and sauté in a little butter until done. Sauté the mushrooms, onion and shallot in the 2 tablespoons of butter until light golden. Place the mushroom mixture on a baking dish and top with the scallops. Coat with the Sauce Duxelles, sprinkle with the crumbs and a little melted butter to moisten and brown in the oven. Serve in the baking dish, hot.

OYSTERS AU GRATIN (or Clams or Mussels)
TO SERVE 4

2 qts oysters
1 cup Duxelles
1 cup Sauce Duxelles
salt and pepper

bread crumbs
butter, melted
lemon wedges
parsley

Preheat oven to 350°. Shell the oysters, reserving their liquid and the bottom halves of their shells. Line these shell halves with the Duxelles and top with the oysters. Boil the oyster liquid down to 1 or 2 tablespoons and blend with the Sauce Duxelles. Use this sauce to top the oysters. Season to taste with salt and pepper. Sprinkle liberally with bread crumbs and a little melted butter and bake in the oven for about 15 minutes, or until the oysters are done and browned. Serve at once, hot, garnished with lemon wedges and sprinkled with parsley.

Before covering with the sauce and crumbs, the oysters are often topped with a slice of raw truffle or mushroom.

CAVIAR AU GRATIN
TO SERVE 4

2 oz heavy cream blended with a
    scant ½ tsp cornstarch
4 Tbs bread crumbs

1 cup caviar
3 eggs, lightly beaten
3 Tbs chives

Preheat oven to 350°. Heat the cream to thicken lightly, but do not boil. Off heat, stir in the crumbs, caviar, eggs and chives, blending well. Pour into a buttered baking dish, cover with foil and bake in the oven for 20 minutes, or until just cooked through. Remove foil and brown lightly. Serve hot.

APRICOTS or PEACHES AU GRATIN
TO SERVE 4

½ cup sugar
1 tsp vanilla extract
¾ cup almonds, toasted in the
    oven
4 cups apricot halves, poached
    in syrup (1 part sugar to 2
    parts water)

2–3 cooking apples, peeled, cor-
    ed, sliced and stewed in sug-
    ared water (1 part sugar to 4
    parts water)
icing sugar

Preheat oven to 350°. Heat the sugar and vanilla in a pan until melted and lightly browned. Add the toasted almonds and mix well. Cool and pound in a mortar until finely ground. This is a praline. Spread the drained, stewed apples in the bottom of a baking dish and top with the drained, poached apricots. Coat with the praline, thinned with a little apricot poaching syrup. Sprinkle with icing sugar and brown lightly in the oven. Serve hot.

Grecque
(GREK)

Means Greek, or Grecian. Food à la Grecque is food as the Greeks would pre-pare it. As we well know, the culture of Greece is quite old. The ancient Greeks, for the most part, ate simply. A hunk of cheese, some olives, bread, and roasted meat or fried fish were standard, though seldom all at one meal.

Although it seems a contradiction to this simple approach to dining, cooking in ancient Greece was considered an art, and was worthy of mention by Sophocles. Men's clubs were frequently the scene of discussions on the merits of particular foods and cooking, both native and foreign, and most of the foods known to the world today were known and used by the Greeks. While the stan-dard fare was simple, the feasts were elaborate. Traditionally, the priests and cooks were one and the same. They alone knew the proper way to butcher for a sacrificial rite.

As a cooking category, Grecque is another of the Mediterranean styles, using olive oil as a fat, and tomatoes, onions and pimientos as typical ingredients. But Grecque also uses lemon juice, lots of it, and this sets its flavor definitely apart. The most distinctive contribution of this cooking mode, however, is its marinated vegetables, as in the recipe for cucumbers and eggplant. The marinating liquids are sometimes boiled down until they are very zippy and sprinkled over the cucumbers, eggplant or whatever vegetables you have prepared.

You can make beefsteaks following the recipe for Lamb Cotelettes, or use slices of beef fillet and follow the Veal Paupiette recipe.

Greek wines are best known in resinated form, like retsina. The resin flavoring takes some getting used to, but it's not as terrible as certain wine connoisseurs make it. I admit it's not a fine table wine, but I also admit that a fine table wine doesn't have the strength to stand up to a lot of recipes à la Grecque, which retsina does. There are also unresinated wines produced in Greece, of which the sweet muscat of Samos is about the best. The Demestica brand is also fairly well known, and not too bad. As a sidelight, the island of Rhodes is so fertile that three vintages are possible in one year.

Greece matches its unusual resinated wine with some unusual cheeses. Casera, which is also produced in Turkey, is a salty, crumbly goat's milk cheese. Feta, best known of Greek cheeses, is a semisoft cheese made from sheep's milk and stored in brine. It is an excellent hors d'oeuvre cheese, and goes wonderfully with retsina wine and olives, especially Greek olives, if you can get them.

To achieve the proper atmosphere for a dish à la Grecque, you could serve bread, preferably unleavened, torn with the hands rather than cut with a knife. The dishes could be pottery, especially with Grecian designs, if available. Cheese, figs and olives make an interesting and authentic relish. Wine and honey were also popular in old Greece. A greek resinous wine would go very well with the relish. Add some bread dipped in a bit of honey, and you've got appetizers right in character.

GRECQUE SAUCE (for Fish)
TO MAKE 2 CUPS

4 Tbs chopped onion
½ celery heart, chopped
2 Tbs butter
½ tsp fennel seed
½ tsp thyme
½ bay leaf

20 coriander seeds
cheesecloth, washed
1 cup white wine
1 cup Sauce Velouté,* prefera-
    bly fish-based
1 cup cream
4 Tbs butter (optional)

Cook the onion and celery in the butter until limp but not browned. Add the fennel, thyme, bay leaf and coriander tied in cheesecloth. Add the wine and cook down to ¹/₃. Add the Velouté and cream and cook down to ²/₃. Add the butter, if desired, and serve hot, discarding the herb bouquet.

TOMATO FONDUE À LA GRECQUE
TO MAKE 2 CUPS

1 Tbs chopped onion
2 Tbs olive oil
6 tomatoes, peeled,* seeded
    and chopped

2 pimientos, chopped
1 garlic clove, minced fine
salt and paprika

Sauté the onion in the oil until tender but not browned. Add the tomatoes, pimientos and garlic and season to taste with salt and paprika. Cook gently until concentrated into a smooth purée, stirring with a wooden spoon. Use as a tomato sauce.

This fondue with 1 teaspoon of tarragon added becomes Fondue a la Niçoise.

TOMATO SALAD À LA GRECQUE
TO SERVE 4

4 tomatoes, peeled* and cut in
    wedges
olive oil, lemon juice, salt and
    pepper
2 tart apples, peeled, cored and
    sliced
1 green pepper, blanched in
    boiling water for 2–3 min,
    seeded and cut in thin
    julienne strips

1 celery stalk, cut in thin julienne
    strips
2 cups lettuce, shredded fine
4 eggs, hard-boiled and sliced
salt and pepper
mayonnaise, preferably
    homemade*
paprika, parsley and chives

Steep the tomatoes in the oil, lemon juice and salt and pepper to taste for 1 hour and chill. Arrange on a cold platter with the apples, pepper and celery on a bed of the shredded lettuce. Garnish with egg slices. Season. Decorate lavishly with little dollops of mayonnaise, or push the mayonnaise through a pastry bag, making designs, flowerets, etc. Sprinkle with paprika, parsley and chives and serve cold. Serve extra mayonnaise separately.

RICE À LA GRECQUE
TO SERVE 4

1 cup rice
2 Tbs butter
2 cups chicken broth
1 tsp parsley
¼ tsp thyme
¼ bay leaf
cheesecloth, washed
1 small onion, chopped and sautéed in butter, hot

3 Tbs pork sausage meat, cooked, crumbled, drained and hot
¼ cup lettuce, shredded and cooked in a little butter, hot
2 Tbs cooked peas, hot
2 Tbs pimientos, diced, simmered in a little butter, hot

Soak the rice in well-salted water for 1 hour. Drain and cook in the butter for several minutes without browning. Add the broth, and the parsley, thyme and bay leaf tied in cheesecloth. Cook, covered, without disturbing until the rice is done and the liquid is absorbed. Discard the herb bouquet and gently stir in all the other ingredients without breaking them. Serve hot.

VEAL PAUPIETTES À LA GRECQUE (Stuffed Slices)
TO SERVE 4

1½ lbs veal slices
salt and pepper
chervil, tarragon and chives, freshly ground
½ lb thin ham slices (same number as the veal slices)
.1 onion, sliced thin

3 or 4 mushrooms, sliced thin
2 oz wine, preferably Cyprus Rosé, or Madeira
1 cup veal or chicken stock,* or broth
1 tsp lemon juice

Pound the veal to flatten and tenderize. Season lightly with salt and pepper and sprinkle with a little chervil, tarragon and chives. Top each veal slice with a ham slice, roll up and tie with string. Line a heavy, buttered casserole with the onion and mushrooms and pack the paupiettes (rolled stuffed veal) in closely. Cover and put over extremely low heat to sweat the flavors together for 1 hour or more, without actually cooking completely. Add the wine, stock and lemon juice, raise heat slightly, re-cover and simmer about 30 minutes, or until done. Serve hot, in the casserole.

LAMB CÔTELETTES À LA GRECQUE (Cutlets)
TO SERVE 4

4 lamb cutlets	olive oil
½ lb lean veal, cubed	2–3 tsp lemon juice
2 oz chicken liver, cubed	salt and pepper
2 oz chipolata sausage, sliced	¾ tsp marjoram, freshly ground
2 oz lean bacon, cubed	

Sauté the lamb, veal, chicken liver, sausage and bacon separately in a little oil until done and browned. Mix in a pan with the lemon juice, salt and pepper to taste and marjoram and simmer until mixed and heated through. Serve the lamb cotelettes topped with the other meats and pan juices on a hot platter.

Parisienne Potatoes are often an accompaninemt to this dish.

CORNISH GAME HENS À LA GRECQUE
TO SERVE 4

4 1-lb birds	butter
salt and pepper	1 recipe Rice à la Grecque, hot
lemon juice	2 cups game stock* or chicken stock,* or broth

Season the birds inside and out with salt and pepper to taste. Sprinkle 1–2 teaspoons of lemon juice in each bird and truss. Sauté the birds in butter, browning lightly. Cover, lower heat and cook until done and tender. Arrange the birds on a hot platter, untruss and pile the hot rice between them. Keep hot. Add the stock to the bird cooking pot and quickly boil down over high heat, scraping up the juices, until reduced to about ½ cup. Strain over the birds and serve hot. If the birds are fatty, spoon off excess fat before adding the stock to the pot.

This is a fine recipe for any bird, large or small, and very simple. Adjust your cooking time to the size of the bird.

FLOUNDER À LA GRECQUE
TO SERVE 4

2 lbs cooked flounder fillets, hot	1 recipe Sauce Grecque, hot
salt, pepper, lemon juice	

Season the fish with salt, pepper and a little lemon juice to taste. Serve with the sauce spooned over the top, or separately, hot.

This recipe is excellent with any white-fleshed fish.

ARTICHOKES À LA GRECQUE (Pickled)
TO MAKE 4 QUARTS

4 qts water	1 tsp peppercorns
1 qt dry white wine	1 tsp thyme
1 pt olive oil	4 bay leaves
1½ Tbs salt	1 tsp fennel seed
2 celery stalks	cheesecloth, washed
juice of 8 lemons	100 tiny artichokes, trimmed*
1½ Tbs coriander	

Mix the water, wine and oil and add the salt, celery and lemon juice. Tie the coriander, peppercorns, thyme, bay leaves and fennel in cheesecloth and add. Boil for 10 minutes. Add the artichokes and boil 8 minutes more. Discard the celery and herb bouquet and let the artichokes and liquid cool. Put the artichokes and liquid in pint or quart canning jars, filling to ½ inch from the top. Seal and boil for 20 minutes for pints and 30 minutes for quarts. Cool and store. Serve chilled.

CELERY À LA GRECQUE (Pickled)
TO MAKE 4 QUARTS

Proceed as for Pickled Artichokes à la Grecque, using stalks of 6 celery bunches, quartered.

CUCUMBERS À LA GRECQUE
TO SERVE 4

3 or 4 celery leaves	2 cups water
½ tsp fennel seed	1 cup olive oil
½ tsp thyme	juice of 2 lemons
½ bay leaf	salt and pepper
½ tsp coriander	2 cucumbers, peeled and cut in
cheesecloth, washed	½-inch-thick slices

Tie the celery, fennel, thyme, bay leaf and coriander in cheesecloth. Put in a pot with the water, oil, lemon juice and salt and pepper to taste. Bring to a boil. Add the cucumbers and boil for 8 minutes. Let cool and steep in the liquids overnight in the refrigerator. Remove the cucumbers to a dish. Discard the herb bouquet. Boil down the remaining stock to ½, chill and pour over the cucumbers. Serve chilled.

Leeks, onions, cauliflower or celery can be made according to this recipe. Use 2 to 3 cups of thickly sliced leek whites, or very small, bite-size onions, or cauliflower flowerets or celery slices in place of the cucumbers.

EGGPLANT À LA GRECQUE
TO SERVE 4–8

2 tsp coriander	cheesecloth, washed
½ tsp peppercorns	2½ qts water
3 or 4 celery leaves	1 cup olive oil
½ tsp thyme	juice of 5 lemons
½ bay leaf	2 tsp salt
½ tsp fennel seed	2 eggplants, peeled and cut in ¾-inch dice

Tie the coriander, peppercorns, celery, thyme, bay leaf and fennel in cheesecloth. Put in a pot with the water, oil, lemon juice and salt. Bring to a boil. Add the eggplant and boil 12 to 15 minutes. Let cool and steep in the liquids overnight in the refrigerator. Arrange the eggplant on a serving dish and strain a little cooking liquid over the top. Serve chilled.

Mushrooms or zucchini may be made following the eggplant recipe. Use about 6 cups of button mushrooms, or zucchini cut in ¾-inch dice, in place of the eggplant.

Hollandaise

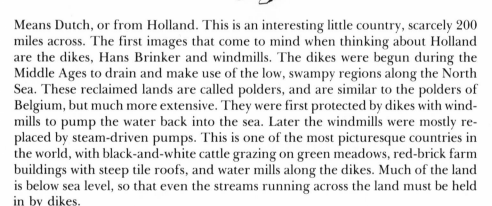

(oh-lahn-DEZ)

Means Dutch, or from Holland. This is an interesting little country, scarcely 200 miles across. The first images that come to mind when thinking about Holland are the dikes, Hans Brinker and windmills. The dikes were begun during the Middle Ages to drain and make use of the low, swampy regions along the North Sea. These reclaimed lands are called polders, and are similar to the polders of Belgium, but much more extensive. They were first protected by dikes with windmills to pump the water back into the sea. Later the windmills were mostly replaced by steam-driven pumps. This is one of the most picturesque countries in the world, with black-and-white cattle grazing on green meadows, red-brick farm buildings with steep tile roofs, and water mills along the dikes. Much of the land is below sea level, so that even the streams running across the land must be held in by dikes.

As a cooking category, Hollandaise revolves around the use of Hollandaise Sauce. It is not very similar to any other category, and Hollandaise Sauce itself is unique. Although the sauce is usually a topping for eggs, fish or vegetables, it is also good with meats, like veal, sweetbreads, pork and even steaks, though you'll seldom see recipes for steak with Hollandaise Sauce! If you like steak and you like Hollandaise Sauce, however, try a grilled steak with Hollandaise Sauce. I guarantee you'll approve.

In the fish recipes any fish may be used, as is typical of most fish recipes.

Generally, Potatoes à l'Anglaise (boiled, seasoned and dressed with butter) are served with dishes à la Hollandaise, but don't feel limited. Parisienne Potatoes are also good, as well as any simply prepared vegetables. The only thing to watch out for is unusually heavy, spicy or vinegary accompaniments that would detract from the rich but delicate flavor of the Hollandaise Sauce.

Anyone who enjoys cheese is probably familiar with the round, red-coated Edam cheeses, as delightful to the eye as they are to the palate. Also from Holland come two unusual cheeses, Komijnikaas, spiced with cumin and anise seeds, and Leden, a spicy, semifirm cheese streaked with green due to cumin seeds having been added to the curds.

For décor, Holland is a snap: tulips in a wooden shoe! Also, Delft porcelain, bright red Edam cheeses and a blue-and-white checkered tablecloth. Since the Dutch are so neat and clean that they actually are known to scrub their streets by hand, the décor should probably reflect this simple, clean feeling. A cluttered table just wouldn't fit.

HOLLANDAISE SAUCE
TO MAKE 1¾ cups

1 Tbs water	¼ tsp white pepper
1 Tbs lemon juice	3 egg yolks
¼ tsp salt	¾ cup butter, melted but cool

Mix the water, lemon juice, salt and pepper. Beat the yolks in a saucepan off heat until thick. Whisk in the lemon juice mixture. Set over very low heat (if too hot, the yolks will curdle) and whisk until very thick. Remove from heat and whisk in the butter a bit at a time. Serve just barely warm, with eggs, fish or vegetables.

It's important to beat in the yolks over a very low heat. If the heat is too high, the yolks will become granular or even scrambled. Often the yolks are beaten in over hot water in a double boiler to eliminate this possibility. When the yolks are well beaten, the butter must be added a bit at a time so that the yolks can absorb each bit completely before more is added.

HOLLANDAISE VARIATIONS

ANCHOVY HOLLANDAISE

Add 2 to 4 teaspoons of anchovy paste and omit the salt from the recipe. Use with fish, especially salmon.

CAPER HOLLANDAISE

Add 2 to 4 ounces of drained capers to the sauce. Very good with fish and light meats.

MUSTARD HOLLANDAISE

Add 4 to 6 teaspoons of Dijon mustard, or to taste. Fine with eggs, fish and light meats, especially when breaded and sautéed or deep-fried.

ORANGE HOLLANDAISE

Use 1 to 2 ounces of orange juice in place of the water, plus the grated rind of 1 or 2 oranges. A different taste with vegetables, especially broccoli and asparagus. This is also called Maltaise Sauce, and is sometimes flavored with a few drops of Curaçao.

SAUCE CHANTILLY (Sauce Mousseline)

Mix 1 part whipped cream to 2 or 3 parts of Hollandaise Sauce. Use for fish, eggs and asparagus.

BLENDER HOLLANDAISE SAUCE
TO MAKE 1¾ CUPS

4 egg yolks	¾ cup butter, melted but cool
1 Tbs lemon juice	white pepper
1 Tbs warm water	

Put the yolks, lemon juice and water in a blender and blend at medium speed for a few seconds. Turn the blender on high and add ½ the melted butter in a slow stream, then the rest of the butter all at once. Season with a little white pepper and blend briefly. Serve just barely warm. Can be used for eggs, fish or vegetables.

VEGETABLES À LA HOLLANDAISE
TO SERVE 4

Use 1½ pounds of peas, celery, asparagus, Swiss chard, broccoli, Brussels sprouts or cauliflower, or 1½ pounds of a combination of vegetables. Boil until tender in water, drain well and season very lightly with salt and white pepper. Serve in a warm bowl topped with 1 cup of just slightly warm Hollandaise Sauce.

ARTICHOKE HEARTS À LA HOLLANDAISE
TO SERVE 4

½ tsp lemon juice	¼ bay leaf
1 onion, sliced	2 peppercorns
1 carrot, sliced	cheesecloth, washed
1 tsp parsley	1½ lbs artichoke hearts
¼ tsp thyme	1 cup Hollandaise Sauce, just barely warm

To 1 quart of lightly salted water, add the lemon juice, onion and carrot. Add the parsley, thyme, bay leaf and peppercorns tied in cheesecloth. Bring to a boil and cook for 20 minutes. Strain, bring back to a boil and add the artichokes. Simmer for about 10 minutes, or until done and tender but not overcooked. Drain the artichokes well and put in a warm bowl. Top with the Hollandaise Sauce and serve.

LETTUCE À LA HOLLANDAISE
TO SERVE 4

Proceed as for Artichokes à la Hollandaise, using 2 small lettuce heads, halved lengthwise and cleaned. Serve each ½ head, after squeezing dry, on a piece of bread sautéed in butter and drained, and top with Hollandaise Sauce.

EGGS HOLLANDAISE (Steamed)
TO SERVE 4

Edam cheese, grated
4 oz lean ham, diced
8 eggs, beaten

1 Tbs chives
½ tsp basil
1 cup Tomato Sauce, preferably
    homemade,* hot

Preheat oven to 350°. Butter a baking dish and coat with some of the grated Edam cheese. Line the bottom with ½ the ham. Pour in the beaten eggs, sprinkle with chives and basil, top with the rest of the ham and sprinkle liberally with more of the grated cheese. Set in a pan of hot water and steam in the oven for about 15 minutes, covered. Test with a cake tester. As soon as it slides in and out clean, the eggs are done. Do not overcook. Serve at once, with the Tomato Sauce served separately, hot.

EGGS BENEDICT
TO SERVE 4

4 slices of bread, trimmed,
    halved diagonally, sautéed
    in a little butter until golden
    and drained
8 slices of cooked ham, cut to
    the shape of the bread and
    lightly sautéed in butter

8 eggs, freshly poached and hot
1½ cups Hollandaise Sauce,
    just warm
parsley sprigs, or chives

Arrange 2 pieces of bread (sautéed bread or English muffins, for variation) on each of 4 hot plates. Top each with a slice of ham and a poached egg. Top with Hollandaise Sauce, decorate with sprigs of parsley or a sprinkling of chives and serve at once.

SALMON STEAKS À LA HOLLANDAISE
TO SERVE 4

3 carrots, sliced
2 onions, sliced
1 celery stalk, sliced
1 bay leaf
1 tsp parsley
¼ tsp thyme
1½ cups dry white wine
3 cups water

1 tsp salt
4 peppercorns
large cheesecloth, washed
4 salmon steaks
1½ cups Hollandaise Sauce,
    just barely warm
chives (optional)

Put all the ingredients down to the cheesecloth in a pot and simmer for 30 minutes. Strain. This is a court bouillon. Put the cheesecloth in a pan so that it covers the bottom and hangs out at either side. Arrange the salmon steaks on the cheesecloth, add the court bouillon, bring to a simmer and cook 20 minutes, or until the salmon is just done. Use the cheesecloth to remove the fish from the pan without breaking the pieces. Arrange on a hot platter and serve topped with dollops of Hollandaise Sauce. Sprinkle with chives if desired and serve at room temperature or chilled.

STUFFED TROUT À LA HOLLANDAISE
TO SERVE 4

4 1-lb trout, whole and cleaned
salt and pepper
1 cup bread crumbs
hot milk (about 1 oz)
2 eggs, beaten
½ cup chopped spinach
1 tsp parsley
½ tsp chervil
¼ tsp tarragon
2 shallots, minced
2 cups dry white wine

1 bay leaf
1 tsp parsley
¼ tsp thyme
¼ tsp rosemary
6 peppercorns
cheesecloth, washed
1½ cups Hollandaise Sauce,
    just barely warm
chives
parsley sprigs

Preheat oven to 350°. Season the fish lightly inside and out with salt and pepper. Moisten the crumbs with the milk and combine with the eggs, spinach, parsley, chervil, tarragon and shallots. Mix well and use to stuff the fish. Tie or sew closed. Place the stuffed trout in a buttered baking dish. Add the wine. Add the bay leaf, parsley, thyme, rosemary and peppercorns tied in cheesecloth. Bring to a simmer over direct heat and put in the oven to bake for 20 minutes, or until the fish flakes easily with a fork and is done. Baste occasionally with the pan juices.

Arrange the cooked fish on a hot platter and keep hot. Discard the herb bouquet. Reduce the cooking juices over high, direct heat to ½ cup. Strain over the fish, decorate with dollops of Hollandaise Sauce, sprinkle with chives and garnish with parsley sprigs. Serve at once, hot.

LOBSTER À LA HOLLANDAISE
TO SERVE 4

4 carrots, sliced
2 onions, sliced
1 bay leaf
10 cups water
1 tsp salt
6 peppercorns

4 1–1½ lb lobsters, preferably live
2 lbs Potatoes à l'Anglaise, hot
large parsley sprigs
1½ cups Hollandaise Sauce,
    just barely warm

Put the first 6 ingredients in a pot, simmer for 30 minutes and strain, to make a court bouillon. Bring the court bouillon to a boil and use to cook the lobsters until bright red and done. Drain. Split in half lengthwise and remove the gritty sac in the head, the intestinal tube and the lungs (stringy, fingerlike sacs in the body). Arrange the lobsters, cut side up, on a hot platter and surround with piles of Potatoes Anglaise. Garnish with parsley sprigs. Put dollops of Hollandaise Sauce on the lobsters and serve hot. If you have not cracked the claws, have tools such as nutcrackers available at the table.

CANAPÉS À LA HOLLANDAISE
TO SERVE 4

8 slices of bread, trimmed, light-
    ly toasted and quartered
3 oz thick Sauce Béchamel
1 oz canned herring fillets,
    washed of salt and dried

32 small strips of anchovy fillet
8 egg yolks, hard-boiled and
    quartered
parsley or watercress sprigs

Blend the Béchamel with the herring into a smooth purée. Spread this purée on the bread pieces. Arrange a strip of anchovy and a yolk quarter on each bread piece, and serve the canapés garnished with sprigs of parsley or watercress.

Hongroise
(ohn-GRWAZ)

Means Hungarian. Hungary, like its food, is a spicy and rich blend of many cultures. Since it lies in the great Alpine depression (once an inland sea, now filled in with the mud and clay of rivers), it was a natural invasion route between the Carpathians, Alps and Dinaric mountains. Mountainous Austria is to the west, Rumania to the east, Yugoslavia to the south and Czechoslovakia to the north. Hungary has always been the easiest route for any invader to use to get from any of these areas to another, and has been invaded successively by the Germans, Huns, Avars and Slavs.

In the sixteenth century the Hungarians were host to the Turks, who introduced the natives to coffee and, more importantly, to paprika. Paprika is now associated more with Hungarian cooking than with Turkish.

The Hungarian cuisine is characterized by the liberal use of cream and paprika. Any category of this importance and scope is naturally rife with variations on the main theme, which generally is food cooked with sautéed onions and tomatoes in a little stock, flavored with paprika. The cooking juices are then mixed with some sour cream and thickened for a sauce.

In the meat dishes (such as the Beef Goulash), celery, carrots and a little garlic are often used instead of the potatoes. Red and green peppers, shredded, are sometimes added. In dishes with lighter meats, such as chicken, slices of green cooking apples are often found, along with celery, peppers and even a few juniper berries on occasion. Tomato paste is often substituted for tomatoes. Garlic and tarragon add interest to Potatoes à la Hongroise. Basil and garlic are also favorite additions to the potato recipe. When using garlic with an herb, like basil, it's generally a good idea to chop or grind them together. It brings out the best flavors of both.

Hongroise dishes made with sweet cream in place of the usual sour cream are called dishes à l'Archiduc (ahr-shee-DEWK), meaning archduke, formerly a prince of the royal family in Austria.

For the wines of Hungary, Tokay is definitely the finest wine made in Eastern Europe today. The best is sweet, fairly old, expensive and known as Aszu. Hungary produces a rosé with a light and refreshing character and a pale tangerine color. The red wines of Hungary are not in the same class with its Tokay, but are acceptable. They are made from the Kadarka grape, and the best Hungarian red wines usually use its name, as in the wine called Nemes Karar, which is exported and available.

Among Hungarian cheeses, Szekeley and Brindza are well worth a mention. Szekeley is a soft sheep cheese in an interesting package, sheep's bladders, and is sometimes smoked. Brindza is made with either sheep's milk or goat's milk, and is sometimes stored in brine and pressed between layers of pine bark, which gives it a resinous flavor.

The national peasant costume is very colorful, and you might turn to this for ideas for décor. Traditionally, the women wore scarves, and many patterns and colors are often evident in a single costume. Hungarian music, whether classical or peasant, is very lively. Brahms, though a German, wrote four books of Hungarian Dances, taken from actual Hungarian tunes that were introduced to Brahms by the violinist Eduarde Reményi. Liszt, a Hungarian-born composer, has been called the most important germinative force in modern music. Perhaps his best-known single piece is the "Second Hungarian Rhapsody."

SAUCE HONGROISE (for Meats and Eggs)
TO MAKE 2 CUPS

6 Tbs chopped onion
butter
1 tsp paprika (more or less as
   desired)
¼ tsp salt
1 cup dry white wine

2 tsp parsley
½ tsp thyme
½ bay leaf
cheesecloth, washed
1½ cups Sauce Velouté*
3–4 Tbs butter (optional)

Sauté the onions in a little butter until limp but not browned. Add the paprika, salt and wine. Add the parsley, thyme and bay leaf, tied in cheesecloth. Boil down to ⅓. Discard the herb bouquet and add the Velouté. Simmer for 5 minutes. Stir in the butter, if desired, and serve hot.

HONGROISE GARNISHES
TO SERVE 4

1. CAULIFLOWER À LA HONGROISE

2 lbs cauliflower flowerets,
   cooked, drained and hot
1 cup Sauce Mornay, hot

paprika
bread crumbs moistened with a
   little melted butter

Preheat oven to 375°. Arrange the cauliflower on a baking dish and coat with the Sauce Mornay. Season to taste with paprika and sprinkle lightly with crumbs. Brown in the oven until golden and serve hot.

2. POTATOES AND CAULIFLOWER À LA HONGROISE

2 lbs Duchesse Potatoes, hot
1 lb cauliflower flowerets,
   cooked, drained and hot

1 cup Sauce Mornay, hot
2 Tbs onion, minced, sautéed
   and seasoned with paprika

Arrange the Duchesse Potatoes on a hot platter in a border of rosettes. Fill the center with the cauliflower. Coat the cauliflower with the Sauce Mornay mixed with the seasoned onion and serve hot. This may be run under the broiler to brown very lightly just before serving.

POTATOES À LA HONGROISE
TO SERVE 4

2 onions, chopped
butter
1 tsp paprika
2 tomatoes, peeled,* seeded
   and chopped
2 lbs potatoes, sliced thin

salt
1 qt unsalted beef stock* or
   broth (if salted, omit preced-
   ing salt)
parsley and/or chives

Sauté the onions in a little butter in a casserole until limp. Add the paprika and stir. Add the tomatoes and stir. Add the potatoes and season with salt if using unsalted stock. Add stock to just cover and simmer until done, uncovered (about 30 minutes). Sprinkle with parsley and/or chives and serve hot, in the casserole.

LENTILS À LA HONGROISE
TO SERVE 4

½ lb lentils, soaked overnight in
   cold water
1 onion, minced
1 oz bacon fat
2 Tbs flour

¼ cup cold water
1 Tbs sugar
1 tsp salt
1 tsp paprika
1 oz cider vinegar

Simmer the lentils in fresh water until tender and drain. Meanwhile, sauté the onion in the bacon fat. Blend in the flour well. Blend in the water, sugar, salt, paprika and vinegar. Cook for a few minutes until smooth. Spoon over the lentils and serve hot.

These lentils are often served on sautéed bread croutons, or small toast squares.

TURNIPS À LA HONGROISE
TO SERVE 4

2 lbs turnips, cut in pieces
½ tsp caraway seeds
boiling, lightly salted water
   (about 1 qt)
½ cup sour cream, scalded and
   hot

salt and red pepper (cayenne)
½ tsp basil, powdered
1 tsp lemon rind, grated
¼ cup bread crumbs
melted butter

Preheat oven to 400°. Put the turnips in a pan with the caraway seeds and enough boiling water to just cover, and boil gently for 20 minutes, or until tender. Drain and put in a buttered casserole. Season the hot sour cream with salt and a little red pepper, and add the basil and lemon rind. Mix well and pour over the turnips. Sprinkle with the crumbs and a few drops of melted butter to moisten, and brown in the oven for about 10 minutes, until golden. Serve hot, in the casserole.

DUMPLINGS À LA HONGROISE
TO SERVE 4

1 lb flour
½ tsp salt
1 egg

cold water
1 Tbs bacon drippings
2 cups chicken stock* or broth

Mix the flour and salt, and make into a pile with a little hollow in the center. Break the egg into this hollow and slowly combine with the flour, adding cold water (as little as possible) to make a stiff paste. Knead well and roll into little balls, ½ inch in diameter. Spread these balls out to dry. Heat the drippings in a pan until lightly browned. Add the stock and bring to a boil. Simmer the dumplings in this stock for 4 to 5 minutes and serve hot with any stew.

These simple dumplings may be kept for several days after drying.

CABBAGE À LA HONGROISE (Stuffed)
TO SERVE 4

1 head green cabbage, core removed	salt, pepper and paprika
2 lbs potatoes	¼ tsp ground bay leaf
1 onion, grated	⅛ tsp grated nutmeg
salt, pepper and grated nutmeg	1 Tbs parsley
½ cup cooked rice	1 garlic clove, minced
2 oz butter, softened	¾ cup chicken stock* or broth
2 onions, sliced thin	1 cup sour cream, scalded and hot

Cook the cabbage in a tightly covered pot with 1 cup of water until tender. Drain and separate the leaves. Grate the potatoes, drain and mix with the grated onion. Season to taste with salt, pepper and nutmeg. Mix well with the rice and butter and use to stuff the cabbage leaves. Stuff about 20 cabbage leaves with the mixture, and chop the remaining cabbage. If necessary, tie the cabbage rolls with string.

Preheat oven to 350°. Line a buttered casserole (with a very tight-fitting cover) with the sliced onion. Sprinkle the chopped cabbage on top of the onion and season lightly with salt, pepper and paprika. Add the bay leaf, cloves, parsley and garlic, sprinkling over the cabbage in the casserole. Arrange the stuffed cabbage leaves on this bed and add the stock. Bring to a simmer, cover tightly and bake in the oven for 40 minutes, or until tender. Uncover, pour on the hot sour cream, and serve in the casserole, hot.

ASPARAGUS À LA HONGROISE
TO SERVE 4

1½ lbs asparagus tips, cooked in water and seasoned lightly with salt and white pepper	1 oz butter, melted
	2 oz sour cream, hot
	bread crumbs

Preheat oven to 425°. Put the cooked asparagus in a buttered baking dish and sprinkle with a little of the melted butter. Coat with sour cream, sprinkle lightly with bread crumbs and dribble on the rest of the butter. Bake in the oven for about 10 minutes, until golden, and serve hot, in the baking dish.

MUSHROOMS À LA HONGROISE
TO SERVE 4

3 oz onion, chopped
butter
1½ lbs small mushrooms

salt and paprika
1 cup sour cream

Sauté the onions in a little butter until limp. Add the mushrooms and sauté gently until done. Season lightly with salt and with paprika to taste. Add the cream and cook down to thicken. Serve hot.

OMELET À LA HONGROISE
TO SERVE 2

4 eggs
salt
2 oz ham, diced
butter

2 oz minced onion
paprika
4 Tbs butter
½ cup Sauce Hongroise, hot

Beat the eggs with salt to taste. Sauté the ham in a little butter. Add the onions and sauté until limp. Season with paprika to taste. Cook the omelet* in very hot butter and fill with the ham and onion mixture. Serve with the Sauce Hongroise, hot.

BEEF ENTRECÔTES À LA HONGROISE (Steaks)
TO SERVE 4

4 steaks
salt and paprika
butter
4 Tbs onion, chopped
butter

salt and paprika
½ cup white wine
½ cup Sauce Velouté* or
    Sauce Béchamel
paprika

Season the steaks with salt and a generous amount of paprika. Sauté in a little butter until about ¾ done. Meanwhile, sauté the onion lightly in a little butter and season lightly with salt and paprika. Add to the steak pan and finish cooking them together. Remove the steaks from the pan and keep hot. Add the wine and boil down, scraping up the juices. Lower the heat and add the Velouté. Blend well, add paprika if needed, pour over the steaks and serve hot.

Boiled potatoes are a standard accompaniment for this dish.

BEEF CUBES À LA HONGROISE
TO SERVE 4

Proceed as for Beef Entrecôtes à la Hongroise, using 2 to 3 pounds of beef in 1½-inch cubes.

BEEF GOULASH À LA HONGROISE
TO SERVE 4

2–3 Tbs lard
½ lb onions, in large dice
1 garlic clove, minced
2–3 lbs lean beef, in 1½-inch
   pieces
salt

¼ tsp marjoram
1 tsp paprika
1 lb tomatoes, peeled,* seeded
   and diced
1 cup water
3 medium potatoes, quartered

Melt the lard and sauté the onions and garlic in it until limp. Add the beef and brown. Season to taste with salt. Add the marjoram and paprika and blend well. Add the tomatoes and water and bring to a boil. Lower heat, cover and simmer gently for 1½ hours. Add the potatoes and a little more water if needed. Simmer for another hour, or until done, and serve hot.

BEEF PAUPIETTES (Stuffed Slices) À LA HONGROISE
TO SERVE 4

¼ lb lean veal, ground
¼ lb pork fat, ground
½ tsp salt
¼ tsp pepper
⅛ tsp ground mace
⅛ tsp grated nutmeg
⅛ tsp ground cloves
⅛ tsp ground cinnamon
⅛ tsp ground bay leaf
⅛ tsp ground sage
⅛ tsp ground marjoram
⅛ tsp ground rosemary
2 oz minced onions, sautéed in
   butter
8 large beef slices, ¼-inch thick,
   seasoned lightly

2 onions, sliced and lightly
   sautéed
salt and paprika
1 cup dry white wine
2 cups Sauce Velouté*
1 tsp parsley
¼ tsp thyme
¼ bay leaf
cheesecloth, washed
20 button mushrooms, lightly
   sautéed in butter
½ cup cream
8 bread slices trimmed into
   ovals
butter

Blend the ground meats, seasonings and minced onions together well and spread on the beef slices. Roll up into paupiettes and secure with string. Brown the paupiettes lightly in butter, if desired. Spread the sliced onion in the bottom of a pan and place the beef paupiettes on this bed. Season lightly with salt and liberally with paprika to taste. Simmer slowly, covered, for 10 minutes. Add the wine and boil down to ½, uncovered. Add the Velouté. Tie the parsley, thyme and bay leaf in cheesecloth and shove this herb bouquet down between the paupiettes. Bring to a boil, cover and simmer very gently over lower heat for 1½ hours. Baste frequently.

Remove the paupiettes and sauce, clean the pan quickly, return the paupiettes and strain the sauce back into the pan over the paupiettes. Add the mushrooms and simmer for 15 minutes more. Add the cream and cook uncovered to thicken. Sauté the bread in a little butter until golden on both sides and drain. Arrange on a hot platter and top each bread slice with a beef paupiette, untrussed. Cover with sauce and mushrooms and serve hot.

BEEF HASH À LA HONGROISE
TO SERVE 4

2 lbs roast beef, diced   1 cup Sauce Hongroise

Heat the beef in the sauce until thickened and serve hot.

VEAL STEW À LA HONGROISE
TO SERVE 4

4 onions, sliced thin
2–3 Tbs lard, or butter
2 tsp paprika
2 lbs lean veal, in pieces
salt and pepper
½ cup hot water
3 tomatoes, peeled,* seeded and chopped

3 green peppers, seeded, cleaned and sliced thin
1 cup mushrooms, sliced
1 cup sour cream, scalded and hot

Brown the onions in the lard and season with the paprika. Add the veal, season lightly with salt and pepper, add the hot water, cover and simmer for 30 minutes. Add the tomatoes, peppers and mushrooms and cook, covered, for 30 minutes more. Stir in the hot sour cream and serve hot.

This dish is generally served with noodles. It can be made with any number of different meats substituted for the veal. Pork, lamb, chicken, duck livers, etc., all make fine dishes. Combinations are good also, such as half veal and half chicken.

MUTTON CHOPS À LA HONGROISE
TO SERVE 4

4–8 mutton chops or cutlets, depending on size
salt and paprika
butter
4 Tbs chopped onion
2 lbs potatoes, in thick slices, boiled and hot

butter
½ cup dry white wine
2 cups heavy cream
2 Tbs butter (optional)
paprika

Season the mutton with a little salt and a generous amount of paprika. Sauté in a little butter until about ¾ done. Discard excess fat, if any. Meanwhile, sauté the onion lightly in a little butter and season lightly with salt and paprika. Add to the mutton pan and finish cooking together. Remove the chops from the pan and keep hot. Toss the cooked potato slices in a little butter and keep hot (season with a little salt and white pepper if desired). Pour the wine into the mutton pan and boil down to ¼, scraping up the cooking juices. Add the cream and simmer until quite thick. Stir in the 2 tablespoons of butter, if desired, and add paprika to taste if needed. Arrange the mutton around the outside of a hot platter, fill the center with the potatoes, pour the sauce over the meat and serve hot.

VEAL CHOPS À LA HONGROISE
TO SERVE 4

Proceed as for Mutton Chops à la Hongroise, using veal in place of the mutton.

HAM MOUSSELINE QUENELLES À LA HONGROISE
(Dumplings)
TO SERVE 4

Proceed as for Ham Mousseline Quenelles à la Florentine, seasoning the quenelle mixture with paprika to taste and eliminating the spinach, Sauce Allemande and grated cheese. Arrange the cooked quenelles in a circle on a hot platter (oven-proof) and cover them with 1 cup of Hongroise Sauce. Fill the center of the platter with hot cauliflower (Hongroise Garnish #1). Brown lightly in a hot oven and serve at once.

CHICKEN À LA HONGROISE
TO SERVE 4

2 small chickens (2–2½ lbs)	butter
salt and pepper	2 oz dry white wine
3 cups rice, ¾ cooked	2 cups Sauce Hongroise
paprika	

Preheat oven to 375°. Season the birds inside and out lightly with salt and pepper. Season the rice with paprika to taste and use to stuff the birds. Sew or skewer closed and truss. Brown in butter in a pot, cover and bake in the oven for 1½ hours, or until done. Put the chickens on a hot platter and untruss. Keep hot. Discard excess fat from the pot, if any. Add the wine to the pot and quickly boil down, scraping up the juices. Add the Sauce Hongroise and bring quickly to a boil. Strain into a hot sauceboat and serve with the chickens, hot.

FLOUNDER À LA HONGROISE
TO SERVE 4

2 lbs fish fillets	½ cup fish fumet* or ¼ cup each
salt and paprika	clam juice and white wine
4 oz chopped onion	4 bread slices, trimmed into 4
butter	heart shapes each
2 tomatoes, peeled,* seeded	butter
and chopped	½ cup cream
paprika	lemon juice

Season the fillets with salt and paprika to taste and fold in half. Sauté the onion in a little butter until almost limp. Add the tomatoes and a little paprika to taste and sauté for 5 minutes more. Place the fillets on this bed of onions and tomatoes and add the fish fumet. Cover and cook for 12 to 15 minutes at a low simmer, or until done. Meanwhile, sauté the bread hearts in butter until golden on both sides. Drain. Arrange the bread hearts on a hot platter with the drained fish fillets, alternating, and keep hot. Add the cream to the fish cooking liquids and quickly boil down to thicken lightly. Season to taste with lemon juice, strain over the fish and bread hearts, and serve hot.

This is a fine recipe for any white-fleshed fish fillets, especially flatfish like sole or halibut.

SALT COD À LA HONGROISE
TO SERVE 4

4 salt cod steaks	1 cup dry white wine
2 large onions, sliced	1 cup mushrooms, coarsely
butter	diced
paprika	¼ cup cream

Soak the cod in cold water overnight and drain dry. Sauté the onions in a little butter until limp and season to taste with paprika. Put ½ the onions in a pan, top with the cod and put the remaining onions on top of the cod. Add the wine and mushrooms and cook at a simmer for 6 minutes. Add the cream and simmer, covered, for 10 minutes more. Uncover and simmer to thicken lightly and serve at once, hot.

STURGEON À LA HONGROISE
TO SERVE 4

4 ½-lb pieces sturgeon	¼ bay leaf
2 onions, diced fine	cheesecloth, washed
butter	1 cup white wine
salt and paprika	1½ cups Sauce Velouté,* pref-
1 tsp parsley	erably fish-based
¼ tsp thyme	1 Tbs butter

Preheat oven to 350°. Sauté the sturgeon and onions in a little butter to brown lightly. Season to taste with salt and paprika. Add the parsley, thyme and bay leaf tied in cheesecloth, and the wine and Velouté. Bring to a boil, cover and cook in the oven for 15 minutes, or until the fish flakes easily with a fork and is done. Uncover and thicken the sauce over direct heat lightly. Add the 1 tablespoon of butter, if desired, discard the herb bouquet and serve hot.

MUSSELS À LA HONGROISE
TO SERVE 4

1 recipe Mussels à la
    Marinière (minus the final
    butter and parsley), hot
1 cup chopped onions
butter

paprika
3 oz Sauce Velouté
1 oz cream
2 Tbs butter (optional)

Season the mussels to taste with paprika and keep hot. Reserve their cooking liquid. Meanwhile, cook the onions in a little butter until limp and season to taste with paprika. Add the mussel cooking liquid. Add the Veloutè and cream and boil down quickly to thicken. Add the butter, if desired, and strain over the mussels. Serve at once, hot.

LIVER DUMPLING SOUP À LA HONGROISE
TO SERVE 4

1½ qts chicken consommé*
¾ cup calf's liver, diced (or beef
    liver)
salt and pepper
butter
1 Tbs butter, softened

4 Tbs onions, minced and lightly
    sautéed
1 tsp parsley
1 egg, beaten
bread crumbs
salt, paprika and grated nutmeg

Heat the consommé to a boil, reduce heat and hold at a very gentle simmer. Meanwhile, season the liver lightly with salt and pepper and sauté until almost done in a little butter, stirring over high heat. Force through a sieve or purée in a blender. Put the liver in a bowl and add the softened butter, onions, parsley, beaten egg and crumbs as needed for a dumpling consistency. Blend well, working with your hands. Season to taste with salt, paprika and nutmeg. Mix well again and shape into very small dumplings (called quenelles). Poach in very gently simmering consommé until just done. Serve hot.

APPLESAUCE À LA HONGROISE
TO SERVE 4

6 cooking apples, peeled, cored
    and sliced
½ cup dry white wine
sugar to taste, depending on the
    apples
1 Tbs lemon juice

1 lemon rind, grated
1 oz brandy
⅛ tsp grated nutmeg
3 egg whites, beaten stiff with a
    tiny pinch of cream of tartar

Steam the apples, covered tightly, in the white wine until tender, about 30 minutes. Drain. Purée in a food grinder, or by forcing through a sieve. Gradually add sugar to taste, lemon juice, lemon rind, brandy and nutmeg and blend well. Fold in the beaten egg whites, chill in individual dishes and serve chilled.

Impératrice

(am-pay-rah-TREESE)

Means Empress. In cooking, it usually applies to fruity desserts based on Rice à l'Impératrice, a dessert rice generally flavored with vanilla but sometimes with orange or lemon. Any fruits can be presented with Rice à l'Impératrice for a splendid dessert. Figs stuffed with almonds make an interesting variations. Anything you do with fruits and unsalted nuts to garnish Rice à l'Impératrice will result in an exquisite dessert.

The keynote here is sweetness, delicacy and elegance. It just wouldn't be fair to the Empress to serve this classy dessert rice in anything but your very best silver or crystal.

RICE À L'IMPÉRATRICE
TO SERVE 4

¼ cup raw rice
7 oz milk scalded with ½ tsp vanilla extract
2 Tbs sugar
1 Tbs butter
few grains of salt
2 egg yolks

4 Tbs finely chopped candied fruit, soaked in Kirsch if desired
1½ cups Custard à l'Anglaise
gooseberry jelly, melted
½ cup stiffly whipped cream (or to taste)

Wash the rice and blanch in boiling water for a few seconds. Drain and rinse in warm water. Drain again. Put in a pot with the milk, sugar, butter and salt. Cook, covered, over very gentle heat for about 35 minutes without disturbing, until the milk is just absorbed and the rice tender. Remove from heat and let cool a bit. Blend in the yolks. Let the rice cool further and mix in the fruit. Add the prepared Custard à l'Anglaise and mix with the cool, cooked rice and fruit.

Meanwhile, line a lightly oiled mold bottom with ¼ inch of gooseberry jelly and chill to set. Fold the whipped cream into the rice mixture and pour into the mold. Chill, covered. Unmold on a serving dish and serve chilled.

This dish is usually served with fruit and/or fruit purées, sweetened to taste. Occasionally it is flavored with fruit liqueurs.

PEACHES or PEARS À L'IMPÉRATRICE
TO SERVE 4

1 pt water
3 cups sugar
½ tsp vanilla extract
2 cups peach (or pear) halves

1 recipe Rice à l'Impératrice, unmolded on a serving dish
raspberry or strawberry jelly
maraschino cherries, halved

Bring the water to a boil and add the sugar. Simmer, making a thick-glazing syrup. Flavor with the vanilla and use to poach the peaches (or pears) for 5 minutes. Drain the fruit and let it cool. Arrange the fruit halves around the rice. Coat the fruit lightly with the jelly or top each piece with a piece of jelly. Decorate the dish with the cherry halves. Serve chilled.

Indienne

(an-D'YEN)

Means Indian. It also means calico or cotton print. This category of course refers to the country of India, whose cuisine is largely misunderstood or, I should say, not understood at all. We can thank the British for this primarily, since they convinced the rest of the world that Indian food is composed of curries. The fact is that in India there is no such thing as a curry. Curry powder itself is a mixture of many spices ground together, a western invention usually containing coriander, fenugreek, turmeric, cumin, pepper, bay leaf, celery seed, nutmeg, cloves, cayenne and ginger. The origin of the word *curry* in English might be from the Tamil word *kari,* which means sauce, or from a spice called kari leaf, or from a north Indian dish of buttermilk and chick peas called *karhi.* The first possibility seems the most logical. At any rate, we've inherited a tremendous misconception. The fact is that Indian food not only doesn't consist of curries, but is probably more varied from one area to another than that of any two countries in all of Europe.

India is a land of seasonings and vegetables by the hundreds, many of which are available and even unknown elsewhere in the world. The most interesting facet of Indian cuisine, however, is their use of whole spices. These will occasionally pop up in sauces, since the Indians do not limit themselves to using just smoothly strained sauces. In any given Indian dish, you might bite right into seeds or pieces of spice. It's a refreshing, if somewhat startling, change of pace. Try it yourself, with any dish: Instead of straining the sauce, let the spices stay in, and use more whole or crushed spices and seeds in cooking instead of their powders, which are usually quite flavorless in comparison anyway.

The recipes that follow of course, are in the French manner, using carefully strained sauces and lots of curry powder. Here the French are just as inaccurate as the British. The French often lose a great deal in their interpretation of foreign dishes by oversimplification, as in this case by using curry powder to flavor everything. It's like putting horseradish on everything. This *is* to say that French recipes à l'Indienne are usually much too limited in their flavorings. Compare the approach and seasonings in the beef and chicken recipes with the suggestions in the notes following each dish, and see how much more alive and exciting the *real* Indian treatment of these dishes can be.

Wine does not fit with any Indian dish, including these curries. Tea is the standard Indian beverage. For dessert, fruits are typical. Loquats, leechees, melons, mangoes, apples, oranges, bananas, guavas and pomegranates are all appropriate. Some of these might help add a bit of flare to a French dish à l'Indienne.

For décor, you might consider Indian prints, such as the fine Madras prints, for tablecloths. The Indians seem to like prints and patterns, and reds, purples, browns and gold are common colors. It must be mentioned here that Indians generally prefer eating with their fingers, and in India that is definitely high class. Also, in India, the women and girls serve the men and boys, and do not eat or converse until they are finished. The Indians also prefer to eat on mats on the floor, often outdoors on the ground. I don't know how you react to all this, but I think it has interesting points and could make for a fun party.

SAUCE INDIENNE (Also Called Curry Sauce)
TO MAKE 2 CUPS

½ cup chopped onion
2 Tbs butter
2 tsp parsley
2 oz celery, chopped fine
½ tsp thyme
½ bay leaf
¼ tsp mace

2 Tbs flour
1 tsp curry powder
2 cups chicken stock* or broth
cheesecloth, washed
½ cup cream
lemon juice (1 tsp)

Cook the onion in the butter until limp. Add the parsley, celery, thyme, bay leaf and mace. Blend in the flour and curry powder and let color lightly. Add the stock, blend well, bring to a boil and simmer slowly for 40 minutes. Strain through cheesecloth and reheat. Stir in the cream and add lemon juice to taste. Serve hot with eggs, chicken, meat and vegetables.

RICE À L'INDIENNE
TO SERVE 4

2 cups rice
4 cups water

2 tsp salt

Cook the rice in the water with the salt at a hard boil for 15 minutes, or until done and tender. Rinse under running cold water and drain well. Wrap loosely in a napkin and put in a very warm place for 15 minutes to dry well. Reheat in a warm oven before serving.

MUSHROOMS À L'INDIENNE
TO SERVE 4

1 lb small mushrooms
butter

2 Tbs chopped onion
¼ cup Sauce Indienne

Sauté the mushrooms in a little butter. Sauté the onions separately, until golden, and add to the mushrooms. Add the sauce, heat well and serve in a hot dish.

BRUSSELS SPROUTS À L'INDIENNE
TO SERVE 4

1½ lbs Brussels sprouts
butter
1 cup Sauce Indienne, hot

1 cup Sauce Indienne, hot
1 recipe Rice à l'Indienne, hot

Simmer the Brussels sprouts in butter until done. Arrange in the center of a hot platter. Top with the sauce, surround with the rice and serve hot.

BEEF À L'INDIENNE
TO SERVE 4

2 lbs beef cubes
½ cup chopped onion
butter
curry powder

1 cup Sauce Béchamel
½ cup cream
1 recipe Rice à l'Indienne, hot

Sauté the beef and onion in a little butter until done to taste and season fairly well with curry powder. Meanwhile, boil the Béchamel and cream down to ½ to make Cream Sauce. When the meat is done, remove excess fat from the pan, if any, and add the Cream Sauce. Blend well. Check the seasoning and add more curry powder if desired. Put the beef and sauce in a hot serving dish and serve the rice separately, hot.

This is the French way to approach Beef à l'Indienne. If you'd like to be more authentic, sauté a little cumin seed, a few peppercorns, 1 small piece of ginger, 1 bay leaf, 1 cardamom pod and a little salt in 2 tablespoons of oil (or a bit more oil, if needed). Let the spices color a bit. Then add the ½ cup of onions and the 2 pounds of beef chunks and sauté, stirring, until done. Cover for the final few minutes. Of course you can vary the spices, but the important thing is that they are sautéed first until lightly colored, then the meat and onions are added and cooked and whatever is left at the end clinging to the meat is the sauce, whole spices and all.

An interesting variation on the spices would be to use 1 piece of cinnamon stick, 2 cloves, 4 peppercorns, ½ bay leaf, 1 teaspoon of ground coriander, ½ teaspoon of ground cumin and ¼ teaspoon of ground turmeric, all sautéed in oil before adding the meat. Garlic may be included with the onion and meat. When the meat is well browned, add ½ cup of water and 1 tablespoon of lemon juice. Cover and simmer for 30 minutes, or until tender, and serve with the pan sauce as is, hot.

VEAL SAUTÉ À L'INDIENNE
TO SERVE 4

2 lbs veal chunks, lean	1 tsp parsley
1½ oz butter	¼ tsp thyme
2 Tbs chopped onion	½ bay leaf
1 tsp curry powder	cheesecloth, washed
1 Tbs flour	1 recipe Rice à l'Indienne, hot
2 cups chicken or veal stock* or broth	

Cook the veal in the butter until about half done. Add the onion and cook for 5 minutes more, stirring. Drain off excess fat, if any. Add the curry powder and flour and stir in well. Cook about 5 minutes more, until the flour starts to turn golden. Add the stock. Add the parsley, thyme and bay leaf tied in cheesecloth. Cover and simmer for 1½ hours. When done, discard the herb bouquet and serve in a hot dish. Serve the rice separately, hot.

This makes a fine dish with lamb. It's at least as good in flavor and much more accurate Indian cooking. In India, lamb and chicken are popular meats. Beef is generally off limits and that covers veal as well. Remember their sacred cows!

CHICKEN À L'INDIENNE
TO SERVE 4

2 small chickens, cut up	¼ tsp thyme
1 large onion, chopped	¼ bay leaf
1 Tbs curry powder	cheesecloth, washed
butter or oil	1 cup chicken or veal stock* or broth, or as needed
1 Tbs flour	1 tsp lemon juice
1 tsp parsley	1 recipe Rice à l'Indienne, hot
½ tsp chervil	

Sauté the chicken pieces, onion and curry powder in a little butter until firm but not browned. Add the flour, stir and cook slowly for 5 minutes. Add the parsley, chervil, thyme and bay leaf tied in cheesecloth, and the stock. Cook, covered, for 45 minutes to 1 hour, until done. Add stock during cooking as needed. Discard the herb bouquet. Blend in the lemon juice and set the chicken and its sauce in a hot serving dish. Serve the rice separately, hot.

To be more true to the Indian spirit, begin by skinning the chicken pieces. Put 2 tablespoons of oil in a pan and use to sauté a little ginger, 1 tablespoon slivered almonds, 1 teaspoon ground coriander, ¼ teaspoon ground cumin, the seeds from 2 cardamom pods and a small pinch each of ground cloves, cinnamon, nutmeg, mace, salt and pepper. Brown very lightly and add the chicken and sauté until done. At the end, add 1 tablespoon of lemon juice, blend well and serve hot, with rice.

CHICKEN LIVERS À L'INDIENNE
TO SERVE 4

1½ lbs chicken livers, halved
salt and pepper
butter
½ lb bacon, cut in ¼-inch-thick,
    1½-inch squares

½ lb small mushroom caps
bread crumbs
1 recipe Rice à l'Indienne, hot
1½ cups Sauce Indienne, hot

Season the livers lightly with salt and pepper and sauté quickly in lots of hot butter to brown. Remove from the pan. Blanch the bacon in boiling water for 5 minutes and drain. Sauté the mushrooms lightly in a little butter in another pan. Thread the livers on 8 small skewers, alternating with the bacon pieces and mushrooms. Dip them in the butter in the liver sauté pan and roll in crumbs to coat. Grill until done over a fire or broil in the oven. Serve the skewers on 4 hot plates on a bed of rice. Pour the sauce over the top and serve hot.

COD À L'INDIENNE
TO SERVE 4

2 lbs cod fillets
salt and pepper
4 Tbs chopped onion, lightly
    sautéed in butter
2 tomatoes, peeled,* seeded
    and chopped

1 garlic clove, minced
1 Tbs parsley
2 Tbs butter, diced
¾ cup dry white wine
2 oz heavy cream
1 recipe Rice à l'Indienne, hot

Preheat oven to 350°. Season the fillets with salt and pepper to taste. Put the onions and tomatoes in a buttered casserole. Sprinkle with the garlic and parsley and top with the cod fillets. Dot the cod with the diced butter. Add the wine and bring to a boil. Cook in the oven for 10 minutes and pour the cream over the cod. Bake 10 minutes more, basting often, or until the fish flakes easily with a fork and is done. Serve hot, with the rice served separately.

This dish may also be served with the fish, drained, set on the rice and topped with Sauce Indienne.

This is a fine recipe for any white-fleshed fish fillets. Eel may also be used, for a bit of a change.

CONSOMMÉ À L'INDIENNE
TO SERVE 4

1 qt chicken consommé,* hot
1–2 tsp curry powder, or to taste

4 Tbs Rice à l'Indienne, hot
½ cup Royale, cut in small dice

Mix the curry powder with the hot consommé. Mix in the rice. Serve hot, garnished with diced Royale.

Soup is not generally prepared in India. This dish is strictly a French idea.

Jardinière

(zhahr-dee-N'YAYR)

Means gardener, or of the garden. Dishes served à la Jardinière are very similar to those served à la Bouquetière (meaning flower girl). They both usually apply to roasts or poultry garnished with bunches of garden vegetables. The only difference is that in Bouquetière every effort is made to arrange the vegetables to look like flower bouquets, while in Jardinière the vegetables are more varied and are simply served in bunches, and the more the merrier. Any meat may be prepared and served garnished with a Jardinière of Vegetables, and you have a dish à la Jardinière.

Jardinière is also similar to other cooking modes, such as Fermière, which feature vegetables of one kind or another. Most other vegetable-oriented categories, however, rely on particular vegetables, or combinations. For instance, Verdurière (vayr-dew E'YAYR), meaning greengrocer, relies primarily on watercress for a leafy-green effect. Jardinière is the most expansive of the vegetable categories. The more variety the better, and there are no vegetables that could be considered inappropriate.

The atmosphere for a dish à la Jardinière could be one of a farm kitchen, or, perhaps better still, of a garden. An ideal setting might be outdoors, in a garden. This would be especially apt if the garden contained a few vegetables, as many beautiful flower gardens do these days.

JARDINIÈRE of VEGETABLES
TO SERVE 4

½ lb carrots, cut in balls
½ lb turnips, cut in balls
salt, sugar, butter
½ lb peas

½ lb small kidney beans
½ lb green beans, sliced
½ lb cauliflower flowerets

Cook the carrots and turnips separately, each in 1 pint of water with ½ teaspoon of salt, ½ teaspoon of sugar and 2 tablespoons of butter. Cook, partially covered, until the water is almost gone, leaving a syrupy liquid. Shake the pans to glaze the vegetables. Cook the peas, kidney beans, green beans and cauliflower as desired and toss in a little butter. Serve all the vegetables hot, together, but in separate bunches.

VEAL ESCALOPES À LA JARDINIÈRE (Slices)
TO SERVE 4

2 lbs veal slices	butter
salt and pepper	1 recipe Jardinière of Vegeta-
2 eggs, beaten (optional)	bles, hot
bread crumbs (optional)	2 cups veal gravy, or Sauce
	Espagnole, hot

Season the veal lightly with salt and pepper. If desired, dip in beaten egg and bread crumbs. Sauté until done in butter. Arrange the veal escalopes in a pile in the center of a hot platter (or, to be more in keeping with the theme of Jardinière, or gardener, perhaps on a warm wooden platter). Surround the veal with separate mounds of the vegetables. Pour the gravy over the veal or serve in a hot dish, separately.

The vegetables here can be varied, and the choice is yours. Any root vegetables like the carrots and turnips here, or onions, should be glazed, as described in Jardinière of Vegetables. If desired, Hollandaise Sauce can be used to top one or more of the nonglazed vegetables.

VEAL BREAST À LA JARDINIÈRE
TO SERVE 4

1 veal breast	1½ cups veal gravy, or Sauce
butter	Espagnole
1 cup chicken stock* or broth	1 recipe Jardinière of Vegeta-
½ cup dry white wine	bles, hot

Preheat oven to 325°. Brown the veal in a little butter. Braise, covered, in the stock until done. *Or* roast in butter, basting, until done. It will take about 30 minutes per pound in the oven. When done, place on a hot platter and keep hot. Add the wine to the pan and quickly boil down, scraping up the juices. Stir in the gravy, blend and heat through. Surround the veal with separate piles of the vegetables. Strain the sauce over the meat or serve separately, hot.

BEEFSTEAKS À LA JARDINIÈRE
TO SERVE 4

Proceed as for Veal Breast à la Jardinière, using a 5- to 6-pound roast of broiled steaks if you prefer. Use Sauce Espagnole or beef gravy rather than veal gravy.

BEEF ROAST À LA JARDINIÈRE

Proceed as for Veal Breast à la Jardinière, using a 5- to 6-pound roast of beef. Cook standing rib roast about 30 minutes per pound, rolled roast or sirloin tip for about 35 minutes per pound. If using a fillet, cook about 1 hour.

LAMB or MUTTON CHOPS À LA JARDINIÈRE
TO SERVE 4

Proceed as for Veal Escalopes à la Jardinière, using 8 to 12 lamb chops, unbreaded. Here you may wish to substitute potatoes for the carrots, and sautéed eggplant for the kidney beans.

LAMB or MUTTON ROAST À LA JARDINIÈRE
TO SERVE 4

Proceed as for Veal Breast à la Jardinière, using a lamb roast. Cook about 35 minutes per pound. You may wish to substitute potatoes for the carrots, and sautéed eggplant for the kidney beans.

Jus

(ZHEW)

Means juice, or gravy, Jus de Veau is the name given to a basic veal stock, which can be used as either a white or brown stock, since the veal flavor acquires the taste of any meat it is used with. For instance, if Jus de Veau is used with chicken, it acquires the light taste of chicken. If it's used with beef, it acquires the full, rich flavor of beef. This makes it the most versatile stock there is for meats.

As a term in cuisine, au Jus is often tacked on the end of a recipe and looks impressive there, but on most menus it means nothing at all except that the dish is juicy. For instance, Prime Ribs au Jus usually means simply prime ribs with their own juice.

This manner can be used to cook virtually anything. In the carrot recipe given here, the sauce is more glaze than juice, but of course, a glaze is nothing more than thickened juice. Onions are also good cooked this way, as are turnips. Cucumber chunks are an excellent substitute in the Brussels sprouts recipe. You can cook any vegetable you wish, following one or another vegetable recipe listed here. The same is true of meats.

JUS DE VEAU (Brown Veal Stock)
TO MAKE 4 QUARTS

6 lbs veal meat and bones (cracked)	2 cups dry white wine
4 carrots, in chunks	5 qts warm water
3 onions, halved	2 tsp salt
2 celery stalks, in chunks	1 Tbs parsley
1 leek, halved (optional)	1 tsp thyme
2 Tbs butter	2 bay leaves
	cheesecloth, washed

Brown the meats and bones in the oven at high heat. Brown the carrots, onions, celery and leek in the butter in a pan. Put the browned vegetables and meats in a large braising pan, or roasting pan, with a tight cover. Cover and put over very low heat for 15 minutes without disturbing. Uncover, add ½ the wine, raise the heat and boil down the wine and juices to a glaze. Add ½ the remaining wine and repeat. Add all the remaining wine and repeat again. Pour in the warm water and salt, and the parsley, thyme and bay leaves tied in cheesecloth. Bring to a boil, lower heat and simmer 6 hours. Strain, forcing all the juices out of the meat and vegetables. Strain again through cheesecloth and cool to room temperature. Refrigerate overnight, and remove the fat layer on the top in the morning. Put the finished Jus de Veau in containers and store or freeze.

Jus can be made with any meats as a base, but when made with veal it has the advantage of versatility. It will "pick" the flavor of the meat it is used with. Jus made with other meats, like beef (Jus de Boeuf), will be limited in their use to whatever their flavor goes well with. Only Jus de Veau will take on the flavors of the dish it accompanies.

CARROTS AU JUS
TO SERVE 4

1½ lbs carrots, cut in large pieces	2 Tbs sugar
1 qt water	6–8 Tbs butter
2 tsp salt	¼ cup rich veal stock,* Jus de Veau or veal gravy, hot

Put the carrots, water, salt, sugar and butter in a pan and boil down until there is just a thick glaze left of the fluid, shaking the pan occasionally. When done, add the stock, shake to glaze well and serve in a hot vegetable dish.

BRUSSELS SPROUTS AU JUS
TO SERVE 4

1½ lbs Brussels sprouts	¼ cup rich veal stock,* Jus de Veau or veal gravy, hot
butter	
salt and white pepper	

Simmer the Brussels sprouts in a little butter until done. Season lightly with salt and white pepper. Toss with the stock and serve in a hot vegetable dish.

CELERY AU JUS
TO SERVE 4

1½ lbs celery, cut in pieces	¼ cup rich veal stock,* or Jus de Veau, or veal gravy, hot
2 Tbs butter	

Cook the celery in simmering, lightly salted water until done. Drain and toss with the butter. Add the stock. Toss and serve in a hot vegetable dish.

ENDIVE AU JUS
TO SERVE 4

1 tsp parsley
¼ tsp thyme
¼ bay leaf
cheesecloth, washed
4 small heads of endive, washed
   and drained

1 cup beef stock* or broth
½ carrot, chopped
½ onion, chopped
½ celery stalk, chopped
¼ cup rich veal stock,* or Jus de
   Veau, or veal gravy, hot

Tie the parsley, thyme, and bay leaf in cheesecloth and put in a pot with the endive, beef stock, carrot, onion and celery. Bring to a boil, cover and lower heat to a simmer. Cook for 40 minutes. Remove the endive, drain and keep hot. Strain the cooking juices and boil down to ½. Blend in the veal stock. Put the endive in a hot vegetable dish, top with the sauce and serve hot.

PUMPKIN AU JUS
TO SERVE 4

1½ lbs pumpkin, peeled, cut in
   cubes, blanched 3 minutes in
   boiling, lightly salted water,
   drained

¼ cup rich veal stock,* or Jus de
   Veau, or veal gravy

Cook the pumpkin in the stock, covered, for 25 minutes at a very low simmer, or until done. Serve in a hot vegetable dish.

WATERCRESS AU JUS
TO SERVE 4

1 lb watercress
butter
3 oz cream, boiling

1–2 oz juice from cutting the finished roast

Blanch the watercress in lightly salted, boiling water for 30 seconds and drain. Simmer in a little butter in a pan until limp. Add the cream and cook down to thicken lightly. Add the juice from the roast and cook to rethicken quickly and lightly. Put in a hot vegetable dish and serve with the roast, hot.

ROAST BEEF AU JUS
TO SERVE 4

1 3-lb beef roast
1 garlic clove, slivered
2 oz brandy
salt and white pepper
¼ lb sliced bacon (optional)
1 cup Madeira wine

1 cup dry red wine
1 cup Jus de Veau, or veal or
   chicken stock*
1 tsp cornstarch
1 Tbs butter (optional)
chives

Preheat oven to 375°. Insert the garlic in the roast with a thin knife. Brush with half the brandy. Season with salt and white pepper. Lay the bacon strips across the roast and fasten with toothpicks. Put on a rack in a roasting pan and moisten with some of the Madeira. Put in the oven and bake for 1 hour, basting alternately with red wine and Madeira every 15 minutes. Lower the heat to 300° and continue cooking for 30 minutes more, or until done, basting frequently and using all the wine. Put the finished roast aside on a hot platter to set the juices for 5 minutes before slicing. Meanwhile, put the pan over medium direct heat, discard excess fat and blend in the Jus de Veau. Blend the cornstarch with the remaining brandy and stir into the pan juice, blending well to thicken lightly. Blend in the butter, if desired. Cut the meat, and serve with the pan sauce strained into a hot sauceboat. Serve the chives separately in a small bowl with a small spoon.

LAMB LEG AU JUS
TO SERVE 4

1 lamb leg, about 5 lbs	1 cup dry red wine
2 garlic cloves, cut in fine strips	1 cup water
1 Tbs basil leaves	1 cup Jus de Veau, or veal or
2 oz brandy	chicken stock*
salt and white pepper	chives

Preheat oven to 400°. Trim any excess fat from the lamb and, using a long, thin knife, insert the garlic strips into the leg. Using the same knife, insert the basil. Brush the lamb with the brandy and rub with salt and pepper liberally. Place on a rack in a pan and brown in the oven. Mix the wine and water. Lower oven to 325° and roast the lamb for about 25 minutes per pound, basting often with the wine and water. When done, set the roast aside for 5 minutes before carving to set the juices.

Meanwhile, put the pan with the cooking juices over medium direct heat and discard excess fat, if any. Add the Jus de Veau and blend well, scraping up the drippings. Boil down to thicken lightly and strain into a hot sauceboat. Serve with the meat, with the chives served separately in a little bowl with its own spoon.

CHICKEN AU JUS
TO SERVE 4

1 4-lb chicken	cheesecloth, washed
salt and white pepper	1 cup Jus de Veau, or veal or
3 bay leaves	chicken stock*
6–8 celery stalk top halves, with	1 oz brandy
leaves	½ tsp tomato paste
1 orange, halved	1 Tbs cornstarch mixed with 2
1 oz butter, melted	Tbs dry white wine
1 cup dry white wine	4 small watercress bunches
1 cup water	

Preheat oven to 375°. Season the chicken inside with salt and white pepper. Put the bay leaves, celery and ½ the orange in the chicken and sew or skewer closed. Rub the chicken outside with the remaining ½ orange several times. Rub well with salt and white pepper. Brush with the melted butter. Mix the wine and water and put ½ in a buttered roasting pan. Add the chicken and roast for 30 minutes. Reduce the heat to 300° and cook about 1 hour and 20 minutes more, or until done. (When the chicken is nicely browned, top with cheesecloth and baste every 8 or 10 minutes with pan juices and the remaining water and wine.) Put the finished chicken on a hot platter and keep hot.

Put the roasting pan over medium direct heat. Discard excess fat, if any, and add the Jus de Veau and brandy. Stir, scraping up the juices. Remove from the heat and blend in the tomato paste and cornstarch mixture. Bring back to a boil quickly to thicken lightly. Strain into a sauceboat and serve with the chicken. Garnish the chicken platter with the watercress bunches, untruss and carve at the table.

Languedocienne

(lahng-duk-S'YEN)

From the large area of southeastern France on the Mediterranean called Languedoc. The old province of Languedoc stretched from Foix, in Gascony, and the eastern Pyrenees along the Mediterranean Sea to the Rhône River, and north along the Rhône nearly to Lyon. Much of the region is covered by the Cevennes Mountains. The landscape goes from seacoast to mountains, and the foods are as varied as the topography. The area was a province of Gaul under the Romans until the fifth century. When Rome disintegrated the area fell to the Visigoths, and the capital was changed from Narbonne to Toulouse. It was called Septimania, since it encompassed the seven cities of Uzes, Nimes, Beziers, Toulouse, Lodeve, Agde and Maguelonne. Three hundred years later it was conquered by the Moors, and in another fifty years the Moors were tossed out by the Franks under King Pepin the Short.

Languedoc has quite a varied history, and a varied cuisine to match. Cooking à la Languedocienne is in the Mediterranean style. Olive oil, tomatoes and onions or garlic are used as a basis. Languedocienne is distinguished from Provençale or Grecque primarily by garlicky sauces flavored with orange rind.

The old Languedoc area is the producer of several wines worth mentioning. Tavel, a rosé, strong and pungent, goes well with a dish à la Languedocienne. Lirac is similar, and comes red as well as rosé. Frontignan, the most famous of France's muscats, is usually sold under the name *Frontignac*. It is more delicate than most muscats, and very sweet. The best white from this area is Limoux, both still and sparkling. The sparkling Limoux is made like champagne, and is known as *Blanquette de Limoux*. Much of the best dessert wine of France, such as the Frontignac, comes from the coastal vineyards of old Languedoc and Lunel.

Only wines with an alcoholic content of a least 15 percent are entitled to the name *Muscate de Lunel,* and they must be made exclusively from grapes from the vineyards of Lunel, Lunel-Viel and Verorgues.

The fine cheese Roquefort has been ripened in natural caverns in the area of old Languedoc for hundreds of years, and is considered the greatest blue cheese made with sheep's milk. Cows cannot subsist on the area's arid pastureland. Roquefort is ripened between layers of bread moldy with penicillium fungus.

SAUCE LANGUEDOCIENNE
TO MAKE 2 CUPS

Blend 2 cups of Demi-Glace Sauce (Sauce Alsacienne) with 2 to 3 tablespoons of tomato paste and 1 teaspoon grated orange rind. Heat and serve hot with meats and poultry.

LANGUEDOCIENNE GARNISHES
TO SERVE 4

1. MUSHROOMS

Sauté 1 pound of small whole mushrooms in ½ butter and ½ oil until done. Drain, and serve hot.

2. EGGPLANT

Peel and slice 2 small eggplants, or cut in large dice. Season lightly with salt and pepper and sauté in oil. Drain, and serve hot.

3. POTATOES

Cut 2 pounds of potatoes like olives and sauté slowly in butter until done. Serve hot, sprinkled with parsley or chives.

TOMATOES À LA LANGUIDOCIENNE (Stuffed)
TO SERVE 4

4 tomatoes, halved and hollowed out	1 tsp parsley
salt and pepper	olive oil
olive oil	4 egg yolks, hard-boiled and mashed
1 Tbs chopped onion	1 lb pork sausage meat, partially cooked and drained
1 garlic clove, minced	

Preheat oven to 325°. Season the tomato halves with salt and pepper to taste and sauté quickly in oil. Drain and set aside. Sauté the onion, garlic and parsley in a little oil until limp. Off heat mix in the yolks and sausage meat. Use this to stuff the tomato halves. Put in the oven on a buttered baking pan and bake for 30 minutes, or until well done. Serve hot.

EGGPLANT GRATIN À LA LANGUEDOCIENNE
TO SERVE 4

2 eggplants
salt
olive oil
1 lb pork sausage meat, cooked
  and drained

1 garlic clove, minced fine
1 Tbs parsley
bread crumbs
butter, melted

Cut the eggplants in half lengthwise and rub with salt. Let stand for 30 minutes. Preheat oven to 350°. Wash off the eggplant halves and dry. Sauté in a little oil until done without damaging the skins. Drain, and scoop out most of the central pulp leaving the skins intact. Mash the pulp and mix with the sausage meat, garlic and parsley. Use this mixture to stuff the eggplants. Place on a buttered baking pan, sprinkle generously with crumbs and a little butter to moisten, and brown until golden in the oven. Serve hot.

EGGS À LA LANGUEDOCIENNE (Sautéed)
TO SERVE 4

1 garlic clove, crushed
2 Tbs butter
1 cup tomatoes, peeled,*
  seeded and diced
1 tsp grated orange rind
salt and pepper

2 oz butter
salt and pepper
lemon juice
8 eggs
8 slices of eggplant
olive oil

Sauté the garlic in the 2 tablespoons butter for a few minutes. Add the tomatoes and orange rind and season to taste with salt and pepper. Simmer to make a smooth fairly thick fondue and discard the garlic. Keep hot. Melt the 2 ounces of butter in a pan and cook until it turns a light brown or hazelnut color. This is Noisette Butter. Season to taste with salt and pepper and a few drops of lemon juice. Keep hot. Sauté the eggs and eggplant slices until done in oil and drain. Season, if desired. Arrange the eggplant slices on a hot platter. Top each slice with a hot egg and sprinkle with the Noisette Butter. Top with the Tomato Fondue and serve at once, hot.

BEEF HASH À LA LANGUEDOCIENNE
TO SERVE 4

2 lbs roast beef, diced
1 cup Sauce Demi-Glace (Sauce
  Alsacienne) or Sauce
  Espagnole
1–2 tsp grated orange rind
1 Tbs parsley
1 small eggplant, peeled and
  sliced thin

olive oil
salt and pepper
1 cup Tomato Fondue,* hot
bread crumbs
Parmesan cheese, grated

Preheat oven to 375°. Heat the diced beef in the Demi-Glace Sauce with the grated orange rind, and season if necessary. Mix in the parsley. Meanwhile, sauté the eggplant in oil until done. Season lightly with salt and pepper and arrange on a buttered baking dish. Top with the beef hash. Cover the hash with the Tomato Fondue. Sprinkle generously with crumbs and cheese, and a little melted butter to moisten, and brown until golden in the oven. Serve hot.

VEAL CHOPS À LA LANGUEDOCIENNE
TO SERVE 4

4 large veal chops	1 garlic clove, minced
goose fat, or butter	1–2 tsp grated orange rind
2 Tbs chopped onion	2 lbs potatoes, cut like olives
2 Tbs ham, diced	butter
12 green pitted olives, sliced	

Sauté the veal in the fat until well browned on both sides. Add the onion and ham and continue sautéing until almost done. Add the olives, garlic and orange rind and finish sautéing together. Meanwhile, sauté the potatoes in butter until done. Set the chops on a hot platter. Top with the onions, ham, olives and garlic from the pan. Surround with the potatoes and serve hot.

PORK LOIN À LA LANGUEDOCIENNE
TO SERVE 4-6

2 garlic cloves, slivered	3 oz dry white wine
1 4–5-lb pork loin	2 Tbs tomato paste
salt and pepper	1–2 tsp grated orange rind
basil and oregano	1½ cups Sauce Demi-Glace
olive oil	(Sauce Alsacienne) or Sauce
	Espagnole

Insert the garlic slivers in the pork with a fine knife. Season to taste with salt and pepper. Sprinkle with basil and oregano liberally. Sprinkle with olive oil generously and marinate for 12 hours, turning occasionally. Preheat oven to 350°. When the roast has marinated, brown quickly on the top of the stove in a roasting pan. Cover, and roast in the oven for 2 hours, or until done. Place the roast on a hot platter and keep hot. Remove excess fat from the pan and add the wine. Boil down quickly over direct heat, scraping up the juices. Add the tomato paste, orange rind and Sauce Demi-Glace. Blend well and heat. Strain into a sauceboat and serve hot, with the roast.

CHICKEN À LA LANGUEDOCIENNE
TO SERVE 4

2 small chickens, cut up
butter
salt and pepper
1 recipe Tomatoes (Stuffed) à
    la Languedocienne, hot
2 oz dry white wine

1 garlic clove, crushed
1½ cups Sauce Demi-Glace
    (Sauce Alsacienne) or Sauce
    Espagnole
1 tsp tomato paste blended with
    ½ tsp grated orange rind

Preheat oven to 325°. Brown the chicken in a little butter in a pot. Season to taste with salt and pepper and bake in the oven for 45 minutes, or until done, covered. Set the chicken on a hot platter, surround with the stuffed tomatoes and keep hot. Add the wine and garlic to the chicken pot over direct heat and boil down, scraping up the juices. Add the Sauce Demi-Glace and tomatoe paste. Blend in well and heat through. Strain over the chicken or serve separately in a sauceboat, hot.

Limousine

(lee-moh-ZEEN)

From the former province of Limousin in central France. Limousin also means stone mason, or a coarse woolen cloak worn by a shepherd. The province took its name from the Lemovices, a Gallic tribe. In the north the territory is a granite plateau, to the south rivers have cut it into deep wide valleys. The abbey of Solignac was founded in Limousin in the seventh century. Its first abbot, St. Eloi, introduced the art of enameling.

Any meat or meats that go well with red cabbage can be served à la Limousine. They should be prepared simply. Veal, mutton, sausages, sweetbreads, kidneys, all are excellent as prepared in the pork chop or pullet recipes. Dishes à la Limousine are typified by red cabbage and chestnuts. This makes the category somewhat similar to Cévenole, which is noted for the use of chestnuts, and also to Alsacienne and Flamande, which use cabbage in one form or another.

Clafouti is a custard-like pancake prepared in Limousin, containing fruit. Black unpitted cherries are the usual ingredient. The simplicity of the dish makes it a fine dessert for a harried entertainer.

The area that was Limousin is not particularly noted for foods and wines today, nor was it ever. The old capital of Limoges on the Vienne River is still an important city, but the whole region is like an unproductive island surrounded by Bordeaux to the southwest, the Dordogne and Garonne valleys to the south, the Rhône Valley far to the east, the Loire valley to the north. So, there aren't any wines to recommend from this area. Here is another fine chance to use an American wine, which is as good as any and much cheaper, especially the better vintages.

RED CABBAGE À LA LIMOUSINE
TO SERVE 4

1 red cabbage, shredded
1 qt chicken or beef
   consommé* or broth
4 Tbs pork fat, chopped

20 chestnuts, boiled for 5
   minutes and peeled
salt and pepper

Put the cabbage, consommé, fat and chestnuts in a pot and season to taste with salt and pepper. Cover and simmer for 1 hour. Drain, and serve hot.

PORK CHOPS À LA LIMOUSINE
TO SERVE 4

8 pork chops
salt and pepper
butter

1 recipe Red Cabbage à la
   Limousine, hot

Season the chops to taste with salt and pepper and sauté in a little butter until done. Serve on a hot platter surrounded with the red cabbage.

PULLETS À LA LIMOUSINE
TO SERVE 4

½ cup chicken stock* or broth
2 pullets, halved lengthwise
salt and pepper
1 oz butter, melted
1 oz olive oil
½ cup Madeira wine
½ cup heavy cream

2 tsp cornstarch blended with 2
   tsp Madeira wine
1 recipe Red Cabbage à la
   Limousine, hot
20 chestnuts, cooked* and reheated in chicken stock* or
   consommé

Preheat broiler. Put the chicken stock in a broiling pan. Season the pullet halves with salt and pepper to taste and brush with some butter and oil. Put in the pan and broil until done, basting frequently and turning to cook evenly (about 30 minutes). When done, place on a hot platter and keep hot. Remove excess fat from the pan and place over direct heat. Add the ½ cup Madeira and boil down, scraping up the juices. Blend in the cream. Lower heat and simmer a few minutes. Use the cornstarch and Madeira slurry to thicken the pan sauce if needed. Serve the pullet halves hot, with the sauce poured over the top, and surrounded by the red cabbage and chestnuts.

CORNISH GAME HENS À LA LIMOUSINE
TO SERVE 4

Proceed as for Pullets à la Limousine, using four halved Cornish game hens, and adjusting cooking time, if necessary, to the smaller birds (about 25 minutes).

CHERRY CLAFOUTI À LA LIMOUSINE
TO SERVE 4

¾ cup flour
1 cup cold milk
3 cups milk flavored with 1 tsp
   vanilla extract

¾ cup sugar mixed with 1/16 tsp
   salt
4 eggs, beaten
1 lb unpitted black cherries

Preheat oven to 325°. Blend the flour with the cold milk, adding a bit at a time. Scald the 3 cups of milk flavored with vanilla, then blend in the flour and cold milk slurry slowly and cook to thicken, stirring. Remove from heat. Add the sugar to the beaten eggs gradually, beating until well mixed and fluffy. Gradually add the flour and milk mixture, blending over low heat. Do not allow to boil. Pour half this mixture into a buttered and lightly floured baking dish, sprinkle on the cherries. Pour the remaining custard on top. Set in a pan with 1 inch of water and bake until done, about 50 minutes. Serve hot or at room temperature. This dish is often sprinkled with confectioner's sugar just before serving.

This is excellent made with purple plums, and of course with red cherries. Traditionally, this Clafouti is made with unpitted cherries, which provides a slightly more interesting flavor. However, pitted cherries are almost as flavorful, if not as authentic, and a whole lot easier eating!

Lyonnaise
(lee-ohn-NEZ)

After the former province of Lyonnais, and its capital, Lyon. Lyon is still an important city in France, and because of its cuisine is considered by many the gastronomic capital of all France.

Although the area around Lyon is largely industrial, the fertile plains it does have are put to fine use growing excellent vegetables and fruits. The Beaujolais Mountains rise to some three thousand feet and are wooded right to the top. Pine and chestnut forests thrust up from meadows and hills apparently at random in a helter-skelter pattern. There are virtually no people to be seen in this beautiful and seldom-visited area except around an occasional village. On its mountainsides chestnut trees bear sweet nuts known around the world. The district is known for fine pork, fish and game. But most noteworthy are the famous sausages of Lyon.

The cooking of Lyon is strongly individual. Food à la Lyonnaise is prepared with a bit of vinegar to add zip. If prepared with lots of onions and seasoned with a dash of vinegar, virtually anything you care to cook can legitimately be called a dish à la Lyonnaise. The acme of Lyonnaise flavor is Lyonnaise Sauce, a good brown Espagnole or Demi-Glace flavored with onion, a little wine and that dash of vinegar. Exquisite and extremely distinctive. Lyonnaise cooking reinforces the concept that great cooking need not be especially difficult. It simply needs to have individual character and good taste.

Beaujolais is the wine of the area, and a short distance away are the wines of Burgundy and the Rhône. Beaujolais is commonly known as a red wine, and it should be, for it is constantly in demand and its best reds are excellent. Beaujolais also comes in white, however, which is dry and fairly strong in flavor but not up to the standard of the red. Actually, no wine will stand up well with a dish that contains vinegar, as do many dishes à la Lyonnaise. But if you feel a wine is a must, then I would recommend that the wine be served with separate courses not containing vinegar before a dish à la Lyonnaise is served.

SAUCE LYONNAISE
TO MAKE 2 CUPS

1½ onions, minced	2 oz white wine vinegar
1½ Tbs butter	1½ cups Sauce Espagnole, or
3 oz dry white wine	beef gravy

Sauté the onion in the butter until limp but not browned. Add the wine and vinegar and boil down until almost gone. Add the Espagnole and simmer slowly for 15 minutes, blending well and thickening lightly. Serve hot with meats, stews and leftovers.

SALAD À LA LYONNAISE (Also Called Salad a la Demi-Deuil)
TO SERVE 4

1 lb boiled potatoes, cut in small strips	2 Tbs heavy cream
1 lb lightly sautéed truffles, cut in small strips	1 small potato, boiled and sliced
2 Tbs prepared mustard	2 truffles, sliced and lightly sautéed in butter

Mix the potatoes and truffles cut in strips with the mustard blended with the cream (use more or less mustard and cream, to taste). Pile in the center of a serving dish and surround with the slices of potato and truffle. Serve at room temperature.

To be properly called Salad à la Demi-Deuil, this must be made with black truffles, since Demi-Deuil means "in half-mourning."

POTATOES À LA LYONNAISE
TO SERVE 4

1½ lbs boiled potatoes, sliced	butter
salad oil	1 tsp vinegar
1 cup chopped onions	salt and pepper
	chives and/or parsley

Gently sauté the potato slices in a little oil until golden on both sides without breaking the slices. Meanwhile, sauté the onions in a little butter until golden brown and add the vinegar. Season to taste with salt and pepper. Drain the potato slices on paper towels and toss gently with the onions without breaking. Serve hot, sprinkled with chives and/or parsley.

WHITE BEANS À LA LYONNAISE (Dried)
TO SERVE 4

½ recipe White Beans à la
    Bretonne, hot
1½ cups onions, sliced fine and
    sautéed in butter, hot

2 Tbs parsley

Mix the ingredients together over medium heat and serve hot.

MUSHROOMS À LA LYONNAISE
TO SERVE 4

1½ lbs button mushrooms
1½ cups chopped onions
butter

lemon juice
parsley

Sauté the mushrooms and onions in a little butter, separately, until done and tender. Mix in a hot serving bowl, and season with a few drops of lemon juice to taste. Sprinkle with parsley and serve hot as a vegetable or an hors d'oeuvre.

GREEN BEANS À LA LYONNAISE
TO SERVE 4

1 lb string beans
¾ cup onions, sliced thin
butter

salt and pepper
1–2 tsp parsley
1 tsp vinegar (or more to taste)

Cook the beans in lightly salted water and drain. Sauté the onions in a little butter until lightly browned. Add the beans, season to taste with salt and pepper, and cook until the beans are just slightly browned. Mix in the parsley and vinegar and cook a few minutes to blend the flavors. Serve hot.

BEETS À LA LYONNAISE
TO SERVE 4

4 Tbs chopped onions
3 Tbs butter
1½ lbs beets, almost completely
    cooked, peeled and sliced

salt and pepper (optional)
1 cup Sauce Espagnole, or veal
    gravy

Sauté the onions in the butter gently for 3 minutes, stirring. Add the beets and continue cooking gently until tender but not browned. Season lightly with salt and pepper, if desired, and add the Espagnole. Simmer 3 minutes and serve hot.

GREEN PEPPERS À LA LYONNAISE
TO SERVE 4

¼ cup bacon drippings, or lard
6 green peppers, sliced in ½-
 inch rings, seeds and membranes removed

1 onion, halved and sliced thin

Heat the bacon drippings in a pan. Mix the pepper rings and onions and sauté in the hot fat slowly, covered, stirring occasionally, until just soft (about 15 minutes). Serve hot, as a garnish with meat or fish.

TOMATO SAUTÉ À LA LYONNAISE
TO SERVE 4

6 medium-small tomatoes,
 peeled* and halved
salt and pepper
butter

¾ cup chopped onions, sautéed
 in butter
parsley

Season the tomato halves with salt and pepper to taste and sauté in a little butter until done and tender. Arrange on a hot serving dish and keep hot. Add the onions to the tomato sauté pan and heat quickly. Pour the onions and juices over the tomatoes, sprinkle with parsley and serve hot.

ARTICHOKES À LA LYONNAISE (Stuffed)
TO SERVE 4

4 artichokes, cleaned and
 trimmed*
salt and pepper
½ lb pork sausage meat
2 oz onions, chopped and lightly
 sautéed
2 tsp parsley
4 bacon strips
4 Tbs butter
1 onion, sliced

1 carrot, sliced
salt and pepper
1 tsp parsley
¼ tsp thyme
½ bay leaf
1 oz dry white wine
2 oz veal stock* or gravy
1 cup Sauce Espagnole, or beef
 gravy

Blanch the artichokes for 5 minutes in boiling water, rinse in cold water and drain dry. Remove the hairy chokes from inside the artichokes and discard. Season to taste with salt and pepper and stuff with a mixture of the sausage meat, onions and parsley. Preheat oven to 350°. Wrap each stuffed artichoke in a strip of bacon and secure with string. Melt the butter in a pan and add the onion, carrot, salt and pepper to taste, parsley, thyme and bay leaf. Place the artichokes on this bed and simmer, covered, for 3 minutes. Add the wine and simmer a few minutes more. Add the stock and braise in the oven, covered, for 1 hour. Baste frequently, adding more butter if needed. Remove the artichokes and set on a hot platter. Keep hot. Untie the string and discard it and the bacon. Skim any excess fat from the pan and add the Sauce Espagnole. Mix well, heat through, and strain over the artichokes and serve hot. If necessary, boil down the pan sauce quickly to thicken a bit before serving.

OMELET À LA LYONNAISE
TO SERVE 2

4 Tbs chopped onion, sautéed
   lightly in butter and ¼ tsp
   vinegar, drained
4 eggs, beaten

½ tsp parsley
salt and pepper
4 Tbs butter

Mix the onion with the eggs. Add the parsley and salt and pepper to taste. Cook the omelet* in hot butter and serve at once.

BEEF ENTRECÔTE À LA LYONNAISE (Steak)
TO SERVE 4

4 steaks
butter
4 Tbs chopped onion
2 Tbs white wine vinegar, or
   cider vinegar

4 Tbs dry white wine
1½ cups Sauce Espagnole, or
   beef gravy
salt and pepper
2 Tbs parsley

Sauté the steaks in a little butter. When half done add the onions and finish together. Set the steaks aside and keep hot. Add the vinegar and wine to the sauté pan and quickly boil down, scraping up the juices. Blend in the Espagnole, season with salt and pepper if necessary, add the parsley. Pour over the steaks and serve hot.

BEEF CHUNKS À LA LYONNAISE
TO SERVE 4

Proceed as for Beef Entrecôte à la Lyonnaise, using 2 pounds of lean beef chunks. If the beef is not tender, boil or braise partially first to tenderize.

BEEF HASH À LA LYONNAISE
TO SERVE 4

2 lbs roast beef, diced`
2 cups Sauce Lyonnaise
1 recipe Duchesse Potatoes, hot

1 onion, sliced in rings, sautéed
   in butter and hot

Heat the beef in the sauce and cook until thick. Put the hash on a hot platter and surround with a ring of the Duchesse Potatoes. Top the hash with the onion rings and serve hot.

VEAL CHOPS or CUTLETS À LA LYONNAISE
TO SERVE 4

4 or 8 veal chops
salt and pepper (optional)
butter
4 Tbs chopped onions

2 cups veal stock* or broth
2 Tbs white wine vinegar, or
    cider vinegar
1 Tbs parsley

Season the veal lightly with salt and pepper, if desired. Begin sautéing the veal in a little butter. Sauté the onions in a little butter until limp. Add to the veal and finish together. Meanwhile, boil the veal stock down to 2 ounces, making a veal glaze. When the veal and onions are done, set on a hot platter and keep hot. Add the veal glaze, vinegar and parsley to the pan, blend with the cooking juices of the veal and onion, pour over the veal and serve hot.

PORK CHOPS or CUTLETS À LA LYONNAISE
TO SERVE 4

Proceed as for Veal Chops à la Lyonnaise using 8 thin pork chops.

CALF'S LIVER À LA LYONNAISE
TO SERVE 4

2 lbs calf's liver, in small slices
    and well trimmed
salt and pepper
flour
butter

2 onions, sliced in rings,
    sautéed in butter and hot
2 oz veal stock* or gravy
1 tsp vinegar
parsley

Season the liver to taste with salt and pepper and dredge in flour, shaking off the excess. Sauté in a little butter until done and arrange on a hot platter. Top with the sautéed onion rings and keep hot. Add the veal stock and vinegar to the liver sauté pan and stir over high heat. Dribble over the liver and onions and serve hot, sprinkled with parsley.

CHICKEN DEMI-DEUIL
TO SERVE 4

2 small young chickens
salt
2 black truffles, sliced fairly thin
3 carrots, sliced
2 onions, sliced
2 leek whites, sliced
1 celery stalk, sliced
1 tsp parsley
½ tsp basil
½ tsp chervil
1 bay leaf
cheesecloth, washed
2 tsp salt

10 peppercorns
1½ cups Sauce Velouté*
½ cup mushrooms, sliced and
   sautéed
2 egg yolks, beaten
½ cup heavy cream
1 Tbs brandy
1 oz Madeira wine
1 black truffle, chopped
20 small mushroom caps
1 oz butter
½ tsp lemon juice
salt and white pepper

Rub the chickens with a little salt, inside and out. Loosen the skin from the flesh of the chickens as much as possible without breaking the skin. Slip the black truffle slices between the skin and flesh all over the bird, through slits as small as possible. This veil of black truffles seen through the skin is what gives the dish the name Demi-Deuil, meaning "half-mourning," as if the birds were covered with mourning veils. Truss the legs and wings to the chickens' bodies. Place the birds in a well-buttered pot and just cover with water. Slowly bring to a boil, reduce heat and simmer. Skim. Add carrots, onions, leeks and celery. Then add the parsley, basil, chervil and bay leaf tied in cheesecloth. Add the salt and peppercorns. Simmer gently until done, partially covered (about 50 minutes). Remove to a hot platter, untruss and keep hot. Strain the cooking stock and reserve.

Heat the Sauce Velouté with 1½ cups of reserved cooking liquid and boil down to half. Add the mushroom slices. Remove from heat. Blend the yolks, cream, brandy and Madeira. Add a little Velouté to the yolk mixture and blend, then pour into the Velouté slowly, mixing well. Add the chopped truffle and reheat but do not boil. Meanwhile, sauté the mushrooms in the butter with the lemon juice, and season lightly with salt and white pepper. Pour a little Velouté mixture over the chickens and garnish with the mushrooms. Serve the rest of the sauce separately, hot.

This is a specialty of Lyonnaise cooking. Any bird can be cooked this way, simply by adjusting the cooking time to the bird's size. The term Demi-Deuil (half-mourning) is also applied to braised light meats, like veal, that are served covered with Sauce Suprême* containing sliced or chopped black truffles.

CHICKEN SAUTÉ À LA LYONNAISE
TO SERVE 4

2 small chickens, cut up
salt and pepper
butter
2 onions, chopped

2 Tbs vinegar
1½ cups Sauce Espagnole, or
   veal gravy
parsley

Season the chickens to taste with salt and pepper and sauté in a little butter until half done. Add the onions and finish cooking together. Put the chicken and onions on a hot platter and keep hot. Remove the excess fat from the pan, if any, and add the vinegar. Boil down, scraping up the drippings. Add the Espagnole and blend, heating quickly. Strain over the chicken, sprinkle with parsley and serve hot.

FROG'S LEGS À LA LYONNAISE
TO SERVE 4

Proceed as for Chicken Sauté à la Lyonnaise, using 8 sets of frog's legs (16 legs). Flour the frog's legs lightly before sautéing.

HERRING SAUTÉ À LA LYONNAISE
TO SERVE 4

Proceed as for Chicken Sauté à la Lyonnaise using 2 pounds of fresh small herring, cleaned but whole.

MACKEREL FILLETS À LA LYONNAISE
TO SERVE 4

2 lbs mackerel fillets
salt and pepper
1 cup sliced onions
butter
2 Tbs vinegar

½ cup dry white wine
bread crumbs
2 Tbs butter, diced
parsley

Preheat oven to 350°. Season the mackerel fillets to taste with salt and pepper. Sauté the onions in a little butter until limp and stir in the vinegar. Spread ½ the onion mixture in the bottom of a buttered baking dish. Top with the mackerel fillets. Top the mackerel with the remaining onion mixture. Add the wine, sprinkle generously with crumbs and dot with butter. Bake in the oven for 20 minutes, or until done. Sprinkle with parsley and serve hot.

PIKE QUENELLES À LA LYONNAISE (Dumplings)
TO SERVE 4

3 cups soft white bread crumbs
¾ cup milk
1 lb pike flesh, flaked
2 tsp salt
½ tsp white pepper
⅛ tsp grated nutmeg
2 Tbs butter, softened
1 whole egg

1 egg white (if needed)
1½ cups thin Sauce Espagnole
24 button mushrooms, sautéed
    in butter
24 pitted black olives, blanched
    30 seconds in boiling lightly
    salted water
24 truffle slices

Make a bread panada (thickening paste) by pounding the crumbs with the milk in a bowl. Pound the fish with the salt, pepper and nutmeg in a mortar or bowl with a pestle or other blunt shaft until well blended. Blend with the panada. Blend in the butter, then the whole egg. Add the egg white if the mixture will take it without becoming too liquid to form quenelles. Blend well. Shape into 1½-inch quenelles and place in a buttered pan. Cover gently with boiling lightly salted water, place over direct heat and simmer gently until done (about 10 minutes). Drain on paper towels. Put the quenelles into a casserole with the Espagnole, mushrooms, olives and truffles. Simmer gently for 10 minutes, covered. Serve right in the casserole, hot, or arrange the quenelles, etc., on a hot platter and pour the sauce over the top.

Macedoine

(mah-say-D'WAHN)

Means a mixture of vegetables or fruits, raw or cooked, served hot or cold. The name *Macedoine* is derived from Macedonia, which was a collection of states united by Alexander the Great in the Balkan area of present-day Yugoslavia, Greece and Bulgaria. Alexander, king of Macedonia, was certainly its most famous and influential citizen. He extended Macedonia's rule over half the known world, reaching as far east as India. After his death in 323 B.C., at only 33 years of age, Macedonia splintered and was constantly at war, until in about 197 B.C. the Romans ended Macedonia's power for all time.

A Macedoine of Vegetables differs from a Vegetable Mirepoix in ingredients and use. A Mirepoix contains carrots, onions and celery, the ingredients so common to braising, stocks and sauces, and is usually used to enhance flavors in meat and seafood dishes. A Macedoine of Vegetables, on the other hand, is generally made of carrots and turnips, either diced or scooped into small balls, plus diced green beans, peas and diced asparagus tips, etc., and is used as a vegetables dish in its own right. Of course the vegetables, or fruits, in a Macedoine can be varied, and often are, according to taste or availability.

Meats are often served with a Macedoine of Vegetables garnishing the platter, such as Beef Fillet à la Macedoine, which is a beef fillet cooked as desired and served on a hot platter surrounded with a border of hot Vegetable Macedoine. Roasts may be prepared à la Macedoine.When cooked, cut off the top ¾ of an inch and set it aside. Then hollow out the roast, leaving 1-inch side and bottom walls. The removed meat is cut in small slices or large dice. Then a lay of Vegetable Macedoine is spread in the bottom of the roast shell, and topped with a layer of the cut-up roast, then another layer of Macedoine and so on, alternating layers of meat and Macedoine and ending with the top slice as a lid. Top with a final layer of Macedoine, return to the oven for a few minutes to reheat well and serve. This is a Roast of Beef (of whatever) à la Macedoine. Some meats are excellent served with a Macedoine of Fruit, omitting the sugar syrup and moistening with a little fruit cordial, such as Curaçao. Cold chicken breast meat is very good this way. Or, the fruits can be added to the chicken sauté pan, just before the chicken is done, and they can simmer together for the final few minutes and be served hot. Other light meats, such as pork or veal are also good with a Macedoine of Fruit.

Finally, poached or soft-boiled eggs, freshly cooked and hot, are often served on a bed of Vegetable Macedoine, and topped with a small dollop of mayonnaise.

MACEDOINE of FRUIT (Fruit Salad)

Put various cleaned and sliced fruits in a silver or glass bowl. You may use any combination you like—pears, apples, bananas, cherries, apricots, strawberries—and add some almonds if desired. Pour on some sugar syrup to sweeten (½ water, ½ sugar) and flavor with a few teaspoons of fruit liqueur like Kirsch or Curaçao. Stir gently and chill well before serving.

This is attractive when made in a clear glass bowl in layers. Each layer may be individually sweetened with syrup or plain sugar to taste. Or, the layers may be molded in gelatin flavored with ⅓ cup of fruit liqueur for each 3 cups of unflavored gelatin. Or, you may wish to use gelatin, or a combination of different flavored gelatins. The Macedoine of Fruit may also be unmolded on a platter before serving.

MACEDOINE of VEGETABLES
TO SERVE 4

½ lb carrot balls	½ lb peas
½ lb turnip balls	butter
½ lb green beans, diced	salt and pepper
½ lb asparagus tips, diced	

Boil all the vegetables in water separately until done. Heat together adding butter, salt and pepper to taste, and serve in a hot vegetable dish.

COLD MACEDOINE of VEGETABLES
TO SERVE 4

Proceed as for Macedoine of Vegetables, omitting the butter, and seasoning with oil, vinegar, salt and pepper to taste. Or, season with salt, pepper and mayonnaise to taste. Serve chilled, as a salad or hors d'oeuvre.

CREAMED MACEDOINE of VEGETABLES
TO SERVE 4

Proceed as for Macedoine of Vegetables, dressing the cooked vegetables in cream cooked down until lightly thickened and seasoned with salt and pepper.

MACEDOINE of VEGETABLES EN GELÉE (In Jelly)
TO SERVE 4

Proceed as for Macedoine of Vegetables, using unflavored gelatin with clear chicken or veal stock* for the aspic jelly, molding the vegetables.

Madère

(mah-DAYR)

Is French for Madeira. The Madeira Islands are a small archipelago lying in the Atlantic about five hundred miles west of Casablanca. They were discovered by the Portuguese early in the fifteenth century. The largest island is Madeira, approximately three hundred square miles. It is volcanic in origin and mountainous, rising over four thousand feet above the sea with beautiful scenery and an equable climate. Prince Henry the Navigator ordered the virgin forest that covered the entire island burned off to fertilize the volcanic soil with ash, and make it suitable for vineyards. The island became the greatest vineyard in the world, and remained so until the vines were hit by phylloxera in the nineteenth century. The industry was eventually revived, but would never regain its former greatness.

Madeira wine has a somewhat sweet, but sharp and smoky character. It can find its way into all sorts of recipes. For a change, try using Madeira in place of the dry white wine in recipes and sauces. These then become dishes au Madère, if the Madeira is the distinctive feature in the dishes. You'll have a fuller, more rounded flavor in the dish with Madeira than with any white table wine. I can't understand why Madeira takes second fiddle to sherry in cooking. In most recipes, Madeira is a vast improvement over sherry. (By the way, when using wines for cooking, never, under any circumstances, use cooking wine. This product is not only inferior to begin with, but is also salted heavily to make it undrinkable so it can be sold as a grocery item. How could anyone think of using this undrinkable horror in cooking? To add injury to insult, the price of "cooking wine" is more than that of the average good table wine!)

Sauce Madère is absolutely excellent with grilled steaks. It is also theeasiest of compound sauces to make, once you have prepared Sauce Espagnole in advance. Add a little Madeira wine to the Espagnole and have Sauce Madère done before you can grill a rare steak! And there is really nothing better than Steak au Madère, that is, Steak with Sauce Madère.

As a cooking mode, Madere is similar to those categories that feature wine as its hallmark, especially Porto and Xérès, which use port and sherry, respectively. Madeira, port and sherry are all fortified wines. That is, they all have brandy added, which raises their alcohol level and keeps them from "turning" soon after opening, as do the table wines which quickly become vinegary.

SAUCE MADÈRE
TO MAKE 2 CUPS

2 cups Sauce Espagnole   2–3 oz Madeira wine

Bring the Espagnole to a boil and stir in the Madeira. Cook to thicken lightly if necessary and serve hot with grilled and roast meats. A teaspoon or two of fresh Madeira is often stirred into the sauce just before serving if the sauce and Madeira need to be cooked to thicken. This will freshen the flavor. This sauce is excellent with mushrooms. Use about half a cup of sliced, sautéed and drained mushrooms in the sauce.

VEAL KIDNEYS AU MADÈRE
TO SERVE 4

2 veal kidneys, fat removed,   ½ cup Sauce Espagnole, or beef
   membranes removed, sliced   or veal gravy
salt and pepper   ¼ tsp sugar
1 oz peanut oil   1 oz brandy
2 oz butter   4 bread slices, trimmed, quar-
½ lb mushrooms, sliced   tered diagonally, sautéed in
4 shallots, chopped   butter, drained and hot
1 cup Madeira wine   chives

Season the kidney slices lightly with salt and pepper and sauté quickly until just done in the oil and butter. Set aside and keep hot. Sauté the mushrooms in the same pan, stirring, until done and set with the kidneys and keep hot. Sauté the shallots in the pan until very limp but not browned and sprinkle over the kidneys and mushrooms and keep hot. Add the Madeira, Espagnole and sugar to the pan and boil down to ½. Add the brandy and blend. Return the kidneys, mushrooms and shallots to the pan and heat through. Arrange the hot bread diamonds on a hot platter and top with the kidneys, mushrooms, shallots and sauce. Sprinkle with chives and serve hot.

DUCK AU MADÈRE
TO SERVE 4

1 5-lb duck   ½ onion, chopped
salt, pepper, ground thyme,   ½ cup chopped celery leaves
   ground mace   1 cup Jus de Veau, veal stock*
1 duck liver   or veal gravy
1 tsp shallot, minced   ½ cup Madeira wine
1 tsp chives   2 egg yolks
1 bay leaf   1 oz butter
1 tsp parsley   1 oz Madeira wine
2 cloves

Season the duck inside with salt and pepper to taste and a little thyme and mace. Mash the liver with the shallots and chives and put in the cavity. Sew or skewer closed, truss and place in a pot. Add the bay leaf, parsley, cloves, onion, celery leaves, Jus de Veau and Madeira. Bring to a boil, lower heat and simmer, covered, 2 hours. Set the duck on a hot platter, discard trussings, and keep hot. Remove excess fat from the pot and strain the sauce into a pan. Boil quickly down to ½ and remove from the heat. Let cool just a bit and beat in the yolks, one at a time. Beat in the butter, then the Madeira. Pour a little sauce over the duck and serve the rest, separately, hot.

Maître d'Hôtel

(maytr d'oh-TEL)

Nowadays this term is applied to the man in charge of the dining room in a hotel or restaurant. In noble households of the past, the office of Maître d'Hôtel was always held by a person of high rank, sometimes princes of royal blood. Although the office had little work attached to it, the Maître d'Hôtel was, at least in name, in charge of all departments of the royal household. Today, although the term hardly denotes a man of royal blood, a Maître d'Hôtel must be an accomplished chef, administrator and diplomat.

In cuisine, Maître d'Hôtel is the name of a seasoned butter used with grilled meats and fish. Any small cut of meat may be prepared a la Maître d'Hôtel by following the steak recipe, or by sauteing such meats as chicken, liver or sweetbreads and topping with a dollop of Maître d'Hôtel Butter just melting on the hot meat or meats. The same is true of any fish, which is especially good coated in egg and bread crumbs, sautéed, and served with a dollop of Maître d'Hôtel Butter melting on the hot fish. Any plainly cooked vegetable served hot and topped by melting Maître d'Hôtel Butter becomes a vegetable à la Maître d'Hôtel. As with all plain cooking styles, this style is versatile. Any dish à la Maître d'Hôtel makes a fine accompaniment for a great many other dishes.

MAÎTRE D'HÔTEL BUTTER
TO MAKE 1 CUP

¾ cup butter, somewhat softened
1½ Tbs parsley

salt and pepper to taste
a few drops of lemon juice

Stir all the ingredients together into a smooth paste. Serve chilled with grilled meats, grilled fish, fried fish or vegetables.

POTATOES À LA MAÎTRE D'HÔTEL
TO SERVE 4

2 lbs potatoes, unpeeled
1 qt boiling milk
2 oz Maître d'Hôtel Butter

salt and pepper
parsley (optional)

Boil the potatoes in lightly salted water until almost done. Drain, peel and slice. Put the potatoes into a pan over medium heat and add the boiling milk. Add the Maître d'Hôtel Butter, season to taste with salt and pepper, and cook slowly until the liquid is reduced almost to nothing. Put in a warm bowl, sprinkle with parsley if desired, and serve hot.

GREEN BEANS À LA MAÎTRE D'HÔTEL
TO SERVE 4

1½ lbs greens beans   2 oz Maître d'Hôtel Butter
salt and pepper

Cook the beans in boiling water until just done. Season to taste with salt and pepper and toss with the Maître d'Hôtel Butter. Serve hot.

ZUCCHINI À LA MAÎTRE D'HÔTEL
TO SERVE 4

4 zucchini   1 Tbs parsley
2 oz butter   lemon juice
salt and pepper

Blanch the zucchini, whole, in slowly boiling lightly salted water for 10 minutes. Drain, trim and cut in large dice. Melt the butter in a pan and gently brown the zucchini. Season to taste with salt and pepper, and stir in the parsley. Let simmer gently a few minutes. Remove from heat, season with a few drops of lemon juice to taste and serve hot.

STEAK À LA MAÎTRE D'HÔTEL
TO SERVE 4

4 steaks   ½ cup Maître d'Hôtel Butter
salt and pepper

Season the steaks with salt and pepper to taste and grill or broil, as desired. When done to taste serve on hot plates topped with dollops of Maître d'Hôtel Butter just melting on the hot steaks.

Marengo
(mah-REN-goh)

From the battle of Marengo, in northern Italy, in which Napoleon defeated the Austrians on June 14, 1800. The name of the battle was given to a chicken dish cooked right on the battlefield by Napoleon's chief, Dunand. Napoleon, who hadn't eaten all day, came to Dunand when the battle was over and asked him to prepare dinner. There was no food at hand, so the master chef sent men from the quartermaster's staff and the ordnance corps to find provisions. All they could find were three eggs, four tomatoes, six crayfish, a small hen, a little garlic, oil and a saucepan. Dunand jointed the chicken and browned it in oil, then fried the eggs in the same oil with the tomatoes and a little garlic. He then poured some water, laced with some of the general's brandy, over the mixture, and set the crayfish on top to steam. The dish was served on a tin plate, with the chicken pieces garnished with the eggs and crayfish and the tomato sauce poured over the top. When Napoleon finished eating he said to Dunand, "You must feed me like this after every battle!" Later, Dunand added wine to the recipe in place of the water, and mushrooms. When he served it without the crayfish Napoleon was upset, and said, "You have left out the crayfish, and it will bring me bad luck. I don't want any of it." Or words to that effect. The result was that crayfish was restored to the recipe, and they have been the traditional garnish for Chicken à la Marengo to this day..

Other meats may be cooked in this manner, as shown in the veal recipe, but the classic dish remains Chicken Marengo. The distinguishing characteristic is of course the serving of crayfish tails with the chicken by simmering them together for the final minutes of cooking so their flavors mingle, making an excellent and unique flavor combination. Often veal stock* or Jus de Veau is added to the pan juices as in the veal recipe. If you'd like to try other meats cooked à la Marengo, follow either the chicken or veal recipes, and use light meats such as turkey or pork.

CHICKEN MARENGO
TO SERVE 4

2 small chickens, cut up
salt and pepper
2 oz olive oil (or as needed)
8 mushroom caps
1 Tbs flour
1 garlic clove, crushed
½ cup dry white wine
½ cup thick rich veal gravy
1 Tbs tomato paste
3 tomatoes, peeled,* seeded and
    sliced
1 Tbs parsley

½ tsp thyme
8 crayfish tails, cleaned (or
    shrimp, or baby lobster tails)
4 bread slices, trimmed in 4
    heart shapes each
butter
4 eggs
olive oil
8 truffle slices, tossed in butter,
    hot
parsley and chives

Season the chicken with salt and pepper to taste and sauté in the oil until golden and almost done. Set aside and keep hot. Sauté the mushrooms in the same oil. Set aside and keep hot. Blend the flour in the pan juices, stirring well. Season with salt and pepper to taste. Add the garlic and simmer for 2 minutes. Add the wine, veal gravy and tomato paste and blend well. Add the tomatoes, parsley and thyme and simmer 5 minutes more. Meanwhile, cook the crayfish in boiling lightly salted water until just done. Arrange the chicken and mushrooms in a casserole, pour over the pan sauce, top with the crayfish and gently simmer covered for 10 minutes. Discard the garlic. While the casserole is simmering, sauté the bread in a little butter and the eggs in a little oil. Pile the finished chicken on a hot platter and surround with the bread hearts, mushrooms and crayfish tails, alternating. Put the fresh-cooked eggs on top of the chicken and decorate with the truffles. Pour the sauce over all, sprinkle with fresh parsley and chives and serve at once, hot. Everything should wind up being done at the same time, so that the mushrooms, and even more particularly the eggs, don't have to be kept hot until the other ingredients are finished.

VEAL À LA MARENGO
TO SERVE 4

1½ lbs veal chunks, lean
salt and pepper
1 garlic clove, crushed
olive oil
2 Tbs onions, chopped
4 oz white wine
3 cups rich veal stock* or broth
1 cup Tomato Sauce, preferably homemade*
1 tsp parsley

¼ tsp thyme
½ bay leaf
cheesecloth, washed
12 small onions
12 mushrooms, sautéed in olive oil
4 bread slices, trimmed in 4 heart shapes each
butter
parsley

Season the veal lightly with salt and pepper and sauté with the garlic in a little oil in a casserole until browned and half cooked. Add the onions and simmer for a few minutes. Add the wine, stock and Tomato Sauce. Then add the parsley, thyme and bay leaf tied in cheesecloth. Cover partially and cook slowly for 1½ hours. Drain the veal. Remove the excess fat from the casserole, if any, and strain the cooking juices. Discard the herb bouquet. Put the veal back in the casserole with the onions, mushrooms and the strained sauce. Simmer for 15 minutes. The sauce should be a medium-thick consistency. Meanwhile, sauté the bread hearts in a little butter until golden on both sides, and drain. Set the veal, onions, mushrooms and bread hearts decoratively on a hot platter. Pour a little of the sauce over the top, and serve the rest separately. Sprinkle with parsley and serve hot.

This dish is customarily garnished with crayfish tails and fried eggs, as in the Chicken Marengo recipe. If you wish to include them, cook the crayfish and add to the casserole for the final 10 minutes of cooking. When you add the crayfish, start to sauté the eggs in olive oil so they will be done at the same time as the casserole. Serve together, hot, as in the Chicken Marengo recipe.

Marinière

(mah-ree-N'YER)

Means *bargeman* and pertains to seamen. In cooking it is a method of preparing mussels and other shellfish, and also applies to fish cooked in white wine and garnished with mussels. This is strictly a seafood category, and is based on Mussels à la Marinière, or a mussel-flavored sauce (Marinière Sauce) for use with fish, especially fillets. Since Marinière is characterized by the use of seafood, it is similar to Dieppoise, Nantua and many more, but is generally distinguished by the addition of mussels.

The natural theme here is the sea, and all the things that relate to the sea come to mind: sailing ships, nets, shells, floats, any touch to spark the table and set the mood of the sea. If you have a cottage by the water, it would be the ideal place for a dish a la Marinière. If your cottage happens to be on the ocean, you might dig your own clams, and work up an appetite of which any seaman would be proud. If you stand in well with the local weatherman, perhaps you can arrange to have a howling nor'easter and lots of whitecaps, for a fitting background.

SAUCE MARINIÈRE
TO MAKE 2 CUPS

1 cup Sauce Bercy
2 oz mussel liquor (liquid from
    freshly opened mussels), or
    clam liquor

1 egg yolk

Heat the Sauce Bercy, and cook with the mussel liquor, reducing slightly to thicken. Remove from heat, let cool to just below a simmer, and beat in the yolk. Serve hot, but do not reboil after adding the yolk, or it will curdle. If you make this sauce in advance, reheat carefully so it warms slowly and thoroughly without approaching a simmer. Serve with poached seafood, especially mussels.

MUSSELS À LA MARINIÈRE
TO SERVE 4

butter
2 Tbs chopped shallots, or on-
    ion
1 tsp parsley
¼ tsp thyme
1 bay leaf
cheesecloth, washed

2 qts mussels, scraped and
    washed well (discard any that
    are open)
2 Tbs butter, diced
1 cup dry white wine
2 Tbs butter
1 Tbs parsley
French or Italian bread

Butter a sauce pan. Sprinkle in the shallots. Tie the parsley, thyme and bay leaf in cheesecloth and add. Put in the mussels, sprinkle with the diced butter and add the wine. Cook, covered, over a high flame. When the mussels are fully open they are done. Set the mussels in 4 hot bowls and keep hot. Discard the herb bouquet. Add the butter and parsley to the cooking stock over medium heat, blend well and pour over the mussels. Serve hot, with crusty French or Italian bread.

When this sauce is finished by adding the butter and parsley (after cooking the mussels), it is often further enriched with ½ cup of fish-based Sauce Velouté,* and seasoned with a few drops of lemon juice to taste.

CLAMS or OYSTERS À LA MARINIÈRE
TO SERVE 4

Proceed as for Mussels à la Marinière, using 2 quarts of clams or oysters.

FLOUNDER À LA MARINIÈRE
TO SERVE 4

8 fish fillets, equal in size and
   shape
salt and white pepper
butter
1 onion, chopped
½ cup dry white wine
½ cup fish fumet,* clam juice or
   water
1 tsp parsley
¼ tsp thyme
¼ bay leaf

cheesecloth, washed
1 qt mussels, scraped and
   washed well
1 lb crayfish tails, or shrimp,
   shelled and cleaned
1 cup Sauce Velouté,* preferably fish-based
2 egg yolks
3 Tbs butter (optional)
1 Tbs parsley

Season the fillets lightly with salt and white pepper. Carefully fold them in half, skin side in. Butter a pan and add the onion, wine, fish fumet, and the parsley, thyme and bay leaf tied in cheesecloth. Lay the folded fillets on this braising bed and simmer gently, covered, for about 10 minutes, depending on their thickness. When the fillets flake easily with a fork, they are done. Do not overcook. Set the fish very carefully on a hot platter in a ring with the points outward and a space in the center. Keep hot. Add the mussels to the fish-braising pan and cook quickly over high heat until all the shells are open, about 5 minutes. Remove from the shells. Meanwhile, cook the crayfish in lightly salted boiling water until they are pink and done, also about 5 minutes. Drain. Pile the crayfish in the open center of the fish platter, and put the mussels around the crayfish in a ring on top of the fish fillets. Keep hot. Strain the flounder-braising liquid and quickly boil down to ½. Lower the heat below a simmer. Add the Velouté, yolks and butter and blend. This is Sauce Marinière. Pour over the crayfish and fish fillets and serve hot, sprinkled with parsley.

The final step of boiling down the cooking liquids and finishing the sauce should be done quickly, so the seafood doesn't cool, or dry and toughen in a holding oven. For best results, cover the platter lightly with foil, put in a warm but turned-off oven, and finish the sauce as quickly as possible. This is an excellent method for any fish—sole, turbot, halibut, trout, perch, whiting or any others, including eel.

CRAYFISH TAILS À LA MARINIÈRE
TO SERVE 4

3 lbs crayfish tails, cleaned	2 cups dry white wine
butter	1 cup Sauce Velouté,* prefera-
salt and white pepper	bly fish-based
¼ tsp thyme	3 Tbs butter (optional)
½ bay leaf	1 Tbs parsley

Sauté the crayfish tails in a little butter until just pink. Season to taste with salt and white pepper and add the thyme, bay leaf and wine. Cover and boil for 10 minutes, or until just done. Set the crayfish tails on a hot platter and keep hot. Quickly boil down the braising stock to ¼ of its volume and strain. Add the Velouté, stir in well and remove from the heat. Blend in the butter, if desired. Pour over the crayfish, sprinkle with parsley and serve hot.

LOBSTER TAILS, SCALLOPS, CRABMEAT CHUNKS À LA MARINIÈRE
TO SERVE 4

Proceed as for Crayfish Tails à la Marinière, using 3 pounds of baby lobster tails, or 2 pounds of scallops or crabmeat chunks.

Matelote
(maht-LOHT)

Means a fish stew made with red or white wine. Matelotes are also called *Meurettes* (Matelotes à la Bourguignonne) or *Pochouses* (Matelotes with white wine, and eel predominating), depending on the method of preparation and the district where they are prepared. Matelotes are generally made with the freshwater fish of a given area. The exception is Matelote à la Normande, which is made with saltwater fish, usually sole, eel and gurnet, and laced with cider in place of wine. The term Matelote is often applied incorrectly to dishes made with light meats, such as veal or chicken. Matelotes are generally garnished with mushrooms and onions (which are cooked with the fish), freshwater crayfish and small buttered croutons.

MATELOTE GARNISHES
TO SERVE 4

1. FRESHWATER CRAYFISH TAILS

16 crayfish tails (or more if small)	1 onion, sliced thin
1½ qts water	1 tsp parsley
salt and pepper	¼ tsp thyme
1 carrot, sliced thin	½ bay leaf

Make an incision along the backs of the crayfish tails. Remove the intestinal tract and wash out well, but leave the shells on the crayfish. Put all the other ingredients in a pot and simmer for 30 minutes, making a court bouillon. Plunge the crayfish into this simmering court bouillon and cook, covered, at a low simmer for 6 to 8 minutes, until the crayfish are red. Let stand in the court bouillon to keep hot, if necessary, otherwise serve at once to garnish the Matelote. (This can be made using shrimp, if desired.)

2. Bread Croutons

4–6 bread slices   butter

Trim the bread slices, toast, butter and trim into diamonds or heart shapes (4 per bread slice). Or, trim and sauté in a little butter until golden on both sides, drain and serve hot.

The mushrooms and onions, which complete the garnish, are cooked with the Matelote, as described in the recipes.

MATELOTE À LA BOURGUIGNONNE
TO SERVE 4

½ cup onions, chopped	cheesecloth, washed
1½ cups tiny whole onions	2½–3 lbs fresh fish, in pieces for
2 small carrots, sliced	a stew (any combination of
2 Tbs peanut oil	freshwater bass, perch, cat-
2 Tbs flour	fish, eel, pike, trout, etc.)
2 cups red Burgundy wine	1 oz brandy
2 cups fish fumet* or clam juice	1 lb mushrooms (button or
(more if needed)	caps) of equal size, sautéed
2 garlic cloves	in butter
salt and pepper	4 bread slices, trimmed, cut in
1 tsp parsley	triangles, sautéed in butter
½ tsp basil	and drained
¼ tsp thyme	1 recipe Matelote Garnish #1,
1 bay leaf	hot
	parsley and chives

Sauté the chopped onion, whole onions and carrots in the oil until tender and lightly browned. Blend in the flour and brown lightly. Add the wine, fumet and garlic. Season to taste with salt and pepper and mix well. Add the parsley, basil, thyme and bay leaf tied in cheesecloth. Bring to a boil and simmer slowly for 30 minutes. Bring to a boil again and add the fish. Flame with the brandy. If necessary add a bit more stock to just cover the fish. Bring back to a boil and simmer for about 10 minutes, or until the fish is just done. Do not overcook. When done discard the herb bouquet and garlic. Arrange the fish carefully on a hot serving dish, cover, and keep hot. Skim fat from the pot, if any, and quickly boil down the juices to thicken lightly. Add the mushrooms and simmer for 2 minutes. Uncover the fish on the serving dish, pour over the sauce with its mushrooms, onions and carrots, garnish with the croutons and Matelote Garnish #1, sprinkle with parsley and chives and serve hot.

If you wish to thicken the sauce a bit, add 1 to 2 tablespoons each of butter and flour kneaded together (this is a *beurre manie*) to the sauce after removing the fish, and cook to thicken as you wish.

MATELOTE À LA MARINIÈRE
TO SERVE 4

Proceed as for Matelote à la Bourguignonne, using white wine in place of the red Burgundy. The carrots are sometimes omitted as well.

MATELOTE À LA MEUNIÈRE
TO SERVE 4

Proceed as for Matelote à la Bourguignonne, using only one kind of fish, usually eel. This is sometimes made with several kinds of fish, but if so should be mostly comprised of eel.

MATELOTE À LA NORMANDE
TO SERVE 4

Proceed as for Matelote à la Bourguignonne, using saltwater fish such as flounder, cod, haddock, eel, halibut, sea bass, etc., in place of the freshwater fish. Substitute hard cider for the wine and omit the carrots.

Matignon

(mah-tee-N'YON)

Matignon is a vegetable fondue served as a garnish for a number of dishes. A typical Matignon would contain carrots, onions and celery, and be seasoned with thyme, bay leaf, salt and sugar. Occasionally, lean ham is included. Matignon also refers to a garnish for meats consisting of artichoke hearts stuffed with a

Matignon Fondue sprinkled with crumbs and browned in the oven, plus braised stuffed lettuce.

A Matignon Fondue differs from a Mirepoix of Vegetables because of the addition of Madeira wine, which is optional, the extra cooking time to allow for the absorbtion of the wine, and, primarily, in the reduction of thevegetables to a smooth fondue texture. The Matignon Fondue can be used with almost any food. It makes an excellent garnish for eggs, or vegetables such as artichokes or celery. When used as a coating for meats, as in the beef fillet and chicken recipes, it lends a distinctive flavor while helping keep the meat moist. Matignon Fondue can be used with any meat, large cut or small, following the beef and chicken recipes here as a general guideline. The Matignon Garnishes alone will turn any ordinary main course, such as pork roast or chops, mutton, etc., into a delightful dish à la Matignon.

MATIGNON FONDUE
TO MAKE 2 CUPS

8 small carrots, diced	½ tsp thyme
3 oz celery, diced	⅛ tsp sugar
3 oz onion, sliced fine	salt
2 oz butter	1 cup Madeira wine
1 bay leaf	

Cook the carrots, celery and onion in the butter gently in a pan until softened somewhat but not browned at all. Add the bay leaf, thyme and sugar. Season lightly with salt and continue cooking over very low heat until fully tender but not browned. Add the Madeira and boil down until almost evaporated. When the mixture is thickened and smooth discard the bay leaf and serve hot as a garnish for meats. This is occasionally puréed by rubbing through a sieve before being used as a garnish.

MATIGNON with MEAT
TO MAKE 2½ CUPS

Proceed as for Matignon Fondue, adding 6 ounces of cooked ham, sliced very fine at the very beginning, to cook with the vegetables.

MATIGNON GARNISHES
TO SERVE 4

1. ARTICHOKE HEARTS À LA MATIGNON

8 artichoke hearts	butter, melted
2 cups Matignon Fondue	1 cup Sauce Madère, hot
bread crumbs	

Preheat oven to 350°. Cook the artichoke hearts in boiling lightly salted water until just done. Drain, fill with the fondue, sprinkle liberally with crumbs and a little melted butter to moisten and brown in the oven. Serve hot.

2. LETTUCE À LA MATIGNON (Stuffed)

1 small head of lettuce, cleaned
  and cored
2 cups chicken stock* or broth
½ lb sausage meat, partially
  cooked and drained
¼ lb ground veal
1 cup chopped sautéed
  mushrooms

1 carrot, chopped
1 onion, chopped
1 celery stalk, chopped
2 tsp butter, chopped
1 tsp parsley
½ tsp oregano
¼ tsp thyme
1 bay leaf
cheesecloth, washed

Simmer the lettuce in the stock until limp. Squeeze dry, reserving the stock. Separate the leaves and spread with a mixture of the sausage meat, veal and mushrooms. Roll up and arrange in a pan. Sprinkle with the chopped carrot, onion, celery and butter. Tie the parsley, oregano, thyme and bay leaf in cheesecloth and push down between the lettuce rolls. Add the reserved stock to just cover. If necessary add a bit of water. Cover with a lid and simmer about 30 minutes, or until the stuffing is done. Serve hot.

You might like to try this using a mixture of ½ pound of ground ham and ¼ pound of ground ham fat in place of the sausage meat and veal. The ham and lettuce make an excellent combination.

BEEF FILLET À LA MATIGNON
TO SERVE 4–8

½ lb salt beef tongue, cut in
  strips (optional)
¼ lb truffles, cut in strips
1 beef fillet
2 cups Matignon Fondue
½ lb thin bacon strips
1 oz butter
2 carrots, diced
2 onions, diced
2 celery stalks, diced

2 tsp parsley
½ tsp thyme
½ tsp chervil
½ bay leaf
cheesecloth, washed
1 cup Madeira wine
2 cups Sauce Espagnole, or
  beef gravy
Matignon Garnishes #1 and 2,
  hot (optional)

Preheat oven to 350°. Insert the salt tongue and truffles into the fillet with a larding needle or thin knife. Coat the fillet with the Matignon Fondue. Wrap with the bacon strips and secure with string. In a braising pan or dutch oven melt the butter and lightly brown the carrots, onions and celery. Add the parsley, thyme, chervil and bay leaf tied in cheesecloth. Place the fillet on the vegetables, add the wine, bring to a boil, cover and place in the oven for about 50 to 60 minutes, depending on the thickness of the fillet. When done, place the fillet on a hot platter and discard the string and bacon. Glaze in the oven for a few minutes. Meanwhile, remove any fat from the pan and strain the cooking juices. Boil down quickly to ½ and blend in the Sauce Espagnole. Heat through and spoon a little of this sauce over the glazed fillet. Serve the rest in a hot sauceboat. Arrange the Matignon Garnishes on the platter with the fillet and serve hot.

CHICKEN À LA MATIGNON
TO SERVE 4

Begin 1 day in advance
½ lb lean veal, ground
¼ lb beef fat, ground
2 eggs
1 tsp salt
½ tsp white pepper
grated nutmeg to taste
2 ice cubes
¼ lb pork fat, diced
2 Tbs butter
½ lb chicken liver
¼ cup minced mushroom peels
    (or mushrooms)
1½ Tbs chopped shallots
1 tsp salt
½ tsp pepper
¼ tsp ground cloves
¼ tsp thyme

⅛ tsp ground bay leaf
2 oz dry white wine
1 small egg yolk
2 2-lb chickens
2 cups Matignon Fondue
2 very thin sheets of pork caul,
    or salt pork
1 carrot, chopped
1 onion, chopped
1 tsp parsley
½ tsp chervil
¼ tsp thyme
1 cup Madeira wine
2 cups Sauce Espagnole, or veal
    gravy
Matignon Garnishes #1 and 2,
    hot

Pound the veal and fat, separately, in a mortar or bowl until well mashed. Blend together, add the eggs and pound into a smooth paste. Season with salt, pepper and nutmeg. Spread out on a board or plate and refrigerate overnight. The next day pound again in a bowl. Add the ice cubes and work with your hands until the ice melts and the water is absorbed. This is a quenelle forcemeat (stuffing). Brown the pork fat in a tablespoon of the butter in a pan. Remove and brown the liver in the same pan. Return the pork fat to the pan, add the mushroom peels, shallots, salt, pepper, cloves, thyme and bay leaf. Cook over high heat for 2 minutes, stirring. Remove the livers and add the wine. Cook down until the wine is gone, chop the liver fine and blend into the pan mixture. Remove from the heat and add the yolk and remaining butter. Blend until smooth. This is a gratin forcemeat (stuffing). Preheat oven to 400°. Blend the two stuffings together and use to stuff the chickens. Sew or skewer closed and truss. Brown the chickens in the oven. Coat the browned chickens with the Matignon Fondue (puréed), wrap in pork caul and tie securely with string. Put the chickens in a braising pan on top of the carrot, onion, parsley, chervil and thyme. Add the Madeira. Bring to a boil on top of the stove, cover and cook in the oven for about 1¼ hours, or until done. Remove the chickens from the pan and skim off any excess fat. Boil down the juices to ⅓ of a cup and strain. Add the Espagnole and blend and heat well. Meanwhile, remove the trussings and pork caul from the chickens and discard. Set the birds on a hot platter and surround with the artichokes and lettuce. Pour a little sauce over the chickens and serve the rest in a sauceboat, hot.

The difference between a quenelle forcemeat and a gratin forcemeat is twofold: texture and ingredients. The quenelle forcemeat is a thick purée of veal, fat and eggs with seasoning. It is also known as a *godiveau,* and is used for stuffings or to make dumplings. It is texture is completely smooth. The texture of a gratin forcemeat is that of finely minced meats and vegetables bound with yolks and butter, and its ingredients are liver of one kind or another with fat (instead of veal and fat), plus mushrooms, shallots, butter, yolks, seasonings and white wine. The gratin forcemeat is used in stuffings and for borders and pâtés.

CORNISH GAME HENS À LA MATIGNON
TO SERVE 4

Proceed as for Chicken à la Matignon, using four 1-pound birds. Adjust the cooking time to about 50 minutes.

Mayonnaise

(my-oh-NEZ)

The name of a well-known sauce. Unfortunately, many of us are only aware that it is something that comes in a jar. To the harried housewife or househusband that's fine, and a real convenience. However, to properly appreciate what Mayonnaise is supposed to be, one should make some from scratch at least once. It isn't hard, and the result is so superior that a comparison would be an insult. The term *Mayonnaise* is confused historically. Some experts say it should be called *Bayonnaise,* because it was conceived in Bayonne and has been merely corrupted to Mayonnaise. I lean toward this genesis, but the fact is that no one really knows. At one time it was called *Mahonnaise,* again no one knows why. To me this sounds like a snobbish way of pronouncing *Mayonnaise,* and nothing more. Careme stated that the real experts, meaning the great chefs of his time, always pronounced it *Magnonnaise,* derived from the verb *manier,* meaning *to stir*—which is what you do plenty of when you make Mayonnaise. Still another view is that *Mayonnaise* is a popular corruption of moyeunaise, derived from the good old French word moyeu, meaning the *yolk of an egg,* because the sauce Mayonnaise is an emulsion of yolks and oil. Aside from being just the name of a sauce, Mayonnaise also means a dish of cold fish, shellfish or poultry, often leftovers, covered with Sauce Mayonnaise and garnished with lettuce hearts, hard-boiled eggs, anchovy fillets, olives and capers. Some of the following dishes are called à la Mayonnaise, and others simply Mayonnaise. If the term is used as in the chicken recipe it should be called Chicken Mayonnaise, since this is a specific term meaning chicken served in this manner (which includes all the garnishes). However, if the dish is simply served with a Sauce Mayonnaise, then it is called à la Mayonnaise, as in the cauliflower recipe. Virtually any foods can be served with one or another of the Mayonnaise sauces, generally chilled. Vegetables, such as peas or broccoli, should be cooked simply, drained and tossed with a bit of Mayonnaise. Or they may be prepared and served as in the cauliflower or asparagus recipes.

SAUCE MAYONNAISE
TO MAKE 2 CUPS

4 egg yolks
½ tsp salt
⅓ tsp white pepper
3 tsp white wine vinegar

2 cups oil, preferably the best ol-
    ive oil, or salad oil, or half
    and half
2 Tbs lemon juice
2 Tbs boiling water

Beat the yolks, salt, pepper and vinegar with a whisk. Add the oil, drop by drop, beating constantly. As the sauce thickens you may add the oil a bit faster. (If the oil is added too quickly the sauce will separate.) When the oil is all incorporated, add the lemon juice (more or less ot taste) and the boiling water. Beat in very well and refrigerate for several hours before using with vegetables, salads, meats, eggs and fish.

Olive oil is generally preferred here, provided it's the very best pure olive oil, because of its distinctive flavor. For a milder flavor, mix with some salad oil, or use just salad oil.

Some chefs use a little pinch of dry mustard in preparing Mayonnaise, or 1 to 2 teaspoons of prepared mustard. Some also use red pepper (cayenne) in place of the white pepper.

GREEN MAYONNAISE

Color regular Mayonnaise with the juices from fresh parsley and watercress, using twice as much parsley as watercress. Break the leaves in pieces, pulverize in a mortar and squeeze through cheesecloth. Use as much of this liquid blended with the Mayonnaise as needed to get the depth of green desired. Artificial coloring can be used, but is less attractive gastronomically. Capers are sometimes added, about 2 tablespoons per cup of Mayonnaise. They should first be rinsed off and well drained.

DILL or WATERCRESS MAYONNAISE
TO MAKE 2 CUPS

Mix 2 cups of Mayonnaise with ½ cup of chopped fresh dill or watercress and 2 to 4 teaspoons of finely minced scallions. Serve chilled with cold fish, especially salmon.

AVOCADO MAYONNAISE
TO MAKE 2 CUPS

2 cups Mayonnaise
⅔ tsp grated lime rind

⅔ cup avocado pulp, mashed
    and strained
2 Tbs lime juice

Blend all the ingredients until smooth and serve chilled with cold shellfish, eggs, salmon or red snapper.

ASPIC MAYONNAISE
TO MAKE 2 CUPS

2 cups Mayonnaise, lukewarm   1 envelope unflavored gelatin

Let the gelatin stand in a few tablespoons of water for 5 minutes. Heat it until the gelatin granules are thoroughly dissolved and mix with the Mayonnaise. Let cool until the Mayonnaise begins to set and use to coat cold foods such as chicken, fish, scallops, olives, artichoke hearts, etc. Chill to set fully and serve chilled.

SAUCE GRIBICHE
TO MAKE 2 CUPS

2 cups Mayonnaise   2 Tbs parsley, fresh and minced
4 Tbs minced dill pickles   2 Tbs tarragon, fresh and
4 Tbs minced capers   minced
                                     2 Tbs chives, fresh and minced

Blend all the ingredients and serve chilled with cold fish and shellfish.

SAUCE MOUSQUETAIRE (Musketeer Sauce)
TO MAKE 2 CUPS

½ cup dry white wine   2 tsp meat glaze*
2 Tbs minced shallots   2 cups Mayonnaise

Heat the wine, shallots and meat glaze and cook down to 2 tablespoons. Cool and blend with the Mayonnaise. This is served chilled, with cold meats, eggs, salads and hors d'oeuvres, and sometimes seasoned with a bit of red pepper (cayenne).

CAULIFLOWER À LA MAYONNAISE
TO SERVE 4

2 lbs cauliflower flowerets,   ½ cup Mayonnaise
    cooked and cooled   1 egg white, beaten stiff
½ cup Vinaigrette Dressing

Season the cauliflower with the Vinaigrette Dressing. Mix the Mayonnaise and beaten egg white, spread on the seasoned cauliflower and serve chilled.

ASPARAGUS À LA MAYONNAISE
TO SERVE 4

1 cup Mayonnaise, at room tem-   salt and white pepper
    perature   1½ lbs asparagus, cooked and
2 oz whipped heavy cream   warm

Mix the Mayonnaise with the whipped cream and season to taste with salt and white pepper. Use to coat the asparagus and serve as is or lightly chilled.

CHICKEN MAYONNAISE
TO SERVE 4

4 tiny lettuces
salt, pepper, oil and vinegar
2 lbs cooked chicken, sliced
1 cup Mayonnaise (or more if needed)
4 hard-boiled eggs, quartered lengthwise

12 anchovy fillets
12 green olives, pitted
12 black olives, pitted
4 tsp capers

Remove the outer leaves from the lettuces, leaving just the hearts intact. Shred the loose leaves and arrange as a bed on a platter. Season to taste with salt, pepper, oil and vinegar. Top with the sliced chicken and season with salt, pepper, oil and vinegar to taste. Coat the chicken with the Mayonnaise. Garnish the platter with the lettuce hearts, egg quarters, anchovies, olives and four little piles of capers. Season the lettuce and egg quarters with salt, pepper, oil and vinegar to taste and serve chilled.

Milanaise

(mee-lahn-NEZ)

After the city of Milan in northern Italy's Lombard region, between the alpine foothills and the Po River. Until World War I, when Rome surpassed it, Milan was the largest city in Italy. Milan was called *Mediolanum* by the Romans, a name of Celtic origin. It became a large Christian center in the late days of the Roman Empire until the Germanic invasions reduced it to a village. Gradually it grew back to an important city until Frederick Barbarossa besieged and practically destroyed the city twice, in 1158 and 1162. After World War I Milan was the center of the fascist movement in Italy, led by Benito Mussolini, who proceeded to Rome in 1922 to form his first ministry. But his career was to have a grisly end back in Milan, where his body and that of his mistress were dishonored by the populace after their execution in April 1945, at Dongo on Lake Como. Today, Milan is a cultural center of universities, institutes, learned societies and academies. It also has its share of monuments. The Cathedral of Milan, in the center of the city, is an awesome example of Italian Gothic architecture. The city grew outward from this center beyond two sets of walls, and a ring of canals, and now reaches five miles or more in all directions. Milan is the home of Da Vinci's *Last Supper,* and the famous opera house La Scala.

Food prepared à la Milanaise is marked by dipping in beaten egg, then coating with bread crumbs and cheese, and sautéing in butter. This mixture of cheese with the bread crumbs adds a zest to the finished dish which sets Milanaise apart from any other style based on sautéed breaded foods, such as Anglaise or Villeroi. Tomato flavoring or sauce will also usually be found with a dish à la Milanaise.

There are two wines worth mentioning produced in the Milan area, Frecciarossa and Chiaretto. Frecciarossa, which means red arrow, is a brand name for a good light red wine from Casteggio, and is labeled as Château Bottled Vintage Claret. Chiaretto is perhaps the best of Italian pink wines, more a light red than a rosé. The finest Chiaretto comes from a tiny walled town called Moniga. Moniga is on the southwest shore of Lake Garda, and its walls are surrounded by the vineyards that produce its fine wine. This wine goes excellently with any dish à la Milanaise, and is sold as Moniga del Garda Chiaretto. As with the majority of the imported wines, however, most of the best is kept at home, and the wine available here is generally not so good in quality, but very good in price. If you can find a decent Chiaretto, it might be worthwhile, but it won't be cheap.

There is a small village near Milan that gives its name to a great cheese, a semisoft, almost creamy cheese, the most delicate of the natural blues, Gorgonzola.

In honor of La Scala, you could play some operas for background music. As far as décor for a dish à la Milanaise is concerned, you might take a hint from some of the products the city has been known for: textiles, leather goods and woodwork.

SAUCE MILANAISE

This is Jus de Veau, or veal stock* or gravy strongly flavored with Tomato Sauce* or purée, which is well seasoned with salt and pepper. It is served hot with meats.

MILANAISE GARNISH
TO SERVE 4

2 cups cooked macaroni
1 cup ham, cut in small strips
1 cup mushrooms, sliced and sautéed
½ cup pickled tongue, cut in strips (optional)

1 truffle, cut in small strips (optional)
1½ cups thick Jus de Veau, or veal stock,* or gravy

Mix all the ingredients together, making a coarse julienne bound with Jus de Veau, and heat gently. Serve hot with meats, especially breaded veal cutlets.

PASTA À LA MILANAISE
TO SERVE 4

1 lb spaghetti, macaroni or other
  pasta
2 oz butter
½ cup grated Gruyère cheese
  (or to taste)
½ cup grated Parmesan cheese
  (or to taste)
salt and grated nutmeg

3 oz Sauce Espagnole, or Sauce
  Demi-Glace (Sauce Alsa-
  cienne)
1 Tbs tomato paste
3 oz shredded ham, or
  shredded pickled tongue
3 oz mushrooms, chopped and
  lightly sautéed

Cook the pasta in boiling lightly salted water until done to taste. Do not overcook. Drain well, and dry by shaking over very low heat. Still keeping the pot over the direct heat, blend in the butter, then the cheeses, and season to taste with salt and nutmeg. Add the Espagnole, tomato paste, ham and mushrooms. Mix and heat well and serve hot.

RICE À LA MILANAISE
TO SERVE 4

4 Tbs onion, chopped
1 Tbs butter
1 cup rice
2 cups vegetable stock* or broth
1 tsp salt (omit if using salted
  stock)

1 Tbs butter
6 Tbs grated Parmesan cheese
½ cup ham, cut in small strips
½ cup mushrooms, cut in small
  strips and sautéed
½ cup thick Sauce Espagnole,
  or beef gravy

In a pot cook the onion in the butter until limp but not browned. Add the rice and cook over low heat until all the rice is infused with the butter. Add the stock, and the salt if necessary, cover and simmer for 15 minutes, or until the stock is completely absorbed and the rice is done. When the rice is cooked add the remaining ingredients and toss over low heat to blend and heat through. Serve hot.

Often 2 ounces each of pickled tongue and truffles, cut in small strips, are added to this recipe.

STUFFING À LA MILANAISE
TO MAKE 3 CUPS

2 cups cooked macaroni
½ cup Tomato Sauce, preferably homemade*
1 cup mushrooms, sliced and
  sauteed

½ cup chopped lean raw beef
salt and pepper

Mix the first 4 ingredients and season well with salt and pepper. Use as a stuffing for fowl.

BRUSSELS SPROUTS À LA MILANAISE
TO SERVE 4

1½ lbs Brussels sprouts
salt

Parmesan cheese, grated
butter, melted

Preheat oven to 375°. Cook the Brussels sprouts in boiling water until just done and tender. Season lightly with salt. Arrange on a buttered baking dish and sprinkle generously with cheese. Dribble a little melted butter on the cheese to just moisten and brown in the oven until golden. Serve at once, hot.

This is often served garnished with 2 freshly fried eggs per serving.

BROCCOLI, CAULIFLOWER, ASPARAGUS, SWISS CHARD À LA MILANAISE
TO SERVE 4

Proceed as for Brussels Sprouts à la Milanaise, using 1½ pounds of the vegetable of your choice.

EGGS À LA MILANAISE (Fried)
TO SERVE 4

½ recipe Pasta à la Milanaise,
  hot (made with macaroni)
8 eggs

olive oil
1 cup Tomato Sauce, preferably
  homemade,* hot

Spread the pasta on 4 hot plates and keep hot. Sauté the eggs in a little oil until done to taste and place 2 on each plate of pasta. Top with the sauce and serve at once, hot.

VEAL CHOPS or CUTLETS À LA MILANAISE
TO SERVE 4

4 or 8 veal chops or cutlets,
  preferably boneless and
  pounded thin
salt and pepper
2 eggs, beaten
bread crumbs mixed with
  grated Parmesan cheese, 4
  parts to 1
clarified butter*

1 recipe Pasta à la Milanaise,
  made with macaroni, hot
4 or 8 lemon slices, peeled and
  seeded
2 oz butter (optional)
lemon juice (optional)

Season the veal to taste with salt and pepper. Dip in the beaten eggs and coat with the crumb mixture. Sauté until just done in clarified butter. Arrange the finished veal around the outside of a hot serving dish and fill the center with the pasta. Top each veal cutlet with a lemon slice. Meanwhile, if you wish, brown the optional 2 ounces of butter in a pan quickly until golden brown and season with a few drops of lemon juice to taste (this is Noisette Butter). Sprinkle over the chops and serve hot.

Interestingly, this dish is generally prepared in Italy using sautéed potatoes instead of the macaroni.

PORK or LAMB CHOPS or CUTLETS À LA MILANAISE
TO SERVE 4

Proceed as for Veal Chops à la Milanaise, using 8 pork or 12 lamb chops. Do not use the optional butter at the end, as the pork or lamb chops are more fatty than the veal. Instead, you may sprinkle them with a liberal amount of chives just before serving.

CHICKEN À LA MILANAISE
TO SERVE 4

1 chicken	2 oz dry white wine
1 recipe Milanaise Stuffing	2 cups veal gravy, or Sauce
salt and pepper	Espagnole
2 oz butter	1–3 Tbs tomato paste

Stuff the chicken with the Milanaise Stuffing and sew or skewer closed. Truss the legs and wings to the body with string. Rub the chicken with salt and pepper to taste and brown well in the butter in a pot. Cover and simmer, basting with butter occasionally (add more butter if needed) until done (about 35 minutes per pound.) Place the bird on a hot serving dish. Discard the trussings. Spoon excess fat from the pot, if any, and add the wine. Place over direct heat and boil down, scraping up the drippings. Add the gravy and tomato paste, blend well and strain some over the bird. Serve the rest separately, hot.

CORNISH GAME HEN À LA MILANAISE
TO SERVE 4

Proceed as for Chicken à la Milanaise using 4 hens. These may take a bit longer per pound than the chicken because of their chunkiness. Allow about 45 minutes total cooking time.

TURKEY À LA MILANAISE
TO SERVE 4

Proceed as for Chicken à la Milanaise, allowing 1 recipe of Milanaise Stuffing for every 5 pounds of bird.

SQUAB À LA MILANAISE (Pigeon)
TO SERVE 4

Proceed as for Chicken à la Milanaise, using 8 pigeons and cooking for about 30 minutes, or until done.

DUCK or GOOSE À LA MILANAISE
TO SERVE 4 OR MORE

Proceed as for Chicken à la Milanaise, using 1 recipe of Milanaise Stuffing for every 4 to 5 pounds of bird.

COD À LA MILANAISE
TO SERVE 4

Proceed as for Veal Chops à la Milanaise, using 2 pounds of rather thick cod fillets in place of the veal. This is excellent with any fish fillets, but expecially with solid fleshed fish such as swordfish or haddock.

Mirepoix

(meer-PWAH)

The name of a mixture of vegetables and herbs cooked in butter, sometimes with the addition of diced ham. A Mirepoix is used to enhance meats, fish, shellfish, sauces and stuffings.

Mirepoix has a great many uses in sauces, stuffings and as an aromatic bed of vegetables for braising. Fish, pork chops, veal or lamb breast, all may be stuffed with a Mirepoix, as may tomatoes, eggplant or onions. In fact, anything that can be stuffed can be stuffed with a Mirepoix and becomes a dish au Mirepoix. The finest use for Mirepoix, however, remains as a braising bed that is often strained from the dish's finished sauce, rather than as a main ingredient.

MIREPOIX with MEAT
TO MAKE 2 CUPS

2 small carrots, diced
½ cup diced onions
¼ cup diced celery
4 oz diced ham

2 Tbs butter
¼ tsp ground thyme
¼ bay leaf

Put all the ingredients in a pan and simmer slowly until very tender, but not browned. Discard the bay leaf.

VEGETABLE MIREPOIX
TO MAKE 1½ CUPS

Proceed as for the Mirepoix with Meat, omitting the ham and adding a little salt to taste.

A Vegetable Mirepoix is often called a *Brunoise*.

CORNISH GAME HENS AU MIREPOIX
TO SERVE 4

4 1-lb game hens
salt and pepper
3 cups Mirepoix with Meat
butter

2 oz Madeira wine
2 cups Sauce Espagnole or veal
   gravy

Preheat oven to 350°. Season the birds inside and out with salt and pepper to taste and stuff with the Mirepoix. Sew or skewer closed, truss, and brown in a little butter in a roasting pan. Cover and bake in the oven for 1 hour or until the birds are done, adding butter if needed. Set the finished birds on a hot platter and untruss. Quickly remove excess fat from the pan, add the wine and boil down, scraping up the drippings. Add the Espagnole, blend and heat well, and strain a little over the birds. Serve the rest in a sauceboat, hot.

CHICKEN, SQUAB or QUAIL AU MIREPOIX
TO SERVE 4

Proceed as for Cornish Game Hens au Mirepoix, using 2 small chickens, 4 squab, or 8 quail. Cook the chickens about 1½ hours, the squab about 1 hour, and the quail about 40 minutes, or until done.

FROG'S LEGS AU MIREPOIX
TO SERVE 4

12 sets of frog's legs (24 legs)
salt and pepper
flour
butter

2 cups Vegetable Mirepoix
1½ cups Sauce Espagnole, hot
parsley or chives

Season the frog's legs with salt and pepper to taste. Dredge in flour, shaking off the excess. Sauté gently in a little butter until done and golden. Add the Vegetable Mirepoix and continue cooking to mix well and heat through. Heap the frog's legs and Mirepoix on a hot serving dish. Add the Sauce Espagnole to the pan, blend in well and pour over the frog's legs. Sprinkle with parsley or chives and serve hot.

Montmorency

(mohn-mohr-ahn SEE)

Named after the Montmorency Cherry, cultivated near Paris. This is a completely distinctive cooking mode. It relies on the use of cherries for its character, and is therefore not similar to other styles. Any dish that features cherries as a main ingredient is a dish à la Montmorency, and any dish that does not feature cherries is not a dish à la Montmorency, regardless of what it says on a menu or in a cookbook.

If you want to create the mood, decorate with cherry blossoms, cherry wood bowls, cherry red and cherry cordial.

TOURNEDOS À LA MONTMORENCY (Beef Fillets)
TO SERVE 4

4 beef fillets
salt and pepper (optional)
butter
2 oz Madeira wine
1½ cups Sauce Espagnole, or
    beef gravy, hot

2 Tbs red currant jelly
1 Tbs horseradish
¾ cup red cherries, pitted,
    soaked in warm water 8
    minutes and drained

Season the fillets with salt and pepper, if desired. Sauté in a little butter until done to taste and set aside. Keep hot. Add the Madeira to the sauté pan and quickly boil down, scraping up the juices. Blend in the Espagnole, red currant jelly, horseradish and cherries. Heat through quickly, blending, and serve with the fillets, hot.

It is very important when making a sauce in the pan used for a steak to move quickly so the steak doesn't have to be kept hot any longer than absolutely necessary. This whole process of sauce-making should take only about 1 minute. Have the Madeira, Espagnole, jelly, horseradish and cherries right next to the pan while you sauté the steaks. While the steaks are still in the pan put the flame on high, set the steaks aside on a hot plate and pour in the wine. It should boil at once and be almost gone in a few seconds. Add the other ingredients, which should be hot, or at least warm, and blend, and you should be done within a minute.

HAM STEAK À LA MONTMORENCY
TO SERVE 4

1 thick 2½-3-lb ham steak (lean)
pepper
2 lemon slices, seeded
1 bay leaf
1 clove
1 garlic clove
4 thin onion slices
¼ cup chopped mushrooms

½ cup dry red wine
½ cup strained canned cherry
    juice
1 Tbs butter kneaded with 1 Tbs
    flour (this is a *beurre manié*)
1 cup canned cherries, pitted
    and drained

Preheat broiler. Season the ham with pepper to taste and brown under the broiler lightly. Lower the heat in the oven to 350°. Put the ham in a casserole and add the lemon, bay leaf, clove, garlic, onions and mushrooms. Add the wine and cherry juice, cover and bake for about 1 hour, turning the ham once when half done. Place the ham on a hot platter and slice as you would a beef brisket, on a slant. Keep hot. Strain the casserole juices into a pan and blend in the *beurre manié*. Bring to a boil and cook to thicken lightly. Stir in the cherries, remove from the heat, and let stand for 30 seconds to blend the flavors. Pour a bit of this sauce over the ham slices and serve the rest separately, hot.

DUCKLING À LA MONTMORENCY
TO SERVE 4

1 4–5 lb duck
pepper
1 cup pitted red cherries
2 oz butter, melted
2 cups pitted red cherries

2 oz Madeira wine
2 oz Kirsch liqueur (optional)
2 cups Sauce Espagnole, or veal
    gravy, blended with 1 Tbs red
    currant jelly

Preheat oven to 325°. Remove all the fat you can from the duck and prick its skin all over with a fork so the fat can escape during cooking. Rub with pepper to taste. Put the cherries in the duck and sew or skewer closed. Truss the legs and wings to the body with string. Put the duck on a rack in a roasting pan and brush with melted butter. Bake uncovered for 2 hours, basting occasionally with butter and pan juices. Transfer the duck to a casserole and add the cherries. Put the roasting pan, minus the rack, over direct heat and spoon off the excess fat. Add the Madeira and Kirsch and boil down somewhat, scraping up the drippings. Stir in the Espagnole, blend well and pour over the duck in the casserole. Bake for ½ hour more, uncovered. Baste several times. Serve right in the casserole, hot.

RICE À LA MONTMORENCY
TO SERVE 4

Prepare Rice à l'Impératrice, and serve as a dessert decorated with banana slices alternating with large red cherries poached in syrup. Make the syrup with 1 cup each of sugar and water, plus 2 ounces of Kirsch liqueur.

Montrouge

(mohn-ROOZH)

Means red mountain. The name comes from the suburb of Montrouge, just to the south of Paris. Among the industries of Montrouge are the production of cheeses, preserves and chocolates. In culinary terms *Montrouge* connotes the use of mushrooms in one form or another, but usually in purée. A dish à la Montrouge is sometimes incorrectly garnished with a purée of potatoes and carrots, often in a mound, like an orange-tinted mountain. However, if you use a purée of potatoes and carrots in a pile you're making a Montorange, not a Montrouge.

The color to use here is obviously red, after the name of the category, *Montrouge*. A red tablecloth with white flowers, like the snows on a mountaintop, would be striking. You might also use a sprinkling of paprika on a finished dish for a touch of red color.

MUSHROOM PURÉE
TO MAKE 2 CUPS

¾ lb white mushrooms, sliced
  cup Sauce Béchamel
1½ Tbs cream

salt and white pepper
1 Tbs butter

Rub the mushrooms through a sieve into the Sauce Béchamel. Put in a pan with the cream and boil down until thickened. Season with salt and white pepper to taste, remove from the heat and stir in the butter. Serve hot, as a garnish or filling.

EGGS À LA MONTROUGE (Poached or Soft-Boiled)
TO SERVE 4

2 cups Mushroom Purée, hot
4 individual baked pastry
  crusts,* hot

8 eggs, freshly poached or soft-
  boiled, hot
1 cup Sauce Suprême,* hot

Put the Mushroom Purée in the bottoms of the crusts, top with the freshly cooked eggs, pour on the Sauce Suprême and serve at once, hot.

LAMB CHOPS À LA MONTROUGE
TO SERVE 4

8 to 12 lamb chops
3 eggs, beaten
bread crumbs
butter

½ lb button mushrooms
1 cup thick Sauce Espagnole, or
  beef gravy, hot

Dip lamb in beaten egg and coat with crumbs. Sauté in a little butter until done and drain. Meanwhile, sauté the mushrooms in a little butter. Arrange the chops around a hot platter and fill the center with the sautéed mushrooms. Pour the Sauce Espagnole on top of the chops in a ring and serve hot.

This recipe can be used for any small cuts of meat, from pork chops to steaks or veal cutlets.

FLOUNDER À LA MONTROUGE
TO SERVE 4

2 lbs flounder fillets
salt and white pepper
dry white wine
butter

½ lb button mushrooms, sautéed in butter, hot
1 recipe Mushroom Purée, hot

Season the fish lightly with salt and white pepper. Sprinkle well with white wine to moisten. Let stand for a few moments to soak in and sprinkle with wine again. Sauté in butter very gently until done, without letting the fillets break. When just done, arrange on a hot platter, keeping the fillets whole. Garnish the platter with the button mushrooms, coat the fish with the Mushroom Purée, and serve hot.

This is an excellent recipe for any fish fillets, including eel. The mushrooms make a very nice change.

MORNAY

(mohr-NAY)

After Philippe de Mornay. Mornay was a French Huguenot leader, born in Buhy, Normandy, in 1549. He escaped the St. Bartholomew's Day Massacre in 1572 and went to England, returning to France a year later to join the army of Henry of Navarre. He was Henry's agent in England and the Low Countries from 1577 to 1582. About 1588 de Mornay became the protestant leader of France, and was known as "The Huguenot Pope." He became the governor of Saumur, where he founded a Protestant University in 1593.

In cuisine, the term Mornay is the name of one of France's greatest sauces, and the name is applied to any dish served with Sauce Mornay. Practically any combination of foods can be finished with Sauce Mornay as in the following recipes. Salmon and broccoli make an interesting combination, as do shrimp and artichoke hearts. Combine the foods you like best. Precook them separately, put in a buttered casserole, or one lined with Sauce Mornay, top with more Sauce Mornay, sprinkle generously with grated Parmesan cheese and an ounce of melted butter to moisten and brown until golden in the oven. Then serve at once, while it's hot. These are all dishes that can be done long ahead, and just put together and browned in the oven for a few minutes. Excellent for company, when you'd rather be socializing than cooking. Mornay is a truly great sauce, in its flavor as well as its versatility. Use it well, which is about the only way it can be used as far as I'm concerned.

SAUCE MORNAY
TO MAKE 2 CUPS

2 cups Sauce Velouté* or
   Sauce Béchamel
½ cup grated Swiss cheese

¼ cup grated Parmesan cheese
salt, pepper, grated nutmeg
red pepper (cayenne), optional

Bring the Sauce Velouté to a boil. Stir in the cheeses and cook, mixing, until melted and blended. Season to taste with salt, pepper and nutmeg. Add a tiny pinch of red pepper, if desired, and serve hot with eggs, meats, fish or vegetables.

CAULIFLOWER À LA MORNAY
TO SERVE 4

1½ lbs cauliflower flowerets
2 Tbs butter, or more if needed

1 cup Sauce Mornay
Parmesan cheese, grated
1–2 oz butter, melted

Preheat oven to 500°. Blanch the cauliflower in boiling lightly salted water for 30 seconds and drain. Finish cooking in the butter in a pan, tossing carefully without breaking the delicate flowerets. Place in a baking dish, cover with the Sauce Mornay, sprinkle generously with cheese, dribble on the melted butter to moisten, and brown in the oven. Serve right in the baking dish, hot.

This is an excellent method for preparing almost any hot vegetable.

ENDIVE À LA MORNAY
TO SERVE 4

4 endives
1 Tbs lemon juice
1 oz butter
½ tsp salt

1 cup water
1½ cups Sauce Mornay
1 Tbs butter, diced fine

Preheat broiler. Put the endive, lemon juice, butter and salt in a pot with the water. Cook covered for 30 to 40 minutes, until tender, and drain. Place in a buttered baking dish, top with the Sauce Mornay and sprinkle with the diced butter. Run under the broiler until lightly browned and serve hot.

This method is good for any leafy vegetables, such as spinach.

EGGS À LA MORNAY (Poached or Soft-Boiled)
TO SERVE 4

1 cup Sauce Mornay, hot
8 eggs, freshly poached or soft-
    boiled, hot

Parmesan cheese, grated
butter, melted (optional)

Preheat oven to 350°. Put half the Sauce Mornay in the bottom of a casserole, top with the eggs, top the eggs with the remaining sauce, sprinkle liberally with cheese, and a little butter to moisten, if desired, and brown in the oven. Serve at once, hot.

FLOUNDER À LA MORNAY
TO SERVE 4

1 cup Sauce Mornay, hot
2 lbs flounder fillets
salt and pepper
2 diced carrots
2 diced onions
butter
1 tsp parsley
¼ tsp thyme

¼ bay leaf
cheesecloth, washed
1 cup fish fumet* or ½ cup each
    of clam juice and dry white
    wine
Parmesan cheese, grated
butter, melted (optional)

Preheat oven to 350°. Put half the Sauce Mornay in a casserole and keep hot. Season the fillets with salt and pepper to taste. Meanwhile, in a separate casserole or pot, sauté the carrots and onions in a little butter until limp but not browned. Add the parsley, thyme and bay leaf tied in cheesecloth. Fold the fillets in half and lay them on the vegetables. Pour in the fish fumet and bring to a boil over direct heat. Cover and braise in the oven for 10 minutes, or until the fish flakes easily with a fork and is done. Do not overcook. Raise the oven to 500°. Remove the fillets from the casserole or pot and place on the Sauce Mornay in the other casserole. Handle carefully so the fillets do not break. Cover with the remaining Sauce Mornay, sprinkle liberally with cheese, and dribble on a little butter if desired. Brown in the oven until golden and serve right in the casserole, hot.

This is an excellent method for fillets of any white-fleshed fish, especially flat fish such as sole and halibut.

CHICKEN À LA MORNAY
TO SERVE 4

Proceed as for Flounder à la Mornay, using 2 small cut-up chickens in place of the fish fillets. Cook as directed, but for about 30 minutes, or until the chicken cooks fully. Use chicken stock* plus 3 or 4 ounces of dry white wine instead of the fish fumet. You may wish to add grated nutmeg to the seasonings for the chicken.

This is especially good using chicken suprêmes (boned, skinned breasts).

Use 6 breasts for 4 people. After boning and skinning you will have 12 suprêmes, or 3 per person. The suprêmes will cook in about 15 minutes.

Another good variation is to use halved Cornish game hens, especially when the rib bones are removed and the birds slightly flattened prior to cooking. Of course these will take longer than the suprêmes, more like ½ hour.

COD À LA MORNAY
TO SERVE 4

1 cup Sauce Mornay, hot
4 individual buttered baking
   shells, or baked piecrusts,*
   hot

2 lbs cooked cod, in chunks (leftover cod is fine)
Parmesan cheese, grated
butter, melted

Preheat oven to 375°. Put half the Sauce Mornay in the bottoms of the shells. Fill with the cod and cover with the remaining sauce. Top generously with cheese and dribble on a little butter to moisten. Brown in the oven until golden and serve hot.

Any fish can be made following the Cod Mornay recipe, but it is especially good with firm-fleshed fish, like salmon, or haddock or swordfish.

FROG'S LEGS À LA MORNAY
TO SERVE 4

8 sets of frog's legs (16 legs)
salt and pepper
2 oz dry white wine
3 oz butter
1 Tbs lemon juice

1 cup Sauce Mornay, hot
1 recipe Duchesse Potatoes, hot
1 egg, beaten
Parmesan cheese, grated
butter, melted

Preheat oven to 375°. Season the frog's legs with salt and pepper to taste. Simmer in the wine, butter and lemon juice until just cooked and drain. Put half the Sauce Mornay in the center of a buttered baking dish and top with the frog's legs. Surround with the Duchesse Potatoes. Coat the potatoes with the beaten egg. Meanwhile, quickly boil down the frog's leg cooking juices and stir in the remaining Sauce Mornay. Pour over the frog's legs. Sprinkle generously with cheese and a little melted butter to moisten. Brown in the oven until golden and serve hot.

LOBSTER À LA MORNAY
TO SERVE 4

4 1–1½-lb lobsters, live
1½ cups diced mushrooms,
   sautéed in butter
¾ cup diced truffles, sautéed
   in butter

2 cups Sauce Mornay
4 oz raw truffles, sliced thin
Parmesan cheese, grated
butter, melted
parsley sprigs

Preheat oven to 400°. Plunge the lobsters head first into rapidly boiling lightly salted water and cook until red and done. Drain. Split in half lengthwise down the back and cut off all the claws. Remove all the flesh, cutting the tail meat into slices and the rest into dice. Mix the diced lobster with the diced mushrooms and truffles and ½ cup of the Sauce Mornay to bind. (If necessary, use a bit more sauce to bind the ingredients.) Add the soft parts of the lobster (the livers and coral, or roe) to the diced mixture and blend well. Clean out the body shells well, wash and dry. Discard the small leg shells, but reserve the large claw shells. Fill the halved body and tail shells with the diced mixture and place on a baking pan, using the large claw shells to prop them up if necessary. Lay the sliced lobster on the partly filled shells, alternating with slices of truffle. Pour over the remaining sauce, sprinkle generously with cheese and a little butter and brown in the oven. Serve hot, garnished with parsley.

SCALLOPS AND MUSHROOMS À LA MORNAY
TO SERVE 4

1½ lbs cooked scallops, hot   Parmesan cheese, grated
½ lb sautéed mushrooms, hot   butter, melted
1 cup Sauce Mornay, hot

Preheat oven to 350°. Mix the scallops and mushrooms and place in a buttered casserole. Top with the Sauce Mornay and a liberal amount of grated cheese. Sprinkle with a little melted butter to moisten, brown in the oven and serve hot.

Dishes like this, that combine different ingredients, are an excellent way to use leftovers. You could, for instance, combine a pound of leftover scallops with ½ pound each of leftover cod and chicken. Warm them, mix them and put in a buttered baking dish, top with Sauce Mornay, grated Parmesan cheese and a little melted butter and brown in the oven. All sorts of combinations are possible, depending primarily on what you happen to have in the refrigerator at the moment.

CLAMS or OYSTERS À LA MORNAY
TO SERVE 4

24 medium clams or large   Parmesan cheese, grated
   oysters, preferably alive   1–2 oz melted butter
1 cup Sauce Mornay

Preheat oven to 400°. Cook the clams in lightly salted water until they are open and are done. Drain well. Remove from the shells and discard the top halves of the shells. Wash and dry the bottom shell halves and reserve. Put 1 teaspoonful of Sauce Mornay in each shell bottom, set a clam in each, and top with another teaspoonful of sauce. Arrange the clams on a baking sheet covered with rock salt. The rock salt will hold the shells level while cooking and keep the clams hot after they are taken from the oven. If you use individual baking dishes, spread them with rock salt and place 6 clams on each. Sprinkle the clams with cheese liberally and dribble on a little butter to moisten. Brown until golden in the oven and serve at once, hot.

Mousseline

(moos-sah-LEEN)

Means muslin, which is often used as a fine strainer. In cuisine, *Mousseline* refers to foods blended with whipped cream or beaten egg white to make them light and frothy, such as potatoes, mashed and mixed with whipped cream. Mousseline also refers to little molds of puréed game, fish or poultry, enriched with cream. Hollandaise Sauce mixed with whipped cream becomes Hollandaise Mousseline Sauce. Mayonnaise mixed with beaten egg white becomes Mayonnaise Mousseline Sauce. An omelet made with eggs blended with whipped cream or beaten egg white becomes a Mousseline Omelet. Finally, *Mousseline* is the name of a particular cake.

To prepare any fish Mousseline, first poach the fish gently in a court bouillon. (To make a court bouillon for poaching fish, combine 1 sliced carrot, 1 sliced onion, 1 tablespoon parsley, 1 bay leaf, ½ teaspoon thyme, salt and pepper to taste, and 1 quart of water in a pot and simmer for 25 minutes. Strain and use to poach the fish.) If using for salmon add 1 tablespoon of lemon juice or cider vinegar to the court bouillon. A delicate fish, such as sole, may be poached in lightly salted water alone. The finished fish is then drained and served on a hot platter topped with a Mousseline Sauce. For vegetables, cook until just tender, and serve hot topped with Hollandaise, Mayonnaise or Blue Cheese Mousseline Sauce.

HOLLANDAISE MOUSSELINE SAUCE
TO MAKE 2½ CUPS

1½ cups Hollandaise Sauce   ½ cup whipping cream

Whip the cream and fold into the Hollandaise Sauce just before serving. This is also called Sauce Chantilly. Serve with vegetables, eggs, fish or fowl.

MAYONNAISE MOUSSELINE SAUCE
TO MAKE 2½ CUPS

2 cups Mayonnaise, preferably   1 egg white
  homemade*

Beat the egg white until stiff and fold into the Mayonnaise just before serving with vegetables, eggs, fish or meats.

Mayonnaise Mousseline Sauce is often made with whipped cream rather than beaten egg white. If you prefer this, use 1½ cups of Mayonnaise mixed with ½ cup of cream, whipped.

BLUE CHEESE MOUSSELINE SAUCE
TO MAKE 2 CUPS

Crumble 3 to 4 tablespoons of blue cheese fine and blend into 2 cups of Hollandaise Mousseline Sauce.

This Blue Cheese Mousseline Sauce is especially good with braised leafy vegetables such as lettuce. To braise, line a pot with sliced onion and carrot, and a little bacon rind if desired. Lay the lettuce on this bed. Cover with meat stock* or broth, or water. Bring to a boil, cover securely and braise in a 350° oven for about 45 minutes. Halve, drain well and separate the leaves. Serve with Blue Cheese Mousseline Sauce.

CAVIAR MOUSSELINE SAUCE
TO MAKE 2 CUPS

Mix 3 to 4 tablespoons of caviar with 2 cups of Hollandaise Mousseline Sauce. Serve with eggs or fish, especially salmon.

MOUSSELINE OMELET
(2 EGGS TO SERVE 1)

Proceed as for any omelet, adding 1 stiffly beaten egg white, or an equal volume of whipped cream (1 to 2 ounces) for every 2 eggs used in the omelet. Fold into the eggs for the omelet* just before cooking. Thus, an omelet à la Lyonnaise, with the addition of beaten egg whites or whipped cream, becomes a Mousseline Omelet à la Lyonnaise. Mousseline Omelets are also made by separating the yolks and whites, and beating the yolks lightly with seasonings, etc. The whites are beaten until stiff and then folded into the yolks. The omelet is prepared at once.

MOUSSELINE POTATOES
TO SERVE 4

4 potatoes, baked	salt, pepper, grated nutmeg
2 Tbs butter, or to taste	½ cup cream, whipped
2 egg yolks	1 oz butter, melted

Preheat oven to 400°. Remove the pulp from the potatoes and rub through a sieve. Put it in a pan over very low heat and stir, blending in the butter and yolks. (If the heat is too high, the yolks will curdle.) Season to taste with salt, pepper and a little nutmeg. Remove from the heat and fold in the whipped cream. Pile in a dome on a buttered baking dish. Sprinkle with the melted butter and brown in the oven. Serve at once, hot.

Nage

(NAHZH)

Means swimming or rowing, and a dish à la Nage is seafood (lobster, crayfish or shrimp in particular) cooked in a boiling court bouillon of water, wine, garlic, herbs, carrots and onions, and served "swimming" in its cooking liquid. The prime difference between a dish à la Nage and à la Marinière is that in Marinière the stock is thickened with Velouté and served hot over the shellfish, while in Nage the shellfish is left to cool in the cooking stock, unthickened, and usually served cool, stock and all. A little fennel is often added to the herbs in a dish à la Nage. Shellfish à la Nage, after cooling in the cooking stock, is sometimes served with White Wine Sauce.* Whatever sauce is served with a dish à la Nage, it should be in small, shallow, individual dishes, so everyone can dip the shellfish right into the sauce. The shellfish is served in a bowl—court bouillon, vegetables and all, like a soup. Discard the bay leaf and garlic before serving.

CRAYFISH TAILS, LOBSTER TAILS, or SHRIMP À LA NAGE
TO SERVE 4

2 lbs shellfish	¼ tsp thyme
3 carrots, sliced	1 bay leaf
1 onion, sliced	4 cups dry white wine
2 shallots, sliced (optional)	2 cups water
2 garlic cloves, crushed	salt and pepper
1 tsp parsley	red pepper (cayenne)
½ tsp basil	

Clean the shellfish by cutting through the bottoms of the shells and removing the central vein (intestine). Wash thoroughly, but leave the shells otherwise intact. Prepare a court bouillon by putting the carrots, onion, shallots, garlic, herbs, wine and water in a pot, seasoning with salt and pepper to taste, and simmering 15 minutes. Bring to a boil and use to cook the shellfish until bright red and done (about 10 minutes). Season with a little red pepper, discard the garlic and bay leaf, and let cool to room temperature. Serve in bowls at room temperature or lightly chilled, stock and all.

This can be done with the shellfish in their shells, as in the recipe, or shelled, as you prefer. If they are left in their shells, however, the dish will be more accurate, technically, and will also have more flavor, since the shells will definitely enhance the flavor of the court bouillon. Generally, this is served with Mayonnaise, Aioli or Tartare Sauce.

Nantua

(nahn-tew-AH)

After the city of Nantua in the former French province of Frenche-Comte, between the city of Dijon and the Swiss border. Nantua and the Jura Mountains along the Swiss border have long been famous for their freshwater crayfish. These crayfish come from the streams of the Jura, where numerous caverns, underground rivers and copious springs have cut through the rocks. This is very rugged country, and the main industries have long been based on the wood from its forests. Furniture, clockmaking and toymaking are typical.

In cuisine, the name *Nantua* is given to dishes that are garnished with freshwater crayfish tails or crayfish purée. Any recipe that calls for the use of Crayfish à la Nantua can be made with either Lobster or Shrimp à la Nantua. Crayfish, especially freshwater crayfish, are often very hard to come by. Whichever you do prepare, Caryfish, Lobster or Shrimp à la Nantua, be sure to make more than you need, so the leftovers can be used in other recipes. The Crayfish and Sauce freezes well, and can be kept in usable portions in the freezer for months. For a real gourmet's delight all you need do is defrost some Crayfish (and sauce) à la Nantua and use it in one of the recipes, such as the Sole à la Nantua. Crayfish à la Nantua can be combined with a wide variety of foods to make exquisite dishes. Almost any seafood (eel to pike quenelles) is beautifully enhanced by the accompaniment of Crayfish à la Nantua.

For a wine typical of the area, the finest and most characteristic are the Vins Jaunes, which are fairly strong and more like an apertif than a table wine, and consequently go rather poorly with a dish à la Nantua. A better choice would be one of the Jura's white table wines, known as Côtes du Jura. There is also Arbois Blanc, a fairly strong wine which is better suited to meats than seafood. The Jura also produces fine rosé wines. The main town of the Jura is Arbois, and the best rosés are called Rosé d'Arbois, the lesser rosés are called Rosé du Jura. Of course the quality varies considerably from brand to brand.

Any handmade wooden items would be appropriate décor for this cooking mode.

CRAYFISH TAILS, LOBSTER TAILS or SHRIMP À LA NANTUA
TO SERVE 4

¼ cup diced carrots
¼ cup diced onions
¼ cup diced celery
½ tsp thyme
1 bay leaf
2 Tbs butter
salt and pepper
2 lbs crayfish or lobster tails, or shrimp, washed
1 cup dry white wine

½ cup Sauce Béchamel
1 small pinch red pepper (cayenne)
1 Tbs butter
1 Tbs flour
3 Tbs brandy
½ cup cream
2 Tbs butter (optional)

Cook the carrots, onions, celery, thyme and bay leaf in the butter until tender but not browned. Season to taste with salt and pepper and toss the crayfish int the mixture to blend. Add the wine, cover, and cook for about 10 minutes, or until done. Remove the crayfish and shell. Put the cooking liquid and all its ingredients in a blender, setting the crayfish aside, and blend well. Strain into a bowl. Mix in the Sauce Béchamel and red pepper to taste and you have Sauce Nantua. Clean the crayfish. Melt the butter in a pan and add the cleaned crayfish and heat without browning. Sprinkle in the flour and blend. Blend in the brandy and slowly add the cream. Simmer very slowly for 8 minutes and mix in the Sauce Nantua. Heat thoroughly. Remove from the heat and blend in the optional butter, if desired, and serve hot.

If you have no blender, you can proceed as they did in the old days. That is, put the cooking stock and its ingredients in a mortar and pound, or grind in a food grinder, and strain to make the Sauce Nantua.

Baked potatoes, halved, hollowed out and stuffed with Crayfish à la Nantua and reheated become Potatoes Georgette. This is usually made with small potatoes and served as an hors d'oeuvre. Top each of these stuffed potatoes with a small hot poached egg and you have Eggs Georgette.

EGGS À LA NANTUA (Poached or Soft-Boiled)
TO SERVE 4

4 individual baked pastry shells,* hot
¼ recipe Crayfish à la Nantua, hot

8 eggs, freshly poached or soft-boiled, hot
1 truffle, sliced, lightly sautéed, and hot

Line the pastry shells with the crayfish tails (without their sauce), top with 2 eggs per dish. Pour the sauce over the eggs, and decorate with truffle slices. Serve at once, hot.

OMELET À LA NANTUA
TO SERVE 2

4 eggs
salt and white pepper
4 Tbs butter

1 recipe Crayfish à la Nantua,
    hot
4 thin truffle slices, lightly sautéed

Beat the eggs with salt and white pepper to taste. Cook the omelet* in hot butter, filling with the Crayfish à la Nantua but reserving most of the sauce. Place the omelet on a hot plate, top with the reserved sauce and garnish with the truffles. Serve at once, hot.

CHICKEN À LA NANTUA
TO SERVE 4

1 4-lb chicken
salt and white pepper
3 cups cooked shrimp meat
1 truffle, minced
1 cup Sauce Velouté*
2 qts chicken stock* or broth (or
    more if needed)

1½ cups Sauce Suprême,
    hot
1 oz shrimp meat kneaded with
    1 oz butter into a smooth
    paste

Season the chicken inside with salt and white pepper. Mix the shrimp, truffle and Velouté over medium heat until blended and thickened, and use to stuff the chicken. Sew or skewer closed and truss the legs and wings to the body. Season the trussed chicken with salt and white pepper to taste. Put the chicken in a deep pot and just cover with the stock. Poach at a gentle simmer, covered, for about 2 hours. When almost done, heat the Sauce Suprême with the shrimp butter and cook to thicken lightly. When the chicken is done, drain, untruss, place on a hot platter, and cover with the sauce, or serve the sauce separately, hot.

SOLE À LA NANTUA
TO SERVE 4

2 lbs sole fillets
salt and white pepper
1 cup fish fumet,* or, ½ cup
    each clam juice and dry
    white wine

½ recipe Crayfish à la Nantua,
    hot
1 truffle, sliced and lightly
    sautéed

Preheat over to 350°. Season the fillets lightly with salt and white pepper and put in a buttered baking dish. Add the fish fumet and cover. Bake in the oven for 12 minutes, or until the fish flakes easily with a fork and is done. Arrange the fillets carefully on a hot platter in a circle, with the crayfish (drained of their sauce) in the center. Cover the fish and crayfish with the sauce, decorate the fillets with the truffle slices and serve hot.

This recipe is fine for any white-fleshed fish fillets, especially mild-flavored fish like flounder or fresh water perch.

COD EN COQUILLES (Shells) À LA NANTUA
TO SERVE 4

4 individual buttered baking shells, or baked piecrusts*	2 lbs cooked cod, in chunks (leftover cod is fine)
1 recipe Sauce Nantua (see Crayfish à la Nantua)	Parmesan cheese, grated
	butter, melted

Preheat oven to 375°. Put half the Sauce Nantua in the bottom of the shells. Top with the cod. Top the cod with the remaining Sauce Nantua. Sprinkle liberally with cheese and a little butter to moisten. Brown in the oven and serve hot.

SALMON STEAKS À LA NANTUA
TO SERVE 4

Proceed as in the Sole à la Nantua using 4 salmon steaks, but cook them slightly longer according to their thickness. If desired, before cooking, halve the 4 salmon steaks into cotelettes (cutlets) by removing the bones and skin, leaving 8 cutlet-shaped salmon pieces.

OYSTERS À LA NANTUA
TO SERVE 4

4 individual size baked pie crusts* or buttered baking dishes	12 oysters, cooked in boiling lightly salted water until open and done
½ recipe Crayfish à la Nantua, hot	Parmesan cheese, grated

Preheat oven to 375°. Drain the crayfish from their sauce and put them in the bottoms of the piecrusts. Put 3 freshly cooked oysters in each tart on the crayfish. Top with the Sauce Nantua, sprinkle liberally with cheese, brown in the oven and serve at once, hot.

Niçoise
(nee-SWAZ)

After the city of Nice on the French Riviera's Bay of Angels. Nice dates back to the Greeks, when it was known as Nicaea. The climate is warm and sunny, helping make Nice a favorite of tourists in Europe, and it is well known for such attractions as carnivals, auto races, flower spectacles and regattas.

This is a complete and important French cooking mode, the best known of all the Mediterranean styles, using olive oil, tomatoes and garlic in a wide range of dishes. The general use of potatoes in these dishes is what sets a dish à la Niçoise apart from other Mediterranean styles such as Provençale. In fact, while other dishes may not necessarily have to include potatoes, the salad must or it isn't a Salade Niçoise.

Flowers and fruits are grown in abundance here, and this should spur ideas for décor to accompany a dish à la Niçoise. The mood that reflects this international playground is casual and opulent. A perfect setting would be on a patio, lazing in the sun, or around a pool. Another perfect setting would be on a boat or yacht. While the atmosphere is casual and relaxed, the ideal utensils would be silver, gold and crystal.

SAUCE NIÇOISE
TO MAKE 2 CUPS

2 cups Mayonnaise, preferably homemade*
4 pimientos, chopped
3 Tbs tomato purée

1 tsp chopped tarragon leaves, or ½ tsp dried tarragon heated in 2 tsp of Madeira wine

Mix all the ingredients well and let stand for a few hours in the refrigerator to blend the flavors before using. Serve chilled.

Jus de Veau or veal gravy, heavily flavored with Tomato Sauce or Tomato Fondue à la Niçoise, is often used as a sauce with Niçoise dishes.

TOMATO FONDUE À LA NIÇOISE
TO MAKE 2 CUPS

2 Tbs olive oil
1 Tbs chopped onion
6 tomatoes, peeled,* seeded and chopped

2 pimientos, minced
2 garlic cloves, minced
salt and paprika to taste
1 tsp tarragon

Put the oil in the pan and use to cook the onion until soft but not browned. Add the remaining ingredients and cook gently until smooth and concentrated.

This fondue without the tarragon is Tomato Fondue à la Grecque.

NIÇOISE GARNISHES

1. TOMATOES SIMMERED IN BUTTER

Peel* 2 pounds of very small tomatoes and simmer them in butter, whole, with 2 minced garlic cloves and salt and pepper to taste. Serve hot with meats and poultry.

2. SAUTÉED ZUCCHINIS

Peel 2 pounds of tiny zucchinis, season to taste with salt and pepper, dredge in flour and sauté in olive oil until done. Drain and serve hot.

3. ARTICHOKES SIMMERED IN BUTTER

Trim* 8 very small artichokes. Halve them and simmer in butter until tender. Season lightly with salt and pepper and serve hot.

4. POTATOES SIMMERED IN BUTTER

Trim 2 pounds of potatoes into olive shapes or little balls and simmer in butter until done. Drain, season with salt and pepper to taste, sprinkle with chives and serve hot.

5. STRING BEANS SIMMERED IN BUTTER

Blanch 1 pound of string beans in boiling water for 30 seconds. Drain, simmer in butter until just done, season lightly with salt and pepper and serve hot.

NIÇOISE GARNISH FOR FISH

Serve freshly cooked fish on a hot platter garnished with black and green pitted olives (blanched for 30 seconds in boiling water), little piles of capers and strips of anchovy fillet laid across the fish fillets. Serve hot Tomato Fondue à la Niçoise separately.

SALADE NIÇOISE
TO SERVE 4

1 lb potatoes, boiled and diced
1 lb green beans, boiled and diced
olive oil, white wine vinegar, salt, pepper
1 can anchovy fillets, drained, rinsed and dried

24 pitted black olives
24 pitted green olives (optional)
2–4 Tbs small capers
4 tomatoes, cut in wedges
fresh chervil and tarragon, chopped (or freshly ground dried herbs)

Mix the potatoes and beans and season to taste with oil, vinegar, salt and pepper. Pile in a neat mound on a platter and decorate with anchovy fillets. Surround with piles of black and green olives and capers. Garnish with the tomato wedges. Season the tomato wedges with oil, vinegar, salt and pepper to taste, and sprinkle them with chervil and tarragon. Serve at room temperature.

Drained canned tuna chunks are often added to the garnish of this salad. If you wish to include the tuna, arrange it with the olives and capers in little piles around the mound of potatoes and beans, and season to taste with oil, vinegar, salt and pepper.

While wine vinegar is generally considered the classic seasoning with olive oil, salt and pepper for a Salade Niçoise, I prefer the milder flavor of cider vinegar.

RATATOUILLE À LA NIÇOISE (Coarse Stew)
TO SERVE 4

1 onion chopped
2 garlic cloves, minced
½ tsp oregano
¼ tsp thyme
1 gay leaf
½ cup olive oil
2 small eggplants, peeled and
 cut in ¾-inch cubes
2 sweet red peppers, seeded
 and cut in strips or small
 pieces

2 green peppers, seeded and
 cut in strips or small pieces
2 zucchinis, cut in ¼-inch-thick
 slices
5 tomatoes, peeled,* seeded
 and chopped
salt and pepper

Sauté the onion, garlic, oregano, thyme and bay leaf in a little of the oil in a casserole for 5 minutes without browning. Meanwhile, sauté the eggplant in some of the oil in a pan and add to the casserole. Then sauté the red peppers, green peppers and zucchini in turn, adding oil as needed and adding each to the casserole when lightly sautéed. (The red and green peppers will take about 10 minutes each, and the zucchini 3 minutes.) Add the tomatoes to the casserole, season to taste with salt and pepper, toss without breaking the vegetables and simmer very gently for 45 minutes. Discard bay leaf and serve hot.

BROCCOLI À LA NIÇOISE
TO SERVE 4

1½ lbs broccoli flowerets
4 bacon strips, fairly lean
¼ cup bread crumbs
2 Tbs olive oil

½ cup minced onion
2 garlic cloves, minced
salt and pepper

Drop the broccoli into rapidly boiling water. Return to boiling and boil slowly for 5 minutes, or until just tender, and drain at once. Cook the bacon in a pan until fairly crisp, drain and crumble. Sauté the bread crumbs in the bacon fat, stirring, until lightly browned and set aside on a dish. Add the oil to the pan and sauté the onions until tender but not browned. Add the garlic, stir in gently and add the broccoli. Season to taste with salt and pepper and toss gently over medium heat. When heated through add the crumbs and bacon, toss for a few minutes, and serve hot.

CAULIFLOWER À LA NIÇOISE
TO SERVE 4

Proceed as for Broccoli à la Niçoise, using 1½ pounds of cauliflower flowerets, and cooking in the boiling water for about twice as long, or until tender.

With the addition of 2 or 3 more mashed garlic cloves, the broccoli or cauliflower becomes a dish à la Catalane.

PEAS À LA NIÇOISE
TO SERVE 4

2 cups peas
2 cups tiny potato balls
1 tsp parsley
½ tsp chervil
¼ tsp savory
¼ tsp thyme

cheesecloth, washed
salt, pepper, grated nutmeg
½ cup tomato juice (more if
   needed)
3 Tbs butter kneaded with 1 Tbs
   flour, diced

Put the peas and potato balls in a pot with the parsley, chervil, savory and thyme tied in cheesecloth. Add salt, pepper and nutmeg to taste, and pour in the tomato juice. Cover tightly and cook slowly for 40 minutes, or until tender, shaking the pot occasionally. If necessary add a bit more juice during cooking. Uncover and discard the herb bouquet. Add the diced butter and flour, bit by bit, blending thoroughly to thicken lightly and serve hot.

STRING BEANS À LA NIÇOISE
TO SERVE 4

Proceed as for Peas à la Niçoise using 2 cups of string beans sliced in 1-inch pieces in place of the peas.

TOMATOES, or ONIONS À LA NIÇOISE (Stuffed)
TO SERVE 4

4 large tomatoes halved and
   scooped out, leaving the
   skins and outer flesh intact
   (when using onions, halve,
   remove outer skin and central portion, leaving outer 3
   layers intact.)
salt and pepper
olive oil

2 cups cooked rice (cooked in
   beef stock* or broth)
1 cup eggplant, sautéed in olive oil, drained and chopped
1 cup bread crumbs
1 Tbs parsley
1 garlic clove, minced fine
bread crumbs

Preheat oven to 350°. Season the tomatoes with salt and pepper to taste and sauté lightly in a little oil. Drain. Mix the rice, eggplant, crumbs, parsley and garlic and season well with salt and pepper. Use to stuff the tomatoes. Place on a buttered baking sheet, sprinkle generously with crumbs and a few drops of oil to moisten and bake in the oven until golden brown. Serve hot.

ARTICHOKE HEARTS À LA NIÇOISE (Stuffed)
TO SERVE 4

¼ cup flour
1 Tbs lemon juice
salt and pepper
8 artichoke hearts
4 Tbs butter
2 oz ham or prosciutto, minced
1 onion, minced

4 tomatoes, peeled,* seeded
   and chopped
1 Tbs parsley
1 garlic clove, minced
pepper
bread crumbs
butter, melted

Preheat oven to 375°. Blend the flour with a little cold water until smooth. Pour into a pan and blend in water to make 3 cups. Add the lemon juice and season lightly with salt and pepper. Add the artichoke hearts and simmer, covered, for 20 minutes. Drain. Melt the butter in a pan, add the artichokes, and simmer for 5 minutes. Put the ham, onion, tomatoes, parsley and garlic in a casserole and stir over medium heat into a smooth paste. Season with pepper if necessary. Put the artichoke hearts on a buttered baking dish and top with the tomato mixture. Sprinkle liberally with crumbs and a little melted butter to moisten and brown in the oven. Serve hot.

These artichoke hearts are often prepared simply by blanching in boiling water for 3 minutes, sauteing until tender in butter, topping with Tomato Fondue à la Niçoise, coating with crumbs and a little melted butter, then browning in the oven.

BEEF ENTRECÔTES À LA NIÇOISE (Steaks)
TO SERVE 4

2 lbs new potatoes, peeled
butter
salt and pepper
24 pitted black olives
4 steaks
salt and pepper
1 oz each, butter and olive oil

2 oz Madeira wine
1½ cups Sauce Espagnole, or
   veal gravy
1 Tbs tomato paste
½ cup thick Tomato Fondue à
   la Niçoise, hot

Prepare Château Potatoes by boiling the new potatoes in lightly salted water until half done. Drain and finish cooking in butter. Season to taste with salt and pepper and keep hot. Blanch the olives in boiling water for a few seconds and keep hot. Season the steaks with salt and pepper to taste and sauté in the butter and oil until done to taste. Set on 4 hot plates and keep hot. Add the wine to the steak pan and boil down quickly, scraping up the juices. Add the Espagnole and tomato paste and heat, blending in well. Season if necessary with salt and pepper. Garnish the steaks with the Château Potatoes and olives, strain the sauce over them, and put a dab of Tomato Fondue on the center of each steak, and serve at once, hot.

LAMB CHOPS or NOISETTES À LA NIÇOISE (Thin Fillets)
TO SERVE 4

Proceed as for Beef Entrecôtes à la Niçoise, using 12 lamb chops or noisettes.

LAMB LOIN À LA NIÇOISE
TO SERVE 4

1 lamb loin
1 Tbs butter (more if needed)
1 zucchini, diced
1 Tbs melted butter
2 tomatoes, peeled,* seeded
   and diced

1 Tbs olive oil
20 small new potatoes, peeled
salt and pepper
parsley or chives

Brown the lamb until golden in the butter in a casserole. Preheat oven to 300°. Toss the zucchini in the melted butter. Sauté the tomatoes lightly in the oil. Place the zucchini, tomatoes and potatoes in the casserole with the lamb and season to taste with salt and pepper. Cook covered in the oven until done, about 1 hour. Sprinkle with parsley or chives and serve in the casserole, hot.

CHICKEN SAUTÉ À LA NIÇOISE
TO SERVE 4

1 Tbs vinegar
4 small artichokes, trimmed*
salt and pepper
2 Tbs butter, melted
4 small zucchini
salt and white pepper
flour
1 oz each butter and olive oil
3 cups small new potatoes,
   peeled

2–3 Tbs butter
24 pitted black olives
2 small young chickens, cut up
salt and pepper
olive oil
1 cup dry white wine
1½ cups Tomato Fondue à la
   Niçoise

Bring a quart of water mixed with a tablespoon of vinegar to a boil and use to blanch the artichokes for 6 minutes. Rince under running cold water and drain. Season lightly with salt and pepper and put in a well-buttered pan with 2 ounces of water. Pour the melted butter on the artichokes, bring to a boil, cover and simmer slowly for 35 minutes. Meanwhile, slice the zucchini rather thickly. Season lightly with salt and white pepper, dredge lightly in flour and sauté in the butter and oil until golden and tender. Drain and keep hot. Cook the potatoes gently in the butter until done and season with salt and white pepper to taste. Blanch the olives in boiling lightly salted water for 30 seconds and drain. Keep all the vegetables hot. Meanwhile, season the chicken to taste with salt and pepper and sauté in a little oil until golden. Set the chicken on a hot platter and surround with the artichokes, little piles of potatoes, and little piles of zucchini. Garnish with the olives and keep hot. Remove excess fat from the chicken sauté pan, and add the wine. Boil down quickly, scraping up the juices. Add the Tomato Fondue. Blend and heat quickly. Strain over the chicken and serve hot.

This is often made using 2 small roasting chickens. They are roasted, basting with butter, and served surrounded with vegetables as in the Chicken Sauté recipe. Serve ½ Tomato Fondue à la Niçoise and ½ Sauce Espagnole (or veal gravy) mixed as a sauce, hot.

SOLE À LA NIÇOISE
TO SERVE 4

2 lbs sole fillets	2 oz olive oil (more if needed)
salt and pepper	1 cup Tomato Fondue à la
2 Tbs lemon juice	Niçoise, hot
2 onions, chopped	Niçoise Garnish for Fish, hot

Season the fillets with salt and pepper to taste and sprinkle with the lemon juice. Let stand for 10 minutes. Sauté the onion lightly in the oil and add the fillets. Sauté until golden, pushing the onions aside. Serve on a hot platter, topped with the onions and Tomato Fondue, decorated with the Nicoise Garnishes for fish, hot.

This is a fine recipe for any white-fleshed fish fillets, including eel, but particularly for flatfish fillets such as flounder or halibut.

FROG'S LEGS À LA NIÇOISE
TO SERVE 4

8 sets of frog's legs (16 legs)	½ cup Tomato Fondue à la
salt and pepper	Niçoise
flour	½ cup thick Sauce Espagnole,
butter	or veal gravy
	parsley

Season the frog's legs lightly with salt and pepper and dredge in flour, shaking off the excess. Sauté in a little butter until golden. Add the Tomato Fondue and simmer for 5 minutes. Add the Espagnole and simmer 3 minutes more to blend. Arrange on a hot platter, sprinkle with parsley and serve hot.

Normande
(norh-MAHND)

Means Norman. The Normans were Scandinavian invaders who settled Normandy from 841 to 966. In 1066 the Scandinavian duke William of Normandy invaded England, defeated and killed King Harold at Hastings, and was crowned king. Later the Normans made conquests in Ireland, Wales and Scotland. They also conquered southern Italy and Sicily. They left a lasting impression of their vigor and warlike tendencies, but always adopted the ways of the conquered peoples and were absorbed into their cultures. Normandy was a northern province of France, on the English Channel, and this is where the Allied invasion of Europe began during World War II.

As a coastal area, Normandy's cuisine is naturally of the sea, but it also has fine cattle, salt-meadow sheep and excellent orchards. Fish and shellfish abound, and the game of Normandy is prized. Food à la Normande is typically braised fish garnished with any combination of oysters, shrimp, mussels, fried smelt, and freshwater crayfish. Mushrooms, truffles and bread fried in butter are also standard, but not as typical of the seaside atmosphere. Meats and fowl are usually cooked in cider. The wide use of apples, Calvados and cider set this style apart from any other major mode of French cooking. If you're looking for a French cooking style that is quite unusual, this is it. While neighboring Brittany has a similar cooking style, it is less common there. The cooking of Brittany, called Bretonne, is generally noted for the use of white beans, not apple products. Dishes garnished with Sauce Normande plus oysters are called à la Cancalaise (kahn-kah-LEZ), after the fishing port of Cancale on the north coast of Brittany, which is famous for its plump oysters.

The region has no vineyards, and wine is seldom drunk by its people. Hard cider and perry (made like cider but from fermented pear juice) are wine's substitutes at the table, and after dinner the celebrated Bénédictine liqueur of Fécamp is fitting. Another drink worthy of mention is Calvados, a spirit made from cider.

Normandy may not produce wines, but it certainly produces fine cheeses. Pont-l'eveque, a soft cheese sold in boxes, has a pungent flavor caused by a mold peculiar to the locale. It was well known as early as 1230, when it was called *Angelot*. Rollot is a small disk-shaped cheese produced in Normandy. And, finally, there is the great Camembert, a soft cream cheese invented by a Norman peasant woman named Marie Harel.

A table in Normandy might be quite rough, as in any coastal fishing area. This would be an interesting theme for a dinner. Anything from the sea would fit, such as a large net instead of a tablecloth, possibly complete with cork floats. Hard cider with the meal and Bénédictine afterward would be completely authentic.

SAUCE NORMANDE #1
TO MAKE 2 CUPS

1 cup Sauce Velouté,* preferably fish-based
½ cup fish fumet* or clam juice
½ cup canned mushroom juice, boiled down to ½
2 egg yolks
2–3 oz cream

½ cup mussel or oyster liquor (the liquid from inside the mussels shells), optional
2–3 Tbs butter (optional)
lemon juice (optional)
salt and pepper

Mix the Velouté, fish fumet, mushroom juice and mussel liquor in a pan and boil down by $^1/_3$. Remove from the heat and blend in the yolks and cream. Blend in the butter, if desired, season with lemon juice and salt and pepper to taste, and serve hot with fish.

This Sauce Normande plus poached oysters becomes Sauce Laguipière. If sliced truffles soaked in Madeira wine are added to the Sauce Laguipière it becomes Sauce Joinville.

SAUCE NORMANDE #2
TO MAKE 2 CUPS

1 onion, sliced fine
3 Tbs butter
2 Tbs flour
1 cup hard cider

salt, pepper, grated nutmeg
1½ cups heavy cream
lemon juice

Sauté the onion in the butter in a pan until limp but not browned. Blend in the flour and cook gently 3 minutes more. Blend in the cider and cook until thickened, stirring. Season to taste with salt, pepper and nutmeg. Blend in the cream, cook down to thicken and add a little lemon juice to taste. Serve hot with eggs, meat or poultry.

NORMANDE GARNISHES

Normande garnishes consist of a selection of poached oysters, poached mussels, cooked shrimp, sautéed button mushrooms, shredded truffles sprinkled over the finished dish, cooked crayfish tails, and often small bread pieces shaped like hearts or diamonds and sautéed lightly in butter, hot.

WHITE BEANS À LA NORMANDE
TO SERVE 4

1 lb dried white beans, soaked
  in cold water for 10 hours,
  drained
1 onion, stuck with 2 cloves
¼ lb ham, diced
2 garlic cloves
1 tsp parsley

1 bay leaf
¼ tsp thyme
cheesecloth, washed
salt and pepper
2 cups Sauce Normande #1, hot
2 Tbs chives

Put the beans in a casserole and cover with warm water. Add the onion, ham and garlic. Add the parsley, bay leaf and thyme tied in cheesecloth. Season to taste with salt and pepper. Bring to a boil, lower heat, and simmer covered for about 40 minutes, or until tender. If necessary add a little water during cooking. Discard the onion, garlic and herb bouquet. Drain the beans, mix with the Sauce Normande, and toss over low heat for a few minutes. Put in a hot serving dish, sprinkle with the chives and serve hot.

TURNIPS À LA NORMANDE
TO SERVE 4

2 lbs turnips, peeled and cut in   1½ cups Sauce Normande #2
   large dice

Preheat oven to 400°. Blanch the turnips in boiling lightly salted water for 10 minutes and drain. Put in a buttered baking dish. Pour the sauce over the top and bake for 15 minutes, or until tender. Serve hot, right in the baking dish.

EGGS À LA NORMANDE (Poached or Soft-Boiled)
TO SERVE 4

1½ cups mussels   8 eggs, freshly poached or soft-
1½ cups shrimp   boiled, hot
½ cup chopped mushrooms   8 oysters, poached in lightly
butter   salted water, cleaned and hot
1 cup Sauce Normande #1, hot   8 truffle slices (optional)

Boil the mussels and shrimp separately in lightly salted water until just done and drain. Clean and chop. Sauté the mushrooms in a little butter until tender, and drain. Mix the mussels, shrimp and mushrooms with ½ of the Sauce Normande, making a salpicon of chopped mussels, shrimp and mushrooms bound with Sauce Normande. Spread the salpicon on 4 hot plates, top with 2 eggs per plate, top the eggs with the oysters and spoon the remaining Sauce Normande over the top. Decorate each dish with 2 truffle slices and serve at once, hot.

This is often served with scrambled eggs in place of poached or soft-boiled eggs. For an omelet for 2, quarter the ingredients in the salpicon and halve the rest of the ingredients. Prepare the omelet* in 4 tablespoons of hot butter, filling with the salpicon of mussels, shrimp and mushrooms bound with Sauce Normande. Serve the finished omelet topped with the oysters, spoon over the remaining Sauce Normande, decorate with the truffle slices and serve at once, hot.

APPLE OMELET À LA NORMANDE
TO SERVE 2

4 eggs   ¼ tsp vanilla extract
1½ Tbs sugar   1 Tbs cream
2 oz cream   1 Tbs Calvados (apple brandy)
1 apple, peeled, cored and   or cider
   sliced   4 Tbs butter
1 Tbs butter   2 oz Cream Sauce, hot (op-
1 tsp sugar   tional)

Beat the eggs with sugar and cream. Sauté the apple lightly and slowly in the butter with the sugar and vanilla. As soon as the apples are cooked and limp add the cream and Calvados and cook down to thicken. Melt the 4 tablespoons of butter in a pan and have very hot. Use to cook the omelet,* filling with the apple mixture. Or, mix the egg and apple mixtures and use the hot butter to prepare a flat omelet.* Serve at once, topped with the Cream Sauce, hot.

PORK CHOPS À LA NORMANDE
TO SERVE 4

4 double-thick pork chops
salt and pepper
2 apples, peeled, cored and
    sliced
1 tsp sugar mixed with ½ tsp
    cinnamon
2 tsp diced butter

1 bay leaf
1 Tbs grated onion
2 cloves
½ cup hard cider
½ cup chicken stock* or broth

Preheat oven to 400°. Season the chops with salt and pepper to taste and arrange in a buttered casserole. Cover with the apple slices, and sprinkle with the mixed sugar and cinnamon. Dot with the butter pieces. Add the bay leaf, grated onion, cloves, cider and stock. Cover tightly (if necessary seal the lid with a flour and water paste) and bake for 1½ hours. Remove the cover and bake for about 15 minutes more, to brown the apples. Discard cloves and bay leaf. Serve hot, right in the casserole.

CORNISH GAME HEN or SQUAB À LA NORMANDE
TO SERVE 4

4 1-lb birds
salt and pepper
butter
2 oz butter
2 lbs cooking apples, peeled,
    cored and sliced

1 cup cider (hard or sweet)
    blended with ½ tsp ground
    cinnamon
½ cup cream

Preheat oven to 350°. Truss the birds and season to taste with salt and pepper. Brown them in a little butter in a casserole. Melt the 2 ounces of butter in a pan and toss the apples in the hot butter to coat. Remove the birds from the casserole, put in ½ the apples, top with the birds, add the rest of the apples and the cider. Cover and bake until done, about 30 to 40 minutes. Put the birds on a hot platter and keep hot. If any liquid remains in the casserole boil it down until almost absorbed by the apples. Add the cream and blend, without breaking the apples. Pile the apple mixture around the birds on the platter and serve hot.

CHICKEN À LA NORMANDE
TO SERVE 4

Proceed as for Cornish Game Hen à la Normande, cooking the chicken for about 30 minutes per pound.

DUCKLING À LA NORMANDE
TO SERVE 4

1 4–5-lb duckling
salt and white pepper
1 cup Muscadet wine (Muscadet
   is the name of a particular
   type of grape, which is quite
   distinctive. For the best flavor
   do not substitute another
   wine.)

¼ cup Calvados (apple brandy)
1 cup heavy cream
3 apples, peeled, cored and
   sliced
2 Tbs butter

Preheat oven to 325°. Remove all fat from inside of the duckling. Season inside and out with salt and pepper to taste, and truss. Prick the skin all over with a fork to allow the fat to escape during cooking. Roast in the oven for about 2 hours, or until done. If the duck begins to brown too much cover loosely with foil. Put the duck on a hot platter and keep hot. Remove all fat from the roasting pan. Add the Muscadet wine and cook over direct heat, scraping up the pan juices, until almost completely gone. Add the Calvados and cream and blend well. Cook until lightly thickened and remove from the heat. Meanwhile, sauté the apples in the butter until golden and slightly limp, but not mushy. Carve the duckling into quarters, coat with the sauce, surround with the apples and serve hot.

In this recipe the apples are sometimes seasoned with a little mixed sugar and cinnamon.

FLOUNDER À LA NORMANDE
TO SERVE 4

2 lbs flounder fillets
salt and pepper
½ cup hard cider
½ cup water
1 cup sliced mushrooms
2 oz butter
2 Tbs flour

1 egg yolk
1 tsp lemon juice
16 small mussels, steamed
salt and pepper
chives
watercress

Preheat oven to 350°. Season the fillets lightly with salt and pepper and place in a buttered casserole. Add the cider and water. Bring to a boil, cover, and bake about 10 minutes, or until the fish is just done. Set the fillets on a hot platter and keep hot. Sauté the mushrooms in the butter until tender and lightly browned. Remove with a slotted spoon and keep hot. Add the flour to the pan and blend well. Stir in the fish cooking liquid and blend well. Bring to a boil and simmer until lightly thickened, stirring. Remove from the heat, let cool just below a simmer, and beat in the yolk. Add the lemon juice, mussels, mushrooms and salt and pepper to taste. Reheat without boiling. Pour over the fish, sprinkle with chives, garnish with little bunches of watercress and serve hot.

APPLE MOUSSE À LA NORMANDE
TO SERVE 4

2 lbs apples, peeled, cored and
   sliced
½ orange rind, grated
2 Tbs sugar
2 Tbs orange marmalade
1 Tbs butter (unsalted)
2 eggs
2 egg yolks
2 Tbs sugar
1 envelope unflavored gelatin
   completely dissolved in 2 Tbs
   hot orange juice

½ cup whipped cream
2 oz Calvados (apple brandy)
4 Tbs orange marmalade
4 Tbs water
skinless sections of 2 tangerines
   or 2 temple oranges
1 crisp eating apple, peeled,
   cored and sliced thin

Cook the apples, orange rind, sugar and orange marmalade in a pan over very low heat, stirring until soft. Force through a strainer to purée. Blend in the butter. Put the eggs, yolks and sugar in a mixer and beat until light and thick. Blend in the dissolved gelatin. Fold in the apple purée, whipped cream and Calvados. Pour this mousse into a serving dish and chill to set. Meanwhile, cook the marmalade and water until melted, strain and cool. When the mousse is chilled and set, decorate with the tangerine and apple slices. Coat with the orange marmalade syrup and serve chilled.

This is also made in a mold, chilled, unmolded, decorated with the tangerine and apple slices, coated with the syrup and served chilled.

CRÊPES À LA NORMANDE
TO SERVE 4

1½ lbs crisp apples, peeled,
   cored and chopped
¼ cup sugar
1 Tbs heavy cream
¼ tsp almond extract
1 oz Calvados (apple brandy) or
   other brandy

6 cooked crêpes*
4 Tbs ground almonds
1½ Tbs butter, melted
1½ Tbs sugar
2 oz Calvados, or other brandy,
   warm

Cook the apples in water in a covered pan very gently for 20 minutes, or until tender but not colored. Blend in the sugar, bring to a boil and cook, stirring, for about 5 minutes, until you have a thick applesauce. This must not be runny. Remove from the heat and blend in the cream, almond extract and Calvados. Preheat oven to 375°. Place a crêpe on a buttered baking dish, top with ⅓ of the applesauce, and sprinkle with ⅓ of the ground almonds. Repeat with layers of crêpes, applesauce and almond, ending with a crêpe on top. Pour the butter over the top and sprinkle with the sugar. Bake on a high rack in the oven for about 30 minutes. Take to the table, pour on the warm Calvados and flame, spooning the flaming brandy over the crêpes until the fire dies. Slice like a cake and serve at once, hot.

Orange
(oh-RAHNZH)

Means orange, as in English. Orange is a city in southern France, but as far as food goes, the term a l'Orange means a dish using oranges in one way or another. Oranges are the fruit of several species of evergreen tree of the rue family, and are native to southeast Asia. There are three distinct types of oranges: (1) Sweet oranges (*Citrus sinensis*) were introduced to Europe in Spain in about 1100. This is the most common commercial orange and has many variations, such as navel oranges and the blood oranges of the Mediterranean (so called because of red streaks of pigment in the flesh). The most important variety is the Valencia orange. (2) Mandarin oranges (*Citrus nebilis*) are noted for their loose peel. Tangerines are the most noted variety. Mandarin oranges are grown widely in China and Japan. (3) Sour oranges (*Citrus aurantium*), or Seville oranges, are used primarily for commercial marmalade. Bitter orange peel comes from sour oranges. King and Temple oranges are natural hybrids between sweet and Mandarin oranges.

Oranges can lend a nice change of pace to an ordinary dish. Simply add orange sections, membranes and seeds removed, to a sauce at the end of cooking, along with a little orange juice or Curaçao, and you have a fresh-tasting and distinctive dish. It goes well with any meat, especially with game birds sautéed in butter. Sautéed chicken is also good with oranges. The orange sections, always without their seeds and membranes, can be warmed in a little butter and used as a simple garnish. Easy and effective, both visually and for the palate. Tangeries can be used in place of the oranges, in which case the finished dish would be called à la Mandarine, which means tangerine.

For décor with a dish à l'Orange, what could be more appropriate than the color orange? A small branch or two of an orange tree would also be nice, if available, especially if it had either oranges or blossoms on it.

POTATOES À L'ORANGE
TO SERVE 4

2 lbs potatoes, mashed	1–2 Tbs butter
1 orange rind, grated	1 oz hot cream blended with
1 egg	1/8 tsp ground cinnamon
salt and pepper	

Blend the mashed potatoes with the orange rind and beat in the egg. Season to taste with salt and pepper. Beat in the butter and cream. Squeeze through a pastry tube onto a buttered pan in rosettes and brown until golden in the oven. Or form the potato mixture into croquettes by rolling into cork shapes (dust your hands with flour to prevent sticking). Roll them in flour, brush with beaten egg and roll in bread crumbs. Deep-fry in hot oil until golden and drain on paper towels. Arrange the rosettes or croquettes around a main course and serve hot.

These potatoes are excellent with Duckling à l'Orange.

PORK CHOPS À L'ORANGE
TO SERVE 4

4 thick pork chops
salt and pepper
flour
1 Tbs butter
6 oz orange juice
½ tsp salt
1½ tsp sugar
1 orange peel, grated
½ lemon peel, grated
½ tsp paprika
⅛ tsp pepper
½ tsp ground cinnamon

¼ tsp ground nutmeg
⅛ tsp ground cloves
2 oz Curaçao liqueur
1 orange, in sections, with membranes and seeds discarded, tossed lightly in a little butter and hot
½ cup Jus de Veau, or veal or chicken stock* or gravy
1 Tbs flour blended with 2 Tbs cold water

Season the chops with salt and pepper to taste. Dredge in flour, shaking off the excess, and sauté in the butter until browned on both sides. Mix orange juice and all the seasonings, except the Curaçao, and when the chops are browned, add to their pan. Bring to a boil. Reduce heat to a very low simmer. Simmer covered for 45 minutes, or until the chops are done. When done, pour on the Curaçao and flame, stirring until the fire dies. Arrange the chops on a hot platter surrounded with the orange sections and keep hot. Skim the fat from the pan and add the Jus de Veau. Blend in the flour and water slurry and cook until thickened. Strain over the chops and serve hot.

CALF'S LIVER À L'ORANGE
TO SERVE 4

4 calf's liver slices, about ½ lb each
salt and pepper
flour
2 Tbs butter
1 oz dry white wine
2 Tbs butter
2 Tbs minced onion
2 garlic cloves, minced

½ tsp ground cinnamon
¼ tsp nutmeg
⅛ tsp ground cloves
2 oz chicken stock* or broth
2 Tbs oil
1 orange, peeled, in seeded sections (membranes removed)
1–2 Tbs sugar

Season the liver to taste with salt and pepper and dredge in flour, shaking off the excess. Sauté in 2 tablespoons of butter until done. Arrange on a hot platter and keep hot. In the same pan, heat the wine and add 2 tablespoons butter. Add the onion and simmer until just limp. Add the garlic and simmer for 1 minute. Blend in the cinnamon, nutmeg, cloves and stock, simmer a few minutes, pour over the liver and keep hot. Add the oil to the pan and when hot, use to heat the orange sections quickly on both sides. Sprinkle with the sugar to form a glaze and use to garnish the liver. Serve hot.

This dish is often served with rice, or rice pilaf, and the liver is sometimes seasoned with a little dry mustard or chili powder, or both, before dredging in the flour and sautéing.

DUCKLING À L'ORANGE
TO SERVE 4

14–5-lb duck	3 Tbs white wine vinegar
salt and pepper	2 cups Sauce Espagnole
ground cinnamon	1 Tbs cornstarch mixed with ½
2 oranges	tsp ground cinnamon
½ lemon	2 oz Curaçao liqueur
4 oranges, peeled	1 Tbs red currant jelly
3 Tbs sugar	3 oz dry white wine

Preheat oven to 325°. Remove all fat from inside the duck. Season it inside and out with salt and pepper to taste and inside with cinnamon lightly. Prick the skin all over with a fork to allow the fat to escape during cooking. Roast in the oven for 2 hours, or until done. If it browns too much, cover loosely with foil until done. Set the duck on a hot platter and keep hot. Pour off all the fat in the roasting pan.

Meanwhile, peel the 2 oranges and ½ lemon and separate the outer skin zest from the peel's white part. Cut the zest in very fine strips and blanch in boiling water for 3 minutes and drain. Squeeze the juice from the oranges and ½ lemon, combine and reserve. Separate the 4 peeled oranges into sections and remove and discard the membranes and seeds. Melt the sugar in a pan. When it turns pale brown, blend in the reserved orange-lemon juice, then the vinegar. Cook down to ½. Blend in the Sauce Espagnole and bring to a gentle simmer. Blend the cornstarch and cinnamon with the Curaçao. Blend in the currant jelly.

When the duck is set aside and the fat removed from the pan, add the wine to the pan and boil down, scraping up the juices. Strain into the sauce, which should be simmering slowly. Sprinkle the duck with the blanched orange and lemon strips and surround with the orange sections. Blend the cornstarch mixture with the sauce and simmer until lightly thickened. This is Sauce Bigarade. Spoon some sauce over the duck and serve the rest separately, hot.

CRÊPES À L'ORANGE (Crêpes Suzette)
TO SERVE 4

2 Tbs sugar
10 drops vanilla extract
½ lemon rind (the colored zest without the white), in very fine strips
½ orange rind (the colored zest without the white), in very fine strips

12 fresh-cooked crêpes, folded in half, then again into triangles, hot*
8 oz butter, unsalted
3 oz Curaçao
3 oz Grand Marnier
additional Curaçao and Grand Marnier

Begin 1 day ahead. Blend the sugar and vanilla extract. Blend in the lemon and orange strips and refrigerate, tightly sealed, for 1 day or more.

Heat the butter in a pan, or at the table in a chafing dish. When the butter bubbles, add the Curaçao and Grand Marnier and flame. Stir until the flame dies and strain in the stored sugar and blend in well. Put some folded crêpes into the sauce and turn carefully, adding more Curaçao and Grand Marnier to taste and flaming at once. Serve immediately, spooning a little flaming liquid over the crepes (3 per person).

These crêpes are usually made with a fairly thin batter, to produce thin finished crêpes.

Parisienne

(pah-ree-Z'YEN)

After Paris. The city of Paris lies in the basin of the River Seine and is surrounded by low hills. A map of Paris somewhat resembles a web, with streets radiating from the Île de la Cité (island of the city), in the Seine where the original settlement stood. In the first century B.C. a Gallic tribe known as the Parisii lived on this island in the Seine where they were discovered by Roman soldiers. Their settlement, called Lutetia, became a Roman town. Christianity was introduced to the inhabitants about 250, but Roman power was unbroken until the fourth century, when the Burgundians, Franks and Visigoths invaded the area.

Hugh Capet, Duke of France, founded the Capetian dynasty in 987 and made Paris the chief city of France. The power of his duchy gradually spread over the rest of France during the time of discord associated with the first three Crusades. The Sorbonne, built in 1253, brought students from all over Europe. From then on, the influence of Paris steadily grew to its present-day position as a leader in European politics, business and culture. Paris is best known for its gowns, millinery, jewelry, perfumes and glassware, all luxury items, but it is also a leading industrial city.

Dishes à la Parisienne are primarily meats and poultry, with various garnishes, but almost always with Potatoes à la Parisienne. Braised lettuce and braised artichokes are typical garnishes. This is an elegant cooking mode, as one would expect. Many of the dishes are served chilled, and the sauces are often enriched with egg yolk. This category is similar to Allemande in that the sauces Parisienne and Allemande are identical. Many of the individual dishes are also interchangeable.

The main difference between these cooking modes is the kinds of food prepared. Allemande dishes often lean to the heavier foods, such as rabbit with sour cream or sauerkraut salad with vinegar dressing. Parisienne dishes, on the other hand, should generally be more delicate foods. As I said, many of these recipes are interchangeable, and you'll find them listed as Parisienne in one place and as Allemande in another.

For wines typical of Paris, we have all of France to choose from, since Paris is the cosmopolitan center of the country. But the wine that is typical of the area around Paris is champagne.

The Île-de-France area, just north of Paris, produces exceptionally fine cheeses, such as Brie, which is delicate, soft and creamy, one of the world's greatest cheeses and a favorite of many French kings. Coulommiers is a velvety-soft dessert cheese much like a small Brie. And La Feuille de Dreux, also similar to Brie, is sold wrapped in chestnut leaves.

For background music and décor, Paris has so much to choose from. Draw ideas from the sidewalk cafe, the Left Bank, the Moulin Rouge, checkered tablecloths, candlelight, fine wines and music ranging from the cancan to that of the Paris-born composers Georges Bizet, Camille Saint-Säens, Charles Gounod, Paul Dukas, Ernest Chausson and Vincent d'Indy. Then there's always the American popular music about Paris, like "April in Paris."

A fine place to serve a dish à la Parisienne would be on a patio or terrace, particularly in a city. I once enjoyed Lamb Chops à la Parisienne on a rooftop terrace behind a friend's apartment in New York, late in the evening, when the street noises had died to a murmur, and I thought I was in Paris.

SAUCE PARISIENNE
TO MAKE 2 CUPS

2 oz veal or chicken glaze*	1–2 egg yolks
1¾ cups Sauce Velouté*	2 Tbs butter, diced (optional)

Blend the veal glaze and Velouté and simmer for several minutes. Blend in the yolks off heat, so they won't boil and curdle. Add the butter, if desired, and serve hot. Do not reboil after adding the yolks. This is the same as Sauce Allemande, and can be used for meats, fowl, vegetables and eggs.

PARISIENNE GARNISHES
TO SERVE 4

1. BRAISED LETTUCE

1 large head of lettuce
1 carrot, sliced
1 onion, sliced

1 cup beef or chicken stock* or
broth

Blanch the lettuce in boiling, lightly salted water for 5 minutes. Drain well. Put the carrot and onion in a pot just large enough to hold the lettuce. Top with the lettuce and add the stock. Bring to a boil, lower heat and simmer covered for 45 minutes. Remove the lettuce, quarter and remove the central core. Boil down the cooking stock to ½ cup, if necessary, and pour over the lettuce quarters. Serve hot.

2. BRAISED ARTICHOKES

12 small trimmed* artichokes, with the central hairy chokes removed
vinegar
1 carrot, sliced
1 onion, sliced

1 tsp parsley
½ tsp thyme
½ bay leaf
cheesecloth, washed
1 cup beef or chicken stock* or
broth

Blanch the artichokes in boiling, lightly salted water with a few drops of vinegar added for 1 minute. Drain well. Put the carrot and onion in a pot. Add the parsley, thyme and bay leaf tied in cheesecloth. Add the artichokes and stock and bring to a boil. Lower heat and simmer until tender, about 10 minutes. Remove the artichokes, boil down the cooking stock to ½ cup, if necessary, and strain over the artichokes. Serve hot.

Vegetable stock* is often used in preparing the braised lettuce or artichokes.

SALAD À LA PARISIENNE
TO SERVE 4

2 cups Macedoine of Vegetables
1 cup Mayonnaise, preferably homemade* (or to taste)
1 lb cooked lobster meat, in slices or chunks

4 hard-boiled eggs, quartered lengthwise
2 very small lettuces, cooked as in Parisienne Garnish #1

Mix the vegetables, Mayonnaise and lobster meat well and arrange in a pile on a serving dish. Garnish with the egg and lettuce quarters alternating around the salad and serve chilled.

POTATOES À LA PARISIENNE
TO SERVE 4

2 lbs tiny potatoes
3 oz butter

1 oz beef glaze*
parsley or chives

Sauté the potatoes over very low heat in the butter until just done. Shake the pan occasionally, rather than stirring, to cook evenly without breaking up the potatoes. When the potatoes are done, toss gently with the beef glaze, sprinkle with parsley or chives and serve hot.

ONIONS À LA PARISIENNE (Stuffed)
TO SERVE 4

8 medium onions
2 cups mushrooms, chopped,
   sautéed and drained

1 cup cooked ham, chopped
pepper
chicken stock* or broth

Preheat oven to 375°. Remove the brown onion skins and cut off their top thirds. Blanch the onions in lightly salted boiling water for 10 minutes and drain. Remove the inside of the onions, leaving 2 layers of outside thickness intact. Chop ½ the onion centers fine, sauté lightly and mix well with the mushrooms and ham. Season lightly with pepper. (Discard remaining onion centers.) Use this mixture to stuff the onions and place them in a buttered baking dish. Add enough stock to half cover the onions, bring to a boil over direct heat, and cook in the oven for 15 minutes. Drain, and serve hot.

TOMATOES À LA PARISIENNE (Stuffed)
TO SERVE 4

8 small tomatoes
salt and pepper
olive oil
1 onion, minced
1½ cups cooked chicken,
   chopped

1 cup mushrooms, minced
½ cup truffles, minced
2 oz butter
1 cup bread crumbs
butter, melted

Preheat oven to 375°. Cut the tops off the tomatoes and scoop out the insides. Season inside with salt and pepper to taste and sauté very lightly in oil. Turn upside down to drain. Mix the onion, chicken, mushrooms and truffles and sauté lightly in the butter. Season to taste with salt and pepper and mix well. Use this mixture to stuff the tomatoes. Place on a buttered baking sheet, top with the crumbs, dribble on a little butter to moisten and bake in the oven until hot through and golden brown. Serve hot.

ARTICHOKE HEARTS À LA PARISIENNE
TO SERVE 4

1½ lbs artichoke hearts   1 cup Sauce Parisienne, hot
butter

Blanch the artichoke hearts in boiling water for 30 seconds. Drain. Sauté in a little butter very gently until done and tender. Place in a hot vegetable dish, top with the sauce and serve hot.

This recipe is excellent using asparagus in place of the artichoke hearts.

EGGS À LA PARISIENNE (Baked)
TO SERVE 4

2 oz chopped cooked chicken   2 oz chopped mushrooms
2 oz chopped pickled tongue   salt and pepper
2 oz chopped truffles   8 eggs
                                     ¾ cup Sauce Espagnole, hot

Preheat oven to 500°. Mix the chicken, tongue, truffles and mushrooms and season lightly with salt and pepper. Use to line the bottoms of 4 buttered individual baking dishes. Add 2 eggs to each dish, being careful not to break their yolks. Season lightly with salt and pepper and bake on a high rack in the oven for 4 minutes, or until the whites are just set and the yolks still soft. Top with the Sauce Espagnole and serve at once, in the baking dishes, hot.

OMELET À LA PARISIENNE
TO SERVE 2

4 eggs   4 Tbs butter
salt and pepper   4 chipolata sausages (or small
1 Tbs chopped onion, sautéed   cocktail sausages), cooked
2 Tbs chopped mushrooms,   and hot
   sautéed   2 oz thick veal gravy or Jus de
                                        Veau,* hot

Beat the eggs with salt and pepper to taste. Blend in the onion and mushrooms. Cook the omelet in very hot butter, flat.* Serve on a hot plate, garnished with the sausages and topped with the gravy, hot.

BOILED BEEF À LA PARISIENNE (Cold)
TO SERVE 4

2 lbs lean cold boiled beef, sliced

1½ lbs potatoes, sliced rather thin and boiled until just done

3 tomatoes, sliced thin

1 lb green beans, cooked, and whole if possible

4 hard-boiled eggs, quartered lengthwise

watercress

2 onions, sliced in very thin rings

oil, vinegar, salt, pepper

parsley, chervil, tarragon

Arrange the slices of beef in an overlapping row down the center of a long platter. Alongside, arrange separate groups of potatoes, tomatoes and beans. Garnish with the egg quarters and small bunches of watercress. Top the meat with the onion rings. Season everything with oil, vinegar, salt and pepper to taste. Sprinkle with parsley, chervil and tarragon and chill. Serve chilled.

These are the typical vegetables used with Cold Beef à la Parisienne, but of course you may wish to substitute your own. Use what you like. The potatoes are always a good basic, and with them almost anything—cooked cauliflower, asparagus spears, peas—would be fine.

VEAL CUTLETS À LA PARISIENNE
TO SERVE 4

4 large veal cutlets, pounded thin

salt and pepper

flour

3 Tbs butter

2 Tbs oil

3 oz Madeira or Port wine

1 cup heavy cream

½ cup Sauce Espagnole, Jus de Veau* or veal gravy

8 slices of black truffle

Season the veal lightly with salt and pepper. Dredge in flour, shaking off the excess, and sauté in hot butter and oil until done and golden, about 5 minutes per side. Set on a hot platter and keep hot. Add the Madeira to the pan and boil down until amost gone, scraping up the juices. Add the cream and Espagnole and blend well, heating through and thickening lightly. Strain over the veal cutlets, decorate with the truffle slices and serve hot.

LAMB CHOPS À LA PARISIENNE
TO SERVE 4

1 lb mushrooms, sliced	12 lamb chops
salt and pepper	4 eggs, beaten
2 oz butter	4 oz butter, clarified*
1 pt cream, boiling	2 oz dry white wine
1 lb asparagus tips	2 cups Jus de Veau* or veal gra-
butter	vy, hot
2 cups bread crumbs	1 recipe Potatoes à la Par-
4 Tbs truffles, minced very fine	isienne, hot

Season the mushrooms lightly with salt and pepper and sauté in the butter for 8 to 10 minutes. Add the cream and boil down until it is almost gone. Cook the asparagus in boiling, lightly salted water until done and toss in a little butter. Keep the mushrooms and asparagus hot.

Meanwhile, mix the bread crumbs with the truffles. Dip the lamb chops in the egg and coat with the crumb mixture. Sauté in the clarified butter until done. Arrange in a ring on a hot, round serving dish and fill the center with the mushrooms in cream. Arrange the asparagus tips around the outside of the lamb with the points outward and keep hot. Meanwhile, add the wine to the lamb sauté pan and boil down, scraping up the juices. Blend in the Jus de Veau. Strain a little over the lamb chops and serve the rest separately. Serve the potatoes separately, hot.

It's important to finish cooking all these ingredients as closely together as possible. Be especially careful not to finish the mushrooms and asparagus too far ahead of the lamb and potatoes, for the longer they are kept hot, the more limp they become. Ideally, they should be served immediately upon completion. This is also true of the lamb and potatoes, but to a lesser degree.

MUTTON CHOPS À LA PARISIENNE
TO SERVE 4

Proceed as for Lamb Chops à la Parisienne, being careful to remove all excess fat from the mutton sauté pan before adding the wine and finishing the sauce.

CHICKEN SUPRÊMES À LA PARISIENNE
TO SERVE 4

4 chicken breasts, skinned, boned and halved, making 8 suprêmes	salt, pepper, grated nutmeg
	1 egg, beaten
salt and pepper (optional)	1½ lbs asparagus tips
butter	butter
1½ lbs potatoes, mashed	2 oz dry white wine
4 Tbs butter	2 cups Jus de Veau,* or veal gravy, hot

Preheat oven to 400°. Season the chicken to taste with salt and pepper if desired and sauté in a little butter until done. Meanwhile, mix the mashed potatoes with the 4 tablespoons of butter and season to taste with salt, pepper and nutmeg. Shape into a large patty about ½ inch thick and place on a well-buttered baking dish. Brush with the beaten egg and brown in the oven. Top with the chicken and keep hot.

Meanwhile, cook the asparagus in lightly salted water until tender and toss in a little butter. Arrange on the dish around the potatoes and chicken. Keep hot. Add the wine to the chicken sauté pan and boil down, scraping up the juices. Blend in the Jus de Veau and strain into a sauceboat, or pour over the chicken, and serve hot.

SOLE À LA PARISIENNE
TO SERVE 4

1 oz butter
2 oz water, lightly salted
2 tsp lemon juice
1 lb mushroom caps
2 lbs sole fillets
salt and pepper

¾ cup dry white wine
1 oz butter
1½ cups White Wine Sauce*
12 truffle slices
4 giant shrimp, cooked and hot

Put the butter, water and lemon juice in a pot and bring to a boil. Add the mushrooms and boil, stirring, for 8 to 10 minutes. Set the mushrooms aside and keep hot. Reserve the cooking juices. Season the sole to taste with salt and pepper and poach in the white wine with the butter and mushroom cooking liquid. Set on a hot platter and keep hot. Add the White Wine Sauce to the pan juices and cook down to thicken. Pour over the fish, garnish with the mushrooms, truffle slices and shrimp, and serve hot.

This is an excellent recipe for any white-fleshed fish fillets or scallops, but is most typical of the Parisienne mode when using delicate fish like sole, flounder or freshwater perch.

SALMON GLACÉ À LA PARISIENNE (Glazed Salmon)
TO SERVE 4

4 salmon steaks, skinned (about ½ lb each)
salt and white pepper
2 cups fish fumet* or 1 cup each clam juice and dry white wine
2 oz pickled tongue, sliced thin (or ham or prosciutto)
2 oz truffles, sliced thin

1 pkg. unflavored gelatin
4 hard-boiled eggs, halved lengthwise
Parisienne Garnish #1, using 2 very small lettuces, cooked and drained
1 recipe Potatoes à la Parisienne

Season the salmon lightly with salt and white pepper and simmer in the fish fumet, covered, until done. Let cool in the juices. Drain and arrange carefully on a platter. Decorate with the tongue and truffle slices, cut in interesting shapes if desired. Add the gelatin to the fish cooking juices and let stand for 5 minutes. Slowly bring to a boil and simmer for 5 minutes, or until all the gelatin granules are completely dissolved. Let cool until ½ set. Meanwhile, arrange the eggs, lettuce quarters and potatoes in separate piles or groups around the salmon. Coat the fish and garnishes with the ½-set gelatin. Chill the platter to set the gelatin, keeping the remaining gelatin just warm enough to prevent further setting. When the platter is cooled and the glaze·set, coat with ½-set gelatin again and chill to set again. Repeat once more. Chill the remaining gelatin separately and when set fully, cut into cubes and add the gelatin cubes to the platter's garnishes. Serve chilled.

This is a fine recipe for chilled, glazed fish of any kind. Use thick ½-pound fillets of the fish of your choice in place of the salmon.

LOBSTER À LA PARISIENNE
TO SERVE 4

2 Tbs parsley
2 tsp chervil
2 tsp tarragon
½ tsp thyme
2 bay leaves
4 peppercorns, crushed
cheesecloth, washed
2 onions, sliced
2 carrots, sliced
2 celery stalks, sliced
2 onions, stuck with 4 cloves each
2 garlic cloves, crushed
3 tsp salt
4 qts water

2 oz lemon juice (optional)
4 1½-lb lobsters, live if possible sible
1 recipe Salad à la Parisienne, made with the chopped body and claw meat
salt and white pepper
1½ cups Aspic Mayonnaise, ½ set
4 hard-boiled eggs, quartered lengthwise
4 lettuce hearts, cooked whole as for Parisienne Garnish #1
2 truffles, sliced thin

Tie the parsley, chervil, tarragon, thyme, bay leaves and peppercorns in cheesecloth and put in a pot with the onions, carrots, celery, the onions stuck with cloves, garlic, salt and water. Boil for 30 minutes and add the lemon juice if desired. Plunge the lobsters into this boiling court bouillon headfirst, 1 or 2 at a time, and cook until the shells are bright red and the lobsters are done. Drain and cool. When cool, split lengthwise and discard their intestinal tracts. Slice the tail meat rather thickly. Remove the remaining meat from the body (except the head sacs and lungs) and from all the claws and chop coarsely.

Put the Salad Parisienne (made using the chopped claw and body meat) in the center of a serving dish in a neat pile. Surround with the lobster tail slices, lightly seasoned with salt and white pepper and coated with ½-set Aspic Mayonnaise. Garnish with hard-boiled eggs and lettuce hearts. Decorate the lobster tail slices with small truffle slices and serve lightly chilled.

This is, of course, the French idea of how to cook lobster. The lobsters they use, however, are inferior in delicacy and flavor to our New England lobsters, hence the use of all the seasonings. American lobsters can instead be boiled in lightly salted water for a lighter and more fresh-tasting dish. They are also excellent as prepared in this recipe, and very flavorful.

CONSOMMÉ À LA PARISIENNE
TO SERVE 4

1 egg	salt and grated nutmeg
1 egg yolk	1 qt chicken consommé
3 oz heavy cream	2 tsp chervil

Preheat oven to 350°. Beat the egg, yolk and cream together and season lightly with salt and a little nutmeg. Strain. Put in a buttered baking dish sized so that the mixture is ¼ inch deep. Bake in the oven for about 10 minutes. Unmold and cut in tiny circles or other shapes. This is called Royale. Heat the consommé and serve hot, garnished with the pieces of Royale and the chervil.

This is often served garnished with a few tablespoons of sautéed, chopped vegetables as well, but I think it is more appropriate to the Parisienne mode with just the Royale and chervil as garnishes.

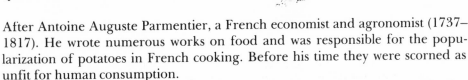

Parmentier

(pahr-mahn-T'YAY)

After Antoine Auguste Parmentier, a French economist and agronomist (1737–1817). He wrote numerous works on food and was responsible for the popularization of potatoes in French cooking. Before his time they were scorned as unfit for human consumption.

In cuisine, the use of the word *Parmentier* means that potatoes will be included in the dish in one form or another. If a dish has no potatoes and is called *Parmentier,* it is misnamed. This is a simple cooking mode, but one that can be dressed up as much as you wish without deviating from its character as long as the potatoes remain a prime feature of the finished dish. Usually the potatoes are mashed, or diced and sautéed. Some other modes that rely on potatoes as their distinguishing feature are Anna and Duchesse.

You could do something quite unusual for a dish Parmentier in the way of decor. In honor of potatoes, or Parmentier, various types of potatoes could be used as part of your centerpiece. There are the typical tan-colored potatoes, the red potatoes, and you could stretch things a bit and use the yellow or orange sweet potatoes, or yams, even though they are tuberous roots, not potatoes. The cinnamon vine, or Chinese yam (*Dioscorea batatas*) grows as far north as New York and is known for its striking foliage and fragrant flowers. True potatoes are members of the nightshade family, *Solanum tuberosum,* and are native to the elevated valleys of the Andes Mountains of South America. They were introduced to Europe in about 1580.

POTATOES PARMENTIER
TO SERVE 4

2 lbs potatoes, diced	salt and pepper
butter	parsley

Sauté the potatoes in a little butter until done and golden. Season to taste with salt and pepper, sprinkle with parsley and serve hot.

POTATOES PARMENTIER (Stuffed)
TO SERVE 4

4 baked potatoes	¼ tsp oregano
salt and pepper	½ cup Sauce Espagnole, or beef
1 lb lean beef leftovers, diced	gravy
½ tsp basil	Parmesan cheese, grated
	butter, melted

Halve the potatoes and scoop out some of the pulp from each half. Season the scooped-out potato shells with salt and pepper to taste. Mix the beef, basil, oregano and Espagnole in a pan and cook until thickened. Use to stuff the potatoes. Preheat oven to 350°. Top the stuffed potatoes liberally with cheese and dribble on a little melted butter to moisten. Place on a buttered baking sheet and bake in the oven until golden brown. Serve hot.

TURNIPS PARMENTIER
TO SERVE 4

4–5 cups mashed cooked turnips	salt and pepper
2 cups mashed cooked potatoes	chives
2 Tbs softened butter	

Blend the turnips and potatoes over very low heat until completely mixed and fairly dry. Do not allow to burn or brown at all. Blend in the butter off heat and season to taste with salt and pepper. Sprinkle with chives and serve hot.

EGGS PARMENTIER (Poached or Soft-Boiled)
TO SERVE 4

3 potatoes, peeled and cut in small thin strips	4 eggs, freshly poached or soft-boiled and hot
3 Tbs oil, preferably peanut	½ cup Sauce Velouté* cooked with ¼ cup heavy cream until thick, hot
3 Tbs butter	

Put the potatoes in 4 mounds in the hot oil and butter in a pan and squeeze lightly with a spatula to make 4 thick cakes. When they are lightly browned turn and brown on the other side. Push a spoon down onto the potato cakes making a depression in the middle of each to hold the eggs. These are called potato barquettes (little boats). Cook until done. Drain. Serve on hot plates, with a freshly cooked egg in the center of each barquette. Top with the Cream Sauce Velouté and serve at once, hot.

EGGS PARMENTIER (Baked)
TO SERVE 4

2 cups diced potatoes	8 eggs
butter	salt and pepper
salt and pepper	4 Tbs cream (optional)

Sauté the potatoes in a little butter until just done and golden. Use to line 4 buttered individual baking dishes. Season with salt and pepper to taste. Preheat oven to 500°. Break 2 eggs carefully into each baking dish and season with salt and pepper to taste. Top with the cream, if desired, and bake on a high rack in the oven for 4 minutes, or until the whites are just set and the yolks still soft. Serve at once, hot.

OMELET PARMENTIER
TO SERVE 2

4 eggs	1 tsp parsley
4 Tbs diced potatoes	salt and pepper
butter	4 Tbs butter

Beat the eggs. Sauté the potatoes in a little butter until golden. Add to the eggs with the parsley and season to taste with salt and pepper. Cook in very hot butter as a flat omelet.*

This is sometimes prepared as a filled omelet, using the sautéed potatoes and parsley as the filling.

BEEF MIROTON PARMENTIER (Meat and Onion Ragout)
TO SERVE 4

2 onions, sliced
butter
1 cup Sauce Lyonnaise, hot
2 lbs leftover beef, sliced and
    hot

2 oz beef stock* or broth
2 lbs potatoes, mashed and hot
parsley

Preheat oven to 350°. Sauté the onions in a little butter until limp and golden, and keep hot. On an oblong baking dish, spread a mixture of the sautéed onions and half the Sauce Lyonnaise. Top with the beef slices moistened with the stock. Top the beef with the remaining Sauce Lyonnaise, and put the potatoes in a ring around the meat. Put in the oven to brown lightly, sprinkle with parsley and serve hot.

MUTTON CHOPS, or CUTLETS PARMENTIER
TO SERVE 4

2 lbs potatoes, diced
salt and pepper
butter
8 mutton chops
salt and pepper

butter
2 oz dry white wine
1 cup Sauce Espagnole, or beef
    gravy
parsley

Season the potatoes with salt and pepper to taste and sauté in a little butter until ¾ done. Season the mutton with salt and pepper to taste and sauté separately until nicely browned on both sides. Add the potatoes to the mutton pan and finish cooking together. Arrange the mutton chops around the outside of a hot serving dish, and pile the potatoes in the center. Keep hot. Discard excess fat from the pan, if any, and add the wine, boiling down and scraping up the juices. Add the Espagnole, heat and blend well, strain over the mutton and potatoes, sprinkle with parsley and serve hot.

VEAL CHOPS, or CUTLETS PARMENTIER
TO SERVE 4

Proceed as for Mutton Chops Parmentier using veal stock* or gravy in place of the Sauce Espagnole.

VEAL SAUTÉ PARMENTIER
TO SERVE 4

Proceed as for Mutton Chops Parmentier, using 2 pounds of lean veal, in bite-size pieces, and veal stock* or gravy in place of the Sauce Espagnole. Serve the veal and potatoes mixed together.

LAMB SAUTÉ PARMENTIER (or Chops or Cutlets)
TO SERVE 4

Proceed as for Mutton Chops Parmentier using 2 pounds of lean lamb pieces (or 8 to 12 chops), but sauté the lamb in a mixture of equal parts of butter and olive oil (or vegetable oil). Add 1 crushed garlic clove with the wine. Also add 1 to 2 ounces of tomato purée to the pan sauce. Serve the lamb chops and potatoes separately, but serve the lamb pieces mixed with the potatoes.

LAMB LOIN PARMENTIER
TO SERVE 4

1 lamb loin	2 oz butter, melted
butter	2 oz dry white wine
salt and pepper	1 cup thickened veal stock* or
2 potatoes, diced	veal gravy
salt and pepper	parsley

Preheat oven to 325°. In a casserole brown the lamb in a little butter and season to taste with salt and pepper. Add the potatoes and season with salt and pepper to taste. Sprinkle with the butter and bake in the oven for about 1 hour, or until golden. Arrange the lamb and potatoes on a hot serving dish. Add the wine to the casserole and boil down, scraping up the juices. Blend in the veal stock and heat through. Strain over the lamb and potatoes, sprinkle with parsley and serve hot.

CHICKEN SAUTÉ PARMENTIER
TO SERVE 4

Proceed as for Mutton Chops Parmentier using 2 small cut-up chickens. Substitute veal gravy for the Sauce Espagnole.

SOLE PARMENTIER
TO SERVE 4

2 lbs sole fillets	butter
salt and pepper	salt and pepper
1 cup fish fumet* or ½ cup each	1 cup Sauce Mornay
clam juice and dry white wine	Parmesan cheese, grated
1 lb potatoes, diced	butter, melted

Preheat oven to 375°. Season the fillets with salt and pepper to taste. Put in a buttered casserole and add the fish fumet. Bring to a boil over direct heat, cover, and bake in the oven for 10 minutes, or until the fish flakes easily with a fork and is done. Meanwhile, sauté the potatoes in a little butter until golden. Season to taste with salt and pepper. Arrange in a shallow baking dish and top with the fish, being careful not to break the fillets. Boil down the fish cooking liquid to 2 tablespoonfuls and mix with the Sauce Mornay. Top the fish with this sauce, sprinkle generously with cheese and dribble on a little melted butter to moisten. Brown in the oven and serve at once, right in the baking dish, hot.

This is an excellent recipe for fillets of any fish, or eel.

COD PARMENTIER
TO SERVE 4

2 lbs cooked cod
½ recipe Duchesse Potatoes, or
   mashed potatoes

¼ cup heavy cream
Parmesan cheese, grated
butter, melted

Preheat oven to 375°. Put the cod in a buttered casserole and top with the potatoes blended with the cream. Sprinkle liberally with cheese and a little butter to moisten, and bake in the oven until golden brown. Serve hot, right in the casserole.

This recipe is excellent for any leftover fish, especially firm fleshed fish such as haddock or swordfish.

POTATO STICKS PARMENTIER
TO MAKE 60

1½ cups mashed potatoes, dry
½ cup flour
2 Tbs butter, softened
2 Tbs cream (or as needed for a
   smooth consistency)

1 cup Gruyère cheese, grated
salt, white pepper, grated
   nutmeg
¼ tsp ground turmeric

Preheat oven to 400°. Beat the potatoes and flour until completely blended. Mix in the butter, little by little, until completely blended. Blend in the cream, then the cheese, and season with salt, white pepper, nutmeg and the turmeric. Using a pastry bag squeeze the mixture onto well-buttered baking tins, in ½-inch-thick strips about 1½ inches long. Leave some room around the strips for expansion during cooking. Bake until golden brown, about 12 minutes, and serve hot as an hors d'oeuvre.

These can be prepared ahead, and baked whenever desired.

PARMENTIER SOUP (Purée of Potato Soup)
TO SERVE 4

1 leek white, shredded	2 Tbs cream
1 Tbs butter	2 Tbs butter (optional)
1½ cups diced potato	1½ tsp chervil
2 cups chicken consommé* or broth	½ cup small croutons, sautéed in butter, or buttered and baked
salt and pepper	

Sauté the leek white lightly in the butter. Add the potatoes and consommé season to taste with salt and pepper, and boil until the potatoes are done and tender. Purée the potato mixture in a blender or rub through a fine sieve. Add the cream. Add the butter, if desired. Add the chervil and keep hot for 8 to 10 minutes to blend the flavors. Serve hot, garnished with the croutons.

Périgourdine

(pay-ree-goor-DEEN)

After the old French department of Périgord, and its capital Périgueux. During Roman times the city was known as Vesuna. In the ninth century it became the capital of Périgord. Today, Périgueux is the capital of the department of Dordogne. As one of the seats of French Protestantism, Périgueux suffered during the religious wars of the late sixteenth century and during the war of the Fronde, from 1651–1653.

In cooking the term Périgourdine connotes a liberal use of pâté de foie gras (fat goose liver) and truffles, and especially the use of foie gras as a stuffing for fowl. If foie gras is unavailable, use chicken liver. If truffles are unavailable use mushrooms. Stuffed dishes are most unusual in this mode, and if they are cooked for the final 20 to 30 minutes with added truffles and sealed in a crust they become dishes Souvarov. If these same dishes are sealed in pieces of buttered white parchment instead they become dishes a la Strasbourgeoise (strahs-boor-ZHWAZ), after the city of Strasbourg on the Ill River. Souvarov dishes (soo-vah-ROFF), after a Russian prince and general, Alexandre Vassilievitch Souvarov are simply an embellishment to dishes à la Périgourdine, rather than a distinct cooking style. The reason for the additional truffles and crust is so that the dish can be served at the table unbroken, and when the crust is pierced the aromas will fill the room.

For wine, the area around Périgueux is noteworthy indeed. Toward the west is the Bordeaux area, and you just can't do any better than that for fine wines.

Since Périgueux still retains much of its Roman character, and dishes à la Périgourdine are invariably expensive, it might be appropriate to present these dishes as in a Roman feast. The more opulent the décor the better. Perhaps you could serve several courses over a period of a few hours, with wines and fruits between. More than one main course would be quite fitting.

SAUCE PÉRIGUEUX
TO MAKE 2 CUPS

4 Tbs diced truffles
salt and pepper
2 tsp butter
2 Tbs Madeira wine

2 cups Sauce Espagnole, or
    thick beef stock* or gravy
2 oz Madeira wine

Season the truffles lightly with salt and pepper and sauté gently in the butter. Remove the truffles from the pan and reserve. Add the 2 tablespoons of Madeira to the pan and simmer a few minutes. Add the Espagnole and simmer a few minutes more. Return the truffles to the pan, lower the heat below a simmer, and add the 2 ounces of Madeira. Keep hot, but do not allow to boil after putting the truffles in the sauce. Serve hot with eggs or meat.

EGGS À LA PÉRIGOURDINE (Baked)
TO SERVE 4

1 cup pâté de foie gras
8 eggs
salt and pepper

3 tsp butter, diced fine
¾ cup thick Sauce Périgueux,
    hot

Preheat oven to 500°. Put the pâté in the bottoms of 4 buttered individual baking dishes. Top with 2 eggs per dish, being careful not to break the yolks. Season lightly with salt and pepper, and sprinkle the butter on the yolks. Bake on a high rack in the oven for 4 minutes, or until the whites are just set and the yolks still soft. Serve at once, topped with the Sauce Périgueux.

EGGS À LA PÉRIGOURDINE (Scrambled)
TO SERVE 4

3 oz goose or chicken liver,
    chopped
1 oz chopped truffles

butter
8 eggs
salt and pepper

Sauté the liver and truffles lightly in butter and drain. Meanwhile, beat the eggs and season to taste with salt and pepper. Scramble the eggs in hot butter, and mix with the liver and truffles. Serve at once, hot.

This is the same as Scrambled Eggs Rossini, except that Madeira Sauce is usually served when the dish is called Rossini.

BEEF FILLET À LA PÉRIGOURDINE
TO SERVE 8

½ lb truffles, cut in thick slivers
1 beef fillet, whole
2 oz butter (more if needed)
pepper
1 lb bacon, sliced
1 carrot, diced
1 onion, diced
1 celery stalk, diced
1 tsp thyme
1 bay leaf

1 cup Madeira wine
1 cup beef stock* or broth
1 lb truffles, diced
4 oz Madeira wine
4 oz Sauce Espagnole, or beef
    gravy
8 small baked tartlet crusts,* hot
4 oz butter
1 lb pâté de foie gras, in small
    slices

Preheat oven to 375°. Using a thin knife, insert the truffle slivers through the entire beef fillet. Brown the fillet in ½ the butter in a pan, and season with pepper to taste. Blanch the bacon in boiling water for 5 minutes, drain, and wrap around the fillet and secure with string. Melt the remaining butter in a braising pan or stewing pot. Add the carrot, onion and celery and brown lightly. Add the thyme and bay leaf, and lay the browned fillet on this braising bed of vegetables. Add the Madeira and stock, and cover. Place in the oven and braise for about 30 to 45 minutes, until done to taste (30 minutes should be fairly rare). Meanwhile, cook the truffles in the Madeira until the wine is absorbed. Add the Espagnole and cook down until thickened enough to hold the truffles together lightly. Fill the tartlets with this truffle salpicon and keep hot. Melt the butter in a pan and toss the pâté de foie gras slices in it lightly to heat and coat. Do not stir with a spoon, and use a very low heat, or the foie gras slices will break. When the fillet is done, set it on a hot platter, discarding the bacon and strings. Surround it with the truffle-filled tartlets and 8 piles of foie gras slices, alternating around the fillet. Keep hot. Quickly remove excess fat from the braising pan, if any, and boil down the juices to half. Strain over the meat and serve hot.

For 4 guests, use ½ beef fillet and halve the other ingredients, but cook for the same time.

TOURNEDOS À LA PÉRIGOURDINE (Beef Fillets)
TO SERVE 4

4 beef fillets
salt and pepper (optional)
butter
16 truffle slices

4 bread slices, trimmed
2 oz Madeira wine
1½ cups Sauce Espagnole, or
    beef gravy, hot

Season the fillets with salt and pepper if desired. Sauté in butter until done to taste, remove from the pan and keep hot. In the same pan quickly sauté the truffles lightly. Remove them and keep them hot. Add the bread to the pan and sauté quickly until golden. Place a slice of sautéed bread on each of 4 hot plates and top with the fillets. Top each fillet with 4 truffle slices and keep hot. Add the wine to the sauté pan and boil down quickly, scraping up the juices. Add the Espagnole and blend well. Strain over the fillets and serve hot.

PORK FORCEMEAT
TO MAKE 2 CUPS

1 lb ground pork	½ tsp basil
1 tsp salt	¼ tsp sage
¼ tsp pepper	¼ tsp mace
½ tsp thyme	¼ tsp coriander
¼ tsp ground bay leaf	

Mix all the ingredients well and let stand for a few hours before using, to blend the flavors.

LAMB CHOPS À LA PÉRIGOURDINE
TO SERVE 4

8–12 lamb chops	1½ cups Sauce Périgueux, hot
butter	
8–12 Tbs Pork Forcemeat mixed with 4–6 Tbs minced truffles	

Preheat oven to 350°. Sauté the chops on one side in a little butter until almost all done. Put the chops, raw side down, on a buttered baking sheet. Top each with 1½ tablespoons of mixed Pork Forcemeat and truffles. Cook in the oven for 7 to 8 minutes, until done. Arrange the chops on a hot platter, spoon a little Périgueux Sauce over the chops and serve the rest separately, hot.

LAMB CRÊPINETTES À LA PÉRIGOURDINE (Flat Sausages)
TO SERVE 4

8 boneless lamb cutlets	½ cup pâté de foie gras
salt and pepper	2 truffles, minced
butter	1 cup Pork Forcemeat
1 carrot, diced	8 thin sheets of pork caul, or of
1 onion, diced	salt pork blanched in boiling
1 celery stalk, diced	water 5 minutes
1 tsp thyme	2 oz melted butter
½ cup Madeira wine	bread crumbs
1 cup beef stock* or broth	

Preheat oven to 350°. Season the lamb with salt and pepper to taste and brown in a little butter. Melt 1 ounce of butter in a braising pan or stewing pot. Add the carrot, onion and celery and brown. Add the thyme and lamb cutlets. Pour in the wine and stock, bring to a boil and cover. Braise in the oven for 20 minutes. Remove the pot from the oven and let the lamb cool in the juices. Mix the pâté de foie gras and truffles with the Pork Forcemeat and blend well. Drain the lamb cutlets and dry on paper towels. Coat them on both sides with the forcemeat mixture. Wrap the coated cutlets separately in pieces of pork caul. Brush with the melted butter and roll in crumbs, pressing them into the surface to adhere. Broil under a low flame until golden on both sides, and serve hot.

BABY LEG of LAMB À LA PÉRIGOURDINE
TO SERVE 4

1 lb pork sausage meat
¼ lb ground goose liver, or
  chicken liver
2 truffles, minced
1 egg
1 boned baby leg of lamb,
  browned in the oven

thin sheets of pork caul, or of
  salt pork
pie crust for a 12-inch pie*
1 egg, beaten
2 cups Sauce Périgueux

Mix the sausage meat, goose liver, truffles and egg well and use to coat the lamb. Preheat oven to 350°. Wrap the coated leg of lamb in pork caul. Roll out the pie crust and use to wrap the lamb, so that the seam is on the bottom of the roast. Place on a buttered baking dish. Remove a small circle of crust from the top to let the steam escape during cooking, about 1 inch across. If desired, decorate the pastry with strips of leftover pastry. Brush with the beaten egg. Bake in the oven for about 35 minutes per pound. When the lamb is almost done warm the Sauce Périgueux but do not boil. When the lamb is done pour the sauce in the hole in the top of the pastry and serve right in the baking dish, hot.

LAMB PIE À LA PÉRIGOURDINE
TO SERVE 4

pie crust for a 12-inch pie*
1 cup Pork Forcemeat
4 oz ground veal
1 egg
¼ cup brandy

2 lbs lamb, sliced thin
½ lb pâté de foie gras, sliced
  thin
2 truffles, sliced thin
butter

Preheat oven to 425°. Roll out ½ the pie crust and use to line a 12-inch pie pan. Roll out the rest of the crust for a top crust. Mix the Pork Forcemeat with the veal, egg and brandy until well blended. Line the pie dish with ⅔ of this mixture on the sides and bottom and reserve the remaining ⅓. Sauté the lamb, pâté de foie gras and truffles separately in a little butter until lightly browned. Put ½ the lamb in the bottom of the pie dish. Top with ½ the pâté de foie gras. Then top with the truffles, then with the remaining lamb and the remaining foe gras. Top with the reserved Pork Forcemeat mixture and cover with the top crust, crimping the crust's edges together. Poke a few holes in the top crust for steam to escape during cooking and bake in the oven for 35 to 45 minutes, until golden brown. Serve hot. If desired, cover the edges of the crust with foil for the first 20 minutes of baking to prevent overbrowning.

CHICKEN À LA PÉRIGOURDINE
TO SERVE 4

2 cups diced pâté de foie gras	1 4–5-lb chicken
1 cup diced truffles	butter
1 oz brandy	1 cup sliced truffles
salt and pepper	4 oz Madeira wine
	1½ cups Sauce Espagnole, hot

Preheat oven to 375°. Mix the pâté de foie gras, truffles and brandy. Season to taste with salt and pepper, and use to stuff the bird. Sew or skewer closed and truss. Brown in a little butter in a roasting pan, cover, and cook in the oven for about 2½ hours, or until done. Add the truffles and cook covered for 10 minutes more. Put the chicken on a hot platter with the truffles, discard the trussings, and keep hot. Remove excess fat from the pan, add the wine and quickly boil down, scraping up the juices. Add the Espagnole and blend well. Strain a little sauce over the bird and serve the rest separately, hot.

If cooked until almost done, then sprinkled with truffles and finished sealed in a pot with a crust, this dish becomes Chicken Souvarov.

This dish is often made with Cornish game hens or other fowl. Simply adjust the cooking time to the size of the bird. For stuffed one-pound game hens, the time would be about 45 minutes. For any other fowl, about 30 minutes per pound.

Piémontaise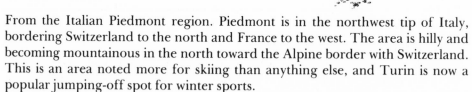

(p'ee-mohn-TEZ)

From the Italian Piedmont region. Piedmont is in the northwest tip of Italy, bordering Switzerland to the north and France to the west. The area is hilly and becoming mountainous in the north toward the Alpine border with Switzerland. This is an area noted more for skiing than anything else, and Turin is now a popular jumping-off spot for winter sports.

A dish cooked à la Piémontaise is generally accompanied by rice and white, or Piedmont, truffles and cheese. Any meat, including kidneys or sweetbreads (sweetbreads must be soaked in cold water, changed often, for 4 hours to cleanse) can be made into a fine dish à la Piémontaise if sliced, sautéed in butter, and served with Rice à la Piémontaise and Sauce Espagnole, Jus de Veau, or a gravy flavored with tomato paste. Truffle essence (made from truffle peelings cooked in a little Madeira wine until the wine is reduced to about ¼ and strained) is often added to the sauce.

The wines of Piedmont are some of Italy's finest, particularly the red wines. Among white wines, Cortese is the best known. It is dry, light and savory. Some of the best Cortese is sold as Gavi Bianco, named after the village of Gavi. Other whites of the area are Coronata, Portofino, Vermentino and Cinqueterre, all somewhat dry and not bad. The red wines of this area are the ones most worthy of notice, however. A good aged Barolo is very rich and almost spicy. Barbaresco has a less all-around character than Barolo, but because of this needs less aging, and is a fine choice. Both of these reds fall into what the Italians call "Great Roast Wines," meaning they are good with roasts.

There is also a very interesting cheese produced in Piedmont, a firm cheese called Bra.

The Piedmont region is alpine and this could be kept in mind for the dinner setting.

TOAST À LA PIÉMONTAISE
TO SERVE 4

4 bread slices, toasted, cut in triangles and buttered

Swiss cheese, grated

Preheat broiler. Sprinkle the toast with cheese and brown quickly under the broiler. Serve hot.

GNOCCHI À LA PIÉMONTAISE
TO SERVE 4

1 lb potatoes, boiled and
mashed dry
¾ cup flour mixed with ½ tsp
oregano freshly ground in a
mortar
1 egg
1 egg yolk

salt and pepper
grated nutmeg
salted water, or chicken stock*
1 cup Sauce Espagnole blended
with 2 Tbs tomato paste, hot
Swiss or Parmesan cheese,
grated

Blend the potatoes, flour, egg and yolk thoroughly and season well with salt and pepper, and with a little nutmeg. Chill. Shape the dough in little cylinders or balls (gnocchi) using wet hands, and rinsing your hands in cold water after forming each shape. Cook the gnocchi in very gently simmering lightly salted water or chicken stock until done. About 10 minutes. Serve hot, with the Espagnole. Serve cheese separately, in a little bowl with its own spoon.

RICE À LA PIÉMONTAISE
TO SERVE 4

4 Tbs chopped onion
1 Tbs butter
1 cup raw rice
2 cups vegetable stock* or broth

½ tsp salt (omit if using salted
stock)
1 Tbs butter
6 Tbs grated Parmesan cheese

Cook the onion in the butter in a pot until limp but not browned. Add the rice and cook over very low heat until all the rice is well colored with the butter. Add the stock, and the salt if necessary. Cover and simmer for 20 minutes, or until the stock is completely absorbed and the rice is done. When the rice is done, mix in the butter and cheese and serve hot.

This rice is often prepared with chopped and sautéed ham, mussels or truffles, or cooked green peas.

TOMATOES À LA PIÉMONTAISE (Stuffed)
TO SERVE 4

4 large tomatoes	grated Parmesan cheese
salt and pepper	butter, melted
3 cups Rice à la Piemontaise, hot	1 cup Tomato Sauce, preferably homemade,* hot
1 Tbs tomato purée	

Preheat oven to 375°. Cut the tops off the tomatoes and scoop out the inside pulp and seeds. Season the tomatoes inside with salt and pepper to taste. Mix the rice and tomato purée and use to stuff the tomatoes. Sprinkle liberally with cheese and a little butter to moisten and bake on a buttered baking sheet in the oven for about 15 minutes, until browned. Serve at once, hot, with the sauce served separately.

To help the tomatoes hold their shape while baking, wrap each in a cup of foil around the bottom and sides. Otherwise they have a tendency to collapse, and are extremely hard to handle after baking. This dish is also called Stuffed Tomatoes à l'Italienne.

PEPPERS À LA PIÉMONTAISE
TO SERVE 4

8 sweet peppers	Parmesan cheese, grated
2 cups chicken stock* or broth	butter, melted
1 recipe Rice à la Piémontaise, hot	

Preheat oven to 375°. Clean and seed the peppers and cut in strips, about 1 by 2 inches. Cook in the stock until tender, about 15 minutes, and drain. Arrange a layer of ⅓ of the peppers in a buttered baking dish. Top with ½ the rice. Sprinkle generously with cheese. Add another layer of ⅓ of the peppers, the remaining rice, another liberal sprinkling of cheese and a final layer of the remaining peppers. Sprinkle with cheese again, and dribble on a little melted butter to moisten. Bake in the oven until golden brown and serve hot.

TOMATO TORTE À LA PIÉMONTAISE
TO SERVE 4

pie crust for a 9-inch pie*   butter
4–5 tomatoes, sliced thick   sugar
salt and pepper   1 oz butter, melted
corn meal

Preheat oven to 450°. Roll out the pie crust and use to line the bottom of a 9-inch pie pan or layer cake pan. Season the tomatoes to taste with salt and pepper and dredge in corn meal. Sauté in hot butter slowly, until golden, without allowing them to break. Put them carefully in the pie pan, sprinkling each tomato slice with a few grains of sugar. When the pie pan is filled with the tomato slices dribble the melted butter over the top and bake in the oven for 10 minutes. Lower the heat to 325° and bake for 15 minutes more. Serve hot, right in the pie dish.

ARTICHOKE HEARTS À LA PIÉMONTAISE
TO SERVE 4

8 large artichoke hearts   Parmesan cheese, grated
salt and pepper   butter, melted
butter
1 recipe Rice à la Piémontaise, hot

Preheat oven to 375°. Season the artichoke hearts with salt and pepper to taste and simmer in a little butter until tender. Arrange the artichokes on a buttered baking dish. Pile the rice on the artichoke hearts and sprinkle generously with cheese. Dribble on a little melted butter to moisten and bake in the oven until golden brown. Serve hot.

EGGS À LA PIÉMONTAISE (Scrambled)
TO SERVE 4

8 eggs, beaten lightly   salt and pepper
½ cup grated Parmesan cheese   4 Tbs butter
   (or to taste)   8 white truffle slices, tossed in
1–1½ Tbs white truffles, grated   butter and hot

Mix the eggs with the cheese and grated truffles and season with salt and pepper to taste. Scramble the mixture in the butter until done and serve garnished with the truffle slices, hot.

TOURNEDOS À LA PIÉMONTAISE (Beef Fillets)
TO SERVE 4

4 beef fillets
butter
salt and pepper
4 baked individual tart crusts,
    hot*

1 recipe Rice à la Piémon-
    taise mixed with 2 minced
    white truffles, hot

Sauté the fillets in butter until done to taste and season with salt and pepper. Fill the tarts with the rice and top with the fillets. Dribble the pan juices over the top and serve hot.

VEAL CHOPS À LA PIÉMONTAISE
TO SERVE 4

8–12 veal chops, or cutlets
salt and pepper
2 eggs, beaten
bread crumbs mixed with
    grated Parmesan cheese (4
    to 1)
4 oz butter, preferably clarified*

1 recipe Rice à la Piémon-
    taise, hot
1½ cups Sauce Espagnole, or
    beef gravy
1½ Tbs tomato paste, or purée

Season the veal with salt and pepper to taste. Dip in the beaten eggs, and coat with the crumb mixture. Sauté until done in the butter. Arrange the veal in a ring on a hot platter and fill the center with the rice. While the veal is cooking, heat the Sauce Espagnole with the tomato paste, blending. Pour over the finished veal on the platter and serve hot.

These chops are often stuffed with ham, Swiss cheese and chopped white truffles before breading and cooking.

CHICKEN À LA PIÉMONTAISE
TO SERVE 4

3 cups Rice à la Piémontaise
4 oz white truffles, chopped (or
    ½ lb sauteed chopped
    mushrooms)
1 4-lb chicken

salt and pepper
4 oz butter
2 oz dry white wine
2 cups veal gravy

Preheat oven to 375°. Mix the rice and truffles. Stuff the chicken with the rice mixture and sew or skewer closed. Truss. Rub with salt and pepper to taste. Melt the butter in a roasting pan, add the chicken and bake in the oven for about 2¼ hours, or until golden brown. If the chicken begins to brown too much, cover loosely with foil until finished. Place the chicken on a hot platter and keep hot. Discard the trussings. Discard excess fat from the roasting pan, if any, and add the wine, scraping up the juices over medium heat. Stir in the gravy, blend and heat well and strain into a sauceboat. Serve hot, with the chicken.

This chicken can also be stuffed with a mixture of onion, chicken liver, chicken meat, veal, pork and bacon, all chopped and sautéed in butter and mixed together. Blend in 2 eggs, a couple ounces of brandy and salt and pepper to taste. The proportions of onions and meats are up to you. You'll need a little over 3 cups total stuffing for a 4-pound chicken. You may also use a little minced bread, soaked in milk and squeezed almost dry, in the stuffing. If you use this alternate stuffing, serve the rice and truffle mixture in a ring around the finished chicken, hot, and moisten the rice with some of the sauce.

CORNISH GAME HEN À LA PIÉMONTAISE
TO SERVE 4

Proceed as for Chicken à la Piémontaise, using 4 game hens and cooking for about 45 minutes.

TURKEY À LA PIÉMONTAISE
TO SERVE 4 OR MORE

Proceed as for Chicken à la Piémontaise, figuring the other ingredients at 1 recipe per four pounds. That is, for an 8-pound turkey double the other ingredients; for a 12-pound turkey triple them. Bake an 8-pound turkey about 3½ hours; a 12-pound turkey about 4½ hours.

FLOUNDER À LA PIÉMONTAISE
TO SERVE 4

1 recipe Polenta*	salt and white pepper
2 lbs flounder fillets	olive oil
salt and pepper	4 oz dry white wine
flour	2 oz tomato purée
butter	1 oz butter (optional)
4 white truffles, sliced	

Pour the Polenta into a buttered mold and chill. Unmold, slice, and sauté in butter until golden brown on both sides. Drain and keep hot. Meanwhile, season the fish to taste with salt and pepper. Dredge in flour, shaking off the excess, and saute in butter until golden brown. Keep hot. Season the truffles lightly and sauté gently in oil. Drain and keep hot. Arrange the Polenta slices on a hot platter, top with the fish and decorate the fish with the truffle slices. Keep hot. Add the wine to the fish sauté pan and boil down quickly, scraping up the juices. Add the tomato purée. Add the butter, if desired. Blend and heat through well. Strain over the fish and serve hot.

A good and unusual recipe for any white-fleshed fish fillets.

MACKEREL À LA PIÉMONTAISE
TO SERVE 4

2 lbs mackerel fillets
salt and pepper
beaten egg
bread crumbs
butter

1 recipe Rice à la Piémontaise, hot
1 cup Tomato Sauce, preferably
homemade,* hot

Season the fillets with salt and pepper to taste and dip in the beaten egg. Coat with crumbs and sauté in butter until golden. Serve the mackerel on the hot rice, topped with the Tomato Sauce, hot.

Another fine recipe for any white-fleshed fish fillets.

Poivrade

(pwahv-RAHD)

Means Pepper Sauce. *Poivre* means pepper. Pepper used in cooking should always be ground fresh from peppercorns. There are two reasons for this: 1) Preground pepper can easily be adulterated with anything from cheaper spices to powdered fruit pits, and often is. 2) The flavor quickly escapes from pepper once the peppercorns are ground, while on the other hand the peppercorns themselves maintain their flavor almost indefinitely. If you wish the dish you are preparing to have the pungency of pepper, the pepper should be ground freshly into the dish and cooked with it. If you want only the pepper's aroma, and not its pungency, this is best achieved by grinding the pepper on the dish at the end of cooking. There is a distinct difference in these two approaches to using pepper, and the only way to learn the difference is to try it both ways. You might cook 2 batches of eggs, one cooked with the pepper, and the other cooked and seasoned with the pepper at the end, and taste the difference. Then you'll be able to decide how you prefer to use pepper in any dish.

Black and white peppercorns come from the same vine (*Piper nigrum*). Black peppercorns are produced from the green berries of the vine, which are simply dried. White peppercorns come from the same plant, after the berries ripen. The flesh and skin of the berries is removed and the corns are dried, producing white peppercorns.

A dish served with Sauce Poivrade is called à la Poivrade, while one cooked with ground peppercorns is called au Poivre. Sauce Poivrade is excellent with game, such as rabbit or venison. Rack of lamb, with its rather strong flavor, is also enhanced by Sauce Poivrade. The sauce is also good with strongly flavored vegetables, such as cooked celery, carrots or Brussels sprouts. Finally, steak coated with coarsely ground peppercorns and sautéed in butter (Steak au Poivre) is excellent served with a hearty sauce, such as Sauce Béarnaise, and would be called Steak au Poivre à la Béarnaise.

SAUCE POIVRADE
TO MAKE 2 CUPS

½ cup Vegetable Mirepoix
2 oz white wine vinegar, or cider vinegar
2 oz white wine

1 cup Sauce Espagnole
1 cup chicken stock,* Jus de Veau, or veal stock*
6 peppercorns, crushed

Mix the Vegetable Mirepoix with the vinegar and wine and boil the liquid down to ½. Add the Espagnole and stock and simmer gently for 1 hour, reducing to 1 cup. Add more stock during the simmering if needed. Add the crushed peppercorns 5 minutes before finishing. Strain and serve hot with meat or vegetables.

SAUCE MIGNONNETTE (Coarse-ground Pepper Sauce)
TO MAKE 2 CUPS

½ cup minced shallots
6 Tbs white peppercorns, coarsely ground

2 cups cider vinegar
2 Tbs olive oil, or salad oil
salt

Blend the shallots, ground peppercorns, vinegar and oil over low heat. Season lightly with salt and serve over freshly cooked clams or oysters, hot.

TOURNEDOS AU POIVRE (Beef Fillets)
TO SERVE 4

2 Tbs peppercorns, crushed
4 beef fillets
3 Tbs butter
2 oz brandy

¼ tsp salt
dry mustard (about 1–2 tsp)
¼ cup heavy cream
1 cup Sauce Espagnole

Press the crushed peppercorns into the steaks firmly and sauté in the butter until done to taste. Pour on the brandy and flame, spooning over the steaks until the fire dies. Remove the steaks and keep hot. Add the salt and mustard to taste and blend. Add the cream and Espagnole, blend and heat through quickly. Spoon over the steaks and serve hot.

STEAK AU POIVRE
TO SERVE 4

3 carrots, chopped
2 onions, chopped
1 Tbs peanut oil
1 Tbs butter
1 Tbs flour
3 tomatoes, peeled,* seeded
   and chopped
1 tsp parsley
¼ tsp thyme
½ bay leaf
cheesecloth, washed
1½ cups water
1½ cups dry white wine

salt
4 steaks
4 Tbs crushed peppercorns
1 Tbs peanut oil
2 Tbs butter
1 cup Port wine
1 Tbs heavy cream
1 tsp brandy
½ cup dry white wine
¼ cup heavy cream
1 oz brandy
salt and white pepper

Simmer the carrots and onions in the oil and butter until lightly browned. Blend in the flour. Add the tomatoes. Add the parsley, thyme and bay leaf tied in cheesecloth. Add the water and wine and season lightly with salt. Cover and simmer 1 hour. Uncover and cook until thick. Discard herb bouquet and purée in a blender. Press the crushed peppercorns firmly into the steaks. Sauté them in hot oil and butter until done to taste. Put the cooked steaks on a hot platter and keep hot. Add the port to the steak pan and boil down to ½. Add the purée and blend well. Blend in the cream and brandy, pour over the steaks and keep hot. Add the wine to the same pan and reduce to ½. Add the cream and reduce to ½ again. Blend in the brandy and season lightly with salt and white pepper. Remove from the heat. Spoon a little cream sauce on each sauce-covered steak, making a round bull's-eye of sauce within sauce. Serve at once, hot.

DUCKLING AU POIVRE
TO SERVE 4

1 5-lb duckling
6 Tbs peppercorns, crushed
3 oz brandy

1½ cups Jus de Veau, or veal
   stock* or gravy
½ cup heavy cream

Preheat oven to 325°. Remove interior fat from the duckling and prick the skin all over with a fork so remaining fat can escape during cooking. Put 1 tablespoon of peppercorns in the duck's cavity and truss. Roast on a rack over a pan in the oven for 1½ hours, covering loosely with foil as soon as it browns lightly. Remove the foil, press the remaining peppercorns into the skin firmly, and bake for another 30 minutes. Remove all fat from the pan and flame with the brandy. When the fire dies set the duckling on a hot platter. Add the Jus de Veau and cream to the pan and heat well, scraping up the juices, over direct heat. Strain the pan sauce into a sauceboat and serve with the duckling, hot.

Porto

(pohr-TOH)

Means port wine. Port is a sweet red wine evolving from a rather poor Portuguese background. Portuguese red wine was traditionally strong and unpleasant. At the beginning of the eighteenth century French wines were excluded from England. This precipitated the birth of the port wine we know today. In England's search for substitute wines, experiments were made with the inferior strong red wine of Portugal. It was blended with brandy before all its rich sugars were fermented, thus halting fermentation and preserving some of the wine's sweetness. If the Portuguese wine was left to ferment completely, the result was so strong as to be actually unpleasant. The simple addition of brandy at the right moment during fermentation saved the wine's sweetness while enriching its flavor. Port, with its brandy addition, is a fortified wine, and will not turn quickly to vinegar after opening as will a table wine. Red port wine, being quite hearty, goes best with flavorful foods, as in the duck recipe listed here. For lighter foods, tawny port is generally used, as in the fish recipe. Actually, any port wine is strongly flavored, and this should be kept in mind when using it in cooking. Port combines well with orange juice and grated orange peel in spicy brown sauces. A little red currant jelly is sometimes included when the sauce is used with roast fowl or game. When making Sauce au Porto, it is definitely best to use a Sauce Espagnole that has no Madeira wine in it, as the Madeira and port flavors do not enhance each other. Try a simple grilled steak with Sauce au Porto. No guest could ask for more. You can prepare the sauce days ahead if you wish, and reheat it while the steaks cook.

Porto as a cooking style is most closely related to Madère and Xérès. Port, Madeira and sherry wines are all fortified, and so produce quite a different effect from the usual red or white table wines.

SAUCE AU PORTO (Port Sauce)
TO MAKE 2 CUPS

2 cups Sauce Espagnole   2–3 oz port wine

Bring the Sauce Espagnole to a boil and stir in the port wine. Serve hot with meat and fowl.

TRUFFLES AU PORTO (or Mushrooms)
TO SERVE 4

½ lb lean ham, minced
¼ lb fresh pork fat, minced
1 oz olive oil
1 oz butter
1 celery stalk, chopped
2 carrots, chopped
1 onion, chopped
1 tsp parsley
¼ tsp thyme

1 bay leaf, crumbled
¼ tsp tarragon
2 garlic cloves, minced
1 tsp cloves, ⅛ tsp cinnamon,
   both ground
salt, pepper, grated nutmeg
1 lb truffles (or mushrooms)
1½ cups port wine

Sauté the ham and pork fat lightly in the oil and butter in a pot. Add the celery, carrot, onion, parsley, thyme, bay leaf, tarragon, garlic, cloves and cinnamon. Blend well and simmer until just browned lightly. Season to taste with salt, pepper and nutmeg. Add the truffles and port wine and simmer covered for 15 minutes. Set the truffles aside. Purée the pot sauce and vegetables in a blender. Return to the pot and bring to a gentle simmer. Add the truffles to warm through and serve hot.

DUCKLING AU PORTO
TO SERVE 4

2 cups port wine
½ cup chopped dried figs
½ cup chopped onion
1 tsp parsley
¼ tsp thyme
½ tsp chervil
1 bay leaf, crumbled
¼ cup chopped green pepper

2 garlic cloves, chopped
1 5-lb duck
brandy
salt and pepper
2 Tbs butter
salt and pepper
1½ cups Sauce Espagnole
chives

Start 1 to 2 days ahead of time. Mix all the stock ingredients (up through the garlic) and bring to a boil. Remove from heat, cool and store in a covered jar in the refrigerator for a day or two. Shake occasionally. Then strain. Reserve liquid. Remove all the fat from inside the duck and prick its skin all over with a fork to allow its fat to escape during cooking. Rub the duck liberally with brandy inside and out, then season inside with salt and pepper, lightly. Truss. Brown the duck in the butter in a pot. Add the strained port liquid (the stock) and simmer 2 minutes. Season with salt and pepper to taste and cook slowly, covered, for 2 hours, or until done. Place the duck on a hot platter and skim all the fat from the pot. Blend the Espagnole with the remaining pot juices over low heat. Pour a little of this sauce over the duck and serve the rest separately. Sprinkle the duck with chives and serve hot.

COD AU PORTO
TO SERVE 4

2 lbs cod fillets
salt and pepper
1 onion, chopped
3 tomatoes, peeled,* seeded
  and chopped
1 garlic clove, chopped

1 cup white port wine
¼ cup heavy cream blended
  with 1 Tbs cornstarch
1 Tbs lemon juice (or to taste)
chives

Preheat oven to 400°. Season the fillets with salt and pepper to taste. Sprinkle the onions, tomatoes and garlic in the bottom of a well-buttered baking dish. Lay the fillets on this bed and add the port wine. Cover loosely with foil and bake in the oven for 10 to 15 minutes, or until the fish flakes easily with a fork. Set the fillets carefully on a hot platter and keep hot. Strain the pan sauce and reduce slightly over direct heat. Blend in the cream and lemon juice and cook to thicken quickly. Pour the sauce over the fillets and sprinkle them with chives. Serve hot.

This is an excellent recipe for any white-fleshed fish fillets, but is especially good for firm-fleshed fish such as haddock.

SABAYON AU PORTO
TO SERVE 4

4 egg yolks
4 Tbs sugar

2 oz port wine

Put the yolks, sugar and port wine in the top of a double boiler and heat over gently simmering water, beating with an electric mixer. The water in the bottom of the double boiler must not touch the top part of the double boiler, or the eggs will curdle. Beat the mixture until it becomes light and frothy. It will about triple in volume. Serve at once, warm, in fine glass stemware. Or, set the top of the double boiler in cold water and continue beating the Sabayon mixture to cool, and serve cooled at once.

Provençale

(proh-vahn-SAHL)

After the old province of Provence, in southeastern France, bordering the Mediterranean Sea and running from the Alps in the east to the Rhone River in the west. Its capital was Aix. The area of old Provence includes the French Riviera, Nice, Antibes, Cannes, St. Raphael, St. Tropez and Marseilles, magnificent beaches, yachts, dark palms and the sun-flat Mediterranean.

The cuisine of this area is definitely Mediterranean, and uses olive oil, tomatoes and garlic generously. Provençale cooking is generally spicy and garlicky, and usually includes herbs such as tarragon, basil, chervil, thyme, marjoram, parsley or chives. Provençale cooking could be considered the classic of Mediterranean styles, while all the other are variations. For example, Niçoise is basically the same, but makes wide use of potatoes; Catalane used much more garlic. Sole à la Provençale is often called Sole à la Niçoise, because the recipes always include tomatoes, usually in the form of a fondue. Because the styles overlap, the names are sometimes interchangeable.

The wines of Provence are not in a class with the finest Bordeaux, but are rather strong in comparison, which is more compatible with the cooking of the area. The *Côtes de Provence* name is allowed for all the wine from the coastal area. Of these, cassis is best known, and very good to quench the thirst following a spicy dish. Cassis, however, is a name that causes considerable confusion. First, it is a black currant liqueur made in Burgundy, as well as a Burgundian wine. *Vin Blanc de Cassis* is a white wine with a fresh flavor from the Cassis district near Marseilles. A *Vin Blanc Cassis,* on the other hand, is an apéritif made by putting a tablespoonful of Cassis liqueur in a wine glass and filling with white Cassis wine. The rosé wines of the area are quite dry and strong. There are two Bandols (red wines) exported: Domaine Tempier, quite light for a southern wine, and Château Pradeaux, strong and typical of southern wines, but quite good, especially with Mediterranean foods which generally defeat more subtle wines.

Finally, there is a cheese called *Cachat* produced in Provence that is quite unusual. It is made from goat or sheep's milk, ripened in vinegar, and sometimes blended with wine or brandy.

Darius Milhaud was born in Aix, in Provence. He is known as a turbulent modern master, and became the foremost composer of his country after the death of Maurice Ravel in 1937. What could be more appropriate to this style of cuisine that Milhaud's *Suite Provençale?*

SAUCE PROVENÇALE
TO MAKE 2 CUPS

2 Tbs minced onion
olive oil
2 large tomatoes, peeled,*
    seeded and chopped
1 small garlic clove, crushed

salt and pepper
3 oz dry white wine
¾ cup Jus de Veau, or veal
    stock* or gravy
½ tsp parsley

Sauté the onion gently in a little oil until just tender but not browned. Add the tomatoes and garlic and season to taste with salt and pepper. Simmer for 3 minutes. Add the wine and boil 3 minutes. Add the Jus de Veau and cook very slowly for 10 to 15 minutes, blending well. Discard the garlic, add the parsley and serve hot with eggs, fish, meat, fowl, vegetables.

TOMATO FONDUE À LA PROVENÇALE
TO MAKE 2 CUPS

½ onion, minced fine
1 Tbs olive oil
3 tomatoes, peeled,* seeded
  and diced, the juice reserved

salt and pepper
1 garlic clove, minced fine
1 tsp parsley

Sauté the onion in the oil until tender but not browned. Add the tomatoes and their juice, season to taste with salt and pepper, and add the garlic. Cook gently until smooth and thickened. Just a minute before serving stir in the parsley. Use at once, hot. If this is to be reheated, add the parsley then, letting it cook in the fondue for a minute before serving.

This fondue is sometimes called Sauce Provençale.

AÏOLI (Garlic Mayonnaise)
TO MAKE 2 CUPS

3 egg yolks
4–5 garlic cloves, minced
2 tsp lemon juice
1 tsp cider vinegar

salt and pepper
1 cup olive oil
3 Tbs boiling water

Put the yolks, garlic, lemon juice, vinegar and salt and pepper to taste (about ¼ teaspoon each) in a blender and blend well. Add a little of the oil and blend until thickened. Add the remaining oil slowly, until completely blended and thick. Add the boiling water and blend again. Chill and serve as a very garlicky Mayonnaise with fish and shellfish.

Aïoli seems to belong under Mayonnaise, or even Catalane because of the garlic, but is listed here because it is thought to have originated in Provence.

PROVENÇALE GARNISHES
TO SERVE 4

1. EGGPLANT À LA PROVENÇALE

2 lbs eggplant, skinned and cut
  in cubes
1 recipe Tomato Fondue à la
  Provençale

bread crumbs
olive oil

Preheat oven to 350°. Mix the eggplant and Tomato Fondue and put in a buttered shallow baking dish. Sprinkle liberally with crumbs and a little oil to moisten and bake in the oven for about 20 minutes, until golden brown. Serve hot.

2. GREEN BEANS À LA PROVENÇALE

1½ lbs green beans, cooked in water and lightly seasoned

olive oil
1–2 garlic cloves, crushed
2 tsp parsley

Sauté the beans in a little hot oil with the garlic and parsley. Discard the garlic, if desired, and serve hot. Do not use too much oil.

3. POTATOES

Use 2 pounds of potatoes, cut like olives and sauté in butter until golden brown. Shake the pan from time to time to brown evenly without breaking the potato ovals.

POTATOES À LA PROVENÇALE (Stuffed)
TO SERVE 4

4 potatoes, baked and halved lengthwise
2 egg yolks, hard-boiled and mashed
4 Tbs Tomato Fondue à la Provençale
4 anchovy fillets, mashed
4 green olives, minced
2 oz tuna fish, minced

salt and pepper
2 Tbs olive oil
1 Tbs parsley
1 tsp chives
½ tsp oregano
½ tsp chervil
½ tsp basil
¼ tsp thyme

Preheat oven to 375°. Hollow out the potato halves, leaving the skins and about ½ inch of their pulp intact. Mix the yolks, Tomato Fondue, anchovies, olives and tuna and mash with the scooped-out potato pulp. Season with salt and pepper to taste and use to stuff the potato shells. Arrange them on a buttered baking sheet. Sprinkle with the olive oil and bake in the oven for 15 minutes. Sprinkle with the herbs and bake a few minutes more and serve hot.

The herbs can be sprinkled on after baking, if desired. If using dried herbs, cook them in a little white wine for a few minutes until limp, and drain before using.

MUSHROOMS À LA PROVENÇALE
TO SERVE 4

½ lb sliced mushrooms, or whole button mushrooms
2 Tbs olive oil
¼ tsp lemon juice
salt and pepper

1 garlic clove, minced
1 Tbs chopped onion, lightly sautéed in olive oil
¼ tsp thyme

Sauté the mushrooms in the oil and lemon juice until limp. Season to taste with salt and pepper. Add the garlic, onion and thyme, and sauté until done. Serve hot.

TOMATOES À LA PROVENÇALE
TO SERVE 4

4 large tomatoes	2 Tbs fresh parsley
salt and pepper	2 Tbs olive oil
½ cup bread crumbs	
3 garlic cloves, minced fine	

Preheat oven to 350°. Cut the top quarter off the tomatoes and place on a buttered baking sheet. Season well with salt and pepper. Mix the crumbs, garlic, parsley and oil and pile on the cut tops of the tomatoes. Bake in the oven for about 15 minutes, until nicely browned, and serve hot.

ZUCCHINI À LA PROVENÇALE
TO SERVE 4

4 zucchini, cut in thick slices	4 tomatoes, sliced thick and well
salt and pepper	salted
flour	2 garlic cloves
olive oil	chives

Season the zucchini with salt and pepper to taste and dredge in flour, shaking off the excess. Sauté in hot oil until just golden. Add the tomatoes and simmer together for 10 minutes, turning the zucchini and tomatoes carefully. Arrange on a hot platter, grate the garlic over the top, sprinkle with chives and dribble on the pan juices. Serve hot.

EGGS À LA PROVENÇALE (Poached or Soft-Boiled)
TO SERVE 4

8 tomato slices	8 eggs, freshly poached or soft-boiled, hot
olive oil	
salt and pepper	1 cup Tomato Fondue à la Provençale, hot
1 cup eggplant, peeled and diced	parsley

Sauté the tomato slices in a little oil and season with salt and pepper to taste. Keep hot. Meanwhile, sauté the eggplant in a little oil, season and keep hot. Prepare the eggs. Put 2 tomato slices on each of 4 hot plates. Top with the hot eggs, garnish with the eggplant (drained), cover the eggs with the Tomato Fondue, sprinkle with parsley and serve hot.

EGGS À LA PROVENÇALE (Fried)
TO SERVE 4

12 parsley sprigs	8 eggplant slices
olive oil	salt and pepper
8 tomato slices	8 eggs

Sauté the parsley in a little oil and drain on paper towels. Sauté the tomato and eggplant slices in the same oil and season with salt and pepper to taste. Arrange the tomato slices on 4 hot plates and keep hot. Top with the eggs, seasoned and fried in the same oil. Set the eggplant around the eggs. Garnish each dish with 3 of the sautéed parsley sprigs and serve hot.

OMELET À LA PROVENÇALE
TO SERVE 2

1 tomato, peeled,* seeded and diced
olive oil, or half oil and half butter
salt and pepper

½ garlic clove, minced fine
4 eggs
1 tsp parsley

Simmer the tomato in a little oil for 5 minutes. Season to taste with salt and pepper and add the garlic. Simmer 5 minutes more. Beat the eggs with the parsley, add to the pan and make a flat omelet.* Serve hot.

TOURNEDOS À LA PROVENÇALE (Beef Fillets)
TO SERVE 4

4 thin strips of pork or ham fat, fresh, not smoked
4 beef fillets
1 tsp basil
½ tsp oregano

¼ tsp thyme
¼ tsp marjoram
¼ tsp powdered bay leaf
olive oil
salt and pepper

Secure a strip of fat around each fillet with string, leaving the two flat sides of each fillet uncovered. Mix the herbs and rub into the fillet's flat sides. Brush with oil and season to taste with salt and pepper. Grill under a broiler until done to taste. Discard fat and string and serve hot.

BEEF DAUBE À LA PROVENÇALE (Stew)
TO SERVE 4

1 garlic clove, crushed
1 cup dry white wine
½ cup brandy
1 carrot, sliced
1 onion, sliced
1 sprig of parsley
1 sprig of thyme
1 bay leaf
3 Tbs olive oil
2 lbs lean beef cubes
flour

½ lb sliced bacon, blanched 2 minutes in boiling water
½ lb carrots, cut in rounds
½ lb small onions
½ lb sliced mushrooms sautéed lightly in goose fat or butter
½ lb pitted black olives
2 tomatoes, peeled,* seeded and diced
3 garlic cloves, crushed
½ cup veal stock* or gravy

Mix all the marinating ingredients (up through olive oil) and marinate the beef for 2 hours, tossing occasionally. Remove the beef and dry on paper towels. Reserve the marinade. Preheat oven to 325°. Dredge the meat in flour, shaking off the excess. Put in a stewing pot. Add the bacon, carrots, onions, mushrooms, olives, tomatoes and garlic. Mix gently. Strain the marinade and add. Add the stock. Cook covered in the oven for 2 hours, stirring occasionally and checking the level of the liquid. Add a bit more stock if needed. When done skim off excess fat, if any, and serve right in the pot, hot.

VEAL CHOPS or CUTLETS À LA PROVENÇALE
TO SERVE 4

8 tomatoes, hollowed out and
   salted inside
2 cups Duxelles, hot
Parmesan cheese, grated
8–12 veal chops or cutlets

salt and pepper
1 oz olive oil
2 oz dry white wine
1 cup Tomato Fondue à la
   Provençale, hot
parsley

Preheat oven to 350°. Stuff the tomatoes with the Duxelles, sprinkle generously with cheese, and bake in the oven on a buttered baking sheet for 20 to 25 minutes, until golden. To help support the tomatoes while they bake, wrap them in foil cups around bottom and sides. Meanwhile, season the veal with salt and pepper to taste and sauté in the oil until done. Drain on paper towels and place in the center of a hot platter. Surround with the stuffed tomatoes and keep hot. Add the wine to the veal sauté pan and boil down, scraping up the juices. Stir in the Tomato Fondue and blend until well heated. Strain over the veal, sprinkle with parsley and serve hot.

VEAL BREAST À LA PROVENÇALE
TO SERVE 4

Proceed as for Veal Chops à la Provençale, browning a veal breast in olive oil and then simmering it slowly, covered, for 1 to 1½ hours, or until done. Use the veal breast in place of the chops.

PORK or LAMB CHOPS or CUTLETS À LA PROVENÇALE
TO SERVE 4

Proceed as for Veal Chops à la Provençale, or Mutton Chops à la Provençale. These recipes for small cuts of meat are interchangeable. For added variation you may use sautéed eggplant slices or cubes, sautéed mushroom caps, or black olives lightly sautéed or blanched in boiling water. Any combination of these items with potatoes as in Provençale Garnish #3, plus Tomato Fondue à la Provençale or Sauce Provençale is fitting for a dish à la Provençale. Anchovy strips are also appropriate.

PORK LOIN À LA PROVENÇALE
TO SERVE 4–8

1 tsp sage leaves
1 pork loin
salt, thyme, powdered bay leaf

12 garlic cloves, crushed
olive oil

Insert the sage leaves into the roast with a thin knife, and rub with salt, thyme and powdered bay leaf to taste. Sprinkle liberally with olive oil and marinate for 12 hours with the garlic. Preheat oven to 325°. Roast the pork for about 35 minutes per pound, basting with the marinade liquid and garlic until browned, then finish the cooking covered. Put the finished roast on a hot platter, remove the excess fat from the roasting pan, and strain the juices over the roast. Serve hot.

CHICKEN SAUTÉ À LA PROVENÇALE
TO SERVE 4

2 small chickens, cut up
salt and pepper
olive oil
1 Tbs chopped onion
4 tomatoes, peeled,* seeded
    and chopped
1 garlic clove, crushed

½ cup dry white wine
3 Tbs thick veal gravy
20 pitted large black olives
12 small mushrooms
olive oil
8 anchovy fillets
1–2 tsp parsley

Season the chicken with salt and pepper to taste. Sauté in a little oil until about ⅔ done. Add the onion and finish sautéing. Remove the chicken from the pan and drain on paper towels. Arrange on a hot platter and keep hot. Add the tomatoes and garlic to the pan and simmer for 10 minutes. Add the wine and boil down to ½. Add the gravy, blend in well to thicken, season if needed and pour over the chicken. Keep hot. Meanwhile, blanch the olives in boiling water for 30 seconds. Sauté the mushrooms in hot oil until lightly browned, and drain. Wash the anchovies to remove most of the salt and oil, and dry. Arrange the olives and mushrooms around the chicken, and decorate it with the anchovy fillets. Sprinkle with parsley and serve hot.

SOLE À LA PROVENÇALE
TO SERVE 4

2 lbs sole fillets
salt and pepper
flour
olive oil

1 cup Tomato Fondue à la
    Provençale, hot
bread crumbs
1–2 tsp parsley

Preheat oven to 375°. Season the fish fillets with salt and pepper to taste. Dredge in flour, shaking off the excess. Sauté in hot oil until done, and drain. Arrange on a buttered baking dish, cover with the Tomato Fondue, sprinkle generously with crumbs and a few drops of olive oil to moisten. Bake in the oven until golden. Sprinkle with parsley and serve hot.

This is an excellent recipe for any white-fleshed fish fillets, especially saltwater fish.

TUNA À LA PROVENÇALE
TO SERVE 4

8 anchovy fillets, drained
4 tuna steaks
olive oil, lemon juice, salt and
  pepper
1 onion, chopped and lightly
  sautéed in butter or oil,
  drained
4 tomatoes, peeled,* seeded
  and chopped

2 garlic cloves, crushed
1 Tbs parsley
½ tsp thyme
½ tsp chervil
½ bay leaf
cheesecloth, washed
1 cup white wine
1½ cups Sauce Espagnole

Insert 2 anchovy fillets into each tuna steak with a larding needle or thin knife. Marinate the tuna in a little oil, lemon juice, salt and pepper for 1 hour. Drain, put in a pan and sauté in a little olive oil until just colored on both sides. Add the onion, tomatoes and garlic. Add the parsley, thyme, chervil and bay leaf tied in cheesecloth. Add the wine and simmer partly covered until done, basting often. Arrange the steaks on a hot platter and keep hot. Discard the garlic and herb bouquet from the pan juices and blend in the Sauce Espagnole. Cook to thicken lightly, pour over the tuna and serve hot.

SALMON COQUILLES À LA PROVENÇALE
TO SERVE 4

2 lbs cooked salmon, in chunks,
  hot
20 truffles, chopped, lightly
  sautéed in butter, hot
20 pitted black olives, coarsely
  chopped
8 mushrooms, coarsely
  chopped, sauteed in butter,
  hot

1 cup Tomato Fondue à la
  Provençale
bread crumbs
olive oil
8 anchovy fillets, drained

Preheat oven to 375°. Mix the salmon, truffles, olives and mushrooms by tossing gently, without breaking the salmon pieces. Use this mixture to fill 4 buttered baking shells. Top with the Tomato Fondue, sprinkle liberally with crumbs, and dribble on a little oil to moisten. Bake in the oven until golden brown and serve decorated with anchovies, hot.

FROG'S LEGS À LA PROVENÇALE
TO SERVE 4

8 sets of frog's legs (16 legs)	olive oil
salt and pepper	2–4 garlic cloves, crushed
flour	1 Tbs parsley

Season the frog's legs to taste with salt and pepper and dredge in flour, shaking off the excess. Sauté in a little oil until golden, adding the garlic and parsley 5 minutes before finishing. Serve on a hot platter.

This is often prepared with 1 cup of chopped tomato pulp (skinless and seedless) added to the pan juices after the frog's legs are done, mixed with the pan juices, and poured over the frog's legs on the platter.

MUSSELS À LA PROVENÇALE
TO SERVE 4

2 qts mussels, scrubbed well	1 garlic clove, minced
2½ oz olive oil	¾ cup dry white wine
1 Tbs parsley	1 oz fish fumet,* or clam juice
1 Tbs chives	pepper
2 Tbs minced mushrooms	1½ tsp lemon juice
2 Tbs minced truffles	salt

Put the mussels in a pan and heat. When they open they are done. Discard the top shells and strain the liquor from the opened mussels and reserve. Put the oil, parsley, chives, mushrooms, truffles and garlic in another pan and gradually heat until very hot. Add the wine, fish fumet and mussel liquor and boil until the mixture thickens lightly. Season to taste with pepper. Add the mussels on their half shells and heat through. When heated, sprinkle with the lemon juice and season lightly with salt. Serve hot.

ESCARGOTS À LA PROVENÇALE (Snails)
TO MAKE 36 SNAILS, ALLOW 6–8 PER SERVING

36 snails in their shells (Snails are usually sold in the U.S. canned, with the shells separate. If using these canned snails eliminate the long soaking in water, salt, vinegar and flour.)	1 Tbs minced shallots
	2 garlic cloves, grated
	2 tsp flour
	1 cup dry white wine
	salt, pepper, grated nutmeg, red pepper (cayenne)
	2 egg yolks, lightly beaten
1 oz olive oil	rock salt
1 tsp parsley	bread crumbs
2 Tbs minced mushrooms	olive oil
2 Tbs minced green pepper	

Wash the snails in water several times, and soak in lightly salted water with several drops of vinegar and a small pinch of flour for 2 hours. Wash again well, and blanch in boiling water for 5 minutes. Drain and cool under running cold water. Remove the snails from their shells and trim off the black part at their ends known as the *cloaca*. Boil their shells in water with ¼ teaspoon of baking soda for 30 minutes, drain and dry. Preheat oven to 425°. Heat the oil in a pan and add the parsley, mushrooms, peppers, shallots and garlic. Cook slowly for 5 minutes, stirring constantly. Blend in the flour well, and slowly add the wine. Season to taste with salt and pepper, a little nutmeg, and a little red pepper. Boil 2 minutes and remove from the heat. Let cool just a bit and beat in the yolks. Add the snails and heat through very slowly without boiling. Fill the shells with the snails and the sauce, and place on a flat baking dish on a layer of rock salt to hold the snails erect during baking. Top the snails liberally with crumbs and a little oil to moisten and bake in the oven until golden brown. Serve at once, hot.

A nice way to serve these is on individual baking dishes, or snail dishes. If using regular baking dishes, the rock salt holds the snails erect while cooking, and also retains the heat when serving.

Rouennaise

(roo-ahn-NEZ)

After the city of Rouen on the Seine river near the English Channel. *Rouennerie* is a name given to the textiles of Rouen, especially the coarse cotton prints so typical of the area. (This suggests an idea for your décor.) The city of Rouen is an important industrial center and port, and is the capital of the department of Seine-Inferieur. Rouen's best-known industry is textiles, but it is also a large dealer in cattle, grain, wine and spirits.

In Roman times this was a Celtic settlement known as *Rotomagus*. When Rollo the Northman became duke of Normandy in 912 it was his capital. It was here at Rouen that Joan of Arc was held captive in the tower, and later burned at the stake in 1431. Rouen suffered heavily during the Wars of Religion, the sixteenth-century conflict between Catholics and Protestants. Although Rouen was severely damaged during World War II, it is still rich in Gothic architecture. The Rouen Cathedral is one of the finest Gothic structures in all Europe.

Rouennaise cooking revolves around the famous Rouen ducks, which are among the finest in the world, and their livers. These livers are the common characteristic for Rouennaise dishes, usually with red wine, and sometimes with brandy. The most common dish is Duck à la Rouennaise. There are innumerable recipes for this famous dish, and two quite different ones are included here. In the omelet recipe I like to use chives, either mixed with the liver purée filling, or sprinkled on the omelet's sauce at the end. An interesting variation in flavor is had by cooking ¼ teaspoon of crushed fennel seed in the wine and mixing it with the sauce while heating. Strain out the seeds before serving.

There are no great wines to recommend from the Rouen area. The closest wine-producing area is the Champagne district, some two hundred miles to the east.

The cooking mode Périgourdine is similar to Rouennaise in that it also stuffs birds with liver, but Périgourdine generally uses goose liver as a stuffing for chickens, while in Rouennaise dishes duck liver is used to stuff ducks.

SAUCE ROUENNAISE
TO MAKE 2 CUPS

2 raw duck livers (or 4 raw chicken livers)	2 cups Sauce Bordelaise

Force the livers through a fine sieve and blend with the Sauce Bordelaise. Heat enough to poach the liver purée in the sauce, but do not boil or cook too long. The liver should not be overcooked. Serve very warm with duckling or eggs.

EGGS À LA ROUENNAISE (Baked)
TO SERVE 4

½ cup duck livers	¼ tsp ground thyme
¼ cup diced pork fat	¼ tsp ground bay leaf
2 oz butter	¼ cup dry white wine
¼ cup diced mushrooms	1 egg yolk
1 Tbs minced shallot	8 eggs
salt and pepper	3 tsp butter, diced
¼ tsp ground cloves	¾ cup Sauce Bourguignonne, hot

Preheat oven to 500°. Sauté the livers and pork fat in the butter until just barely done. Add the mushrooms, shallots, salt and pepper to taste, cloves, thyme and bay leaf. Cook for 3 minutes, stirring. Remove the livers from the pan, add the wine and boil until almost gone, blending. Remove the pan from the heat, return the livers and rub through a sieve to purée. Add the egg yolk and beat until smooth. Put this purée in the bottoms of 4 individual buttered baking dishes and top with 2 eggs each, being careful not to break the yolks. Season lightly with salt and pepper and dot with the diced butter. Bake on a high rack in the oven for 4 minutes, or until the whites are just set and the yolks still soft. Serve at once, topped with the sauce, hot.

OMELET À LA ROUENNAISE
TO SERVE 2

4 eggs	4 Tbs butter
salt and pepper	2 oz dry red wine
1 duck liver, or chicken liver	3 oz Sauce Espagnole, or beef gravy

Beat the eggs lightly with salt and pepper to taste. Force the liver through a sieve to purée. Prepare an omelet* in hot butter, filling with the liver purée. Meanwhile, in a separate pan boil the wine until almost gone, blend in the Espagnole and heat well. Put the finished omelet on a hot serving dish, top with the sauce and serve at once, hot.

DUCKLING À LA ROUENNAISE #1
TO SERVE 4

1 onion, minced
1 lb duck liver, chopped (or
   chicken liver)
2 Tbs parsley
2 oz fresh pork fat, chopped
butter
salt and pepper

1 4–5-lb duck, all interior fat removed
2 oz butter
1 onion, chopped
2 carrots, sliced
1 celery stalk, sliced
½ cup Madeira wine

Sauté the onion, liver, parsley and pork fat in butter for 5 minutes, remove from heat, season to taste with salt and pepper and cool. Use to stuff the duck. Truss and prick the skin all over with a fork to allow the fat to escape during cooking. Brown the duck well in the butter in a pot. Remove all the excess fat from the pot. Add the onion, carrot, celery and wine, reduce the heat and simmer covered for about 2 hours, or until done. Add more wine during cooking, if needed. When done, place the duck on a hot platter and untruss. Skim excess fat from the pot, strain the sauce and serve hot with the duck.

DUCKLING À LA ROUENNAISE #2
TO SERVE 4

½ lb lean bacon, diced
2 Tbs butter
16 small onions
2 garlic cloves, crushed
1 4–5-lb duck, cut in pieces
2 oz brandy
¼ cup flour
3 cups dry red wine
1 cup chicken stock* or broth
salt and pepper

1 tsp parsley
1 bay leaf
1 tsp basil
½ tsp sage
cheesecloth, washed
½ lb mushrooms, sliced
1 minced raw duck liver (or 2
   chicken livers)
3 Tbs flour kneaded with 3 Tbs
   butter (this is a *beurre manié*)

Sauté the bacon in a casserole until crisp, remove with a slotted spoon, and reserve. Add the butter to the casserole and use to brown the onions and garlic lightly. Remove and reserve. Add the duck and brown, adding butter if needed. Flame with the brandy, stirring until the fire dies. Blend in the flour. Slowly blend in the wine and stock and cook, stirring, until smooth. Return the bacon, onions and garlic to the casserole. Season to taste with salt and pepper. Add the parsley, bay leaf, basil and sage tied in cheesecloth. Cover and simmer gently for 1 hour. Add the mushrooms and cook 30 minutes more. Discard the herb bouquet, and arrange the duck, onions and mushrooms on a hot platter and keep hot. Add the liver and *beurre manié* to the sauce over very low heat to blend and thicken the sauce, but do not boil. Pour over the duck and serve hot.

Half a lemon peel and ½ an orange peel are often cooked with the duck and discarded before serving. Sometimes ½ to 1 cup of duck blood is added to the sauce at the end over very low heat with the liver and *beurre manié* and heated without boiling for 4 to 5 minutes before pouring the sauce over the duck.

Royale

(roy-AHL)

Means royal, kingly. In cooking it is a term given to various preparations, such as Royale Soup Garnish, which is a custard cut in decorative shapes and used to garnish soup. It is also applied to poultry poached in a little liquid and coated in a Cream Sauce Velouté with truffle purée. Chicken à la Royale can be made by preparing chicken breasts, as in Chicken Suprêmes au Blanc, and serving with Sauce Velouté* and cream blended together (half and half) and cooked down to thicken, in place of the Beurre Blanc in the recipe. This sauce is usually blended with a little truffle purée (1 to 2 ounces of truffles rubbed through a sieve).

This is not an especially individual or important cooking category, but it does add one very nice touch to the French Grande Cuisine, the Royale Soup Garnishes. These are tasty, attractive and quite a classy variation for soups. Royal custard shapes are sometimes dipped in frying batter* and quickly deep-fried in hot fat, drained and used at once to garnish soup.

SAUCE ROYALE
TO MAKE 2 CUPS

2 cups Sauce Velouté*
1 cup chicken stock* or broth
1 cup heavy cream

4 Tbs truffles, rubbed through a
  sieve
2 Tbs butter
2 Tbs sherry wine

Mix the Velouté and stock and boil down to ½. Add the cream and simmer until quite thick. Stir in the truffles, butter and sherry, blend well and serve hot with eggs or chicken (especially poached).

ROYALE SOUP GARNISH
TO MAKE ¾ CUP

1 egg
1 egg yolk
3 oz heavy cream
salt

grated nutmeg (or ground coriander, ground cinnamon,
ground cardamon)

Preheat oven to 350°. Beat the egg, yolk and cream together and season lightly with salt and a little nutmeg to taste. Put in a buttered baking dish, of a size so that the mixture is ¼ of an inch deep in the pan. Bake in the oven for about 12 minutes, or until firm. Cool. Unmold and cut in tiny decorative shapes.

Royales may be made with various flavorings and colorings by substituting a purée for ½ of the cream. For a tomato-flavored red Royale substitute thick tomato purée. For green, use pea or asparagus purée. For a warm gray, use truffle purée.

The addition of 2 tablespoons of ground cooked chicken to the mixture makes a Chicken Royale. The addition of ½ minced carrot, cooked in butter and puréed, makes a Royale à la Crécy.

COFFEE ROYALE
TO SERVE 4

2 cups strong coffee, hot, sweetened to taste
4 warmed demitasse cups

2 oz whiskey of your choice,
warm

Pour the coffee into the warm cups, one by one. Float the whiskey on top of each and flame individually, stirring until the fire dies. Or, let everyone flame and stir their own.

SWEET POTATOES À LA ROYALE
TO SERVE 4

2 cups mashed sweet potatoes,
hot
2 cups mashed cooked
chestnuts,* hot

2 oz unsalted butter, melted and
hot
2 oz light rum
2 oz brandy

Mix the mashed potatoes and chestnuts and blend well with the butter, preferably in a hot chafing dish. Set on the table, hot. Mix the rum and brandy in a metal long-handled warmer and heat just a bit. Ignite, and pour the flaming liquor over the potato-chestnut mixture and serve immediately, while still flaming.

EGGS À LA ROYALE (Poached or Soft-Boiled)
TO SERVE 4

½ cup Sauce Espagnole
4 oz Madeira wine
4 oz truffles, chopped
4 individual pastry shells, baked and hot*

8 eggs, freshly poached or soft-boiled and hot
1 cup Sauce Velouté*
½ cup cream

Mix the Espagnole, ½ the Madeira and the truffles in a pan and cook down until thickened. Pour into the bottoms of the pastry shells. Place 2 hot eggs in each. Meanwhile, mix the Velouté, cream and the remaining 2 ounces of Madeira and cook down until thickened. Pour over the eggs and serve hot.

Soubise

(soo-BEEZE)

After the Soubise family, prominent in France from the 1500s through the late eighteenth century. Benjamin de Rohan de Soubise was chief of the Protestant party under Louis XIII. Madame Soubise, wife of Francis de Rohan, was a paramour of Louis XIV. Charles de Rohan de Soubise, French prince and marechal, had the Hotel Soubise built in Paris, and today it houses the National Archives.

In cuisine Soubise is the name of a purée of onions, usually bound and thickened with rice but sometimes with mashed potatoes. Purée Soubise is used as an accompaniment to meats, large cuts or small, with eggs, and for stuffings. A thin Soubise is used as a sauce for eggs, meats and fowl. Dishes à la Maintenon (man-tuh-NOHN) are simply variations on dishes Soubise with other sauces, like Velouté, added to the Soubise along with other ingredients such as pickled tongue.

SAUCE SOUBISE
TO MAKE 2 CUPS

2 cups minced onions
1 Tbs butter
1 cup Sauce Béchamel

salt and white pepper
a few grains of sugar (optional)
2–4 tsp heavy cream, hot

Blanch the onions in lightly salted boiling water for 10 seconds, drain and squeeze dry. Cook them in the butter in a pan until limp but not browned. Add the Sauce Béchamel, season with salt and pepper to taste, and with sugar if desired. Cook very gently for 30 minutes, or until the onions are soft, and rub through a sieve or purée in a blender. Mix in the cream and serve hot with eggs, meats or fowl.

PURÉE SOUBISE
TO MAKE 2½ CUPS

Prepare 1 recipe of Sauce Soubise and add ½ cup of mashed cooked rice (or as needed) to thicken and bind. Or bind with ½ cup of dry mashed potatoes. Serve hot with meats, eggs and in stuffings. For smooth mashed rice or potatoes, rub through a sieve.

ARTICHOKE PURÉE SOUBISE
TO MAKE 2 CUPS

Mix about 1⅓ cups of artichokes (cooked in vegetable broth, drained and puréed in a blender or by rubbing through a sieve) with ⅔ cup of Purée Soubise. Serve hot with meats or eggs.

POTATOES SOUBISE (Stuffed)
TO SERVE 4

4 baked potatoes, hot	bread crumbs
1 cup Sauce Soubise, hot	butter, melted

Preheat oven to 375°. Halve the potatoes lengthwise and hollow out. Mash the removed potato pulp and mix with the Sauce Soubise. Use to stuff the potatoes. Sprinkle generously with crumbs and dribble on a little melted butter to moisten. Brown in the oven and serve hot.

EGGS SOUBISE (Baked)
TO SERVE 4

8 eggs	2 oz beef glaze,* hot (optional)
1½ cups Sauce Soubise	
salt and pepper	

Preheat oven to 350°. Line 4 individual buttered baking dishes with ½ Sauce Soubise. Break 2 eggs carefully into each. Season with salt and pepper to taste and spoon the remaining sauce over them. Bake in the oven until just done, about 8 minutes. Serve in the baking dishes with the meat glaze spooned on top, hot.

EGGS SOUBISE (Hard-Boiled)
TO SERVE 4

8 eggs, hard-boiled and halved lengthwise	1 cup Purée Soubise
	½ cup Cream Sauce

Preheat oven to 400°. Put the Purée Soubise in the bottom of a buttered baking dish. Place the halved hard-boiled eggs on the Soubise, and top with the Cream Sauce. Bake in the oven until lightly browned and heated through, and serve hot.

TOURNEDOS SOUBISE (Beef Fillets)
TO SERVE 4

4 beef fillets

1½ cups Sauce Soubise, or
Purée Soubise, hot

Grill the fillets to taste. Serve at once, topped with Soubise, hot.

LAMB CHOPS SOUBISE
TO SERVE 4

8–12 lamb chops (depending on
   their size), seasoned
1 oz butter (more if needed)
1 onion, sliced
salt and pepper
1 tsp parsley

1 bay leaf
½ cup dry white wine
1½ cups Sauce Soubise, hot
1 cup onion rings, dredged in
   flour, sautéed, drained and
   hot

Sauté the lamb in the butter until well browned. Set the chops aside, add the onion to the sauté pan, and sauté until golden. Season with salt and pepper to taste. Add the parsley, bay leaf and wine and mix. Return the chops to the pan, spoon over some pan sauce, cover, and simmer 15 to 20 minutes, until done. Arrange the chops on a hot platter. Discard the bay leaf and the excess fat from the pan. Add the Sauce Soubise and blend with the pan juices. Pour over the lamb, garnish with the sautéed onion rings, and serve hot.

This recipe is also fine for mutton chops. Or, either lamb or mutton chops, or any other small cut of meat, can be sautéed, broiled or grilled, topped with Sauce or Purée Soubise and served hot for a fine dish Soubise.

Talleyrand

(tah-lay-RAHND)

After Charles Maurice de Talleyrand-Périgord, French bishop, politician and diplomat, and one of the greatest French gastronomes. He was born in Paris on February 13, 1754. At twenty-one he became abbot of Saint-Denis, and by the time he was thirty-five, was bishop of Autun. But high ecclesiastical office didn't keep him from a wordly life. His lack of moral scruples and aptitude for intrigue enabled him to retain his prominence throughout the Revolution, the Directory, the Empire and the Restoration, with only short periods of reversal. The splendor of his table was well known in the Court, and at the time of the First Empire his chef was the great Careme. Talleyrand felt that in cases of diplomacy, a good table was an important tool. Once on leaving for the Congress of Vienna, where he hoped to gain diplomatic advantages for France, he said to Louis XVIII, "Sire, I have more need of casseroles than of written instructions." Talleyrand was eventually excommunicated, but apparently cared little, and continued to live life to the hilt to the fairly ripe age of eighty-four.

Macaroni Talleyrand is the standard accompaniment for a dish Talleyrand. Virtually any meat can be prepared and served with this accompaniment. Usually the meat is cooked in a pan, covered or not, as desired, but finished uncovered with a little Madeira wine, to which is added cream plus Sauce Velouté* or Sauce Espagnole. This sauce is then served with the meat and macaroni. Truffles and pickled tongue are often added to the sauce as a garnish. Sauce Périgueux is frequently served with Beef Talleyrand. Use cream with Velouté to finish sauces for light meats such as chicken. Use cream with Purée Soubise, or Espagnole Sauce for darker meats such as beef.

An appropriate atmosphere would be eighteenth-century posh, but most important, fine cuisine and wines.

SAUCE TALLEYRAND
TO MAKE 2 CUPS

1½ cups Sauce Velouté*
1½ cups chicken stock* or broth
3 oz cream
½ cup Madeira wine
4 Tbs butter

2 Tbs minced truffles
2 Tbs minced pickled tongue
2 Tbs minced carrot, onion and
   celery, mixed and simmered
   in butter, drained

Bring the Velouté and stock to a boil and add the cream and Madeira. Cook down to ½. Stir in the butter, truffles, tongue and vegetables and serve hot.

MACARONI TALLEYRAND
TO SERVE 4

1 lb macaroni, cooked, drained
   and hot
1 oz butter
¾ cup Gruyère or Parmesan
   cheese, grated, or half and
   half (or to taste)

½ cup truffles, in small strips,
   simmered in Madeira wine,
   drained
½ cup pâté de foie gras,
   chopped, simmered in butter, drained and hot

Mix the macaroni and butter. Toss with the cheese, or cheeses. Mix in the truffles and pâté de foie gras and serve hot.

VEAL CUTLETS TALLEYRAND
TO SERVE 4

4 large veal cutlets, lightly seasoned and pounded flat
1 oz butter
½ cup chopped mushrooms
2 tsp shallots, minced
3 oz heavy cream

1 tsp lemon juice
1 tsp parsley
½ tsp basil
salt and pepper
2 egg yolks, beaten with a fork
1 recipe Duchesse Potatoes, hot

Brown the veal in the butter. Set aside and keep hot. Add the mushrooms and shallots to the pan and simmer a few minutes without coloring, adding butter if needed. Add cream and heat. Return veal to the pan and simmer until done. Stir in the lemon juice, parsley, basil and salt and pepper to taste, and simmer 1 minute more. Remove from the heat and let stand for a minute. Beat in the yolks, blending well. Make a bed of the potatoes on a hot platter, top with the veal and sauce and serve hot.

LAMB CHOPS TALLEYRAND
TO SERVE 4

12 lamb chops	1 cup diced mushrooms
salt and pepper (optional)	½ cup diced truffles
butter	2 oz sherry wine
2 cups Purée Soubise, hot	1 cup heavy cream

Season the lamb lightly with salt and pepper, if desired. Sauté in butter until done to taste. Drain, and arrange on a hot platter in a ring. Fill the center of the ring with the Purée Soubise and keep hot. Discard excess fat from the lamb sauté pan and add the mushrooms and truffles. Sauté lightly, adding butter as needed. Add the sherry and cook a few minutes more, stirring up the juices. Add the cream and simmer a few minutes to blend and thicken. Spoon the sauce over the lamb and serve hot.

Turque
(TEWRK)

Means Turkish, and is also spelled *Turc*. The Turkish people are believed to have come from a region in Asia between the Ural and Altai mountains, where they were already mixed with Mongols. These nomads became Moslems during their westward migration. The position of Turkey, at the crossroads between Europe and Asia, has prompted extensive intermingling of different peoples. The early inhabitants of the area were apparently similar to the ancient Alpine subrace of Europe, but modified by later infiltrations of Gauls and Semites. Later the country was subject to the Macedonian, Roman, Byzantine and Ottoman empires, each introducing fresh strains to the people already there. With the fall of Constantinople in 1453 the Turks accelerated their settlements throughout the Balkan area, but were strongly resisted by the Christians. Even the Balkan groups who adopted Islam—the Bosnian Slavs, Albanians and Bulgarian Pomaks—were not assimilated by the Turks, and thus Turkish influence declined in the nineteenth century.

In cuisine, the Middle Eastern effect begins in Greece, and strengthens through Turkey and around the east of the Mediterranean, with the height of

Middle Eastern cuisine found in Beirut, Lebanon, which definitely equals Paris as the capital of a particular cuisine. In Middle East cookery lemon juice is a popular substitute for vinegar, and as far as I'm concerned the result is much lighter and more refreshing. We're all familiar with shish-kebab, which should really be spelled *seekh kebab*. It originated in India, not the Mideast. In Hindu or Urdu a *seekh* is a thin metal rod with a loop at one end for a finger hold and a point at the other, and a *kebab* is a meatball. A favorite meat throughout the Middle East is lamb, and in a seekh kebab, marinated lamb is far superior to beef in flavor, and should be cooked as you would beef; that is, pink and juicy inside, to taste, but never overdone. The staple starch here is rice, and olives and egg-plant are common garnishes. This category is basically the same as any other Mediterranean cooking style, relying on olive oil, tomatoes, onions and garlic as its most typical ingredients, although butter is sometimes found in recipes à la Turque, such as in the recipe for Chicken Medaillons. The only really distinctive feature of this mode is the Rice Pilaf à la Turque with its chick peas, pine kernels or currants. This pilaf is served with all sorts of Turque dishes. In fact, without this distinctive pilaf as an accompaniment, a dish à la Turque could as well be called by any other Mediterranean cooking style's name. The only exception to this is a particular dish, the Salad à la Turque, with its characteristic lemony dressing.

Turkey produces some very interesting cheeses: Casera, a salty, crumbly cheese made from goat's milk; Pennich, made from sheep's milk and packed in sheep's or lamb's skin to cure; and, Edirne, a semifirm white cheese made from sheep's milk; very good in green salads.

Turkey is certainly not noted as a wine producer, but does have an interesting native drink to offer. It is called Ouzo, or Rakhi, and is a colorless but anise-flavored liquid.

If you mix Ouzo with water, it becomes an opaque milky fluid, and is more potent than brandy. French equivalents are Pernod, Ricard and Pastis.

A Turkish theme in décor can be great fun, and a real change of pace. Flowing silks, elaborate candelabra, Middle Eastern water pipes, intricate de-signs in fabrics, tapestries and china, and the tiny cups for Turkish coffee. I once planned a party for a group of friends and business associates with this theme. The décor was based on a 3-foot-wide rolls of red and white crêpe paper, hung across wires from the center of the ceiling draped down to about 5 feet high along the walls and then straight down to the floor, in alternating red and white stripes like inside of a tent. The effort was not great, but the result was. The doors to the room were hung with beads from a costume supply (stage props). The décor was augmented by miscellaneous Middle Eastern items I scrounged from a few friends, and a huge water pipe rented from an import store for a few dollars. Greek salad was served from a 3-foot wooden bowl borrowed from a restaurant, and a small group of Lebanese students provided music with Middle Eastern instruments. All-in-all the effort was well spent. Of course, you needn't be so extravagant; any little touch that creates an unusual atmosphere helps immense-ly. Zeus and Heimdall save me from the typical cocktail party, where everyone stands awkwardly clutching a drink, trying desperately to think of something clever to say.

TOMATO FONDUE À LA TURQUE
TO SERVE 4

1 Tbs minced onions
2 Tbs olive oil
6 tomatoes, peeled,* seeded
   and chopped

2 garlic cloves, finely minced (or
   grated)
salt and paprika
lemon juice

Cook the onions in the oil until limp but not browned. Add the rest of the ingredients, seasoning to taste with salt and paprika, and a few drops of lemon juice. Simmer until well blended and concentrated. Use as a sauce or garnish, hot.

SALAD À LA TURQUE

Use your preferred greens, with lots of fresh parsley, and dress with olive oil, lemon juice, salt and pepper. You may add oregano, beaten egg, and even grated Parmesan or blue cheese. In Turkey, sliced cucumbers, chopped walnuts and chopped green peppers are favorites. Fresh mint may be substituted for the parsley. A favorite ploy in the Middle East is to mix the olive oil and lemon juice with just a touch of vinegar and use it to marinate 1 or 2 crushed garlic cloves for a few hours. Then they discard the garlic and proceed with making the salad, tossing in the oil mixture, seasoning and serving at once. This is consistent with the French idea that a salad should be made at the table with its dressing and eaten at once. Neither the salad nor the dressing should be prepared ahead for best results.

This is also called Salad à la Grecque.

RICE PILAF À LA TURQUE
TO SERVE 4

1 cup raw rice
2 Tbs butter
2 cups chicken broth
1 tsp parsley
¼ tsp thyme

¼ bay leaf
cheesecloth, washed
1 cup chick peas, pine kernels
   or currants

Soak the rice in well-salted water for 1 hour. Drain, and cook in the butter for several minutes without browning. Add the broth. Add the parsley, thyme and bay leaf tied in cheesecloth. Cook covered without stirring until done and the liquid is absorbed. Discard the herb bouquet. Meanwhile, cook the chick peas or pine kernels and brown in the oven, or plump the currants in hot water. Mix the chick peas, pine kernels or drained currants with the rice and serve hot.

PEPPERS À LA TURQUE
TO SERVE 4

1 cup Rice Pilaf à la Turque
1 lb mutton or lamb, cooked and chopped
2 garlic cloves, minced fine
4 Tbs tomato purée

salt and pepper
8 sweet green peppers
2 onions, diced
olive oil
3 oz Tomato Sauce, preferably homemade*

Mix the pilaf, mutton, garlic and tomato purée and season to taste with salt and pepper. Preheat oven to 350°. Remove the tops from the peppers and clean out the inside membranes and seeds. Blanch for 3 to 5 minutes in boiling water, and drain. Stuff with the pilaf mixture. Meanwhile, sauté the onions lightly in olive oil, drain, and use to line the bottom of a buttered baking dish. Place the stuffed peppers on this bed. The dish should be just big enough to hold the peppers rather tightly. Moisten the peppers with the Tomato Sauce. Bake covered in the oven for 30 to 35 minutes. Serve on a hot vegetable dish, topped with the cooking juices, hot.

EGGPLANT IMAM BAALDI À LA TURQUE
TO SERVE 4

2 small eggplants, halved lengthwise
2 tomatoes, peeled,* seeded and chopped
1 onion, diced

½ cup currants
olive oil
salt and pepper
thyme, ground
bay leaf, ground

Preheat oven to 350°. Scoop out most of the pulp from the eggplant halves, leaving the skins intact. Chop the scooped-out pulp and mix with the tomatoes, onion and currants. Sauté in a little olive oil until limp but not browned. Season to taste with salt and pepper and use to stuff the eggplant shells. Sprinkle with a little thyme and bay leaf. Sprinkle with olive oil, to moisten well. (Use only the finest pure olive oil.) Bake in the oven for about 40 minutes. Cool, and serve chilled. This is often served with yogurt, particularly in Turkey.

Imam Baaldi means *the priest has fainted* in Turkish. There is a folk tale of a priest (Imam) who came to dinner, and when he entered the home he was so moved by the aroma of this dish that he fainted.

TOMATOES À LA TURQUE
TO SERVE 4

Proceed as for Tomato Fondue à la Turque, cutting the tomatoes into large dice. Cook the rest of the ingredients as described in the recipe, without the tomatoes. Add the tomatoes at the end of cooking for just a few minutes to cook lightly. Serve hot as a vegetable.

LAMB NOISETTES À LA TURQUE (Thin Fillets)
TO SERVE 4

2 lbs lamb slices
salt and pepper
butter
1 recipe Rice Pilaf à la Turque,
   hot

1 eggplant, peeled, diced,
   sautéed in olive oil, drained,
   lightly seasoned and hot
1 Tbs tomato purée
1 cup veal stock* or broth, or
   beef stock* or broth

Season the lamb lightly with salt and pepper and sauté in butter. Put the pilaf on a hot platter and top with the lamb slices. Surround with the eggplant and keep hot. Add the tomato purée and stock to the lamb sauté pan and quickly thicken, scraping up the juices. Strain over the lamb and serve hot.

CHICKEN MEDAILLONS À LA TURQUE (Round Slices)
TO SERVE 4

2 lbs chicken breasts, skinned,
   boned and cut in round or
   oval slices
paprika
butter

1 recipe Rice Pilaf à la Turque,
   hot
2 oz dry white wine
1½ cups veal gravy
1–2 Tbs tomato paste

Season the chicken with paprika to taste and sauté in butter until done. Do not overcook. Put the pilaf on a hot platter, top with the chicken and keep hot. Add the wine to the sauté pan and boil down, scraping up the juices. Add the gravy and tomato paste, blend well and heat through. Strain over the chicken and rice and serve hot.

A fruity variation I enjoy is made by skipping the tomato paste in the sauce, and substituting ½ cup of halved seedless grapes. Cook the grapes in the sauce, after straining it, for just a few minutes to blend the flavors. Do not cook the grapes more than a few minutes, or they will lose their delicate flavor and freshness. Spoon over the chicken and serve at once, hot.

BEURRECKS À LA TURQUE
TO SERVE 4

1 cup Gruyère cheese,
   chopped fine
½ cup thick Sauce Béchamel

½ cup noodle paste*
butter

Mix the cheese and Béchamel and chill. Divide in ½ ounce pieces and shape each like a small cigar. Roll out the noodle paste in wafer-thin pieces, just large enough to wrap the cheese shapes. Wrap each cheese shape in noddle paste, seal the edges and sauté in butter until golden brown. Drain, and serve at once, hot, as hors d'oeuvres.

COFFEE À LA TURQUE (Turkish Coffee)
TO SERVE 4

4 tiny slivers of lemon rind (yellow part only)
5 tsp sugar

1½ cups water
5 Tbs coffee, finely ground

Heat 4 demitasse cups and put a piece of lemon rind in each. Bring the sugar and water to a boil in a pan. Slowly sift in the coffee. Raise and lower the heat several times, each time letting the coffee foam up, then subside. Do not stir. Strain through cheesecloth into the heated cups, swirl with the lemon rind and serve at once, hot.

Viennoise

(vee-enn-NWAZ)

After the city of Vienna, in Austria. Vienna is situated on the Danube River, at the junction of the Alps and Carpathian mountains, where the Danube enters the Hungarian plain. Originally founded by the Celts, Vienna became a military frontier station called Vindobona in the Roman campaigns against the marauding Germanic tribes. Marcus Aurelius was killed here in 180. In the middle of the fifth century, Vienna was destroyed by invading Huns under Attila.

Vienna has rivaled Paris as the center of European culture and entertainment. Waltzes are practically synonymous with Vienna, and among the city's national monuments are the homes of the great composers Beethoven, Haydn, Schubert and Mozart. The city's museums are among the finest in the world. It was in Vienna that Sigmund Freud lived and did much of his work, until he fled from the Nazi occupation in 1938. Vienna is the industrial, financial and political heart of Austria. It deals in iron, leather goods, textiles, chemicals, furniture and fine art objects.

Cooking à la Viennoise is typified by garnishes of chopped hard-boiled egg whites and yolks, anchovy fillets, olives, lemon slices, capers and parsley, all around a dish of meat or poultry usually dipped in egg, coated with crumbs and sautéed. The most typical Viennoise dishes are the schnitzels of Austria, thin veal cutlets coated with egg and crumbs and cooked in innumerable variations, often with cheeses, or ham. This cooking mode is similar to the categories Anglaise, Milanaise and Villeroi in that they all use coatings on foods in the preparation of their dishes.

Most French categories that deal with foods of a foreign country are second-rate copies of the particular country's cuisine, such as the use of curry powder in the category Indienne. This is not so true of the category Viennoise. These dishes are probably the best effort by the French to represent accurately a foreign cuisine.

Unfortunately, almost none of the fine wine of Austria is exported today. If any is available, however, look for the names Krems, Durnstein and Loiben, fine wine-producing towns. Usually the only Austrian wine available is the very run-of-the-winery Schluck.

To get in the mood for a dish à la Viennoise, we should take a mental trip back to a grand ball in Vienna, where elaborately dressed guests would be dancing to the latest hit, a waltz by Johann Strauss.

VIENNOISE GARNISH

This consists of separate small piles of chopped hard-boiled egg whites and yolks, capers, anchovies, olives and lemon wedges, all arranged around the main course.

BEEF ENTRECÔTES À LA VIENNOISE (Steaks)
TO SERVE 4

8 small beefsteaks, boneless	2 cups onion rings
salt and paprika	1 oz butter, melted
flour	cider vinegar
butter and olive oil, ½ and ½	

Pound the steaks to tenderize and flatten. Season with salt and paprika to taste and dredge in flour, shaking off the excess. Sauté in hot butter and oil until done to taste and drain. Meanwhile, sauté the onion rings in butter and oil separately until done and golden and drain. Arrange the steaks on a hot platter surrounded with the onion rings. Dress with the melted butter and a few drops of vinegar to taste and serve at once, hot.

Boiled potatoes are often served with this dish.

VEAL ESCALOPES À LA VIENNOISE (Slices)
TO SERVE 4

2 lemons, peeled, sliced and seeded	parsley
green olives, pitted	2 lbs veal escalopes
anchovy fillets, drained	salt and pepper
6 eggs, hard-boiled, yolks and whites separated	3 eggs, beaten
capers	bread crumbs
	butter

Have the lemons, olives, anchovies, eggs, capers and parsley ready, so the finished veal can be garnished and served quickly, without cooling. The egg whites and yolks should be chopped separately.

Pound the veal to flatten and tenderize and season lightly with salt and pepper. Dip in beaten egg and coat with crumbs. Sauté in hot butter until done and golden brown. Do not overcook. Set on a hot platter and place the lemon slices on top of the veal. Put an olive ringed with an anchovy fillet on each lemon slice, and arrange little piles of egg white, egg yolk, capers and parsley around the dish decoratively. Serve at once, hot.

This dish is excellent prepared with veal chops, or very thin boneless pork fillets. If using pork, cut into a piece to be sure it is done before serving.

LAMB LOIN À LA VIENNOISE
TO SERVE 4

1 tsp salt	1 Tbs parsley
½ tsp pepper	flour
1 lamb loin, boned and halved lengthwise (milk-fed or baby lamb only)	3 eggs, beaten bread crumbs butter, preferably clarified*
1 cup olive oil	2 lemons, quartered
½ cup lemon juice	

Rub the salt and pepper into the lamb and marinate it in the oil, lemon juice and parsley for 1 hour, turning occasionally. Drain the lamb and dry. Dredge in flour and shake off the excess. Coat with the beaten egg and crumbs, pressing the crumbs into the flesh to adhere. Sauté until done and nicely browned in butter. Drain. Serve at once on a hot platter garnished with the lemon wedges.

CHICKEN SUPRÊMES À LA VIENNOISE
TO SERVE 4

To make chicken suprêmes, take 6 breasts, halve, skin and bone. You now have 12 supremes. Proceed as for Beef Entrecôtes à la Viennoise, using the suprêmes in place of the steaks.

CHICKEN SAUTÉ À LA VIENNOISE
TO SERVE 4

2 small tender chickens, cut up	1 Tbs olive oil
salt and pepper	bread crumbs
flour	butter, preferably clarified*
3 eggs	2 lemons, quartered

Season the chicken lightly with salt and pepper and dredge in flour, shaking off the excess. Beat the eggs with the oil and season with salt and pepper to taste. Dip the chicken pieces in the beaten egg, coat with crumbs, and sauté until done and nicely browned in butter. Serve garnished with the lemon quarters, hot.

An interesting garnish for a chicken dish à la Viennoise is peeled and quartered cucumbers, boiled in lightly salted water until tender and tossed in butter, served hot.

A nice sauce may be made for the Chicken Sauté à la Viennoise after the chicken is done. Arrange the chicken with the lemon quarters on a hot platter and keep hot. Discard excess fat from the sauté pan. Add 2 ounces of dry white wine to the pan and quickly boil down, scraping up the juices. Add 1 cup of heavy cream and blend in and heat. Season with about 1 teaspoon of lemon juice. Blend in 1 to 2 teaspoons butter, if desired. Strain over the chicken and serve hot.

CORNISH GAME HENS or SQUAB À LA VIENNOISE
TO SERVE 4

Proceed as for Chicken Sauté à la Viennoise, using 4 1-pound birds halved lengthwise.

NOODLE CASSEROLE À LA VIENNOISE
TO SERVE 4

1 lb noodles, cooked and drained, hot
1 cup lean cooked ham, ground

1½ cups sour cream, well seasoned with salt and pepper
½ lb cottage cheese, drained and forced through a sieve

Preheat oven to 300°. Mix the noodles with the ham and sour cream well. Put in a buttered casserole. Top with the cottage cheese and bake in the oven for 20 minutes. Serve hot, as a main course.

CUSTARD À LA VIENNOISE
TO SERVE 4

¼ cup sugar
1 oz dry white wine
¾ cup sugar
2 cups scalded milk, hot
2 tsp vanilla extract
⅛ tsp salt

2 eggs
4 egg yolks
½ cup heavy cream
confectioners' sugar
1 oz coffee liqueur

Preheat oven to 300°. Make a caramel by heating the ¼ cup of sugar in a pan, then blending in the wine slowly. Use this caramel to coat a 1-quart mold. Chill in refrigerator to set quickly. Cook the ¾ cup of sugar in another pan until it is a very light caramel. Blend in the milk, slowly at first, Add the vanilla and salt. Remove from heat. Mix the eggs and extra yolks and beat. Blend in the milk mixture slowly, beating, so its heat doesn't curdle the eggs. Strain this custard mixture into the mold, place mold in a pan of water and bake in the oven in the water bath for about 40 minutes, or until done. Unmold. Whip the cream with a little confectioners' sugar to taste and with the coffee liqueur. Serve the custard cool, topped with the whipped cream.

Vigneronne

(veen-nayr-ROHN)

Means vine dresser, one who tends grapes. Grapes are the fruit of any species of the *Vitis* genus of the vine family. Grapes are the only important commercial fruit produced by a climbing plant. The vines can grow up to 30 feet in one summer, and all grapes are edible, except for a few decorative Japanese varieties. The color of cultivated grapes ranges through red, pink, blue, purple, black, golden, green and white. Grapes were among the earliest of cultivated plants.

Any bird may be cooked à la Vigneronne, as well as any meats, especially small cuts like chops or fillets. Usually, however, this approach is used with game birds. This category, in using fresh grapes cooked with the main course for the final few minutes, is unique. Although fresh grapes may occasionally be used in this manner in other recipes and categories, this is the only category that uses grapes in this manner as its hallmark.

Here again the theme is grapes and wines, as in Bourguignonne and Bordelaise. The main difference is that in dishes à la Vigneronne the foods are actually cooked with grapes. So, lots of different colored grapes with various flowers would be perfect for décor.

CORNISH GAME HEN, PARTRIDGE, SQUAB or CHICKEN À LA VIGNERONNE
TO SERVE 4

4 1-lb game hens, partridges or squab, or 2 small chickens	1 lb peeled, seeded grapes (or seedless grapes)
salt and pepper	½ cup chicken broth
butter	1–2 oz brandy

Season the birds with salt and pepper to taste inside and out and truss. Brown well in butter in a casserole and cook covered until done—about 45 minutes for game hens or squab, 30 minutes for partridge or 1½ hours for chickens. When done, discard excess fat and add the grapes, broth and brandy. Cover and simmer 10 minutes more. Serve at once, in the casserole, uncovering it at the table so the fresh aroma of the grapes will fill the room.

This dish is often made with the birds stuffed with chopped goose or chicken liver mixed with about ½ as much chopped truffles and mushrooms and a bit of brandy and salt and pepper to taste. Pâté de foie gras is sometimes used in place of the livers.

CHICKEN SUPRÊMES À LA VIGNERONNE
TO SERVE 4

Proceed as for Game Hens à la Vigneronne, using 6 chicken breasts. To make suprêmes, halve the breasts, then skin and bone them. That will yield 12 suprêmes. Simmer the suprêmes in butter until just barely done. Then add the grapes, broth and brandy and simmer covered for 10 minutes more and serve hot, as in the game hen recipe.

When a bird has been cooked à la Vigneronne, a fine sauce can be made in the casserole or pot after removing the bird or birds. Set them on a hot platter and keep hot. Add ½ cup of white wine to the pot and boil down, scraping up the juices. Add ¾ cup of Jus de Veau, veal stock,* chicken stock* or broth and blend well. Add ½ cup of heavy cream and blend. Cook over fairly high heat to thicken lightly, stirring. Flame the birds on the platter with ½ cup of warm champagne, strain on the pot sauce when the flame dies, and serve at once, hot.

A nice accompaniment is a garnish of toast triangles spread with pâté de foie gras, or chicken liver pâté, with a very thin round slice of raw mushroom on each triangle.

PORK CHOPS or VEAL CHOPS À LA VIGNERONNE
TO SERVE 4

Proceed as for Game Hens à la Vigneronne, using 2 pounds of well-trimmed chops, lightly seasoned and simmered in butter until done. Then add the grapes, broth and brandy and simmer covered for 10 minutes more. Serve hot, as in the game hen recipe.

Villeroi

(veel-rWAH)

Ville means town or city and *roi* means king, but the food category Villeroi is named after Nicholas de Villeroi, a marshal of France born in Paris in 1598. He was a governor under Louis XIV. Villeroi's son Francois, born in Paris in 1644, was also a marshal of France, but was considered a poor general, being beaten in Italy in 1701 and 1702, then losing again at Ramillies in 1706. Nonetheless, he was made governor of the young King Louis XV by the will of Louis XIV. Louis the XV was the grandson of Louis the XIV, not the son as one might expect.

In cuisine, the term Villeroi is applied to a particular sauce, used to coat foods to be sautéed or deep-fried, and to any foods prepared in that manner. This category lends itself to a wide variety of dishes. Anything that can be breaded and sautéed can be dipped in Sauce Villeroi and sautéed or deep-fried, breaded or not, as desired. Chicken suprêmes (boned, skinned breasts) are excellent, as are sliced sweetbreads. The variety of combinations of foods that can be prepared à la Villeroi is endless. Use the foods you prefer, separately or in combination.

Villeroi is a fine variation for fried foods. Other categories that use coated foods as keynotes are Anglaise, Milanese and Viennoise.

SAUCE VILLEROI
TO MAKE 1½ CUPS

2 cups Sauce Allemande
½ cup chicken or veal stock*

½ cup mushroom fumet (juice from cooked mushrooms) or canned mushroom juice

Combine the ingredients and cook down until quite thick, about 1½ cups. Use as a coating for foods to be prepared à la Villeroi.

Depending on the food to be coated, this sauce may be flavored with 1 to 2 ounces of tomato purée, or 2 to 4 ounces of Purée Soubise, or chopped truffles.

MUTTON CHOPS or CUTLETS À LA VILLEROI
TO SERVE 4

1 carrot, chopped
1 onion, chopped
1 celery stalk, chopped
1 tsp parsley
¼ tsp thyme
¼ bay leaf
cheesecloth, washed
1 oz butter
8 mutton chops, lean
salt and pepper

1 cup beef stock* or broth
2 cups Sauce Villeroi
3 eggs, beaten
bread crumbs
butter, preferably clarified*
4 small parsley bunches
fat for deep-frying, very hot
2 cups Sauce Périgueux, or Tomato Sauce,* hot

Preheat oven to 350°. Put the carrot, onion and celery in a pot. Add the parsley, thyme and bay leaf tied in cheesecloth. Add the butter and brown the vegetables. Season the mutton with salt and pepper to taste and lay on the vegetables in the pot. Add the stock, bring to a boil, cover and cook in the oven for about 30 minutes, or until the mutton is just done. Let the mutton cool in the stock. Drain and remove any excess fat. Chill.

Dip the chilled mutton chops in the Sauce Villeroi, then in the beaten eggs, then coat with crumbs and sauté until golden brown in butter. Meanwhile, deep-fry the parsley bunches in the hot fat until just crisp and drain. Serve the mutton on a hot platter garnished with the parsley, with the sauce served separately, hot.

LAMB CHOPS or CUTLETS À LA VILLEROI
TO SERVE 4

Proceed as for Mutton Chops à la Villeroi, using 12 lean lamb chops.

CALF'S SWEETBREADS À LA VILLEROI
TO SERVE 4

Proceed as for Mutton Chops à la Villeroi, using 2 pounds of calf's sweetbreads. Before using, soak the sweetbreads in cold water for 4 hours, changing the water often. Slice the sweetbreads and trim away central tubes.

CORNISH GAME HEN, SQUAB or QUAIL À LA VILLEROI
TO SERVE 4

4 1-lb birds
salt and pepper
butter
2 cups Sauce Villeroi

3 eggs, beaten
bread crumbs
2 cups Sauce Périgueux, hot

Split the birds in half lengthwise and remove all interior bones. Flatten. Season lightly with salt and pepper and sauté until just done in butter. Drain. Chill under weights to flatten further. Coat with the Sauce Villeroi, dip in beaten egg and coat with crumbs. Sauté in butter until golden brown. Serve with the Sauce Périgueux, hot. Small bunches of parsley deep-fried in hot fat and drained are typical as a garnish.

This recipe may also be used for chicken suprêmes (boned, skinned breasts).

CLAMS À LA VILLEROI
TO SERVE 4

1 qt live clams
1 cup Sauce Villeroi
2 eggs, beaten
bread crumbs

butter, or hot fat for deep-frying
parsley

Put the clams in a pot with 1 cup of water and boil, covered. When the clams open, they are done. Discard the shells and put the clams on small metal skewers. Coat with the Sauce Villeroi and chill. Dip in egg and crumbs and sauté in hot butter, or deep-fry in hot fat, until golden. Drain and serve hot, sprinkled with parsley.

This recipe may also be used for oysters or mussels.

ATTEREAU (Small Skewers) À LA VILLEROI

This is a method of cooking meats on small skewers. The ingredients are all precooked, cut in uniform pieces and chilled. They are then arranged on small skewers, coated with Sauce Villeroi and with bread crumbs, sautéed in butter until golden brown and served at once, hot, as an hors d'oeuvre.

Sometimes these small skewers are also dipped in beaten egg, after coating with Sauce Villeroi and crumbs, and coated with crumbs again before sautéing. Use precooked brains, cockscombs and cock's kidneys, sweetbreads, liver, mushrooms, truffles, artichoke hearts, tongue, ham, poultry meat or whatever you prefer, in any combination, but in equal small pieces. These should be small, as a delicate appetizer, not as a meal in themselves.

Vinaigrette

(vee-nay-GRET)

Means vinegar sauce. *Vinaigre* means vinegar. Vinegar itself was certainly discovered accidentally, since any table wine left uncorked soon begins to turn bitter and become vinegar. Therefore we can assume with reasonable certainty that vinegar is as old as wine and dates back at least to the ancient Egyptians and Persians. The Greeks were producing wine in France as early as 600 B.C., near Marseille. Where there's wine there's vinegar, and where there's vinegar there's probably a vinaigrette dressing of some kind. All the ancient wine producers were familiar with olive oil, and it's hard to imagine that they would overlook as natural a combination as vinegar and olive oil for a dressing. So, when we talk about Sauce Vinaigrette, we're talking about one of the truly ancient sauces.

This category is simply a method of using a salad dressing, namely Vinaigrette, or French dressing, in a variety of ways with a variety of foods. Lightly cooked vegetables such as peas, beans, thin carrot slices, asparagus tips, diced turnips, diced beets, sliced mushrooms, or whatever else you like *are* very French. Especially interesting would be a combination of vegetables, cooked separately, and served mixed or separately, seasoned with Vinaigrette.

There are also innumerable variations on the Vinaigrette given here. Chopped hard-boiled eggs may be added, whites, yolks, or crumbled bacon. Lemon juice may be used in place of some or all the vinegar. Or use different vinegars, for example tarragon wine vinegar, or different oils, like walnut oil, a real taste treat, but expensive and hard to find. Even the different combinations of green herbs you can use is tremendous. For an unusual menu, even though you may not wish to overdo dishes à la Vinaigrette, you might try an appetizer of frog's legs à la Vinaigrette as a first course, followed by vegetables of your choice, preferably including boiled rice or any other starch, with hot Roast Beef à la Vinaigrette as the main course. It makes an excellent meal, right out of history, or perhaps prehistory. If you feel that's too much Vinaigrette, use a different appetizer. Nuts and cheeses would fit in well.

For décor when serving a Vinaigrette dish, you might take a cue from ancient times. The table would need no cloth, the implements would be simple and basic. Though forks were used at the table as early as the tenth century in Byzantium, they were nothing but a curiosity in most of Europe until the eighteenth century. Spoons were used, but primarily for cooking. The standard implement was the knife, and most people carried their own. It was of a dagger shape, a general-purpose tool. Juices were mopped up with bread, usually unleavened bread, since raised, or leavened, bread as we know it today was a very uncertain thing then, depending on airborne yeast cells to get in the dough by chance and make it rise. The plates and bowls you use should be simple to enhance this theme, and the wine served in bowl-like cups. If you've invited fun-loving guests, this approach can lead to a relaxed, informal affair. If you're skeptical, think of how much better a piece of fried chicken tastes eaten in the hand than it does on a plate with a knife and fork.

SAUCE VINAIGRETTE
TO MAKE 2 CUPS

1½ cups pure olive oil, or salad
   oil
½ cup cider vinegar or wine
   vinegar

salt and pepper

Mix the oil and vinegar and season to taste with salt and pepper. This is a basic Sauce Vinaigrette, or dressing, for salads and marinades. For a sharper flavor, use just a bit more vinegar; for a milder flavor, a bit less. As with all salad dressings, this is best freshly made.

My preference in Vinaigrette is the very best olive oil, and cider vinegar. To me, wine vinegar is too distinctive to blend well with olive oil, and a dressing with a bland salad oil in place of the fine olive oil is completely uninteresting. If salad oil is all that's available, then I prefer using wine vinegar to give it all the flavor it can get.

This dressing is usually flavored with green herbs, about 4 to 6 tablespoons of mixed fresh herbs or 4 to 6 teaspoons of dried herbs. Parsley, chives, basil, tarragon, chervil and thyme are most commonly used, in any proportions you prefer.

SAUCE VINAIGRETTE À LA MOUTARDE
TO MAKE 2 CUPS

Prepare a basic Sauce Vinaigrette and blend 3 to 4 teaspoons of dry mustard. Use for cold meats or vegetables.

SAUCE RAVIGOTE
TO MAKE 2 CUPS

1¼ cups basic Sauce
   Vinaigrette
1 onion, minced
2 Tbs minced capers

1 Tbs minced fresh chervil
1 Tbs minced chives
2 tsp fresh minced parsley
2 tsp fresh minced tarragon

Blend all the ingredients and use at once for hot or cold beef, chicken, fish, vegetables or pig's feet. If you must use dried herbs, use about 1/3 as much, and let them stand in the Sauce Vinaigrette for 15 minutes, shaking occasionally to blend the flavors.

AVOCADOS À LA VINAIGRETTE
TO SERVE 4

lettuce leaves
2 avocados, peeled and halved
   lengthwise, with the stones
   removed

½ cup Sauce Vinaigrette, or to
   taste

Arrange very green lettuce leaves on 4 plates and top with ½ an avocado each, cut side up. As soon as the avocados are cut, rub the cut edges with a little Vinaigrette or lemon juice to prevent discoloring. Pour the Vinaigrette into the holes left by the stones and serve chilled.

This dish is often served with ½ pound tiny shrimp mixed with the Sauce Vinaigrette and piled on top of the avocado halves.

Young artichokes eaten raw with a peppery Sauce Vinaigrette are called Artichokes à la Poivrade, as are young artichokes with Sauce Poivrade.

CAULIFLOWER À LA VINAIGRETTE
TO SERVE 4

1½ lbs cauliflower flowerets,
   cooked and drained
½ cup Sauce Vinaigrette, or to
   taste

1 Tbs chives
1 Tbs parsley

Toss the cauliflower in the Vinaigrette with the chives and parsley. Let marinate for 1 hour and serve chilled.

This dish is often served with 1 or 2 ounces of heavy cream, or sour cream, blended into the dressing.

LEEKS À LA VINAIGRETTE
TO SERVE 4

1½ lbs leek whites
salt
olive oil

cider vinegar
pepper

Simmer the leek whites in lightly salted water until done and tender. Drain, arrange in a serving dish and dress with oil, vinegar and pepper to taste. Serve at room temperature or chilled.

PEPPERS À LA VINAIGRETTE
TO SERVE 4

1 lb small sweet peppers, quar-
    tered or sliced, seeded
olive oil
cider vinegar

salt and pepper
parsley
chervil

Arrange the peppers in a serving dish and season to taste with oil, vinegar and salt and pepper. Sprinkle with a little parsley and chervil and serve at room temperature.

This dish is sometimes served with the addition of 4 to 6 small quartered tomatoes, 1 sliced onion and 2 chopped hard-boiled eggs. The onions and tomato quarters are arranged in the dish with the peppers. After seasoning the dish with oil, vinegar, salt and pepper, the chopped egg is sprinkled on top with the parsley and chervil.

TOMATOES À LA VINAIGRETTE
TO SERVE 4

1½ lbs tomatoes, peeled,*
    sliced and seeded
salt
olive oil

cider vinegar
pepper
parsley
chervil or tarragon

Season the tomatoes with a little salt and let stand on paper towels for 10 minutes, to drain. Arrange the tomato slices in a serving dish and season with oil, vinegar and pepper to taste. Sprinkle with parsley, and a little chervil or tarragon, and chill. Serve chilled as a vegetable or hors d'oeuvre.

BEEF À LA VINAIGRETTE
TO SERVE 4

3 lbs boiled beef, or cold cooked
    beef, or reheated leftover
    beef, sliced or in chunks
olive oil
salad oil
wine vinegar

cider vinegar
salt and pepper
minced onion
parsley
chives

Serve the sliced beef with the oil and vinegar in separate cruets along with the salt and pepper in grinders or shakers. Serve small separate bowls of onion, parsley and chives, each with its own small serving spoon.

ROAST BEEF À LA VINAIGRETTE
TO SERVE 4 OR MORE

Roast the beef in one piece and serve hot. If you wish, let everyone cut off chunks of meat, as the ancients did, with their own knives and proceed with knives and fingers, holding the meat in bread slices and seasoning it with oil, vinegar and salt and pepper to taste.

TONGUE À LA VINAIGRETTE
TO SERVE 4

Proceed as for Beef à la Vinaigrette, using cold, cooked sliced tongue.

FROG'S LEGS À LA VINAIGRETTE
TO SERVE 4

4 sets of frog's legs (8 legs)	parsley
2 cups white wine	olive oil
1 Tbs lemon juice	cider vinegar
salt and pepper	

Simmer the frog's legs in the wine and lemon juice until done and tender. Season to taste with salt and pepper and sprinkle with parsley. Place on 4 hors d'oeuvre plates and serve hot or chilled, with cruets of oil and vinegar served separately.

Xérès

(kser-RES)

Means sherry, sherry wine. Sherry is a fortified wine produced mostly from the Palomino grape in the area around the city of Jerez de la Frontera in the extreme south of Spain near Gibraltar. The English name, sherry, is taken from the old Moorish name for the city, Sheris. The wine produced is strong and sweet, and belongs to a class known as sack, hence the names Dry Sack sherry, etc.

Sherry wines are extremely varied, from almost clear white to nearly black in color, and ranging from extreme sweetness to almost acid in flavor. The dry sherries include Fino, Vino de Pasto, Manzanilla, and an older and darker variety called Amontillado. A bit sweeter are Oloroso and Amoroso. The darker and sweeter types are cream, brown and East India. Spanish sherries undergo a special process of fermentation, ageing and blending, which imparts a quality unequalled anywhere in the world.

Sherry is a very versatile wine and for that reason is used in cooking. A little sherry added to almost any saute pan will improve an otherwise prosaic dish. I happen to prefer Madeira to sherry, in just about anything, but that's a matter of individual preference. What isn't a matter of individual preference is the subject of "cooking sherry." This terrible invention is so adulterated as to be considered undrinkable, and therefore can be sold as a grocery item. Cooking sherry will certainly destroy any dish it is added to, and actually costs more than good sherry wines from a liquor store.

MUSHROOM OMELET AU XÉRÈS
TO SERVE 2

½ cup sliced mushrooms
1 Tbs butter
1 Tbs sherry
4 eggs
salt and pepper

4 Tbs butter
4 medium mushroom caps,
   sautéed in butter, hot
watercress sprigs

Simmer the sliced mushrooms in the butter and wine until done and tender. Keep hot. Meanwhile, beat the eggs with salt and pepper to taste and prepare an omelet in very hot butter,* filling with the mushroom-wine mixture. Serve at once, hot, topped with the sautéed mushroom caps and garnished with watercress sprigs.

CHICKEN AU XÉRÈS
TO SERVE 4

1 4-lb chicken
salt and pepper
2 Tbs peanut oil
3 Tbs butter
2 oz brandy

3 oz sherry
½ cup heavy cream
1 cup Sauce Espagnole, or veal
   gravy
1–2 Tbs butter (optional)

Preheat oven to 325°. Season the chicken inside and out with salt and pepper to taste. Truss. Brown the chicken in the oil and butter in a casserole. Put in the oven and roast for 1½ hours, uncovered, basting. Discard excess fat and trussing strings and roast for 30 minutes more, basting, or until done. Remove excess fat from the casserole. Flame with the brandy, stirring until the fire does. Add the sherry, cover and cook in the oven for 5 minutes more. Remove the chicken to a hot platter and keep hot. Add the cream and Sauce Espagnole to the casserole and bring to a boil, blending with the cooking juices. Blend in the butter if desired. Strain into a sauceboat and serve hot.

OYSTERS AU XÉRÈS
TO SERVE 4

2 oz butter	1 tsp lemon juice
¼ tsp anchovy paste	2 tsp grated onion
2 cups tiny cubes crustless	2 oz heavy cream
French or Italian bread	2 Tbs sherry
salt and pepper	¼ cup bread crumbs tossed in a
1 pt oysters, drained	very little butter
1 Tbs chives	¼ cup grated Parmesan cheese
1 Tbs parsley	melted butter
1 tsp minced garlic	

Preheat oven to 300°. Blend the butter and anchovy paste in a pan over low heat. Add the bread cubes and sauté until golden, tossing occasionally. Season to taste with salt and pepper. Put ½ of this mixture into a buttered casserole. Top with ½ the oysters. Sprinkle with ½ the chives, parsley, garlic, lemon juice and onion. Repeat with the other ½ of these ingredients. Blend the cream and sherry and pour over the mixture in the casserole. Mix the crumbs and cheese and sprinkle over the top. Sprinkle with a little melted butter to moisten and bake in the oven for 30 minutes, or until done and golden brown. Serve at once, hot.

FRYING BATTER AU XÉRÈS

1¼ cups flour	2 eggs
2 tsp baking powder	1 oz sherry
⅛ tsp salt	¼ cup heavy cream
grated nutmeg	½ cup milk

Mix the flour, baking powder, salt and a little nutmeg to taste in a bowl. Beat the eggs and sherry together, and add to the flour mixture little by little, alternating with the cream. Mix well. Add the milk and beat until smooth. To use, dip the food to be deep-fried into the batter, then into bread crumbs, if desired, and deep-fry in hot fat. Drain and serve hot. Excellent for small pieces of chicken (precooked), quenelles, balls of thick vegetable purée or any other kinds of fritters.

Zingara
(zen-gah-RAH)

Meaning gypsy, from the Italian word *zingaro*. Gypsies originated in the northwest of India, and were first noted in the Byzantine Empire about the ninth century. By the fourteenth century they were known in the Balkans, and a hundred years later in Germany, Italy, Switzerland and France. They spread to England by about the sixteenth century. Their language is a neo-Indic dialect, but has been affected by Armenian and Iranian influences during the course of their travels. Gypsies are still to be found throughout Europe, and in the United States, and have always remained somewhat seclusive.

The distinctive characteristics of this category are its sauce and garnish, and the use of ham in many of the recipes, but nonetheless it's quite a hodge-podge. The paprika is reminiscent of Hungarian cooking. The ham is typical of Bayonne cooking. And Rice à l'Indienne often appears in recipes à la Zingara. It's a hard category to pin down, like a gypsy.

Any small cuts of meat can be made following the veal or chicken recipes. Use about 2 pounds of boneless meat, or 3 pounds of steaks or chops with bones, to serve 4. Any eggs served on bread croutons with sautéed ham and Sauce Zingara becomes a dish à la Zingara.

This theme lends itself easily to décor. We're all familiar with Gypsy fortunetellers, brightly colored fabrics, crystal balls and the soft lighting of candles or kerosene lamps. Wild gypsy violin music would be great in the background, and a colorful sash around your waist, or even a bright scarf knotted at the back of your head would be appropriate, as would a gold loop earring.

As a cooking category, Zingara is the same as Bohémienne. This is the name of a garnish to accompany small cuts of meat and poultry. It consists of finely chopped shredded ham, tongue, truffles and mushrooms held together by a thick brown sauce such as Espagnole, with tomato and tarragon flavoring.

SAUCE ZINGARA
TO MAKE 2 CUPS

2 cups Sauce Espagnole, or
 beef gravy
2 oz Tomato Sauce, preferably
 homemade*
2 oz mushroom juice (juice from
 cooking mushrooms, or
 canned mushroom juice)

2 Tbs ham, minced or shredded
2 Tbs pickled tongue, minced or
 shredded
2 Tbs finely sliced mushrooms
2 tsp finely sliced truffles (optional)
paprika

Heat the Espagnole in a pan. Add the Tomato Sauce and mushroom stock and simmer for a few minutes. Add the ham, tongue and mushrooms and cook for about 5 minutes. Stir in the truffles, lower the heat below a boil, season to taste with paprika and serve hot with eggs or meats.

ZINGARA GARNISH
TO SERVE 4

½ cup Sauce Espagnole, or beef
 gravy, thick
¼ cup lean ham
¼ cup pickled tongue (optional)
¼ cup mushrooms

1 Tbs butter
¼ cup truffles
½ tsp tarragon
1 Tbs Tomato Sauce or purée
paprika

Heat the Sauce Espagnole in a pan. Chop or shred the ham and tongue fine and add to the pan. Sauté the mushrooms in the butter, drain and chop very fine with the truffles. Add to the pan. Add the tarragon, Tomato Sauce and paprika to taste and cook, but do not boil, for 5 minutes. Serve hot with small cuts of meat and poultry.

EGGS À LA ZINGARA (Poached or Soft-Boiled)
TO SERVE 4

4 bread slices, trimmed, sautéed in butter, drained and hot
4 ham slices, hot

8 eggs, freshly poached or soft-boiled and hot
1 cup Sauce Zingara, hot

Arrange the bread croutons on 4 hot plates. Top each with a ham slice and 2 eggs. Pour on the sauce and serve at once, hot.

VEAL CHOPS or CUTLETS À LA ZINGARA
TO SERVE 4

8–12 veal chops
salt and paprika
flour (optional)

butter
8–12 ham slices
2 cups Sauce Zingara, hot

Season the veal with salt and paprika to taste. Dredge in flour if desired, shaking off the excess. Sauté in butter until done and nicely browned. Meanwhile, sauté the ham lightly in butter. Place the finished veal on 4 hot plates, top with the ham and sauce and serve hot.

CHICKEN BREASTS À LA ZINGARA
TO SERVE 4

6 chicken breasts, halved and boned, skin intact
salt and paprika
butter
½ cup Madeira wine
1 tsp paprika
1 tsp tarragon
1 cup heavy cream

¼ cup pimientos, cut in strips
16 mushroom caps, sautéed and hot
1 recipe Rice à l'Indienne, cooked in chicken stock* or broth, hot
1 Tbs cornstarch blended with 2 Tbs cold water (optional)

Season the chicken lightly with salt and paprika and sauté until almost done in butter. Add the Madeira, paprika, tarragon and cream and simmer 15 minutes more. Arrange the chicken on a hot platter and decorate with the pimiento strips. Garnish with the mushrooms and piles of rice. If the sauce in the pan needs thickening, slowly blend in as much of the cornstarch slurry as needed, strain over the chicken and serve hot.

CHICKEN SAUTÉ À LA ZINGARA
TO SERVE 4

2 small chickens, cut up
salt and paprika
olive oil, or vegetable oil
½ recipe Zingara Garnish
¼ cup Madeira wine
1½ cups Sauce Espagnole, or
  veal gravy

2 Tbs Tomato Sauce, preferably
  homemade*
4 pieces of toast, trimmed, buttered and hot
4 ham slices, same size as toast
  slices, sautéed in butter, hot

Season the chicken with salt and paprika to taste and brown in a little oil. Lower the heat and finish cooking slowly in the pan until done. Discard excess fat from the pan. Add the garnish and stir with the chicken for a few minutes until heated through. Set the chicken on a long hot platter, arranged down the center, with a pile of the garnish at each end. Keep hot. Add the Madeira to the pan and boil down, scraping up the juices. Add the Espagnole and Tomato sauces, blend in and heat well. Meanwhile, top the toast with the ham and quarter diagonally, making 16 ham-topped toast triangles. Arrange them in an overlapping row on each side of the chicken on the platter. Strain the pan sauce over the chicken and serve hot.

APPENDIX

General Recipes

STOCKS, GLAZES, ASPICS

BEEF STOCK (Brown Stock, Meat Stock)
TO MAKE 5–6 QUARTS

6–8 lbs beef: meat, bones, trimmings
4–5 lbs veal: meat, bones, trimmings
6 carrots, quartered
4 onions, each stuck with 1 clove
1 veal knuckle, quartered
6 qts water
4 scallions

6 leek whites
3 celery stalks
1 small turnip, halved (optional)
1 Tbs salt (omit if stock is to be
  reduced to a glaze)
1 Tbs parsley
1 tsp thyme
1 bay leaf
cheesecloth, washed

Preheat oven to 400°. Put the beef, veal, carrots and onions in a pan and brown in the oven for 35 minutes. Blanch the veal knuckle in boiling water for a few seconds and drain. Put all the bones and meats in a large pot, cover with the water and bring to a boil. Meanwhile, dissolve the caramelized juices in the browning pan with a little boiling water and add to the stock pot. Skim. Add the scallions, leeks, celery, turnip and salt. Add the parsley, thyme and bay leaf tied in cheesecloth and skim again. Simmer for at least 6 hours, maintaining the liquid level by adding boiling water when needed. Strain the finished stock through a sieve, then through cheesecloth, into a deep bowl or bowls and refrigerate overnight, covered. All the fat will rise to the top and solidify into a hard layer. The next day, remove the fat layer and discard. The stock should be lightly jelled from the collagen in the connective tissues, which dissolves when heated. This dissolved collagen gives the stock, and any finished sauce made from it, its consistency. If the stock is frozen, it will keep for many months, but must be boiled at once upon defrosting.

CHICKEN STOCK (White Stock)
TO MAKE 4 QUARTS

2 tsp parsley	5 carrots, coarsely sliced
½ tsp thyme	4 onions, coarsely sliced
1 bay leaf	3 celery stalks, coarsely sliced
cheesecloth, washed	4 leek whites
6 lbs chicken backs, necks and giblets (except livers), or 2 4-lb stewing chickens	2 cloves
	8 qts cold water
	salt (optional)
2 veal knuckles, quartered, or 2 lbs veal bones and trimmings (optional)	

Tie the parsley, thyme and bay leaf in cheesecloth. Put all the ingredients in a large pot and bring slowly to a boil, skimming. Lower the heat and simmer very gently for 5 hours, skimming when needed. After 5 hours the stock should be reduced by ½. If the stock begins to reduce to less than ½, add boiling water as needed. Strain through a sieve, then through a sieve lined with cheesecloth. Season lightly with salt if desired, but do not season with salt if the stock is to be reduced to a glaze. Refrigerate overnight. The next day, remove the fat layer on top of the stock and discard. This stock will keep frozen for many months. After defrosting, boil at once.

COURT BOUILLON
TO MAKE 1 QUART

1 carrot, sliced	½ tsp thyme
1 onion, sliced	salt and pepper
1 Tbs parsley	1 qt water
1 bay leaf	

Combine all the ingredients and simmer for 25 minutes. Strain and use to poach fish. (If using for salmon add 1 tablespoon of lemon juice or cider vinegar.)

FISH FUMET (Fish Stock)
TO MAKE 1 QUART

1 onion, sliced
1 carrot, sliced
1 celery stalk, sliced
1 oz butter
2 lbs fish, bones and trimmings
   from lean fish like sole (not
   fatty fish like herring,
   mackerel or trout)

1 cup dry white wine
1 qt cold water
1 tsp parsley
¼ tsp thyme
½ bay leaf
cheesecloth, washed
salt (optional)

Sauté the onion, carrot and celery in the butter until tender and just a bit golden. Add the remaining ingredients, with the parsley, thyme and bay leaf tied in cheesecloth. Simmer for 30 minutes, skimming. Strain through a sieve. Then strain through a sieve lined with cheesecloth. Season lightly with salt, except if the stock is to be reduced to a glaze. Refrigerate overnight, discard the fat that solidifies at the top and freeze if you wish to keep the stock more than a couple of days. This stock does not last long unfrozen. When defrosting, boil and use at once.

Fish fumet can be made with red wine, for use in aspics and glazes.

GAME STOCK (Game Fumet)
TO MAKE 5–6 QUARTS

Proceed as for Beef Stock, substituting the bones, meat and trimmings of the particular game for the beef and veal. Add several juniper berries and a sage leaf to the herb bouquet if desired.

MUSHROOM FUMET (Mushroom Stock)
TO MAKE 1¼ CUPS

2 cups mushrooms, trimmings,
   peelings, stems, etc., minced
1 tsp parsley
¼ tsp thyme
¼ bay leaf

1 clove
cheesecloth, washed
2 cups cold beef stock*
2 Tbs chopped onion
½ tsp chopped garlic

Put the mushrooms in a pot. Tie the parsley, thyme, bay leaf and clove in cheesecloth and add. Add the stock, onion and garlic and bring slowly to a boil. Cook down to ½, about 1¼ cups of liquid. Strain through cheesecloth. When cold, seal and store or freeze. This stock will keep in the refrigerator for several weeks, or frozen for several months. Boil at once when defrosting. Use for flavoring soups or sauces.

VEAL STOCK (Jus de Veau, Brown Veal Stock)
TO MAKE 4 QUARTS

See listed under the category JUS.

VEGETABLE FUMET (Vegetable Stock)
TO MAKE 2 QUARTS

3 carrots, sliced	2½ qts cold water
2 onions, sliced	1 tsp parsley
4 green onions, green and white parts, sliced	¼ tsp thyme
	¼ tsp chervil
4 leeks, green and white parts, sliced	¼ bay leaf
	cheesecloth, washed
1 celery stalk, sliced	
1 oz butter, preferably unsalted	

Sauté the carrots, onions, green onions, leeks and celery in the butter in a pot until limp but not browned. Add the water and bring slowly to a boil. Skim. Add the parsley, thyme, chervil and bay leaf tied in cheesecloth. Simmer gently for about 1½ to 2 hours, until the stock is reduced to 2 quarts. Strain through cheesecloth and store in the refrigerator or freeze. This stock will keep for several weeks in the refrigerator, or several months frozen.

CLARIFYING STOCKS
TO CLARIFY 1 QUART

CLARIFYING ANY STOCK

Beat 2 egg whites with their crumbled shells. Slowly blend in 1 quart of lukewarm stock with the beaten egg mixture. Pour into a pot and bring slowly to a bare simmer. Simmer gently for 15 minutes, stirring occasionally. Strain through cheesecloth.

TO CLARIFY BEEF STOCK

Add 2 ounces of finely minced lean beef, ¼ cup minced leek greens, 2 tablespoons fresh parsley and a couple of sprigs of fresh chervil or tarragon to the egg whites and their shells and beat together. Add the lukewarm stock and proceed as in Clarifying Any Stock.

TO CLARIFY CHICKEN STOCK

Proceed as for Clarifying Beef Stock, using lean chicken meat in place of the beef.

TO CLARIFY FISH STOCK

Use only the beaten egg whites and their crumbled shells.

TO CLARIFY GAME STOCK

Proceed as for Clarifying Beef Stock, using the particular game (lean) in place of the beef.

TO CLARIFY VEAL STOCK

Proceed as for Clarifying Beef Stock, using lean veal in place of the beef.

GLAZES

Any stock cooked down to about becomes a glaze. For example, 1 cup of beef stock cooked down to 1 ounce is a beef glaze. The stock used should be clear, and must not be salted or peppered.

GRAVIES

Any stock may be thickened with flour or cornstarch to make gravy. Use 1 to 2 tablespoons cornstarch or 2 to 3 tablespoons of flour per cup. To prevent lumping, first mix starch with an equal amount of liquid such as water or wine. Then add slowly to very hot stock, stirring continously until mixture is thickened to desired consistency.

ASPICS (To Coat Foods in Aspic Jelly)
TO MAKE 2 CUPS

BROWN VEAL ASPIC

Boil down 4 cups of clear veal stock to 2 cups. Let cool. When half set, use to coat chilled foods lightly with a brush. Chill the coated foods to quickly set the thin film of aspic, keeping the remaining aspic just warm enough to remain half set. When the first coat has set, coat again. Coat 2 to 4 times for a nice even aspic.

CHICKEN ASPIC

Soften 1 envelope of unflavored gelatin in a little cold water. Blend with 2 cups of clear chicken stock, and heat gently until all the gelatin granules are dissolved completely. Cool and use as in Brown Veal Aspic.

BEEF ASPIC

Proceed as for Chicken Aspic, using clear beef stock.

FISH ASPIC

Boil 4 cups of clear fish stock down to half, cool and use as in Brown Veal Aspic.

RED FISH ASPIC

Proceed as for Fish Aspic, using fish stock made with dry red wine. This aspic has an excellent color.

PORT, SHERRY or MADEIRA ASPICS

Proceed as for Brown Veal or Beef Aspic, adding 2 ounces of wine to the stock. These are colorful as well as flavorful aspics.

SAUCES

LOBSTER SAUCE (For Seafood)
TO MAKE 2 CUPS

2 cups White Wine Sauce #1 or #2
liver from a 1-lb lobster (optional)
coral (eggs) from a 1-lb lobster (optional)

2 Tbs butter, softened
2–3 Tbs lobster meat, mashed until pulpy
red pepper (cayenne)

Blend all the ingredients together and season with a very little red pepper. Serve hot, but do not boil.

ROEBUCK SAUCE (Chevreuil Sauce)

for small cuts of meat
TO MAKE 2 CUPS

6 cups Sauce Poivrade
1 cup dry red wine

red pepper (cayenne)

Boil the Sauce Poivrade down to $^1/_3$, adding the wine little by little during cooking. Season with a very little red pepper. Strain through cheesecloth and serve hot.

SAUCE SUPRÊME
TO MAKE 2 CUPS

1½ cups Sauce Velouté*
1½ cups chicken stock*

1½ cups cream
2 Tbs butter (optional)

Mix the Velouté and stock in a pot and boil down to ½. Add the cream and cook down to 2 cups. Blend in the butter, if desired, and serve hot with eggs, poultry, vegetables and variety meats.

TARTARE SAUCE (For Fish, Meats, Eggs)
TO MAKE 2 CUPS

2 cups Mayonnaise, preferably
    homemade
2 Tbs minced dill pickles

2 Tbs minced capers
2 Tbs minced chives

Blend all the ingredients and serve at room temperature or chilled.

This sauce can be flavored with prepared mustard to taste, preferably Dijon.

TOMATO SAUCE
TO MAKE 2 CUPS

1 large onion, minced
1½ oz butter
2 Tbs flour
2 lbs tomatoes, peeled,* seeded
    and puréed in a blender
½ tsp sugar

salt and pepper
1 tsp parsley
¼ tsp thyme
½ tsp chervil
½ bay leaf
cheesecloth, washed

Sauté the onion in the butter until limp but not browned. Blend in the flour well. Add the tomatoes, sugar and salt and pepper to taste (check the seasoning when finished cooking). Add the parsley, thyme, chervil and bay leaf tied in cheesecloth. Simmer gently, partially covered, for 1 hour, stirring occasionally. Discard herb bouquet and serve hot.

SAUCE VELOUTÉ
TO MAKE 2 QUARTS

1 cup butter
1 cup flour
4 qts chicken stock,* hot
1 cup mushroom stems and
    pieces, chopped
1 tsp parsley

¼ tsp thyme
½ bay leaf
½ tsp chervil
4 peppercorns
cheesecloth, washed

Melt the butter in a large pan and blend in the flour, making a roux. Cook for 10 minutes without coloring. Blend in 3 quarts of the hot stock slowly and bring to a boil. Add the mushrooms. Add the parsley, thyme, bay leaf, chervil and peppercorns tied in cheesecloth. Reduce the heat and simmer gently for 30 minutes. Skim. Add the remaining stock and bring to a boil again. Lower the heat to a simmer, and simmer until reduced to 2 quarts, skimming until fat-free. Strain and let cool to room temperature. Store in tight jars or plastic containers. Freeze in plastic containers, if desired. This is a basic, or "mother" sauce.

SAUCE VELOUTÉ, FISH-BASED (For Seafood)
TO MAKE 2 CUPS

2 oz butter	¼ tsp grated orange rind
4 Tbs flour	½ tsp basil
2 cups fish fumet*	salt and white pepper
½ tsp anchovy paste	2 Tbs butter (optional)

Melt the butter in a pan and blend in the flour. Cook for 10 minutes without coloring, making a blond roux. Blend in the fish fumet. Bring to a boil and add the anchovy paste, orange rind and basil. Lower the heat and simmer for 5 minutes. Skim if necessary. Season with salt and pepper to taste. Blend in the butter, if desired, and serve hot.

WHITE WINE SAUCE #1 (For Seafood)
TO MAKE 2 CUPS

1½ cups fish fumet* made with white wine	8 oz butter, melted
4 egg yolks	salt and white pepper
	lemon juice

Boil the fish fumet down to 1/3. Let cool a bit off heat and add the yolks, beating until the sauce thickens. Gradually blend in the butter. Season to taste with salt, pepper, and a few drops of lemon juice. Strain and serve hot. Do not reboil after adding the yolks, or they will curdle.

Mushroom skins and stems are often boiled with the fish fumet to enhance the flavor of this sauce.

WHITE WINE SAUCE #2 (For Seafood)
TO MAKE 2 CUPS

Blend 2 cups of Hollandaise Sauce with 2 to 4 teaspoons of fish glaze.★ Season if necessary with salt and white pepper and serve hot.

WHITE WINE SAUCE #3 (For Coating)
TO MAKE 2 CUPS

1 cup fish-based Sauce Velouté*	4 egg yolks
1 cup fish fumet* made with white wine	4 oz butter, diced
	salt and white pepper

Mix the Velouté and fish fumet in a pan and boil down to ½. Remove from the heat, let cool just a bit and blend in the yolks, beating until thick. Return to very low heat and do not let boil after adding the yolks. Blend in the butter, piece by piece. Season with salt and white pepper if needed and strain. Use hot, to coat cooked fish. Run them under the broiler to glaze and serve at once, hot.

CONSOMMÉS AND SOUPS

BEEF CONSOMMÉ
TO MAKE 1½ QUARTS

3 qts water (more if needed)
1 lb lean beef, cubed
1 lb veal, cubed
2 lbs beef bones, cracked
1 veal knuckle, cracked (or other veal bones)
½ tsp salt
3 carrots, chopped
3 celery stalks, chopped
2 leek whites, chopped (optional)
1 turnip, chopped (optional)
2 onions stuck with 1 clove each
1 tsp parsley
¼ tsp thyme
½ tsp chervil
½ bay leaf
cheesecloth, washed

Put the water, meats and bones in a large pot and bring slowly to a boil. Skim. Add the salt and skim again. Add the carrots, celery, leeks, turnip and onions. Add the parsley, thyme, chervil and bay leaf tied in cheesecloth. Bring slowly back to a boil and skim. Simmer very slowly for 4 to 5 hours, reducing liquids by ½. Skim occasionally and add a bit of water if needed. Strain through a sieve lined with cheesecloth. Degrease if necessary by laying paper towels just on the surface of the consommé, to absorb the fat without actually getting in the consommé. If the consommé is cloudy, clarify as in Clarifying Beef Stock.

CHICKEN CONSOMMÉ
TO MAKE 1½ QUARTS

Proceed as for Beef Consommé, using the veal meat and knuckle, with 2 pounds of chicken parts in place of the beef and beef bones. If necessary, clarify as in Clarifying Chicken Stock.

The chicken meat may be removed from the consommé after 1½ hours of cooking and used elsewhere, returning all the bones and trimmings to the consommé to finish cooking.

FISH CONSOMMÉ

This is the same as Fish Stock.

VEGETABLE CONSOMMÉ
TO MAKE 1½ QUARTS

1½ qts vegetable stock   2 envelopes unflavored gelatin

Let the gelatin soften in a little cold stock for 10 minutes. Bring slowly to a simmer and simmer until the gelatin granules are completely dissolved, about 5 minutes. Blend with the rest of the stock.

When served hot, consommés should be very hot. When served chilled, they should be lightly jelled, to melt quickly in the mouth. If chilled consommé is jelled too hard it is very unpleasant and rubbery, and needs to be reheated with a little plain thin stock so it will gel lightly when rechilled.

CHICKEN VELOUTÉ SOUP
TO MAKE 1½ QUARTS

5 cups Chicken Consommé*   4 Tbs butter
1 lb chicken necks and wings   ¼ cup heavy cream
4 Tbs flour   salt and white pepper

Simmer the consommé with the chicken necks and wings until they are cooked, and let cool until lukewarm. Meanwhile, mix the flour and butter in a pan over fairly low heat until well blended but not colored. Gradually blend in the consommé and simmer for 30 minutes. Strain through cheesecloth. Mix in the cream and season with salt and white pepper to taste just before serving. Serve hot.

EGGS

CODDLED (Soft-Boiled)

Bring water to a good boil in a pot and plunge the eggs into the water. Cover and remove from the heat. Let stand for 4 to 7 minutes, depending on how well you like them done. I like mine at 5½ minutes. Pour off the hot water and put the eggs under running cold water to stop the cooking.

This is by far the best way to soft-boil or coddle eggs. They have a soft and fine texture unattainable by any other method. They are excellent on toast, with a little caviar stirred into them. If you use eggs at room temperature, they will cook fairly evenly. If you use chilled eggs, the whites will cook faster than the yolks.

FRIED (Sautéed)

The more gently the eggs are sautéed, the softer and more delicate their texture will be. Use plenty of butter, and have it hot before adding the eggs to the pan, but then lower the heat to cook the eggs very slowly.

HARD-BOILED (Hard-Cooked)

Proceed as for coddled eggs, letting the eggs rest in the water off heat for 15 minutes. These eggs will be smooth-textured and not rubbery, as are the ones hard-cooked in continuously boiling water.

OMELETS

Season the eggs for the omelet lightly with salt and pepper to taste. Mix in any herbs to be used, as well as a little heavy cream, if desired. Beat the eggs lightly. For each egg in the omelet, melt 1 tablespoon of butter in a pan. Have the butter very hot, pour in the egg mixture and let stand for 5 seconds. Then beat air into the omelet mixture with a fork, without breaking the film of solidified egg on the bottom of the pan, if possible. This beating will allow the eggs to cook evenly. Stop beating with the fork when the eggs begin to set. If the omelet is to be filled, this is the time to fill it, before it is completely done. Arrange the filling down the center of the omelet, tilt the pan forward steeply so the omelet slides forward and part way up the front of the pan. Fold the front third of the omelet back over the filling. Tilt the pan backward and fold the back third of the omelet over the fillings, and hold in place for a few seconds with a spatula to set in place. Slide onto a hot plate and serve at once, hot.

Do not overbeat the eggs to be used in an omelet, and use eggs at room temperature so they will cook evenly and quickly. The longer and slower an omelet cooks, the more rubbery it will be.

POACHED

Eggs should be poached in water with a little vinegar and salt. For each quart of water, add 1 tablespoon of vinegar and 1 teaspoon of salt. Fresh eggs make much better poached eggs than eggs that have been standing around for weeks. The older the eggs, the more they will disperse in the water while cooking. The water should not be boiling, but just barely trembling. Eggs poached free in the water, or with a French egg poacher (a spoonlike affair with a long handle that sticks straight up out of the water) have the finest texture. The typical household poacher, in which the eggs sit in individual round cups held by a rack over boiling water, is the worst possible implement for cooking eggs. They are not poached at all, but steamed, and consequently have a texture somewhere between rubber and plastic.

SHIRRED (Baked)

The faster the eggs are baked, the better the texture. Use eggs at room temperature. Bake the eggs in buttered dishes on a high rack in a 500° oven. They will cook quickly, and from the bottom up, thus keeping the yolks soft while the whites set. If desired, baste with melted butter when half done. Serve in the baking dishes, as soon as cooked, hot.

Shirred eggs are often topped with 1 tablespoon of heavy cream each, or with a sprinkling of grated cheese, before baking.

For added flavor and aroma, rub the egg-baking dishes with a piece of cut garlic before buttering them.

DOUGHS

BRIOCHE
TO MAKE 2 LARGE OR UP TO 12 SMALL BRIOCHES

1 cup flour	2 Tbs sugar
2 pkgs dry yeast, mixed with 3 oz warm water	½ cup milk, lukewarm
lukewarm water	6 eggs, at room temperature
4 cups flour	½ cup butter, softened
2 tsp salt	½ cup butter, softened
	1 egg, beaten

Put the 1 cup of flour in a bowl and make a depression in its center. Pour in the yeast mixture and stir into the flour, forming a dough. Knead it and form into a ball. Cover this dough ball (sponge) completely with lukewarm water and set in a warm place until it expands and rises to the surface. Then remove the dough ball from the water at once and set aside. Meanwhile, put the 4 cups of flour in a very large bowl and make a depression in its center. Put the salt, sugar, milk, 6 eggs and ½ cup of butter in this well and blend with the flour. Then knead in the dough ball (sponge) that was set aside. Knead until smooth and elastic, about 12 minutes. Knead in the remaining ½ cup butter until completely incorporated and the dough is smooth again. Put the dough in another, buttered, bowl. Drape a cloth over it and set in a warm place to double in size. Punch down, and let double in size again. Punch down again. Put in refrigerator, punch down after 2 hours, then return to refrigerator for several hours more, or overnight.

TO BAKE 2 LARGE BRIOCHES

Take 2 pieces of dough the size of pullet eggs and shape into 2 balls. Form the remaining dough into 2 perfect balls and place in 2 buttered 4-cup molds. They should more than half fill the molds. Push a hole in the top center of each dough ball and insert the small dough balls so they're about ⅓ of the way in. Place the molds in a warm place until the dough doubles in size. Brush with the beaten egg. Bake each in the center of a 400° oven until done, about 40 minutes, and unmold as soon as baked to cool on a rack. (It's better to bake them separately, one after the other, than together and off center in the oven. Ideally, 2 ovens should be used, or one of the brioches kept cool to rise slower than the other so it can be baked after the first.)

TO BAKE SMALL BRIOCHES

Proceed as for the large brioches, reserving about ⅕ of the dough for making the small dough balls that are inserted in the top of the brioches. Bake at 400° for about 15 to 30 minutes, depending on their size.

CHOU PASTE (Pâté a Choux)
TO MAKE 12 CREAM PUFFS OR ABOUT 35 PROFITEROLES (LITTLE PASTRY PUFFS)

1 cup milk	2 tsp sugar
6 Tbs butter	1½ cups flour
½ tsp salt	6–8 eggs, lightly beaten

Bring the milk, butter, salt and sugar to a boil in a pot. Remove from heat and beat in the flour all at once. Stir until it forms a ball. Put over medium heat and dry the batter as much as possible without browning, by pressing down with a wooden spoon and flipping the batter over in the pot continuously (do this for 6 to 8 minutes). Put the batter in a bowl. When cooled a little, put in the eggs with a pastry blender one at a time, using as many as the batter will absorb. (The more milk steamed from the batter during drying, the more eggs can be absorbed and the lighter the cream puffs will be.) Beat until smooth after each egg addition. It should be fairly thick to just hold its shape during baking.

FOR CREAM PUFFS

Squeeze out the dough through a ¾-inch pastry tube into 2-inch mounds on a buttered baking tin. Bake in a 400° oven for 20 minutes. Remove from the oven and make a slit in their sides to allow steam to escape. Turn off the oven and return the puffs to dry with the door ajar—about 10 minutes. Cool completely before filling.

FOR PROFITEROLES

Proceed as for cream puffs, using a ½-inch pastry tube and making small 1-inch mounds on the baking sheet. Bake at 400° for 20 minutes.

FOR ÉCLAIRS

Proceed as for cream puffs, squeezing the paste into éclair shapes, 1 inch thick and 4 to 6 inches long.

CRÊPE BATTER
TO MAKE 18–24 CRÊPES

¾ cup flour
3 eggs
1 cup milk, scalded

2 Tbs butter, melted
¼ tsp salt

Put the flour in a bowl and make a well in its center. Break in the eggs and mix with a whisk or mixer until blended. Do not overbeat. Slowly blend in the milk. Blend in the butter and salt. Strain and let stand for 30 minutes before using.

DESSERT CRÊPE BATTER
TO MAKE 18–24 CRÊPES

¾ cup flour
⅛ tsp salt
1 Tbs confectioners' sugar
2 eggs
1 egg yolk

1 cup milk, scalded
3 Tbs butter, melted
1 oz liqueur of your choice
    (Curaçao, Kirsch, etc.)

Mix the flour, salt and sugar in a bowl and make a well in the mixture's center. Add the eggs and yolk and blend with the flour mixture. Slowly blend in the milk, then the melted butter and liqueur. Strain and let stand for 30 minutes before using.

COOKING CRÊPES

Melt about 3 tablespoons of butter in a 5 to 6-inch diameter pan. Pour off the excess butter and reserve, leaving the pan's bottom well coated with butter. Return the pan to the heat for a moment, pour in a scant ¼ cup of crêpe batter, and quickly tilt the pan in a circular motion to spread the batter evenly. Cook for about 1 minute. Shake the pan to loosen the crêpe, turn and cook the other side for about ½ minute. This is called the second side, and is usually inferior in coloring to the side cooked first and is served down or folded in, presenting the more perfect, first side to be seen. Add a little reserved melted butter to the pan, heat quickly, add more batter and make another crêpe, and so on until all the batter is used. Crêpes may be kept warm if used soon, or reheated for later use by freezing or storing separately in foil and reheating in a 400° oven in the foil for about 5 to 6 minutes. Crêpes should be wrapped in the foil while still warm and stored or frozen at once.

FRYING BATTER
TO MAKE 2½ CUPS

1½ cups flour
½ tsp salt
a tiny pinch of white pepper
1 Tbs peanut oil
2 egg yolks

1 whole egg
½ cup beer
¾ cup milk
2 egg whites, beaten stiffly

Blend the flour, salt, pepper, oil, yolks and whole egg in a bowl with a pastry blender. Mix in the beer and milk. Put in a blender and blend until smooth. Pour into a clean bowl, fold in the beaten egg whites and use as a batter to coat foods to be deep-fried.

NOODLE PASTE
TO MAKE NOODLES FOR 4

3 cups flour
4 eggs

½ tsp salt dissolved in 3 Tbs
    water

Put the flour in a bowl and make a well in its center. Put the eggs and salted water in the well. Work with your hands, kneading the eggs into the flour until you have a smooth dough. Set it aside for 1 hour. Divide the dough in ½s or ¼s and roll out separately on a floured surface as thin as you can, about 1/16 inch thick. Fold the rolled-out dough several times and cut in strips to any width you prefer. Spread the dough strips out on a floured surface or cloth and dry for 6 hours or more.

PASTRY CRUST
TO MAKE 1 2-CRUST 9 or 10-INCH PIE

1½ cups flour
4 Tbs cold water
½ tsp salt

10 Tbs butter, cold and cut into
    small pieces

Put the flour in a bowl and make a well in its center. Put 1 teaspoon of the water in this well with the salt and butter. Cut the butter pieces into the flour with a pastry blender to make a gritty mixture (or work by hand). Add the remaining water 1 teaspoon at a time, mixing in lightly by hand. By now the ingredients should form one large lump of dough. If the dough seems soft, refrigerate before rolling out. Using the palm of your hand, push the dough out in one direction on a floured surface, flattening as for a thick crust. Then roll the dough out to make 2 crusts with a rolling pin.

For a sweet crust, reduce the salt to ¼ teaspoon and mix 1½ teaspoons of sugar with the flour before mixing with the other ingredients.

For a caramelized crust, sprinkle with a little sugar before baking.

For a 1-crust pie, use ½ of the recipe. Also use a ½ recipe for 4 to 8 individual-size tart crusts, or individual pastry shells.

To prebake the crusts, line the pie or tartlet shells with crust. Prick with a fork and refrigerate for 1 hour or more. Bake at 425° for 7 to 8 minutes. If the crusts lift from the pan during baking, prick with a fork again. To prevent the crusts from lifting from the pie pans during baking, fit a piece of foil snugly into the unbaked crusts and fill them with dried beans to hold the crust down and in place. Then bake for 7 minutes. Remove the beans and foil and finish baking until lightly browned, about 4 to 5 minutes more.

PUFF PASTRY
TO MAKE 2 8–9-INCH PASTRY CRUSTS, OR 10–20 INDIVIDUAL-SIZE TART CRUSTS

1 ¾ cups butter, chilled	¼ cup butter, softened
4 cups flour (preferably bread flour)	1¼ cups cold water

Knead the 1¾ cups of chilled butter until smooth and waxy. If it warms during the kneading, chill lightly. This butter should be at a temperature that's moderately cool, and have a consistency of a dough, neither cold and hard nor warm and soft. Separately, blend the flour with the ¼ cup of softened butter in a bowl, using a pastry blender. Blend very well. Make a well in the center and add the cold water and blend with the flour, making a semifirm dough. Knead this dough for 3 to 5 minutes, until it becomes a solid ball. Remove from the bowl and knead on a floured working surface for 10 minutes more. If it becomes too soft, chill lightly.

Roll out the dough on a floured surface (many chefs use a well-floured pastry cloth) into a rectangle about 8 by 16 inches. Take the kneaded 1¾ cups of butter and form into a flat rectangle about 4 by 5 inches, and place crosswise on the rectangle of dough, about 2 inches from one of the short ends. Fold the dough in half, making an 8 by 8-inch dough package with the butter inside, in the center. Press the edges of the dough together so the butter is securely enclosed and will not ooze out while the dough is being rolled. Flop the dough over and give it a half turn, so one of the crimped edges is toward you and the one solid side where the dough was folded is pointing away from you. Roll out into a rectangle about 8 by 16 inches. Fold the ⅓ of the dough closest to you over the top, making a 3-layer folded dough. Give this a ½ turn so the folds run away from you and roll out again. Fold up into ⅓ again and chill for 30 minutes. Each time you fold and roll out the dough is called a "turn." After chilling for 30 minutes, roll out and fold twice more; that is, take 2 more "turns." Chill again for 30 minutes. Repeat, making 6 turns in all. This should be done in a cool room, on a cool surface, or the butter might soften and break through the dough, ruining the crust. Even the rolling pin should be chilled to prevent this.

When rolling and folding is completed, you will have a crust with 1,459 alternating fine layers of dough and butter. To use, roll out to about ⅓ inch thick and cut into 2 rounds, larger than the pastry dish to be lined. Place in buttered pastry tins, trim away excess dough around the edges and chill, or, even better, freeze. This will help keep the dough from collapsing while baking. Bake at 450° for 10 minutes, reduce heat to 350° and bake 15 to 20 minutes (only about 10 minutes more at 350° for smaller, individual-size crusts).

It is better to prebake this crust as directed than to fill it and then bake it, as it tends to become soggy easily. Also, to keep the dough from collapsing during cooking, you might cook it in a dish with sloping sides rather than sides that are straight up and down.

When the crust is baked, remove the center of the top crust and the moist layers below it, leaving a perfect shell.

Another method is to cut a round of rolled-out dough to the desired size, then another equal in size, and remove the center of the second crust, all but 1 inch or so of the edge, leaving a doughnutlike ring. Set the ring on the first crust, crimp their outer edges together with shallow vertical knife cuts about ½ inch apart and bake on a buttered cookie sheet. Remove the central crust layers that are moist and raised after baking and before filling.

General Procedures

ALMONDS

TO TOAST ALMONDS (or Any Other Nuts)

Spread almonds on a cookie tray and toast in a 325° oven, tossing often to toast evenly. Do not overbrown; they will toast very quickly once they start to color.

ARTICHOKES

TRIMMING AN ARTICHOKE

Have a lemon handy. Use it to rub all surfaces of the artichoke as soon as it is cut, to prevent discoloring. Cut the stem from the artichoke. Remove the tough outer leaves. Cut the top ⅓ off the artichoke. Cut the sharp points off the leaves that remain. If the artichokes are to be stuffed, remove the central hairy "chokes" by scooping out with a spoon.

PREPARING ARTICHOKE HEARTS

These are also called artichoke bottoms. Remove the stems, all the leaves and the "chokes" from the artichokes and rub the remaining disklike hearts quickly with lemon juice to prevent discoloring.

BLANCHING

Blanching is plunging food into boiling water for anywhere from a few seconds to several minutes. It is done to soften and cleanse foods, not to cook them. The time required for blanching depends on the food's original toughness and how tender you want it after blanching. Dried vegetables are usually blanched by immersing in cold water and bringing to a boil. Fresh vegetables are plunged directly into boiling water. Meats are also blanched, usually to remove excessively strong flavors. The particular type of blanching to be used will be given in the individual recipe.

BONING BIRDS

Bone birds by cutting along the back from the neck to the tail. Carefully trim the skin and meat away from the backbone and ribs, keeping the skin and flesh intact. Remove the backbone, the ribs, the remaining interior bones and finally the leg and wing bones, which are out around the joints from the inside to free them. Generally the leg and wing bones are left in to hold the shape of the legs and wings. The removed bones may be reserved for use in stocks.

BUTTER

KNEADED BUTTER AND FLOUR (Beurre Manié)

This is a mixture of butter and flour, usually in equal parts, kneaded together so they will blend easily into sauces, and is used for thickening. For thickening 1 cup of sauce, use 1 tablespoon each of butter and flour kneaded together for a medium sauce, 2 tablespoons of each for a thicker sauce.

CLARIFYING BUTTER

Melt the butter to be clarified over medium heat. Set aside and let stand for 30 minutes. Spoon off the foamy crust (composed of casein) and discard, or reserve and use on vegetables. Spoon out the clear, golden liquid butter fat without disturbing the whey gathered at the bottom of the pan. This whey is then discarded.

CHESTNUTS, SHELLING

To shell chestnuts, cut an X in the flat side of each chestnut with a heavy, sharp knife, being careful not to cut your fingers. The chestnut shells are very hard, and they tend to slip easily from your grasp. The X cut in the chestnuts should go just through the shells, but not deeply into the chestnuts. Place the chestnuts in a pot of water, bring to a boil, boil for 1 minute, and remove from the heat. Take 3 to 4 chestnuts from the water with a slotted spoon and peel, removing the shell and dark skin from the chestnuts. Leave the remaining chestnuts in the hot water while you peel each small batch so they stay hot. If they cool too much, the shells and skins will not come off cleanly.

DEGLAZING

Deglazing is a term applied to pans which have cooking juices solidified and stuck on their bottoms. Excess fat is removed from the pan and a liquid is added, usually wine or stock, and cooked down over high heat, while you scrape up the solidified cooking juices (glazes) on the pan's bottom. This releases the full flavor of the cooking juices for use in whatever sauce will be prepared.

MUSHROOM COOKING LIQUOR (Mushroom Cooking Juice)
TO COOK 2 POUNDS OF MUSHROOMS FOR HORS D'OEUVRES

2 lbs mushrooms (for hors d'oeuvres, use small whole mushrooms)
1/3 cup water

½ tsp salt
2 oz butter
1–2 Tbs lemon juice

Trim the mushroom stalks off flush with the caps. Put the water, salt, butter and lemon juice in a pan and bring to a boil. Add some of the mushroom caps and simmer for 5 minutes. Drain the mushrooms and put in a hot bowl. Cover with a wet cloth and keep hot. Cook the remaining mushrooms in batches until all are done, and serve at once, hot. If they must be kept, reheat them while still covered and serve at once, hot. These cannot be kept for any great length of time successfully.

OYSTERS POACHED in THEIR OWN JUICE

Open the oysters and reserve their juice. Poach them in their juice, just below a simmer, until they swell—about 3 to 4 minutes. Drain and use at once, hot.

POLENTA
TO SERVE 4

1 cup yellow cornmeal
4 cups boiling lightly salted water

2 Tbs butter
Parmesan cheese, grated

Gradually mix the cornmeal into the boiling, lightly salted water, whisking constantly to prevent lumping. Cook until done and very thick. Add the butter and blend well. Sprinkle with cheese and serve hot. Or, chill, slice and sauté in butter and serve hot, sprinkled with cheese.

SLURRIES

Slurries are mixtures of starch and a little cold liquid, and are used for thickening sauces. They are indispensable for last-minute additions to sauces that turn out too thin. To use, mix a little cornstarch, flour, arrowroot or potato starch with a little cold water (or wine) and add as much as needed to your sauce, a bit at a time, to thicken as desired. Generally, if the liquid is completely unthickened, 1 tablespoon of cornstarch will thicken 1 cup of liquid. You will need less cornstarch slurry if the liquid is already somewhat thickened. Potato starch or arrowroot takes only about ½ as much to thicken the same amount as cornstarch. Using cornstarch to thicken sauces results in the most stable gel but this gel is somewhat opaque. Arrowroot gel is not so opaque, but somewhat filmy. Potato starch gel is the smoothest and clearest.

SWEETBREADS

CLEANING SWEETBREADS

To clean sweetbreads, soak them in cold water for 4 hours, changing the water often. After soaking, place the sweetbreads in cold, fresh water in a pot and blanch by letting the water heat to a boil slowly. Let them boil for 2 minutes if they are to be braised whole, and 5 minutes if they are to be sliced and sautéed. Drain and rinse under cold running water. Cut away all their tubes and sinews, but do not remove the membrane that encloses them, or they will fall apart. Braise whole, or slice and sauté.

TOMATOES

PEELING

To peel tomatoes, plunge them into boiling water for a few seconds, run under cold water so you can hold them, remove the stem area with a sharp knife, and the peel will come off the tomatoes very easily. This same method can be used with peppers.

TOMATO FONDUE
TO MAKE 2 CUPS

3 lbs tomatoes, peeled,*
    seeded, drained and
    chopped

2 Tbs butter or oil

Simmer the chopped tomatoes in the butter or oil until tender and rub through a sieve. This is seasoned in various ways, depending on your intended use. Salt and pepper, and minced garlic cooked with the tomatoes, is most typical. But all kinds of green herbs might be desired, or a dash of lemon juice or a substitution of some pimentos for some of the tomatoes. The variations are endless, but the basic fondue is just tomatoes, butter, salt and pepper, and garlic if desired.

TRUFFLES

PREPARATION

Since we use canned truffles here (they do not grow in the United States), their flavor should be revived before use. For black truffles, peel and slice or dice and steep in warm Madeira wine. For white truffles, whose taste is more delicate (they are often best eaten raw), steep for just a few seconds in to heat through just before serving.

TRUFFLE PURÉE
TO MAKE 1 CUP

¼ lb raw truffles, rubbed through a sieve
¾ cup thick Sauce Béchamel

1 oz heavy cream
salt and white pepper
butter (optional)

Mix the truffles, Sauce Béchamel and cream and season lightly with salt and white pepper. Heat without boiling and add a little butter, if desired. Blend well.

VANILLA SUGAR

Place 2 vanilla beans, cut open along the side, in a 1-quart jar and fill with sugar. Seal tightly and store for future use.

VEAL MOUSSE (For Stuffing)
TO MAKE 3 CUPS

4 bread slices, trimmed
milk
1 lb lean veal, ground several times

2 egg whites
¾ cup cream
½ tsp salt
white pepper

Soak the bread in milk and squeeze dry. Mix with the veal and put through a meat grinder and into a metal bowl. Blend in the egg whites well. Put the metal bowl holding the veal mixture in a larger bowl with ice water and ice cubes and gradually beat the cream into the veal mixture. The veal mousse will be cooled by the ice water as you blend in the cream. Season with the salt, and with white pepper to taste.

VEGETABLES

COOKING

While vegetables are usually cooked in lightly salted water, they retain much more of their food value if cooked in fresh, unsalted water. Cook quickly until just done, drain and season at once with salt and pepper to taste. Serve at once, hot.

GLAZING
TO GLAZE 2 POUNDS OF VEGETABLES

Cut the vegetables into equal-size pieces, or use similarly sized onions, etc. Bring to a boil in water and drain. Just cover with fresh water, and add 2 tablespoons sugar, 2 ounces butter and a very little salt and white pepper to taste. Boil uncovered, until the liquid is almost gone, except for the butter and sugar, which will glaze the vegetables. Shake the vegetables to coat with the glaze and serve at once, hot.

VEGETABLE FONDUE
TO MAKE 2 CUPS

2 carrots, sliced
1 turnip, diced
1 leek white, sliced
1 onion, chopped
¼ celery root, or 1 celery stalk, chopped

salt to taste
½ tsp sugar
1 Tbs butter
½ cup veal stock*

Put all the ingredients except the veal stock in a pot, cover and simmer gently until very soft. Uncover and simmer with the veal stock until thickened. Rub through a sieve and use hot.

WHIPPING CREAM

For best results, the cream and everything it touches—the beater as well as the bowl—should be chilled beforehand. Place the bowl to contain the cream in a deep pan filled with ice cubes and water to keep the cream cold while it is being whipped. Also, try to introduce as much air into the whip as possible by moving the beaters around. The whole process should take only a few minutes.

French Cooking Terms and Ingredients

Generally, pluralized words are pronounced the same as when singular. For example, *escargot* and *escargots* are both pronounced "ess-kar-GOH."

Abricot (ah-bree-KOH)   Apricot

Agneau (ahn-N'YOH)   Lamb

Ail (EYEa)   Garlic

Aïoli (ay-oh-IEE) — A garlicky mayonnaise

à la (ah LAH) — In the manner of

Ananas (ah-nah-NAH) — Pineapple

Anchois (ahn-SHWAH) — Anchovy

Anguille (ahn-GEEya) — Eel

Artichaut (ahr-tee-SHOW) — Artichoke

Asperge (ah-SPERZH) — Asparagus

Aspic (ahs-PEEK) — Aspic jelly

Attereaux (ah-tay-ROW) — Small skewers

au (oh) — Contraction of *à le* (masculine form *à la*), can also mean with

Aubergine (oh-bare-ZHEEN) — Eggplant

aux (oh) — Plural of *au* and *à la*

Ballottine (bah-luh-TEEN) — A piece of meat that is boned, stuffed and rolled

Banane (bah-NAHN) — Banana

Barquette (bahr-KET) — Small pastry shaped like a boat

Bavaroise (bah-vahr-WAHZ) — A hot beverage of tea, eggs, milk and liqueur

Betterave (bee-TRAHV) — Beet

Beurre (BEHR) — Butter

Beurre Manié (behr mah-NEE) — Flour and butter kneaded together, used for thickening sauces

Blanquette (blahn-KET) — A white ragout bound with eggs and cream

Boeuf (BUF) — Beef

Bouillabaisse (boo-yah-BESS) — A fish soup

Bouquet (boo-KAY) — Bouquet, aroma

Bouquet Garni (boo-KAY gahr-NEE) — A selection of herbs tied in cheesecloth, used as a seasoning

Braise (Brez) — To cook covered, usually in a little fluid or sauce

Brandade (brahn-DAHD)	A blend of pounded salt cod, garlic and oil
Brioche (bree-AWSCH)	A rich egg bread
Café (kah-FAY)	Coffee
Caille (KI-ya)	Quail
Canapé (kah-nah-PAY)	Crustless bread spread with or holding various foods, used as an appetizer or garnish
Canard, Caneton (kah-NAHR, kah-neh-TOH)	Duck, duckling
Carbonnade (kahr-bohn-AHD)	Thin slice
Carotte (kah-ROHT)	Carrot
Carpe (KAHRP)	Carp
Cassolette (kah-soh-LET)	A small casserole
Céleri (sel-leh-REE)	Celery
Cervelle (sehr-VEL)	Brain
Champignon (shahm-pee-N'YOHN)	Mushroom
Chapon (shah-POH)	Capon
Château (shah-TOH)	Castle, mansion
Châteaubriand (sha-toh-bree-AHND)	A preparation of beef fillet invented by Montmireil while chef to Chateaubriand
Chiffonnade (sheef-fohn-AHD)	Finely cut vegetables, usually simmered in butter, especially lettuce and sorrel
Chocolat (shoh-koh-LAH)	Chocolate
Chou, Choux (SHOO)	Cabbage, also a type of pastry
Choucroute Garnie (shoo-KROOT gahr-NEE)	Garnished sauerkraut
Chou-Fleur (shoo-FLEH)	Cauliflower
Citron (see-TROHn)	Lemon
Civet (see-VET)	Red wine ragout of furred game, such as rabbit
Clafouti (klah-foo-TEE)	A black cherry pastry specialty of Limousin

Concombre (kohn-KOH-Bra)   Cucumber

Confit d'Oie (kohn-FEE D'WAH)   Goose cooked and preserved in its own fat

Consommé   (kon-so-MAY)   A rich clarified stock

Coquilles Saint-Jacques (koh-KEEya san ZHAK)   Scallops

Côtelette (koh-tuh-LET)   Cutlet, chop

Cotriade (koh-tree-AHD)   A Breton fish soup

Courgettes (koor-ZHET)   Zucchini

Court Bouillon (koort boo-YOHNG)   An aromatic liquid for cooking meats, fish and vegetables

Crème   (KREM)   Cream

Crêpe   (KREHP)   Pancake

Crépinette (krayp-en-NET)   A small, flat sausage

Crevette (kre-VET)   Shrimp

Croquette (kroh-KET)   Croquette

Croûte   (KROOT)   Crust; piecrust

Cuisses de Grenouilles (kwees duh gren-N'OYa)   Frog's legs

Daube (DOHB)   Stew

Demi-glace (duh-mee-GLAHSS)   Half-glaze

Demitasse (duh-mee TAHSS)   A very small cup, or black coffee

Dinde, Dindon, Dindonneau (DAHND, dahn-DOHN, dahn-doh-NOH)   Hen turkey, cock turkey, young turkey

Duxelles (dewk-SEL)   A mixture of chopped mushrooms, onion, shallots, and seasonings, sautéed

Écrevisse (ay-creh-VEECE)   Crayfish

En Gelée (ahn Zha-LAY)   In jelly

Entrecôte (ahn-tray-KOHT)   Steak, generally meant as a cut taken from between two ribs of beef

Entrée (ahn-TRAY)   Although it literally means *beginning* in French, it generally means the main or third course of a meal

Épinard (ay-pee-NAHR)	Spinach
Escalop (ays-kahl-LOHP)	Slice
Escargot (ess-kar-GOH)	Snail
Faisan (fay-ZAHN)	Pheasant
Fève (FEV)	Bean
Fillet (fi-LAY)	Generally a small boneless cut of meat or fish
Foie (FWAH)	Liver
Foie Gras (fwah GRAH)	Fat liver
Fondue (fohn-DEW)	Fondue
Fraise (FREZ)	Strawberry
Framboise (frahm-B'WAZ)	Raspberry
Fromage (fro-MAZH)	Cheese
Fumet (few-MAY)	A liquid prepared by cooking foods, such as fish, in stock or wine, an aromatic liquid
Garni, Garnie (gahr-NEE)	Garnished, trimmed
Gelée (zha-LAY)	Jelly
Génoise (zhen-WAZ)	A type of cake
Glace (GLAHSS)	Ice cream, chilled fruit in syrup, meat or fish extracts
Glacé (glah-SAY)	Frosted, iced, glazed, candied
Gombos (gohm-BOH)	Okra
Haricot (ah-ree-COH)	Kidney bean
Hochepot (ohsh-POH)	Hotchpotch, ragout
Homard (oh-MAHR)	Lobster
Hors d'Oeuvre (or-DERV)	A light snack, hot or cold, formerly called an entrée when served hot preceding a main course
Huile (ooEEL)	Oil
Huître (WHEE-trah)	Oyster
Jambon (zham-BOHn)	Ham

Julienne (zhew-lee-EN)	Finely cut or shredded foods
Lait (LAY)	Milk
Laitue (lay-TOO)	Lettuce
Langue (LAHNG)	Tongue
Lapin (lah-PAHN)	Rabbit
Légume (lay-GOOM)	Vegetable
Lièvre (lee-EVRA)	Hare
Macédoine (mah-say-DWAN)	Medley
Marron (mah-ROHn)	Chestnut
Medaillon (may-dahl-YOHn)	Round or oval slice of meat, a collop
Merlan (mare-LAHN)	Whiting
Mirepoix (meer-PWAH)	A mixture of vegetables and herbs
Miroton (mee-roh-TOHn)	A meat and onion stew
Morue (moh-ROO)	Cod
Moule (MOOL)	Mussel
Mousse (MOOSS)	A finely textured dish, like a purée, usually eaten cold
Mouton (moo-TOHn)	Mutton
Naturel (nah-tewr-REL)	Natural
Navarin (nah-vah-REN)	A mutton ragout
Navet (nah-VAY)	Turnip
Noisette (nwah-ZET)	A small round slice or fillet of meat or a hazelnut
Oeuf, Oeufs (UHF, UH)	Egg, Eggs
Oie (WAH)	Goose
Oignon (oh-N'YOHn)	Onion
Olive (oh-LEEV)	Olive
Omelette (ohm-LET)	Omelet
Orge Perle (OHRZH pair-LAY)	Pearl barley
Pain (PAN)	Bread

Panad (pah-NAHD)	A paste of liquid and starch, such as bread and milk, for thickening soups or to use in stuffings
Pannequet (pahn-neh-KAY)	A pancake spread with a mixture, such as jam, then rolled up, or folded in four, sprinkled with sugar or crushed macaroons and glazed in the oven
Pâté (pah-TAY)	A dough, a pastry case containing meats or fish, the name incorrectly given to various terrines
Pâtissière (pah-tee-S'YAIR)	Pastry cook
Paupiette (poh-P'YET)	A thin slice of meat, stuffed and rolled into a cork shape
Perdrix, Perdeau (pair-DREE, pair-DROH)	Partridge, young partridge
Pilaf (pee-LAHF)	Pilaf, pilau, a method of preparing rice, usually mixed with other ingredients, such as shrimp or livers
Piperade (pee-pay-RAHD)	An egg dish with tomatoes and peppers
Pistache (pees-TAHSH)	Mutton (or partridges or pigeons) prepared with a great many garlic cloves
Poire (PWAHR)	Pear
Poireau (pwah-ROW)	Leek
Pois (PWAH)	Pea, peas
Pois Chiche (pwah SHEESH)	Chick pea
Poisson (pwah-SOHn)	Fish
Pomme (POM)	Apple
Pomme de Terre (pom duh TAIR)	Potato
Porc (PORK)	Pork
Potage (poh-TAZH)	Soup
Pot-au-Feu (poh-toh-FUH)	A broth of soup, meat and vegetables, all in one dish
Poulet, Poularde (poo-LAY, poo-LAHRD)	Chicken, fat pullet
Poupeton (poo-pay-TOHn)	Meats rolled one inside the other

Praline (preh-LEN)	An almond paste
Profiterole (proh-fee-tehr-OHL)	A little ball of chou paste piped through a pastry bag and baked like a tiny cream puff
Purée (pew-RAY)	A thick, smooth pulp
Quenelle (ken-EL)	Dumpling
Quiche (KEESH)	A savory custard tart originated in Lorraine
Radis (rah-DEE)	Radish
Ragôut (rah-GOO)	Ragout, stew
Ratatouille (rah-tah-TEW-ya)	A dish of eggplant, zucchini, peppers and tomatoes cooked with onion and garlic in oil
Ris (REE)	Sweetbread
Riz (REE)	Rice
Rognon (rogn-N'YOHn)	Kidney
Roux (ROO)	Mixture of butter or other fat and flour cooked together
Sabayon (sah-bah-YOHn)	A dessert sauce, called zabaglione in Italian
Salade (sah-LAHD)	Salad
Salpicon (sahl-pee-KOHn)	Diced ingredients bound with a sauce
Sauce (SOHSS)	Sauce
Saumon (soh-MOHn)	Salmon
Sauté (soh-TAY)	Fry, fried
Sucre (SOO-kra)	Sugar
Suprême (soo-PREM)	Supreme, a boned skinned chicken breast half
Sur le Plat (sewr luh PLAH)	On a plate
Terrine (tair-REEN)	Potted meat, a container for potted meat
Thon (TOHN)	Tuna
Timbale (taym-BAHL)	A round metal container, a preparation cooked or served in a piecrust

Tomate (toh-MAHT)	Tomato
Tournedos (toor-neh-DOH)	Beef fillet steaks
Truite (TRWEET)	Trout
Veau (VOH)	Veal
Venaison (ven-ay-ZOHn)	Venison
Viande (vee-AHND)	Meat
Vin (VAN)	Wine
Volaille (voh-LIE)	Poultry

French Wines and Other Beverages

Armagnac (ahr-mahn-YAHK)

Beaujolais (bow-joh-LAY)

Bordeaux (bohr-DOH)

Bourgogne (boor-GOHNya)

Cassis (kah-SEESS)

Chablis (shah-BLEE)

Chambéry (shahm-bay-REE)

Champagne (shahm-PAHNya)

Chinon (she-NOHn)

Cognac (kohn-YAHK)

Cotes de (KOTE duh)

Graves (GRAHV)

Jurançon (zhur-rahn-SOHn)

Lirac (lee-RAHK)

Mâcon (mah-SOHn)

Margaux (mahr-GO)

Médoc, Haut Médoc (may-DOK, oht may-DOK)

Moselle (moh-ZEL)

Muscadet (moose-kah-DAY)

Muscat (moose-KAH)

Rhine (RHAHn)

Rhône (RHOHN)

Sauternes (soh-TEARn)

Tavel (tah-VEL)

Vouvray (voo-VRAY)

Some French Cheeses

Beaufort (boh-FOH)

Brie (BREE)

Cachat (KAHSH-shah)

Camembert (kahm-mum-BEHR)

Cancoillotte (kahn-kwah-LOT)

Cantal (kahn-TAHL)

Carré de l'Est (kah-RAY duh LEST)

Chambérat (shahm-bay-RAH)

Chaource (shah-OORSE)

Comté (cohm-TAY)

Coulommiers (koo-lum-ME'YAY)

Époisses (ay-PWASS)

Fourmes (FOORM)

Gapron (gah-PROHn)

Géromé (zhay-roh-MAY)

La Feuille de Dreux (lah FOYya duh DRUH)

Langres (LANG-ra)

Maroilles (mahr-R'WEEL)

Montereau (mohn-ta-ROW)

Morbier (mohn-B'YAY)

Münster (muhn-STARE)

Nantais (nahn-TAY)

Neufchâtel (nuf-shah-TEL)

Persille des Aravis (pair-see-YAY day zah-rah-VEE)

Pithiviers (pee-tee-V'YAY)

Pont l'Évêque (poe lay-VECK)

Port-Salut (pohr sal-LOO)

Reblochon (ruh-bloh-SHOWn)

Rocroi (rok-rWA)

Rollot (roh-LOH)

Roquefort (ruk-FOHR)

Saint-Marcellin (sahn mahr-suh-LAHn)

Saint-Nectaire (sahn nek-TAIR)

Sassenage (sah-suh-NAZH)

Soumaintrain (soo-man-TRAN)

Tomme (TOHM)

Vachard (vah-SHAR)

Vacherin (vahsh-RAHN)

Vendômois (vahn-dohm-WAH)

Index